Globalisation, Economic Growth, and Employment in India

Sankar Kumar Bhaumik

Globalisation, Economic Growth, and Employment in India

PETER LANG

Chennai · Berlin · Bruxelles · Lausanne · Oxford · New York

Bibliographic information published by the Deutsche Nationalbibliothek. The German National Library lists this publication in the German National Bibliography; detailed bibliographic data is available on the Internet at http://dnb.d-nb.de.

A catalogue record for this book is available from the British Library.

Library of Congress Cataloging-in-Publication Data
Library of Congress Control Number: 2025049347

ISBN 978-1-80584-138-8 (Print)
ISBN 978-1-80584-139-5 (E-PDF)
ISBN 978-1-80584-140-1 (E-Pub)
DOI 10.3726/b23218

Published by Peter Lang Pvt Ltd, Chennai (India)

info@peterlang.com

This publication has been peer reviewed.

www.peterlang.com

Dedicated to
My beloved students, Dr Atreyee Pal and Dr Sk. Abdul Rashid

Contents

Figures

Tables

Acknowledgements

This book draws on my research into employment in India over the past decade and a half. I must begin by expressing my gratitude to my mentor, the late Professor G. K. Chadha, former Vice Chancellor of Jawaharlal Nehru University and former President of the South Asian University, New Delhi. He first introduced me to issues of growth and employment in India in the 1980s when I was his research student. Although my initial research under his guidance focused on agrarian issues, he fostered in me a deep interest in crucial aspects of the Indian economy, such as employment and unemployment, which I ultimately came to regard as one of my favourite research areas.

Over the years, I have gained valuable insights into employment issues in India through my participation in various conferences organised by the Indian Society of Labour Economics. I sincerely thank Dr Alakh N. Sharma, Director of the Institute for Human Development in New Delhi, for inviting me to these events. The works of many senior researchers on growth and employment have shaped my thinking and guided my research. Notably, I must acknowledge distinguished economists such as the late Dr Ajit K. Ghose, the late Dr T. S. Papola, Dr C. Rangarajan, Dr Rizwanul Islam, Dr Santosh Mehrotra, Dr Praveen Jha, Dr K. P. Kannan, and Dr Amit Basole.

Much of this work was carried out while I was at the University of Calcutta, the Central University of South Bihar, and the Patliputra School of Economics. All my colleagues there supported me in many different ways, which helped me to complete this rather challenging task.

I received assistance from many of my students with data processing tasks at different times. I would like to specifically thank Ankita De Sarkar, Jiten Giri, and Suraya Roy for their assistance. However, the most valuable support came from two of my research students, Dr Atreyee Pal and Dr Sk. Abdul Rashid, who not only motivated me to complete this work but also carefully read the manuscript, provided helpful comments and identified several errors in data presentation and interpretation. Without their support, this work would not have come to fruition; for this reason, I dedicate it to them.

Some parts of this work were prepared with the support of the Indian Council of Social Science Research, New Delhi, through a research project grant, for which I am grateful.

I appreciate the two anonymous referees for their helpful and constructive comments, which contributed to the improvement of the manuscript.

As always, my wife, Bidisha, and my daughter, Jayini, remain my main inspirations for undertaking serious academic research. I am deeply grateful to them.

I want to express my gratitude to Ms Indrani Dutta, Acquisitions Editor at Peter Lang International Academic Publishers, for her guidance and inspiration in preparing this manuscript. I also appreciate the assistance and support of their editorial and production teams.

Sankar Kumar Bhaumik

Introduction

1.1 Background to the Study

The primary goal of any nation, particularly in the developing world, is to promote rapid economic growth and generate sufficient employment opportunities. These objectives become increasingly vital when the aim is to achieve inclusive growth, which emphasises creating employment opportunities alongside higher economic growth, as measured by national income growth. Nonetheless, it is crucial to recognise that higher economic growth and employment generation do not always co-occur, a phenomenon that has sparked substantial interest in the economic literature. In this context, Keynes (1936) and Kalecki (1944) noted that the relationship between income growth and employment growth is primarily determined by aggregate demand. According to them, increasing income stimulates aggregate demand in the domestic market, fostering employment and enhancing economic output. Their perspective highlights the government's crucial role in stimulating aggregate demand through effective monetary and fiscal policies. Conversely, neoclassical economists argue that employment creation is more closely linked to the structural features of the labour market than to demand alone. Following this, new classical or supply-side economists argue that economic growth is best achieved by increasing the aggregate supply of goods and services. This is often achieved through policies such as tax cuts, deregulation, and free trade, which aim to stimulate production and investment, ultimately leading to increased employment. However, they acknowledge that short-term unemployment may occur when proper price signals are lacking, often due to insufficient information or excessive government intervention. In such cases, they remain optimistic that the economy's self-correcting nature will eventually reduce long-term unemployment, provided there is a steady flow of information.[1]

During the 1960s, the relationship between income growth and employment was described by 'Okun's Law', which indicated a negative correlation between the unemployment rate and GDP (income) growth, while accounting for population growth rates. Kaldor (1955) identified that the difference between output and productivity growth determines employment growth. Thus, while increased output growth typically boosts employment growth, the opposite can occur if productivity rises. Although Purfield (2006) supported Kaldor's viewpoint, researchers such as Khan (2001, 2007) and Islam (2006, 2010), having examined various Asian countries, argue that employment growth is not necessarily inversely related to increases in labour productivity. They suggest that a high economic growth rate (output growth) can promote increased employment and labour productivity, particularly when it arises from expanding labour-intensive sectors.

An analysis of the Indian economy's development since independence reveals that employment was initially regarded as a byproduct of economic growth during the country's planning phase (Papola, 2008; Bhaumik, 2013). Consequently, development policies focused more on achieving higher GDP growth rates rather than on implementing distinct strategies for employment expansion.[2] Furthermore,

---

1 The debate regarding the relative efficacy of demand-side and supply-side policies is essential for developing effective economic strategies within a nation. In India, economists such as Amit Bhaduri, Prabhat Patnaik, and Deepak Nayyar strongly advocate for demand-side policies, emphasising their capacity to create jobs and enhance living standards for a broader segment of the population. Conversely, proponents of supply-side policies, including Jagdish Bhagwati and Arvind Panagaria, present persuasive arguments in their favour. Since the onset of liberalisation and globalisation, subsequent governments have primarily focused on supply-side measures. However, analysing the growth transitions from 1950 to 2020, Balakrishnan et al. (2021) argue that while liberalising reforms have accelerated growth in India, persistent obstacles to growth still exist that cannot be addressed solely by neo-liberal or supply-side policies. They suggest that the growth experiences of East Asian countries may offer insights into how to tackle the challenge of low per capita income levels in India, even amidst ongoing and accelerating growth.

2 The evolution of employment strategies in post-independence India is influenced as much by socio-economic challenges as by the ideological predilections of the policy planners. Here's a summary of the approach to employment since the start of the planning era: In the initial four Five-Year Plans, spanning the period until the early 1970s, employment was viewed as a derivative of economic growth. Achieving high GDP growth was anticipated to create more employment opportunities, reducing the need for specific employment strategies. The Fifth Five-Year Plan (1974–1979) marked a shift by aligning developmental policies with employment-focused growth, introducing various anti-poverty initiatives and employment generation programmes. This focus persisted until approximately the mid-1980s. Notably, for the first time, the Seventh Five-Year Plan (1985–1990) positioned

these strategies were primarily grounded in a state-led growth policy that, due to various intrinsic inefficiencies, ultimately led to a severe balance of payments crisis and macroeconomic instability in the 1980s. In response to these crises, India implemented economic reforms since July 1991, embracing 'liberalisation and globalisation',[3] a strategy akin to the 'Washington Consensus' that strongly advocates for freer markets and a reduced role for the state. It is worth noting that the twin phenomena of liberalisation and globalisation are closely interlinked (Sikdar, 2006). Liberalisation led to a significant decrease or steady removal of the state's involvement in economic activities, allowing market forces to operate independently and encouraging the private sector to thrive and prosper the economy. Liberalisation comprised two aspects: internal and external. Following internal liberalisation, India aimed to implement reforms granting private-sector producers greater decision-making freedom. External liberalisation involved the gradual easing of state regulation over foreign trade, investment, and capital movement

---

employment as a central component of the development strategy, establishing a declared objective of achieving a 4 % annual growth rate in employment. The Eighth Five-Year Plan (1992–1997), coinciding with the implementation of economic reform policies, conducted a comprehensive assessment of employment and unemployment trends in the country. This plan was the first to address employment as a separate chapter within the document. It set a target for annual employment growth of 2.6 % to 2.8 % to achieve 'employment for all' by 2002. The Ninth Five-Year Plan (1997–2002) adopted an employment-led growth strategy and recognised employment as one of the critical dimensions of state policy. Nevertheless, by the late 1990s, it became apparent that the nation was facing significant employment challenges, particularly in rural areas, despite achieving higher GDP growth. In response, the Tenth Five-Year Plan (2002–2007) aimed to further realign the growth strategy to enhance its employment content. This plan's employment policy is primarily guided by the report titled "Special Group on Targeting Ten Million Employment Opportunities Per Year" (Government of India, 2002). A pivotal development during this period was the enactment of the National Rural Employment Guarantee Act (NREGA) by the first United Progressive Alliance government. The Eleventh Five-Year Plan (2007–12) adopted the strategy of 'inclusive growth', emphasising the effective reduction of poverty by creating productive employment opportunities accessible to all citizens. The Twelfth Five-Year Plan (2012–2017) continues with 'inclusive growth' as a key development goal. The current government's approach, encapsulated by the mantra *Sabka Saath, Sabka Vikas, and Sabka Vishwas*, also highlights the significance of expanding employment opportunities.

Thus, there has been no shortage of efforts at the policy-making level to improve the employment situation in India. Despite these efforts, employment remains a significant concern. This understandably raises questions about the effectiveness of neo-liberal economic policies, pursued with increasing vigour by successive governments since the early 1990s, in addressing the employment issue.

3 There are many studies that provide detailed accounts of India's reforms and globalisation. See, for instance, Srinivasan (2000); Kotwal et al. (2011); Panagaria (2008); Nayyar (2017); and Ahluwalia (2020).

in and out of the country (Ibid.). An alternative term for external liberalisation is globalisation, which seeks to achieve greater economic integration with the rest of the world in trade, assets, technology, knowledge, information, and ideas across national boundaries. It is worth noting, however, that India took a gradual approach to liberalisation and globalisation (Ahluwalia, 2002), thereby protecting its economy from global shocks such as the 2008 financial crisis.

Several past studies have investigated the impact of liberalisation and globalisation policies in India,[4] especially in areas such as economic growth, regional or interstate disparities, employment, unemployment, and poverty. Focusing on the effect of globalisation on economic growth, Ahluwalia (2002) reported that India's annual gross domestic product (GDP) growth rate increased from 3.2 % between 1971 and 1981 to 5.7 % from 1998 to 2003. Although this view has been disputed by Nagaraj (2000), subsequent scholars provided ample evidence that GDP growth accelerated during the period following liberalisation and globalisation (Shetty, 2003; Ahmed, 2007; Ahluwalia, 2002a, 2011; Bhandari & Kale, 2019; Panagaria et al., 2014).

While the era of globalisation saw the country's GDP growth rate outpace that of the pre-globalisation period, scholars have expressed concerns about rising inequality among states in per capita net state domestic product (NSDP) growth. Given that states begin with different structural weaknesses and natural resource endowments and often implement varying policy regimes, it is only to be expected that they will exhibit differing growth performances. Whether this contributes to the widening inequality between them is a vital issue for investigation. To investigate this, scholars have examined the hypotheses of 'beta-convergence' and 'sigma-convergence' (Barro & Sala-i-Martin, 1995). Within this context, although some researchers have identified evidence of conditional convergence among Indian states in terms of per capita net state domestic product (PCNSDP) growth rates, the majority have backed the hypothesis of divergence (Dholakia, 1994; Cashin & Sahay, 1996; Bajpai & Sachs, 1996; Marjit & Mitra, 1996; Ahluwalia, 2000; Dasgupta et al., 2000; Aiyar, 2001; Nayyar, 2008; Chikte, 2011; Kumar & Subramanian, 2012; Sanga & Shaban, 2017; Ghosh & Kaustabh, 2025), suggesting an increase in inequality among the states in terms of PCNSDP growth.

There is now a broad consensus that, despite the Indian economy's higher GDP growth rates since the reforms, employment growth has been inadequate, resulting in a period of jobless growth. Data from the quinquennial employment/unemployment surveys and the Periodic Labour Force Survey (PLFS) of 2017–18,

---

[4] In this study, the terms 'economic reforms' and 'liberalisation and globalisation' are employed interchangeably.

conducted by the National Sample Survey Office (NSSO), indicate that India's annual employment growth rate sharply declined after the adoption of economic reforms and globalisation policies. Moreover, there are variations in employment performance across states, arising from differences in NSDP growth, the pace of employment diversification, informal versus formal employment structures, urbanisation, and levels of infrastructural development. The sluggish growth of the manufacturing sector and excessive reliance on informal sector employment have posed challenges in generating stable and higher-quality employment (Sharma, 2024). It has also been observed that rural areas have consistently fallen behind urban areas in employment performance since liberalisation and globalisation, prompting some scholars to describe the situation as a 'setback' (Bhalla, 2007; Chadha, 2001, 2009; Himanshu, 2011).

Moreover, concerns regarding the nature and quality of employment in India persist during the era of globalisation, particularly in rural areas where many workers are self-employed or engage in casual work. According to the latest figures, approximately three-quarters of India's workforce is self-employed, with a significant portion involved in subsistence and low-productivity work. As globalisation has advanced, many producers have gradually adopted strategies that favour informalisation and casual employment, aiming to reduce production costs and compete globally. The presence of casual or contract workers, who are not subject to restrictive labour laws, provides greater flexibility to the labour market (Rajeev, 2006). Consequently, the number of casual and contract labourers in India has increased, particularly since the early 1990s when the country began implementing economic reforms. There is also rising concern regarding the decline of formal jobs in the organised sector and the informalisation of formal employment (Ghose, 2016a, 2016b). According to current statistics, fewer than one in ten employed individuals in India are part of the formal sector (Sharma & Mehta, 2024). Even public sector enterprises have reduced their workforce to alleviate financial pressures resulting from macroeconomic stabilisation policies. This trend has led to a decline in 'white-collar' employment opportunities.

Another significant trend in India following globalisation is the increasing proportion of females in the labour force (Sharma, 2024; IHD-ILO, 2024). However, this growth has primarily taken place in informal and irregular sectors, raising concerns about the quality and stability of such employment (Ghose, 2004; Lingam, 2006). This development may be due to females often accepting lower wages than their male counterparts, enabling employers to cut costs. In addition to examining the gender aspect of employment, researchers have shown growing interest in the composition of the labour force across religious groups, social categories, and age brackets within the context of globalisation. The available data suggest that the employment rate (or worker-population ratio) is highest among Hindus, while Christians experience the highest unemployment rates, followed by Muslims. Similarly, while labour force participation rates are higher for lower-caste groups than for upper-caste groups, the quality of employment they undertake also raises concerns. There is also considerable concern about the low employment rate among young people in India.

While India has consistently maintained high GDP growth rates since adopting globalisation policies, it continues to face widespread unemployment and underemployment. In other words, the employment-generating capacity of higher economic growth during the globalisation era has diminished, as shown by researchers who calculated employment elasticity values. The income elasticity of employment was found to be considerably lower in the post-globalisation era compared to the pre-globalisation era. Therefore, although GDP growth increased, employment growth either declined or failed to keep pace (Bhalla & Hazell, 2003; Islam, 2004). Given these circumstances, it is vital to analyse the employment elasticity using the latest data to understand the employment-promoting effects of the country's recent growth processes, including those at the state level. Such analysis is crucial for making better-informed policy decisions aimed at improving future employment outcomes nationwide.

Against this backdrop, this study aims to shed light on the growth processes in India's economy during the era of globalisation, focusing on whether these growth trajectories can generate employment. By analysing growth trends and employment outcomes at both the national and state levels throughout the globalisation period, and comparing them with the pre-globalisation phase, the study seeks to explore the relationship between economic growth and employment and assess the potential for increased economic growth to create meaningful employment opportunities. What sets this work apart from previous studies is its analysis of growth and employment trends in India and its states over more than forty years, using the latest available data and providing a detailed breakdown by region (rural/urban), sectors, gender, age, education level, and social and religious demographics.

Specifically, this book aims to provide empirical answers to the following research questions, which are crucial for gaining a clear understanding of India's economic and employment dynamics in the context of globalisation: How has the growth performance of the Indian economy during the globalisation period compared with that in the pre-globalisation period? Which sectors or sub-sectors have contributed to higher income growth during the era of globalisation? Have the states in India converged or diverged in terms of economic growth during globalisation? What are the characteristics of the emerging employment scenarios in India? Which sectors or sub-sectors have experienced faster employment growth during globalisation? What is the degree of employment diversification among workers? What are the determinants of employment diversification? How have modes of employment (an indicator of employment quality) changed during the period of globalisation? What determines the workers' choice of mode of employment? Has there been any change in the age composition of workers in the era of globalisation? Have female workers faced discrimination in employment? What accounts for many women abstaining from the labour force in recent years? What has been the employment growth for workers from various social and religious groups during globalisation? What have the values of employment elasticities been in different sectors during globalisation? What are the emerging sectors of the economy that favour employment expansion? What is the relationship between income growth and employment in India? What has been the employment performance of the states when considered separately from the quantitative and qualitative dimensions of employment? What are the implications of current growth processes for the future expansion of productive employment?

1.2 Data Sources and Methodology

Our study relies entirely on secondary data. We examined issues such as income growth, interstate disparity, and sectoral performance using GSDP/NSDP data from the Reserve Bank of India (RBI) from 1980–81 to 2023–24. The analysis of employment-related issues spans the period from 1983 to 2023–24. We utilise data from the reports along with the 'unit-level' data from the employment and unemployment surveys for the 38th (1983), 50th (1993–94), 55th (1990–00), and 68th (2011–12) rounds, conducted by the National Sample Survey Office (NSSO). Additionally, unit-level data from the Periodic Labour Force Surveys (PLFS), also conducted by the NSSO, for 2017–18 and 2023–24 are used.[5] An advantage of the employment data from NSSO surveys is that they have generally utilised a common conceptual framework for estimating the number of employed and unemployed individuals across all their surveys, facilitating inter-temporal comparisons of employment outcomes.[6] Furthermore, unlike the Census of India data,

5 The unit-level data from the PLFS used in this study pertained to the first visits of the surveys.

6 The sample selection methodology differs between the employment/unemployment surveys till 2011–12 and the Periodic Labour Force Surveys since 2017–18. Hence, some scholars have been sceptical about the comparability of these two data sets. However, on closer scrutiny of the data collection methodologies of these surveys, it has been noted that there is no problem with attempting cross-sectional comparisons by regions, states, gender, caste,

the NSSO's estimates of employed individuals or workers are comprehensive and include most workers who contribute to the production of goods and services in the country, thereby alleviating concerns about underestimating any worker group in the context of the NSSO data.[7]

The following methodological aspects of this study are worth noting:

- Firstly, as the GSDP/NSDP data are available at different base year prices, we have reconstructed the series for our entire study period (1980–81 to 2023–24) in 2011–12 base year prices using the 'splicing method'. This has facilitated the inter-temporal comparison of the growth of GSDP/NSDP, which we calculated for various periods.
- Second, the NSSO data on employment and unemployment are available according to three definitions: usual status (US), current weekly status (CWS),[8] and current daily status (CDS).[9] The employed individuals in the US are further categorised into usual principal status (US-PS) workers and usual subsidiary status (US-SS) workers. Those classified as employed according to US-PS are individuals engaged in any economic activity for a relatively longer duration during the 365 days preceding the survey date. In contrast, individuals classified as employed according to the US-SS were categorised as unemployed under the US-PS definition but engaged in some economic activity in a subsidiary capacity. In this study, we have considered data based on the usual principal plus subsidiary status (UPSS) to enhance our understanding of the evolving employment scenarios in India and its states. This is because data based on this concept are considered more helpful for understanding inter-temporal changes in employment characteristics than those derived from a weekly or daily status basis (Chadha, 2000).
- Third, for the analysis, we calculated the absolute numbers of employed (or workers) at our selected time points after adjusting the data obtained from NSSO reports or estimates generated using 'unit-level' data. This is necessary because

---

religious groups, etc. Even a time-series comparison may be attempted for key indicators of employment, especially when considering the rural and urban areas combined and using PLFS data from the survey's first visit (Jajoria and Jatav, 2020; Jatav and Jajoria, 2022).

7 Another limitation of Census data is that it lacks information for the period after 2011, rendering it unsuitable for evaluating recent changes in employment trends in the post-globalisation era.

8 A person is designated as employed as per the CWS concept if he/she was engaged in any economic activity for at least one hour on any day of the week preceding the survey.

9 The CDS concept gives an idea about the level of employment on each day for the week preceding the survey date. A person is designated as employed under CDS on a day if he/she has worked for four hours or more during that day. However, if he/she worked for one hour or more but less than four hours, this is considered a half-day of employment.

NSSO data underestimates the country's population during survey years, and NSSO reports on employment/unemployment provide data in the form of 'rates' – labour force participation rate, workforce participation rate, and unemployment rate. To determine the absolute numbers of employed and unemployed individuals across India and its states, we first calculated population levels at the midpoints of our selected years (i.e., on 1 July 1983, 1 January 1994, 1 January 2000, 1 January 2012, 1 January 2018, and 1 January 2024).[10] For this purpose, we used population data from the reports/website of the Census of India for the years 1981, 1991, 2001 and 2011, as well as the report titled *Population Projections for India and States 2011–2036*, released by the Ministry of Health & Family Welfare, Government of India, New Delhi. Using these data, we calculated the annual compound growth rates of population for the decades between 1980 and 2030, which we subsequently used to estimate, by interpolation, the population figures corresponding to the midpoints of the reference years. After obtaining the population figures, we utilised the NSSO data on the 'rates' to ascertain the absolute numbers in the labour force and workforce, separately for each gender, region, caste, and religion. These absolute figures have been used to calculate growth rates for the pre- and post-globalisation periods, as well as for various sub-periods of the post-globalisation era.

- Fourth, in contrast to studies that consider the population aged 15 and over,[11] this study considers the entire population to understand the changes in employment scenarios. We do this because participation in the labour force and workforce is not necessarily absent for those under fifteen. Moreover, considering the entire population helps to obtain a more complete picture of the subject of our enquiry.
- Fifth, to ensure inter-temporal comparability among the states regarding employment, we adjusted data from 2011–12 onwards. As the states of Jharkhand, Uttarakhand, Chhattisgarh, and Telangana were carved out of Bihar, Uttar Pradesh, Madhya Pradesh, and Andhra Pradesh, respectively, we merged Bihar with Jharkhand, Uttar Pradesh with Uttarakhand, Madhya Pradesh with Chhattisgarh, and Andhra Pradesh with Telangana. These merged states are considered for analysis from 1983 to 2017–18 (Chapters 3–6). However, in Chapter 7, while analysing the most recent changes in employment from 2017–18 to 2023–24, we provided information on the merged and unmerged states.
- Sixth, although this study's reference period extends from 1980–81 to 2023–24, limited by the years of NSSO surveys, the employment issues have been analysed

---

10 The method was first suggested by Sundaram (2001) and followed by subsequent researchers.

11 Recent examples are Sharma & Mehta (2024) and IHD-ILO (2024).

from 1983 to 2023–24. The period before 1993–94 is regarded as pre-globalisation, while the period following 1993–94 is termed post-globalisation. However, in Chapters 3 through 6, we have compared the periods from 1983 to 1993–94 and from 1993–94 to 2017–18, as some striking changes in employment scenarios seem to be emerging after 2017–18.[12] Consequently, we have dedicated a separate chapter (Chapter 7) to provide a thorough overview of employment changes between the 2017–18 and 2023–24 periods.

- Throughout this study, except for 1983, where the NSSO survey's reference period was January to December, the latest calendar year has been reported for all years (for example, 1994 for 1993–94, 2012 for 2011–12, and so on) for brevity.
- Lastly, it is essential to clarify that our study is empirical and aims to understand the changing employment scenarios at the all-India and state levels during the era of globalisation. We will compare these scenarios with those that existed before the adoption of economic reforms and globalisation policies. This approach provides a concrete understanding of how globalisation has transformed the country's employment landscape. The empirical data we used have been analysed rigorously, including the application of statistical and econometric tools where necessary.

[12] For instance, the labour force and workforce participation rates have been rising gradually after 2017–18, especially for females. This marks a departure from the trends observed in the country following liberalisation and globalisation. Of course, to what extent this indicates improvement in the employment situation in the country, especially regarding the generation of productive employment opportunities, becomes an issue for serious investigation.

Economic Growth and Interstate Disparity in India

2.1 Introduction

Following independence, India focused its planning efforts on accelerating economic growth to achieve social and economic development. Policymakers believed that breaking the profoundly entrenched cycle of poverty and inequality, which had resulted from centuries of colonial rule, required the establishment of strong and sustainable economic growth (Bhagwati, 1998). They recognised that merely redistributing income would only offer a temporary solution. The state-led initiatives during this period underperformed, resulting in an average annual growth rate of approximately 3.5 % until the 1970s. However, over the following decades, significant political and economic changes at the national and international levels substantially increased the growth rate. Despite this growth, it proved unsustainable, leading to a severe balance of payments crisis and an external debt trap. Various policies and corrective measures were introduced in the early 1990s under the guidance of the World Bank and the International Monetary Fund to revive the economy during this crisis. These initiatives were part of India's broader efforts to globalise its economy. The aim was to implement substantial structural changes, stimulate sustainable and robust economic growth, and address socio-economic challenges to promote overall development.

Research indicates that the period following the globalisation of the Indian economy, also known as the adoption of economic reform policies since the early 1990s, is characterised by a significantly increased growth rate, as evidenced by studies conducted by Ahluwalia (2000, 2001), Shetty (2003), Ahmed (2007), Kumar & Subramanian (2012), Raju (2012), Rangarajan & Srivastava (2017), Balakrishnan et al. (2021), amongst others. These reforms, which included liberalisation, privatisation, and deregulation, effectively spurred economic activity and led to a surge in gross domestic product growth. However, as time progressed, it became evident that this impressive growth momentum did not align with broader socio-economic objectives, such as poverty alleviation, income equality, and improved living standards for all citizens. This compelled the government to redirect its policies towards fostering pro-poor growth, ensuring that the benefits of economic growth were deliberately and strategically allocated to uplift marginalised and underprivileged groups. However, fulfilling this vision proved challenging in the long term, mainly because of the large scale and diversity of the targeted populations. As a result, India adopted an 'inclusive growth strategy' since the Eleventh Five-Year Plan, a multifaceted approach aimed at involving all social segments in the development process. This strategy emphasised the importance of creating opportunities for everyone to participate in economic activities, especially for those traditionally excluded from the growth narrative. By promoting equitable access to resources, education, skills training, employment opportunities, health, and other essential services, the inclusive growth strategy aimed to ensure that the benefits of economic expansion were broadly shared, thereby fostering a more balanced and sustainable development framework throughout the country.

As economic reform policies were introduced, the economy evolved into a market-driven system with limited government intervention. This change heightened competition and exacerbated inequality among states, regions, and social groups. Research conducted by Bhattacharya & Sakthivel (2004), Ramaswamy (2007), Kar & Sakthivel (2007), Bakshi et al. (2015), Ghose (2023), Bharti et al. (2024), among others, has established clear evidence of increasing inequality across various states and segments of the population. Furthermore, by using the neoclassical growth model as a guiding framework, researchers have employed statistical methods to examine whether growth rates across states converge or diverge. In the early years following the reforms, two notable studies by Cashin & Sahay (1996) and Nagaraj et al. (1997) provided evidence of convergence. In contrast, later research by Marjit and Mitra (1996), Ghosh et al. (1998), Rao et al. (1999), Dasgupta et al. (2000), and Sanga & Shaban (2017) indicated a clear divergence among Indian states.

Given the vastness and diversity of the Indian economy, a comprehensive investigation into issues related to reform-driven growth at both aggregate and disaggregate levels, utilising recent data, is essential. This chapter analyses the gross domestic product (GDP), net state domestic product (NSDP), and per capita NSDP (PCNSDP) data available from the Reserve Bank of India (RBI) website to examine the growth dynamics of the Indian economy and its major states from 1981 to 2024, focusing mainly on the post-globalisation period. We aim to identify the sectors and sub-sectors that influence changes in income growth, if any, at the national level and within individual states. Additionally, we assess the extent of interstate disparity and explore whether there is regional convergence or divergence in the growth rates of per capita net state domestic product, while identifying factors that explain the disparities in PCNSDP between states.

Using the 'splicing method', the entire series of the NSDP and PCNSDP has been adjusted to a base of 2011–12 at constant prices. The growth rates have been estimated by fitting two-kink exponential or simple exponential models, following the methodology developed by Boyce (1987). In this chapter, the period from 1981 to 1993 is referred to as the pre-globalisation period, and the period from 1994 to 2024 is the post-globalisation period. The post-globalisation period has been divided into two sub-periods, 1994–2011 and 2012–2024, to determine whether growth performance has changed over time during the post-globalisation phase.[1]

2.2 Growth of Net State Domestic Product (NSDP)

Economic growth refers to the increase in the market value of goods and services produced by a nation over a specific period. Although it does not fully capture the population's overall well-being, it provides insights into the nation's economic conditions. Table 1 illustrates economic growth by showing the growth rates of NSDP in India and the individual states during the pre- and post-globalisation periods. During the pre-globalisation period (1981–1993), the national GDP growth rate was 4.93 %, significantly higher than the average 3.5 % growth rate experienced during the first three decades following independence, commonly referred to as the 'Hindu rate of growth'. Between 1981 and 1993, the state with the highest growth rate was Maharashtra, at 6.07 %. Other states that achieved growth rates above the national average included Rajasthan (5.82 %), Andhra Pradesh (5.42 %), Tamil Nadu (5.04 %), and Haryana (4.97 %). Conversely, the state with the lowest growth rate was Bihar (1.88 %), while additional states that exhibited low growth rates during this period included Odisha (2.59 %), Jammu & Kashmir (2.59 %), Assam (2.82 %), and Kerala (3.36 %).

---

1 The selected periods for growth calculation are based on our analysis of India's GDP series, which identifies 1993 and 2012 as two trend-breaking years within the series spanning from 1981 to 2024.

Table 1: Annual Growth Rates of NSDP in Major States

State	1981–1993		1994–2011		2012–2024		1994–2024		1981–2024	
	Gr. Rate	Rank	Gr. Rate	Rank	Gr. Rate	Rank	Gr. Rate	Rank	Gr. Rate	Rank
Andhra Pradesh	5.42	3	6.13	9	6.40	8	6.24	7	6.00	5
Assam	2.82	14	3.53	20	6.79	6	4.88	18	4.28	15
Bihar	1.88	17	5.42	11	6.35	9	5.80	11	4.66	14
Gujarat	4.78	7	7.63	1	8.87	1	8.14	1	7.16	1
Haryana	4.97	5	7.38	2	6.82	4	7.15	2	6.51	2
Himachal Pradesh	4.65	8	6.90	4	5.86	11	6.47	4	5.94	6
Jammu & Kashmir	2.59	15	4.83	17	4.15	18	4.55	19	3.98	17
Karnataka	4.60	9	6.29	7	6.58	7	6.41	6	5.88	7
Kerala	3.36	13	4.53	19	4.08	19	4.34	20	4.06	16
Madhya Pradesh	4.05	11	5.31	14	6.97	2	6.00	8	5.43	8
Maharashtra	6.07	1	7.17	3	5.43	14	6.45	5	6.34	3
Odisha	2.59	16	5.34	13	6.80	5	5.94	9	4.96	11
Punjab	4.53	10	4.96	16	5.33	15	5.11	15	4.94	12
Rajasthan	5.82	2	5.41	12	4.53	16	5.04	16	5.27	9
Tamil Nadu	5.04	4	6.90	5	6.83	3	6.87	3	6.34	4
Uttar Pradesh	3.88	12	4.56	18	5.67	13	5.02	17	4.69	13
West Bengal	4.93	6	6.18	8	3.90	20	5.24	14	5.15	10
Jharkhand	–	–	5.04	15	5.81	12	5.36	13	–	–
Chhattisgarh	–	–	5.49	10	6.23	10	5.80	12	–	–
Uttarakhand	–	–	6.84	6	4.41	17	5.83	10	–	–
Telangana	–	–	–	–	6.52	–	–	–	–	–
Major States (NSDP)	4.90		6.32		5.62		6.03		6.18	
All-India (GDP)	4.93		6.29		5.85		6.11		5.91	

Source: Author's computation using NSDP data for the states and GDP data for India, obtained from the RBI website.

Notes: (i) Growth rates for 1981–1993, 1994–2011 and 2012–2024 are computed by fitting the two-kink exponential model; (ii) growth rates for 1994–2024 are weighted averages of growth rates of 1994–2011 and 2012–2024; (iii) growth rates for 1981–2024 are weighted averages of previous three sub-periods; and (iv) for Telangana, the growth rate, computed by fitting an exponential function, refers to 2005–2024.

Adopting macroeconomic stabilisation programmes and policies that induced structural changes in the early 1990s marked the beginning of the post-globalisation era, raising the country's GDP growth rate to 6.29 % between 1994 and 2011. All states, except Rajasthan, experienced higher growth rates in NSDP than in the pre-globalisation period (1981–1993). During this period (1994–2011), Gujarat recorded the highest NSDP growth rate at 7.63 %. Other states that recorded NSDP growth rates higher than the national average during this period include Haryana (7.38 %), Maharashtra (7.17 %), Himachal Pradesh (6.90 %), Tamil Nadu (6.90 %), and Uttarakhand (6.84 %). However, the growth rate of NSDP was the lowest in Assam (3.53 %) during this period; other relatively low-growth states, with growth rates below 5.0 %, include Kerala, Uttar Pradesh, Jammu & Kashmir, and Punjab.

In the second sub-period of the post-globalisation era (2012–2024), India's GDP growth declined to 5.85 % per annum.[2] However, eleven states showed an improvement in NSDP growth rates during this period, while nine states registered a decline. During this period, Gujarat (8.87 %) remained the leading state in NSDP growth, while West Bengal (3.90 %) remained at the bottom. Other states that recorded impressive (more than 6.0 %) NSDP growth are Madhya Pradesh (6.97 %), Tamil Nadu (6.83 %), Haryana (6.82 %), Odisha (6.80 %), Assam (6.79 %), Karnataka (6.58 %), Andhra Pradesh (6.40 %), Bihar (6.35 %), and Chhattisgarh (6.23 %). On the other hand, some other states reporting relatively low (less than 5.0 %) NSDP growth include Kerala (4.08 %), Jammu & Kashmir (4.15 %), Uttarakhand (4.41 %), and Rajasthan (4.53 %).

Throughout the post-globalisation period (1994–2024), India's annual GDP growth rate stands at 6.11 %, 1.18 percentage points higher than its pre-globalisation level. It is also encouraging to note that all states except Rajasthan recorded higher growth rates in NSDP during the post-globalisation period

---

2 This development occurred in the aftermath of the global financial crisis of 2008, which may have had a delayed impact on the Indian economy. However, due to restrictions on the Indian banking sector and the influx of foreign capital into the capital account, the economy grew at an impressive 5.85 % during this period. This growth rate was among the highest in the world, second only to China's, leading some commentators to refer to China and India as the 'dragon' and 'elephant' of the global economy. The occurrence of the COVID-19 pandemic towards the end of this sub-period also hindered the country's GDP growth during this period.

(1994–2024) than during the pre-globalisation period (1981–1993). From 1994 to 2024, the highest NSDP growth was recorded in Gujarat (8.14 %), followed by Haryana (7.15 %), Tamil Nadu (6.87 %), Himachal Pradesh (6.47 %), Maharashtra (6.45 %), Karnataka (6.41 %), and Andhra Pradesh (6.24 %). In these states, the growth rates exceeded the national average. Conversely, NSDP growth during 1994–2024 was the lowest in Kerala (4.34 %), while two other states, Jammu & Kashmir and Assam, recorded NSDP growth below 5.0 %.

The above analysis indicates that globalisation has enhanced the growth performance of the Indian economy, and all states (except Rajasthan) are experiencing higher growth rates compared to the pre-globalisation era, although the extent varies. However, the growth benefits of globalisation have been more evident in states such as Gujarat, Tamil Nadu, Maharashtra, and Haryana, which are renowned for their industrial development. In examining the factors driving this significant growth during the post-globalisation period, some researchers have emphasised the roles of increased productivity and investment in states that have experienced more substantial growth (see, for example, Goldar & Mitra, 2002; Rodrick & Subramaniam, 2004; Rangarajan & Srivastava, 2017).

2.3 Growth of Per Capita Net State Domestic Product

The per capita net state domestic product (PCNSDP) reflects the average economic production for each individual in a given state, considering the net worth of goods and services generated within the state's boundaries. In addition to examining the growth rate of NSDP, an analysis of per capita NSDP is necessary, as it provides an index for comparing the extent of economic prosperity across states and for assessing changes in inter-temporal economic stability within a given state. Table 2 indicates that, at the all-India level, per capita net national product (NNP) growth has significantly improved from 2.68 % in the pre-globalisation period to 4.38 % during the post-globalisation period. Even at the state level, PCNSDP growth rates have improved across all states in the post-globalisation period, with Bihar, Odisha, Jammu & Kashmir, Gujarat, and Assam demonstrating more than a 3.0 percentage-point improvement. During the post-globalisation period, Bihar recorded the most impressive improvement in PCNSDP growth, rising by 4.4 percentage points, while Punjab recorded the smallest, increasing by 0.88 percentage points.

Table 2: Annual Growth Rates of Per Capita NSDP in Major States

	1981–1993		1994–2011		2012–2024		1994–2024		1981–2024	
State	Gr. Rate	Rank	Gr. Rate	Rank	Gr. Rate	Rank	Gr. Rate	Rank	Gr. Rate	Rank
Andhra Pradesh	3.22	5	5.09	8	5.83	5	5.40	6	4.76	4
Assam	0.52	15	2.01	20	5.74	6	3.55	16	2.67	16
Bihar	-0.41	17	3.35	14	4.90	11	3.99	14	2.70	15
Gujarat	2.85	6	5.87	4	7.59	1	6.58	1	5.49	1
Haryana	2.47	10	5.25	7	5.55	8	5.37	7	4.52	8
Himachal Pradesh	2.68	7	5.37	6	5.22	9	5.31	8	4.54	7
Jammu & Kashmir	-0.14	16	2.87	17	3.68	20	3.21	20	2.23	17
Karnataka	3.42	3	5.09	9	6.23	3	5.56	4	4.93	3
Kerala	2.51	9	6.07	2	4.59	14	5.46	5	4.59	6
Madhya Pradesh	1.64	13	3.35	15	5.58	7	4.27	12	3.50	11
Maharashtra	3.71	1	5.45	5	4.52	15	5.07	9	4.67	5
Odisha	0.70	14	4.00	11	5.98	4	4.82	10	3.61	10
Punjab	2.61	8	3.13	16	4.01	19	3.49	17	3.24	12
Rajasthan	3.37	4	4.04	10	4.63	13	4.28	11	4.02	9
Tamil Nadu	3.67	2	6.03	3	6.34	2	6.16	3	5.43	2
Uttar Pradesh	1.74	12	2.66	19	4.26	17	3.32	18	2.86	14
West Bengal	1.99	11	2.75	18	4.13	18	3.32	19	2.93	13
Jharkhand	–	–	3.36	13	4.38	16	3.78	15	–	–
Chhattisgarh	–	–	3.71	12	4.74	12	4.14	13	–	–
Uttarakhand	–	–	7.48	1	4.98	10	6.45	2	–	–
Telangana	–	–	–	–	6.03	–	6.49	–	–	–
All-India (NNP)	2.68		4.43		4.31		4.38		4.04	

Source: Same as Table 1.
Note: Same as Table 1.

The examination of PCNSDP growth rates across sub-periods of the post-globalisation era reveals that between 1994 and 2011, Uttarakhand (7.48 %) and Assam (2.01 %) recorded the highest and lowest growth rates, respectively. Additionally, aside from Uttarakhand, eight other states recorded a growth rate of more than 5.0 % per annum in PCNSDP during this sub-period: Kerala, Tamil Nadu, Gujarat,

Maharashtra, Himachal Pradesh, Haryana, Andhra Pradesh, and Karnataka. In the subsequent sub-period, from 2012 to 2024, Gujarat led with a PCNSDP growth rate of 7.59 %, while Jammu and Kashmir had the lowest rate at 3.68 %. Alongside Gujarat, the other states that maintained a growth rate exceeding 5.0 % during this period include Tamil Nadu, Karnataka, Telangana, Odisha, Andhra Pradesh, Assam, Madhya Pradesh, Haryana, and Himachal Pradesh. It is noteworthy that sixteen states improved their PCNSDP growth rates in the second sub-period compared to the first, while four states (Uttarakhand, Kerala, Maharashtra, and Himachal Pradesh) did not sustain their growth momentum, thus recording reduced PCNSDP growth rates in the second sub-period relative to the first. However, among the states that recorded improved growth rates in the second sub-period of the post-globalisation era are both the formerly backward (BIMARU) states and the more developed ones.

2.4 Growth Scenarios Across Various Production Sectors

The country's economy can be divided into nine sectors: agriculture and allied activities; mining and quarrying; manufacturing (both registered and unregistered); electricity, gas, water supply, and other utility services; construction; trade, hotels, and restaurants; transport, storage, and communication, financial, real estate, and professional services; and public administration. These sectors can be categorised into three broad groups: primary, secondary, and tertiary. The primary sector comprises agriculture and other allied activities such as forestry, logging, and fishing. The secondary sector includes mining and quarrying, manufacturing, electricity, gas, water supply, other utility services, and construction. Conversely, the tertiary sector encompasses transport, storage, communication, trade, hotels and restaurants, financial services, real estate, professional services, and public administration.

Tables 3 and 4 illustrate each sector's contribution to the economy and the growth rates before and after globalisation. As shown in Table 3, the share of 'agriculture and allied activities' in gross value added (GVA) has declined significantly between 1981 and 2024. From 41.2 % of the GVA in 1981, this sector's share decreased to 14.5 % by 2024. This decline is accompanied by an increase in the share of GVA for all non-agricultural sectors except 'mining and quarrying' and 'transport, storage, and communication'. Among the non-agricultural sectors, the most significant increase in the share of GVA has occurred in the 'financial, real estate, and professional services' sector, which rose from 11.1 % in 1981 to 23.3 % in 2024. Next is 'manufacturing', which increased its share of GVA from 13.8 % in 1981 to 17.3 % in 2024. The secondary sector as a whole experienced an increase from 27.1 % to 30.9 % between 1981 and 2024. Meanwhile, the tertiary sector experienced a significant rise, from 31.7 % in 1981 to 54.6 % by 2024. The tertiarisation of the economy has progressed more rapidly in India over the past four and a half decades, particularly during the period of globalisation.

Table 3: Contribution of Major Production Sectors to Gross Value Added (GVA) in India (%)

Year	Agriculture & allied activities (Primary)	Mining & quarrying	Manufacturing	Electricity, gas, water supply & other utility services	Construction	Secondary	Trade, hotels & restaurants	Transport, storage & communication	Financial, real estate & professional services	Public administration	Tertiary
1981	41.2	4.0	13.8	1.6	7.7	27.1	2.1	9.0	11.1	9.6	31.7
1982	40.6	4.3	14.1	1.6	7.7	27.7	2.1	8.9	11.3	9.2	31.6
1983	39.4	4.7	14.2	1.7	7.0	27.5	2.2	9.1	12.0	9.7	33.1
1984	40.1	4.5	14.4	1.6	6.8	27.4	2.2	8.8	12.2	9.3	32.5
1985	39.3	4.4	14.5	1.8	6.8	27.4	2.3	8.8	12.6	9.7	33.4
1986	37.9	4.4	14.4	1.8	6.9	27.5	2.4	9.1	13.2	9.9	34.6
1987	36.2	4.8	14.5	1.9	6.8	28.0	2.5	9.2	13.9	10.2	35.9
1988	34.4	4.8	14.8	2.0	6.9	28.5	2.6	9.4	14.5	10.6	37.1
1989	35.9	5.0	14.5	2.0	6.7	28.2	2.3	9.1	14.3	10.2	35.9
1990	34.3	5.1	14.9	2.1	6.7	28.8	2.3	9.3	14.9	10.4	36.9
1991	33.8	5.3	14.8	2.1	7.1	29.4	2.3	9.2	15.1	10.2	36.9
1992	32.6	5.4	14.3	2.3	7.2	29.1	2.4	9.2	16.3	10.3	38.3
1993	33.1	5.2	14.0	2.3	7.0	28.5	2.4	9.2	16.5	10.4	38.5
1994	32.4	5.0	14.4	2.3	6.7	28.4	2.5	9.4	17.2	10.2	39.3
1995	31.9	5.2	15.0	2.4	6.7	29.2	2.5	9.7	16.8	9.8	38.9
1996	29.8	5.1	16.2	2.4	6.6	30.4	2.8	10.3	17.0	9.9	39.9

(Continued)

Table 3. *(Continued)*

Year	Agriculture & allied activities (Primary)	Mining & quar-rying	Manu-facturing	Electricity, gas, water supply & other utility services	Cons-truction	Secondary	Trade, hotels & restau-rants	Transport, storage & commu-nication	Financial, real estate & profes-sional services	Public admini-stration	Tertiary
1997	30.4	4.8	16.6	2.4	6.3	30.0	2.8	10.4	16.7	9.8	39.6
1998	28.5	5.1	15.9	2.4	6.7	30.1	2.9	10.6	17.6	10.3	41.4
1999	28.5	4.9	15.4	2.5	6.7	29.4	3.1	10.6	17.8	10.7	42.1
2000	27.1	4.7	15.1	2.4	6.7	28.9	3.4	10.8	18.7	11.1	44.0
2001	26.1	4.7	15.6	2.4	6.8	29.4	3.7	10.9	18.8	11.1	44.5
2002	26.3	4.5	15.1	2.3	6.8	28.7	4.1	11.0	19.0	11.0	45.0
2003	23.8	4.7	15.7	2.3	7.1	29.8	4.5	11.3	19.6	11.0	46.4
2004	24.1	4.5	15.5	2.3	7.4	29.7	4.8	11.5	19.2	10.7	46.2
2005	22.6	4.6	15.6	2.3	8.1	30.5	5.2	11.6	19.4	10.8	46.9
2006	21.9	4.5	15.7	2.2	8.4	30.9	5.3	11.6	19.6	10.7	47.2
2007	20.9	4.3	17.2	2.2	8.6	32.4	5.4	11.8	19.5	10.2	46.8
2008	20.5	4.2	17.1	2.3	9.0	32.5	5.5	11.6	19.5	10.3	47.0
2009	19.6	3.9	17.1	2.3	9.1	32.4	5.5	11.2	19.7	11.5	47.9
2010	18.2	3.9	17.8	2.3	9.1	33.0	5.7	11.0	19.6	12.5	48.8
2011	18.3	4.1	17.8	2.2	8.9	33.0	6.1	11.2	19.0	12.4	48.7
2012	20.1	3.5	18.8	2.5	10.4	35.2	6.8	12.1	11.8	14.0	44.7

(Continued)

Table 3. *(Continued)*

Year	Agriculture & allied activities (Primary)	Mining & quarrying	Manufacturing	Electricity, gas, water supply & other utility services	Construction	Secondary	Trade, hotels & restaurants	Transport, storage & communication	Financial, real estate & professional services	Public administration	Tertiary
2013	19.2	3.3	18.8	2.4	9.8	34.3	7.1	12.4	12.4	14.5	46.5
2014	19.1	3.1	18.6	2.4	9.5	33.6	7.4	12.2	12.3	15.3	47.3
2015	16.5	3.0	17.3	2.2	8.6	31.1	7.2	11.4	21.4	12.4	52.4
2016	15.4	3.0	18.2	2.1	8.3	31.6	7.4	11.6	21.9	12.2	53.0
2017	15.2	3.1	18.1	2.2	8.1	31.5	7.7	11.3	22.0	12.3	53.3
2018	15.3	2.7	18.4	2.3	8.0	31.4	10.4	9.3	21.1	12.6	53.3
2019	14.8	2.6	18.3	2.3	8.1	31.2	11.2	8.8	21.3	12.8	54.0
2020	15.1	2.4	17.1	2.3	7.9	29.6	11.5	8.9	21.9	13.1	55.3
2021	16.4	2.3	18.4	2.3	7.9	30.8	9.5	7.4	23.3	12.6	52.9
2022	15.6	2.2	18.5	2.3	8.6	31.6	9.7	8.2	22.5	12.4	52.8
2023	15.4	2.1	16.9	2.4	8.8	30.2	10.0	8.7	23.0	12.7	54.4
2024	14.5	2.1	17.3	2.4	9.1	30.9	9.8	8.9	23.3	12.7	54.6

Source: Reserve Bank of India

Table 4: Growth Rates of Major Production Sectors in India

Sector	Annual Growth rate during				
	1981–1993	**1994–2011**	**2012–2024**	**1994–2024**	**1981–2024**
Agriculture & allied activities **(Primary)**	3.21	2.72	3.98	3.24	3.09
Mining & quarrying	6.98	4.00	0.87	2.70	3.97
Manufacturing	5.21	7.05	5.95	6.59	6.44
Electricity, gas, water supply & other utility services	8.46	5.72	6.05	5.86	6.36
Construction	3.67	7.99	5.05	6.77	6.46
Secondary	5.32	6.75	5.26	6.13	6.13
Transport, storage & communication	5.68	7.35	2.44	5.32	5.97
Trade, hotels & restaurants	5.72	11.64	9.94	10.94	10.04
Financial, real estate & professional services	8.96	5.79	8.54	6.93	7.03
Public administration	5.20	7.17	6.26	6.79	6.57
Tertiary	6.79	7.16	6.93	7.06	7.03

Source: Same as Table 2
Note: Same as Table 1

Table 4 presents the growth rates of various production sectors across different periods. Agriculture and allied activities experienced a decline in growth rate during the initial phase of the post-globalisation period (1994–2011) compared to the pre-globalisation phase (1981–1993). As shown in the table, the annual growth rate in this sector decreased from 3.21 % in the previous period to 2.72 % in the later period. However, agriculture and allied activities improved their growth rate during the second phase of globalisation, reaching 3.98 %, close to the 4.0 % target set at the beginning of the Twelfth Five-Year Plan. Moreover, when comparing the pre-globalisation period with the whole post-globalisation period, it is noted that the growth rate of agriculture and allied activities was marginally higher (3.24 %) in the latter period than in the former.

Table 4 further indicates that, during 1994–2011, the highest growth was achieved in 'trade, hotels, and restaurants' (11.64 %), followed by 'construction'

(7.99 %), 'transport, storage, and communication' (7.35 %), 'public administration' (7.17 %), and 'manufacturing' (7.05 %). All these sectors experienced higher growth rates than in the pre-globalisation period (1981–1993). However, in the second phase of the globalisation era, all sectors, except 'agriculture and allied activities', 'electricity, gas, water supply, and other utility services', and 'financial, real estate, and professional services' experienced a decline in growth rates compared to the first phase of the globalisation period. In this latter phase, the highest growth was once again recorded by 'trade, hotels, and restaurants' (9.94 %), followed by 'financial, real estate, and professional services' (8.54 %), 'public administration' (6.26 %), 'electricity, gas, water supply and other utility services' (6.05 %), 'manufacturing' (5.95 %), and 'construction' (5.05 %). A comparison of the pre-globalisation period with the entire globalisation period reveals that all non-agricultural sectors, aside from 'mining and quarrying', 'electricity, gas, water supply, other utility services', 'transport, storage, and communication', and 'financial, real estate and professional services' experienced higher growth rates in the latter period than in the former. The most impressive growth performance from 1994 to 2024 is demonstrated by the 'trade, hotels, and restaurants' sector, which expanded at nearly 11 % annually. Other sectors achieving notable output growth of over 6.0 % during the same period include 'financial services, real estate, professional services', 'public administration', 'construction', and 'manufacturing'. Another vital point to note is that, as expected, the tertiary sector's output has grown at a higher rate in both the pre- and post-globalisation periods than the secondary sector's. This explains why the tertiary sector contributed nearly 55 % of the country's GVA in 2024.

Focusing on the individual states (Table 5), it is evident that ten states experienced a decline in the primary sector's output growth rate during the first part of globalisation (1994–2011) compared to the pre-globalisation period (1981–1993). These states comprise a mix of developed and underdeveloped states. While Jharkhand recorded the highest growth rate in the primary sector during the first phase of globalisation, at 5.81 %, Kerala experienced the lowest, at −0.91 %. The situation changed in the second phase of globalisation (2012–2024) when thirteen out of twenty states reported higher output growth rates for the primary sector than in the first part of globalisation. The most notable achievement during this period was recorded by Madhya Pradesh, with a primary sector output growth rate of 8.22 %, followed by Andhra Pradesh, Chhattisgarh, and Tamil Nadu, all of which recorded output growth rates of over 5.0 % in this sector. However, Kerala continued to experience the lowest and most negative growth in this sector during the second part of globalisation. Among the seventeen states we considered from 1981 to 2024, eight saw an improvement in their primary sector growth rates between 1994 and 2024 compared to the period from 1981 to 1993. Among these states, the most impressive improvement in the growth rate of primary sector output occurred in Gujarat (3.32 percentage points), followed by Andhra Pradesh (3.19 percentage points), Bihar (3.03 percentage points), Odisha (2.89 percentage points), Madhya Pradesh (2.83 percentage points), Jammu and Kashmir (1.35 percentage points), Assam (0.83 percentage points), and Himachal Pradesh (0.49 percentage points). However, from 1994 to 2024, Andhra Pradesh recorded the highest growth in primary sector output, at 5.36 %, while Kerala recorded the lowest growth, at –1.08 %.

Regarding the secondary sector, Table 5 indicates that most states experienced higher output growth rates during the first sub-period of the post-globalisation era than during the pre-globalisation period. During the first sub-period of the post-globalisation era, Himachal Pradesh recorded the highest growth rate (8.91 %) in secondary-sector output, while Assam recorded the lowest (0.67 %). Other states that recorded impressive growth (more than 6 %) in secondary sector output during this period include Uttarakhand (8.27 %), Gujarat (7.56 %), Punjab (7.03 %), Madhya Pradesh (7.02 %), and Karnataka (6.20 %). The ranking of states by secondary sector output growth during the second sub-period of the post-globalisation era changed, with Gujarat recording the highest growth of 10.18 % and Rajasthan the lowest at 3.03 %. During this sub-period, other states demonstrating impressive growth in secondary sector output include Bihar (9.03 %), Assam (8.83 %), Himachal Pradesh (6.93 %), Tamil Nadu (6.87 %), Haryana (6.47 %), and Uttar Pradesh (6.29 %). It is also evident from Table 5 that eleven states (out of twenty considered) improved their growth rates of secondary sector output during the second sub-period of the post-globalisation period compared to the first. It is indeed encouraging to note that the improvement in the growth rate of secondary sector output between these sub-periods has been more pronounced in less developed states such as Assam, Bihar, and Odisha (each recording an increase of more than 4.0 percentage points) compared to Gujarat (3.81 percentage points).

Table 5: Growth Rates of Sectoral NSDP in Major States

Sector	State	1981–1993		1994–2011		2012–2024		1994–2024		1981–2024	
		Gr. Rate	Rank	Gr. Rate	Rank	Gr. Rate	Rank	Gr. Rate	Rank	Gr. Rate	Rank
Primary	Andhra Pradesh	2.17	11	3.69	3	7.72	2	5.36	1	4.22	1
	Assam	1.92	12	1.54	17	4.46	9	2.75	12	2.24	15
	Bihar	0.13	16	2.89	7	3.55	13	3.16	10	2.45	12
	Gujarat	0.93	15	3.98	2	4.63	6	4.25	4	3.47	5
	Haryana	4.23	5	2.52	10	3.62	12	2.98	11	3.11	7
	Himachal Pradesh	1.86	13	2.42	11	2.24	15	2.35	16	2.27	14
	Jammu & Kashmir	1.23	14	3.11	5	1.82	16	2.58	15	2.44	13
	Karnataka	3.69	8	2.23	12	4.63	7	3.22	9	3.04	8
	Kerala	4.01	7	–0.91	20	–1.32	20	–1.08	20	0.04	17
	Madhya Pradesh	2.28	10	2.92	6	8.22	1	5.11	2	3.90	3
	Maharashtra	4.39	4	2.87	8	4.58	8	3.58	6	3.55	4
	Odisha	–0.14	17	1.65	16	4.31	10	2.75	13	1.83	16
	Punjab	4.74	2	1.91	14	1.71	18	1.83	18	2.46	11
	Rajasthan	4.21	6	3.19	4	4.83	5	3.88	5	4.16	2
	Tamil Nadu	4.57	3	1.45	19	5.90	4	3.29	8	3.04	8
	Uttar Pradesh	2.83	9	2.21	13	3.49	14	2.74	14	2.61	10
	West Bengal	5.89	1	2.64	9	1.77	17	2.28	17	3.14	6
	Jharkhand	–	–	5.81	1	3.73	11	4.95	3	–	–
	Chhattisgarh	–	–	1.71	15	6.02	3	3.49	7	–	–
	Uttarakhand	–	–	1.54	18	0.84	19	1.25	19	–	–
	Telangana	–	–	–	–	–	–	4.53	–	–	–

(Continued)

Table 5. *(Continued)*

Sector	State	1981–1993		1994–2011		2012–2024		1994–2024		1981–2024	
		Gr. Rate	Rank	Gr. Rate	Rank	Gr. Rate	Rank	Gr. Rate	Rank	Gr. Rate	Rank
Secondary	Andhra Pradesh	7.20	3	5.40	10	4.64	14	5.09	12	5.62	6
	Assam	3.61	15	0.67	20	8.83	3	4.05	17	3.01	16
	Bihar	1.64	17	4.64	13	9.03	2	6.46	4	4.93	12
	Gujarat	3.75	14	7.56	3	10.18	1	8.64	1	7.31	2
	Haryana	4.34	13	5.50	9	6.47	6	5.90	7	5.46	9
	Himachal Pradesh	8.45	1	8.91	1	6.93	4	8.09	2	8.40	1
	Jammu & Kashmir	6.04	5	1.73	18	5.02	11	3.09	19	3.33	15
	Karnataka	4.93	10	6.20	6	5.70	9	5.41	9	5.51	7
	Kerala	4.95	9	5.55	8	4.63	15	5.17	11	5.23	11
	Madhya Pradesh	4.59	11	7.02	5	4.59	16	6.01	6	6.00	5
	Maharashtra	5.67	7	4.76	12	4.12	17	4.50	16	4.82	13
	Odisha	6.02	6	1.04	19	5.17	10	2.75	20	2.95	17
	Punjab	5.41	8	7.03	4	4.76	13	6.09	5	6.22	4
	Rajasthan	7.44	2	5.87	7	3.03	20	4.68	15	6.44	3
	Tamil Nadu	7.18	4	4.35	15	6.87	5	5.39	10	5.48	8
	Uttar Pradesh	4.44	12	5.16	11	6.29	7	5.63	8	5.25	10
	West Bengal	2.22	16	4.53	14	4.96	12	4.71	14	4.13	14
	Jharkhand	–	–	2.81	17	3.91	19	3.27	18	–	–
	Chhattisgarh	–	–	4.35	16	5.79	8	4.95	13	–	–
	Uttarakhand	–	–	8.27	2	4.11	18	6.53	3	–	–
	Telangana	–	–	–	–	–	–	4.12	–	–	–

(Continued)

Table 5. *(Continued)*

Sector	State	1981–1993		1994–2011		2012–2024		1994–2024		1981–2024	
		Gr. Rate	Rank	Gr. Rate	Rank	Gr. Rate	Rank	Gr. Rate	Rank	Gr. Rate	Rank
Tertiary	Andhra Pradesh	5.87	2	8.19	6	6.29	11	7.40	6	7.30	4
	Assam	3.73	14	5.61	19	5.23	17	5.45	18	5.14	15
	Bihar	3.19	15	7.03	10	6.58	7	6.84	9	6.13	10
	Gujarat	5.12	5	8.34	4	7.75	1	8.10	2	7.54	1
	Haryana	4.80	7	8.38	3	7.53	2	8.03	3	7.45	2
	Himachal Pradesh	3.94	12	6.23	14	5.89	13	6.09	15	5.68	13
	Jammu & Kashmir	2.78	16	6.23	15	3.92	20	5.27	20	5.02	16
	Karnataka	5.53	4	8.05	7	7.38	3	7.77	4	7.38	3
	Kerala	3.93	13	7.14	9	5.79	14	6.58	11	6.50	8
	Madhya Pradesh	4.99	6	5.93	16	6.47	8	6.15	14	5.85	12
	Maharashtra	5.59	3	6.91	11	6.18	12	6.61	10	6.48	9
	Odisha	4.31	9	6.85	13	5.37	15	6.24	13	6.01	11
	Punjab	2.07	17	4.95	20	6.45	9	5.57	17	4.66	17
	Rajasthan	6.30	1	7.23	8	5.33	16	6.43	12	6.67	7
	Tamil Nadu	3.97	11	8.23	5	6.67	6	7.58	5	7.01	5
	Uttar Pradesh	4.04	10	5.67	18	6.45	10	5.99	16	5.49	14
	West Bengal	4.46	8	8.84	2	4.05	19	6.86	8	6.91	6
	Jharkhand	–	–	6.89	12	7.37	4	7.09	7	–	–
	Chhattisgarh	–	–	5.75	17	5.02	18	5.45	19	–	–
	Uttarakhand	–	–	9.62	1	7.03	5	8.55	1	–	–
	Telangana	–	–	–	–	–	–	8.38	–	–	–

Source: Same as Table 2

Note: Growth rates are determined by fitting an exponential function to the data.

However, when considering the entire post-globalisation period (1994–2024), Table 5 shows that Gujarat topped the list of states for growth in secondary sector output, while Odisha remained at the bottom. The other states that experienced over 6.0 % growth in secondary sector output during the post-globalisation period from 1994 to 2024 include Himachal Pradesh, Uttarakhand, Bihar, Punjab, and Madhya Pradesh. Furthermore, ten of the seventeen states for which data are available from 1981 to 2024 improved their secondary-sector output growth rates between 1994 and 2024 compared to the period from 1981 to 1993. Notably, the most significant improvement in this growth rate has been in Gujarat (4.89 percentage points), followed by Bihar (4.82 percentage points), a less developed state.

Regarding growth in the tertiary sector, all states showed improvement during the first sub-period of the post-globalisation era compared to the pre-globalisation era. Uttarakhand recorded the highest growth in this sector during this sub-period at 9.62 %, while Punjab recorded the lowest at 4.95 %. Furthermore, it appears that the increase in the growth rate of this sector during this sub-period is significant not only compared to the pre-globalisation period in most states, but also that it surpassed 6.0 % in three-fourths of the states for which growth calculations have been conducted. In the second sub-period of the post-globalisation era, the growth rates of the tertiary sector declined in most states compared to the previous sub-period. However, they continued to exceed the growth rates observed during the pre-globalisation period in all states except Rajasthan and West Bengal. Gujarat recorded the highest growth in tertiary sector output during this second sub-period, at 7.75 %, while Jammu & Kashmir recorded the lowest, at 3.92 %. Comparing the pre- and post-globalisation periods, it can be concluded that all states in India experienced significantly higher growth in tertiary-sector output in the latter period than in the former. This is evident from the fact that sixteen of the twenty states achieved growth of more than 6.0 % in tertiary sector output from 1994 to 2024. The state with the highest growth rate in the tertiary sector during this period is Uttarakhand, at 8.55 %, while Jammu & Kashmir ranks last at 5.27 %. The tertiarisation of economies has progressed more rapidly during the post-globalisation period, both in advanced and certain less developed states. However, the front-runners were developed states, such as Gujarat, Haryana, Karnataka, Tamil Nadu, and Andhra Pradesh, alongside the less developed states of Jharkhand and Bihar.

2.5 Interstate Disparity

The preceding discussion establishes that, although the economy's overall growth rate has risen in the era of globalisation, not all states and sectors have benefited equally from this growth. Some researchers have observed that interstate and interregional disparities have widened in India following globalisation. This trend contradicts the country's fundamental principle of development planning and hinders the attainment of an inclusive growth regime. In other words, the issue of regional imbalance remains a significant concern, underscoring the persistent structural constraints that prevent all regions and states from achieving similar levels of development, thereby obstructing inclusiveness. It is therefore essential to re-examine the pattern of interstate disparity in the country during the era of globalisation, compared to the pre-globalisation period.

To begin with, we examine interstate disparity in India from 1981 to 2024 by examining inter-temporal changes in the coefficient of variation (CV) and the Gini coefficient of PCNSDP across states. It is evident from Figure 1 and Table 6 that, apart from inevitable mild fluctuations in some years, the values of both the CV and Gini coefficient, computed from the PCNSDP, have steadily increased over time since the early 1980s. The higher values observed in recent years indicate a widening interstate disparity in the post-globalisation era. Further scrutiny regarding this can be carried out by analysing the stability of the rankings of the states based on their PCNSDP. For this purpose, we have applied Kendall's test of concordance of ranks to the states in different years of the pre-globalisation and post-globalisation periods. The results of the concordance test are shown in Table 7. This table displays the mean rank values for various states during these periods, along with the values of Kendall's W-statistic. The first point to note is that during the pre-globalisation period, the mean rank value was lowest in Punjab, indicating that it ranked first among the states in per capita NSDP. The states following Punjab to secure the second and third positions are Haryana and Jammu & Kashmir. In contrast, Bihar has the highest mean rank value, making it the lowest state in terms of PCNSDP during the pre-globalisation period. Uttar Pradesh and Madhya Pradesh follow Bihar in this ranking. During the post-globalisation period, the ranking shifts slightly, with Haryana recording the lowest mean rank value and emerging as the highest-ranking state for PCNSDP, followed by Maharashtra and Kerala. However, Bihar still has the highest mean rank value, placing it at the bottom of the PCNSDP during this period, with Uttar Pradesh and Madhya Pradesh following. Over the entire period from 1981 to 2024, the top three states in terms of PCNSDP are Haryana, Punjab, and Maharashtra (in ascending order of mean rank value), while Bihar, Uttar Pradesh, and Madhya Pradesh occupy the bottom three positions (in descending order of mean rank value). The second point to note from Table 7 is that the calculated values of Kendall's W statistic are statistically significant at the 1 % level across all periods – pre-globalisation, post-globalisation, and the entire duration. This indicates strong concordance among states' PCNSDP ranks in India, suggesting that states with higher PCNSDP at the start of the study period have generally maintained this status in subsequent years, with no evident reduction in interstate disparity.

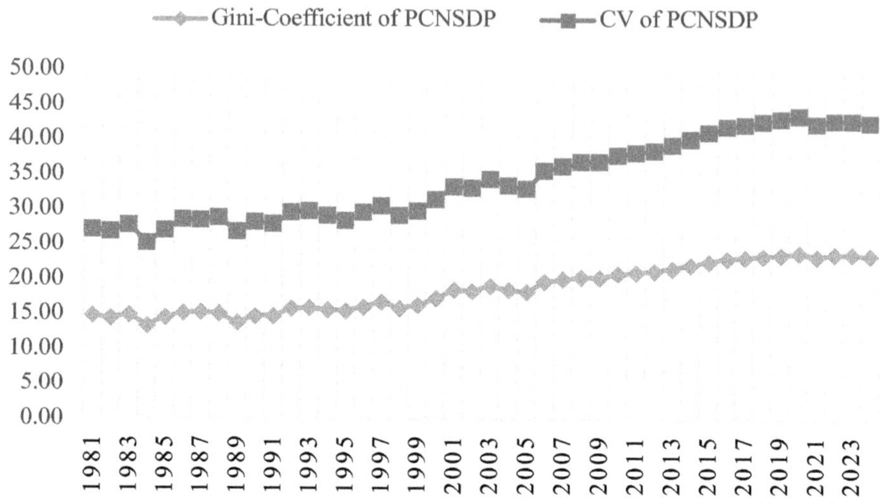

Figure 1: Gini Coefficient and CV of PCNSDP Across Years
Source: Drawn by author using the PCNSDP data available from the RBI.

Table 6: Changes in Values of Gini-Coefficient and CV of PCNSDP in India

Year	Gini-Coefficient of PCNSDP	CV of PCNSDP	Year	Gini-Coefficient of PCNSDP	CV of PCNSDP
1981	0.149	27.18	2003	0.191	34.39
1982	0.145	26.92	2004	0.185	33.48
1983	0.150	27.85	2005	0.183	33.01
1984	0.135	25.23	2006	0.197	35.60
1985	0.146	27.09	2007	0.201	36.23
1986	0.153	28.63	2008	0.204	36.90
1987	0.153	28.56	2009	0.203	36.86
1988	0.152	28.95	2010	0.208	37.80
1989	0.139	26.89	2011	0.210	38.17
1990	0.148	28.26	2012	0.212	38.47
1991	0.148	27.98	2013	0.216	39.22
1992	0.159	29.67	2014	0.221	40.11
1993	0.160	29.79	2015	0.226	41.05
1994	0.157	29.20	2016	0.231	41.92
1995	0.155	28.50	2017	0.233	42.23
1996	0.161	29.68	2018	0.235	42.69
1997	0.168	30.54	2019	0.236	42.98

(Continued)

Year	Gini-Coefficient of PCNSDP	CV of PCNSDP	Year	Gini-Coefficient of PCNSDP	CV of PCNSDP
1998	0.159	29.21	2020	0.239	43.44
1999	0.164	29.80	2021	0.234	42.33
2000	0.173	31.48	2022	0.237	42.79
2001	0.185	33.33	2023	0.237	42.75
2002	0.184	33.14	2024	0.235	42.46

Source: Same as in Figure 1

Table 7: Results of Kendall's Test of Concordance of Ranks in PCNSDP Across States

State	Mean rank		
	1981–1993 (Pre-globalisation)	**1994–2024 (Post-globalisation)**	**1981–2024 (Entire period)**
Andhra Pradesh	12.2	10.3	10.1
Assam	7.4	15.7	11.6
Bihar	17.0	20.0	17.0
Gujarat	10.2	6.3	7.0
Haryana	2.4	1.7	1.9
Himachal Pradesh	5.2	6.3	5.7
Jammu & Kashmir	4.4	12.2	9.0
Karnataka	5.0	4.6	4.1
Kerala	6.7	4.5	5.0
Madhya Pradesh	15.2	17.2	15.1
Maharashtra	5.3	3.8	4.1
Odisha	11.9	14.5	12.3
Punjab	1.0	5.4	3.8
Rajasthan	13.5	12.8	11.9
Tamil Nadu	11.8	6.9	8.0
Uttar Pradesh	15.8	19.0	15.9
West Bengal	8.2	13.2	10.6
Jharkhand	–	16.8	–
Chhattisgarh	–	12.4	–
Uttarakhand	–	6.5	–
Kendall's W	0.925	0.892	0.822
Degrees of freedom	16	19	16
Asymp. significance	0.00	0.00	0.00

Source: Author's computation using PCNSDP data obtained from the RBI website

Since diminishing marginal returns on production inputs are a fundamental aspect of neoclassical economics, poorer regions are expected to grow faster than more prosperous regions. This is because they initially have less per capita capital and enjoy a higher return on capital, assuming diminishing marginal returns to capital. This enables them to catch up with the more prosperous regions – a phenomenon known as convergence (Solow, 1956). In examining interstate disparity in India, we investigate whether poorer states have experienced faster growth over time, thereby narrowing the gap with wealthier states and supporting the convergence hypothesis. This is achieved by estimating the following two equations:

$$\text{Growth Rate}_{\text{PCNSDP}} = \alpha + \beta \ln (\text{PCNSDP}_{\text{Base year}})$$
$$\ln (\text{SD}_{\text{PCNSDP}}) = \delta + \sigma \text{T}$$

where PCNSDP signifies per capita net state domestic product, SD denotes standard deviation, and T refers to the year. While the first equation tests for the presence of 'unconditional β-convergence',[3] the second investigates the existence of 'σ-convergence'. The presence of the first would require obtaining a statistically significant estimate of β with a negative sign. In contrast, the latter would require a negative, statistically significant estimate of σ. Positive signs for the slope coefficients, along with their statistical significance, would suggest divergence among the states.

Table 8 presents the results of the convergence tests using state-level PCNSDP data. We examined convergence separately during the pre-globalisation, post-globalisation, and the entire periods. The results almost unanimously reject the hypotheses of both β-convergence and σ-convergence. All slope coefficients are positive, and all but one in the β-convergence test are statistically significant for the pre-globalisation period. Rejecting the β-convergence hypothesis leads to the conclusion that states with higher initial levels of PCNSDP have grown faster, suggesting divergence among states. Furthermore, rejecting the σ-convergence hypothesis indicates that states have diverged over time in their PCNSDPs, thereby increasing interstate disparity. These conclusions remain valid regardless of the period considered. The adoption of globalisation policies since the early 1990s has not reduced interstate (per capita) income disparity in India.

---

3 Incorporating socio-economic factors as determinants of PCNSDP growth in this equation allows for testing 'conditional β-convergence'. However, our test is limited to examining the presence of 'unconditional β-convergence'.

Table 8: Regression Analysis Results for Convergence Tests in India

Test	Period	Intercept		Slope		R^2	F-stat
		Estimate	t-stat	Estimate	t-stat		
β-convergence	Pre-glo-balisation (1981–1993)	1.49	1.02	0.000031	0.49	0.019	0.60
	Post-glo-balisation (1994–2024)	5.35	11.20*	0.000016	0.89	0.023	0.42
	Entire period (1981–2024)	3.85	4.59*	0.000003	0.09	0.0003	0.01
σ-convergence	Pre-glo-balisation (1981–1993)	8.59	350.40*	0.03438*	12.21*	0.945	190.78*
	Post-glo-balisation (1994–2024)	8.91	238.89*	0.06554*	29.99*	0.988	2466.49*
	Entire period (1981–2024)	8.37	121.24*	0.05558*	22.92*	0.970	1634.13*

Source: Author's computation
*Notes: (i) t-stats are computed using heteroskedasticity and autocorrelation corrected (HAC) standard errors, and (ii) * indicates significance at the 1 per cent level.*

Having observed that, as in the pre-globalisation period, the post-globalisation period has not fostered convergence among states in their PCNSDP, thereby perpetuating divergence, it may be intriguing to explore the factors influencing interstate variation in PCNSDP. We have employed the panel regression technique to shed light on this issue using data on twenty-one states from 2012 to 2024. In our panel regression, PCNSDP is regressed on variables such as the ratio of NSDP from the secondary sector to the primary sector (secpri), the ratio of NSDP from the tertiary sector to the primary sector (terpri), the rate of urbanisation (urban), defined as the ratio of the urban population to the total population, the literacy rate among individuals aged seven and above (lit), the per capita availability of power in kilowatt-hours (power), the credit-deposit ratio according to the place of utilisation (credit), and a COVID dummy (covid), which was assigned the value '0' for the years 2021 and 2022 and '1' for others. The selection of these variables is based on the understanding that the extent of income diversification (captured by secpri and terpri), urbanisation, education and skills of the population (proxied by lit), infrastructure development (proxied by power), institutional support for development (proxied by cd), and natural calamities (covid) are significant factors, among others, that determine PCNSDP in the states. More specifically, we hypothesise that the relationship between PCNSDP and each explanatory factor is positive.[4] Before presenting our regression results, it is worth noting that our dataset had a few gaps, as information on some variables was unavailable for one state and specific years. However, we have filled most of these gaps using the interpolation method, and where it failed (for example, in Telangana), we applied the 'row-deletion' method. This provided us with an unbalanced panel comprising 262 observations, which were used to estimate the 'Panel Random Effects GLS Regression' model.

The panel regression results (Table 9) support our hypothesis, as the estimated coefficients for all variables, except 'covid', are statistically significant and positive. Consequently, states with higher PCNSDP are more diversified and urbanised, have better-educated populations, boast improved infrastructure, and provide better institutional support for economic activities. The two alternative models that we estimated demonstrated overall statistical significance. Consequently, the findings of this exercise can be regarded as drawing policy lessons to enhance PCNSDP in underperforming states and reduce interstate disparity. The apparent policy lessons suggest that implementing proactive strategies to promote the secondary and tertiary sectors, improving infrastructure, encouraging urbanisation, and enhancing the educational base of the population may enable such states to catch up with developed states that have enjoyed higher PCNSDP growth.

4 The choice of explanatory variables in this analysis is well-founded, as the separately computed multiple correlation coefficient between PCNSDP and all the explanatory factors combined is 0.91. This means that 91 % of the total variation in the PCNSDP series is explained by these factors, leaving only 9 % attributable to omitted variables.

Table 9: Factors Explaining Interstate Variation in Per Capita NSDP: Results of Panel Random Effects GLS Regression

	Model 1			Model 2		
Variable	**Est. Coeff.**	***z*-value**	***p*-value**	**Est. Coeff.**	***z*-value**	***p*-value**
secpri	16918.65	5.12	0.00	9467.19	7.12	0.00
terpri	6927.58	2.69	0.01	–	–	–
urban	–	–	–	1255.36	6.48	0.00
lit	–	–	–	975.05	3.49	0.00
power	–	–	–	52.30	16.30	0.00
cd	275.91	2.24	0.03	–	–	
covid	–	–		978.08	0.65	0.52
constant	20827.41	1.79	0.07	–101412.10	–4.86	0.00
Adjusted-R^2		0.29			0.86	
Wald χ^2		110.30 (df = 3)			1117.85 (df = 5)	
p-value (χ^2)		0.00			0.00	
Total observations		262			262	

Sources: Author's computation using data from RBI (2024), Handbook of Statistics on Indian States 2023–24; Ministry of Health & Family Welfare, GoI, Population Projection Report 2011–2036; and NSSO conducted employment/unemployment survey 2011–12 and PLFS (2017–18 through 2023–2024).

Note: Alternative models have been estimated to avoid the multicollinearity problem

2.6 Summary of Findings

Comparing the growth rates of GDP in the country during the pre-globalisation and post-globalisation periods, we observed that they improved significantly in the latter, despite a decline in the growth rate during the second sub-period of the post-globalisation phase relative to the first sub-period. It is encouraging to note that all major states in India have enhanced their NSDP growth rates during the post-globalisation phase, although the extent of improvement varied across states. As expected, the states that are benefiting the most from improvements in their NSDP growth rates during the era of globalisation are the developed ones, such as Gujarat, Haryana, Tamil Nadu, Himachal Pradesh, Maharashtra, Karnataka, and Andhra Pradesh (in descending order of their growth rates).

Like the NSDP, the annual growth rate of PCNSDP significantly improved in the country and all states during the post-globalisation period compared to the pre-globalisation period. At the national level, it rose from 2.68 % in the pre-globalisation period to 4.38 % in the post-globalisation period. During the post-globalisation period, while Gujarat ranked highest in PCNSDP growth, Jammu & Kashmir ranked lowest. Notably, the most significant improvement in PCNSDP between these periods occurred in Bihar, which had ranked lowest in this respect during the pre-globalisation period. Moreover, when we compared the growth rates of PCNSDP across the two sub-periods of the post-globalisation period, it was found that sixteen out of twenty states improved their growth rates in the second sub-period compared to the first. Furthermore, the former BIMARU states and more developed states were among these sixteen states.

The process of income diversification in the Indian economy has progressed swiftly during our study period, resulting in a decline in the share of the primary sector (agriculture and allied activities) in gross value added (GVA), while the shares of the secondary and tertiary sectors have risen. In 1981, the primary sector accounted for nearly 41 % of GVA; however, by 2024, its share had decreased to 14.5 %. Conversely, the shares of the secondary and tertiary sectors increased from 27 % and 32 % in 1981 to 31 % and 55 % in 2024, respectively. Therefore, the expansion of the tertiary sector has been considerably more pronounced than that of the secondary sector, indicating a greater level of tertiarisation of the economy over time.

Upon examining the growth rates of output from the primary, secondary, and tertiary sectors, it became evident that, at the all-India level, the primary sector experienced a decline during the first sub-period of the post-globalisation era, compared to the pre-globalisation period, followed by a recovery in the second sub-period. The picture is somewhat different in the secondary and tertiary sectors, where output growth rates increased during the first sub-period of the post-globalisation era, compared to the pre-globalisation period, before declining. This trend is evident across all sub-sectors of the secondary and tertiary sectors, except for 'mining and quarrying', 'electricity, gas, water supply, and other utility services' and 'financial, real estate, and professional services'. During the post-globalisation period, the primary, secondary, and tertiary sectors recorded growth rates of 3.24 %, 6.13 %, and 7.06 %, respectively. Among the sub-sectors, the highest growth (10.94 %) during this period was attained by 'trade, hotels and restaurants', followed by 'financial, real estate and professional services' (6.93 %), 'public administration' (6.79 %), 'construction' (6.77 %), and 'manufacturing' (6.59 %).

Regarding the states, the growth rate of the primary sector's output was higher in the post-globalisation period (1994–2024) than in the pre-globalisation period in eight of the seventeen states for which such a comparison is feasible. During the post-globalisation period, Andhra Pradesh recorded the highest growth in primary sector output among the states, at 5.36%, while Kerala recorded the lowest, at –1.08 %. Three other states that recorded impressive growth in the primary sector during this period are Madhya Pradesh (5.11 %), Jharkhand (4.95 %), and Gujarat (4.25 %).

The growth rate of secondary sector output exceeded that of the primary sector during the post-globalisation period in all states except Andhra Pradesh, Jharkhand, and Telangana. Nonetheless, all states recorded higher growth in the tertiary sector than in the primary sector during this period. Furthermore, in ten out of seventeen states, secondary sector output increased more during the post-globalisation period than during the pre-globalisation period, except in Andhra Pradesh, Himachal Pradesh, Jammu & Kashmir, Maharashtra, Odisha, Rajasthan, and Tamil Nadu. In contrast, the tertiary sector expanded more rapidly in all states during the post-globalisation period than during the pre-globalisation period. The most significant improvements in the growth rates of the secondary and tertiary sectors during the post-globalisation period, compared to the pre-globalisation period, are observed in Gujarat and Bihar, respectively. It is also noteworthy that while Gujarat recorded the highest growth in secondary sector output (8.64 %) during the post-globalisation period, Uttarakhand holds the distinction for the tertiary sector, with 8.55 %. Overall, although the tertiary sector has been the main driver of growth in the NSDP across most states in the post-globalisation period, the secondary sector has also played a role.[5]

---

5 In a recent paper, Goldar (2024) argued that, contrary to established wisdom, India's economic growth in recent years has been driven by manufacturing rather than services. He contends that the perception of services-led growth in India arises from the failure to employ the 'double deflation method for national accounts'. However, his perspective seems only partially valid when one notes a mere 2.9 percentage-point increase in manufacturing's share of the country's GVA between 1994 and 2024, compared to a 15.3 percentage-point increase for the services sector as a whole. Furthermore, the growth rates of these two sectors during this period were 6.13 % and 7.06 %, respectively (see Tables 3 and 4). It can also be posited that even if there were an overvaluation of services-sector output and an undervaluation of manufacturing output, this would not affect the growth rates calculated. Our view is that the CSO's income accounting method may have affected the output values of these sectors to some degree. However, the substantial difference between them in terms of shares of GVA, as revealed by the CSO data, casts doubt on the acceptability of the 'manufacturing-led economic growth' argument. Ultimately, this matter warrants further research.

Noting that Indian states have had differing growth rates over time, we aimed to statistically investigate whether there is any indication of convergence in their PCNSDP, which would suggest a decrease in interstate disparity. To this end, we assessed the trends in the coefficients of variation (CV) and Gini coefficients (GC) of PCNSDP. Additionally, we employed panel regression techniques to evaluate the validity of the unconditional-β and σ-convergence hypotheses. Our findings indicate that the CV and GC values have increased over time, with no evidence that this trend reverses in the post-globalisation period. Kendall's test of concordance of ranks for the states' PCNSDPs indicated that states with higher PCNSDPs continued to rank higher during our study period (1981–2024). This finding is further supported by the regression analysis, which tests the convergence hypotheses and suggests a scenario of divergence among the states during our study period. Focusing solely on the post-globalisation period, the divergence among the states becomes even more evident.[6]

What factors influence the PCNSDP across various states? This question warrants exploration to inform policy formulation and mitigate interstate disparity. To achieve this, we estimated the Panel Random Effects GLS Regression Model using data from twenty-one states over the period from 2012 to 2024. In this model, the dependent variable is PCNSDP, while the explanatory variables proxy for income diversification, urbanisation, infrastructure, education, and natural disasters. The results indicated that the PCNSDP is higher in states with higher urbanisation rates, characterised by a predominance of the secondary and tertiary sectors over the primary sector, improved infrastructure, enhanced education for the populace, and better institutional support for the development of economic activities. Notably, when all these factors are considered collectively, they can account for as much as 91 % of the total interstate variation in the PCNSDP. The policy implications of this result are, therefore, evident. By promoting economic diversification, supporting further urban development, increasing investment in both physical and human capital, and strengthening institutional support, lagging states might be able to catch up with leading states, thereby reducing disparity between them in the future.

---

6 The hypotheses of divergence or convergence could also be tested using indicators other than the PCNSDP of the states. For example, in a recent study, Mahapatra and Sahu (2025) considered the values of a multidimensional index calculated from state-level data on socio-economic and fiscal indicators for 2011–12 to 2017–18. Their observation is that although disparities in development levels among states persist, they decrease over time, indicating convergence. Fiscal and health indicators primarily drive this convergence, and it would have been even more evident if economic (per capita GSDP) and educational indicators had not diverged.

Labour Force Participation Patterns in India

3.1 Introduction

In a developing country like India, achieving inclusive growth necessitates the creation of employment opportunities. Economic growth, as indicated by gross domestic product (GDP) growth and employment creation, fosters pro-poor growth and ultimately reduces poverty. For this reason, the focus on attaining higher GDP growth rates and expanding employment has been significant since the onset of the planning era, particularly during the Eleventh and Twelfth Five-Year Plans. The Twelfth Five-Year Plan viewed inclusive growth as a multifaceted concept that can be realised by establishing sufficient job opportunities. The current Central Government's approach to establishing the *Sabka Saath, Sabka Vikas, Sabka Vishwas* regime recognises the importance of employment expansion in the country. This is particularly relevant, given that the country has been experiencing a 'jobless growth' phase for some time. Stressing the necessity for employment expansion, Ghose (2019, p. 1) correctly observed that employment forms the vital link between wealth and welfare, as well as between economic growth and enhancements in the living standards of a country's population. Economic growth enhances living standards when accompanied by a substantial increase in employment opportunities for adults.

It is essential to note that the interaction between the demand and supply sides of the labour market determines overall employment opportunities. While the potential for gainful employment largely depends on demand, the supply side also plays a significant role in determining employment levels. A consistent supply of workers with the appropriate knowledge and skills can enhance their productivity and marketability. This, in turn, helps the economy move toward full-employment equilibrium.

In India, most individuals in the labour force lack the basic skills and expertise necessary to secure gainful employment. Furthermore, population expansion results in a continuous influx of unskilled labour into the labour market, creating excessive pressure and widening the gap from a full-employment equilibrium. This gap is exacerbated by demand-side constraints, primarily due to stringent labour laws that regulate the labour market. Three major categories of labour laws that influence employers' decisions to hire more labour are (i) those about the payment of reasonable compensation to workers in the event of enterprise closures, (ii) those concerning the establishment of minimum wages, and (iii) 'Others', which relate to the permanence of casual and contract workers after a specified period (Ghose, 2004). Additionally, the government's singular focus on formulating strategies and policies to enhance GDP growth, treating employment merely as a secondary consideration, has also been a key reason for the resultant environment lacking adequate employment opportunities (Papola, 2008a, 2008b; Bhaumik, 2013).

The trend in the Indian labour market since the implementation of globalisation (or economic reform) policies in the early 1990s has been somewhat concerning. The growth rate of the labour force has declined during the post-globalisation period. This has raised several questions because, unlike employment, which results from the interaction of labour supply and demand in the economy, the growth of the labour force reflects only the supply side. The decline in labour force participation and growth rates may stem from socio-economic challenges. Some scholars have also posited that the decrease in labour force growth could result from an increased valuation of leisure and domestic activities relative to external work. Alternatively, it may also be due to discouragement in joining the labour force, stemming from prior knowledge of a lack of suitable employment opportunities. The drop in the labour force growth rate may also result from an unfavourable demographic transition within the economy, particularly in age composition, leading to a decreased proportion of the working-age population. Therefore, while the first two factors suggest that the decline in labour force growth is linked to a reduction in the labour force participation rate (LFPR), the third factor explains the phenomenon in terms of demographic transition.

In light of the above context, this chapter examines the evolving patterns of labour force participation and its growth rate in India and its seventeen major states from 1983 to 2018,[1] utilising data from the NSSO surveys on employment and unemployment,

[1] The major or relatively larger states are considered for analysis, as the estimates may not be accurate for smaller states due to their limited sample sizes.

and the first Periodic Labour Force Survey (2017–18[2]).[3] This discussion is conducted at both aggregated and disaggregated levels. Moreover, this chapter aims to identify the key factors influencing labour force participation nationwide.

This chapter is structured as follows: Section 3.2 discusses the trends in labour force participation in India at aggregated (all individuals and all regions) and disaggregated levels (male and female, and rural and urban). Section 3.3 examines changes in labour force participation rates (LFPR) across different age groups, while Section 3.4 addresses the same issue by educational categories. Sections 3.5 and 3.6 explore the LFPR among various social and religious groups. Section 3.7 examines the growth of the labour force in India from 1983 to 2018, as well as its sub-periods, categorised by region (rural/urban), gender, age, education, social class, and religious affiliation. Section 3.8 analyses the composition of individuals out of the labour force to illuminate the phenomenon of 'missing labour'. Section 3.9 highlights evolving labour market conditions in seventeen major states by analysing two key indicators: labour force participation rates and labour force growth. Section 3.10 aims to identify significant determinants of labour force participation in India. Finally, Section 3.11 summarises the key findings of this chapter.

3.2 Trends of Labour Force Participation in India

3.2.1 The Size of the Labour Force

To understand the changes in labour force participation patterns at the all-India level from 1983 to 2018, we examine the size of the labour force (in terms of numbers). A person becomes part of the labour force when working or seeking work. Conversely, a person not currently seeking work due to attending an educational institution, engaged in domestic duties, or unavailable for work due to a specific illness or disability is excluded from the labour force. Thus, the labour force comprises both the employed and unemployed. It reflects the size of the labour supply available to produce goods and services (ILO, 2013).

Regarding the estimates of the labour force (i.e. individuals participating in the labour market), we adhere to the definition adopted in the NSSO surveys on employment and unemployment, as well as Periodic Labour Force Surveys. The NSSO surveys enable us to estimate the labour force using various concepts. However, as noted in Chapter 1, we evaluate the size of the labour force under the usual principal and subsidiary status (UPSS), which combines the labour force under the usual principal status (UPS) and the usual subsidiary status (USS).

---

2 This year is referred to as 2018 throughout this study using the last calendar year.

3 Chapter 7 discusses the changes in labour market scenarios between 2018 and 2024.

Table 10 shows that, as anticipated, the country's total labour force (under the UPSS concept) gradually increased over time. The total labour force was approximately 312 million in 1983, rising to 382 million in 1994, 407 million in 2000, 484 million in 2012, and 502 million in 2018. Considering average annual changes in the labour force, the highest rate of increase occurred from 1983 to 1994, at 6.59 million per year. It experienced a significant decline in the subsequent period from 1994 to 2000 (4.24 million). However, it increased again by 6.4 million from 2000 to 2012, followed by a decline from 2012 to 2018 (3.08 million). When comparing the entire pre-globalisation period (1983–1994) with the post-globalisation period (1994–2018), it is clear that the yearly increase in the labour force size was lower in the latter (5.03 million) than in the former (6.59 million).

Table 10. Size of Labour Force (UPSS Basis) in India

Year / Period	Rural			Urban			Rural + Urban		
	Male	Female	Male + Female	Male	Female	Male + Female	Male	Female	Male + Female
				Number in Labour Force [in million]					
1983	159.4	91.1	250.5	49.1	12.8	61.9	208.5	103.9	312.3
1994	190.4	105.6	296.0	67.3	18.3	85.6	257.7	123.9	381.6
2000	202.0	106.8	308.8	78.9	19.3	98.2	281.0	126.1	407.0
2012	238.9	103.5	342.4	112.7	28.8	141.5	351.6	132.3	483.9
2018	254.1	79.8	333.9	133.6	35.2	168.7	387.1	115.3	502.4
				Average Yearly Change in Labour Force [in million]					
1983 to 1994	2.96	1.38	4.34	1.73	0.53	2.26	4.68	1.91	6.59
1994 to 2000	1.94	0.20	2.13	1.94	0.16	2.11	3.88	0.36	4.24
2000 to 2012	3.07	−0.27	2.80	2.81	0.79	3.60	5.88	0.52	6.40
2012 to 2018	2.52	−3.95	−1.42	3.48	1.06	4.54	5.92	−2.84	3.08
1994 to 2012	2.69	−0.12	2.58	2.52	0.58	3.10	5.22	0.47	5.68
1994 to 2018	2.65	−1.07	1.58	2.76	0.70	3.46	5.39	−0.36	5.03

Source: Author's computation using unit-level data from NSSO employment/unemployment surveys (38th, 50th, 55th and 68th rounds) and PLFS 2017–18

When considering rural and urban areas separately, the overall size of the labour force (males and females combined) expanded over time in both regions until 2012. However, this upward trend in the size of the labour force persisted only in urban areas after 2012, whereas it declined in rural areas. Between 1983 and 1994 (the pre-globalisation period), the average annual increase in the labour force was higher in rural India (4.34 million) than in urban India (2.26 million). Nonetheless, this trend reversed from 1994 to 2018 (the post-globalisation period), when the yearly increases in the labour force in rural and urban areas were 1.58 million and 3.46 million, respectively.

We may also examine the labour force size in all-India separately for males and females, as outlined in Table 10. The size of the male labour force (rural and urban areas combined) increased steadily during our study period, rising from approximately 209 million in 1983 to 258 million in 1994, 281 million in 2000, 352 million in 2012, and 387 million in 2018. Although the same upward trend continued for females until 2012, it declined in 2018. Thus, the female labour force in all-India rose from about 104 million in 1983 to 124 million in 1994 and 132 million in 2012. However, it decreased to 115 million in 2018. Consequently, while the average yearly increase in the male labour force during the post-globalisation period (1994 to 2018) was as high as 5.39 million, the average annual decrease for females was 0.36 million.

An important point to emphasise here is that the decline in the absolute number of females in the labour force, as observed during the post-globalisation period in India, has occurred solely due to the decrease among rural females. As indicated in Table 10, the size of the female labour force in rural areas declined significantly from 105.6 million in 1994 to 79.8 million by 2018. Conversely, the female labour force in urban areas increased from 18.3 million to 35.2 million during this timeframe. Furthermore, analysis of various years (1994, 2000, 2012, and 2018) in the post-globalisation era reveals that the most substantial decline in the female labour force in rural areas occurred in 2018 compared to the preceding years. Thus, 2018 has been the most severe year for rural females in terms of labour force size. Section 3.8 examines the reasons for the withdrawal or absence of 23.7 million rural females from the labour force over just six years (2012–2018).

3.2.2 Share of Rural Areas in the Total Labour Force

Table 11 presents data on the share of rural areas in the total labour force in India, separated by gender. The first point to note is a steady decline in the share of the rural areas within the total labour force. While the rural share of the total labour force was 80.2 % in 1983, it fell to 77.6 % in 1994, 70.8 % in

2012, and 70.8 % in 2018 (including males and females). Secondly, the decline in the share of rural areas in the total labour force is apparent for both males and females. Thirdly and importantly, throughout 1983–2018, the share of rural females in the labour force has consistently been higher than that of rural males. This suggests that the female labour force in India is more rural than the male labour force.

Table 11. Share of Rural Areas in Total Labour Force in India (UPSS Basis)

Year	Male	Female	Male + Female
1983	76.4	87.7	80.2
1994	73.9	85.2	77.6
2000	71.9	84.7	75.9
2012	68.0	78.2	70.8
2018	70.1	73.3	70.8

Source: Same as Table 10

3.2.3 Share of Females in the Total Labour Force

In Table 12, we present information on the proportion of females in the total labour force in India, separately for rural and urban areas. Three important points emerge: (i) The females' share in the total labour force (considering rural and urban areas together) has declined steadily across all-India from 1983 to 2018, with a particularly sharp decrease observed after 2000. Specifically, the female proportion of the total labour force was 32.5 % in 1994 and 31 % in 2000, decreasing to 27.3 % in 2012 and 22.9 % in 2018. (ii) When considering rural and urban areas separately, we find that the rural females' share in the labour force has consistently been significantly higher than that of their counterparts in urban areas, although the gap between the two narrowed considerably in 2018; and (iii) The overall decline in the females' share in the labour force across all-India is primarily driven by reductions in rural areas, particularly in 2018. A significant number of rural females were missing from the labour force in 2018 compared to 2012, leading to a noticeable decline in their share. As shown in Table 12, in rural areas the share of females in the total labour force decreased from 30.2 % in 2012 to 23.9 % in 2018, while the corresponding figures for urban females were 20.4 % and 20.8 %, respectively.

Table 12. Share of Females in Total Labour Force in India (UPSS Basis)

Year	Rural	Urban	Rural + Urban
1983	36.4	20.6	33.2
1994	35.7	21.4	32.5
2000	34.6	19.6	31.0
2012	30.2	20.4	27.3
2018	23.9	20.8	22.9

Source: Same as Table 10

3.2.4 Labour Force Participation Rates

We will now examine the trends in the labour force participation rate (LFPR) in India by region (rural/urban) and gender (male/female) from 1983 to 2018. The LFPR is defined as the proportion of individuals entering the labour market (i.e. employed plus unemployed) relative to the total population. It is one of the key indicators of prevailing conditions in an economy's labour market. Table 13 presents data on the LFPR (under the UPSS concept) for all-India at various time points, by region and sex of individuals. The main points emerging from this table are the following:

- At the all-India level, considering males, females, and rural and urban areas, the LFPR has continuously declined from 1983 to 2018. As shown in the table, the LFPR decreased from 43.5 % in 1983 to 42.7 % in 1994, 40.5 % in 2000, 39.4 % in 2012, and 36.9 % in 2018. Thus, the decline in the LFPR was most pronounced in 2018.
- The decline in the country's LFPR is primarily due to decreasing LFPR among females. Table 13 indicates that the LFPR for males, which was 56.1 % in 1983, decreased only marginally, even after nearly 35 years, to 55.6 %. Conversely, the LFPR for females has been consistently declining since 2000. As illustrated in the table, females' LFPR was 30 % in 1983, falling to 26 % in 2000, 22.2 % in 2012, and 17.5 % in 2018. Thus, it is evident that the females' LFPR was significantly lower than that of the males throughout 1983–2018, and the gap between these two segments of the population has widened over time. It is abundantly clear that during the decline in the country's LFPR, females exited the labour market in large numbers, accounting for the significant reduction in their LFPR in 2018.

- The LFPR has declined over time in rural areas. This decline has been noticeably more significant, particularly in 2018. On the other hand, the LFPR in urban areas did not show any considerable change over the period from 1983 to 2018. It is also noteworthy that while the LFPR for rural individuals has consistently been higher than that of their urban counterparts, the gap between the two has gradually narrowed over time, to the extent that the difference in LFPR for rural and urban individuals became almost negligible in 2018 (37 % and 36.8 %, respectively). Thus, in relative terms, rural India experienced a more significant decline in the LFPR from 1983 to 2018 than urban areas.

Table 13. Labour Force Participation Rates (%) in India (UPSS Basis)

	Rural			Urban			Rural + Urban		
Year	Male	Female	Male + Female	Male	Female	Male + Female	Male	Female	Male + Female
1983	56.8	34.2	45.8	53.9	15.9	36.1	56.1	30.0	43.5
1994	56.1	33.1	44.9	54.3	16.5	36.4	55.6	28.8	42.7
2000	54.0	30.2	42.4	54.2	14.7	35.5	54.1	26.0	40.5
2012	55.3	25.3	40.7	56.3	15.5	36.7	55.6	22.2	39.4
2018	54.9	18.2	37.0	57.0	15.9	36.8	55.6	17.5	36.9

Source: Same as Table 10

- Table 13 also presents information on the LFPR for males and females separately. The LFPR for rural males has declined marginally, while that for urban males has increased slowly. Conversely, the LFPR for rural females has decreased significantly over time, with the most significant drop occurring between 2012 and 2018. However, the LFPR remained unchanged for urban females from 1983 to 2018. Another important point is that the LFPR for females has consistently lagged far behind that of males in rural and urban areas. In 2018, the LFPR for rural males and females was 54.9 % and 18.2 %, respectively. In urban areas, the corresponding figures were 57 % and 15.9 %, respectively. In rural areas, the female LFPR is approximately one-third that of the male LFPR, and it is even lower in urban areas.

3.3 Labour Force Participation Across Age Groups in India

Labour force participation rates for various age groups and changes over time are essential issues in discussions of shifts in labour market scenarios. To emphasise these issues, we compiled LFPR data for six age groups at our selected time points.

These age groups are 0–4, 5–14, 15–24, 25–34, 35–59, and 60 and above. The data presented in Table 14 lead to the following observations:

- At the all-India level, the LFPR across age groups follows an inverted U-shaped curve. This indicates that the LFPR increases as we move to higher age groups and begins to decline after reaching its peak, typically occurring in the 35–59 age group. This pattern holds in both rural and urban areas, as well as for males and females.
- The LFPR (considering both rural and urban areas, as well as males and females) has declined over time across all age groups. However, this decline is most pronounced among the 5–14 and 15–24 age groups. While the LFPR for these two age groups in 1983 was 11.4 % and 58.5 %, respectively, by 2018, these figures had fallen drastically to 0.8 % and 28.9 %, respectively. Interestingly, the decline in the LFPR nationwide began with more individuals in the 5–14 age group withdrawing from the labour force. Over time, an increasing number of individuals from the 15–24 age group also started to exit the labour force. By 2018, this group had become the most significant contributor to the country's overall decline in the LFPR. Conversely, although the LFPR for the 35–59 age group also declined over time, the extent of this decline was considerably less than that of the previously mentioned age groups. This age group consistently maintained the highest LFPR throughout the period studied. As for the LFPR among older adults (aged 60 and above) across all-India, it is noteworthy that, although it too declined over time, 29.1 % remained part of the labour force in 2018.
- The significant decline in the LFPR observed for the age groups 5–14 and 15–24 at the all-India level is also evident for both males and females. Table 14 illustrates that males and females aged 15–24 experienced a loss of approximately thirty percentage points in the value of LFPR from 1983 to 2018. However, the LFPR for males in this age group was nearly four times that of females. When comparing rural and urban areas, although the LFPR declined over time for the age groups 5–14 and 15–24, the decline was more pronounced in the former than in the latter. Between 2012 and 2018, while the rural population in the 15–24 age group experienced a 9.3 percentage-point decrease in LFPR, the corresponding decline in the urban population was only 2.8 percentage points. Another point to consider is that, in 2018, across all age groups, the LFPR was highest in rural areas for the 35–59 age group, while it was highest in urban areas for the 25–34 age group. Younger individuals in urban areas tend to join the labour force earlier than their counterparts in rural areas.

Table 14. Labour Force Participation Rates (%) by Age Groups in India (UPSS Basis)

Region	Sex	Age groups	1983	1994	2000	2012	2018
Rural	Male	0–4	0.2	0.0	0.0	0.0	0.0
		5–14	13.6	7.3	4.8	1.6	1.2
		15–24	79.9	73.2	68.8	52.8	45.1
		25–34	98.6	98.4	98.0	97.6	96.2
		35–59	97.1	97.9	97.2	97.9	97.0
		60 & above	66.6	69.8	63.1	64.9	52.1
		All ages	55.4	56.1	54.0	55.3	54.9
	Female	0–4	0.1	0.0	0.0	0.0	0.0
		5–14	12.5	7.3	4.9	1.6	0.3
		15–24	47.9	42.0	36.9	22.7	11.5
		25–34	57.6	55.7	52.6	39.9	28.7
		35–59	58.8	57.5	55.1	46.5	35.1
		60 & above	22.6	24.1	21.5	21.3	11.7
		All ages	34.2	33.0	30.2	25.3	18.2
	Male + Female	0–4	0.1	0.0	0.0	0.0	0.0
		5–14	13.1	7.3	4.9	1.6	0.8
		15–24	63.9	58.2	53.2	38.5	29.2
		25–34	77.7	76.5	74.5	67.4	61.4
		35–59	78.0	78.1	76.6	72.5	66.0
		60 & above	44.7	47.4	42.4	43.1	32.4
		All ages	45.0	44.9	42.3	40.6	37.0
Urban	Male	0–4	0.2	0.0	0.0	0.0	0.0
		5–14	6.6	3.7	2.9	1.9	1.0
		15–24	65.2	57.3	54.7	45.4	42.4
		25–34	97.9	97.0	96.5	96.9	96.0
		35–59	95.9	96.3	95.6	96.6	95.2
		60 & above	50.4	44.2	39.7	36.5	35.8
		All ages	53.9	54.3	54.2	56.3	57.0
	Female	0–4	0.1	0.0	0.0	0.0	0.0
		5–14	3.8	2.6	2.0	0.5	0.2
		15–24	19.4	18.4	15.5	14.5	12.8
		25–34	25.8	26.5	22.9	25.6	27.0
		35–59	29.3	29.9	27.1	25.1	25.4
		60 & above	13.8	11.3	9.3	7.7	7.5
		All ages	15.9	16.5	14.7	15.5	15.9
	Male + Female	0–4	0.1	0.0	0.0	0.0	0.0
		5–14	5.3	3.2	2.4	1.3	0.6
		15–24	43.8	39.1	36.4	31.0	28.2
		25–34	64.1	62.8	60.0	61.6	61.5
		35–59	64.7	65.3	63.6	62.0	60.3
		60 & above	31.2	27.3	23.8	21.8	21.4
		All ages	35.8	36.3	35.4	36.7	36.8

(Continued)

Table 3. *(Continued)*

Region	Sex	Age groups	1983	1994	2000	2012	2018
Rural + Urban	Male	0–4	0.2	0.0	0.0	0.0	0.0
		5–14	12.1	6.4	4.4	1.7	1.2
		15–24	75.8	68.8	64.7	50.5	44.3
		25–34	98.4	98.0	97.6	97.4	96.1
		35–59	96.8	97.5	96.8	97.5	96.5
		60 & above	63.4	64.3	57.9	57.0	47.4
		All ages	55.0	55.6	54.0	55.6	55.5
	Female	0–4	0.1	0.0	0.0	0.0	0.0
		5–14	10.6	6.2	4.3	1.3	0.3
		15–24	40.6	35.8	31.1	20.2	11.9
		25–34	49.8	48.2	44.7	35.5	28.1
		35–59	52.1	50.6	47.8	40.1	32.1
		60 & above	20.7	21.1	18.5	17.4	10.4
		All ages	29.9	29.0	26.3	22.5	17.5
	Male + Female	0–4	0.1	0.0	0.0	0.0	0.0
		5–14	11.4	6.3	4.3	1.5	0.8
		15–24	58.5	53.0	48.5	36.2	28.9
		25–34	74.2	72.8	70.5	65.5	61.4
		35–59	74.9	74.8	73.1	69.3	64.2
		60 & above	41.9	42.9	38.1	37.1	29.1
		All ages	42.8	42.8	40.6	39.5	36.9

Source: Same as Table 10

- When considering males and females separately in rural and urban areas, it becomes evident that the decline in the LFPR for those aged 15–24 has been significantly more pronounced in rural areas than in urban areas. Specifically, rural males and females in this age group experienced a decrease in LFPR of approximately 24 and 25 percentage points, respectively, from 2000 to 2018. In contrast, the declines for urban males and females during this period were only 12 and 2 percentage points. Additionally, it is noteworthy that in rural and urban areas, the LFPR for males has remained exceedingly high (over 95 %) for the age groups 25–34 and 35–59 from 1983 to 2018. Conversely, for rural females, the LFPR was highest in the 35–59 age group during this period, whereas for urban females, the LFPR peaked in the 25–34 age group in recent years (2012 and 2018).
- The LFPR for older individuals (60 and above) is significantly higher in rural areas compared to urban areas, particularly for males. Table 14 indicates that as many as 52.1 % of rural males aged 60 and above were part of the labour force in 2018, whereas the corresponding figure for urban areas was 35.8 %. Among females in this age group, 11.7 % in rural areas and 7.5 % in urban areas participated in the labour force in the same year.

In the context of the discussion on LFPR by age groups, examining the shares of different age groups in the total labour force may be worthwhile.[4] The information presented in Table 15 demonstrates the predominance of the 35–59 age group at the all-India level, in terms of its share in the country's total labour force. It is evident from the table that the share of this age group in the total labour force gradually increased over time, reaching a point where, by 2018, half of the country's labour force belonged to this group alone. Notably, this group, along with the age groups 15–24 and 25–34, comprised about 92 % of the total labour force in the same year. It should also be noted that the share of elderly persons (aged 60 and above) increased over time, albeit marginally, standing at 7.8 % in 2018.

When we compare the rural and urban distributions of the labour force across age groups, the picture is essentially the same: one-half of the labour force belongs to the 35–59 age group alone. However, comparing males and females, the share of the 35–59 age group in the total labour force is slightly higher for females than for males in all years since 1983, except in 2000. In 2018, across rural and urban areas, the female labour force, comprising 54.4 % of the total, was concentrated in the 35–59 age group, whereas the corresponding share of the male labour force was 49.2 %.

4 According to the Period Labour Force Survey (PLFS) 2018 data, the shares of these age groups in the total population of India are 7.82 %, 18.27 %, 19.13 %, 15.95 %, 28.99 %, and 9.84 %, respectively.

Table 15. Percentage Shares in Total Labour Force by Age Groups in India (UPSS Basis)

Sex	Age groups	Rural					Urban					Rural + Urban				
		1983	1994	2000	2012	2018	1983	1994	2000	2012	2018	1983	1994	2000	2012	2018
Male	0–4	0.0	0.0	0.0	0.0	0.0	0.0	0.0	0.0	0.0	0.0	0.0	0.0	0.0	0.0	0.0
	5–14	6.9	3.3	2.4	0.7	0.5	3.0	1.6	1.2	0.7	0.3	6.0	2.8	2.1	0.7	0.4
	15–24	24.7	23.9	22.4	18.0	16.2	25.3	21.9	20.8	16.2	14.4	24.8	23.4	22.0	17.5	15.7
	25–34	23.5	25.0	25.5	24.6	25.4	28.4	28.8	28.4	29.4	29.0	24.7	25.9	26.3	26.0	26.5
	35–59	36.8	39.4	41.4	47.3	48.7	38.4	43.2	45.3	48.8	50.2	37.2	40.3	42.4	47.8	49.2
	60 & above	8.0	8.4	8.3	9.4	9.2	4.9	4.5	4.3	4.9	6.1	7.3	7.5	7.3	8.1	8.3
	All ages	100	100	100	100	100	100	100	100	100	100	100	100	100	100	100
Female	0–4	0.1	0.0	0.0	0.0	0.0	0.0	0.0	0.0	0.0	0.0	0.1	0.0	0.0	0.0	0.0
	5–14	9.6	5.1	4.0	1.4	0.3	6.0	3.5	3.0	0.6	0.2	9.1	4.9	3.9	1.2	0.3
	15–24	24.9	23.0	21.3	16.0	11.8	24.8	22.5	20.6	17.9	14.9	24.9	22.9	21.2	16.4	12.6
	25–34	23.9	26.7	27.6	25.4	25.5	24.9	26.9	26.6	30.1	30.4	24.0	26.8	27.4	26.3	26.8
	35–59	37.1	40.1	41.9	50.1	56.1	38.8	42.7	45.3	47.1	49.7	37.3	40.5	42.4	49.5	54.4
	60 & above	4.5	5.0	5.2	7.1	6.3	5.5	4.4	4.5	4.3	4.9	4.6	5.0	5.1	6.6	5.9
	All ages	100	100	100	100	100	100	100	100	100	100	100	100	100	100	100
Male + Female	0–4	0.0	0.0	0.0	0.0	0.0	0.0	0.0	0.0	0.0	0.0	0.0	0.0	0.0	0.0	0.0
	5–14	7.9	3.9	3.0	0.9	0.4	3.6	2.0	1.5	0.7	0.3	7.1	3.5	2.6	0.8	0.4
	15–24	24.8	23.6	22.0	17.4	15.2	25.2	22.0	20.7	16.6	14.5	24.8	23.3	21.7	17.2	15.0
	25–34	23.6	25.6	26.2	24.8	25.4	27.7	28.4	28.1	29.5	29.3	24.4	26.2	26.7	26.1	26.5
	35–59	36.9	39.7	41.5	48.2	50.5	38.5	43.1	45.3	48.5	50.1	37.2	40.4	42.4	48.3	50.4
	60 & above	6.7	7.2	7.2	8.7	8.5	5.0	4.5	4.4	4.8	5.8	6.4	6.6	6.6	7.7	7.8
	All ages	100	100	100	100	100	100	100	100	100	100	100	100	100	100	100

Source: Same as Table 10

3.4 Labour Force Participation Across Education Levels in India

To understand the relationship between labour force participation and educational levels, we present LFPR data by educational level in Table 16 for our selected years. Six distinct educational groups have been identified: illiterate, below primary, primary, middle, secondary/H.S., and graduate & above. The table shows that, at the all-India level, the LFPR tends to rise with higher levels of education. This is true for both males and females in rural and urban areas. For the country as a whole, the LFPR in 2018 nearly doubled, rising from the illiterate group (32.5 %) to the graduates and above group (61.7 %). Another point to note is that illiterate males have a significantly higher LFPR compared to illiterate females across all regions (rural and urban). Moreover, the gap in LFPR between illiterate males and females has widened over time in rural and urban settings. This may have occurred as more illiterate females withdrew from the labour force. Another interesting observation is that during the sub-period from 2012 to 2018, the LFPR for males with primary and middle-level education improved in both rural and urban areas. However, this trend is only evident among females with primary education in urban areas.

Table 16. Labour Force Participation Rates (%) by Educational Levels in India (UPSS Basis)

Region	Sex	Edn Level	1983	1994	2000	2012	2018
Rural	Male	Illiterate	53.0	53.8	51.4	53.7	50.2
		Below Primary	43.7	41.1	35.6	34.8	25.1
		Primary	62.9	60.4	55.1	53.6	54.3
		Middle	69.4	69.5	68.9	67.8	68.4
		Secondary / H.S.	77.6	75.2	76.2	66.4	62.6
		Graduate & above	85.8	90.9	91.2	81.3	81.9
		All	55.4	56.1	54.0	55.3	54.9
	Female	Illiterate	37.0	37.8	35.7	31.5	22.4
		Below Primary	18.4	17.8	15.3	13.8	9.4
		Primary	29.4	26.7	24.9	22.4	15.6
		Middle	26.9	25.8	25.3	23.7	16.4
		Secondary / H.S.	32.9	28.8	26.9	21.9	15.5
		Graduate & above	36.3	47.8	44.3	36.7	31.6
		All	34.2	33.0	30.2	25.3	18.2

(Continued)

Table 16. *(Continued)*

Region	Sex	Edn Level	1983	1994	2000	2012	2018
Rural	Male + Female	Illiterate	43.7	44.4	42.2	40.4	33.9
		Below Primary	34.7	31.8	26.9	25.1	17.7
		Primary	51.5	47.6	42.7	39.3	35.7
		Middle	58.1	55.2	53.2	49.4	46.1
		Secondary / H.S.	68.3	62.9	61.3	49.7	44.1
		Graduate & above	75.1	82.9	81.0	67.3	63.7
		All	45.0	44.9	42.3	40.6	37.0
Urban	Male	Illiterate	40.3	41.0	39.6	39.5	42.8
		Below Primary	36.5	33.2	29.3	28.0	21.7
		Primary	58.1	54.1	50.7	50.1	52.4
		Middle	66.8	65.3	65.3	66.6	68.8
		Secondary / H.S.	72.8	68.9	68.3	64.0	61.5
		Geaduate & above	86.8	86.2	85.9	81.3	81.5
		All	53.9	54.3	54.2	56.3	57.0
	Female	Illiterate	19.0	19.9	17.9	16.3	15.8
		Below Primary	8.6	8.9	7.4	8.8	7.4
		Primary	11.8	12.7	10.7	13.1	13.6
		Middle	10.9	12.2	11.6	13.8	12.7
		Secondary / H.S.	19.1	16.5	14.2	11.8	11.9
		Graduate & above	34.6	36.6	32.0	32.0	34.4
		All	15.9	16.5	14.7	15.5	15.9
	Male + Female	Illiterate	27.7	28.5	26.8	25.7	27.1
		Below Primary	23.9	22.2	19.1	19.0	14.8
		Primary	37.9	34.9	31.8	32.6	33.3
		Middle	45.1	42.7	41.8	42.3	42.2
		Secondary / H.S.	54.5	48.5	46.3	40.3	38.8
		Graduate & above	71.0	68.9	66.0	61.9	60.4
		All	35.8	36.3	35.4	36.7	36.8

(Continued)

Table 16. *(Continued)*

Region	Sex	Edn Level	1983	1994	2000	2012	2018
Rural + Urban	Male	Illiterate	51.1	51.8	49.6	51.0	48.7
		Below Primary	41.9	39.2	34.2	33.2	24.2
		Primary	61.5	58.7	54.0	52.7	53.8
		Middle	68.5	68.2	67.8	67.5	68.5
		Secondary / H.S.	75.2	72.4	72.8	65.5	62.2
		Graduate & above	86.5	87.9	87.8	81.3	81.7
		All	55.0	55.6	54.0	55.6	55.5
	Female	Illiterate	34.2	35.0	32.9	28.7	21.1
		Below Primary	15.2	15.3	13.2	12.6	8.9
		Primary	22.8	22.0	20.5	19.9	15.1
		Middle	19.1	20.2	20.2	20.6	15.2
		Secondary / H.S.	23.6	21.7	20.0	17.3	14.1
		Graduate & above	35.0	38.6	34.5	33.4	33.4
		All	29.9	29.0	26.3	22.5	17.5
	Male + Female	Illiterate	41.3	42.0	39.8	37.6	32.5
		Below Primary	31.7	29.3	25.0	23.6	16.9
		Primary	47.2	43.8	39.7	37.6	35.1
		Middle	52.9	51.0	49.4	47.3	45.0
		Secondary / H.S.	60.6	55.9	54.2	45.9	42.2
		Graduate & above	72.2	73.2	70.6	63.7	61.7
		All	42.8	42.8	40.6	39.5	36.9

Source: Same as Table 10

When discussing labour force participation across educational groups, we should also consider each group's share of the total labour force.[5] The information presented in Table 17 indicates that the proportion of lower educational groups within the total labour force has declined significantly over time, while that of higher educational groups has increased for both males and females in both rural and urban areas. Nevertheless, the category of illiterates (considering all areas and all individuals together) has represented the highest percentage of the labour force throughout the period we considered, which was 26.4 % in 2018. However, differences exist between rural and urban areas regarding the share of illiterates in the total labour force. In 2018, illiterates comprised 30.9 % of the labour force in rural areas (considering both males and females), whereas the corresponding figure in urban areas was 15.3 %. Another notable point is that the share of illiterates among the total female labour force has consistently been higher than that among the total male labour force in rural and urban areas. This suggests that the female labour force in India is relatively less educated and skilled than its male counterpart.

5 According to the PLFS 2018, these groups represented 29.95 %, 13.32 %, 13.54 %, 17.27 %, 18.22 %, and 7.70 % of India's total population, respectively.

Table 17. Percentage Shares in Total Labour Force by Education Levels in India (UPSS Basis)

Sex	Edn level	Rural					Urban					Rural + Urban				
		1983	1994	2000	2012	2018	1983	1994	2000	2012	2018	1983	1994	2000	2012	2018
Male	Illiterate	52.3	43.6	39.4	27.5	24.8	22.3	18.2	15.9	11.1	12.8	45.2	37.4	33.3	22.7	21.2
	Below Primary	14.4	15.1	13.9	12.7	6.5	12.5	11.7	9.6	7.5	4.7	13.9	14.3	12.8	11.2	6.0
	Primary	15.0	14.0	13.6	14.9	14.2	17.8	14.0	12.2	11.3	11.1	15.7	14.0	13.2	13.8	13.3
	Middle	10.6	13.5	16.1	19.0	24.2	18.0	17.4	18.8	17.3	21.0	12.4	14.5	16.8	18.5	23.3
	Secondary / H.S.	6.2	11.0	13.7	19.5	22.1	19.5	24.4	26.4	27.3	26.1	9.4	14.3	17.0	21.8	23.3
	Graduate & Above	1.4	2.7	3.4	6.4	8.2	9.8	14.3	16.9	25.5	24.3	3.4	5.6	6.9	12.1	13.0
	All	100	100	100	100	100	100	100	100	100	100	100	100	100	100	100
Female	Illiterate	84.3	77.7	72.8	55.4	50.3	57.1	46.2	41.8	26.7	24.6	81.0	73.3	68.4	49.8	43.4
	Below Primary	5.6	7.8	8.2	10.0	7.0	9.1	9.4	8.5	8.4	5.4	6.0	8.1	8.3	9.7	6.6
	Primary	6.1	6.9	8.0	11.9	12.0	10.5	10.3	9.3	10.5	10.3	6.6	7.4	8.2	11.6	11.6
	Middle	2.5	4.4	6.2	10.9	13.8	7.0	8.7	10.4	12.1	13.1	3.1	5.0	6.8	11.1	13.6
	Secondary / H.S.	1.2	2.7	3.9	8.8	11.3	9.9	13.5	15.2	16.5	15.7	2.2	4.2	5.5	10.3	12.5
	Graduate & Above	0.3	0.5	0.9	3.0	5.7	6.4	11.8	14.9	25.9	30.9	1.0	2.1	2.8	7.5	12.4
	All	100	100	100	100	100	100	100	100	100	100	100	100	100	100	100
Male + Female	Illiterate	64.3	55.8	51.0	36.0	30.9	29.6	24.2	21.1	14.3	15.3	57.4	49.1	44.4	30.2	26.4
	Below Primary	11.1	12.5	11.9	11.9	6.6	11.8	11.2	9.4	7.7	4.8	11.2	12.3	11.3	10.8	6.1
	Primary	11.7	11.4	11.6	14.0	13.7	16.3	13.2	11.6	11.1	10.9	12.6	11.8	11.6	13.2	12.9
	Middle	7.6	10.3	12.7	16.5	21.7	15.6	15.5	17.2	16.2	19.3	9.2	11.4	13.7	16.4	21.0
	Secondary / H.S.	4.3	8.0	10.2	16.2	19.5	17.5	22.0	24.2	25.1	23.9	7.0	11.0	13.3	18.6	20.8
	Graduate & Above	1.0	2.0	2.5	5.4	7.6	9.1	13.8	16.5	25.6	25.7	2.6	4.5	5.6	10.8	12.9
	All	100	100	100	100	100	100	100	100	100	100	100	100	100	100	100

Source: Same as Table 10

3.5 Labour Force Participation Among Social Groups in India

This section discusses labour force participation patterns among various social groups during the period under study. In the NSSO survey, the population is categorised into four social groups – Scheduled Tribes (ST), Scheduled Castes (SC), Other Backward Classes (OBC), and 'Others' (which includes those not belonging to the preceding three categories, referred to as general castes). Based on our estimates using unit-level data from the 2017–18 Periodic Labour Force Survey, we found that the shares of these categories in the total population were 9.3 %, 19.6 %, 42.8 %, and 28.2 %, respectively.

Information on LFPR for different social groups is presented in Table 18. At the all-India level (including males and females across rural and urban areas), the LFPR has consistently been highest for ST, followed by SC, OBC, and 'Others'. In 2018, the LFPR for the ST was 41.8 %, while it was 37.6 % for SC, 36.2 % for OBC, and 35.9 % for 'Others'. It also appears that, although the LFPR declined over time across all social categories, in line with the country's general trend, the decline has been relatively more pronounced for the ST, SC, and OBC categories than for 'Others' between 2000 and 2018. However, it should be noted that, despite this decline, the weaker social categories (SC, ST, and OBC) have retained a higher LFPR than 'Others'.

Another point to note from Table 18 is that across all social categories, the LFPR has been significantly lower for females than for males. Furthermore, regarding the LFPR of males, there is little difference across social groups. Conversely, the LFPR for females from weaker social groups was higher than for the 'Others' group. In 2018, while the LFPR for females from the ST category stood at 26.6 %, the corresponding figures for SC, OBC, and 'Others' were 18.2 %, 17.1 %, and 14.7 %, respectively. When considering the LFPR of different social groups in rural and urban areas, a consistent conclusion emerges regarding the superiority of weaker social groups, particularly for females. Another observation is that while the LFPR for males across social groups does not differ much between rural and urban areas, the LFPR of rural females from weaker social groups is higher than that of urban females in the same categories. Moreover, in rural areas, concerning the extent of the decline in LFPR over time, rural females from weaker social groups have faced greater losses than those from the 'Others' group. Conversely, in urban areas, there appears to be a trend in which ST females are losing ground, while those from SC, OBC, and 'Others' are gaining ground in LFPR in recent years.

Table 18. Labour Force Participation Rates (%) by Social Groups in India (UPSS Basis)

Region	Sex	Social groups	1983	1994	2000	2012	2018
Rural	Male	ST	59.0	59.5	56.4	56.5	56.6
		SC	55.5	56.0	54.2	55.0	55.9
		OBC	–	–	54.1	54.7	53.6
		Others	54.8*	55.6*	53.2	56.2	55.6
		All	55.4	56.1	54.1	55.3	54.9
	Female	ST	47.9	48.3	44.1	36.9	27.6
		SC	38.3	35.6	32.6	26.5	18.0
		OBC	–	–	30.5	24.3	17.4
		Others	31.2*	30.0*	22.8	20.6	15.0
		All	34.2	33.0	30.0	25.3	18.2
	Male + Female	ST	53.5	54.0	50.3	46.9	42.5
		SC	47.1	46.2	43.7	41.1	37.3
		OBC	–	–	42.6	39.8	36.0
		Others	43.2*	43.2*	38.3	38.9	35.9
		All	45.0	44.9	42.3	40.6	37.0
Urban	Male	ST	55.5	54.5	50.1	53.8	53.7
		SC	51.6	52.9	53.1	56.3	57.3
		OBC	–	–	55.1	56.1	57.2
		Others	54.2*	54.5*	54.5	56.8	57.0
		All	53.9	54.3	54.3	56.3	57.0
	Female	ST	25.9	23.8	20.9	20.2	18.4
		SC	21.1	20.8	19.3	18.1	19.2
		OBC	–	–	16.8	15.9	16.1
		Others	14.7*	15.6*	11.8	13.8	14.2
		All	15.9	16.5	14.8	15.5	15.9
	Male + Female	ST	42.0	39.8	35.8	38.0	36.6
		SC	37.2	37.8	37.1	37.7	38.6
		OBC	–	–	36.7	36.7	36.9
		Others	35.4*	36.0*	34.1	36.3	36.0
		All	35.8	36.3	35.4	36.7	36.8

(Continued)

Table 18. *(Continued)*

Region	Sex	Social groups	1983	1994	2000	2012	2018
Rural + Urban	Male	ST	58.7	59.1	55.7	56.1	56.2
		SC	54.8	55.5	54.0	55.3	56.2
		OBC	–	–	54.3	55.1	54.6
		Others	54.7*	55.3*	53.7	56.5	56.2
		All	55.0	55.6	54.2	55.6	55.5
	Female	ST	46.0	46.3	41.5	35.1	26.6
		SC	35.4	33.1	30.2	24.7	18.2
		OBC	–	–	27.5	22.1	17.1
		Others	26.9*	26.0*	19.0	17.8	14.7
		All	29.9	29.0	26.2	22.5	17.5
	Male + Female	ST	52.5	52.8	48.7	45.9	41.8
		SC	45.4	44.8	42.5	40.4	37.6
		OBC	–	–	41.2	38.9	36.2
		Others	41.1*	41.1*	36.8	37.8	35.9
		All	42.8	42.8	40.6	39.5	36.9

Source: Same as Table 10
*Note: * for 1983 and 1994, the category of 'Others' included the OBC*

We also have data on the percentage shares of various social categories in the country's total labour force. The information presented in Table 19 shows that in 2018, the largest proportion of the labour force across the country belonged to the OBC category (42 %), followed by 'Others' (27.4 %), SC (20 %), and ST (10.6 %). From 2000 to 2018, although the share of OBC individuals appears to have increased within the total labour force, that of the 'Others' has declined. Nevertheless, the shares of SC (approximately 20 %) and ST (around 10 %) in the total labour force have remained relatively stable. When we examine the percentage distribution of the labour force among various social groups separately for rural and urban areas, it becomes evident that the shares of weaker groups (ST, SC, and OBC) in the total labour force are higher in rural areas compared to urban areas. A contrasting scenario exists for the 'Others' category, for whom the share of the labour force is higher in urban areas. The same conclusion holds when comparing the labour force shares of males and females separately in rural and urban settings.

Table 19. Percentage Shares in Total Labour Force by Social Groups in India (UPSS Basis)

Region	Sex	Social groups	1983	1994	2000	2012	2018
Rural	Male	ST	10.7	10.8	11.0	11.1	12.1
		SC	18.6	20.4	21.6	20.6	21.9
		OBC	–	–	37.1	44.4	42.5
		Others	70.7*	68.9*	30.4	24.0	23.5
		All	100	100	100	100	100
	Female	ST	14.2	15.2	15.8	15.8	17.8
		SC	20.4	21.6	23.0	21.7	21.4
		OBC	–	–	37.5	43.6	41.7
		Others	65.4*	63.2*	23.7	18.9	19.1
		All	100	100	100	100	100
	Male + Female	ST	12.0	12.3	12.7	12.5	13.5
		SC	19.3	20.8	22.1	20.9	21.8
		OBC	–	–	37.2	44.1	42.3
		Others	68.8*	66.8*	28.0	22.4	22.5
		All	100	100	100	100	100
Urban	Male	ST	3.5	2.9	3.5	3.3	3.4
		SC	11.9	12.5	14.2	14.2	14.9
		OBC	–	–	31.5	41.1	41.2
		Others	84.6*	84.6*	50.7	41.5	40.5
		All	100	100	100	100	100
	Female	ST	5.0	4.2	5.6	4.3	4.1
		SC	16.3	16.0	18.7	17.0	17.9
		OBC	–	–	35.6	42.6	42.0
		Others	78.7*	79.7*	40.1	36.1	35.9
		All	100	100	100	100	100
	Male + Female	ST	3.8	3.2	3.9	3.5	3.6
		SC	12.9	13.2	15.1	14.7	15.6
		OBC	–	–	32.4	41.4	41.4
		Others	83.4*	83.6*	48.6	40.4	39.5
		All	100	100	100	100	100

(Continued)

Table 19. *(Continued)*

Region	Sex	Social groups	1983	1994	2000	2012	2018
Rural + Urban	Male	ST	8.9	8.8	9.1	8.8	9.5
		SC	17.0	18.4	19.7	18.7	19.8
		OBC	–	–	35.6	43.4	42.1
		Others	74.1*	72.8*	35.7	29.1	28.6
		All	100	100	100	100	100
	Female	ST	13.1	13.6	14.3	13.6	14.2
		SC	19.9	20.9	22.4	20.7	20.5
		OBC	–	–	37.2	43.4	41.8
		Others	67.0*	65.5*	26.0	22.3	23.6
		All	100	100	100	100	100
	Male + Female	ST	10.3	10.4	10.7	10.1	10.6
		SC	18.0	19.2	20.5	19.3	20.0
		OBC	–	–	36.1	43.4	42.0
		Others	71.7*	70.4*	32.6	27.2	27.4
		All	100	100	100	100	100

Source: Same as Table 10
Note: Same as Table 18

3.6 Labour Force Participation Among Religious Groups in India

We now examine India's labour force participation rates across different religious groups. Firstly, it is worth noting that, according to the PLFS 2018 data, Hindus comprise 81.7 % of the total population in India, followed by Muslims (12.7 %), Christians (2.2 %), and 'Others' (3.4 %). Since Hindus and Muslims together account for approximately 94 % of the total population, our discussion on LFPR for various religious groups will primarily focus on a comparison between these two groups.

The LFPR information for different religious groups is presented in Table 20. At the all-India level, the LFPR has been the highest for Christians throughout our study period. However, when we compare the LFPR of Hindus and Muslims, it appears that the former enjoyed superiority compared to the latter in all the years considered by us. This observation holds true irrespective of the region (rural/urban) and sex (male/female) of the persons considered. In 2018, across all persons, including rural and urban areas, the LFPR for Hindus and Muslims was 37.7 % and 31.2 %, respectively. However, it is worth noting that the LFPR gap for these two religious groups has been gradually reduced over time. Thus, while the LFPR of Hindus exceeded that of Muslims by 8.8 percentage points in 1983, it exceeded that of Muslims by 6.5 percentage points in 2018.

As we consider the LFPR for males and females from various religious groups, it becomes evident that Muslim females lag significantly behind their male counterparts when compared to Hindu females. Thus, at the all-India level (rural and urban combined) in 2018, while the male-female difference in LFPR for Muslims was 42.3 percentage points, the corresponding figure for Hindus was 37.4 percentage points. Table 20 also indicates that the male-female gap in LFPR for Muslims is more pronounced in urban areas than in rural areas. This suggests that Muslim females in urban settings find themselves in a more disadvantaged position relative to males compared to their counterparts in rural areas.

Table 20. Labour Force Participation Rates (%) by Religious Groups in India (UPSS Basis)

Region	Sex	Religious groups	1983	1994	2000	2012	2018
Rural	Male	Hindus	55.7	56.7	54.7	55.8	55.4
		Muslims	51.8	50.5	48.9	51.1	50.4
		Christians	54.7	57.6	58.3	56.0	56.3
		Others	58.6	56.6	54.2	57.9	58.0
		All	55.4	56.1	54.1	55.3	54.9
	Female	Hindus	35.6	34.9	31.6	26.4	19.1
		Muslims	20.5	16.5	16.7	15.9	10.5
		Christians	39.1	37.6	34.1	30.4	22.8
		Others	34.1	31.2	31.3	30.1	18.2
		All	34.2	33.0	30.0	25.3	18.2
	Male + Female	Hindus	45.8	46.1	43.4	41.5	37.7
		Muslims	36.3	33.9	32.8	33.7	30.7
		Christians	46.9	47.6	46.1	43.1	39.6
		Others	46.8	44.4	43.2	44.7	38.8
		All	45.0	44.9	42.3	40.6	37.0

(Continued)

Table 20. *(Continued)*

Region	Sex	Religious groups	1983	1994	2000	2012	2018
Urban	Male	Hindus	54.5	54.8	54.9	56.5	57.4
		Muslims	51.7	51.7	52.2	55.3	55.1
		Christians	52.8	54.3	52.1	56.5	55.2
		Others	52.6	54.1	52.9	56.4	57.5
		All	53.9	54.3	54.3	56.3	57.0
	Female	Hindus	16.6	17.1	15.4	16.1	17.1
		Muslims	11.5	12.8	10.7	10.9	8.2
		Christians	24.0	24.7	25.0	27.7	22.8
		Others	12.5	12.6	12.3	14.5	17.1
		All	15.9	16.5	14.8	15.5	15.9
	Male + Female	Hindus	36.6	37.0	36.1	37.2	37.7
		Muslims	32.3	33.2	32.4	34.2	32.0
		Christians	38.9	39.6	38.5	41.7	38.5
		Others	33.6	34.1	33.5	36.4	37.6
		All	35.8	36.3	35.4	36.7	36.8
Rural + Urban	Male	Hindus	55.4	56.2	54.7	56.0	55.9
		Muslims	51.8	51.0	50.0	52.6	52.1
		Christians	54.1	56.6	56.4	56.2	55.9
		Others	56.8	55.9	53.8	57.4	57.8
		All	55.0	55.6	54.2	55.6	55.5
	Female	Hindus	31.5	30.9	27.8	23.6	18.6
		Muslims	17.4	15.3	14.8	14.2	9.9
		Christians	34.7	33.8	31.3	29.4	22.8
		Others	27.9	25.9	25.7	25.1	17.9
		All	29.9	29.0	26.2	22.5	17.5
	Male + Female	Hindus	43.8	44.0	41.7	40.3	37.7
		Muslims	34.9	33.6	32.7	33.9	31.2
		Christians	44.5	45.2	43.8	42.6	39.2
		Others	43.0	41.5	40.3	42.0	38.5
		All	42.8	42.8	40.6	39.5	36.9

Source: Same as Table 10

In Table 21, we have presented information on the shares of different religious groups in the total labour force. In 2018 (considering males and females and rural and urban areas together), as against 83.4 % of the total labour force being Hindus, the percentage of Muslims in the labour force was 10.7%. It, however, needs to be mentioned that the share of Hindus in the labour force has been declining over time, and that of Muslims is increasing. This declining trend in the labour force share is also evident among Christians.

Table 21. Percentage Shares in Total Labour Force by Religious Groups in India (UPSS Basis)

Region	Sex	Religious groups	1983	1994	2000	2012	2018
Rural	Male	Hindus	85.8	86.1	84.9	84.0	84.1
		Muslims	8.8	8.8	9.8	11.3	10.2
		Christians	2.2	2.1	2.2	1.9	1.9
		Others	3.2	3.0	3.0	2.8	3.7
		All	100	100	100	100	100
	Female	Hindus	88.8	89.8	88.1	86.7	87.5
		Muslims	5.7	5.0	6.3	7.9	6.6
		Christians	2.6	2.4	2.5	2.3	2.5
		Others	2.9	2.8	3.1	3.0	3.5
		All	100	100	100	100	100
	Male + Female	Hindus	86.9	87.4	86.0	84.8	84.9
		Muslims	7.7	7.4	8.6	10.3	9.4
		Christians	2.3	2.2	2.3	2.0	2.1
		Others	3.1	2.9	3.0	2.9	3.7
		All	100	100	100	100	100
Urban	Male	Hindus	78.1	79.2	78.2	78.1	78.7
		Muslims	15.2	14.8	15.7	15.2	15.4
		Christians	2.9	2.6	2.6	2.9	2.6
		Others	3.8	3.5	3.6	3.8	3.3
		All	100	100	100	100	100

(Continued)

Table 21. *(Continued)*

Region	Sex	Religious groups	1983	1994	2000	2012	2018
Urban	Female	Hindus	80.4	81.0	80.3	80.4	83.2
		Muslims	11.9	12.0	11.7	11.9	9.1
		Christians	4.6	4.2	5.0	4.6	4.2
		Others	3.0	2.8	3.0	3.0	3.6
		All	100	100	100	100	100
	Male + Female	Hindus	78.6	79.6	78.6	78.6	79.7
		Muslims	14.5	14.2	14.9	14.5	14.1
		Christians	3.3	2.9	3.0	3.3	2.9
		Others	3.6	3.4	3.5	3.6	3.4
		All	100	100	100	100	100
Rural + Urban	Male	Hindus	83.9	84.4	83.2	82.1	82.5
		Muslims	10.4	10.3	11.3	13.0	11.8
		Christians	2.3	2.2	2.3	2.0	2.1
		Others	3.3	3.2	3.2	2.9	3.6
		All	100	100	100	100	100
	Female	Hindus	87.7	88.6	87.0	85.4	86.3
		Muslims	6.5	6.0	7.1	8.8	7.3
		Christians	2.9	2.7	2.9	2.8	2.9
		Others	2.9	2.8	3.1	3.0	3.5
		All	100	100	100	100	100
	Male + Female	Hindus	85.2	85.7	84.4	83.0	83.4
		Muslims	9.0	8.9	10.0	11.9	10.7
		Christians	2.5	2.4	2.5	2.2	2.3
		Others	3.2	3.0	3.1	2.9	3.6
		All	100	100	100	100	100

Source: Same as Table 10

When we consider males and females separately in rural areas, the same declining trend in the share of the total labour force is evident among Hindus for both groups. On the other hand, both males and females among Muslims in rural areas have improved their positions in terms of shares in the total labour force. In urban areas, the proportion of male Hindus and Muslims in the urban labour force remained nearly unchanged from 1983 to 2018. However, while Hindu females in urban areas have improved their share of the total urban labour force (especially in 2018 compared to preceding years), Muslim females seem to have lost somewhat.

Considering both males and females together, it can be said that in rural areas, while Hindus experienced a decline in their share of the total labour force, Muslims improved their position in this regard. In contrast, in urban areas, while Hindus appear to have increased their share of the total labour force, Muslims' position has remained relatively unchanged.

3.7 Growth of the Labour Force in India

3.7.1 All-India Scenario

We now examine the growth of the labour force in India across all possible levels of disaggregation – region, sex, age groups, education levels, social categories, and religious affiliations – from 1983 to 2018. To enhance our understanding of labour force growth, we have divided the entire period into four sub-periods: 1983–1994, 1994–2000, 2000–2012, and 2012–2018. In addition to these sub-periods, we have calculated growth rates from 1994 to 2018, which can be termed the post-globalisation era in India, and compared them with the period from 1983 to 1994, referred to as the pre-globalisation era.

Table 22 presents data on the annual compound growth rates of the labour force in all-India for males, females, and persons in rural, urban, and combined areas. The growth rate of the rural labour force decreased from 1.60 % annually between 1983 and 1994 to 0.50 % from 1994 to 2018. In the final sub-period, from 2012 to 2018, the growth rate fell to –0.44 %. Although labour force growth rates during the post-globalisation period have been lower for both males and females in rural areas than during the pre-globalisation period, the decline has been more pronounced for females than for males. As indicated in the table, from 1983 to 1994, males and females in rural areas recorded labour force growth rates of 1.71 % and 1.42 %, respectively; these figures declined to 1.21 % and –1.16 %, respectively, from 1994 to 2018. Another noteworthy point is that rural women began withdrawing from the labour force in large numbers after 2000, resulting in a negative growth rate of –0.26 % for this category from 2000 to 2012. This trend was further pronounced in the subsequent sub-period (2012 to 2018), as evidenced by a labour force growth rate of –4.24 % for rural women.

Table 22. Annual Growth Rates (%) of Labour Force in India (UPSS Basis)

Region	Sex	Annual growth rate (%) during				
		1983 to 1994	**1994 to 2000**	**2000 to 2012**	**2012 to 2018**	**1994 to 2018**
Rural	Male	1.71	0.99	1.41	1.03	1.21
	Female	1.42	0.18	−0.26	−4.24	-1.16
	Male + Female	1.60	0.71	0.86	−0.44	0.50
Urban	Male	3.04	2.70	3.01	2.87	2.90
	Female	3.51	0.87	3.39	3.39	2.75
	Male + Female	3.14	2.32	3.09	2.87	2.84
Rural + Urban	Male	2.04	1.45	1.89	1.62	1.71
	Female	1.70	0.29	0.40	-2.27	-0.30
	Male + Female	1.93	1.08	1.45	0.55	1.13

Source: Same as Table 10

The growth of the labour force in urban areas differs significantly from that in rural areas for both males and females. The first observation from comparing rural and urban areas is that the growth of the labour force in the former has been lower than in the latter in all sub-periods for both males and females. The growth rate of the urban labour force for both males and females decreased slightly in the post-globalisation period compared to the pre-globalisation period. As shown in Table 22, while the growth rates for urban males and females between 1983 and 1994 were 3.04 % and 3.51 %, respectively, the corresponding rates from 1994 to 2018 are 2.90 % and 2.75 %, respectively. Another notable point is that during the last sub-period, 2012–2018, when rural females experienced a significant decline in labour force growth, urban females not only showed remarkable growth (3.39 %) but also surpassed urban males (2.87 %) in this regard. Recent developments in rural labour markets have not favoured females, resulting in a substantial decline in both the growth rate and the absolute numbers of the labour force.

Considering both rural and urban areas, it is again noted that the labour force growth for both males and females declined during the post-globalisation period compared to the pre-globalisation period. However, the decline in growth rate has been more significant among females than among males. Females recorded a negative labour force growth rate of −0.30 % during the post-globalisation period, whereas the growth rate was impressive during the pre-globalisation period at

1.70 %. On the other hand, in combined rural and urban areas, the male labour force growth rate decreased from 2.04 % during the pre-globalisation period to 1.71 % in the post-globalisation period. When considering both males and females together across the combined (rural plus urban) areas, the labour force growth rate declined from 1.93 % between 1983 and 1994 to 1.13 % between 1994 and 2018.

3.7.2 Labour Force Growth Rates by Age Groups

Table 23 presents labour force growth rates in all-India across various age groups. The overall labour force growth rate, across all regions and genders, has decreased over time across all age categories. However, this decline is less pronounced among older age groups (25–34, 35–59, and 60 and above) than younger groups (5–14 and 15–24). This trend is evident in both rural and urban areas, as well as among males and females, with few exceptions (male, female, and male plus female in urban areas with the age group 60 and above, where the labour force growth rate increased over time). The table further reveals that the decrease in the labour force growth rate during the post-globalisation period, compared to the pre-globalisation period, was more pronounced for females than for males across most age groups in both rural and urban contexts. This decline has been notably more significant for rural females in the post-globalisation era than for their urban counterparts. As shown in the table, all age groups for rural females (except 35–59) experienced negative growth rates of the labour force from 1994 to 2018, while these rates were high and positive from 1983 to 1994 (except rural females in the 5–14 age group, which recorded a high negative growth rate of –4.4 %).

Table 23. Annual Growth Rates of Labour Force (UPSS) in India by Age Groups

Region	Sex	Age groups	1983 to 1994	1994 to 2000	2000 to 2012	2012 to 2018	1994 to 2018
Rural	Male	5–14	-5.3	–4.2	-8.8	-5.4	-6.8
		15–24	1.4	–0.1	–0.4	–0.7	-0.4
		25–34	2.3	1.4	1.1	1.5	1.3
		35–59	2.4	1.8	2.5	1.5	2.1
		60 & above	2.2	0.8	2.5	0.7	1.6
		All ages	1.7	1.0	1.4	1.0	1.2

(Continued)

Table 23. *(Continued)*

Region	Sex	Age groups	1983 to 1994	1994 to 2000	2000 to 2012	2012 to 2018	1994 to 2018
Rural	Female	5–14	−4.4	−3.8	−8.9	−24.8	−11.9
		15–24	0.7	−1.1	−2.6	−9.0	−3.9
		25–34	2.5	0.7	−0.9	−4.2	−1.4
		35–59	2.2	0.9	1.2	−2.4	0.2
		60 & above	2.4	0.8	2.3	−6.1	−0.2
		All ages	1.4	0.2	−0.3	−4.2	−1.2
	Male + Female	5–14	−5.0	−4.0	−8.8	−11.9	−8.4
		15–24	1.1	−0.5	−1.1	−2.7	−1.3
		25–34	2.4	1.1	0.4	−0.1	0.5
		35–59	2.3	1.5	2.1	0.3	1.5
		60 & above	2.3	0.8	2.4	−0.8	1.2
		All ages	1.6	0.7	0.9	−0.4	0.5
Urban	Male	5–14	−3.2	−1.9	−1.8	−11.0	−4.2
		15–24	1.6	1.8	0.9	0.8	1.1
		25–34	3.2	2.5	3.3	2.7	2.9
		35–59	4.2	3.5	3.7	3.4	3.5
		60 & above	2.3	2.0	4.1	6.7	4.2
		All ages	3.0	2.7	3.0	2.9	2.9
	Female	5–14	−1.6	−1.7	−9.4	−15.7	−9.2
		15–24	2.5	−0.6	2.2	0.2	1.0
		25–34	4.3	0.7	4.5	3.5	3.3
		35–59	4.5	1.9	3.7	4.3	3.4
		60 & above	1.4	1.1	3.0	5.7	3.2
		All ages	3.5	0.9	3.4	3.4	2.8
	Male + Female	5–14	−2.6	−1.9	−4.0	−11.9	−5.5
		15–24	1.8	1.3	1.2	0.6	1.1
		25–34	3.4	2.1	3.5	2.7	3.0
		35–59	4.3	3.2	3.7	3.4	3.5
		60 & above	2.1	1.8	3.9	6.4	4.0
		All ages	3.1	2.3	3.1	2.9	2.8

(Continued)

Table 23. *(Continued)*

Region	Sex	Age groups	1983 to 1994	1994 to 2000	2000 to 2012	2012 to 2018	1994 to 2018
Rural + Urban	Male	5–14	-5.0	-3.8	-7.3	-6.7	-6.3
		15–24	1.5	0.4	0.0	-0.2	0.0
		25–34	2.5	1.7	1.8	1.9	1.8
		35–59	2.8	2.3	2.9	2.1	2.6
		60 & above	2.3	1.1	2.8	2.0	2.2
		All ages	2.0	1.5	1.9	1.6	1.7
	Female	5–14	-4.2	-3.5	-8.9	-23.5	-11.5
		15–24	0.9	-1.0	-1.7	-6.5	-2.8
		25–34	2.8	0.7	0.1	-2.0	-0.3
		35–59	2.5	1.1	1.7	-0.7	0.9
		60 & above	2.3	0.8	2.5	-3.9	0.5
		All ages	1.7	0.3	0.4	-2.3	-0.3
	Male + Female	5–14	-4.6	-3.6	-8.0	-11.9	-7.9
		15–24	1.3	-0.1	-0.5	-1.8	-0.7
		25–34	2.6	1.4	1.3	0.8	1.2
		35–59	2.7	1.9	2.6	1.3	2.1
		60 & above	2.3	1.0	2.7	0.7	1.8
		All ages	1.9	1.1	1.5	0.5	1.1

Source: Same as Table 10

From 1994 to 2018, the growth of the rural male labour force declined in the 5–14 and 15–24 age groups. For rural females, all age groups except one also experienced negative growth during the same period. In urban areas, males and females experienced negative labour force growth in the 5–14 age group only during the post-globalisation period. Furthermore, the difference in growth rates between males and females in the labour force is considerably smaller in urban areas than in rural areas.

Overall, although the labour force growth rate for both males and females has declined in the post-globalisation period compared to the pre-globalisation period, rural females, especially those from younger age groups, have experienced a more significant reduction.

3.7.3 Labour Force Growth Rates by Educational Groups

We now examine the growth rates of the labour force across different educational groups. Table 24 indicates that, following the overall trend in India, the labour force growth rate declined for nearly all education groups during the post-globalisation period (1994–2018) compared with the pre-globalisation period (1983–1994). The labour force growth rate for illiterates and individuals with below primary education decreased and became negative during the post-globalisation period, across both rural and urban areas. This trend is consistent even when analysing males and females separately. The only segment of the population that experienced a marginal increase in the labour force growth rate during the post-globalisation period is those with primary-level education; however, this observation applies only to males, not to females.

Overall, it seems that at the aggregate level, as well as in rural areas, individuals from lower educational backgrounds (illiterates and those with education below the primary level) suffered the most during the post-globalisation period, experiencing a decline in their labour force growth rates compared to the pre-globalisation era. This conclusion is supported by comparing the growth rates from the last sub-period (2012–2018) with those from earlier sub-periods.

Table 24. Annual Growth Rates of Labour Force (UPSS) in India by Education Groups

Region	Sex	Edn Level	1983 to 1994	1994 to 2000	2000 to 2012	2012 to 2018	1994 to 2018
Rural	Male	Illiterate	−0.03	−0.7	−1.6	−0.7	-1.1
		Below Primary	2.2	−0.5	0.7	-9.6	-2.3
		Primary	1.0	0.5	2.2	0.3	1.3
		Middle	4.1	4.0	2.8	5.2	3.7
		Secondary / H.S.	7.4	4.8	4.5	3.2	4.2
		Graduate & above	8.0	4.8	6.9	5.2	6.0
		All	1.7	1.0	1.4	1.0	1.2

(Continued)

Table 24. *(Continued)*

Region	Sex	Edn Level	1983 to 1994	1994 to 2000	2000 to 2012	2012 to 2018	1994 to 2018
Rural	Female	Illiterate	0.6	-0.9	-2.5	-5.8	-2.9
		Below Primary	4.7	1.0	1.4	-9.8	-1.6
		Primary	2.6	2.8	3.1	-4.2	1.2
		Middle	6.9	6.4	4.4	-0.3	3.7
		Secondary / H.S.	9.9	6.4	6.8	-0.2	4.9
		Graduate & above	7.9	8.1	10.9	6.2	9.0
		All	1.4	0.2	-0.3	-4.2	-1.2
	Male + Female	Illiterate	0.2	-0.8	-2.0	-2.9	-1.9
		Below Primary	2.8	-0.2	0.9	-9.7	-2.1
		Primary	1.4	1.0	2.4	-0.8	1.2
		Middle	4.5	4.3	3.1	4.2	3.7
		Secondary / H.S.	7.7	4.9	4.8	2.7	4.3
		Graduate & above	8.2	5.0	7.5	5.4	6.3
		All	1.6	0.7	0.9	-0.4	0.5
Urban	Male	Illiterate	1.1	0.5	0.0	5.4	1.4
		Below Primary	2.4	-0.6	0.9	-5.0	-1.0
		Primary	0.7	0.4	2.3	2.5	1.9
		Middle	2.7	4.1	2.3	6.3	3.7
		Secondary / H.S.	5.2	4.1	3.3	2.1	3.2
		Graduate & above	6.8	5.6	6.6	2.0	5.2
		All	3.0	2.7	3.0	2.9	2.9

(Continued)

Table 24. *(Continued)*

Region	Sex	Edn Level	1983 to 1994	1994 to 2000	2000 to 2012	2012 to 2018	1994 to 2018
Urban	Female	Illiterate	1.4	−0.8	−0.4	1.9	0.1
		Below Primary	3.9	−0.8	3.2	-3.8	0.4
		Primary	3.3	-1.0	4.5	3.2	2.8
		Middle	5.7	4.0	4.7	4.8	4.5
		Secondary / H.S.	6.6	2.8	4.1	2.6	3.4
		Graduate & above	9.8	4.8	8.3	6.5	7.0
		All	3.5	0.9	3.4	3.4	2.8
	Male + Female	Illiterate	1.2	−0.02	−0.2	4.1	0.9
		Below Primary	2.6	−0.6	1.4	−4.8	−0.7
		Primary	1.1	0.2	2.7	2.5	2.0
		Middle	3.1	4.1	2.6	5.9	3.8
		Secondary / H.S.	5.4	3.9	3.4	2.0	3.2
		Graduate & above	7.3	5.4	6.9	2.9	5.5
		All	3.1	2.3	3.1	2.9	2.8
Rural+Urban	Male	Illiterate	0.2	−0.5	−1.3	0.5	−0.7
		Below Primary	2.3	−0.4	0.8	−8.5	-1.9
		Primary	0.9	0.5	2.2	0.9	1.5
		Middle	3.6	4.0	2.7	5.6	3.7
		Secondary / H.S.	6.2	4.4	4.0	2.8	3.8
		Graduate & above	6.8	5.1	6.7	2.9	5.4
		All	2.0	1.5	1.9	1.6	1.7

(Continued)

Table 24. *(Continued)*

Region	Sex	Edn Level	1983 to 1994	1994 to 2000	2000 to 2012	2012 to 2018	1994 to 2018
Rural+Urban	Female	Illiterate	0.7	−0.9	−2.2	−4.5	−2.5
		Below Primary	4.5	0.7	1.7	−8.4	−1.2
		Primary	2.7	2.1	3.4	−2.4	1.6
		Middle	6.5	5.8	4.5	1.1	4.0
		Secondary / H.S.	8.0	4.7	5.9	0.9	4.3
		Graduate & above	8.9	5.2	9.0	6.3	7.3
		All	1.7	0.3	0.4	−2.3	−0.3
	Male + Female	Illiterate	0.4	−0.6	−1.8	−1.7	−1.5
		Below Primary	2.8	−0.2	1.0	−8.5	−1.8
		Primary	1.3	0.8	2.5	0.1	1.5
		Middle	4.0	4.2	3.0	4.8	3.8
		Secondary / H.S.	6.4	4.4	4.3	2.4	3.9
		Graduate & above	7.2	5.1	7.1	3.5	5.7
		All	1.9	1.1	1.5	0.5	1.1

Source: Same as Table 10

3.7.4 Labour Force Growth Rates Among Social Groups

Let us focus on the labour force growth rates for different social groups at the all-India level. The information presented in Table 25 shows that, in rural areas, from 1983 to 1994 (the pre-globalisation period), the labour force growth rates for backward social groups such as ST and SC were significantly higher than those for the 'OBC+Others' category. This observation holds even when considering rural males and females separately. Although the growth rate of the labour force declined in rural areas for all categories during the post-globalisation period (1994–2018), and more specifically during the sub-period 2012–2018, the rate of decline was comparatively less for the males from the ST and SC categories than for their counterparts in the 'OBC+Others' category. The situation regarding rural females is somewhat different, as the labour force growth rates turned negative during the post-globalisation period, regardless of the social category to which they belonged. However, it should be noted that the magnitude of the decline in the labour force growth rate during the post-globalisation period has been relatively less severe for rural women from the ST and SC categories compared to those from 'OBC+Others'.

Table 25. Annual Growth Rates of Labour Force (UPSS) in India by Social Groups

Region	Sex	Social groups	1983 to 1994	1994 to 2000	2000 to 2012	2012 to 2018	1994 to 2018
Rural	Male	ST	1.81	1.41	1.42	2.54	1.69
		SC	2.59	1.96	1.02	2.06	1.51
		OBC	–	–	2.94	0.30	–
		OBC+Others	1.45	0.63	1.52	0.45	1.03
		All	1.71	0.99	1.41	1.03	1.21
	Female	ST	2.06	0.88	−0.25	−2.33	−0.49
		SC	1.99	1.22	−0.76	−4.40	−1.20
		OBC	–	–	1.00	−4.96	–
		OBC+Others	1.08	−0.36	−0.08	−4.70	−1.32
		All	1.42	0.18	−0.26	−4.24	−1.16
	Male + Female	ST	1.90	1.17	0.74	0.79	0.86
		SC	2.35	1.69	0.42	0.23	0.69
		OBC	–	–	2.31	−1.15	–
		OBC+Others	1.33	0.30	1.04	−0.90	0.37
		All	1.60	0.71	0.86	−0.44	0.50
Urban	Male	ST	1.28	6.04	2.51	3.56	3.65
		SC	3.47	4.99	2.97	3.76	3.67
		OBC	–	–	5.30	2.91	–
		OBC+Others	3.04	2.21	3.04	2.69	2.74
		All	3.04	2.70	3.01	2.87	2.90
	Female	ST	1.83	5.53	1.23	2.55	2.62
		SC	3.32	3.55	2.54	4.35	3.24
		OBC	–	–	4.95	3.15	–
		OBC+Others	3.64	0.00	3.72	3.22	2.65
		All	3.51	0.87	3.39	3.39	2.75
	Male + Female	ST	1.42	5.92	2.15	3.19	3.34
		SC	3.43	4.63	2.86	3.80	3.53
		OBC	–	–	5.22	2.86	–
		OBC+Others	3.16	1.78	3.17	2.68	2.70
		All	3.14	2.32	3.09	2.87	2.84

(Continued)

Table 25. *(Continued)*

Region	Sex	Social groups	1983 to 1994	1994 to 2000	2000 to 2012	2012 to 2018	1994 to 2018
Rural + Urban	Male	ST	1.92	1.92	1.58	2.99	2.02
		SC	2.82	2.56	1.46	2.60	2.02
		OBC	–	–	3.58	1.10	–
		OBC+Others	1.87	1.11	2.04	1.18	1.59
		All	2.04	1.45	1.89	1.62	1.71
	Female	ST	2.12	1.13	-0.06	-1.58	-0.15
		SC	2.15	1.49	-0.24	-2.46	-0.37
		OBC	–	–	1.69	-2.90	–
		OBC+Others	1.47	-0.30	0.72	-2.36	-0.31
		All	1.70	0.29	0.40	-2.27	-0.30
	Male + Female	ST	1.99	1.60	0.93	1.33	1.20
		SC	2.56	2.19	0.92	1.16	1.29
		OBC	–	–	3.02	0.003	–
		OBC+Others	1.75	0.69	1.68	0.26	1.08
		All	1.93	1.08	1.45	0.55	1.13

Source: Same as Table 10
Note: The growth rates for 'OBC' could not be computed for 1983/1994, 1994/2000, and 1994/2018 due to non-availability of separate information for them for 1983 and 1994.

In urban areas, the growth rates of the labour force for males from disadvantaged social categories, such as ST and SC, have improved during the post-globalisation period (as well as during the sub-period 2012–2018) compared to the pre-globalisation period. In contrast, for males from the 'OBC+Others' category, the growth rate of the labour force declined slightly during the post-globalisation period (falling from 3.04 % during 1983–1994 to 2.74 % during 1994–2018). Among urban females, those from the ST category experienced a higher labour force growth rate during the post-globalisation period than during the pre-globalisation period. However, urban females in the SC and 'OBC+Others' categories experienced declining labour force growth rates. When considering urban individuals (males and females combined), it can be concluded that while those from weaker social categories (ST and SC) improved their labour force growth rates during the post-globalisation period, individuals from the 'OBC+Others' category experienced a decline in their growth rate.

Let us consider the rural and urban areas together. There has been an improvement in the labour force growth rate for males from the ST category during the post-globalisation period. However, for all other categories, the growth rate of the labour force has declined, with a more significant decrease observed in the 'OBC+Others' category compared to the SC category. Regarding females, growth rates for all social categories became negative during the post-globalisation era. When considering all individuals combined across rural and urban areas, the SC category ranks first in labour force growth rate, followed by the ST and 'OBC+Others' categories. Even in the last sub-period from 2012 to 2018, which saw a notable decline in the overall labour force growth rate compared to earlier sub-periods, individuals from the ST category recorded a growth rate of 1.33 %. In contrast, those in the SC and 'OBC+Others' categories reported growth rates of 1.16 % and 0.26 %, respectively.

3.7.5 Labour Force Growth Rates Among Religious Groups

Table 26 presents the labour force growth rates by religious groups in India. Considering all individuals across combined areas (rural and urban), it is observed that the growth rate of the labour force among Hindus exceeded that of Muslims during the pre-globalisation period. However, in the post-globalisation period, particularly until 2012, the growth rate of the Muslim labour force continued to rise, while that of the Hindu labour force declined. Across the entire post-globalisation period (1994–2018), it appears that Muslims experienced 1.94 % labour force growth, compared with 1.01 % for Hindus. The observation that Muslims outperformed Hindus regarding labour force growth rates during the post-globalisation period remains valid even when examining males and females separately in the combined areas. The declining labour force growth rate during the post-globalisation period is evident among Christian females. In contrast, Christian males experienced a higher growth rate during this period than before globalisation.

Table 26. Annual Growth Rates of Labour Force (UPSS) in India by Religious Groups

Region	Sex	Religious groups	1983 to 1994	1994 to 2000	2000 to 2012	2012 to 2018	1994 to 2018
Rural	Male	Hindus	1.74	0.77	1.31	1.05	1.11
		Muslims	1.68	2.83	2.64	−0.68	1.84
		Christians	1.27	2.30	−0.18	1.59	0.87
		Others	1.23	0.88	0.76	6.00	2.08
		All	1.71	0.99	1.41	1.03	1.21
	Female	Hindus	1.53	−0.13	−0.39	−4.10	−1.27
		Muslims	0.05	4.16	1.69	−7.08	0.02
		Christians	0.78	0.62	−0.84	−3.39	−1.12
		Others	1.04	1.90	−0.38	−2.07	−0.24
		All	1.42	0.18	−0.26	−4.24	−1.16
	Male + Female	Hindus	1.66	0.44	0.75	−0.42	0.38
		Muslims	1.30	3.15	2.40	−2.01	1.47
		Christians	1.06	1.65	−0.42	−0.04	0.19
		Others	1.18	1.23	0.38	3.72	1.42
		All	1.60	0.71	0.86	−0.44	0.50
Urban	Male	Hindus	3.17	2.48	3.00	3.02	2.88
		Muslims	2.74	3.78	2.74	3.10	3.09
		Christians	1.79	2.78	4.08	0.66	2.89
		Others	2.34	2.84	3.56	0.52	2.61
		All	3.04	2.70	3.01	2.87	2.90
	Female	Hindus	3.58	0.72	3.41	3.96	2.86
		Muslims	3.64	0.40	3.52	−1.09	1.57
		Christians	2.47	3.88	2.78	1.54	2.74
		Others	2.63	2.34	3.41	6.21	3.83
		All	3.51	0.87	3.39	3.39	2.75
	Male + Female	Hindus	3.26	2.11	3.09	3.10	2.84
		Muslims	2.90	3.19	2.86	2.34	2.81
		Christians	1.98	3.16	3.69	0.83	2.83
		Others	2.40	2.75	3.52	1.55	2.83
		All	3.14	2.32	3.09	2.87	2.84

(Continued)

Table 26. *(Continued)*

Region	Sex	Religious groups	1983 to 1994	1994 to 2000	2000 to 2012	2012 to 2018	1994 to 2018
Rural + Urban	Male	Hindus	2.09	1.21	1.77	1.70	1.62
		Muslims	1.96	3.15	3.07	−0.07	2.30
		Christians	1.38	2.45	0.61	2.52	1.54
		Others	1.51	1.45	1.10	5.49	2.27
		All	2.04	1.45	1.89	1.62	1.71
	Female	Hindus	1.79	−0.01	0.25	−2.11	−0.41
		Muslims	0.87	3.15	2.22	−5.21	0.54
		Christians	1.09	1.35	0.29	−1.73	0.04
		Others	1.26	1.97	0.20	0.28	0.66
		All	1.70	0.29	0.40	−2.27	−0.30
	Male + Female	Hindus	1.98	0.81	1.31	0.62	1.01
		Muslims	1.73	3.14	2.90	−1.09	1.94
		Christians	1.26	2.06	0.50	1.02	1.02
		Others	1.44	1.61	0.84	4.06	1.83
		All	1.93	1.08	1.45	0.55	1.13

Source: Same as Table 10

Focusing exclusively on rural males, we observe that the labour force growth rate for Hindus was higher than that of Muslims during the pre-globalisation period. This trend reversed in the post-globalisation period. According to Table 26, the labour force growth rate for Hindu males in rural areas during the pre-globalisation period was 1.74 %, declining to 1.11 % in the post-globalisation period. In contrast, the labour force growth rate for Muslim males in rural areas increased from 1.68 % in the pre-globalisation period to 1.84 % in the post-globalisation period. Regarding Hindu females in rural areas, labour force growth declined sharply in the post-globalisation period, becoming negative across all sub-periods of this era. However, Muslim females in rural areas improved their labour force growth rate in all sub-periods of the post-globalisation era, except for the periods from 2012 to 2018 and 1994 to 2018. For rural populations, it is clear that while Hindus performed better than Muslims in labour force growth during the pre-globalisation period (1.66 % for Hindus and 1.30 % for Muslims), the situation reversed after globalisation, with Muslims showing higher growth than Hindus (1.47 % and 0.38 % respectively).

In urban areas, the labour force growth rate for Hindu males (3.17 %) was higher than that of Muslim males (2.74 %) during the pre-globalisation period.

This trend reversed in the post-globalisation period, when Muslim males recorded a higher growth rate (3.09 %) than Hindu males (2.88 %). A somewhat different picture emerges when comparing the labour force growth rates of Hindu and Muslim females in urban areas. As shown in Table 26, during the pre-globalisation period (1983–1994), the growth rate of the labour force for Hindu females was slightly lower (3.58 %) than that for Muslim females (3.64 %). Conversely, Hindu females experienced a higher labour force growth rate (2.86 %) than Muslim females (1.57 %) in urban areas during the post-globalisation period (1994–2018). The growth rate of the urban labour force indicates that Hindus had an advantage over Muslims during both the pre-globalisation and post-globalisation periods.

Overall, the post-globalisation era in India witnessed a rise in the labour force growth rate for Muslims, while the rate for Hindus decreased, especially among females in rural areas.

3.8 Composition of Persons Outside the Labour Force in India

In the NSSO surveys, individuals who are neither working, seeking work, nor available for work during the reference period for various reasons are categorised as out-of-labour-force persons. Such individuals are classified into the following categories: (1) attended educational institutions (code 91); (2) engaged solely in domestic duties (code 92); (3) involved in domestic duties while also participating in the free collection of goods, sewing, tailoring, weaving, etc. for household use (code 93); (4) rentiers, pensioners, remittance recipients, etc. (code 94); (5) unable to work due to disability (code 95); (6) others (including beggars, prostitutes, etc.) (code 97); (7) casual workers who did not work due to sickness (code 98); and (8) children aged 0–4 years (code 99). An analysis of estimates of the proportion of out-of-labour-force persons in these categories over time would help clarify the primary cause(s) of the declining labour force participation rate among rural females, as well as the significant number of them who have been missing from the labour force in recent years.[6]

It may be worth noting that previous scholars have attempted to explain why many women are withdrawing from the labour force, or why the proportion of women outside the labour force (mainly in rural areas) has been increasing over time. One significant explanation is that females have recently withdrawn from the labour force due to their increased attendance at educational institutions (see,

---

6 In the previous discussion, it was noted that as many as 23.7 million rural females missed out (withdrew) from the labour force within a span of six years (2012 to 2018).

for example, Neff, Sen and Kling, 2012; Hirway, 2012; Rustagi, 2013; Abraham, 2013; Srivastava and Bhaskar, 2020). We can evaluate the validity of this explanation by examining the composition of out-of-labour-force males and females at our selected points in time.

The information on the activity profiles of out-of-labour-force individuals at the all-India level, separately for rural and urban areas and males and females, is presented in Table 27. In rural areas, the primary reason for males not participating in the labour force is their attendance at educational institutions. Another noteworthy point is that the proportion of this activity among rural males has increased substantially over time, rising from 40.72 % in 1983 to 64.72 % in 2018, while the share of 'Others' (including beggars, prostitutes, etc., and children aged 0–4 years) has decreased sharply during this period, falling from 51.63 % in 1983 to 23.56 % in 2018. The situation is quite different for rural females. The main reasons for their absence from the labour force are fulfilling domestic duties and attending educational institutions. Another point worth mentioning is that for rural females, the shares of these activities among total out-of-labour-force females have increased continuously from 1983 to 2012. However, between 2012 and 2018, while the share of females engaged in domestic duties increased, the share of those attending educational institutions declined. In 2018, among out-of-labour-force females in rural areas, 52.83 % reported involvement in domestic duties, while 29.92 % were attending educational institutions. Based on these observations, one might argue that, at present, rural females are underrepresented in the labour force in large numbers primarily because of their greater involvement in domestic duties. The prevailing notion that they are also more engaged in higher education does not appear to hold, according to the 2018 data.

The composition of out-of-labour-force individuals is relatively consistent in urban areas. In 2018, attendance at educational institutions accounted for 63.28 % of out-of-labour-force males in urban areas, followed by 'Others' (including beggars, prostitutes, and children aged 0–4 years), which made up 19.70 %. Furthermore, there is a noticeable trend of increasing attendance at educational institutions (except in 2018) and a decreasing share of 'Others' among urban males.

Conversely, the primary reasons why urban women remain outside the labour force are their domestic responsibilities and their attendance at educational institutions. In 2018, among the total number of urban women who exited the labour force, 55.41 % did so due to domestic duties, while 29.44 % cited attending educational institutions as the reason. Notably, while the proportion of domestic responsibilities gradually increased from 1983 to 2018, the share of those attending educational institutions declined from 2012 to 2018. However, the extent of this decline was considerably lower among urban females than among their rural counterparts.

Table 27. Percentage Distribution of Out-of-Labour-Force Persons (UPSS) Engaged in Different Activities in India

NSS Code	Activity	Year	Rural			Urban			Rural + Urban		
			Male	Female	Male + Female	Male	Female	Male + Female	Male	Female	Male + Female
91	Attended educational institutions	1983	40.72	14.96	25.58	56.49	25.32	37.07	44.65	17.84	28.64
		1994	50.72	22.12	33.85	61.12	29.37	41.34	53.42	24.21	35.92
		2000	53.25	25.97	37.08	61.34	29.42	41.23	55.33	26.97	38.23
		2012	67.01	33.30	46.27	66.73	30.58	43.57	66.93	32.46	45.45
		2018	64.72	29.92	42.68	63.28	29.44	41.16	64.31	29.77	42.23
92	Attended to domestic duties only	1983	0.59	25.50	15.22	0.65	40.36	25.39	0.60	29.63	17.93
		1994	0.55	23.67	14.19	0.60	39.62	24.91	0.56	28.25	17.15
		2000	0.60	25.69	15.47	0.75	43.46	27.66	0.64	30.82	18.84
		2012	0.33	22.42	13.92	0.46	41.87	27.00	0.37	28.45	17.86
		2018	1.19	37.31	24.07	1.48	51.17	33.95	1.27	41.47	26.97
93	Attended domestic duties and also engaged in free collection of goods, sewing, tailoring, weaving, etc. for household use	1983	1.01	16.49	10.10	0.27	9.04	5.73	0.82	14.41	8.94
		1994	0.43	19.85	11.89	0.24	10.36	6.54	0.38	17.12	10.41
		2000	0.39	16.25	9.79	0.10	7.23	4.59	0.31	13.65	8.35
		2012	0.51	24.77	15.44	0.17	12.62	8.15	0.41	21.00	13.24
		2018	0.69	15.52	10.08	0.21	4.24	2.85	0.56	12.14	7.96
92 + 93	Attended different domestic duties (incl. those engaged in free collection of goods, sewing, tailoring, weaving, etc. for household use)	1983	1.60	41.98	25.32	0.91	49.40	31.12	1.43	44.05	26.87
		1994	0.98	43.52	26.08	0.83	49.98	31.46	0.94	45.38	27.57
		2000	0.99	41.94	25.26	0.85	50.69	32.25	0.95	44.47	27.19
		2012	0.84	47.19	29.36	0.63	54.49	35.15	0.78	49.46	31.10
		2018	1.88	52.83	34.15	1.69	55.41	36.80	1.83	53.61	34.93

(Continued)

Table 27. *(Continued)*

NSS Code	Activity	Year	Rural			Urban			Rural + Urban		
			Male	Female	Male + Female	Male	Female	Male + Female	Male	Female	Male + Female
94	Rentiers, pensioners, remittance recipients, etc.	1983	0.47	0.32	0.38	2.16	0.47	1.11	0.89	0.36	0.57
		1994	0.77	0.37	0.53	3.59	0.59	1.72	1.50	0.44	0.86
		2000	1.04	0.53	0.74	4.08	0.70	1.95	1.83	0.58	1.08
		2012	2.50	1.17	1.68	8.00	1.82	4.04	4.08	1.37	2.39
		2018	7.05	4.01	5.12	12.43	4.45	7.21	8.57	4.14	5.74
95	Not able to work due to disability	1983	5.58	6.12	5.90	4.98	4.42	4.63	5.43	5.65	5.56
		1994	1.49	0.82	1.10	1.34	0.53	0.83	1.45	0.74	1.02
		2000	1.72	0.85	1.21	1.64	0.70	1.05	1.70	0.81	1.16
		2012	2.69	1.57	2.00	2.54	1.41	1.82	2.65	1.52	1.95
		2018	2.79	1.02	1.67	2.91	0.97	1.64	2.82	1.01	1.66
97 + 98	Others (incl. beggars, prostitutes, etc.) plus those casual workers who did not work due to sickness	1983	–	–	–	–	–	–	–	–	–
		1994	21.25	17.01	18.75	13.79	8.82	10.69	19.31	14.66	16.52
		2000	17.53	13.69	15.25	11.67	7.67	9.15	16.02	11.95	13.56
		2012	7.44	4.84	5.83	5.28	3.16	3.92	6.82	4.31	5.25
		2018	4.86	2.27	3.22	3.95	1.88	2.61	4.60	2.15	3.04
99	Children of age 0–4 years	1983	–	–	–	–	–	–	–	–	–
		1994	24.79	16.15	19.69	19.33	10.71	13.96	23.37	14.58	18.11
		2000	25.47	17.02	20.46	20.41	10.81	14.37	24.17	15.23	18.78
		2012	19.53	11.93	14.86	16.81	8.53	11.51	18.75	10.88	13.85
		2018	18.70	9.95	13.16	15.75	7.86	10.59	17.87	9.32	12.41

(Continued)

Table 27. *(Continued)*

NSS Code	Activity	Year	Rural			Urban			Rural + Urban		
			Male	Female	Male + Female	Male	Female	Male + Female	Male	Female	Male + Female
97 + 98 + 99	Others (incl. beggars, prostitutes, etc.) plus those casual workers who did not work due to sickness plus children of age 0–4 years	1983	51.63	36.63	42.82	35.46	20.40	26.07	47.60	32.11	38.35
		1994	46.04	33.16	38.44	33.12	19.53	24.65	42.68	29.24	34.63
		2000	43.00	30.71	35.71	32.08	18.48	23.52	40.19	27.18	32.34
		2012	26.97	16.77	20.69	22.09	11.69	15.43	25.57	15.19	19.10
		2018	23.56	12.22	16.38	19.70	9.74	13.20	22.47	11.47	15.45

Source: Same as Table 10

Another important point is that the proportion of rentiers, pensioners, remittance recipients, and Others among the total number of individuals outside the labour force has shown a clear tendency to increase over time for both males and females in rural and urban settings. However, this trend has been more marked among urban males during the last sub-period, 2012–2018.

3.9 Labour Force Participation in Major States

In this section, we aim to explore trends and patterns of labour force participation across India's seventeen major states. To achieve this, two indicators are considered: (i) labour force participation rates and (ii) growth rates of the labour force. The data on these aspects have been compiled separately for males, females, and the combined group (males plus females) in rural, urban, and combined (rural plus urban) areas. The states have also been ranked by their performance on these indicators.

3.9.1 Labour Force Participation Rates by State

Table 28 provides state-level data on labour force participation rates for males, females, and persons, distinguished by rural, urban, and combined areas.

Among rural males, the labour force participation rate was highest in Andhra Pradesh and lowest in Haryana across the three points assessed from 1983 to 2000. However, Karnataka and West Bengal held the top positions in 2012 and 2018, respectively, while Uttar Pradesh and Bihar ranked last. In 2018, the states with labour force participation rates for rural males that exceeded the all-India level include West Bengal, Tamil Nadu, Karnataka, Andhra Pradesh, Assam, Himachal Pradesh, Punjab, Madhya Pradesh, Gujarat, Odisha, Maharashtra, and Jammu & Kashmir (arranged in descending order of the labour force participation rate). The states with a lower labour force participation rate for rural males than the all-India level are Kerala, Haryana, Rajasthan, Uttar Pradesh, and Bihar.

Himachal Pradesh occupied the top position in the rural females' labour force participation rate in 1983. Andhra Pradesh occupied the top position at two points in time between 1994 and 2000 regarding the rural females' labour force participation rate. Assam held the lowest positions in 1983, 1994 and 2000. However, in 2012 and 2018, Himachal Pradesh led, while Bihar remained at the bottom in terms of rural females' labour force participation rates. Furthermore, in 2018, there were nine states (Himachal Pradesh, Andhra Pradesh, Tamil Nadu, Madhya Pradesh, Maharashtra, Jammu & Kashmir, Karnataka, Rajasthan, and Kerala, in descending order of the labour force participation rate) that recorded higher rates of rural females' labour force participation than the all-India average. Conversely, eight other states (Gujarat, West Bengal, Odisha, Punjab, Haryana, Uttar Pradesh, Assam, and Bihar) fell short of the all-India figure.

Regarding rural individuals (males plus females), it is noted that Andhra Pradesh had the highest labour force participation rate in all years until 2000. However, this distinction has shifted to Himachal Pradesh, which maintained the top position in 2012 and 2018. Nine states recorded labour force participation rates for rural individuals that exceeded the all-India level in 2018: Himachal Pradesh, Andhra Pradesh, Tamil Nadu, Madhya Pradesh, Maharashtra, Jammu & Kashmir, Karnataka, Gujarat, and West Bengal, listed in descending order of their labour force participation rates. The states where this fell below the all-India level include Rajasthan, Odisha, Kerala, Assam, Punjab, Haryana, Uttar Pradesh, and Bihar.

In urban areas, the male labour force participation rate was highest in three specific years (1983, 2000, and 2012) in West Bengal, but it peaked in Tamil Nadu in 1994 and in Assam in 2018. Conversely, in all years except 1983, the labour force participation rate of urban males was the lowest in Bihar. The states that recorded a higher urban male labour force participation rate compared to the all-India average in 2018 are Assam, Tamil Nadu, West Bengal, Punjab, Gujarat, Himachal Pradesh, Madhya Pradesh, Andhra Pradesh, Karnataka, Odisha, and Maharashtra (listed in descending order of labour force participation rate). The states where this rate was below the all-India level are Jammu & Kashmir, Haryana, Uttar Pradesh, Kerala, Rajasthan, and Bihar.

Between 1983 and 2000, the urban female labour force participation rate was highest in Kerala at three points. In 2012, it was highest in Himachal Pradesh, whereas in 2018, Tamil Nadu was in the lead. The states where the labour force participation rate for urban females was above the all-India level in 2018 include Tamil Nadu, Andhra Pradesh, Kerala, Himachal Pradesh, West Bengal, Karnataka, Jammu & Kashmir, Madhya Pradesh, and Maharashtra, listed in descending order of their participation rates. The remaining eight states – Punjab, Odisha, Gujarat, Assam, Rajasthan, Haryana, Uttar Pradesh, and Bihar – had rates lower than the all-India level.

Regarding urban areas, Tamil Nadu ranked highest in labour force participation rates in 1983 and 1994, while Kerala ranked highest in 2000. Additionally, Himachal Pradesh ranked highest in 2012 and 2018. Conversely, Bihar ranked lowest among the states throughout 1983–2018. In 2018, eleven states recorded labour force participation rates for urban populations that exceeded the all-India level. These states, listed in descending order of their labour force participation rates, are Himachal Pradesh, Tamil Nadu, Andhra Pradesh, West Bengal, Punjab, Madhya Pradesh, Karnataka, Jammu & Kashmir, Maharashtra, Assam, and Kerala. The six states where the urban population's labour force participation rate fell below the all-India level in 2018 are Gujarat, Odisha, Haryana, Rajasthan, Uttar Pradesh, and Bihar.

Table 28. Labour Force Participation Rates (%) in Seventeen Major States of India (UPSS basis)

State	Year	Rural			Urban			Rural + Urban		
		Male	Female	Male + Female	Male	Female	Male + Female	Male	Female	Male + Female
Andhra Pradesh	1983	61.2 (1)	47.2 (3)	54.2 (1)	53.4 (11)	18.6 (5)	36.4 (6)	59.2 (2)	40.4 (3)	49.9 (2)
	1994	63.5 (1)	52.2 (1)	57.9 (1)	56.0 (5)	20.6 (3)	38.7 (4)	61.5 (1)	43.7 (2)	52.7 (2)
	2000	61.1 (1)	48.0 (1)	54.6 (1)	53.2 (9)	18.5 (4)	36.2 (8)	59.0 (2)	40.1 (2)	49.6 (1)
	2012	61.2 (2)	44.8 (2)	53.0 (2)	57.6 (8)	18.0 (5)	37.9 (8)	60.0 (6)	35.7 (2)	47.9 (2)
	2018	60.4 (4)	36.3 (2)	48.3 (2)	58.0 (8)	22.1 (2)	40.1 (3)	59.5 (4)	31.2 (2)	45.3 (2)
Assam	1983	51.1 (16)	12.9 (17)	32.7 (17)	52.3 (13)	8.6 (17)	32.9 (15)	51.2 (15)	12.5 (17)	32.7 (17)
	1994	54.1 (13)	17.2 (17)	36.3 (16)	55.9 (6)	12.4 (14)	35.9 (10)	54.3 (12)	16.7 (16)	36.2 (16)
	2000	54.6 (9)	16.2 (17)	36.0 (14)	56.6 (4)	13.8 (9)	36.6 (6)	54.9 (10)	15.9 (16)	36.1 (14)
	2012	56.4 (10)	12.9 (16)	35.1 (15)	57.3 (9)	9.7 (16)	34.2 (13)	56.5 (10)	12.4 (16)	35.0 (15)
	2018	59.1 (5)	9.5 (16)	35.7 (13)	61.1 (1)	12.4 (13)	36.9 (10)	59.3 (5)	9.8 (15)	35.8 (14)
Bihar	1983	51.5 (15)	24.9 (14)	38.5 (14)	49.5 (15)	10.7 (15)	31.8 (17)	51.2 (16)	23.2 (13)	37.7 (15)
	1994	52.1 (16)	17.3 (16)	35.4 (17)	47.1 (17)	7.6 (17)	28.9 (17)	51.4 (16)	16.1 (17)	34.5 (17)
	2000	50.3 (14)	17.4 (15)	34.4 (17)	46.6 (17)	8.2 (16)	28.8 (17)	49.8 (15)	16.2 (15)	33.7 (17)
	2012	49.9 (16)	9.0 (17)	30.2 (17)	46.6 (17)	6.2 (17)	27.4 (17)	49.4 (17)	8.6 (17)	29.8 (17)
	2018	46.4 (17)	4.4 (17)	26.7 (17)	47.3 (17)	7.0 (17)	27.9 (17)	46.5 (17)	4.7 (17)	26.8 (17)
Gujarat	1983	55.4 (9)	41.2 (7)	48.4 (8)	54.1 (9)	13.6 (10)	34.9 (11)	55.0 (9)	32.6 (8)	44.1 (8)
	1994	58.2 (5)	39.7 (8)	49.2 (8)	55.2 (8)	14.9 (11)	36.1 (9)	57.1 (8)	31.1 (9)	44.6 (8)
	2000	58.8 (4)	41.3 (5)	50.3 (4)	54.7 (8)	13.8 (10)	35.5 (10)	57.2 (5)	31.4 (8)	44.8 (5)
	2012	60.2 (6)	27.9 (8)	44.5 (6)	60.7 (3)	13.5 (13)	38.6 (7)	60.4 (4)	21.8 (11)	42.0 (7)
	2018	58.5 (9)	17.2 (10)	39.0 (8)	59.2 (5)	12.7 (12)	36.7 (12)	58.8 (7)	15.4 (11)	38.0 (9)

(Continued)

Table 28. *(Continued)*

State	Year	Rural						Urban						Rural + Urban					
		Male		Female		Male + Female		Male		Female		Male + Female		Male		Female		Male + Female	
Haryana	1983	47.9	(17)	23.3	(15)	36.4	(16)	55.8	(5)	11.6	(13)	35.4	(10)	49.7	(17)	20.7	(15)	36.2	(16)
	1994	47.0	(17)	27.2	(11)	37.8	(15)	53.2	(11)	15.7	(10)	35.9	(11)	48.6	(17)	24.2	(12)	37.3	(14)
	2000	48.0	(17)	20.2	(13)	35.1	(15)	52.0	(11)	10.1	(14)	32.7	(14)	49.2	(16)	17.4	(14)	34.4	(15)
	2012	53.2	(14)	16.4	(15)	36.0	(14)	53.5	(13)	10.2	(15)	33.3	(15)	53.3	(14)	14.2	(15)	35.0	(14)
	2018	52.6	(14)	10.8	(14)	32.8	(15)	56.0	(13)	10.5	(15)	34.5	(14)	53.7	(14)	10.7	(14)	33.4	(15)
Himachal Pradesh	1983	53.7	(12)	47.8	(1)	50.8	(5)	57.6	(3)	18.5	(6)	40.2	(3)	54.0	(11)	45.8	(1)	50.0	(1)
	1994	59.5	(4)	52.1	(2)	55.8	(2)	50.5	(13)	20.2	(4)	36.8	(7)	58.7	(4)	49.4	(1)	54.1	(1)
	2000	54.6	(10)	47.3	(2)	51.0	(3)	53.2	(10)	14.1	(7)	35.8	(9)	54.4	(11)	44.4	(1)	49.5	(2)
	2012	54.7	(13)	52.9	(1)	53.8	(1)	61.2	(2)	23.6	(1)	43.8	(1)	55.4	(13)	50.1	(1)	52.8	(1)
	2018	58.7	(6)	41.6	(1)	50.0	(1)	58.7	(6)	19.5	(4)	41.5	(1)	58.7	(8)	39.7	(1)	49.1	(1)
Jammu & Kashmir	1983	55.5	(8)	28.6	(12)	42.7	(12)	55.6	(6)	10.8	(14)	34.6	(12)	55.5	(8)	24.8	(12)	41.0	(12)
	1994	52.4	(15)	39.3	(9)	46.0	(9)	52.2	(12)	14.3	(13)	34.5	(13)	52.3	(14)	33.4	(8)	43.3	(10)
	2000	55.5	(7)	33.1	(9)	44.7	(9)	50.1	(15)	6.8	(17)	30.4	(16)	54.1	(12)	26.8	(10)	41.2	(11)
	2012	55.9	(12)	26.3	(9)	41.9	(10)	56.3	(11)	14.5	(10)	37.2	(11)	56.0	(11)	23.1	(10)	40.6	(10)
	2018	57.3	(12)	24.3	(6)	41.6	(6)	56.6	(12)	18.0	(7)	37.8	(8)	57.4	(12)	22.9	(6)	40.8	(6)
Karnataka	1983	59.2	(4)	38.8	(8)	49.1	(7)	53.5	(10)	20.4	(3)	37.6	(5)	57.5	(4)	33.5	(7)	45.7	(7)
	1994	60.9	(3)	43.2	(6)	52.2	(4)	55.8	(7)	19.2	(5)	38.1	(5)	59.3	(3)	35.7	(6)	47.7	(4)
	2000	60.1	(3)	38.1	(8)	49.2	(5)	56.2	(7)	18.6	(3)	38.0	(4)	58.8	(3)	31.6	(7)	45.5	(4)
	2012	62.0	(1)	28.9	(6)	45.7	(5)	59.4	(6)	17.1	(7)	38.7	(5)	61.0	(2)	24.3	(7)	42.9	(5)
	2018	60.9	(3)	21.9	(7)	41.4	(7)	57.8	(9)	18.1	(6)	37.9	(7)	59.7	(3)	20.4	(8)	40.0	(7)

(Continued)

Table 28. *(Continued)*

State	Year	Rural			Urban			Rural + Urban		
		Male	Female	Male + Female	Male	Female	Male + Female	Male	Female	Male + Female
Kerala	1983	52.3 (14)	33.8 (9)	42.9 (11)	55.1 (7)	25.9 (1)	40.3 (2)	52.8 (14)	32.2 (9)	42.4 (10)
	1994	56.8 (8)	26.4 (12)	41.3 (11)	59.9 (2)	25.0 (1)	42.1 (2)	57.6 (5)	26.0 (11)	41.5 (11)
	2000	58.6 (5)	27.4 (12)	42.6 (11)	59.1 (2)	25.4 (1)	41.8 (1)	58.8 (4)	26.8 (11)	42.4 (8)
	2012	58.3 (7)	25.8 (10)	41.4 (12)	56.7 (10)	22.2 (2)	38.7 (6)	57.5 (8)	24.0 (8)	40.1 (13)
	2018	54.1 (13)	20.7 (9)	36.4 (12)	53.6 (15)	22.1 (3)	36.9 (11)	53.9 (13)	21.3 (7)	36.6 (11)
Madhya Pradesh	1983	56.4 (7)	43.3 (6)	50.0 (6)	49.3 (17)	14.7 (9)	33.0 (14)	54.8 (10)	37.5 (5)	46.5 (5)
	1994	57.6 (7)	41.0 (7)	49.6 (7)	49.7 (16)	14.8 (12)	33.2 (15)	55.7 (10)	35.0 (7)	45.7 (7)
	2000	53.9 (13)	38.3 (7)	46.3 (7)	50.9 (14)	13.6 (11)	33.2 (12)	53.2 (13)	32.3 (5)	43.1 (7)
	2012	56.4 (11)	28.8 (7)	42.9 (8)	52.9 (15)	15.0 (9)	34.7 (12)	55.4 (12)	25.2 (6)	40.7 (8)
	2018	58.5 (8)	29.9 (4)	44.8 (4)	58.2 (7)	17.5 (8)	38.2 (6)	58.4 (9)	27.0 (4)	43.3 (4)
Maharashtra	1983	56.6 (6)	47.3 (2)	52.0 (3)	54.2 (8)	15.7 (7)	36.4 (7)	55.7 (7)	36.5 (6)	46.4 (6)
	1994	55.8 (10)	47.8 (4)	51.9 (5)	55.0 (9)	17.7 (6)	37.6 (6)	55.4 (11)	36.3 (5)	46.2 (6)
	2000	54.1 (12)	43.7 (3)	49.0 (6)	56.4 (6)	14.7 (6)	36.9 (5)	55.1 (8)	31.9 (6)	43.9 (6)
	2012	58.2 (8)	38.9 (3)	48.8 (4)	56.0 (12)	17.2 (6)	37.6 (10)	57.2 (9)	29.2 (5)	43.7 (4)
	2018	57.8 (11)	29.8 (5)	44.2 (5)	57.3 (11)	16.9 (9)	37.4 (9)	57.6 (11)	24.2 (5)	41.2 (5)
Odisha	1983	57.5 (5)	29.5 (11)	43.5 (10)	52.6 (12)	11.8 (12)	33.7 (13)	56.9 (5)	27.5 (10)	42.3 (11)
	1994	57.6 (6)	32.0 (10)	44.9 (10)	54.7 (10)	16.1 (9)	36.7 (8)	57.2 (7)	29.9 (10)	43.7 (9)
	2000	56.5 (6)	30.2 (10)	43.4 (10)	51.1 (13)	15.3 (5)	34.2 (11)	55.6 (7)	28.1 (9)	42.1 (9)
	2012	60.6 (4)	25.1 (11)	43.0 (7)	60.3 (4)	15.8 (8)	38.8 (4)	60.5 (3)	23.6 (9)	42.3 (6)
	2018	58.1 (10)	15.3 (12)	36.6 (11)	57.7 (10)	13.4 (11)	35.1 (13)	58.0 (10)	15.0 (12)	36.4 (12)

(Continued)

Table 28. *(Continued)*

State	Year	Rural			Urban			Rural + Urban		
		Male	Female	Male + Female	Male	Female	Male + Female	Male	Female	Male + Female
Punjab	1983	59.3 (3)	32.4 (10)	46.7 (9)	55.8 (4)	13.5 (11)	36.2 (8)	58.3 (3)	27.1 (11)	43.7 (9)
	1994	55.3 (11)	22.3 (13)	39.8 (12)	57.1 (4)	9.8 (16)	35.2 (12)	55.9 (9)	18.5 (14)	38.4 (13)
	2000	54.2 (11)	28.3 (11)	42.0 (12)	56.5 (5)	12.8 (13)	36.4 (7)	55.0 (9)	23.2 (12)	40.1 (12)
	2012	57.9 (9)	23.7 (12)	41.6 (11)	58.6 (7)	14.1 (12)	37.8 (9)	58.2 (7)	20.1 (12)	40.2 (12)
	2018	58.6 (7)	11.1 (13)	35.6 (14)	60.2 (4)	14.2 (10)	38.4 (5)	59.2 (6)	12.3 (13)	36.7 (10)
Rajasthan	1983	55.3 (11)	46.6 (4)	51.1 (4)	49.5 (16)	19.6 (4)	35.5 (9)	54.0 (12)	41.0 (2)	47.8 (4)
	1994	54.2 (12)	45.7 (5)	50.2 (6)	49.8 (14)	16.4 (8)	34.2 (14)	53.2 (13)	39.1 (4)	46.5 (5)
	2000	50.3 (15)	38.8 (6)	44.8 (8)	49.9 (16)	14.1 (8)	33.1 (13)	50.2 (14)	33.2 (4)	42.0 (10)
	2012	50.0 (15)	34.9 (5)	42.7 (9)	50.7 (16)	14.4 (11)	33.4 (14)	50.2 (16)	29.8 (4)	40.4 (11)
	2018	51.1 (15)	21.8 (8)	36.9 (10)	53.1 (16)	10.8 (14)	33.1 (15)	51.6 (15)	19.3 (9)	36.0 (13)
Tamil Nadu	1983	60.9 (2)	46.0 (5)	53.5 (2)	57.9 (2)	22.5 (2)	40.6 (1)	59.9 (1)	38.3 (4)	49.2 (3)
	1994	61.3 (2)	48.1 (3)	54.7 (3)	60.1 (1)	24.7 (2)	42.7 (1)	60.9 (2)	39.5 (3)	50.3 (3)
	2000	61.0 (2)	43.4 (4)	52.3 (2)	58.4 (3)	22.7 (2)	40.7 (2)	59.9 (1)	34.6 (3)	47.4 (3)
	2012	60.7 (3)	38.6 (4)	49.7 (3)	59.9 (5)	21.1 (3)	40.5 (3)	60.3 (5)	30.0 (3)	45.2 (3)
	2018	61.3 (2)	31.3 (3)	46.1 (3)	60.6 (2)	22.5 (1)	41.3 (2)	61.0 (2)	27.2 (3)	43.9 (3)
Uttar Pradesh	1983	53.5 (13)	25.7 (13)	39.8 (13)	52.3 (14)	9.9 (16)	32.8 (16)	53.3 (13)	22.9 (14)	38.5 (13)
	1994	52.7 (14)	22.0 (14)	38.2 (14)	49.8 (15)	10.3 (15)	31.5 (16)	52.1 (15)	19.6 (13)	36.9 (15)
	2000	48.6 (16)	20.2 (14)	35.1 (16)	51.2 (12)	9.7 (15)	31.8 (15)	49.1 (17)	18.0 (13)	34.4 (16)
	2012	49.5 (17)	18.4 (14)	34.6 (16)	53.2 (14)	10.6 (14)	33.2 (16)	50.3 (15)	16.7 (14)	34.3 (16)
	2018	50.3 (16)	10.0 (15)	30.5 (16)	53.8 (14)	8.3 (16)	32.0 (16)	51.0 (16)	9.6 (16)	30.8 (16)

(Continued)

Table 28 *(Continued)*

State	Year	Rural			Urban			Rural + Urban		
		Male	Female	Male + Female	Male	Female	Male + Female	Male	Female	Male + Female
West Bengal	1983	55.3 (10)	19.6 (16)	37.6 (15)	59.1 (1)	14.8 (8)	39.0 (4)	56.4 (6)	18.4 (16)	38.0 (14)
	1994	56.7 (9)	18.8 (15)	38.3 (13)	58.7 (3)	16.7 (7)	39.2 (3)	57.3 (6)	18.2 (15)	38.6 (12)
	2000	54.9 (8)	16.5 (16)	36.2 (13)	61.1 (1)	12.9 (12)	38.4 (3)	56.7 (6)	15.5 (17)	36.8 (13)
	2012	60.2 (5)	19.4 (13)	40.3 (13)	63.0 (1)	18.6 (4)	41.4 (2)	61.1 (1)	19.1 (13)	40.7 (9)
	2018	61.7 (1)	15.5 (11)	38.9 (9)	60.3 (3)	18.5 (5)	39.6 (4)	61.3 (1)	16.4 (10)	39.1 (8)

Source: Same as Table 10
Note: The figures in parentheses are ranks among 17 major states.

When considering both rural and urban areas, the labour force participation rate for individuals (males and females combined) ranged from 50 % in Himachal Pradesh to 32.7 % in Assam in 1983. Regarding labour force participation rates, Himachal Pradesh ranked first in all years except 2000. Conversely, Bihar consistently recorded the lowest rates, except in 1983. In 2018, nine states reported that labour force participation rates for all individuals were higher than the all-India average. These states are Himachal Pradesh, Andhra Pradesh, Tamil Nadu, Madhya Pradesh, Maharashtra, Jammu & Kashmir, Karnataka, West Bengal, and Gujarat (listed in descending order based on labour force participation rate). In contrast, the states with labour force participation rates for all individuals below the all-India average in 2018 included Punjab, Kerala, Odisha, Rajasthan, Assam, Haryana, Uttar Pradesh, and Bihar.

When considering all males combined (rural and urban), Tamil Nadu and Andhra Pradesh had the highest labour force participation rates until 2000, after which West Bengal took the lead among states. Conversely, Bihar was ranked the lowest in both 2012 and 2018. In 2018, twelve states recorded male labour force participation rates exceeding the all-India level. These states, listed in descending order of their labour force participation rates, are West Bengal, Tamil Nadu, Karnataka, Andhra Pradesh, Assam, Punjab, Gujarat, Himachal Pradesh, Madhya Pradesh, Odisha, Maharashtra, and Jammu & Kashmir. The five states with the lower labour force participation rates for all males relative to the all-India level are Kerala, Haryana, Rajasthan, Uttar Pradesh, and Bihar.

Himachal Pradesh consistently recorded the highest female labour force participation rates from 1983 to 2018, while Bihar had the lowest in recent years (2012 and 2018). In 2018, the states with labour force participation rates for females higher than the all-India level included Himachal Pradesh, Andhra Pradesh, Tamil Nadu, Madhya Pradesh, Maharashtra, Jammu & Kashmir, Kerala, Karnataka, and Rajasthan (listed in descending order of participation rate). Conversely, the states with female labour force participation rates below the all-India level were West Bengal, Gujarat, Odisha, Punjab, Haryana, Assam, Uttar Pradesh, and Bihar.

3.9.2 Ranking of States by Labour Force Participation Rates

Table 28 also presents the rankings of the states regarding labour force participation rates at the five selected time points. We further calculated the average of ranks of the states at those points and re-ranked the states based on these ranks to identify the better and worse performers in this context over the entire period from 1983 to 2018. All this information is displayed in Table 29.

Table 29. Mean of Ranks of the States in Terms of LFPR and Kendall's Coefficients of Concordance (W)

State	Rural			Urban			Rural + Urban		
	Male	Female	Male + Female	Male	Female	Male + Female	Male	Female	Male + Female
Andhra Pradesh	1.8 (1)	1.8 (2)	1.4 (1)	8.2 (9)	3.8 (3)	5.8 (6)	3.0 (2)	2.2 (2)	1.8 (2)
Assam	10.6 (12)	16.6 (17)	15.0 (14)	6.6 (4)	13.8 (15)	10.8 (11)	10.4 (11)	16.0 (17)	15.2 (15)
Bihar	15.6 (16)	15.8 (16)	16.4 (17)	16.6 (17)	16.4 (17)	17.0 (17)	16.2 (17)	15.8 (16)	16.6 (17)
Gujarat	6.6 (5)	7.6 (8)	6.8 (7)	6.6 (5)	11.2 (11)	9.8 (9)	6.6 (6)	9.4 (10)	7.4 (7)
Haryana	15.8 (17)	13.6 (13)	15.0 (15)	10.6 (12)	13.4 (14)	12.8 (14)	15.6 (16)	14.0 (13)	14.8 (14)
Himachal Pradesh	9.0 (8)	1.4 (1)	2.4 (2)	6.8 (6)	4.4 (4)	4.2 (3)	9.4 (10)	1.0 (1)	1.2 (1)
Jammu & Kashmir	10.8 (13)	9.0 (9)	9.2 (9)	11.2 (13)	12.2 (12)	12.0 (13)	11.4 (13)	9.2 (8)	9.8 (10)
Karnataka	2.8 (3)	7.0 (7)	5.6 (5)	7.8 (8)	4.8 (5)	5.2 (5)	3.0 (3)	7.0 (7)	5.4 (4)
Kerala	9.4 (10)	10.4 (10)	11.4 (11)	7.2 (7)	1.6 (1)	4.4 (4)	8.8 (8)	9.2 (9)	10.6 (11)
Maharashtra	9.4 (9)	6.2 (6)	4.6 (4)	9.2 (10)	6.8 (6)	7.4 (7)	9.2 (9)	5.4 (5)	5.4 (5)
Madhya Pradesh	9.2 (11)	3.4 (3)	6.4 (6)	13.8 (14)	9.8 (10)	11.8 (12)	10.8 (12)	5.4 (6)	6.2 (6)
Odisha	6.2 (4)	10.8 (11)	9.6 (10)	9.8 (11)	9.0 (8)	9.8 (10)	6.4 (5)	10.0 (11)	9.4 (9)
Punjab	8.2 (7)	11.8 (12)	11.6 (12)	4.8 (3)	12.4 (13)	8.2 (8)	6.8 (7)	12.4 (12)	11.2 (12)
Rajasthan	13.6 (14)	5.6 (5)	7.4 (8)	15.6 (16)	9.0 (9)	13.0 (15)	14.0 (14)	4.6 (4)	8.6 (8)
Tamil Nadu	2.2 (2)	3.8 (4)	2.6 (3)	2.6 (2)	2.0 (2)	1.8 (1)	2.2 (1)	3.2 (3)	3.0 (3)
Uttar Pradesh	15.2 (15)	14.0 (14)	15.0 (16)	13.8 (15)	15.2 (16)	15.8 (16)	15.2 (15)	14.0 (14)	15.2 (16)
West Bengal	6.6 (6)	14.2 (15)	12.6 (13)	1.8 (1)	7.2 (7)	3.2 (2)	4.0 (4)	14.2 (15)	11.2 (13)
Kendall's coeff.	61.2	94.0	73.7	56.4	66.8	62.7	64.8	74.2	71.9
p-value	0.00	0.00	0.00	0.00	0.00	0.00	0.00	0.00	0.00

Source: Author's computation using information presented in Table 28

Note: The figures in parentheses are ranks among 17 major states based on the mean of ranks for five-time points

The states that ranked higher in labour force participation rates for rural males from 1983 to 2018 are Andhra Pradesh, Tamil Nadu, Karnataka, Odisha, and Gujarat, listed in descending order of their mean ranks across five time points. Conversely, the lower-performing states are Haryana, Bihar, Uttar Pradesh, Rajasthan, and Jammu & Kashmir, listed in ascending order of their mean ranks. The remaining seven states are situated in the intermediate range. The states with higher labour force participation rates for rural females include Himachal Pradesh, Andhra Pradesh, Madhya Pradesh, Tamil Nadu and Rajasthan. The states with lower participation rates are Assam, Bihar, West Bengal, Uttar Pradesh and Haryana. Among rural individuals (male and female combined), the better-performing states are Andhra Pradesh, Himachal Pradesh, Tamil Nadu, Maharashtra, and Karnataka. In contrast, the lower-performing states are Bihar, Uttar Pradesh, Haryana, Assam, and West Bengal.

The ranking pattern of states by labour force participation rates in urban areas from 1983 to 2018 differs somewhat from that in rural areas. Table 29 shows that, among urban males, the top five states in this regard are West Bengal, Tamil Nadu, Punjab, Assam, and Gujarat. On the other hand, the states that appeared to have performed poorly in labour force participation rates for urban males are Bihar, Rajasthan, Uttar Pradesh, Haryana, Madhya Pradesh, and Jammu & Kashmir (mostly the BIMARU states). Among urban females, the five best performers are Kerala, Tamil Nadu, Andhra Pradesh, Himachal Pradesh, and Karnataka; performance is worse in Bihar, Uttar Pradesh, Assam, Haryana, and Punjab. Among urban areas, the overall labour force participation rate from 1983 to 2018 was higher in Tamil Nadu, West Bengal, Himachal Pradesh, Kerala and Karnataka; the worst performers were Bihar, Uttar Pradesh, Rajasthan, Haryana and Jammu & Kashmir.

3.9.3 The Growth of the Labour Force in the States

3.9.3.1 Pre-Globalisation Period (1983 to 1994)

We now examine the growth rates of the labour force in seventeen major Indian states. Table 30 presents this information. It has been observed that from 1983 to 1994 (pre-globalisation), the growth rate was highest for rural males in Uttar Pradesh, followed by Himachal Pradesh, West Bengal, Assam and Bihar. Conversely, the five states with lower labour force growth rates for rural males are Punjab, Tamil Nadu, Kerala, Maharashtra, and Jammu & Kashmir (in ascending order of growth rate). The remaining seven states fell between these two extremes. Among rural females, the labour force growth rate during the pre-globalisation period was highest in Jammu & Kashmir, followed by Assam, Haryana, Andhra

Pradesh, and Himachal Pradesh. In contrast, the five states at the bottom are Punjab, Kerala, Bihar, Uttar Pradesh, and Gujarat. Considering rural males and females together, the top performers in labour force growth during the pre-globalisation period are Jammu & Kashmir, followed by Assam, Himachal Pradesh, Haryana, and West Bengal. The five states at the bottom are Punjab, Kerala, Tamil Nadu, Bihar, and Maharashtra.

In urban areas, the growth rate of the male labour force during the pre-globalisation period was highest in Kerala, followed by Assam, Madhya Pradesh, Andhra Pradesh, and Haryana. During this period, the states with the lowest labour force growth rates among urban males include Himachal Pradesh, Bihar, West Bengal, Tamil Nadu, and Uttar Pradesh. Assam was the top performer for urban females during the pre-globalisation era, followed by Haryana, Jammu & Kashmir, Odisha, and Maharashtra. The states that performed poorly in labour force growth for urban females are Bihar, Punjab, Rajasthan, Karnataka, and Tamil Nadu. Considering urban males and females together, the labour force growth during the pre-globalisation period was highest in Assam, followed by Kerala, Haryana, Odisha, and Jammu & Kashmir. The states with the lowest labour force growth rates among urban residents are Bihar, Himachal Pradesh, West Bengal, Punjab, and Karnataka.

When considering all males (rural plus urban) during the pre-globalisation period, the labour force growth rate was highest in Uttar Pradesh, followed by Himachal Pradesh, Assam, Madhya Pradesh, and West Bengal. The states that ranked lower in this respect were Tamil Nadu, Punjab, Odisha, Jammu & Kashmir, and Kerala. For all females (rural and urban combined), the top-performing state regarding the growth rate of the labour force during the pre-globalisation period has been Jammu & Kashmir, followed by Assam, Haryana, Andhra Pradesh and Himachal Pradesh. Conversely, the states that ranked lower in this regard are Punjab, Bihar, Kerala, Uttar Pradesh, and Gujarat. Regarding the growth of the labour force for all persons (males and females, rural and urban combined), the leading state is Jammu & Kashmir, followed by Assam, Haryana, Himachal Pradesh, and Andhra Pradesh. Meanwhile, the bottom five states in labour force growth for all persons are Punjab, Kerala, Bihar, Tamil Nadu, and Odisha.

Table 30. Annual Growth Rates (%) of Labour Force (UPSS) in Seventeen Major States of India

State	Period	Rural			Urban			Rural + Urban		
		Male	Female	Male + Female	Male	Female	Male + Female	Male	Female	Male + Female
Andhra Pradesh	1983 to 1994	2.0 (9)	2.5 (4)	2.2 (6)	3.5 (4)	4.1 (7)	3.6 (6)	2.3 (9)	2.7 (4)	2.5 (5)
	1994 to 2000	0.6 (15)	−0.1 (9)	0.3 (14)	0.5 (16)	−0.4 (13)	0.3 (17)	0.6 (16)	−0.1 (9)	0.3 (15)
	2000 to 2012	0.2 (16)	−0.2 (7)	0.0 (15)	3.7 (5)	3.0 (10)	3.5 (6)	1.2 (16)	0.2 (10)	0.8 (16)
	2012 to 2018	−0.1 (16)	−3.2 (6)	−1.4 (14)	3.2 (6)	6.8 (4)	4.1 (4)	0.9 (15)	−1.0 (5)	0.2 (10)
	1994 to 2018	0.2 (16)	−0.9 (6)	−0.3 (15)	2.7 (12)	3.1 (7)	2.8 (8)	1.0 (16)	−0.2 (8)	0.5 (16)
Assam	1983 to 1994	2.4 (4)	4.9 (2)	2.9 (2)	3.7 (2)	7.3 (1)	4.2 (1)	2.6 (3)	5.0 (2)	3.1 (2)
	1994 to 2000	1.7 (5)	0.5 (7)	1.4 (6)	3.1 (7)	5.3 (2)	3.5 (2)	1.9 (5)	1.0 (6)	1.7 (5)
	2000 to 2012	1.6 (9)	−0.4 (8)	1.2 (7)	2.5 (16)	0.0 (17)	2.1 (17)	1.7 (13)	−0.3 (14)	1.3 (11)
	2012 to 2018	2.2 (4)	−3.5 (8)	1.7 (2)	3.2 (5)	7.2 (1)	3.8 (5)	2.3 (4)	−2.3 (9)	2.0 (3)
	1994 to 2018	1.8 (2)	−1.0 (7)	1.4 (2)	2.8 (8)	3.1 (6)	2.9 (7)	1.9 (6)	−0.5 (10)	1.6 (4)
Bihar	1983 to 1994	2.4 (5)	−1.5 (15)	1.3 (14)	2.1 (16)	−0.5 (17)	1.7 (17)	2.4 (8)	−1.4 (16)	1.4 (15)
	1994 to 2000	1.7 (4)	2.6 (2)	1.9 (4)	2.3 (14)	4.0 (3)	2.5 (10)	1.8 (6)	2.6 (2)	2.0 (3)
	2000 to 2012	2.1 (2)	−3.4 (17)	1.0 (10)	2.8 (10)	0.7 (16)	2.5 (15)	2.2 (5)	−3.0 (17)	1.2 (13)
	2012 to 2018	0.9 (9)	−9.4 (16)	0.0 (5)	3.1 (8)	5.4 (5)	3.2 (7)	1.2 (13)	−7.5 (17)	0.4 (8)
	1994 to 2018	1.7 (4)	−3.5 (17)	1.0 (5)	2.7 (13)	2.7 (8)	2.7 (10)	1.8 (7)	−2.8 (17)	1.2 (9)
Gujarat	1983 to 1994	2.0 (8)	1.1 (13)	1.6 (12)	3.2 (9)	3.8 (9)	3.3 (9)	2.4 (7)	1.5 (13)	2.1 (12)
	1994 to 2000	1.8 (3)	2.3 (3)	2.0 (3)	2.9 (9)	1.4 (9)	2.6 (8)	2.2 (3)	2.1 (3)	2.2 (2)
	2000 to 2012	1.2 (13)	−2.3 (15)	−0.1 (16)	4.0 (3)	2.9 (13)	3.8 (4)	2.3 (3)	−1.2 (16)	1.3 (12)
	2012 to 2018	0.4 (15)	−6.9 (13)	−1.3 (13)	2.7 (10)	2.1 (12)	2.2 (12)	1.4 (11)	−4.0 (12)	0.2 (11)
	1994 to 2018	1.1 (12)	−2.4 (14)	0.1 (13)	3.4 (4)	2.3 (11)	3.1 (5)	2.0 (4)	−1.1 (14)	1.2 (8)
Haryana	1983 to 1994	1.9 (10)	3.5 (3)	2.4 (4)	3.3 (5)	6.9 (2)	3.9 (3)	2.3 (10)	4.0 (3)	2.8 (3)
	1994 to 2000	2.2 (2)	−3.0 (17)	0.6 (10)	3.9 (2)	−3.4 (16)	2.6 (7)	2.7 (2)	−3.1 (17)	1.2 (8)
	2000 to 2012	1.9 (4)	−0.6 (12)	1.3 (6)	3.9 (4)	4.0 (5)	3.9 (3)	2.5 (2)	0.3 (8)	2.1 (3)
	2012 to 2018	0.7 (12)	−5.7 (10)	−0.6 (8)	4.4 (2)	4.5 (7)	4.3 (2)	1.9 (7)	−2.7 (11)	1.1 (4)
	1994 to 2018	1.7 (6)	−2.5 (15)	0.6 (9)	4.0 (2)	2.2 (13)	3.7 (2)	2.4 (2)	−1.3 (15)	1.6 (3)

(Continued)

Table 30 *(Continued)*

State	Period	Rural						Urban						Rural + Urban					
		Male		Female		Male + Female		Male		Female		Male + Female		Male		Female		Male + Female	
Himachal Pradesh	1983 to 1994	2.7	(2)	2.5	(5)	2.6	(3)	1.8	(17)	4.1	(6)	2.3	(16)	2.6	(2)	2.6	(5)	2.6	(4)
	1994 to 2000	0.0	(16)	−0.1	(10)	0.0	(16)	4.0	(1)	−3.3	(15)	2.4	(11)	0.4	(17)	−0.2	(12)	0.1	(16)
	2000 to 2012	1.2	(12)	2.1	(2)	1.7	(2)	2.5	(15)	6.4	(2)	3.3	(7)	1.4	(15)	2.3	(2)	1.8	(5)
	2012 to 2018	2.4	(1)	−2.8	(3)	−0.1	(6)	0.4	(17)	−1.3	(15)	0.6	(17)	2.2	(5)	−2.6	(10)	0.0	(15)
	1994 to 2018	1.2	(10)	0.3	(2)	0.8	(7)	2.4	(16)	1.9	(14)	2.4	(15)	1.3	(15)	0.4	(4)	0.9	(12)
Jammu & Kashmir	1983 to 1994	1.6	(13)	5.6	(1)	3.0	(1)	3.1	(10)	6.4	(3)	3.6	(5)	1.9	(14)	5.7	(1)	3.1	(1)
	1994 to 2000	3.6	(1)	−0.4	(13)	2.0	(2)	2.8	(10)	−9.3	(17)	1.0	(15)	3.4	(1)	−1.1	(16)	1.8	(4)
	2000 to 2012	2.2	(1)	−0.1	(6)	1.4	(5)	4.1	(2)	9.9	(1)	4.9	(2)	2.7	(1)	0.9	(5)	2.2	(2)
	2012 to 2018	2.3	(2)	0.3	(2)	1.7	(3)	3.1	(7)	7.0	(2)	3.4	(6)	2.6	(2)	1.9	(2)	2.2	(2)
	1994 to 2018	2.6	(1)	−0.1	(4)	1.6	(1)	3.5	(3)	4.1	(3)	3.5	(3)	2.8	(1)	0.7	(3)	2.1	(1)
Karnataka	1983 to 1994	1.8	(11)	2.5	(6)	2.1	(9)	3.0	(12)	2.1	(14)	2.8	(13)	2.1	(12)	2.5	(7)	2.3	(8)
	1994 to 2000	0.9	(11)	−0.9	(15)	0.2	(15)	2.6	(12)	2.1	(5)	2.5	(9)	1.4	(9)	−0.4	(13)	0.8	(14)
	2000 to 2012	1.1	(14)	−1.5	(14)	0.2	(13)	3.1	(7)	2.1	(14)	2.9	(11)	1.8	(11)	−0.7	(15)	1.0	(15)
	2012 to 2018	0.5	(13)	−3.8	(9)	−0.9	(12)	2.2	(14)	3.9	(8)	2.4	(11)	1.1	(14)	−1.4	(7)	0.3	(9)
	1994 to 2018	0.9	(14)	−1.9	(13)	−0.1	(14)	2.8	(9)	2.6	(9)	2.7	(11)	1.5	(12)	−0.8	(11)	0.8	(14)
Kerala	1983 to 1994	1.3	(15)	−1.8	(16)	0.1	(16)	4.5	(1)	3.5	(12)	4.2	(2)	2.0	(13)	−0.8	(15)	1.1	(16)
	1994 to 2000	1.4	(6)	1.7	(4)	1.5	(5)	0.4	(17)	1.1	(10)	0.6	(16)	1.1	(13)	1.5	(4)	1.3	(6)
	2000 to 2012	−2.7	(17)	−3.0	(16)	−2.8	(17)	5.6	(1)	5.2	(4)	5.5	(1)	0.3	(17)	−0.2	(13)	0.1	(17)
	2012 to 2018	−4.2	(17)	−6.4	(12)	−5.0	(17)	5.6	(1)	6.8	(3)	5.9	(1)	0.3	(17)	−0.3	(4)	0.0	(14)
	1994 to 2018	−2.1	(17)	−2.7	(16)	−2.3	(17)	4.3	(1)	4.5	(1)	4.4	(1)	0.5	(17)	0.2	(5)	0.4	(17)

(Continued)

Table 30 *(Continued)*

State	Period	Rural						Urban						Rural + Urban					
		Male		Female		Male + Female		Male		Female		Male + Female		Male		Female		Male + Female	
Madhya Pradesh	1983 to 1994	2.2	(6)	1.4	(11)	1.9	(10)	3.6	(3)	3.6	(11)	3.6	(7)	2.5	(4)	1.6	(12)	2.2	(11)
	1994 to 2000	0.7	(13)	0.7	(6)	0.7	(9)	3.2	(6)	1.5	(8)	2.8	(5)	1.2	(11)	0.8	(7)	1.1	(10)
	2000 to 2012	2.1	(3)	−0.6	(13)	1.1	(8)	2.8	(9)	3.5	(7)	2.9	(10)	2.2	(4)	−0.1	(12)	1.5	(8)
	2012 to 2018	2.3	(3)	2.4	(1)	2.4	(1)	4.1	(3)	5.4	(6)	4.2	(3)	2.8	(1)	3.2	(1)	3.0	(1)
	1994 to 2018	1.8	(3)	0.4	(1)	1.3	(3)	3.2	(5)	3.5	(4)	3.2	(4)	2.1	(3)	0.9	(2)	1.7	(2)
Maharashtra	1983 to 1994	1.6	(14)	1.7	(9)	1.6	(13)	3.3	(7)	4.6	(5)	3.6	(8)	2.2	(11)	2.1	(8)	2.2	(10)
	1994 to 2000	1.0	(9)	−0.2	(11)	0.5	(13)	3.4	(3)	−0.2	(12)	2.7	(6)	2.0	(4)	−0.2	(10)	1.2	(7)
	2000 to 2012	1.7	(8)	0.0	(5)	1.0	(11)	2.1	(17)	3.8	(6)	2.4	(16)	1.9	(10)	0.8	(6)	1.5	(7)
	2012 to 2018	0.9	(8)	−3.5	(7)	−0.7	(10)	2.4	(13)	2.0	(13)	2.0	(13)	1.6	(9)	−1.6	(8)	0.5	(7)
	1994 to 2018	1.3	(8)	−0.9	(5)	0.4	(10)	2.5	(15)	2.3	(12)	2.4	(16)	1.8	(8)	0.0	(6)	1.2	(10)
Odisha	1983 to 1994	1.6	(12)	2.3	(7)	1.9	(11)	3.3	(6)	6.2	(4)	3.8	(4)	1.8	(15)	2.5	(6)	2.1	(13)
	1994 to 2000	1.0	(10)	0.4	(8)	0.8	(7)	1.3	(15)	2.0	(6)	1.5	(14)	1.0	(14)	0.5	(8)	0.8	(12)
	2000 to 2012	1.7	(7)	−0.4	(9)	1.1	(9)	3.7	(6)	3.0	(11)	3.5	(5)	2.0	(6)	−0.1	(11)	1.4	(9)
	2012 to 2018	0.4	(14)	−6.9	(14)	−1.5	(15)	1.4	(16)	−0.2	(14)	0.7	(16)	0.6	(16)	−6.0	(14)	−1.2	(17)
	1994 to 2018	1.2	(11)	−1.9	(11)	0.3	(12)	2.5	(14)	1.9	(15)	2.3	(17)	1.4	(13)	−1.5	(16)	0.6	(15)
Punjab	1983 to 1994	0.8	(17)	−2.0	(17)	0.0	(17)	3.0	(11)	−0.4	(16)	2.5	(14)	1.5	(16)	−1.8	(17)	0.6	(17)
	1994 to 2000	0.8	(12)	5.3	(1)	2.1	(1)	3.2	(5)	7.7	(1)	3.8	(1)	1.6	(7)	5.7	(1)	2.6	(1)
	2000 to 2012	1.3	(11)	−0.6	(11)	0.7	(12)	2.6	(13)	3.4	(9)	2.8	(12)	1.8	(12)	0.3	(9)	1.4	(10)
	2012 to 2018	0.9	(10)	−11.2	(17)	−1.9	(16)	2.7	(11)	2.5	(11)	2.6	(9)	1.5	(10)	−6.6	(15)	−0.2	(16)
	1994 to 2018	1.1	(13)	−1.9	(12)	0.4	(11)	2.8	(11)	4.2	(2)	3.0	(6)	1.7	(10)	−0.2	(9)	1.3	(6)

(Continued)

Table 30 *(Continued)*

State	Period	Rural						Urban						Rural + Urban					
		Male		Female		Male + Female		Male		Female		Male + Female		Male		Female		Male + Female	
Rajasthan	1983 to 1994	2.2	(7)	2.1	(8)	2.2	(7)	3.3	(8)	1.5	(15)	2.8	(10)	2.4	(6)	2.1	(9)	2.3	(7)
	1994 to 2000	1.1	(7)	−0.2	(12)	0.5	(12)	2.7	(11)	0.3	(11)	2.2	(12)	1.5	(8)	−0.2	(11)	0.8	(13)
	2000 to 2012	1.8	(6)	0.9	(4)	1.4	(4)	2.6	(12)	2.9	(12)	2.7	(13)	2.0	(8)	1.1	(4)	1.7	(6)
	2012 to 2018	2.1	(5)	−5.9	(11)	−0.7	(11)	3.3	(4)	−2.0	(17)	2.4	(10)	2.4	(3)	−5.2	(13)	0.0	(13)
	1994 to 2018	1.7	(5)	−1.1	(8)	0.7	(8)	2.8	(7)	1.0	(17)	2.5	(13)	2.0	(5)	−0.8	(12)	1.0	(11)
Tamil Nadu	1983 to 1994	0.8	(16)	1.2	(12)	1.0	(15)	2.6	(14)	3.2	(13)	2.8	(12)	1.4	(17)	1.6	(11)	1.5	(14)
	1994 to 2000	−0.7	(17)	−2.2	(16)	−1.3	(17)	3.0	(8)	2.3	(4)	2.8	(4)	0.8	(15)	−1.1	(15)	0.1	(17)
	2000 to 2012	0.5	(15)	−0.4	(10)	0.1	(14)	2.7	(11)	2.1	(15)	2.6	(14)	1.5	(14)	0.3	(7)	1.1	(14)
	2012 to 2018	0.8	(11)	−2.8	(4)	−0.6	(9)	2.6	(12)	3.6	(9)	2.8	(8)	1.6	(8)	−0.1	(3)	1.0	(5)
	1994 to 2018	0.3	(15)	−1.5	(10)	−0.4	(16)	2.8	(10)	2.5	(10)	2.7	(12)	1.4	(14)	−0.1	(7)	0.8	(13)
Uttar Pradesh	1983 to 1994	2.8	(1)	0.6	(14)	2.1	(8)	2.7	(13)	3.7	(10)	2.8	(11)	2.7	(1)	0.8	(14)	2.2	(9)
	1994 to 2000	0.6	(14)	0.8	(5)	0.7	(8)	3.3	(4)	2.0	(7)	3.1	(3)	1.2	(12)	1.0	(5)	1.1	(9)
	2000 to 2012	1.8	(5)	1.0	(3)	1.6	(3)	2.9	(8)	3.5	(8)	3.0	(9)	2.0	(7)	1.3	(3)	1.9	(4)
	2012 to 2018	1.9	(6)	−8.2	(15)	−0.5	(7)	2.7	(9)	−1.4	(16)	2.0	(14)	2.0	(6)	−7.0	(16)	0.0	(12)
	1994 to 2018	1.5	(7)	−1.4	(9)	0.8	(6)	3.0	(6)	1.9	(16)	2.8	(9)	1.8	(9)	−0.9	(13)	1.2	(7)
West Bengal	1983 to 1994	2.6	(3)	1.5	(10)	2.4	(5)	2.1	(15)	3.8	(8)	2.4	(15)	2.5	(5)	2.0	(10)	2.4	(6)
	1994 to 2000	1.0	(8)	−0.6	(14)	0.6	(11)	2.4	(13)	−2.2	(14)	1.5	(13)	1.4	(10)	−1.0	(14)	0.9	(11)
	2000 to 2012	1.6	(10)	2.2	(1)	1.7	(1)	2.6	(14)	6.0	(3)	3.2	(8)	1.9	(9)	3.2	(1)	2.2	(1)
	2012 to 2018	1.2	(7)	−3.0	(5)	0.1	(4)	1.7	(15)	2.8	(10)	1.9	(15)	1.3	(12)	−1.2	(6)	0.7	(6)
	1994 to 2018	1.3	(9)	0.2	(3)	1.1	(4)	2.3	(17)	3.1	(5)	2.5	(14)	1.6	(11)	1.0	(1)	1.5	(5)

Source: Same as Table 10

Note: The figures in parentheses are ranks among 17 major states

3.9.3.2 Post-Globalisation Period (1994 to 2018)

Focusing on the period from 1994 to 2018, the post-globalisation period, we observed changes in states' performance in labour force growth. During this time, the state reporting the highest labour force growth for rural males is Jammu & Kashmir, followed by Assam, Madhya Pradesh, Bihar, and Rajasthan. Conversely, the growth has been low in Kerala, Andhra Pradesh, Tamil Nadu, Karnataka, and Punjab. Among rural females, the highest labour force growth during the post-globalisation period is observed in Madhya Pradesh, followed by Himachal Pradesh, West Bengal, Jammu & Kashmir, and Maharashtra; the states with the lowest growth in this regard are Bihar, Kerala, Haryana, Gujarat, and Karnataka. Concerning rural persons, Jammu & Kashmir ranked first, followed by Assam, Madhya Pradesh, West Bengal, and Bihar.

In urban areas, the growth rate of the male labour force during the post-globalisation period has been highest in Kerala, followed by Haryana, Jammu & Kashmir, Gujarat, and Madhya Pradesh; conversely, it has been low in West Bengal, Himachal Pradesh, Maharashtra, Odisha, and Bihar. Among urban females, the most significant growth in the labour force is observed in Kerala, followed by Punjab, Jammu & Kashmir, Madhya Pradesh, and West Bengal. The states that have shown low labour force growth among urban females during the post-globalisation period are Rajasthan, Uttar Pradesh, Odisha, Himachal Pradesh, and Haryana (listed in ascending order of growth rate). Among urban areas, Kerala recorded the highest labour force growth during this period, followed by Haryana, Jammu & Kashmir, Madhya Pradesh, and Gujarat. In contrast, the lowest growth has been noted in Odisha, while other states with low labour force growth for urban individuals include Maharashtra, Himachal Pradesh, West Bengal, and Rajasthan.

When considering all males (rural and urban), the labour force growth rate during the post-globalisation period has been highest in Jammu & Kashmir, followed by Haryana, Madhya Pradesh, Gujarat, and Rajasthan. The five states with the lowest labour force growth for males (rural and urban combined) are Kerala, Andhra Pradesh, Himachal Pradesh, Tamil Nadu, and Odisha (in descending order of growth rate). Among all females (rural and urban), the state that reported the highest labour force growth during the post-globalisation period is West Bengal, followed by Madhya Pradesh, Jammu & Kashmir, Himachal Pradesh, and Kerala. Labour force growth among all females during the post-globalisation period was lowest in Bihar; other states with low growth rates include Odisha, Haryana, Gujarat, and Uttar Pradesh. The growth rate of the labour force, including males and females, during the post-globalisation period has been highest in Jammu &

Kashmir, followed by Madhya Pradesh, Haryana, Assam, and West Bengal. Conversely, the five states with the lowest labour force growth during this period are Kerala, Andhra Pradesh, Odisha, Karnataka, and Tamil Nadu (in ascending order of growth rate).

To understand the relative performance (ranks) of the states regarding labour force growth rates from 1983 to 2018, we first computed these growth rates for different sub-periods and ranked the states accordingly. Subsequently, we calculated the mean values of ranks for the states in various sub-periods, which were then used to rank the states again, allowing us to assess the relative performance of the states in terms of labour force growth during the entire period of 1983–2018. This information, presented in Table 31, illustrates that during 1983–2018, the group of front-runners in terms of labour force growth for rural males included mainly the less developed states (Jammu & Kashmir, Bihar, Assam, Rajasthan, Maharashtra, Uttar Pradesh, etc.), with Maharashtra being the notable exception. The states that have fallen behind in growth rates for rural males are Kerala, Tamil Nadu, Andhra Pradesh, Punjab and Karnataka. The top five states in terms of labour force growth for rural females between 1983 and 2018 are Himachal Pradesh, Jammu & Kashmir, Assam, Andhra Pradesh, and West Bengal. Conversely, Bihar, Kerala, Punjab, Karnataka, and Gujarat are the five lowest-performing states. For rural persons, the front-runners in labour force growth during this period appear to be Jammu & Kashmir, Assam, West Bengal, Uttar Pradesh, and Himachal Pradesh; on the other hand, those at the bottom include Tamil Nadu, Kerala, Karnataka, Andhra Pradesh, and Madhya Pradesh.

In urban areas, among males, the states that appear to have achieved superior ranks in labour force growth during 1983–2018 are Haryana, Kerala, Maharashtra, Jammu & Kashmir, and Assam; those ranking poorly in this regard include West Bengal, Himachal Pradesh, Bihar, Tamil Nadu, and Karnataka. For urban females, the top performer appears to be Assam, followed by Jammu & Kashmir, Kerala, Haryana, and Maharashtra. States such as Rajasthan, Gujarat, Uttar Pradesh, Tamil Nadu, and Karnataka performed poorly. Regarding urban persons, the leading five performers are Haryana, Kerala, Assam, Maharashtra, and Jammu & Kashmir; the states at the bottom are West Bengal, Himachal Pradesh, Bihar, Rajasthan, and Karnataka.

Table 31. Mean of Ranks of States Concerning Periodic Growth of LFPR and Coefficients of Concordance (W)

State	Rural			Urban			Rural + Urban		
	Male	Female	Male + Female	Male	Female	Male + Female	Male	Female	Male + Female
Andhra Pradesh	14.0 (15)	6.5 (4)	12.3 (14)	7.8 (6)	8.5 (6)	8.3 (6)	14.0 (16)	7.0 (2)	11.5 (13)
Assam	5.5 (3)	6.3 (3)	4.3 (2)	7.5 (5)	5.3 (1)	6.3 (3)	6.3 (5)	7.8 (4)	5.3 (3)
Bihar	5.0 (2)	12.5 (17)	8.3 (8)	12.0 (15)	10.3 (12)	12.3 (15)	8.0 (8)	13.0 (17)	9.8 (9)
Gujarat	9.8 (10)	11.0 (13)	11.0 (11)	7.8 (7)	10.8 (16)	8.3 (7)	6.0 (4)	11.0 (16)	9.3 (8)
Haryana	7.0 (7)	10.5 (11)	7.0 (6)	3.3 (1)	7.5 (4)	3.8 (1)	5.3 (3)	9.8 (12)	4.5 (2)
Himachal Pradesh	7.8 (9)	5.0 (1)	6.8 (5)	12.5 (16)	9.5 (11)	12.8 (16)	9.8 (11)	7.3 (3)	10.0 (11)
Jammu & Kashmir	4.3 (1)	5.5 (2)	2.8 (1)	7.3 (4)	5.8 (2)	7.0 (5)	4.5 (1)	6.0 (1)	2.3 (1)
Karnataka	12.3 (13)	11.0 (14)	12.3 (15)	11.3 (13)	10.3 (13)	11.0 (13)	11.5 (13)	10.5 (14)	11.5 (14)
Kerala	16.3 (17)	12.0 (16)	13.8 (16)	5.0 (2)	7.3 (3)	5.0 (2)	15.0 (17)	9.0 (8)	13.3 (17)
Maharashtra	6.3 (4)	7.8 (6)	7.0 (7)	5.3 (3)	8.0 (5)	6.3 (4)	5.0 (2)	8.0 (6)	7.5 (5)
Madhya Pradesh	9.8 (10)	8.0 (7)	11.8 (13)	10.0 (10)	9.0 (9)	10.8 (12)	8.5 (9)	8.0 (7)	7.8 (6)
Odisha	10.8 (12)	9.6 (10)	10.5 (10)	10.8 (12)	8.8 (7)	9.8 (11)	12.8 (14)	9.8 (13)	12.8 (16)
Punjab	12.5 (14)	11.5 (15)	11.5 (12)	10.0 (11)	9.3 (10)	9.0 (8)	11.3 (12)	10.5 (15)	11.0 (12)
Rajasthan	6.3 (4)	8.6 (8)	8.5 (9)	8.8 (9)	13.8 (17)	11.3 (14)	6.3 (6)	9.3 (10)	9.8 (10)
Tamil Nadu	14.8 (16)	10.5 (12)	13.8 (17)	11.3 (14)	10.3 (14)	9.5 (10)	13.5 (15)	9.0 (9)	12.5 (15)
Uttar Pradesh	6.5 (6)	9.3 (9)	6.5 (4)	8.5 (8)	10.3 (15)	9.3 (9)	6.5 (7)	9.5 (11)	8.5 (7)
West Bengal	7.0 (7)	7.5 (5)	5.3 (3)	14.3 (17)	8.8 (8)	12.8 (17)	9.0 (10)	7.8 (5)	6.0 (4)
Kendall's Coeff.	53.7	21.4	44.6	33.3	15.6	28.3	46.4	11.5	38.2
p-value	0.00	0.62	0.03	0.17	0.87	0.32	0.02	0.96	0.08

Source: Author's computation using information presented in Table 30

Note: The figures in parentheses are ranks among 17 major states

When considering rural and urban areas combined, for males, the five states showing relatively better performance in the growth of the labour force from 1983 to 2018 are Jammu & Kashmir, Maharashtra, Haryana, Gujarat, and Assam; those performing poorly in this regard are Kerala, Andhra Pradesh, Tamil Nadu, Odisha, and Karnataka. For all females (rural plus urban), the leaders are Jammu & Kashmir, Andhra Pradesh, Himachal Pradesh, Assam, and West Bengal; those at the bottom are Bihar, Gujarat, Punjab, Karnataka, and Odisha. For males and females combined, the state that performed best from 1983 to 2018 was Jammu & Kashmir, followed by Haryana, Assam, West Bengal, and Maharashtra. Conversely, the five states at the bottom are Kerala, Odisha, Tamil Nadu, Karnataka, and Andhra Pradesh. The remaining states occupy a middle position in terms of their ranks based on labour force growth rates from 1983 to 2018.

To what extent have the ranking patterns of the states in different sub-periods concerning the growth rates of the labour force changed? This can be assessed using Kendall's test of concordance. The results of this test, also presented in Table 31, indicate that, unlike the ranking patterns of labour force participation rates, the ranking of the states regarding the growth of the labour force changed significantly for most categories throughout our study, with the exceptions being rural males, rural persons, all (rural plus urban) males, and all persons. The most noticeable point here is that the ranking patterns of the states shift significantly when we consider the growth rates of the female labour force in both rural and urban areas.

In the context of the present discussion, it is noteworthy that the globalisation policies implemented in India since the early 1990s have significantly impacted females in general and rural females in particular, as demonstrated by comparing labour force growth rates before and after their implementation. A close examination of the information presented in Table 31 indicates that the declining growth rates of the labour force for females persisted throughout almost the entire post-globalisation period. Thus, from 1994 to 2000, in twelve out of seventeen major states, rural females experienced a decrease in the labour force growth rate compared to the previous period (1983 to 1994); the corresponding figures for the periods 2000 to 2012 and 2012 to 2018 were twelve and fifteen, respectively. It is abundantly clear that rural females in most states experienced a decline in their labour force growth rates after 1994, with the situation worsening, particularly after 2012. As many as eight states witnessed a decrease of more than five percentage points in the growth rate of rural females' labour force from 2012 to 2018: Bihar, Gujarat, Haryana, Kerala, Odisha, Punjab, Rajasthan, and Uttar Pradesh. A similar picture is observed for rural males, where twelve states experienced a decrease in the labour force growth rate from 1994 to 2000, compared to the previous period, 1983 to 1994. The corresponding figures for the periods from 2000 to 2012 and 2012 to 2018 were twelve and thirteen, respectively. However, in this case, the decline in growth rate was lower than that of their female counterparts.

The situation is somewhat different in urban areas, where nine states demonstrated a slight decline in the male labour force growth rate during the post-globalisation period from 1994 to 2018, while the growth rate increased in the remaining eight states. However, for females, fourteen states showed a decline in the labour force growth rate from 1994 to 2000 compared to the period from 1983 to 1994. The majority of states experienced an increase in the growth rate of the urban female labour force during both the periods of 2000–2012 and 2012–2018, relative to the preceding period. When considering both rural and urban areas together and comparing the entire post-globalisation period (1994 to 2018) with the pre-globalisation period (1983 to 1994), it appears that in fourteen out of seventeen states, the growth rate of the male labour force declined during the post-globalisation period, with the exceptions being Haryana, Jammu & Kashmir, and Punjab. Similarly, fifteen states saw a decline in the growth rate of the female labour force during the post-globalisation period, with Kerala and Punjab as exceptions.

3.10 Determinants of Labour Force Participation: Findings from Logit Regression

This section aims to identify factors influencing a person's decision to join the labour force. Specifically, we have sought to identify various socio-economic factors affecting individuals' choices regarding labour force participation. For this purpose, we have utilised the 'unit-level' data from the PLFS 2018. We assume that an individual's willingness to participate in the labour force is shaped by their surrounding environment, which is often reflected in their socio-economic status.

In our analysis, we have estimated logit regression models separately for rural, urban, and combined areas. The dependent variable is 'labf', a binary variable where a value of '1' indicates that a person has participated in the labour force, and '0' otherwise. Below are the explanatory variables along with their corresponding hypotheses:

Age of the person (age): Individuals' age likely affects their participation in the labour force. While younger people tend to continue their studies, older people are more likely to enter the labour market in search of employment. Thus, we hypothesise a positive relationship between 'labf' and 'age'.

Sex of the person (sex): An individual's sex is likely to play a significant role in determining labour force participation. Women often face discrimination in the labour market within a male-dominated society. Additionally, women may feel compelled to withdraw from the labour force during unfavourable labour market conditions, while their male counterparts may continue working. It is also possible that women leave the labour force when their husbands' incomes increase, as they may be expected to devote more time to their children and domestic responsibilities. In our study, the variable 'sex' is binary, coded as '1' for males and '0' for females. The hypothesis proposes a positive relationship between 'labf' and 'sex'.

Household size (hsize): Household size refers to the total number of individuals residing together in a single dwelling. This size can influence the number of people entering the labour force. In larger households, there may be less pressure for members to join the labour market immediately. Therefore, we can hypothesise that larger households have lower labour force participation.

Marital status (marstat): Married individuals are more likely to participate in the labour force than unmarried individuals, as they need to earn an income to support their families. The variable 'marstat' is a binary variable with value '1' for married individuals and '0' for unmarried individuals. We hypothesise that the relationship between 'labf' and 'marstat' is positive.

Social groups (sg1, sg2 and sg3): This variable examines whether caste differences influence individuals' decisions to join the labour force. The PLFS categorises social groups into four categories: Scheduled Tribe (ST), Scheduled Caste (SC), Other Backward Classes (OBC), and 'Others' (general castes). To investigate how caste status impacts labour force participation, we created three dummy variables for social groups: 'sg1', which takes the value '1' for SC and '0' for all others; 'sg2', which takes the value '1' for ST and '0' for all others; and 'sg3', which takes the value '1' for OBC and '0' for all others. The reference category comprises individuals from the 'Others' (general castes) category. These dummy variables enable us to analyse whether individuals from weaker castes (SC/ST/OBC) are more likely to join the labour force than those from general castes. Based on our earlier findings that labour force participation is higher among individuals from weaker caste groups in India, we anticipate a positive relationship between these dummy variables and labour force participation ('labf').

Religious groups (rel1 and rel2): In the survey mentioned above, eight groups have been formed based on individuals' religions: Hinduism, Islam (Muslim), Christianity, Sikhism, Jainism, Buddhism, Zoroastrianism, and Others. Among these eight groups, Hinduism emerged as the most dominant religion, representing 82 % of the total population, according to the PLFS 2018. Muslims constituted

13 % of the total population, while the remaining six groups accounted for 5 %. We have created two dummy variables, using Hinduism as the reference category for our analysis. The first variable, 'rel1', is assigned a value of '1' if the individual identifies as a Muslim and '0' otherwise. The second variable, 'rel2', is assigned a value of '1' if the individual belongs to a religion other than Hinduism or Muslim and '0' otherwise. Many believe that Muslims in India, along with other religious groups, are at a disadvantage compared to Hindus in areas such as education, health, access to resources, and employment. These dummy variables help evaluate the validity of this hypothesis regarding labour force participation. Specifically, we hypothesise that the relationships between 'labf' and 'rel1' or 'rel2' are negative.

General education groups (gedu1, gedu2, gedu3 and gedu4): Education is crucial for accessing employment opportunities in the labour market, particularly in the non-agricultural sector. The level of education attained affects the quality and skills of the labour force. In the PLFS, education is categorised into twelve distinct levels. To simplify the analysis, we have created four educational dummies, using 'illiterates' as the reference category. These are: 'gedu1' = 1 if the individual's education is up to primary and '0' otherwise; 'gedu2' = 1 for education above primary but up to secondary and '0' otherwise; 'gedu3' = 1 for education above secondary but up to graduation and '0' otherwise; and 'gedu4' = '1' if post-graduate and above and '0' otherwise. We hypothesise that the probability of joining the labour force increases with higher levels of education compared to the 'illiterates'.

Technical education (techedu): Some technical education encourages individuals to enter the workforce. In this context, we have employed a dummy variable, assigning the value '1' to those who have completed technical education (diploma/degree) and '0' otherwise. We hypothesise that there is a positive association between 'labf' and 'techedu'.

Attendance of educational institution (attendcur): Individuals currently enrolled in educational institutions are not expected to enter the labour force. Recent studies have indicated a decline in the labour force participation rate, particularly among females. This decline can be partly attributed to their attendance in educational institutions. To examine the validity of this observation, we employ a dummy variable that takes the value '1' for those currently attending an educational institution and '0' otherwise. We hypothesise a negative relationship between 'labf' and 'attendcur'.

Poverty status (pstat): Joining the labour force is expected to enhance access to employment and income opportunities, helping individuals move out of poverty. Consequently, members of poor households are more likely to participate in the labour force than those from non-poor households. The datasets we utilised enable us to examine the impact of an individual's poverty status on their labour force participation. By analysing data on per capita consumption expenditure (in Rs.) and applying the 'official poverty line' for 2018, we determined the poverty status of each individual.[7] We created a dummy variable to classify individuals by household per capita consumption expenditure. If a person's per capita monthly consumption expenditure falls below the poverty line (in Rs.), the variable is assigned a '0', indicating that the person is classified as 'poor'. Conversely, if the expenditure is greater than or equal to the poverty line, the variable is assigned a '1', labelling the person as 'non-poor'. The hypothesis posits a negative relationship between 'labf' and 'povstat'.

3.10.1 Logit Regression Results

The regression results for rural, urban, and combined areas are presented in Table 32. In rural areas, the estimated coefficients for all explanatory variables, except the two religious dummies (rel1 and rel2), are statistically significant. Based on the signs of the estimated coefficients, we can conclude that the likelihood of an individual participating in the labour force in rural India increases with the individual's age, if the individual is male, married, has obtained technical education, is not currently attending any educational institution, and comes from a poor family. Conversely, the probability of labour force participation decreases if the individual belongs to a household with more members. The estimated coefficients related to social group dummies indicate that individuals from marginalised castes (SC, ST, and OBC) are more likely to participate in the labour force than those from general castes. Additionally, the coefficients for the religious group dummies suggest that individuals from the Muslim community are less likely to participate in the labour force than Hindus; however, the estimated coefficient for this dummy is statistically insignificant. Furthermore, the estimated coefficients of education dummies reveal that individuals with higher levels of general education are more likely to participate in the labour force than those who are illiterate. The observations regarding the factors influencing labour force participation in rural areas also generally apply to urban areas.

The logit regression results for the combined areas (rural plus urban) convey nearly the same message. It is observed that the probability of labour force participation in India increases for males, older individuals, married individuals, more educated individuals, individuals who have received technical training,

[7] We utilised state-specific poverty lines for rural and urban areas for the 2017–18 period, after adjusting the Tendulkar poverty lines for 2011–12 using the suitable price deflators.

and individuals from 'poor' families. Additionally, it is found that individuals from lower-caste families are more likely to be in the labour force than those from higher castes. However, the likelihood of labour force participation is lower for individuals from Muslim and 'Other' groups compared to those from Hindu families.

Table 32. Logit Regression Results of Determinants of Participation in Labour Force in India [Dep. Variable: labf = 1 if participated in labour force; 0 otherwise]

	Rural Areas			Urban Areas			Rural + Urban Areas		
Explanatory variables	**Est. coeffi-cient**	***z*-value**	***p*-value**	**Est. coeffi-cient**	***z*-value**	***p*-value**	**Est. coeffi-cient**	***z*-value**	***p*-value**
age	0.04	68.91	0.00	0.02	36.34	0.00	0.03	77.25	0.00
sex	2.55	177.21	0.00	2.79	160.14	0.00	2.63	239.49	0.00
hsize	−0.03	−12.07	0.00	−0.03	−10.84	0.00	−0.03	−16.64	0.00
marstat	1.41	81.78	0.00	1.32	67.36	0.00	1.35	105.8	0.00
sg1	0.28	16.09	0.00	0.44	22.15	0.00	0.39	30.72	0.00
sg2	0.44	21.56	0.00	0.36	10.99	0.00	0.55	33.61	0.00
sg3	0.19	12.85	0.00	0.27	17.89	0.00	0.27	25.65	0.00
rel1	−0.03	−1.42	0.16	0.02	1.42	0.16	−0.04	−3.35	0.00
rel2	0.03	1.13	0.26	−0.08	−3.18	0.00	−0.06	−3.51	0.00
gedu1	0.54	31.81	0.00	0.53	23.64	0.00	0.44	33.01	0.00
gedu2	1.05	72.13	0.00	1.17	58.75	0.00	0.96	83.83	0.00
gedu3	1.31	71.85	0.00	1.54	71.06	0.00	1.25	92.85	0.00
gedu4	2.36	30.64	0.00	2.44	57.68	0.00	2.08	59.46	0.00
techedu	0.94	15.65	0.00	1.01	25.18	0.00	0.99	30.05	0.00
attendcur	−1.48	−109.62	0.00	−1.65	−103.78	0.00	−1.54	−151.77	0.00
pstat	−0.09	−7.77	0.00	−0.18	−12.08	0.00	−0.16	−17.63	0.00
35 state dummies	Estimated coefficients are not reported								
	Pseudo R^2 = 0.35			Pseudo R^2 = 0.34			Pseudo R^2 = 0.34		
	LR Chi-sq = 50644.4 (df = 51; p-value = 0.00)			LR Chi-sq = 36083.71 (df = 51; p-value = 0.00)			LR Chi-sq = 85030.10 (df = 51; p-value = 0.00)		
	No. of observations = 2,46,783			No. of observations = 1,86,501			No. of observations = 4,33,284		

Source: Author's computation using PLFS unit-level data for 2017–18

Note: z-values are calculated using White's robust standard errors

3.11 Summary of Findings

The overall size of the labour force in India has increased over time, from 312 million in 1983 to 502 million in 2018. However, comparing the period before 1994 with that after, it is clear that the annual increase in the labour force has significantly declined in the latter period. Specifically, after 2012, although the labour force grew in urban areas, it began to decline in rural areas. This decrease is primarily due to a drop in female participation in the rural labour force, with approximately 23.7 million rural women leaving the labour market between 2012 and 2018.

India's labour force participation rate (LFPR) has consistently declined from 1983 to 2018, with a notable acceleration in the rate of decline after 2012. A drop in female participation primarily drove this decrease in the LFPR. The LFPR for females has been significantly lower than that for males, and the gap between the two has widened over time. Evidence indicates that many females exited the labour market, reducing their LFPR from 30.0 % in 1983 to just 17.5 % in 2018. In contrast, the LFPR for males, which stood at 56.1 % in 1983, remained almost unchanged (55.6 %) in 2018. Another observation is that, although the labour force participation rate declined significantly in rural areas, it rose slightly in urban areas during the period 1983–2018, except in 2000.

The LFPR across age groups in India exhibits a negatively skewed distribution. The LFPR rises through the 35–59 age group, then declines. Notably, the LFPR has decreased across all age groups over time, with the most significant reductions observed among the 5–14 and 15–24 age groups for both males and females. When comparing rural and urban areas, the decline in the LFPR for the 15–24 age group is more pronounced in rural areas than in urban areas. In 2018, the 35–59 age group comprised approximately half of the country's labour force.

There is a clear positive correlation between the LFPR and the level of education. For example, in 2018, the LFPR for those with graduate-level education and above was nearly double that of illiterates. However, a comparison of males and females revealed that the LFPR of illiterate males was higher than that of illiterate females. Furthermore, the share of female illiterates in the total female labour force was higher than that of male illiterates in the total male labour force, indicating that the female labour force in India has lower levels of education and skills than their male counterparts. Almost one-quarter of India's total labour force was illiterate in 2018; the shares of male and female illiterates in the total male and female labour force were 21 % and 43 %, respectively.

We also examined labour force participation rates (LFPRs) across various social and religious groups. The LFPR is higher for individuals from lower social groups, such as Scheduled Tribes (ST), Scheduled Castes (SC), and Other Backward Classes (OBC), than for the 'Others' category, which includes individuals from the general caste. This trend is evident in both rural and urban areas, as well as among the total population (male and female combined) and among females specifically. However, the male LFPR exceeds that of females in each social group. Although the LFPR has declined over time for males and females across different social groups, the decline for females from weaker social groups has been more pronounced than for the 'Others' group. Regarding the LFPR among religious groups, our primary finding is that the LFPR for Muslims has consistently been lower than that for Hindus throughout 1983–2018. Nonetheless, the gap in LFPR between these two groups tends to narrow over time. Another noteworthy observation is that Muslim females lag significantly behind their Hindu counterparts concerning the LFPR.

Analysing labour force growth rates, we found that it declined for rural populations from 1.60 % during 1983–1994 to 0.50 % during 1994–2018. This decline was more significant in the sub-period 2012–2018 (–0.44 %). Moreover, due to a substantial withdrawal of rural women from the labour force, their growth rate became negative after 2000, with the most severe decline occurring between 2012 and 2018 (–4.24 %). In urban areas, however, the growth rates of both male and female labour forces declined marginally between 1994 and 2018, compared to the decline observed between 1983 and 1994. We also noted that, although a decrease in the labour force growth rate has been evident across all age groups since 1994, this decline has been particularly pronounced among the younger age groups – specifically 5–14 and 15–24 – among both males and females. Furthermore, individuals with lower educational attainment, especially those who are illiterate or have less than primary education, experienced a larger decline in the labour force growth rate between 1994 and 2018.

The analysis of the growth rates of the labour force by social groups reveals that the ST and SC categories held a superior position during 1983–1994 compared to the OBC and 'Others' categories. During 1994–2018, although the labour force growth rate declined across all categories, the decline was relatively less pronounced for the ST and SC groups. Another important finding is that, unlike males, females from all social groups experienced negative labour force growth during 1994–2018. Regarding labour force growth by religious groups, we found that while Hindus had a clear advantage over Muslims during 1983–1994, the latter surpassed the former during 1994–2018. This is true for both Muslim males and females.

We analysed the reasons behind the recent decline in female labour force participation by examining the composition of women who are 'out of the labour force'. While attending educational institutions and domestic duties were the primary reasons for their withdrawal from the labour force until 2012, the most significant factor thereafter was domestic duties. This is true for both rural and urban females. In contrast, males withdrew from the labour force primarily to attend educational institutions.

We examined the LFPR across different states during five distinct years from 1983 to 2018. Focusing on rural areas and taking an overall perspective, it appears that some of the better-performing states in terms of LFPR during 1983–2018 are Andhra Pradesh, Himachal Pradesh, Tamil Nadu, Maharashtra, and Karnataka, while the underperformers include Bihar, Uttar Pradesh, Haryana, Assam, and West Bengal. However, in urban areas, the LFPR has been higher in states such as Tamil Nadu, West Bengal, Himachal Pradesh, Kerala, and Karnataka. In contrast, it has been low in Bihar, Uttar Pradesh, Rajasthan, Haryana, and Jammu & Kashmir. Himachal Pradesh had the highest LFPR across both rural and urban areas in all years except 2000, whereas Bihar remained at the bottom. Regarding male LFPR, Tamil Nadu is the top performer, while Bihar is the lowest. For female LFPR, Himachal Pradesh is the best performer, and Assam is the worst.

Considering both rural and urban areas, as well as males and females collectively, we found that labour force growth rates declined across all states (except Punjab) during the period from 1994 to 2018 (post-globalisation) compared to the period from 1983 to 1994 (pre-globalisation). In examining the growth of the male labour force, a decline is observed in fourteen of seventeen major states, with Haryana, Jammu & Kashmir, and Punjab being the exceptions. However, in all states except Kerala and Punjab, the growth rate of the female labour force has declined. During the period 1994–2018, the highest and lowest growth rates of the male labour force were recorded in Jammu & Kashmir (2.83 %) and Kerala (0.50 %), respectively; similarly, the highest and lowest growth rates of the female labour force were observed in West Bengal (1.05 %) and Bihar (–2.81 %), respectively. When considering males and females together, Jammu & Kashmir emerged as the best performer in terms of labour force growth rate during 1994–2018 (2.10 %), while Kerala recorded the lowest rate (0.38 %).

These trends suggest that the globalisation of the Indian economy has reduced women's labour-market participation, particularly in rural areas. The decline in the female labour force growth persisted throughout the post-globalisation period and deteriorated after 2012. In seven states (Bihar, Gujarat, Haryana, Odisha, Punjab, Rajasthan, and Uttar Pradesh), rural females experienced a decrease of over five percentage points in their labour force growth rate between 2012 and 2018, compared to the preceding period (2000–2012). Conversely, for rural males, nine states (Bihar, Gujarat, Haryana, Karnataka, Kerala, Madhya Pradesh,

Odisha, Punjab, and West Bengal) experienced a decline in their labour force growth rate during this period, while the growth rate increased in the remaining eight states. Ten states (Andhra Pradesh, Bihar, Gujarat, Haryana, Jammu & Kashmir, Karnataka, Maharashtra, Odisha, Punjab, and Kerala) noted a drop in the male labour force growth rate in urban areas during the post-globalisation era. Similarly, in nine states (Gujarat, Himachal Pradesh, Jammu & Kashmir, Madhya Pradesh, Odisha, Punjab, Rajasthan, Uttar Pradesh, and West Bengal), the growth rate of the labour force for urban females decreased between 2012 and 2018, as well as between 2000 and 2012.

We estimated a logit regression model using unit-level data from the PLFS 2018 to identify factors influencing labour force participation among individuals in India. The results show that the probability of participating in the labour force increases for individuals who are male, older, married, better educated, have received technical training, come from poor families, and belong to socially disadvantaged (lower-caste) backgrounds. However, the probability of labour force participation is lower for individuals from Muslim and other minority backgrounds than for those from Hindu backgrounds.

India's Evolving Employment Landscape: The Quantitative Dimensions

4.1 Introduction

Employment forms the foundation of any economic development, as it is a crucial means of fostering national identity and social equality. It is also a significant source of human dignity and self-respect (Government of India, 2001). Widespread productive employment opportunities are crucial for the sustainable development of an economy and for reducing poverty and promoting equitable income distribution. The issue of employment has not received adequate attention in India since the early years of the planning era. It was assumed that increasing the income growth rate would generate sufficient employment opportunities, thereby reducing poverty, destitution, and socio-economic inequality in the country (Papola, 2008a, 2008b; Bhaumik, 2013). Employment was brought to the forefront for the first time in the Seventh Five-Year Plan, launched in 1985, nearly four decades after India's independence. Discussions surrounding this topic gained momentum following the official introduction of the new economic reforms in July 1991, known as globalisation policies, which represented a paradigm shift in India's economic policy-making. While proponents of the reforms envisioned enhanced employment opportunities arising from implementing these measures, critics argued that the era of reforms would hurt employment. The former group anticipated that increased income through greater export earnings, facilitated by a well-functioning supply side, would improve the economy's employment performance, generating a positive 'employment effect' under economic reforms and globalisation. In contrast, critics contended that the aspects of globalisation, such as liberalisation and privatisation, would create an environment of intensified international competition for firms, potentially causing them to minimise costs through worker retrenchment, thereby exacerbating the existing employment situation in the economy.

Since then, various scholars have endeavoured to analyse employment scenarios during the post-globalisation period compared to the pre-globalisation era, arriving at ambiguous and often contradictory conclusions. This chapter examines the evolution of employment scenarios in the Indian economy from 1983 to 2018, with a focus on the post-globalisation era. Our discussions centre on the quantitative dimensions of employment scenarios, while the qualitative aspects will be addressed in the next chapter. We utilise data from published reports and unit-level data from the NSSO's employment/unemployment surveys for 1983, 1993–94, 1999–2000, and 2011–12, as well as data from the Periodic Labour Force Survey conducted by the NSSO for 2017–18.[1]

At the outset, it is worth noting that achieving high employment growth is likely to depend on expanding both the supply and demand sides of the labour market. In the previous chapter, we examined the changing scenario on the supply side of the Indian labour market. This chapter focuses exclusively on the demand side. As the labour force comprises employed and unemployed individuals, our focus here is solely on employed individuals, referred to as workers. The employed here are those engaged in productive economic activities that provide cash or kind remuneration. In our study, we have considered estimates of employed or workers based on the usual principal and subsidiary status (UPSS) concept.

This chapter comprises ten sections. After providing an introduction in Section 4.1, Section 4.2 examines workforce participation trends across India at both aggregated (for all persons and regions) and disaggregated (male/female and rural/urban) levels. Section 4.3 addresses changes in workforce participation rates (WPR) across different age groups, while Section 4.4 focuses on educational groups. Sections 4.5 and 4.6 examine the WPR for various social and religious groups. Section 4.7 reviews the growth of the workforce in all-India during 1983–2018, as well as in multiple sub-periods, across all possible levels of disaggregation – rural/urban, male/female, age groups, education groups, social groups, and religious groups. Section 4.8 examines the evolving employment scenarios across seventeen major states, focusing on two key indicators: workforce participation rates and workforce growth. Section 4.9 seeks to identify key determinants of employment status (employed or unemployed) in India. Section 4.10 concludes by summarising the main findings of this chapter.

---

[1] For brevity, we refer to the years as 1983, 1994, 2000, 2012, and 2018.

4.2 Trends in Workforce Participation in India

4.2.1 Size of Workforce

To understand the trends in workforce participation at the all-India level during the period from 1983 to 2018, we begin by examining the size (in terms of numbers) of workers (following the UPSS definition) by gender (male/female) and region (rural/urban). The information in Table 33 indicates that the total number of workers increased in rural and urban India over time. While the total number of rural workers was approximately 248 million in 1983, it rose to 292 million in 1994 and 316 million in 2018. However, this rising trend appears to have stagnated after 2012, when the total number of rural workers reached 336 million. In contrast, urban India experienced a consistent increase in the workforce throughout the studied period, rising from 59 million in 1983 to 82 million in 1994 and reaching 154 million by 2018. Due to steady growth in the number of workers in rural and urban India from 1983 to 2012, the total number of workers across the two regions also increased consistently. However, the overall number of workers in India (rural and urban combined) declined slightly by 2.33 million between 2012 and 2018. This decline resulted from a loss of 20.14 million workers in rural India, which outstripped the increase in urban workers by 17.81 million during this period.

Table 33: Size of Workforce/Employed (UPSS Basis) in India

Year / Period	Rural			Urban			Rural + Urban		
	Male	Female	Male + Female	Male	Female	Male + Female	Male	Female	Male + Female
Number of Workers [in million]									
1983	157.14	90.45	247.59	46.62	12.14	58.75	203.76	102.59	306.35
1994	187.74	104.74	292.48	64.58	17.21	81.79	252.32	121.95	374.27
2000	198.61	105.69	304.30	75.38	18.20	93.58	273.99	123.89	397.88
2012	234.59	101.46	336.04	109.28	27.30	136.58	343.87	128.76	472.63
2018	239.25	76.70	315.90	124.10	31.31	154.40	363.35	108.01	470.30
Average Yearly Change in Workers/Employed [in million]									
1983 to 1994	2.91	1.36	4.28	1.71	0.48	2.19	4.63	1.84	6.47
1994 to 2000	1.81	0.16	1.97	1.80	0.17	1.97	3.61	0.32	3.93
2000 to 2012	3.00	−0.35	2.65	2.82	0.76	3.58	5.82	0.41	6.23
2012 to 2018	0.08	−0.41	−0.34	0.25	0.07	0.30	0.32	−0.35	−0.04
1994 to 2012	2.60	−0.18	2.42	2.48	0.56	3.04	5.09	0.38	5.46
1994 to 2018	2.15	−1.17	0.98	2.48	0.59	3.03	4.63	−0.58	4.00

Source: NSSO unit-level data from Employment/Unemployment Surveys for 1983, 1993–94, 1999–2000, 2011–12, and Periodic Labour Force Survey for 2017–18.

When we examine trends in the number of male and female workers separately, we observe that males experienced a steady increase from 1983 to 2018, both in rural and urban areas. The same holds for urban females. However, a noticeable decline in the number of female workers in rural areas was evident in 2000, and this decline has been particularly severe from 2012 to 2018. While the number of rural male workers increased marginally by 4.66 million during this period, the number of rural female workers decreased by 24.76 million from 2012 to 2018 alone. It is also alarming to note that the number of rural female workers in India in 2018 (76.7 million) is significantly lower than in 1983. Thus, it can be said that rural women in India have been the most affected in terms of workforce representation.

Table 33 further illustrates that the rate of increase in the number of workers in rural areas decreased over time for both rural males and females, although this trend is far more pronounced for the latter. Let us compare the pre- and post-globalisation periods (1983–1994 and 1994–2018, respectively). During the former period, the average yearly increase in rural male workers was 2.91 million, whereas in the latter period, it was 2.15 million. In contrast, for rural females, the average yearly increase in workers was 1.36 million during the pre-globalisation period, whereas the average annual decline was 1.17 million during the post-globalisation period. Conversely, in urban areas, males and females experienced a rise in the average yearly change in the number of workers during the post-globalisation period compared to the pre-globalisation period. As shown in Table 33, the average annual increases in the number of workers for urban males were 1.71 million and 2.48 million for the pre- and post-globalisation periods, respectively; the corresponding figures for urban females were 0.48 million and 0.59 million.

When considering both rural and urban areas, it is evident that, while the annual increase in male workers remained constant at 4.63 million during both the pre- and post-globalisation periods, the situation for female workers was starkly different. The yearly increase in female workers was 1.84 million during the pre-globalisation phase, while female workers declined by 0.58 million annually on average during the post-globalisation period. Taking all workers (males and females) together, the average yearly increase in the total number of workers in the country declined appreciably in the post-globalisation period (4.0 million) compared to the pre-globalisation period (6.47 million). Therefore, India witnessed a setback in employment during the post-globalisation period, particularly for rural females.

4.2.2 Share of Females in Total Workforce

The reality that rural females have been the most significant victims of employment loss in the era of globalisation is further emphasised by examining changes in the proportion of females among total workers from 1983 to 2018. The information presented in Table 34 indicates that the percentage of female workers within the total workforce in rural India steadily declined over time, with a notably severe drop after 2012. While 36.53 % of rural workers were female in 1983, this figure declined to 30.19 % in 2012 and further to 24.28 % in 2018. In contrast, urban females retained their share of total urban workers, which remained around 20 % from 1983 to 2018. For all regions combined (rural plus urban), however, a consistent decline in the share of female workers among total workers is evident, with the rate of decline accelerating after 2012.

Table 34: Share of Females in Total Workers (UPSS) in India

Year	Rural	Urban	Rural + Urban
1983	36.53	20.66	33.49
1994	35.81	21.04	32.58
2000	34.73	19.45	31.14
2012	30.19	19.99	27.24
2018	24.28	20.28	22.97

Source: Same as Table 33

4.2.3 Workforce Participation Rates

We now examine changes in workforce participation rates (WPR) in India by sex (male/female) and region (rural/urban). The data presented in Table 35 reveal the following: Firstly, in rural areas, a distinct trend of declining WPR over time is evident for both males and females. However, this decline has been particularly pronounced for rural females, especially after 2000. As indicated in the table, the WPR for rural males was recorded at 54.6 in 1983, 53.1 in 2000, and 51.7 in 2018, while the corresponding figures for rural females were 33.6, 29.9, and 17.5 in these years, respectively. It is abundantly clear that women in rural India have fared significantly worse than their male counterparts in terms of employment during the era of globalisation. As the WPR for rural females sharply declined from 2000 onwards, the WPR for rural persons (males and females combined) also declined. Table 35 illustrates that the WPR for rural persons decreased from 44.5 in 1983 to 41.7 in 2000 and further to 35.0 in 2018.

Table 35: Work Force Participation Rates (%) in India (UPSS)

	Rural			Urban			Rural + Urban		
Year	Male	Female	Male + Female	Male	Female	Male + Female	Male	Female	Male + Female
1983	54.59	33.95	44.45	51.18	15.10	34.03	53.76	29.58	41.98
1994	55.29	32.78	44.36	52.10	15.47	34.70	54.49	28.55	41.96
2000	53.06	29.88	41.72	51.76	13.90	33.67	52.73	25.89	39.67
2012	54.34	24.84	39.92	54.64	14.66	35.47	54.43	21.65	38.64
2018	51.70	17.49	35.02	52.96	14.16	33.90	52.07	16.51	34.69

Source: Same as Table 33

Furthermore, when we limit our comparison to the pre- and post-globalisation periods, we observe that both males and females in rural India experienced a decline in WPR during the post-globalisation period (1994–2018) compared to the pre-globalisation period (1983–1994). Although the decrease in WPR persisted among rural males during the post-globalisation period, rural females experienced a severe decline in WPR. As indicated in Table 35, while the WPR for rural males declined by 3.59 percentage points between 1994 and 2018, the WPR for rural females decreased by 15.29 percentage points during the same period.

The situation in urban India is somewhat different. While urban males appear to have gained marginal improvements in WPR over the years, urban females experienced a slight decline. However, it is worth noting that between 2012 and 2018, both males and females experienced minor losses in WPR. Another significant observation regarding WPR in both rural and urban areas is that the WPR for males in both regions was almost similar in 2018. In contrast, the WPR for urban females is significantly lower than that for rural females.

Considering rural and urban areas collectively, the WPR for males and females remained relatively unchanged from 1983 to 1994. However, during the period from 1994 to 2018, a decline in WPR was observed for both males and females in India. Importantly, this decline has been particularly severe for females, especially in the recent sub-period of 2012–2018. The overall picture presents a clear trend of declining WPR in the country under globalisation.

4.3 Workforce Participation by Age Groups in India

This section examines changes in workforce participation rates (WPR) by age group in India from 1983 to 2018. We consider six age groups (in years): 0–4,

5–14, 15–24, 25–34, 35–59, and 60 and above. The WPR data for these age groups are presented in Table 36.

In rural areas, the WPR declined rapidly and drastically over time, particularly among the 5–14 and 15–24 age groups. Although this trend is evident among both rural males and females, the decline in WPR has been especially pronounced among those aged 15–24 from 2012 to 2018. A similar downward trend in WPR is also noticeable for rural males and females aged 60 and above. While the WPR declined for males aged 25–34 in rural areas, the decrease was less severe than for other age groups. On the other hand, WPR remained almost unchanged among rural males aged 35–59, but declined sharply and steadily among rural females. However, rural females across both higher and lower age groups experienced significant declines in WPR over time, particularly from 2012 to 2018.

In urban areas, the pattern of change in WPR concerning age groups is largely consistent for males. Urban males in younger age groups have experienced a significantly more pronounced decline in WPR over time than those in older age groups. This trend is more pronounced for the period 2012–2018. The same is true for urban females, except that the decline in WPR over time (including the 2012–2018 sub-period) for the age groups 25–34, 35–59, and 60 and above appears to have been marginal compared to their male counterparts and rural females.

Table 36: Workforce Participation Rates (%) by Age Groups in India (UPSS Basis)

Region	Sex	Age groups	1983	1994	2000	2012	2018
Rural	Male	0–4	0.16	0.02	0.00	0.00	0.00
		5–14	13.37	7.19	4.74	1.40	0.92
		15–24	76.71	70.17	65.20	49.15	34.15
		25–34	97.57	96.97	96.36	96.09	90.64
		35–59	96.95	97.83	97.11	97.78	96.42
		60 & above	66.57	69.84	63.03	64.88	51.91
	Female	0–4	0.13	0.05	0.00	0.00	0.00
		5–14	12.47	7.25	4.92	1.49	0.28
		15–24	46.98	41.00	35.64	21.35	9.30
		25–34	57.39	55.27	52.09	39.07	27.22
		35–59	58.73	57.45	55.09	46.40	34.92
		60 & above	22.60	24.09	21.49	21.33	11.72

(Continued)

Table 36 *(Continued)*

Region	Sex	Age groups	1983	1994	2000	2012	2018
Rural	Male + Female	0–4	0.15	0.03	0.00	0.00	0.00
		5–14	12.94	7.22	4.82	1.44	0.63
		15–24	61.84	56.12	50.77	35.92	22.38
		25–34	77.13	75.57	73.40	66.20	57.96
		35–59	77.92	78.01	76.56	72.42	65.61
		60 & above	44.67	47.40	42.40	43.08	32.27
Urban	Male	0–4	0.18	0.00	0.00	0.00	0.00
		5–14	6.04	3.58	2.68	1.83	0.50
		15–24	56.18	50.25	47.38	40.29	31.80
		25–34	94.21	93.25	91.88	93.75	87.78
		35–59	95.32	95.99	94.99	96.26	93.72
		60 & above	50.13	44.14	39.66	36.48	35.44
		0–4	0.05	0.01	0.00	0.00	0.00
	Female	5–14	3.77	2.52	1.93	0.53	0.11
		15–24	16.80	15.07	12.90	12.07	8.44
		25–34	24.53	24.66	21.34	23.94	22.95
		35–59	29.19	29.69	26.89	24.97	24.78
		60 & above	13.81	11.29	9.29	7.75	7.42
	Male + Female	0–4	0.12	0.01	0.00	0.00	0.00
		5–14	4.96	3.09	2.32	1.23	0.32
		15–24	37.75	33.81	31.33	27.15	20.61
		25–34	61.47	59.96	56.93	59.15	55.35
		35–59	64.37	65.04	63.14	61.72	59.26
		60 & above	31.12	27.23	23.74	21.78	21.17
Rural + Urban	Male	0–4	0.17	0.02	0.00	0.00	0.00
		5–14	11.76	6.35	4.27	1.51	0.81
		15–24	70.92	64.66	60.02	46.43	33.48
		25–34	96.65	95.94	95.09	95.30	89.70
		35–59	96.54	97.34	96.51	97.32	95.58
		60 & above	63.26	64.31	57.80	56.95	47.13
	Female	0–4	0.11	0.04	0.00	0.00	0.00
		5–14	10.54	6.12	4.22	1.25	0.24
		15–24	39.24	34.14	29.45	18.59	9.05
		25–34	49.31	47.47	43.94	34.36	25.87
		35–59	52.03	50.55	47.67	40.02	31.79
		60 & above	20.68	21.12	18.51	17.41	10.40

(Continued)

Table 36 *(Continued)*

Region	Sex	Age groups	1983	1994	2000	2012	2018
Rural + Urban	Male + Female	0–4	0.14	0.03	0.00	0.00	0.00
		5–14	11.18	6.25	4.25	1.39	0.55
		15–24	55.34	50.08	45.29	33.27	21.87
		25–34	73.04	71.43	68.88	63.92	57.12
		35–59	74.70	74.67	72.91	69.20	63.65
		60 & above	41.83	42.88	38.04	37.03	28.95

Source: Same as Table 33

When considering rural and urban areas together, it can be observed that males in India aged 5–14 and 15–24 have experienced the most significant decline in WPR compared to those in the 25–34 and 35–59 age groups, especially after 2012. The decrease in WPR for males aged 60 and above during this period has also been considerable. Although males in the 25–34 and 35–39 age groups also experienced a decline in WPR, this decline was less severe than in other age groups. For females, the general trend indicates a reduction in WPR across all age groups, with the pace of decline accelerating after 2000. The most significant decline in this regard is particularly noticeable after 2012.

Overall, at the all-India level, the WPR declined significantly for males and females in the 5–14 and 15–24 age groups. This decline is notably more pronounced in rural areas, especially among females. The age groups that experienced the least decline in WPR are 25–34 and 35–59. Even urban individuals (and also males and females separately) aged 60 and above were not immune to a considerable decline in WPR after 2012.

When comparing the pre-globalisation period (1983–1994) and the post-globalisation period (1994–2018), the conclusion is that the WPR was lower in the latter period than in the former across all age groups, sexes, and regions. However, rural females aged 5–14 and 15–24, as well as urban females aged 15–24, experienced the largest decline in WPR during the post-globalisation period, followed by all other segments. A notable decrease in WPR for those aged 60 and above is also evident at the all-India level in the post-globalisation period.

4.3.1 Shares of Total Workforce (Employed) and Total Population by Age Groups

In the context of the discussion on changes in WPR across age groups, it would be intriguing to examine the proportions of these age groups within the total workforce compared to their representation in the overall population. Information on these aspects is presented in Table 37. The key points to note are as follows:

- Consistent with the pattern of rural males aged 5–14 and 15–24 experiencing a significant decline in the workforce participation rate (WPR) during the post-globalisation period, their shares of total employment also fell at a higher rate than their shares in the total population. As shown in Table 37, for rural males in the 5–14 age group, the ratio of employed to total population decreased from 0.24 in 1983 to 0.13 in 1994 and then to 0.02 in 2018. The decline for rural males aged 15–24 has been even more pronounced in the post-globalisation period, decreasing from 1.41 in 1983 to 1.27 in 1994 and 0.66 in 2018. A similar declining trend in the ratio of employed to population is also evident for rural males aged 60 and above. In contrast, rural males aged 35–59 appear to have experienced a slight improvement in this respect. The situation is primarily the same for rural females. While rural females in the 5–14 and 15–24 age groups experienced significant declines in their respective ratios of workforce share to population share, those in the 35–59 age group appear to have benefited from slight improvements in this ratio. However, like rural males, rural females aged 60 and above also experienced a decline in the ratio of workforce share to population share during the post-globalisation period (especially during 2012–2018). When considering rural individuals (rural males and rural females combined), it can be concluded that those in the age groups 5–14 and 15–24 have suffered the most in terms of declining employment shares over the years, particularly during the period of globalisation. The declining trend in this ratio is also observable for rural individuals aged 60 and above. Conversely, rural individuals in the 35–59 age group recorded some improvement in the ratio of workforce share to population share even during the post-globalisation period.
- In urban areas, for males, although there is a visible decline in the ratio of workforce share to population share across all age groups, this decline is most pronounced among those in the 5–14, 15–24, and 60 and above age groups. For urban females, however, a decrease in the ratio of workforce share to population share is evident across all age groups, albeit at varying rates, except for the 25–34 age group, which appears to retain its share. A similar trend is observed mainly for urban individuals, with the ratio of workforce share to population share decreasing across all age groups, most notably in the 15–24, 60 & above, and 5–14 age brackets.

Table 37. Percentage Shares in Total Workforce (UPSS) and Total Population by Age Groups in India

Region	Sex	Age groups	Share in Employed/Workforce (%)					Share in population (%)					Ratio of workforce share to population share				
			1983	1994	2000	2012	2018	1983	1994	2000	2012	2018	1983	1994	2000	2012	2018
Rural	Male	0–4	0.0	0.0	0.0	0.0	0.0	13.8	12.9	11.7	8.7	8.4	0.00	0.00	0.00	0.00	0.00
		5–14	6.9	3.3	2.4	0.6	0.4	28.2	25.2	26.6	23.7	20.0	0.24	0.13	0.09	0.03	0.02
		15–24	24.0	23.3	21.6	17.0	13.1	17.1	18.3	17.6	18.8	19.8	1.41	1.27	1.23	0.90	0.66
		25–34	23.6	24.9	25.5	24.6	25.4	13.2	14.2	14.1	13.9	14.5	1.79	1.75	1.82	1.77	1.75
		35–59	37.3	39.9	42.0	48.1	51.5	21.0	22.6	23.0	26.7	27.6	1.78	1.77	1.83	1.80	1.87
		60 & above	8.1	8.6	8.5	9.6	9.8	6.7	6.8	7.1	8.0	9.7	1.22	1.26	1.19	1.19	1.00
	Female	0–4	0.1	0.0	0.0	0.0	0.0	13.6	12.8	11.9	8.9	8.1	0.00	0.00	0.00	0.00	0.00
		5–14	9.6	5.1	4.0	1.3	0.3	26.1	23.3	24.6	21.5	18.2	0.37	0.22	0.16	0.06	0.02
		15–24	24.6	22.6	20.8	15.4	9.9	17.7	18.1	17.5	17.9	18.7	1.38	1.25	1.19	0.86	0.53
		25–34	23.9	26.8	27.6	25.2	25.1	14.2	15.9	15.8	16.0	16.2	1.69	1.69	1.74	1.57	1.56
		35–59	37.3	40.4	42.3	50.9	58.1	21.6	23.1	22.9	27.2	29.1	1.73	1.75	1.84	1.87	2.00
		60 & above	4.6	5.1	5.3	7.2	6.6	6.8	6.9	7.3	8.4	9.8	0.67	0.73	0.72	0.86	0.67
	Male + Female	0–4	0.0	0.0	0.0	0.0	0.0	13.7	12.8	11.8	8.8	8.3	0.00	0.00	0.00	0.00	0.00
		5–14	7.9	4.0	3.0	0.8	0.3	27.2	24.3	25.6	22.6	19.1	0.29	0.16	0.12	0.04	0.02
		15–24	24.2	23.0	21.3	16.5	12.3	17.4	18.2	17.5	18.4	19.2	1.39	1.26	1.22	0.90	0.64
		25–34	23.7	25.6	26.3	24.8	25.3	13.7	15.0	14.9	15.0	15.3	1.74	1.70	1.76	1.66	1.66
		35–59	37.3	40.1	42.1	49.0	53.1	21.3	22.8	23.0	27.0	28.3	1.75	1.76	1.84	1.81	1.87
		60 & above	6.8	7.3	7.3	8.9	9.0	6.7	6.8	7.2	8.2	9.8	1.00	1.07	1.02	1.08	0.92

(Continued)

Table 37 *(Continued)*

Region	Sex	Age groups	Share in Employed/Workforce (%)					Share in population (%)					Ratio of workforce share to population share				
			1983	1994	2000	2012	2018	1983	1994	2000	2012	2018	1983	1994	2000	2012	2018
Urban	Male	0–4	0.0	0.0	0.0	0.0	0.0	12.0	10.5	9.3	7.3	6.8	0.00	0.00	0.00	0.00	0.00
		5–14	2.9	1.6	1.2	0.6	0.2	24.7	22.7	22.5	19.4	16.9	0.12	0.07	0.05	0.03	0.01
		15–24	22.9	20.0	18.9	14.9	11.6	20.9	20.8	20.6	20.2	19.3	1.10	0.96	0.92	0.74	0.60
		25–34	28.8	28.8	28.4	29.3	28.6	15.6	16.1	16.0	17.1	17.2	1.84	1.79	1.78	1.72	1.66
		35–59	40.2	44.9	47.1	50.1	53.2	21.6	24.4	25.7	28.5	30.1	1.86	1.84	1.84	1.76	1.77
		60 & above	5.1	4.7	4.5	5.0	6.5	5.2	5.5	5.9	7.6	9.7	0.98	0.85	0.77	0.67	0.67
	Female	0–4	0.0	0.0	0.0	0.0	0.0	12.4	10.6	9.2	7.2	6.6	0.00	0.00	0.00	0.00	0.00
		5–14	6.2	3.7	3.1	0.6	0.1	24.7	22.5	22.3	17.9	15.6	0.25	0.16	0.14	0.04	0.01
		15–24	22.6	19.6	18.2	15.7	11.0	20.3	20.1	19.6	19.0	18.4	1.11	0.97	0.93	0.82	0.60
		25–34	24.9	26.8	26.3	29.7	29.0	15.3	16.8	17.1	18.2	17.9	1.62	1.59	1.53	1.63	1.62
		35–59	40.6	45.2	47.6	49.4	54.5	21.0	23.6	24.6	29.0	31.1	1.93	1.92	1.93	1.70	1.75
		60 & above	5.8	4.7	4.8	4.5	5.5	6.3	6.5	7.1	8.6	10.4	0.91	0.73	0.67	0.53	0.52
	Male + Female	0–4	0.0	0.0	0.0	0.0	0.0	12.2	10.5	9.3	7.3	6.7	0.00	0.00	0.00	0.00	0.00
		5–14	3.6	2.0	1.5	0.6	0.2	24.7	22.6	22.4	18.7	16.3	0.15	0.09	0.07	0.03	0.01
		15–24	22.9	19.9	18.7	15.0	11.5	20.6	20.5	20.1	19.6	18.9	1.11	0.97	0.93	0.77	0.61
		25–34	28.0	28.4	28.0	29.4	28.7	15.5	16.4	16.5	17.6	17.6	1.81	1.73	1.69	1.67	1.63
		35–59	40.3	45.0	47.2	50.0	53.5	21.3	24.0	25.2	28.7	30.6	1.89	1.87	1.87	1.74	1.75
		60 & above	5.2	4.7	4.6	4.9	6.3	5.7	6.0	6.5	8.0	10.0	0.91	0.78	0.70	0.61	0.62

(Continued)

Table 37 *(Continued)*

Region	Sex	Age groups	Share in Employed/Workforce (%)					Share in population (%)					Ratio of workforce share to population share				
			1983	1994	2000	2012	2018	1983	1994	2000	2012	2018	1983	1994	2000	2012	2018
Rural + Urban	Male	0–4	0.0	0.0	0.0	0.0	0.0	13.4	12.3	11.1	8.3	8.0	0.00	0.00	0.00	0.00	0.00
		5–14	6.0	2.9	2.1	0.6	0.3	27.4	24.6	25.5	22.5	19.1	0.22	0.12	0.08	0.03	0.02
		15–24	23.8	22.5	20.9	16.4	12.6	18.0	19.0	18.3	19.2	19.6	1.32	1.19	1.14	0.85	0.64
		25–34	24.8	25.9	26.3	26.0	26.3	13.8	14.7	14.6	14.9	15.3	1.80	1.76	1.80	1.75	1.72
		35–59	38.0	41.1	43.3	48.7	52.0	21.1	23.0	23.7	27.2	28.3	1.80	1.79	1.83	1.79	1.84
		60 & above	7.4	7.6	7.5	8.3	8.8	6.3	6.5	6.8	7.9	9.7	1.18	1.18	1.10	1.05	0.91
	Female	0–4	0.1	0.0	0.0	0.0	0.0	13.3	12.3	11.2	8.4	7.7	0.00	0.00	0.00	0.00	0.00
		5–14	9.2	4.9	3.9	1.2	0.3	25.8	23.1	24.0	20.5	17.4	0.36	0.21	0.16	0.06	0.01
		15–24	24.3	22.2	20.5	15.4	10.2	18.3	18.6	18.0	18.2	18.6	1.33	1.20	1.14	0.85	0.55
		25–34	24.0	26.8	27.4	26.1	26.1	14.4	16.1	16.1	16.7	16.7	1.67	1.66	1.70	1.57	1.57
		35–59	37.7	41.0	43.0	50.6	57.2	21.4	23.2	23.4	27.7	29.7	1.76	1.77	1.84	1.82	1.93
		60 & above	4.7	5.0	5.2	6.7	6.3	6.7	6.8	7.3	8.5	10.0	0.70	0.74	0.72	0.79	0.63
	Male + Female	0–4	0.0	0.0	0.0	0.0	0.0	13.3	12.3	11.2	8.4	7.8	0.00	0.00	0.00	0.00	0.00
		5–14	7.1	3.6	2.7	0.8	0.3	26.6	23.9	24.8	21.5	18.3	0.27	0.15	0.11	0.04	0.02
		15–24	24.0	22.4	20.8	16.1	12.1	18.2	18.8	18.2	18.7	19.1	1.32	1.19	1.14	0.86	0.63
		25–34	24.5	26.2	26.6	26.0	26.3	14.1	15.4	15.3	15.7	16.0	1.74	1.70	1.74	1.65	1.65
		35–59	37.9	41.1	43.2	49.2	53.2	21.3	23.1	23.5	27.5	29.0	1.78	1.78	1.84	1.79	1.83
		60 & above	6.5	6.8	6.7	7.8	8.2	6.5	6.6	7.0	8.2	9.8	1.00	1.02	0.96	0.96	0.83

Source: Same as Table 33

- When examining rural and urban areas combined, it is noted that the workforce shares across India declined at a greater rate than the population share for all age groups, except those aged 35–59 years, particularly in the post-globalisation period. Moreover, among all age groups, those aged 15–24 experienced the largest decline in the ratio of workforce share to population share, followed by the 5–14 and 60 years and above age groups. This trend is broadly consistent for both males and females.

4.4 Workforce Participation by Educational Groups in India

This section explores workforce participation rates among educational groups across India. We have established six educational categories by combining data from twelve educational groups in the NSSO employment/unemployment and Periodic Labour Force surveys. The categories include illiterate, below primary, primary, middle, secondary/HS, and graduate and above. The workforce participation rates (WPR) for these groups at selected time points are presented alongside male/female and rural/urban breakdowns in Table 38.

The WPR was highest among rural males with an educational level of 'graduate and above' and lowest for those with an educational level of 'below primary'. This trend persists throughout the period from 1983 to 2018. Another critical point is that the WPR declined almost uninterruptedly for rural males across all educational groups from 1983 to 2018. However, the rate of decline appears to have been steepest for the 'below primary' category among rural males and least for the 'middle' category. This is particularly true during the sub-period from 2012 to 2018. Furthermore, if we exclude the 'below primary' category from our analysis, we can assert that the WPR of rural males increases with higher educational attainment. This observation holds for all the years considered, except 2018, when the WPR of rural males declined for the 'middle' and 'secondary/H.S.' categories.

For rural females, the WPR appears to be higher in the 'illiterate' and 'graduate & above' categories than in the intermediate categories. As observed among rural males, the WPR for rural females has been lowest in the 'below primary' category. Furthermore, the WPR for all educational categories of rural females has declined over time. However, this decline appears to be relatively more pronounced among rural females from lower educational groups. It is also noteworthy that for all educational groups, the WPR for rural females has been lower than that for rural males.

Among rural persons (males and females), the overall trend mirrors that seen among rural males and females. Consequently, the WPR for rural persons has been highest in the 'graduate and above' category and lowest in the 'below primary' category across all years. The WPR for higher educational levels among rural persons has generally exceeded that for lower educational levels. However, the WPR of rural persons has decreased sharply over time, across all educational groups. Specifically, the 'secondary/H.S.' and 'graduate & above' categories have experienced the most significant drop in WPR in recent years.

Table 38. Workforce Participation Rates (%) by Educational Levels in India (UPSS Basis)

Region	Sex	Edn Level	1983	1994	2000	2012	2018
Rural	Male	Illiterate	52.79	53.63	51.26	53.39	48.38
		Below Primary	43.31	40.91	35.33	34.54	24.64
		Primary	61.96	60.01	54.45	52.87	52.16
		Middle	66.92	67.99	67.33	66.50	64.46
		Secondary / H.S.	72.56	70.97	72.42	64.79	58.09
		Graduate & above	79.15	82.04	83.60	75.28	66.81
		All	54.59	55.29	53.06	54.34	51.7
	Female	Illiterate	36.97	37.76	35.65	31.38	22.22
		Below Primary	18.33	17.78	15.18	13.77	9.342
		Primary	29.21	26.52	24.68	22.28	15.45
		Middle	25.29	25.04	24.53	23.14	15.76
		Secondary / H.S.	26.38	24.92	23.95	20.45	14.25
		Graduate & above	27.65	35.14	30.99	29.77	22.13
		All	33.95	32.78	29.88	24.84	17.49
	Male + Female	Illiterate	43.63	44.35	42.08	40.19	32.86
		Below Primary	34.43	31.69	26.74	24.92	17.38
		Primary	50.80	47.23	42.19	38.90	34.49
		Middle	55.83	54.00	51.87	48.43	43.55
		Secondary / H.S.	62.88	58.80	57.80	48.19	40.84
		Graduate & above	68.07	73.56	72.17	60.98	51.01
		All	44.45	44.36	41.72	39.92	35.02

(Continued)

Table 38 *(Continued)*

Region	Sex	Edn Level	1983	1994	2000	2012	2018
Urban	Male	Illiterate	39.47	40.61	39.08	39.22	36.63
		Below Primary	35.50	32.56	28.57	27.36	20.89
		Primary	55.51	52.55	49.00	49.20	50.22
		Middle	61.86	61.83	61.87	65.09	64.54
		Secondary / H.S.	67.08	64.58	64.15	62.02	57.04
		Graduate & above	81.16	81.32	80.55	77.14	72.31
		All	51.18	52.10	51.76	54.64	52.96
	Female	Illiterate	18.90	19.79	17.81	16.26	14.71
		Below Primary	8.43	8.69	7.30	8.71	7.255
		Primary	11.34	12.22	10.40	12.88	13.38
		Middle	9.34	10.82	10.67	13.38	12.07
		Secondary / H.S.	15.37	13.69	12.26	10.91	10.21
		Graduate & above	28.62	29.69	27.31	28.06	26.98
		All	15.10	15.47	13.90	14.66	14.16
	Male + Female	Illiterate	27.31	28.32	26.52	25.54	23.32
		Below Primary	23.29	21.74	18.64	18.56	14.37
		Primary	36.26	33.84	30.80	32.01	32.12
		Middle	41.46	40.17	39.52	41.29	39.65
		Secondary / H.S.	49.44	44.79	43.02	38.85	35.67
		Graduate & above	65.26	63.34	60.89	57.77	52.71
		All	34.03	34.70	33.67	35.47	33.9
Rural + Urban	Male	Illiterate	50.80	51.66	49.36	50.74	46.16
		Below Primary	41.38	38.92	33.79	32.84	23.65
		Primary	60.11	58.01	53.05	51.94	51.66
		Middle	65.13	66.09	65.68	66.10	64.48
		Secondary / H.S.	69.75	68.15	68.86	63.75	57.73
		Graduate & above	80.50	81.58	81.62	76.44	69.88
		All	53.76	54.49	52.73	54.43	52.07

(Continued)

Table 38 *(Continued)*

Region	Sex	Edn Level	1983	1994	2000	2012	2018
Rural + Urban	Female	Illiterate	34.15	34.98	32.85	28.59	20.74
		Below Primary	15.09	15.23	13.15	12.55	8.788
		Primary	22.49	21.67	20.34	19.76	14.9
		Middle	17.48	19.28	19.38	20.05	14.63
		Secondary / H.S.	18.98	18.36	17.57	16.08	12.64
		Graduate & above	28.39	30.67	28.06	28.57	25.22
		All	29.58	28.55	25.89	21.95	16.51
	Male + Female	Illiterate	41.13	41.89	39.65	37.46	31.01
		Below Primary	31.34	29.15	24.79	23.40	16.58
		Primary	46.15	43.25	39.04	37.10	33.87
		Middle	50.12	49.25	47.81	46.32	42.44
		Secondary / H.S.	55.38	51.97	50.84	44.35	38.96
		Graduate & above	66.09	66.46	64.31	58.88	52.01
		All	41.98	41.96	39.67	38.64	34.69

Source: Same as Table 33

In urban areas, the WPR for males has consistently been highest in the 'graduate & above' category and lowest in the 'below primary' category across all years. Over time, the WPR has declined across all educational groups (except the 'middle' category, where WPR increased) among urban males, with the decline more pronounced among lower educational groups, specifically the 'below primary' category. Urban females with lower educational qualifications have a lower WPR than their counterparts with higher educational qualifications. Additionally, it is noteworthy that the WPR for urban females is lower than that of rural females across all educational groups. Furthermore, mirroring the trend observed in urban males, urban females across all educational groups (except 'primary' and 'middle' categories) have also experienced declines in their respective WPRs.

For urban persons, the prevailing pattern is one of lower WPR for those in lower educational groups and higher WPR for those in higher educational groups. Over time, although the WPR of urban persons declined across all educational groups, the decline was more pronounced for the 'secondary/H.S.' and 'below primary' groups, followed by the 'graduate & above' group. Among all educational groups of urban residents, the WPR was lowest for those in the 'below primary' category and highest for those in the 'graduate & above' group throughout 1983–2018.

When considering rural and urban areas combined, the WPR has been lowest for males and females in the 'below primary' educational group, while it has been highest for the 'graduate & above' group. Although the WPR declined across all educational groups over time, the rate of decline has been highest in the 'secondary/H.S.' group, immediately followed by the 'below primary', 'graduate & above', 'primary', 'illiterate', and 'middle' education groups. Furthermore, the WPR was significantly lower among females than among males across all educational groups.

4.4.1 Shares of Total Workforce (Employed) and Total Population by Educational Groups

Our discussion above noted that the WPR was lowest for those with 'below primary' education and highest for the 'graduate & above' category. This has generally remained true for both males and females in rural and urban areas. We also observed a decline in WPR over time across all educational groups, with the decrease more pronounced in two higher education groups and one lower education group, viz., 'below primary'. We will now examine the shares of various educational groups in total employed and the population. Information on this aspect is presented in Table 39.

A careful review of the data in Table 39 reveals that, for males and females from lower educational groups, the share of the employed was lower than their population share in most of the years studied. This is true in both rural and urban areas. Furthermore, the ratio of employed share to population share declined over time for the lower educational groups, indicating that they experienced a larger decline in their employment share than those from higher educational groups. In contrast, those in the 'graduate & above' category gained the most in increasing their employed share relative to their population share over time. In this context, marginal improvement is observed for the 'middle' education group.

Table 39. Percentage Shares in Total Employed/Workforce (UPSS) to Total Population by Education Groups in India

Region	Sex	Education groups	Share in Employed / Workforce (%)					Share in population (%)					Ratio of workforce share to population share				
			1983	1994	2000	2012	2018	1983	1994	2000	2012	2018	1983	1994	2000	2012	2018
Rural	Male	Illiterate	52.9	44.2	39.9	27.9	24.7	54.7	45.5	41.3	28.4	27.1	0.97	0.97	0.97	0.98	0.91
		Below Primary	14.5	15.3	14.0	12.8	6.8	18.2	20.7	21.0	20.2	14.2	0.79	0.74	0.67	0.64	0.48
		Primary	15.0	14.1	13.7	14.9	14.5	13.2	13.0	13.3	15.3	14.3	1.13	1.09	1.03	0.97	1.01
		Middle	10.4	13.4	16.0	19.0	24.2	8.5	10.9	12.6	15.5	19.4	1.23	1.23	1.27	1.22	1.25
		Secondary/ H.S.	5.9	10.5	13.2	19.4	21.8	4.4	8.2	9.7	16.2	19.4	1.33	1.28	1.36	1.19	1.12
		Graduate & Above	1.4	2.5	3.2	6.1	8.1	0.9	1.7	2.0	4.4	5.5	1.45	1.48	1.58	1.39	1.47
	Female	Illiterate	84.8	78.2	73.5	56.1	51.3	77.8	67.9	61.6	44.5	40.7	1.09	1.15	1.19	1.26	1.26
		Below Primary	5.6	7.9	8.3	10.1	7.2	10.4	14.5	16.3	18.2	13.5	0.54	0.54	0.51	0.55	0.53
		Primary	6.1	6.9	8.0	12.1	12.4	7.1	8.5	9.7	13.5	14.0	0.86	0.81	0.83	0.90	0.88
		Middle	2.4	4.3	6.1	10.8	13.8	3.2	5.6	7.5	11.6	15.4	0.75	0.76	0.82	0.93	0.90
		Secondary/ H.S.	0.9	2.4	3.5	8.4	10.8	1.2	3.1	4.4	10.2	13.2	0.78	0.76	0.80	0.82	0.81
		Graduate & Above	0.2	0.4	0.6	2.5	4.6	0.3	0.4	0.6	2.1	3.3	0.81	1.07	1.04	1.20	1.39

(Continued)

Table 39 *(Continued)*

Region	Sex	Education groups	Share in Employed / Workforce (%)					Share in population (%)					Ratio of workforce share to population share				
			1983	1994	2000	2012	2018	1983	1994	2000	2012	2018	1983	1994	2000	2012	2018
Rural	Male + Female	Illiterate	64.8	56.4	51.7	36.5	31.2	66.1	56.4	51.3	36.2	33.7	0.98	1.00	1.01	1.01	0.92
		Below Primary	11.1	12.6	12.0	12.0	6.9	14.4	17.7	18.7	19.3	13.9	0.77	0.71	0.64	0.62	0.50
		Primary	11.7	11.5	11.7	14.1	14.0	10.2	10.8	11.5	14.4	14.2	1.14	1.06	1.01	0.97	0.99
		Middle	7.4	10.1	12.6	16.5	21.7	5.9	8.3	10.1	13.6	17.4	1.26	1.22	1.24	1.21	1.24
		Secondary/ H.S.	4.0	7.6	9.8	16.0	19.1	2.9	5.7	7.1	13.3	16.4	1.41	1.33	1.39	1.21	1.17
		Graduate & Above	0.9	1.8	2.3	5.0	7.2	0.6	1.1	1.3	3.3	4.4	1.53	1.66	1.73	1.53	1.64
Urban	Male	Illiterate	23.0	18.8	16.5	11.4	10.3	29.9	24.1	21.8	15.8	17.1	0.77	0.78	0.76	0.72	0.60
		Below Primary	12.8	12.0	9.8	7.6	4.9	18.5	19.1	17.8	15.2	12.3	0.69	0.62	0.55	0.50	0.39
		Primary	17.9	14.2	12.4	11.4	11.4	16.5	14.1	13.1	12.7	12.0	1.08	1.01	0.95	0.90	0.95
		Middle	17.5	17.2	18.7	17.4	21.2	14.5	14.5	15.6	14.6	17.4	1.21	1.19	1.20	1.19	1.22
		Secondary/ H.S.	19.0	23.8	26.0	27.2	26.1	14.5	19.2	21.0	24.0	24.2	1.31	1.24	1.24	1.14	1.08
		Graduate & Above	9.7	14.1	16.6	25.0	26.2	6.1	9.0	10.7	17.7	17.0	1.59	1.56	1.56	1.41	1.54

(Continued)

Table 39 *(Continued)*

Region	Sex	Education groups	Share in Employed / Workforce (%)					Share in population (%)					Ratio of workforce share to population share				
			1983	1994	2000	2012	2018	1983	1994	2000	2012	2018	1983	1994	2000	2012	2018
Urban	Female	Illiterate	59.8	49.1	44.0	28.1	24.7	47.7	38.4	34.4	25.3	24.7	1.25	1.28	1.28	1.11	1.00
		Below Primary	9.4	9.8	8.9	8.7	6.0	16.8	17.5	17.0	14.7	11.7	0.56	0.56	0.52	0.59	0.51
		Primary	10.6	10.6	9.6	10.9	11.4	14.1	13.5	12.8	12.4	12.1	0.75	0.79	0.75	0.88	0.95
		Middle	6.3	8.2	10.2	12.3	13.9	10.2	11.8	13.2	13.5	16.3	0.62	0.70	0.77	0.91	0.85
		Secondary/ H.S.	8.4	11.9	13.9	16.1	15.2	8.3	13.5	15.7	21.6	21.1	1.02	0.88	0.88	0.74	0.72
		Graduate & Above	5.6	10.2	13.4	23.9	28.8	2.9	5.3	6.8	12.5	14.3	1.90	1.92	1.96	1.91	2.02
	Male + Female	Illiterate	30.8	25.2	21.9	14.7	13.3	38.4	30.9	27.8	20.4	20.8	0.80	0.82	0.79	0.72	0.64
		Below Primary	12.1	11.5	9.6	7.8	5.1	17.7	18.4	17.4	14.9	12.0	0.68	0.63	0.55	0.52	0.42
		Primary	16.4	13.4	11.8	11.3	11.4	15.4	13.8	12.9	12.6	12.1	1.07	0.98	0.91	0.90	0.95
		Middle	15.2	15.3	17.0	16.4	19.7	12.4	13.2	14.5	14.1	16.9	1.22	1.16	1.17	1.16	1.17
		Secondary/ H.S.	16.7	21.3	23.6	25.0	23.8	11.5	16.5	18.5	22.9	22.7	1.45	1.29	1.28	1.10	1.05
		Graduate & Above	8.8	13.3	16.0	24.8	26.7	4.6	7.3	8.8	15.2	15.7	1.92	1.83	1.81	1.63	1.71

(Continued)

Table 39 *(Continued)*

Region	Sex	Education groups	Share in Employed / Workforce (%)					Share in population (%)					Ratio of workforce share to population share				
			1983	1994	2000	2012	2018	1983	1994	2000	2012	2018	1983	1994	2000	2012	2018
Rural + Urban	Male	Illiterate	46.0	38.0	34.0	23.0	20.4	48.7	40.1	36.3	24.7	24.2	0.94	0.95	0.94	0.93	0.84
		Below Primary	14.1	14.5	12.9	11.3	6.2	18.3	20.3	20.2	18.7	13.7	0.77	0.71	0.64	0.60	0.45
		Primary	15.7	14.1	13.3	13.9	13.6	14.0	13.3	13.3	14.6	13.7	1.12	1.06	1.01	0.95	0.99
		Middle	12.1	14.3	16.7	18.5	23.3	10.0	11.8	13.4	15.2	18.8	1.21	1.21	1.25	1.21	1.24
		Secondary/ H.S.	8.9	13.7	16.5	21.7	23.1	6.9	11.0	12.6	18.5	20.8	1.30	1.25	1.31	1.17	1.11
		Graduate & Above	3.3	5.3	6.6	11.6	13.5	2.2	3.5	4.3	8.3	8.8	1.50	1.50	1.55	1.40	1.52
	Female	Illiterate	81.8	74.4	69.5	50.8	44.6	70.9	60.7	54.8	39.0	36.0	1.15	1.23	1.27	1.30	1.24
		Below Primary	6.1	8.1	8.4	9.9	6.9	11.9	15.3	16.5	17.2	13.0	0.51	0.53	0.51	0.57	0.53
		Primary	6.6	7.4	8.2	11.9	12.1	8.7	9.7	10.5	13.2	13.4	0.76	0.76	0.79	0.90	0.90
		Middle	2.8	4.8	6.7	11.1	13.8	4.8	7.1	8.9	12.1	15.6	0.59	0.68	0.75	0.91	0.89
		Secondary/ H.S.	1.8	3.6	4.9	9.8	11.9	2.9	5.6	7.2	13.4	15.5	0.64	0.64	0.68	0.73	0.77
		Graduate & Above	0.8	1.7	2.3	6.6	10.7	0.9	1.6	2.1	5.1	6.5	0.96	1.07	1.08	1.30	1.64

(Continued)

Table 39 *(Continued)*

Region	Sex	Education groups	Share in Employed / Workforce (%)					Share in population (%)					Ratio of workforce share to population share				
			1983	1994	2000	2012	2018	1983	1994	2000	2012	2018	1983	1994	2000	2012	2018
Rural + Urban	Male + Female	Illiterate	58.3	50.0	45.3	30.7	26.0	59.5	50.1	45.3	31.7	30.0	0.98	1.00	1.00	0.97	0.87
		Below Primary	11.3	12.4	11.5	10.9	6.4	15.2	17.9	18.4	18.0	13.3	0.75	0.69	0.62	0.61	0.48
		Primary	12.6	11.9	11.7	13.3	13.2	11.4	11.5	11.9	13.9	13.5	1.10	1.03	0.98	0.96	0.98
		Middle	8.9	11.2	13.5	16.4	21.1	7.4	9.5	11.2	13.7	17.3	1.19	1.17	1.21	1.20	1.22
		Secondary/ H.S.	6.5	10.4	12.8	18.4	20.5	4.9	8.4	10.0	16.0	18.2	1.32	1.24	1.28	1.15	1.12
		Graduate & Above	2.4	4.1	5.2	10.2	12.8	1.6	2.6	3.2	6.7	7.7	1.57	1.58	1.62	1.52	1.66

Source: Same as in Table 33

4.5 Workforce Participation Among Social Groups in India

In this section, we discuss the patterns and changes in the WPR for various social groups at the all-India level. Both the NSSO employment/unemployment surveys and the PLFS categorised households into four social groups: Scheduled Tribes (ST), Scheduled Castes (SC), Other Backward Classes (OBC), and Others. Table 40 presents information on WPR for these categories at our selected time points. It was found that, in rural areas, the WPR decreases as we move from lower to higher social groups. Consequently, the WPR was highest for the ST category at all timepoints for both males and females in rural areas. Furthermore, the WPR has declined over time across all social groups. When comparing rural males and females, it is notable that the WPR has consistently been lower for rural females than for rural males across all social groups. Moreover, the rate of decline in WPR over time, particularly after 2012, has been significantly greater for rural females across all social groups than for rural males. The overall pattern of changes in WPR for rural persons reveals that the ST category ranks first among the four social groups, followed by SC, OBC, and 'Others'. However, all social group categories of rural persons showed a decline in WPR over time, with the decline being more pronounced during the period from 2012 to 2018.

Table 40: Workforce Participation Rates (%) by Social Groups in India (UPSS Basis)

Region	Sex	Social groups	1983	1994	2000	2012	2018
Rural	Male	ST	58.73	59.08	55.87	55.71	53.81
		SC	54.81	55.40	53.14	53.89	52.33
		OBC	–	–	53.30	53.78	50.54
		Others*	53.95	54.71	51.97	55.18	52.24
		All	54.59	55.29	53.13	54.34	51.70
	Female	ST	47.80	48.19	43.92	36.44	27.02
		SC	38.05	35.49	32.42	26.17	17.39
		OBC	–	–	30.17	23.91	16.76
		Others*	30.82	29.71	22.36	20.08	14.12
		All	33.95	32.78	29.70	24.84	17.49
	Male + Female	ST	53.33	53.74	49.98	46.28	40.76
		SC	46.65	45.80	43.09	40.36	35.22
		OBC	–	–	42.00	39.11	34.08
		Others*	42.57	42.56	37.42	38.15	33.69
		All	44.45	44.36	41.66	39.92	35.02

(Continued)

Table 40 *(Continued)*

Region	Sex	Social groups	1983	1994	2000	2012	2018
Urban	Males	ST	53.11	51.98	47.96	51.97	49.89
		SC	48.92	50.50	50.46	54.54	52.54
		OBC	–	–	52.87	54.65	53.21
		Others*	51.44	52.34	51.89	54.90	53.13
		All	51.18	52.10	51.84	54.64	52.96
	Females	ST	25.48	23.41	20.30	19.24	17.02
		SC	20.48	19.94	18.79	17.24	17.16
		OBC	–	–	15.91	15.12	14.34
		Others*	13.92	14.53	10.91	12.89	12.60
		All	15.09	15.47	13.98	14.66	14.16
	Male + Female	ST	40.55	38.22	34.46	36.61	33.94
		SC	35.53	36.05	35.43	36.41	35.17
		OBC	–	–	35.12	35.62	34.03
		Others*	33.56	34.38	32.34	34.89	33.30
		All	34.03	34.70	33.74	35.47	33.90
Rural + Urban	Males	ST	58.18	58.46	54.99	55.28	53.36
		SC	53.77	54.54	52.63	54.03	52.38
		OBC	–	–	53.20	54.02	51.29
		Others*	53.26	54.02	51.94	55.06	52.61
		All	53.76	54.49	52.79	54.43	52.07
	Females	ST	45.92	46.10	41.34	34.57	25.90
		SC	35.09	32.85	29.90	24.21	17.34
		OBC	–	–	27.02	21.56	16.07
		Others*	26.38	25.43	18.34	17.14	13.48
		All	29.58	28.55	25.75	21.95	16.51
	Male + Female	ST	52.16	52.42	48.26	45.20	39.99
		SC	44.72	44.12	41.65	39.49	35.21
		OBC	–	–	40.46	38.16	34.07
		Others*	40.15	40.22	35.60	36.80	33.53
		All	41.98	41.96	39.64	38.64	34.69

Source: Same as Table 33
*Note: * for 1983 and 1994, the OBCs are included in the category of 'Others'.*

The situation in urban areas differs for males, as the ST category has displayed the lowest WPR since 1994. The WPR for urban males appears similar to that of the other three categories, particularly in 2012 and 2018. When we focus specifically on the period between 2000 and 2018 (when separate data on the WPR of the four social categories are available), all social groups have shown some improvement in male WPR in urban areas. Among urban females, those in the ST category had the highest WPR value until 2012. By 2018, this distinction shifted to the SC women, although the difference between the ST and SC women remained marginal. In any case, SC and ST women in urban areas experienced higher WPR values than those from the OBC and 'Others' categories. A clear trend emerges of declining WPR over time for women across all social groups, although the rate of decline has been more pronounced for those from lower social groups. Additionally, the WPR for urban persons has decreased over time, and it appears to be slightly higher among lower social groups than among higher ones.

When considering both rural and urban areas together, the WPR value is consistently highest for both ST males and females. The overall trend indicates a decline in WPR as we move from lower to higher social groups. Furthermore, the WPR has declined across all social groups over time, with a notably steeper decrease during the sub-period 2012–2018 than in earlier sub-periods. It is also worth noting that the WPR for females has consistently been much lower than that of males at all times and across each social group.

4.5.1 Shares of Total Workforce (Employed) and Total Population by Social Groups

In Table 41, we provide information on the shares of the total employed (workforce) and total population by social groups. It was found that, in rural areas, individuals in the ST category had a higher share of the total employed compared to their share of the total population at all time points. This observation holds for both males and females. Consequently, the ratio of workforce share to population share has been greater than unity for them.

It is also encouraging to note that ST females in rural areas have increased their share of the total workforce over time, compared to their share of the total population. This is evident from the rise in the ratio of their workforce share to population share. However, the opposite has happened for SC females in rural areas. Among other social categories in rural areas, while SC and 'Others' males have largely maintained equal shares in the total workforce and total population from 1983 to 2018, those from the OBC categories have experienced a decline in their share of the total workforce compared to their share in the total population.

The situation is somewhat different in urban areas. Here, ST males and females have observed a decline in the ratio of the total workforce to the total population over time. Nevertheless, ST females in urban areas have maintained a higher share of the employed than their share of the total population. The same holds for SC females in urban areas, although for SC males and OBC males and females, the relationship between workforce and population shares appears to be proportional. For urban males and females in the 'Others' category, the ratio of workforce share to population share has consistently been less than unity, suggesting that their share of the workforce is lower than their share of the population.

Combining the rural and urban areas, it can be said that the persons from the ST and SC categories (both males and females) have maintained their superiority over the OBC and 'Others' categories regarding their share of total employed relative to the total population. Consequently, their ratio of employed share to population share has consistently exceeded unity at all the time points we examined. In contrast, this ratio has remained below unity for males and females from the OBC and 'Others' categories, particularly in recent years. Overall, it can be asserted that, at the all-India level, in terms of share in total employed compared to share in total population, ST and SC men and women hold a superior position relative to their counterparts in the OBC and 'Others' categories. The ST and SC categories have maintained a higher share of total employment in the country than their share of the total population throughout 1983–2018.

Table 41. Percentage Shares in Total Employed/Workforce (UPSS) to Total Population by Social Groups in India

Region	Sex	Social groups	Share in Employed / Workforce (%)					Share in population (%)					Ratio of workforce share to population share				
			1983	1994	2000	2012	2018	1983	1994	2000	2012	2018	1983	1994	2000	2012	2018
Rural	Male	ST	10.76	10.84	11.13	11.10	12.20	10.00	10.15	10.58	10.83	11.72	1.08	1.07	1.05	1.03	1.04
		SC	18.64	20.41	21.53	20.54	21.76	18.56	20.37	21.52	20.71	21.50	1.00	1.00	1.00	0.99	1.01
		OBC	–	–	37.17	44.41	42.56	–	–	37.05	44.88	43.54	–	–	1.00	0.99	0.98
		Others*	70.60	68.75	30.18	23.95	23.48	71.44	69.48	30.85	23.58	23.24	0.99	0.99	0.98	1.02	1.01
	Female	ST	14.25	15.23	15.91	15.90	18.11	10.12	10.36	10.76	10.84	11.72	1.41	1.47	1.48	1.47	1.55
		SC	20.44	21.73	23.11	21.73	21.57	18.24	20.08	21.17	20.63	21.69	1.12	1.08	1.09	1.05	0.99
		OBC	–	–	37.54	43.58	41.67	–	–	36.94	45.29	43.47	–	–	1.02	0.96	0.96
		Others*	65.31	63.04	23.44	18.78	18.66	71.63	69.56	31.13	23.23	23.12	0.91	0.91	0.75	0.81	0.81
	Male + Female	ST	12.07	12.42	12.79	12.56	13.65	10.06	10.25	10.67	10.84	11.73	1.20	1.21	1.20	1.16	1.16
		SC	19.31	20.88	22.08	20.90	21.71	18.40	20.23	21.35	20.67	21.59	1.05	1.03	1.03	1.01	1.01
		OBC	–	–	37.30	44.16	42.34	–	–	37.00	45.08	43.50	–	–	1.01	0.98	0.97
		Others*	68.62	66.69	27.83	22.37	22.30	71.53	69.52	30.99	23.41	23.18	0.96	0.96	0.90	0.96	0.96
Urban	Male	ST	3.48	2.86	3.51	3.28	3.43	3.36	2.87	3.79	3.45	3.64	1.04	1.00	0.93	0.95	0.94
		SC	11.93	12.40	14.18	14.14	14.74	12.48	12.80	14.56	14.17	14.85	0.96	0.97	0.97	1.00	0.99
		OBC	–	–	31.72	41.29	41.23	–	–	31.09	41.29	41.03	–	–	1.02	1.00	1.00
		Others*	84.59	84.73	50.60	41.28	40.61	84.16	84.33	50.55	41.09	40.47	1.01	1.00	1.00	1.00	1.00
	Female	ST	5.22	4.45	5.73	4.35	4.27	3.09	2.94	3.95	3.31	3.55	1.69	1.51	1.45	1.31	1.20
		SC	16.65	16.32	19.30	17.10	18.01	12.27	12.67	14.36	14.54	14.86	1.36	1.29	1.34	1.18	1.21
		OBC	–	–	35.71	42.88	41.97	–	–	31.37	41.58	41.43	–	–	1.14	1.03	1.01
		Others*	78.14	79.23	39.26	35.68	35.75	84.64	84.39	50.32	40.57	40.16	0.92	0.94	0.78	0.88	0.89

(Continued)

Table 41 *(Continued)*

Region	Sex	Social groups	Share in Employed / Workforce (%)					Share in population (%)					Ratio of workforce share to population share				
			1983	1994	2000	2012	2018	1983	1994	2000	2012	2018	1983	1994	2000	2012	2018
Urban	Male + Female	ST	3.85	3.20	3.95	3.49	3.60	3.23	2.90	3.87	3.38	3.60	1.19	1.10	1.02	1.03	1.00
		SC	12.93	13.23	15.19	14.73	15.41	12.38	12.74	14.47	14.35	14.86	1.04	1.04	1.05	1.03	1.04
		OBC	–	–	32.51	41.60	41.38	–	–	31.23	41.43	41.23	–	–	1.04	1.00	1.00
		Others*	83.23	83.57	48.35	40.17	39.61	84.39	84.36	50.44	40.84	40.32	0.99	0.99	0.96	0.98	0.98
Rural + Urban	Male	ST	9.07	8.92	9.19	8.81	9.60	8.38	8.31	8.82	8.67	9.37	1.08	1.07	1.04	1.02	1.02
		SC	17.08	18.48	19.66	18.66	19.67	17.08	18.46	19.72	18.80	19.56	1.00	1.00	1.00	0.99	1.01
		OBC	–	–	35.78	43.50	42.17	–	–	35.51	43.83	42.81	–	–	1.01	0.99	0.99
		Others*	73.84	72.60	35.38	29.03	28.56	74.53	73.23	35.96	28.70	28.27	0.99	0.99	0.98	1.01	1.01
	Female	ST	13.19	13.80	14.52	13.71	14.61	8.49	8.55	9.05	8.70	9.32	1.55	1.61	1.61	1.58	1.57
		SC	19.99	21.02	22.59	20.85	20.67	16.86	18.27	19.46	18.90	19.68	1.19	1.15	1.16	1.10	1.05
		OBC	–	–	37.29	43.45	41.74	–.	–	35.55	44.23	42.87	–	–	1.05	0.98	0.97
		Others*	66.82	65.18	25.59	21.99	22.97	74.65	73.19	35.94	28.17	28.14	0.90	0.89	0.71	0.78	0.82
	Male + Female	ST	10.49	10.53	10.87	10.16	10.77	8.44	8.43	8.93	8.69	9.34	1.24	1.25	1.22	1.17	1.15
		SC	18.08	19.31	20.58	19.27	19.91	16.97	18.37	19.59	18.85	19.62	1.07	1.05	1.05	1.02	1.01
		OBC	–	–	36.26	43.48	42.07	–	–	35.53	44.03	42.84	–	–	1.02	0.99	0.98
		Others*	71.43	70.16	32.28	27.09	27.26	74.59	73.20	35.95	28.44	28.20	0.96	0.96	0.90	0.95	0.97

Source: Same as Table 33

*Note: * for 1983 and 1994, the OBCs are included in the category of 'Others'.*

4.6 Workforce Participation Among Religious Groups in India

Let us focus on the workforce participation rates among various religious groups across India. The NSSO employment/unemployment surveys and PLFS provided data on eight religious groups. Among these, the most dominant group in India is Hindus, followed by Muslims. Hindus and Muslims together accounted for 94.4 % of the country's total population in 2018. Therefore, when comparing the workforce participation rates by religious groups, it is more appropriate to focus specifically on the rates of these two groups.

Information on WPR by religious groups at the all-India level is presented in Table 42. The key points to note are the following:

First, both in rural and urban areas, Muslims lagged behind Hindus in the WPR. For instance, compared to the WPR of 35.77 for Hindus in rural areas in 2018, the corresponding figure for Muslims was 28.69. Similarly, in urban areas, the WPRs for Hindus and Muslims in the same year are 34.83 and 29.28, respectively. Thus, it is evident that Muslims find themselves in a disadvantaged position regarding their WPR. This trend persisted throughout 1983–2018, although there is some evidence that the difference between Hindus and Muslims regarding their WPRs has decreased over time in rural areas, particularly between 2000 and 2018. On the other hand, an opposite trend is observed regarding the WPRs of Hindus and Muslims in urban areas, with the difference widening during the same period. However, when both rural and urban areas are considered together, it emerges that although the gap between the WPRs of Hindus and Muslims increased marginally between 1983 and 2000 (rising from 8.87 percentage points to 9.11 percentage points), this gap declined significantly between 2000 and 2018 (from 9.11 percentage points to 6.7 percentage points).

Secondly, it is evident that although the WPR for females is lower than that for males across all religious groups, it is deficient for Muslim females compared to those from other religious groups, including Hindus. As shown in Table 42, the WPRs for Muslim females in rural and urban areas were 9.92 and 7.52, respectively, in 2018. For their Hindu counterparts, the corresponding figures were 18.45 and 15.36. Additionally, it is essential to note that while the rate of decline in the WPR for Hindu women in rural areas was slightly higher than that for Muslim women during the sub-period 2012–2018, the reverse is true in urban areas, where the decline in the WPR for Muslim women was more significant than that for Hindu women. Contrary to the overall trend during this period, the WPR for Hindu females improved marginally.

Thirdly, focusing on the males, it can be said that, in the rural areas, although both the Hindu and Muslim males suffered a decline in the WPR over time, such a decline has been slightly higher for the Muslims than the Hindus. A similar picture emerges in urban areas when we focus on the sub-period from 2012 to 2018.

Table 42. Workforce Participation Rates (%) by Religious Groups in India (UPSS Basis)

Region	Sex	Religious group	1983	1994	2000	2012	2018
Rural	Male	Hindu	54.93	55.93	53.74	54.91	52.20
		Muslim	50.99	49.48	47.73	49.94	47.02
		Christian	52.34	55.46	56.65	54.08	52.44
		Others	57.78	55.95	53.18	57.07	54.48
		All	54.59	55.29	53.13	54.34	51.70
	Female	Hindu	35.40	34.70	31.36	26.05	18.45
		Muslim	20.31	16.26	16.49	15.30	9.92
		Christian	37.68	36.01	32.03	28.42	20.84
		Others	33.69	31.06	31.19	29.87	17.57
		All	33.95	32.78	29.69	24.84	17.49
	Male + Female	Hindu	45.34	45.63	42.82	40.82	35.77
		Muslim	35.81	33.21	32.15	32.79	28.69
		Christian	45.01	45.75	44.25	41.17	36.68
		Others	46.22	44.05	42.57	44.14	36.69
		All	44.45	44.36	41.66	39.92	35.02
Urban	Male	Hindu	51.74	52.57	52.45	54.99	53.43
		Muslim	49.38	50.01	49.75	53.22	50.93
		Christian	47.31	50.34	48.61	54.03	50.26
		Others	50.22	52.06	50.52	54.54	53.78
		All	51.18	52.10	51.84	54.64	52.96
	Female	Hindu	15.80	16.06	14.59	15.26	15.36
		Muslim	11.25	12.30	9.95	10.46	7.52
		Christian	21.92	21.97	22.95	25.23	19.24
		Others	12.00	11.61	11.76	13.95	14.53
		All	15.09	15.47	13.98	14.66	14.16
	Male + Female	Hindu	34.73	35.27	34.38	35.94	34.83
		Muslim	30.97	32.06	30.76	32.84	29.28
		Christian	35.03	36.27	35.72	39.23	34.29
		Others	32.15	32.56	32.02	35.20	34.42
		All	34.03	34.70	33.74	35.47	33.90

(Continued)

Table 42 *(Continued)*

Region	Sex	Religious group	1983	1994	2000	2012	2018
Rural + Urban	Male	Hindu	54.21	55.13	53.42	54.93	52.54
		Muslim	50.43	49.67	48.43	51.15	48.47
		Christian	50.82	53.93	54.16	54.07	51.64
		Others	55.57	54.85	52.39	56.25	54.29
		All	53.76	54.49	52.79	54.43	52.07
	Female	Hindu	31.21	30.43	27.41	23.14	17.59
		Muslim	17.23	14.93	14.36	13.60	9.02
		Christian	33.13	31.86	29.22	27.29	20.23
		Others	27.48	25.49	25.50	24.74	16.70
		All	29.58	28.55	25.75	21.95	16.51
	Male + Female	Hindu	43.01	43.22	40.80	39.49	35.51
		Muslim	34.14	32.81	31.68	32.81	28.91
		Christian	42.06	42.93	41.61	40.49	35.78
		Others	42.15	40.78	39.45	41.26	36.05
		All	41.98	41.96	39.64	38.64	34.69

Source: Same as Table 33

Overall, it can be stated that the WPR of Muslims has been lower than that of Hindus. However, the WPR for Muslim women has been exceptionally low in comparison to women from Hindu and other religious groups. The general trend indicates that men and women from all religious groups have experienced a decline in WPR over time. Nevertheless, for the country as a whole – encompassing rural and urban areas as well as males and females – there is a distinct trend showing that the gap in WPR values between Hindus and Muslims has reduced over time, suggesting that individuals (particularly males) from the Muslim community are beginning to catch up with their Hindu counterparts.

4.6.1 Shares of Total Workforce (Employed) and Total Population by Religious Groups

In Table 43, we present information on the shares of total employed persons and the total population by religious groups. This information reveals that at all five time points considered, the share of Muslim males and females among the employed was lower than their share of the total population. Consequently, their workforce-to-population share ratio fell below unity. In contrast, Hindu males and females exhibit higher shares in the total workforce than in the population, resulting in ratios greater than unity for them.

Table 43. Percentage Shares in Total Employed/Workforce (UPSS) to Total Population by Religious Groups in India

Region	Sex	Religious group	Share in Employed / Workforce (%)					Share in population (%)					Ratio of workforce share to population share				
			1983	1994	2000	2012	2018	1983	1994	2000	2012	2018	1983	1994	2000	2012	2018
Rural	Male	Hindu	85.86	86.15	84.99	84.07	84.23	85.33	85.17	84.03	83.20	83.44	1.01	1.01	1.01	1.01	1.01
		Muslim	8.82	8.76	9.76	11.29	10.14	9.44	9.78	10.87	12.29	11.15	0.93	0.89	0.90	0.92	0.91
		Christian	2.11	2.03	2.22	1.82	1.90	2.20	2.03	2.08	1.83	1.87	0.96	1.00	1.07	1.00	1.01
		Others	3.21	3.06	3.02	2.81	3.73	3.03	3.02	3.02	2.68	3.54	1.06	1.01	1.00	1.05	1.05
	Female	Hindu	88.87	89.93	88.27	86.98	87.71	85.25	84.97	83.57	82.94	83.15	1.04	1.06	1.06	1.05	1.05
		Muslim	5.73	4.94	6.27	7.75	6.49	9.58	9.95	11.28	12.59	11.44	0.60	0.50	0.56	0.62	0.57
		Christian	2.53	2.35	2.38	2.22	2.33	2.28	2.14	2.21	1.94	1.95	1.11	1.10	1.08	1.14	1.19
		Others	2.87	2.78	3.09	3.05	3.47	2.89	2.93	2.94	2.54	3.46	0.99	0.95	1.05	1.20	1.00
	Male + Female	Hindu	86.99	87.51	86.13	84.96	85.08	85.29	85.07	83.80	83.07	83.30	1.02	1.03	1.03	1.02	1.02
		Muslim	7.66	7.39	8.54	10.21	9.25	9.51	9.87	11.07	12.43	11.29	0.81	0.75	0.77	0.82	0.82
		Christian	2.27	2.15	2.28	1.95	2.00	2.24	2.08	2.14	1.89	1.91	1.01	1.03	1.06	1.03	1.05
		Others	3.08	2.96	3.05	2.89	3.67	2.96	2.98	2.98	2.61	3.50	1.04	0.99	1.02	1.11	1.05
Urban	Male	Hindu	78.12	79.13	78.23	78.12	78.83	77.27	78.42	77.31	77.27	78.14	1.01	1.01	1.01	1.01	1.01
		Muslim	15.32	14.86	15.70	15.32	15.34	15.88	15.48	16.35	15.88	15.95	0.96	0.96	0.96	0.96	0.96
		Christian	2.74	2.47	2.51	2.74	2.50	2.97	2.56	2.67	2.97	2.64	0.92	0.97	0.94	0.92	0.95
		Others	3.81	3.54	3.56	3.81	3.32	3.88	3.54	3.66	3.88	3.27	0.98	1.00	0.97	0.98	1.02
	Females	Hindu	80.28	80.97	80.49	80.28	83.92	76.71	78.03	77.11	76.71	77.34	1.05	1.04	1.04	1.05	1.09
		Muslim	12.20	12.35	11.60	12.20	8.74	16.37	15.54	16.30	16.37	16.45	0.75	0.79	0.71	0.75	0.53
		Christian	4.46	3.95	4.84	4.46	3.94	3.07	2.78	2.95	3.07	2.90	1.45	1.42	1.64	1.45	1.36
		Others	3.06	2.73	3.07	3.06	3.39	3.85	3.64	3.65	3.85	3.31	0.80	0.75	0.84	0.80	1.02

(Continued)

Table 43 *(Continued)*

Region	Sex	Religious group	Share in Employed / Workforce (%)					Share in population (%)					Ratio of workforce share to population share				
			1983	1994	2000	2012	2018	1983	1994	2000	2012	2018	1983	1994	2000	2012	2018
Urban	Male + Female	Hindu	78.58	79.52	78.68	78.58	79.87	77.00	78.24	77.22	77.00	77.74	1.02	1.02	1.02	1.02	1.03
		Muslim	14.67	14.33	14.89	14.67	13.99	16.11	15.51	16.33	16.11	16.20	0.91	0.92	0.91	0.91	0.86
		Christian	3.10	2.78	2.97	3.10	2.80	3.01	2.66	2.80	3.01	2.77	1.03	1.05	1.06	1.03	1.01
		Others	3.65	3.37	3.47	3.65	3.34	3.87	3.59	3.65	3.87	3.29	0.94	0.94	0.95	0.94	1.01
Rural + Urban	Male	Hindu	84.07	84.46	83.27	82.20	82.63	83.36	83.47	82.29	81.45	81.90	1.01	1.01	1.01	1.01	1.01
		Muslim	10.33	10.23	11.27	12.94	11.69	11.01	11.22	12.29	13.77	12.55	0.94	0.91	0.92	0.94	0.93
		Christian	2.26	2.14	2.29	1.97	2.08	2.39	2.16	2.24	1.98	2.09	0.95	0.99	1.03	0.99	0.99
		Others	3.35	3.17	3.16	2.89	3.61	3.24	3.15	3.19	2.79	3.46	1.03	1.01	0.99	1.03	1.04
	Females	Hindu	87.85	88.75	87.21	85.70	86.75	83.27	83.28	81.95	81.28	81.44	1.06	1.07	1.06	1.05	1.07
		Muslim	6.50	5.92	6.99	8.61	7.06	11.16	11.32	12.54	13.89	12.92	0.58	0.52	0.56	0.62	0.55
		Christian	2.76	2.56	2.71	2.68	2.74	2.46	2.30	2.39	2.15	2.23	1.12	1.12	1.13	1.24	1.23
		Others	2.89	2.77	3.09	3.02	3.45	3.11	3.11	3.12	2.68	3.41	0.93	0.89	0.99	1.13	1.01
	Male + Female	Hindu	85.37	85.87	84.52	83.17	83.59	83.32	83.38	82.12	81.37	81.67	1.02	1.03	1.03	1.02	1.02
		Muslim	9.01	8.81	9.92	11.75	10.61	11.08	11.27	12.41	13.83	12.73	0.81	0.78	0.80	0.85	0.83
		Christian	2.43	2.28	2.43	2.16	2.23	2.42	2.23	2.31	2.06	2.16	1.00	1.02	1.05	1.05	1.03
		Others	3.19	3.04	3.14	2.92	3.57	3.18	3.13	3.15	2.74	3.44	1.00	0.97	1.00	1.07	1.04

Source: Same as Table 33

Another striking observation is that the Muslim women's workforce share compared to their population share has been markedly low. In rural areas, the workforce-to-population ratio for Muslim women was 0.57 in 2018, whereas for Hindu women, it was 1.05. Similarly, in urban areas, this ratio for Muslim women was 0.53 in the same year, compared to 1.09 for Hindu women. There is no denying the fact that Muslim women are lagging far behind their Hindu and other religious counterparts regarding employment.

4.7 Growth of the Employment (Workforce) in India

This section examines employment growth rates at the all-India level from 1983 to 2018, as well as across various sub-periods at all possible levels of disaggregation: rural/urban, male/female, age groups, educational groups, social groups, and religious groups. We also discuss the employment growth performance of the Indian economy in the post-globalisation period (1994–2018) compared to the pre-globalisation period (1983–1994).

4.7.1 Growth of Employment Across India

Table 44 illustrates that, for rural males across all-India, the annual (compound) growth rate of employment declined in the post-globalisation period compared to the pre-globalisation period. During the post-globalisation phase, the employment growth rate among rural males was 1.02 % per annum, compared with 1.71 % per annum during the pre-globalisation period. During the sub-period from 2012 to 2018, rural males experienced a significant decline in the annual employment growth rate, which was 0.33 %. The scenario for rural females has been considerably bleaker regarding employment expansion during the post-globalisation period, as they experienced negative employment growth. As the table shows, rural females experienced an annual employment growth rate of 1.41 % during the pre-globalisation period. In contrast, their employment growth rate plummeted to –1.29 % during the post-globalisation period. It is essential to note that the period from 2000 onward brought severe hardships for females in rural areas in terms of employment. Consequently, two sub-periods of the 2000–2018 period recorded negative employment growth for rural females. Notably, the most severe decline in rural female employment occurred between 2012 and 2018, with the employment growth rate turning negative at –4.56 % per annum. Due to this substantial decline in the employment growth rate for rural females, the overall growth rate for rural individuals (males and females combined) also turned negative at –1.04 % during this sub-period. Furthermore, comparing the pre-globalisation period with the entire post-globalisation period, it becomes evident that the annual employment growth rate for rural individuals during the post-globalisation period (0.32 %) is precisely one-fifth of that observed during the pre-globalisation period (1.60 %).

Although urban areas also experienced a decline in the employment growth rate in the post-globalisation period compared to the pre-globalisation period, the rate of decline was less significant than that observed in rural areas. Table 44 shows that urban males had an annual employment growth rate of 3.15 % during the pre-globalisation period, while the corresponding figure during the post-globalisation period was 2.76 %. The annual employment growth rates for urban females during the pre- and post-globalisation periods were 3.38 % and 2.53 %, respectively. It is worth noting that while urban females enjoyed a higher employment growth rate during the pre-globalisation period than urban males, this trend reversed in the post-globalisation period when urban males experienced a higher employment growth rate than urban females. When considering urban males and females together, it can be stated that the employment growth rate was lower during the post-globalisation period compared to the pre-globalisation period. Furthermore, among all sub-periods of the post-globalisation era, the employment growth rate for urban persons was the lowest at 2.06 % per annum during 2012–2018. This figure, however, appears impressive when compared to the negative employment growth of –1.04 % for rural persons during the same period.

Table 44. Annual Growth Rates of Employed/Workforce (UPSS) in India

Region	Sex	1983 to 1994	1994 to 2000	2000 to 2012	2012 to 2018	1994 to 2018
Rural	Male	1.71	0.94	1.40	0.33	1.02
	Female	1.41	0.15	–0.34	–4.56	–1.29
	Male + Female	1.60	0.66	0.83	–1.04	0.32
Urban	Male	3.15	2.61	3.14	2.14	2.76
	Female	3.38	0.94	3.44	2.31	2.53
	Male + Female	3.20	2.27	3.20	2.06	2.68
Rural + Urban	Male	2.06	1.38	1.91	0.92	1.53
	Female	1.66	0.26	0.32	–2.89	–0.50
	Male + Female	1.93	1.02	1.44	–0.08	0.96

Source: Same as Table 33

For combined rural and urban areas, the following observations can be made regarding employment growth at the all-India level: (i) The growth rates of employment for both males and females were lower during the post-globalisation period compared to the pre-globalisation period; (ii) While the growth rate of employed males remained positive in all sub-periods, females experienced a drastic decline in employment growth in the sub-period 2012–2018 and even witnessed a negative growth rate during this time (–2.89 %); (iii) Females in India have always lagged behind males concerning their employment growth rates; (iv) For all individuals (males plus females) and across all areas (rural plus urban), the growth rate of employment at the all-India level was indeed lower in all sub-periods of the post-globalisation era; and (v) The recent sub-period 2012–2018 showed a negative growth rate of employment in India (–0.08 %) when considering all individuals and all regions.

4.7.2 Growth of Employment in India by Age Groups

We now examine the employment growth rates by age group at the all-India level, considering both male and female divisions, as well as rural and urban divisions. Table 45 presents the annual employment growth rates across various age groups during different periods. The following observations can be made in this regard:

- It is found that, for rural males and females, the employment growth rate turned negative for those aged 5–14 during the pre-globalisation period and in all sub-periods of the post-globalisation era. However, the decline in employment growth was greater for rural females than for rural males in this age group. Rural males and females aged 15–24 also experienced an adverse employment growth rate during the post-globalisation period. However, no other age group of rural males experienced negative employment growth, although a decline in their growth rate was evident during the post-globalisation period. Regarding rural females aged 25–34, employment growth turned negative after 1999–2000. It is also observed that during the sub-period 2012–2018, the growth rate of employed rural females across all age groups turned negative. Overall, in rural India, males and females aged 5–14 and 15–24 are the worst affected during the post-globalisation period, as their employment growth rates have turned negative. For rural females, the same holds for all other age groups when we focus on the sub-period from 2012 to 2018.
- In urban areas, the employment growth rate was negative for individuals aged 5–14 in all sub-periods. This holds for both males and females. Apart from this age group, both males and females aged 15–24 experienced

negative employment growth during the sub-period 2012–2018. All other age groups of urban males and females continued to show positive growth rates throughout 1983–2018. However, for most of these groups, the growth rate declined during the post-globalisation period compared to the pre-globalisation period.

- When considering both rural and urban areas, it can be stated that for both males and females, the age group most affected by negative employment growth throughout 1983–2018 is 5–14. Furthermore, the sub-period 2012–2018 witnessed a significant decline in the employment growth rate for this demographic in India. As indicated in Table 45, employment among males in India in the 5–14 age group decreased by 10.76 % per annum, while the decline among females in the same age group was 24.76 % per annum. In the 15–24 age group, male employment growth turned negative after 2000. However, female employment growth became negative after India adopted globalisation policies. Moreover, females experienced negative employment growth across all ages during 2012–2018.

Table 45. Annual Growth Rates of Employed/Workforce (UPSS) by Age Groups in India

Region	Sex	Age groups	1983 to 1994	1994 to 2000	2000 to 2012	2012 to 2018
Rural	Male	0–4	-15.96	-100.00	–	–
		5–14	-5.25	-4.37	-9.43	-8.28
		15–24	1.39	-0.33	-0.58	-4.03
		25–34	2.25	1.34	1.09	0.81
		35–59	2.37	1.81	2.54	1.46
		60 & above	2.23	0.77	2.45	0.65
	Female	0–4	-8.37	-100.00	–	–
		5–14	-4.43	-3.80	-9.37	-25.41
		15–24	0.61	-1.21	-2.83	-11.27
		25–34	2.49	0.65	-1.07	-4.62
		35–59	2.17	0.91	1.21	-2.42
		60 & above	2.47	0.79	2.31	-6.10
	Male + Female	0–4	-12.04	-100.00	–	–
		5–14	-4.90	-4.08	-9.40	-14.46
		15–24	1.11	-0.64	-1.28	-5.81
		25–34	2.34	1.09	0.36	-0.72
		35–59	2.30	1.49	2.10	0.30
		60 & above	2.33	0.76	2.43	-0.82

(Continued)

Table 45 *(Continued)*

Region	Sex	Age groups	1983 to 1994	1994 to 2000	2000 to 2012	2012 to 2018
Urban	Male	0–4	-31.11	-100.00	–	–
		5–14	-2.80	-2.29	-1.77	-19.18
		15–24	1.83	1.59	1.11	-1.99
		25–34	3.17	2.33	3.42	1.71
		35–59	4.24	3.43	3.69	3.15
		60 & above	2.29	2.05	4.08	6.51
	Female	0–4	-13.36	-100.00	–	–
		5–14	-1.60	-1.92	-9.23	-22.28
		15–24	2.00	-0.30	2.16	-3.58
		25–34	4.10	0.66	4.49	1.86
		35–59	4.46	1.81	3.75	3.99
		60 & above	1.40	1.07	3.04	5.53
	Male + Female	0–4	-22.97	-100.00	–	–
		5–14	-2.36	-2.14	-4.00	-19.85
		15–24	1.87	1.21	1.32	-2.41
		25–34	3.35	2.01	3.63	1.63
		35–59	4.29	3.10	3.70	3.21
		60 & above	2.09	1.85	3.88	6.20
Rural + Urban	Male	0–4	-17.59	-100.00	–	–
		5–14	-4.85	-4.01	-7.78	-10.76
		15–24	1.51	0.14	-0.12	-3.42
		25–34	2.48	1.63	1.83	1.08
		35–59	2.83	2.26	2.91	1.98
		60 & above	2.32	1.04	2.77	1.96
	Female	0–4	-8.73	-100.00	–	–
		5–14	-4.15	-3.58	-9.29	-24.76
		15–24	0.78	-1.08	-2.02	-9.27
		25–34	2.70	0.66	-0.09	-2.77
		35–59	2.48	1.05	1.69	-0.77
		60 & above	2.32	0.84	2.48	-3.86
	Male + Female	0–4	-13.15	-100.00	–	–
		5–14	-4.55	-3.78	-8.45	-15.29
		15–24	1.27	-0.25	-0.66	-4.82
		25–34	2.55	1.31	1.25	0.06
		35–59	2.72	1.88	2.55	1.20
		60 & above	2.35	0.98	2.71	0.70

Source: Same as Table 33

- From an overall perspective, it can be stated that not only did individuals aged 5–14 in India endure negative employment growth throughout 1983–2018, but the rate of decline in employment growth also intensified during the post-globalisation era, particularly after 2012. Similarly, those aged 15–24 experienced a comparable decrease after 1994, as their employment growth rate declined at an accelerating pace over time. In contrast, none of the other age groups experienced negative employment growth rates between 1983 and 2018. Nevertheless, the growth rate continued diminishing as we progressed from one sub-period of the post-globalisation phase to the next.

4.7.3 Growth of Employment in India by Educational Groups

Information on the employment growth rates for various education groups is provided in Table 46. The main points to note here are the following:

- In rural areas, the employment growth rate for illiterate males was negative in all sub-periods. The same applies to rural females, except during the pre-globalisation period, when illiterate females experienced positive employment growth. However, the decline in employment growth during the post-globalisation period was significantly greater for illiterate females than for illiterate males in rural areas.
- In the sub-period 2012–2018, both males and females in rural areas with 'below primary' education experienced a significantly negative employment growth rate. The same is true for those with a 'primary' level education. However, for all other (higher) education groups of rural males, the growth rates of employed individuals are positive across all sub-periods, although a decline in growth rate is noticeable in the sub-period from 2012 to 2018, except for those with a 'middle' level of education. In contrast, the employment growth rate for rural females was negative across all education groups except 'graduates and above' during this sub-period.
- If we consider rural persons (males plus females), it becomes evident that the two groups most affected by a significantly negative employment growth rate in the sub-period 2012–2018 of the post-globalisation era are those identified as 'illiterate' and 'below primary'. The individuals in the 'primary' category also experienced a negative employment growth rate during this period. Overall, the decline in employment growth rates in rural areas was more pronounced among individuals with lower educational attainment than among those with higher educational attainment. The available evidence suggests that

rural workers with limited education were the most significantly affected by employment losses, especially during globalisation.

- In urban areas, the situation for males differs in that, except for those with 'below primary' education, the employment growth rates were positive in both the pre-globalisation and post-globalisation periods, regardless of educational levels. However, it should not be overlooked that, across all educational groups except those with a 'middle' level of education, employment growth rates have declined during the post-globalisation period compared to the pre-globalisation period. Overall, it is evident that urban males across all educational groups experienced better employment growth rates than their rural counterparts.
- The employment growth rates for various educational groups of urban females reflect a similar trend. Once again, all educational groups saw positive employment growth rates except those with 'below primary' education. Nevertheless, all urban female educational groups experienced a decline in their employment growth rates in the post-globalisation period compared to the pre-globalisation period.
- Concerning urban persons, it can be noted that only those with 'below primary' education faced negative employment growth rates during the post-globalisation era, while all other educational groups maintained positive growth rates throughout this period. Nonetheless, a general trend of declining employment growth rates for urban individuals is apparent during the sub-period 2012–2018 across all educational groups, except for those with a 'middle' level of education.
- Taking into account both rural and urban areas, it can be stated that 'illiterate' males at the all-India level suffered negative employment growth rates in all the sub-periods of the post-globalisation era. Males with 'below primary' education also experienced negative employment growth, except from 2000 to 2012. The employment growth rates remained positive post-globalisation for all male educational groups. However, a general trend of declining growth rates is observed in this period compared to pre-globalisation, excluding those with a 'middle' level of education. Regarding females at the all-India level, those belonging to the 'illiterate' category faced negative employment growth during the post-globalisation period. In the sub-period from 2012 to 2018, females with 'below primary' and 'primary' levels of education also experienced negative employment growth. Furthermore, females across all educational groups witnessed declining employment growth rates over time during the post-globalisation era. Overall, individuals with weaker educational foundations suffered greater employment losses during the globalisation era, as their growth rates either turned negative or declined in the post-globalisation period.

Table 46. Annual Growth Rates of Workforce/Employed (UPSS) by Education Groups in India

Region	Sex	Edn Level	1983 to 1994	1994 to 2000	2000 to 2012	2012 to 2018
Rural	Male	Illiterate	−0.02	−0.74	−1.60	-1.69
		Below Primary	2.26	−0.56	0.68	-9.82
		Primary	1.11	0.41	2.15	-0.19
		Middle	4.22	3.95	2.82	4.51
		Secondary / H.S.	7.47	4.89	4.68	2.33
		Graduate & above	7.82	5.05	7.01	5.28
	Female	Illiterate	0.63	−0.88	−2.55	-5.98
		Below Primary	4.71	0.98	1.34	-9.80
		Primary	2.60	2.76	3.12	-4.20
		Middle	7.23	6.31	4.48	-0.51
		Secondary / H.S.	10.66	6.90	7.17	-0.46
		Graduate & above	7.58	7.23	12.21	5.38
	Male + Female	Illiterate	0.25	−0.78	−2.06	-3.60
		Below Primary	2.83	−0.22	0.85	-9.82
		Primary	1.47	0.92	2.40	-1.16
		Middle	4.71	4.29	3.14	3.60
		Secondary / H.S.	7.90	5.07	5.04	1.90
		Graduate & above	1.60	0.66	0.83	-1.04
Urban	Male	Illiterate	1.16	0.39	0.00	0.48
		Below Primary	2.46	−0.70	0.95	-5.19
		Primary	0.89	0.31	2.46	2.11
		Middle	2.95	4.09	2.52	5.58
		Secondary / H.S.	5.40	4.13	3.55	1.39
		Graduate & above	6.90	5.47	6.69	2.94
	Female	Illiterate	1.47	−0.87	−0.37	0.16
		Below Primary	3.87	−0.68	3.23	-3.89
		Primary	3.42	−0.85	4.56	3.11
		Middle	6.08	4.51	5.11	4.36
		Secondary / H.S.	6.87	3.50	4.71	1.34
		Graduate & above	9.58	5.62	8.54	5.53

(Continued)

Table 46 *(Continued)*

Region	Sex	Edn Level	1983 to 1994	1994 to 2000	2000 to 2012	2012 to 2018
Urban	Male + Female	Illiterate	1.25	-0.09	-0.19	0.35
		Below Primary	2.70	-0.69	1.41	-4.99
		Primary	1.27	0.12	2.83	2.19
		Middle	3.28	4.13	2.88	5.25
		Secondary / H.S.	5.58	4.04	3.71	1.24
		Graduate & above	7.31	5.48	7.02	3.35
Rural + Urban	Male	Illiterate	0.23	-0.51	-1.34	-1.13
		Below Primary	2.34	-0.53	0.78	-8.71
		Primary	1.04	0.42	2.26	0.48
		Middle	3.75	4.00	2.78	4.86
		Secondary / H.S.	6.32	4.52	4.28	1.93
		Graduate & above	6.80	5.14	6.83	3.41
	Female	Illiterate	0.74	-0.85	-2.27	-4.87
		Below Primary	4.54	0.73	1.70	-8.38
		Primary	2.71	2.12	3.42	-2.43
		Middle	6.86	5.88	4.67	0.90
		Secondary / H.S.	8.52	5.35	6.34	0.34
		Graduate & above	8.65	5.60	9.41	5.39
	Male + Female	Illiterate	0.44	-0.62	-1.79	-2.80
		Below Primary	2.81	-0.27	1.01	-8.66
		Primary	1.40	0.76	2.54	-0.23
		Middle	4.19	4.24	3.12	4.16
		Secondary / H.S.	6.61	4.57	4.58	1.69
		Graduate & above	7.12	5.11	7.26	3.74

Source: Same as Table 33

4.7.4 Growth of Employment in India by Social Groups

Table 47 presents employment growth rates for various social groups at the all-India level, separately for males and females, as well as for rural and urban areas. The main observations are the following:

- Among rural males, the employment growth rates appeared to have declined for all social groups except the STs during the post-globalisation period compared to the pre-globalisation period. Between 2012 and 2018, the growth rate of ST males in rural areas was the highest among all social groups and exceeded that of all previous sub-periods, including the pre-globalisation phase. For SC males in rural areas, the employment growth rate in this period was positive, albeit lower than that recorded in earlier sub-periods. Conversely, while OBC males in rural areas experienced a negative employment growth rate during this period, the growth rate for 'Others' (including general castes) stood at zero. However, the scenario is somewhat different for rural females, whose employment growth rates declined post-globalisation and turned negative in the sub-period 2012–2018, regardless of caste group. Considering rural persons, it can be stated that although all social groups experienced a decline in employment growth rates during the post-globalisation period compared to the pre-globalisation phase, only the STs managed to sustain a positive employment growth rate.
- In urban areas, employment growth rates for males across all social groups are positive in every sub-period. Additionally, STs in urban areas appear to have experienced higher employment growth rates in the sub-period 2012–2018 of the post-globalisation era than in the preceding period. During 2012–2018, employment growth in urban areas was highest among STs, followed by SCs, OBCs, and 'Others'. There is compelling evidence suggesting that, among urban males, those from weaker social groups have outperformed 'Others' in employment growth during 2012–2018. The overall picture for urban females from various social groups indicates that their growth rates remained positive in all sub-periods. Moreover, urban females from weaker social groups (ST, SC, and OBC) have sometimes shown better employment growth rates than their counterparts from the 'Others' category during the entire period. In urban areas, although the growth rates of employed persons across social groups appear to have declined between 2012 and 2018, they still achieved positive, remarkably impressive growth rates compared to their rural counterparts. In this sub-period, among urban persons, the highest employment growth rate is observed among SCs, followed by STs, OBCs, and 'Others'.

Table 47. Annual Growth Rates of Workforce/Employed (UPSS) by Social Groups in India

Region	Sex	Social groups	1983 to 1994	1994 to 2000	2000 to 2012	2012 to 2018
Rural	Male	ST	1.78	1.38	1.38	1.92
		SC	2.59	1.84	1.00	1.30
		OBC	–	–	2.91	-0.38
		Others*	1.45	-12.00	-0.54	0.00
	Female	ST	2.05	0.89	-0.34	-2.47
		SC	2.00	1.18	-0.85	-4.67
		OBC	–	–	0.91	-5.27
		Others*	1.07	-15.07	-2.16	-4.66
	Male + Female	ST	1.88	1.16	0.68	0.34
		SC	2.36	1.60	0.37	-0.41
		OBC	–	–	2.26	-1.73
		Others*	1.33	-12.98	-0.99	-1.09
Urban	Male	ST	1.25	6.15	2.58	2.88
		SC	3.54	4.92	3.12	2.85
		OBC	–	–	5.43	2.12
		Others*	3.17	-5.84	1.41	1.86
	Female	ST	1.83	5.28	1.08	2.01
		SC	3.19	3.80	2.40	3.20
		OBC	–	–	5.03	1.94
		Others*	3.52	-10.21	2.62	2.34
	Male + Female	ST	1.40	5.92	2.15	2.57
		SC	3.43	4.65	2.94	2.84
		OBC	–	–	5.34	1.97
		Others*	3.24	-6.64	1.62	1.82
Rural + Urban	Male	ST	1.89	1.88	1.56	2.34
		SC	2.82	2.43	1.47	1.77
		OBC	–	–	3.58	0.37
		Others*	1.89	-10.07	0.25	0.61
	Female	ST	2.10	1.12	-0.16	-1.74
		SC	2.14	1.48	-0.35	-2.92
		OBC	–	–	1.61	-3.43
		Others*	1.42	-14.20	-0.94	-2.07
	Male + Female	ST	1.97	1.57	0.87	0.88
		SC	2.57	2.11	0.89	0.46
		OBC	–	–	2.99	-0.64
		Others*	1.75	-11.23	-0.03	0.01

Source: Same as Table 33

Note: For 1983 and 1994, 'Others' included 'OBC'

- When considering rural and urban areas together, it is observed that, for males at the all-India level, there is a tendency for the growth rate of employment to decline over time for all social groups, except for the STs, for which the growth rate of employment increased in the sub-period 2012–2018 compared to all preceding sub-periods. Furthermore, the male employment growth rate in this sub-period was highest for the STs, followed by SCs, 'Others' and OBCs. The general trend of declining employment growth during post-globalisation is also evident among females across all social groups. This decline has been so severe since 2000 that their employment growth rates have turned negative. Regarding all persons, it can be stated that social groups in India experienced a significant decline in employment growth rates during the post-globalisation period, particularly after 2000. In the sub-period of 2012–2018, the employment growth rate for the OBCs remained negative (–0.64 % per annum), while that for the 'Others' category was nearly zero (0.01 %). The growth rates for the two other social groups, namely STs and SCs, are low but positive during this period (0.88 % and 0.46 %, respectively).
- Overall, although all social groups in India experienced a decline in employment growth rates during the post-globalisation period, this decline has been relatively more significant for social groups such as OBCs and SCs than 'Others' and STs. It is also noted that the decrease in employment growth rates was more pronounced among females than among males across all social groups. In the sub-period 2012–2018, females across all social groups faced negative employment growth rates. The employment performance of urban persons during the post-globalisation period across various social groups was not as poor as that observed in rural areas, despite a general decline in employment growth rates for all social groups except STs. Rural females across all social groups suffered significantly after 2000 as their employment growth rates turned negative. In contrast, among rural males, while STs appear to have improved their employment growth rate over time (including in the sub-period 2012–2018), other social groups experienced a decline.

4.7.5 Growth of Employment in India by Religious Groups

The annual employment growth rates among religious groups across India are presented in Table 48. Here, we focus on the growth rates of the employed population in two major religious groups (Hindus and Muslims) in India, which together comprise approximately 94 % of the total population, according to the PLFS 2018. The key points to note are as follows:

- In rural areas, employment growth rates for both males and females were higher among Hindus than Muslims during the pre-globalisation phase. From 1994 to 2012, the growth rates for employed Muslim men and women improved and surpassed those of Hindu men and women. However, the rising growth rates for Muslims were not sustained after 2012. From 2012 to 2018, the employment growth rate for Hindu men declined significantly (though it remained positive) compared to the previous sub-period (2000–2012), while the rate for Muslim men became negative. Between 2012 and 2018, there was negative employment growth for rural females across all religious groups. It is important to note that the decline in employment growth rates for Muslim women was much steeper in comparison to that of Hindu women during 2012–2018. In terms of rural persons, while both Hindu and Muslim groups experienced negative growth rates in employment during this sub-period, the decline was more pronounced among Muslims than among Hindus. In urban areas, Muslim males also experienced higher employment growth rates from 1994 to 2012 than in the preceding pre-globalisation period. However, the growth rates of employed Hindu males in urban areas were slightly higher from 1983 to 2018, except for the sub-period from 1994 to 2000. During the sub-period 2012–2018, while Muslim females in urban areas experienced a negative employment growth rate (–3.22 % per annum), their Hindu counterparts witnessed an impressive employment growth rate (3.07 %). Considering the urban persons, it may be observed that Muslims experienced greater employment growth from 1994 to 2000 than Hindus. However, the growth of employed Hindu individuals in urban areas was higher than that of Muslim individuals in the sub-periods of 2000–2012 and 2012–2018. During the post-globalisation period, both Hindu and Muslim persons in urban areas experienced a decline in employment growth rates. However, the magnitude of such a decline has been more pronounced for the latter than the former.

Table 48. Annual Growth Rates of Workforce/Employed (UPSS) by Religious Groups in India

Region	Sex	Religious groups	1983 to 1994	1994 to 2000	2000 to 2012	2012 to 2018
Rural	Male	Hindus	1.74	0.71	1.31	0.36
		Muslims	1.64	2.79	2.63	−1.45
		Christians	1.34	2.46	−0.25	0.97
		Others	1.26	0.75	0.79	5.15
	Female	Hindus	1.52	−0.16	−0.46	−4.42
		Muslims	−0.03	4.21	1.44	−7.34
		Christians	0.71	0.34	−0.91	−3.81
		Others	1.10	1.94	−0.45	−2.47
	Male + Female	Hindus	1.66	0.40	0.71	−1.02
		Muslims	1.24	3.14	2.34	−2.66
		Christians	1.07	1.65	−0.48	−0.57
		Others	1.21	1.16	0.37	2.99
Urban	Male	Hindus	3.28	2.42	3.13	2.30
		Muslims	2.85	3.55	2.94	2.16
		Christians	2.13	2.87	3.91	0.60
		Others	2.42	2.74	3.72	−0.16
	Female	Hindus	3.47	0.84	3.41	3.07
		Muslims	3.50	−0.11	3.87	−3.22
		Christians	2.20	4.41	2.74	0.22
		Others	2.27	2.91	3.41	4.08
	Male + Female	Hindus	3.32	2.09	3.19	2.34
		Muslims	2.97	2.92	3.07	1.26
		Christians	2.14	3.38	3.58	0.32
		Others	2.40	2.76	3.66	0.54
Rural + Urban	Male	Hindus	2.10	1.14	1.80	0.97
		Muslims	1.96	3.04	3.09	−0.81
		Christians	1.53	2.59	0.62	1.79
		Others	1.55	1.31	1.15	4.71
	Female	Hindus	1.76	−0.03	0.18	−2.58
		Muslims	0.76	3.09	2.07	−5.94
		Christians	0.96	1.21	0.21	−2.42
		Others	1.25	2.07	0.13	−0.58
	Male + Female	Hindus	1.98	0.76	1.31	−0.01
		Muslims	1.71	3.04	2.88	−1.77
		Christians	1.30	2.10	0.48	0.41
		Others	1.47	1.55	0.85	3.30

Source: Same as Table 33

- When considering both rural and urban areas, it appears that among males, the employment growth rate was higher for Hindus than for Muslims during the pre-globalisation period. Between 1994 and 2012, in the two sub-periods, Muslim males experienced higher employment growth than Hindu males. However, this trend reversed in the sub-period from 2012 to 2018, during which Muslim males experienced negative employment growth, while Hindu males recorded positive growth. In the case of females, those from the Muslim community exhibited a significantly higher employment growth rate from 1994 to 2012 compared to their Hindu counterparts. Nevertheless, the sub-period 2012–2018 showed negative employment growth rates for females from both religions (Hindus and Muslims). Looking at all individuals (male plus female) at the all-India level, it seems that Hindus experienced a higher employment growth rate during the pre-globalisation period compared to Muslims. This trend reversed in the first two sub-periods of the post-globalisation era. Both Hindu and Muslim males faced negative employment growth in the last sub-period of 2012–2018, with the decline in employment growth for Muslims being more significant than that for Hindus during this time.

4.8 Evolving Employment Scenarios in Major States

This section examines changes in employment scenarios across seventeen major Indian states from 1983 to 2018. Two indicators selected for this purpose are workforce participation rates (WPR) and workforce growth (i.e. the growth in the number of workers or employed individuals). Regarding the WPR, we have compiled data for five points in time: 1983, 1994, 2000, 2012, and 2018. The growth rates have been computed for the pre-globalisation period (1983–1994) and three different sub-periods of the post-globalisation period (1994–2000, 2000–2012, and 2012–2018). Information has been provided separately for males, females, and all persons, as well as for rural, urban, and all areas (rural and urban combined).

4.8.1 Workforce Participation Rates Across the States

The information on workforce participation rates in seventeen major states at our chosen time points is presented in Table 49. The main observations here are the following:

- For rural males, Andhra Pradesh continued to hold the highest position among the states regarding the WPR until 2000, after which Karnataka and West Bengal took over this top position in 2012 and 2018, respectively. Conversely, the poorest performers in this regard were Haryana until 2000 and Bihar in 2012 and 2018. In 2018, the states following West Bengal in terms of rural males' WPR were Karnataka, Andhra Pradesh, Madhya Pradesh, Tamil Nadu, Maharashtra, Jammu & Kashmir, Gujarat, Himachal Pradesh, Assam, Punjab, and Odisha (in descending order of WPR value). In all these states, the WPR for rural males remained above the all-India level. The states with WPR values lower than the all-India level were Kerala, Rajasthan, Haryana, Uttar Pradesh, and Bihar.
- Regarding rural females' WPR, Table 49 shows that while Himachal Pradesh led the list of states in 1983, 2012, and 2018, Assam was the worst performer at the first three time points (1983, 1994, and 2000), and Bihar in the last two time points (2012 and 2018). In 2018, the states following Himachal Pradesh in terms of rural females' WPR were Andhra Pradesh, Madhya Pradesh, Tamil Nadu, Maharashtra, and Jammu & Kashmir (in descending order of WPR). In these states, the WPR remained above the all-India level. In the remaining nine states (including Bihar), the rural females' WPR was lower than the all-India average.
- For rural persons, the WPR appears to be highest in Andhra Pradesh for the first three time points and in Himachal Pradesh for the last two. Aside from Himachal Pradesh, the states that recorded a WPR higher than the all-India level in 2018 include Andhra Pradesh, Madhya Pradesh, Maharashtra, Tamil Nadu, Jammu & Kashmir, Karnataka, West Bengal, Gujarat, and Rajasthan (in descending order of WPR value). Conversely, the WPR of rural individuals is recorded as the lowest in Assam during the first two time points and in Bihar in the last three. In 2018, apart from Bihar, other states with lower WPR values for rural individuals than the all-India level are Uttar Pradesh, Haryana, Kerala, Assam, Punjab, and Odisha. Overall, regarding the WPR of rural persons in 2018, the group of poor-performing states in India appears to include both developed and underdeveloped states.

- In urban areas, the male WPR was highest in West Bengal in 1983 and 2000, Tamil Nadu in 1994, Gujarat in 2012, and Assam in 2018. Conversely, Bihar ranks last at all five time points. The states that recorded a higher WPR than the all-India level in 2018 are Assam, Gujarat, Tamil Nadu, West Bengal, Punjab, Himachal Pradesh, Karnataka, Andhra Pradesh, Madhya Pradesh, Maharashtra, Odisha, and Jammu & Kashmir (listed in descending order of WPR). The WPR is lower than the all-India level in the five remaining states.
- For urban females, the states that held the top position regarding WPR were Kerala in 1983, Tamil Nadu in 1994, 2000, and 2018, and Himachal Pradesh in 2012. The worst performers in this respect have been Assam in 1983, Bihar in 1994, 2012, and 2018, and Jammu & Kashmir in 2000. In 2018, the states that followed Tamil Nadu in terms of urban females' WPR were Andhra Pradesh, West Bengal, Himachal Pradesh, Karnataka, Madhya Pradesh, Kerala, and Maharashtra (in descending order of WPR value). The WPR of urban females remained above the all-India levels in these states. The WPR of urban females in the other nine states remained below the all-India WPR.
- When considering urban persons, Tamil Nadu has consistently topped the list of states regarding WPR, except in 2012, when Himachal Pradesh occupied the highest position. Conversely, Bihar ranked last in this regard at all time points we examined. The states following Tamil Nadu in terms of the WPR of urban persons in 2018 are Himachal Pradesh, West Bengal, Andhra Pradesh, Punjab, Karnataka, Madhya Pradesh, Gujarat, Maharashtra, Assam, and Jammu & Kashmir (listed in descending order of WPR value). In the remaining six states, the WPR of urban persons remained below the all-India average.
- Considering all areas (rural and urban) collectively, it is found that although the male WPR was recorded as the highest in Andhra Pradesh in 1983 and 1994, it peaked in Tamil Nadu in 2000, in Gujarat in 2012, and in West Bengal in 2018. Conversely, the states with the lowest male WPR (considering all areas) were Haryana in 1983 and 1994, Uttar Pradesh in 2000, and Bihar in 2012 and 2018. In addition to West Bengal, as many as eleven states in 2018 recorded a higher male WPR than the level observed for all of India. These states are Karnataka, Tamil Nadu, Andhra Pradesh, Gujarat, Madhya Pradesh, Punjab, Assam, Himachal Pradesh, Jammu & Kashmir, Maharashtra, and Odisha (arranged in descending order of WPR value). Apart from Bihar, Uttar Pradesh, Rajasthan, Haryana, and Kerala, exhibit a male WPR lower than the national average in 2018.

- Concerning the WPR of females in combined (rural plus urban) areas, it is observed that while Himachal Pradesh ranked first among 17 major states at all time points, Assam held the last position in 1983, 1994, and 2000, while Bihar did so in 2012 and 2018. In addition to Himachal Pradesh, the states that recorded a female WPR above the all-India level in 2018 (for combined areas) include Andhra Pradesh, Madhya Pradesh, Tamil Nadu, Maharashtra, Jammu & Kashmir, Karnataka, Rajasthan, Kerala, and West Bengal. This figure is lower in seven states than the all-India level in the same year: Bihar, Assam, Uttar Pradesh, Haryana, Punjab, Odisha, and Gujarat.
- When we consider both males and females and rural and urban areas together, it appears that, among 17 major states of India, Himachal Pradesh came first in WPR in 1994, 2012, and 2018; the same position went to Andhra Pradesh in 1983 and 2000. On the other hand, the state that performed worst in the WPR was Bihar at all times except in 1983, when Assam appeared to be the worst performer. As many as ten major states in India (out of seventeen major states considered) recorded a higher value of WPR in 2018 compared to the same for the all-India level, which are Himachal Pradesh, Andhra Pradesh, Madhya Pradesh, Tamil Nadu, Maharashtra, Jammu & Kashmir, Karnataka, West Bengal, Gujarat, and Rajasthan. On the other hand, seven states recorded WPR values below the national average in 2018: Bihar, Uttar Pradesh, Haryana, Kerala, Assam, Odisha, and Punjab.

Table 49: Workforce Participation Rates (%) in Major States of India (UPSS Basis)

State	Year	Rural						Urban						Rural + Urban					
		Male		Female		Male + Female		Male		Female		Male + Female		Male		Female		Male + Female	
Andhra Pradesh	1983	60.6	(1)	47.1	(3)	53.9	(1)	50.9	(10)	18.0	(5)	34.9	(6)	58.2	(1)	40.2	(3)	49.3	(1)
	1994	63.1	(1)	52.1	(1)	57.7	(1)	54.4	(5)	19.9	(4)	37.5	(3)	60.7	(1)	43.5	(2)	52.2	(2)
	2000	60.5	(1)	47.8	(1)	54.2	(1)	51.1	(9)	17.8	(3)	34.8	(8)	57.9	(2)	39.7	(2)	48.9	(1)
	2012	60.2	(2)	44.5	(2)	52.4	(2)	55.4	(8)	17.0	(5)	36.3	(9)	58.6	(6)	35.2	(2)	46.9	(2)
	2018	57.1	(3)	35.2	(2)	46.1	(2)	54.1	(8)	19.8	(2)	36.9	(4)	56.0	(4)	29.6	(2)	42.7	(2)
Assam	1983	50.0	(15)	12.6	(17)	32.0	(17)	50.1	(13)	7.8	(17)	31.3	(16)	50.0	(15)	12.1	(17)	31.9	(17)
	1994	51.6	(15)	15.9	(17)	34.3	(17)	52.8	(8)	9.2	(16)	32.8	(13)	51.7	(13)	15.2	(17)	34.2	(16)
	2000	52.9	(13)	15.1	(17)	34.6	(16)	52.2	(8)	11.2	(13)	33.1	(10)	52.8	(12)	14.6	(17)	34.4	(14)
	2012	54.0	(13)	12.2	(16)	33.6	(16)	54.2	(11)	9.0	(16)	32.3	(14)	54.0	(13)	11.7	(16)	33.4	(16)
	2018	54.7	(10)	8.1	(16)	32.7	(13)	57.8	(1)	11.0	(13)	34.6	(10)	55.0	(8)	8.4	(16)	32.9	(13)
Bihar	1983	50.8	(14)	24.8	(14)	38.1	(14)	47.0	(17)	10.5	(14)	30.4	(17)	50.3	(14)	23.1	(13)	37.1	(14)
	1994	51.1	(16)	17.2	(16)	34.8	(16)	43.9	(17)	6.9	(17)	26.9	(17)	50.1	(16)	15.9	(16)	33.8	(17)
	2000	49.2	(15)	17.3	(15)	33.8	(17)	43.2	(17)	7.5	(16)	26.6	(17)	48.4	(16)	16.0	(15)	32.8	(17)
	2012	48.6	(17)	8.4	(17)	29.3	(17)	44.5	(17)	5.4	(17)	25.9	(17)	48.0	(17)	8.0	(17)	28.8	(17)
	2018	43.0	(17)	4.3	(17)	24.8	(17)	42.8	(17)	6.4	(17)	25.2	(17)	43.0	(17)	4.5	(17)	24.8	(17)
Gujarat	1983	55.0	(10)	41.1	(7)	48.2	(8)	51.7	(7)	13.2	(9)	33.4	(11)	53.9	(10)	32.4	(8)	43.5	(8)
	1994	57.4	(5)	39.6	(8)	48.7	(8)	53.5	(7)	14.2	(11)	34.9	(9)	56.0	(5)	30.8	(9)	43.9	(8)
	2000	58.4	(4)	41.3	(5)	50.1	(4)	53.6	(6)	13.5	(8)	34.8	(6)	56.6	(4)	31.2	(8)	44.4	(5)
	2012	59.9	(3)	27.8	(8)	44.3	(6)	60.3	(1)	13.3	(12)	38.3	(4)	60.1	(1)	21.7	(10)	41.7	(6)
	2018	55.3	(8)	16.5	(10)	37.0	(9)	56.7	(2)	12.2	(11)	35.1	(8)	55.8	(5)	14.7	(11)	36.2	(9)

(Continued)

Table 49 *(Continued)*

State	Year	Rural						Urban						Rural + Urban					
		Male		Female		Male + Female		Male		Female		Male + Female		Male		Female		Male + Female	
Haryana	1983	46.4	(17)	23.2	(15)	35.6	(16)	53.3	(5)	10.9	(13)	33.8	(10)	48.0	(17)	20.5	(15)	35.2	(16)
	1994	46.3	(17)	27.1	(11)	37.4	(15)	51.9	(10)	15.2	(8)	34.9	(8)	47.7	(17)	24.0	(11)	36.8	(14)
	2000	47.5	(17)	20.2	(13)	34.8	(14)	50.6	(10)	9.8	(14)	31.9	(14)	48.4	(15)	17.3	(14)	34.0	(15)
	2012	51.8	(14)	16.2	(15)	35.1	(14)	51.4	(14)	9.7	(15)	32.0	(15)	51.7	(14)	13.9	(15)	34.0	(14)
	2018	47.8	(15)	9.6	(15)	29.7	(15)	52.3	(13)	9.3	(15)	32.0	(13)	49.4	(14)	9.5	(14)	30.5	(15)
Himachal Pradesh	1983	53.0	(13)	47.6	(1)	50.3	(5)	53.3	(6)	17.1	(6)	37.1	(2)	53.0	(12)	45.4	(1)	49.3	(2)
	1994	59.0	(4)	52.0	(2)	55.5	(2)	48.8	(14)	20.1	(3)	35.9	(7)	58.0	(4)	49.4	(1)	53.7	(1)
	2000	53.6	(9)	47.1	(2)	50.4	(3)	49.9	(11)	13.0	(10)	33.5	(9)	53.2	(9)	44.1	(1)	48.7	(2)
	2012	54.1	(12)	52.4	(1)	53.3	(1)	60.0	(3)	21.2	(1)	42.1	(1)	54.7	(11)	49.5	(1)	52.1	(1)
	2018	55.1	(9)	40.0	(1)	47.4	(1)	54.3	(6)	16.9	(4)	37.9	(2)	55.0	(9)	38.0	(1)	46.4	(1)
Jammu & Kashmir	1983	55.2	(8)	28.5	(12)	42.5	(11)	53.8	(4)	10.1	(15)	33.3	(12)	54.9	(6)	24.5	(12)	40.5	(11)
	1994	51.9	(14)	39.1	(9)	45.7	(9)	49.1	(12)	13.0	(13)	32.3	(14)	51.2	(15)	33.0	(8)	42.5	(10)
	2000	54.8	(7)	32.7	(9)	44.2	(9)	47.8	(15)	6.2	(17)	28.9	(16)	53.0	(11)	26.4	(10)	40.4	(10)
	2012	54.7	(11)	25.5	(9)	40.9	(10)	53.9	(12)	11.7	(13)	34.6	(11)	54.5	(12)	21.8	(9)	39.2	(12)
	2018	55.4	(7)	22.9	(6)	39.9	(6)	53.2	(12)	13.9	(9)	34.0	(11)	54.9	(10)	21.0	(6)	38.6	(6)
Karnataka	1983	58.7	(3)	38.6	(8)	48.8	(7)	51.2	(9)	19.5	(3)	36.0	(3)	56.5	(5)	33.1	(7)	45.0	(7)
	1994	60.4	(2)	43.0	(6)	51.8	(4)	54.2	(6)	18.1	(5)	36.8	(4)	58.4	(3)	35.2	(6)	47.0	(4)
	2000	59.5	(2)	38.0	(8)	48.9	(5)	54.5	(5)	17.8	(4)	36.7	(3)	57.8	(3)	31.3	(6)	44.8	(4)
	2012	61.2	(1)	28.7	(7)	45.2	(5)	57.9	(6)	16.3	(7)	37.5	(5)	59.9	(2)	23.9	(7)	42.2	(5)
	2018	58.5	(2)	21.1	(8)	39.8	(7)	54.1	(7)	16.8	(5)	35.4	(6)	56.8	(2)	19.5	(7)	38.1	(7)

(Continued)

Table 49 *(Continued)*

State	Year	Rural						Urban						Rural + Urban					
		Male		Female		Male + Female		Male		Female		Male + Female		Male		Female		Male + Female	
Kerala	1983	48.6	(16)	31.4	(10)	39.9	(12)	50.0	(14)	21.9	(1)	35.8	(4)	48.9	(16)	29.5	(9)	39.0	(12)
	1994	53.7	(12)	23.8	(12)	38.4	(12)	55.9	(2)	20.3	(2)	37.7	(2)	54.3	(10)	22.9	(12)	38.3	(11)
	2000	55.3	(5)	23.8	(12)	39.1	(12)	55.8	(3)	20.3	(2)	37.6	(2)	55.4	(5)	22.9	(12)	38.7	(12)
	2012	56.5	(9)	22.1	(12)	38.6	(13)	55.2	(9)	19.1	(3)	36.3	(10)	55.9	(9)	20.6	(11)	37.5	(13)
	2018	50.9	(13)	16.7	(9)	32.7	(14)	50.0	(14)	16.0	(7)	32.0	(14)	50.5	(13)	16.4	(9)	32.4	(14)
Madhya Pradesh	1983	56.2	(6)	43.3	(6)	49.9	(6)	47.7	(16)	14.5	(8)	32.1	(14)	54.4	(7)	37.5	(5)	46.2	(5)
	1994	57.2	(6)	41.0	(7)	49.3	(7)	47.1	(16)	14.2	(12)	31.5	(15)	54.8	(9)	34.8	(7)	45.1	(7)
	2000	53.6	(8)	38.2	(7)	46.1	(7)	48.8	(13)	13.4	(9)	32.0	(12)	52.4	(13)	32.2	(5)	42.6	(7)
	2012	56.0	(10)	28.8	(6)	42.7	(7)	51.5	(13)	14.4	(9)	33.6	(12)	54.8	(10)	25.0	(6)	40.3	(8)
	2018	56.1	(4)	29.5	(3)	43.4	(3)	53.9	(9)	16.1	(6)	35.3	(7)	55.6	(6)	26.3	(3)	41.5	(3)
Maharashtra	1983	56.1	(7)	47.3	(2)	51.7	(3)	51.3	(8)	15.1	(7)	34.6	(8)	54.3	(8)	36.3	(6)	45.6	(6)
	1994	55.1	(9)	47.7	(4)	51.5	(5)	52.6	(9)	16.9	(6)	35.9	(6)	54.1	(11)	35.9	(5)	45.3	(6)
	2000	53.1	(11)	43.4	(3)	48.3	(6)	53.2	(7)	13.7	(7)	34.8	(7)	53.1	(10)	31.3	(7)	42.7	(6)
	2012	57.6	(7)	38.8	(3)	48.5	(4)	54.9	(10)	16.6	(6)	36.7	(8)	56.4	(8)	28.8	(5)	43.1	(4)
	2018	55.8	(6)	28.9	(5)	42.7	(4)	53.8	(10)	14.9	(8)	34.6	(9)	54.9	(11)	22.8	(5)	39.2	(5)
Odisha	1983	57.5	(5)	29.4	(11)	43.5	(10)	50.2	(11)	11.1	(12)	32.1	(13)	56.6	(4)	27.3	(10)	42.1	(10)
	1994	56.6	(7)	31.7	(10)	44.2	(10)	51.0	(11)	15.1	(9)	34.3	(10)	55.8	(6)	29.5	(10)	42.9	(9)
	2000	55.1	(6)	29.9	(10)	42.6	(10)	47.5	(16)	14.5	(5)	31.9	(13)	53.9	(7)	27.7	(9)	41.0	(9)
	2012	59.2	(5)	24.6	(10)	42.0	(9)	57.9	(5)	15.5	(8)	37.4	(6)	59.0	(5)	23.1	(8)	41.2	(7)
	2018	53.8	(12)	14.4	(12)	34.1	(11)	53.5	(11)	11.7	(12)	32.1	(12)	53.7	(12)	14.0	(12)	33.8	(12)
Punjab	1983	58.1	(4)	31.9	(9)	45.8	(9)	53.8	(3)	12.9	(11)	34.8	(7)	56.9	(3)	26.6	(11)	42.7	(9)
	1994	54.6	(10)	22.0	(13)	39.3	(11)	55.3	(3)	9.3	(15)	34.0	(11)	54.8	(8)	18.1	(14)	37.7	(12)
	2000	53.0	(12)	28.0	(11)	41.2	(11)	54.9	(4)	12.5	(11)	35.4	(5)	53.6	(8)	22.9	(11)	39.3	(11)

(Continued)

Table 49 *(Continued)*

State	Year	Rural						Urban						Rural + Urban					
		Male		Female		Male + Female		Male		Female		Male + Female		Male		Female		Male + Female	
Punjab	2012	56.6	(8)	23.4	(11)	40.8	(11)	57.0	(7)	13.6	(11)	36.8	(7)	56.8	(7)	19.7	(12)	39.3	(11)
	2018	54.3	(11)	9.9	(13)	32.8	(12)	56.3	(5)	12.3	(10)	35.5	(5)	55.1	(7)	10.8	(13)	33.8	(11)
Rajasthan	1983	55.0	(9)	46.6	(4)	51.0	(4)	47.7	(15)	19.5	(4)	34.5	(9)	53.4	(11)	40.9	(2)	47.4	(4)
	1994	54.0	(11)	45.7	(5)	50.0	(6)	49.0	(13)	16.3	(7)	33.7	(12)	52.8	(12)	39.1	(3)	46.3	(5)
	2000	50.0	(14)	38.8	(6)	44.6	(8)	48.6	(14)	13.8	(6)	32.2	(11)	49.7	(14)	33.1	(4)	41.7	(8)
	2012	49.5	(15)	34.7	(5)	42.4	(8)	49.0	(16)	14.1	(10)	32.3	(13)	49.4	(16)	29.6	(3)	39.9	(9)
	2018	48.2	(14)	21.5	(7)	35.2	(10)	49.5	(15)	9.8	(14)	30.7	(15)	48.5	(15)	18.8	(8)	34.2	(10)
Tamil Nadu	1983	59.5	(2)	45.5	(5)	52.6	(2)	54.0	(2)	21.2	(2)	37.9	(1)	57.7	(2)	37.5	(4)	47.7	(3)
	1994	60.2	(3)	47.8	(3)	54.1	(3)	57.5	(1)	23.0	(1)	40.5	(1)	59.2	(2)	38.7	(4)	49.1	(3)
	2000	59.4	(3)	43.0	(4)	51.2	(2)	56.3	(2)	21.5	(1)	39.1	(1)	58.1	(1)	33.9	(3)	46.1	(3)
	2012	59.5	(4)	37.8	(4)	48.7	(3)	58.7	(4)	20.1	(2)	39.4	(3)	59.1	(4)	29.1	(4)	44.2	(3)
	2018	55.9	(5)	29.4	(4)	42.5	(5)	56.7	(3)	20.4	(1)	38.3	(1)	56.3	(3)	25.3	(4)	40.6	(4)
Uttar Pradesh	1983	53.1	(12)	25.7	(13)	39.6	(13)	50.2	(12)	9.6	(16)	31.5	(15)	52.5	(13)	22.8	(14)	38.1	(13)
	1994	52.2	(13)	21.9	(14)	37.9	(13)	48.2	(15)	10.2	(14)	30.6	(16)	51.4	(14)	19.6	(13)	36.4	(15)
	2000	48.1	(16)	20.1	(14)	34.8	(15)	49.0	(12)	9.4	(15)	30.5	(15)	48.3	(17)	17.9	(13)	33.9	(16)
	2012	48.9	(16)	18.3	(14)	34.3	(15)	51.1	(15)	10.1	(14)	31.8	(16)	49.4	(15)	16.4	(14)	33.7	(15)
	2018	47.2	(16)	9.8	(14)	28.8	(16)	48.7	(16)	7.3	(16)	28.9	(16)	47.5	(16)	9.3	(15)	28.8	(16)
West Bengal	1983	53.9	(11)	19.3	(16)	36.7	(15)	54.2	(1)	13.1	(10)	35.6	(5)	54.0	(9)	17.7	(16)	36.4	(15)
	1994	55.7	(8)	18.5	(15)	37.6	(14)	55.0	(4)	14.3	(10)	36.1	(5)	55.5	(7)	17.4	(15)	37.2	(13)
	2000	53.4	(10)	16.0	(16)	35.2	(13)	56.7	(1)	11.7	(12)	35.5	(4)	54.3	(6)	14.8	(16)	35.3	(13)
	2012	58.6	(6)	18.9	(13)	39.3	(12)	60.2	(2)	17.4	(4)	39.4	(2)	59.1	(3)	18.4	(13)	39.3	(10)
	2018	59.0	(1)	15.2	(11)	37.4	(8)	56.3	(4)	17.4	(3)	37.0	(3)	58.2	(1)	15.9	(10)	37.3	(8)

Source: Same as Table 33

Note: The figures in parentheses are ranks among seventeen major states.

4.8.2 Overall Performance of States Regarding Workforce Participation Rates

We calculated the mean of the ranks of the states in various years based on their workforce participation rates. We again ranked the states to determine their overall performance in workforce participation rates from 1983 to 2018. We have also examined whether there has been a change in the ranking patterns of states over time regarding WPR by conducting Kendall's concordance test. The results of these are presented in Table 50.

It is clear that, as regards the WPR of rural males, considering the entire period of our study, the best performer has been Andhra Pradesh. The next five states to follow in this regard are Karnataka, Tamil Nadu, Gujarat, Madhya Pradesh and Odisha. The worst performers in this regard have been Haryana, followed by Bihar, Uttar Pradesh, Assam, Rajasthan, and Kerala. The remaining five states (West Bengal, Maharashtra, Punjab, Himachal Pradesh, and Jammu & Kashmir) ranked as medium performers in the WPR from 1983 to 2018.

As regards the WPR of rural females, Himachal Pradesh has been the best performer, followed by Andhra Pradesh, Madhya Pradesh, Tamil Nadu, Rajasthan, and Maharashtra. Assam is the worst-performing state; other poor-performing states include Bihar, West Bengal, Uttar Pradesh, Haryana, Punjab, and Kerala. The remaining states fell into the middle category.

When considering males and females together in rural areas from 1983 to 2018, Andhra Pradesh stands out as the top performer in WPR, followed by Himachal Pradesh, Tamil Nadu, Madhya Pradesh, Karnataka, and Maharashtra. Conversely, the states that performed relatively poorly in WPR for rural persons include Bihar (the worst performer), Assam, Haryana, Uttar Pradesh, Kerala, and West Bengal. States categorised between these groups include Gujarat, Rajasthan, Jammu and Kashmir, Odisha, and Punjab.

In urban areas, Tamil Nadu leads the list of states in WPR for males, females, and persons, while Bihar ranks last. Other states that perform better in terms of the WPR of urban males include West Bengal, Punjab, Gujarat, Karnataka, and Andhra Pradesh. Besides Tamil Nadu, the WPR of urban females is notable in Kerala, Andhra Pradesh, Himachal Pradesh, Karnataka, and Madhya Pradesh. For urban persons, the states following Tamil Nadu are West Bengal, Himachal Pradesh, Karnataka, Andhra Pradesh, and Kerala.

Table 50. Mean of Ranks of the States in terms of WPR and Kendall's Coefficients of Concordance (W)

State	Rural						Urban						Rural + Urban					
	Male		Female		Male + Female		Male		Female		Male + Female		Male		Female		Male + Female	
Andhra Pradesh	1.6	(1)	1.8	(2)	1.4	(1)	8.0	(6)	3.8	(3)	6.0	(5)	2.8	(2)	2.2	(2)	1.6	(2)
Assam	13.2	(14)	16.6	(17)	15.8	(16)	8.2	(8)	15.0	(15)	12.6	(14)	12.2	(13)	16.6	(17)	15.2	(16)
Bihar	15.8	(16)	15.8	(16)	16.2	(17)	17.0	(17)	16.2	(17)	17.0	(17)	16.0	(17)	15.6	(16)	16.4	(17)
Gujarat	6.0	(4)	7.6	(8)	7.0	(7)	4.6	(4)	10.2	(11)	7.6	(8)	5.0	(4)	9.2	(9)	7.2	(7)
Haryana	16.0	(17)	13.8	(13)	14.8	(15)	10.4	(11)	13.0	(13)	12.0	(11)	15.4	(16)	13.8	(13)	14.8	(14)
Himachal Pradesh	9.4	(10)	1.4	(1)	2.4	(2)	8.0	(7)	4.8	(4)	4.2	(3)	9.0	(8)	1.0	(1)	1.4	(1)
Jammu & Kashmir	9.4	(11)	9.0	(9)	9.0	(9)	11.0	(13)	13.4	(14)	12.8	(15)	10.8	(12)	9.0	(8)	9.8	(10)
Karnataka	2.0	(2)	7.4	(7)	5.6	(5)	6.6	(5)	4.8	(5)	4.2	(4)	3.0	(3)	6.6	(7)	5.4	(4)
Kerala	11.0	(12)	11.0	(11)	12.6	(13)	8.4	(9)	3.0	(2)	6.4	(6)	10.6	(11)	10.6	(11)	12.4	(13)
Maharashtra	8.0	(8)	5.8	(6)	6.0	(6)	13.4	(14)	8.8	(9)	12.0	(12)	9.0	(9)	5.2	(5)	6.0	(6)
Madhya Pradesh	6.8	(5)	3.4	(3)	4.4	(4)	8.8	(10)	6.8	(6)	7.6	(9)	9.6	(10)	5.6	(6)	5.4	(5)
Odisha	7.0	(6)	10.6	(10)	10.0	(10)	10.8	(12)	9.2	(10)	10.8	(10)	6.8	(7)	9.8	(10)	9.4	(9)
Punjab	9.0	(9)	11.4	(12)	10.8	(11)	4.4	(3)	11.6	(12)	7.0	(7)	6.6	(6)	12.2	(12)	10.8	(11)
Rajasthan	12.6	13	5.4	(5)	7.2	(8)	14.6	(16)	8.2	(8)	12.0	(13)	13.6	(14)	4.0	(4)	7.2	(8)
Tamil Nadu	3.4	(3)	4.0	(4)	3.0	(3)	2.4	(1)	1.4	(1)	1.4	(1)	2.4	(1)	3.8	(3)	3.2	(3)
Uttar Pradesh	14.6	(15)	13.8	(14)	14.4	(14)	14.0	(15)	15.0	(16)	15.6	(16)	15.0	(15)	13.8	(14)	15.0	(15)
West Bengal	7.2	(7)	14.2	(15)	12.4	(12)	2.4	(2)	7.8	(7)	3.8	(2)	5.2	(5)	14.0	(15)	11.8	(12)
Kendall's W	0.78		0.94		0.92		0.70		0.81		0.78		0.79		0.93		0.92	
Chi-Square	62.49		75.12		73.71		55.95		64.80		62.70		63.25		74.49		73.30	
Degrees of freedom	16		16		16		16		16		16		16		16		16	
Asymp. Sig.	0.00		0.00		0.00		0.00		0.00		0.00		0.00		0.00		0.00	

Source: Author's computation using information presented in Table 49

Note: The figures in parentheses are ranks among 17 major states on the basis of mean of of ranks for five time points.

When considering both rural and urban areas, the states performing relatively well in male WPR from 1983 to 2018 are Tamil Nadu (the top performer), Andhra Pradesh, Karnataka, Gujarat, West Bengal, and Punjab. Conversely, the states that have performed relatively poorly in this regard are Bihar (the worst performer), Haryana, Uttar Pradesh, Rajasthan, Assam, and Jammu & Kashmir. Regarding the female WPR, when rural and urban areas are combined, Himachal Pradesh leads the list, followed by Andhra Pradesh, Tamil Nadu, Rajasthan, Maharashtra, and Madhya Pradesh. The states that perform relatively poorly in terms of female WPR are Assam, Bihar, West Bengal, Uttar Pradesh, Haryana, and Punjab. When considering both males and females together across all areas (rural and urban), it is found that during the period 1983–2018, the state with the highest WPR value has been Himachal Pradesh, followed by Andhra Pradesh, Tamil Nadu, Karnataka, Madhya Pradesh, and Maharashtra. The states that have lagged in this regard are Bihar (the worst performer), Assam, Uttar Pradesh, Haryana, Kerala, and West Bengal. The five states that fall between these groups are Gujarat, Rajasthan, Odisha, Jammu & Kashmir, and Punjab.

Table 50 also presents the results of the Kendall's concordance test. Here, our null hypothesis is that 'the ranks of the states at five different points in time do not indicate a significant level of agreement.' It is found that for males, females, and persons in rural, urban, and combined areas, the null hypothesis is rejected at the 1 % level of significance. This implies that the ranking pattern of states on the WPR did not change significantly between 1983 and 2018. Consequently, the states of India that exhibited relatively higher values of WPR in the early 1980s (e.g. Himachal Pradesh, Andhra Pradesh, Tamil Nadu, Karnataka, Madhya Pradesh, etc.) have continued, more or less, to do so over the next three and a half decades. Similarly, the states lagging in this regard (e.g. Bihar, Assam, Uttar Pradesh, Haryana, Kerala, West Bengal, etc.) have not attained any significant gain in their ranks over time concerning the WPR value, which is why the computed values of Kendall's 'W' and 'Chi-square' turned out to be statistically significant. This conclusion applies to all worker categories (male, female, and persons) in both rural and urban areas.

4.8.3 Growth of the Workforce in the States

In Table 51, we present the annual growth rates of employed in seventeen major states of India for five different periods: 1983–1994, 1994–2000, 2000–2012, 2012–2018, and 1994–2018. The growth rates have been calculated separately for males, females, and persons in rural, urban, and all areas (rural plus urban).

4.8.3.1 Period: 1983 to 1994 (Pre-Globalisation)

It appears from Table 51 that, among the seventeen major states of India, the growth rate of employed rural males during this period has been highest in Uttar Pradesh and lowest in Tamil Nadu. Other states that ranked high in rural male employment growth include Himachal Pradesh, West Bengal, Bihar, Madhya Pradesh, and Rajasthan. In this regard, the states that ranked low (following Tamil Nadu) are Punjab, Kerala, Odisha, Maharashtra, and Jammu & Kashmir. The remaining five states (Assam, Haryana, Andhra Pradesh, Gujarat, and Karnataka) are situated between these two groups. Regarding rural females, it is found that Jammu & Kashmir tops the list of states, followed by Assam, Haryana, Himachal Pradesh, Andhra Pradesh, and Karnataka. Conversely, the growth rate of employed rural females has been the lowest in Kerala during this period. The other states with low rankings are Punjab, Bihar, Uttar Pradesh, Gujarat, and Tamil Nadu. When considering rural persons, it is evident that while Jammu & Kashmir leads the list, Punjab remains at the bottom. The states enjoying relatively higher ranks are Himachal Pradesh, Assam, Haryana, West Bengal, and Andhra Pradesh. In contrast, those with relatively low growth rates in the employed rural population are Kerala, Tamil Nadu, Bihar, Gujarat, and Maharashtra.

In urban areas, concerning the growth rate of employed males, Kerala topped the list of states, followed by Andhra Pradesh, Assam, Haryana, Rajasthan, and Maharashtra. The state with the lowest rank in this regard is Bihar. Other states performing relatively poorly in terms of growth in employed urban males include Himachal Pradesh, West Bengal, Uttar Pradesh, Jammu & Kashmir, and Tamil Nadu. Regarding the employment growth rate among urban females, Haryana leads the list, while Bihar ranks last. Other states that perform better regarding urban females' employment growth rate are Jammu & Kashmir, Odisha, Assam, Himachal Pradesh, and Maharashtra. Aside from Bihar, Punjab, Rajasthan, Karnataka, Kerala, and Tamil Nadu have shown poor performance in urban female employment growth. Concerning urban persons, Kerala ranks first, while Bihar ranks last in terms of the employment growth rate during this period. Other better-performing states in terms of growth in employed urban residents are Haryana, Assam, Andhra Pradesh, Odisha, and Maharashtra. Conversely, the states performing poorly in this regard (after Bihar) are Punjab, West Bengal, Himachal Pradesh, Karnataka, and Uttar Pradesh.

Table 51: Annual Growth Rates of Workforce/Employed (UPSS) in Major States of India

State	Period	Rural			Urban			Rural + Urban		
		Male	Female	Male + Female	Male	Female	Male + Female	Male	Female	Male + Female
Andhra Pradesh	1983 to 1994	2.0 (9)	2.6 (5)	2.2 (6)	3.6 (2)	4.1 (7)	3.7 (4)	2.4 (8)	2.7 (4)	2.5 (5)
	1994 to 2000	0.5 (15)	−0.1 (9)	0.2 (14)	0.3 (17)	−0.5 (12)	0.1 (17)	0.5 (16)	−0.2 (9)	0.2 (15)
	2000 to 2012	0.2 (16)	−0.2 (5)	0.0 (15)	3.7 (6)	2.8 (12)	3.5 (7)	1.2 (15)	0.2 (9)	0.8 (15)
	2012 to 2018	−0.8 (16)	−3.6 (7)	−2.0 (13)	2.6 (7)	5.9 (4)	3.4 (4)	0.3 (15)	−1.6 (6)	−0.4 (10)
	1994 to 2018	0.0 (15)	−1.1 (6)	−0.4 (15)	2.6 (13)	2.7 (7)	2.6 (8)	0.8 (16)	−0.4 (7)	0.3 (16)
Assam	1983 to 1994	2.2 (7)	4.3 (2)	2.6 (3)	3.6 (3)	5.3 (4)	3.8 (3)	2.3 (9)	4.3 (2)	2.7 (3)
	1994 to 2000	1.9 (3)	0.7 (6)	1.7 (5)	2.7 (10)	6.9 (2)	3.3 (2)	2.0 (4)	1.2 (4)	1.9 (4)
	2000 to 2012	1.5 (9)	−0.3 (6)	1.2 (6)	2.7 (14)	1.1 (15)	2.4 (16)	1.7 (12)	−0.1 (10)	1.3 (10)
	2012 to 2018	1.6 (4)	−5.1 (9)	1.0 (4)	3.2 (4)	6.3 (1)	3.7 (3)	1.8 (4)	−3.8 (10)	1.4 (4)
	1994 to 2018	1.7 (2)	−1.3 (8)	1.3 (2)	2.8 (6)	3.8 (3)	3.0 (6)	1.8 (5)	−0.7 (10)	1.5 (3)
Bihar	1983 to 1994	2.4 (4)	−1.5 (15)	1.3 (14)	1.9 (17)	−1.3 (17)	1.5 (17)	2.3 (10)	−1.5 (16)	1.3 (15)
	1994 to 2000	1.7 (5)	2.6 (2)	1.9 (4)	2.2 (14)	4.2 (3)	2.4 (10)	1.7 (6)	2.7 (2)	2.0 (3)
	2000 to 2012	2.0 (3)	−3.8 (16)	0.9 (11)	3.0 (8)	0.3 (17)	2.7 (13)	2.2 (5)	−3.5 (17)	1.1 (13)
	2012 to 2018	0.1 (9)	−8.9 (16)	−0.7 (6)	2.1 (9)	6.2 (3)	2.5 (8)	0.4 (14)	−7.1 (15)	−0.3 (9)
	1994 to 2018	1.5 (5)	−3.6 (17)	0.8 (5)	2.6 (12)	2.7 (8)	2.6 (10)	1.6 (8)	−2.9 (17)	1.0 (10)
Gujarat	1983 to 1994	1.9 (10)	1.1 (13)	1.6 (13)	3.3 (8)	3.7 (9)	3.4 (7)	2.4 (7)	1.4 (13)	2.1 (12)
	1994 to 2000	1.9 (4)	2.3 (3)	2.1 (1)	3.0 (9)	1.8 (8)	2.8 (6)	2.3 (3)	2.2 (3)	2.3 (2)
	2000 to 2012	1.2 (12)	−2.3 (14)	−0.1 (16)	4.1 (2)	3.0 (10)	3.9 (3)	2.3 (3)	−1.3 (15)	1.3 (11)
	2012 to 2018	−0.5 (14)	−7.5 (14)	−2.1 (14)	2.1 (10)	1.6 (12)	1.6 (13)	0.6 (12)	−4.6 (12)	−0.5 (11)
	1994 to 2018	0.9 (12)	−2.5 (14)	−0.1 (13)	3.3 (4)	2.3 (11)	3.1 (5)	1.9 (4)	−1.2 (14)	1.1 (6)

(Continued)

Table 51 *(Continued)*

State	Period	Rural						Urban						Rural + Urban					
		Male		Female		Male + Female		Male		Female		Male + Female		Male		Female		Male + Female	
Haryana	1983 to 1994	2.1	(8)	3.5	(3)	2.5	(4)	3.5	(4)	7.2	(1)	4.1	(2)	2.4	(5)	4.0	(3)	2.9	(2)
	1994 to 2000	2.3	(2)	−3.0	(17)	0.7	(7)	3.9	(1)	−3.3	(15)	2.6	(7)	2.8	(2)	−3.0	(17)	1.2	(6)
	2000 to 2012	1.7	(6)	−0.7	(12)	1.2	(7)	3.8	(5)	3.8	(5)	3.8	(5)	2.4	(2)	0.2	(8)	1.9	(3)
	2012 to 2018	−0.5	(13)	−7.3	(11)	−1.8	(12)	3.9	(2)	3.1	(9)	3.8	(2)	1.0	(8)	−4.3	(11)	0.1	(6)
	1994 to 2018	1.3	(6)	−3.0	(15)	0.3	(10)	3.8	(2)	1.8	(13)	3.5	(2)	2.2	(2)	−1.7	(16)	1.3	(5)
Himachal Pradesh	1983 to 1994	2.8	(2)	2.6	(4)	2.7	(2)	2.2	(16)	4.9	(5)	2.8	(14)	2.7	(2)	2.6	(5)	2.7	(4)
	1994 to 2000	−0.1	(16)	−0.2	(10)	−0.1	(16)	3.4	(2)	−4.6	(16)	1.7	(12)	0.2	(17)	−0.3	(11)	0.0	(17)
	2000 to 2012	1.3	(10)	2.1	(2)	1.7	(2)	2.9	(10)	6.2	(3)	3.6	(6)	1.5	(14)	2.2	(2)	1.8	(5)
	2012 to 2018	1.5	(5)	−3.3	(5)	−0.8	(7)	−0.5	(17)	−2.0	(14)	−0.3	(17)	1.3	(6)	−3.1	(9)	−0.7	(13)
	1994 to 2018	1.0	(10)	0.2	(3)	0.6	(7)	2.2	(17)	1.3	(16)	2.1	(17)	1.1	(15)	0.2	(4)	0.7	(12)
Jammu & Kashmir	1983 to 1994	1.6	(12)	5.6	(1)	3.0	(1)	2.8	(13)	6.2	(2)	3.3	(8)	1.8	(14)	5.6	(1)	3.1	(1)
	1994 to 2000	3.5	(1)	−0.5	(13)	2.0	(3)	3.1	(8)	−9.2	(17)	1.3	(15)	3.4	(1)	−1.2	(16)	1.8	(5)
	2000 to 2012	2.1	(1)	−0.3	(7)	1.3	(5)	4.1	(3)	8.8	(1)	4.7	(2)	2.6	(1)	0.5	(5)	2.0	(2)
	2012 to 2018	2.1	(1)	−0.1	(3)	1.4	(2)	2.8	(5)	6.2	(2)	2.8	(6)	2.4	(1)	1.4	(2)	1.9	(2)
	1994 to 2018	2.4	(1)	−0.3	(4)	1.5	(1)	3.5	(3)	3.4	(5)	3.4	(3)	2.7	(1)	0.3	(3)	1.9	(1)
Karnataka	1983 to 1994	1.8	(11)	2.5	(6)	2.1	(9)	3.1	(9)	1.9	(14)	2.8	(13)	2.2	(13)	2.4	(7)	2.3	(8)
	1994 to 2000	0.9	(8)	−0.9	(15)	0.2	(15)	2.6	(11)	2.3	(5)	2.5	(8)	1.4	(9)	−0.3	(13)	0.8	(11)
	2000 to 2012	1.0	(13)	−1.5	(13)	0.1	(13)	3.2	(7)	2.1	(14)	2.9	(11)	1.8	(10)	−0.7	(14)	1.0	(14)
	2012 to 2018	0.0	(10)	−4.3	(8)	−1.4	(10)	1.5	(14)	3.4	(8)	1.8	(10)	0.6	(13)	−1.9	(7)	−0.2	(8)
	1994 to 2018	0.7	(14)	−2.1	(11)	−0.2	(14)	2.6	(9)	2.5	(9)	2.5	(11)	1.4	(12)	−0.9	(12)	0.6	(13)

(Continued)

Table 51 *(Continued)*

State	Period	Rural						Urban						Rural + Urban					
		Male		Female		Male + Female		Male		Female		Male + Female		Male		Female		Male + Female	
Kerala	1983 to 1994	1.4	(15)	−2.1	(17)	0.2	(16)	4.8	(1)	3.1	(13)	4.3	(1)	2.2	(12)	−1.1	(15)	1.1	(16)
	1994 to 2000	1.4	(6)	1.1	(4)	1.3	(6)	0.6	(16)	0.9	(10)	0.7	(16)	1.1	(12)	1.0	(5)	1.1	(7)
	2000 to 2012	−2.5	(17)	−3.1	(15)	−2.7	(17)	5.9	(1)	5.8	(4)	5.9	(1)	0.5	(17)	−0.2	(13)	0.3	(16)
	2012 to 2018	−4.7	(17)	−7.4	(12)	−5.6	(17)	4.9	(1)	3.8	(7)	4.5	(1)	−0.3	(17)	−2.2	(8)	−0.9	(15)
	1994 to 2018	−2.1	(17)	−3.2	(16)	−2.5	(17)	4.3	(1)	4.1	(1)	4.2	(1)	0.5	(17)	−0.4	(8)	0.2	(17)
Madhya Pradesh	1983 to 1994	2.2	(5)	1.4	(11)	1.9	(10)	3.3	(7)	3.4	(11)	3.3	(9)	2.4	(6)	1.6	(12)	2.1	(11)
	1994 to 2000	0.7	(12)	0.7	(7)	0.7	(9)	3.4	(3)	1.9	(7)	3.1	(3)	1.3	(10)	0.8	(7)	1.1	(8)
	2000 to 2012	2.1	(2)	−0.6	(11)	1.1	(8)	2.9	(11)	3.3	(7)	3.0	(10)	2.3	(4)	−0.1	(11)	1.5	(7)
	2012 to 2018	1.7	(3)	2.1	(1)	2.0	(1)	3.3	(3)	4.6	(5)	3.4	(5)	2.1	(2)	2.9	(1)	2.4	(1)
	1994 to 2018	1.6	(3)	0.4	(1)	1.2	(3)	3.1	(5)	3.3	(6)	3.1	(4)	2.0	(3)	0.8	(2)	1.6	(2)
Maharashtra	1983 to 1994	1.5	(13)	1.6	(9)	1.6	(12)	3.4	(6)	4.5	(6)	3.6	(6)	2.2	(11)	2.1	(8)	2.2	(10)
	1994 to 2000	0.9	(9)	−0.2	(12)	0.4	(13)	3.2	(5)	−0.6	(13)	2.4	(9)	1.8	(5)	−0.3	(12)	1.0	(10)
	2000 to 2012	0.5	(15)	−3.9	(17)	−1.1	(7)	1.6	(17)	0.5	(16)	1.1	(17)	1.0	(16)	−2.3	(16)	−0.1	(17)
	2012 to 2018	1.8	(2)	0.0	(2)	1.1	(3)	2.4	(8)	4.0	(6)	2.7	(7)	2.1	(3)	0.9	(3)	1.7	(3)
	1994 to 2018	1.2	(8)	−1.0	(5)	0.3	(9)	2.4	(15)	2.0	(12)	2.2	(14)	1.7	(6)	−0.2	(5)	1.1	(7)
Odisha	1983 to 1994	1.5	(14)	2.3	(7)	1.7	(11)	3.1	(10)	6.1	(3)	3.6	(5)	1.7	(15)	2.5	(6)	1.9	(13)
	1994 to 2000	0.9	(10)	0.3	(8)	0.7	(10)	1.3	(15)	2.1	(6)	1.5	(14)	0.9	(14)	0.4	(8)	0.8	(14)
	2000 to 2012	1.8	(5)	−0.5	(8)	1.0	(10)	4.0	(4)	3.3	(9)	3.8	(4)	2.1	(6)	−0.1	(12)	1.4	(8)
	2012 to 2018	−0.5	(15)	−7.5	(13)	−2.4	(15)	0.8	(16)	−2.1	(15)	−0.1	(16)	−0.3	(16)	−6.7	(14)	−2.0	(17)
	1994 to 2018	1.0	(11)	−2.1	(12)	0.1	(12)	2.5	(14)	1.6	(14)	2.2	(16)	1.2	(13)	−1.7	(15)	0.4	(15)
Punjab	1983 to 1994	0.9	(16)	−2.0	(16)	0.0	(17)	3.0	(11)	−0.4	(16)	2.5	(16)	1.5	(17)	−1.8	(17)	0.7	(17)
	1994 to 2000	0.7	(13)	5.3	(1)	2.0	(2)	3.2	(4)	8.3	(1)	3.9	(1)	1.5	(7)	5.8	(1)	2.6	(1)

(Continued)

Table 51 *(Continued)*

State	Period	Rural			Urban			Rural + Urban		
		Male	Female	Male + Female	Male	Female	Male + Female	Male	Female	Male + Female
Punjab	2000 to 2012	1.3 (11)	−0.6 (10)	0.7 (12)	2.6 (15)	3.3 (8)	2.7 (12)	1.8 (11)	0.2 (7)	1.4 (9)
	2012 to 2018	0.0 (11)	−12.6 (17)	−2.9 (16)	2.0 (11)	0.7 (13)	1.7 (11)	0.7 (10)	−8.2 (17)	−1.2 (16)
	1994 to 2018	0.8 (13)	−2.3 (13)	0.1 (11)	2.6 (10)	3.9 (2)	2.8 (7)	1.4 (11)	−0.6 (9)	1.0 (8)
Rajasthan	1983 to 1994	2.2 (6)	2.1 (8)	2.2 (7)	3.5 (5)	1.5 (15)	3.0 (10)	2.4 (4)	2.1 (9)	2.3 (7)
	1994 to 2000	1.1 (7)	−0.2 (11)	0.5 (11)	2.6 (12)	0.0 (11)	2.0 (11)	1.4 (8)	−0.2 (10)	0.8 (12)
	2000 to 2012	1.7 (7)	0.9 (4)	1.4 (4)	2.6 (16)	2.9 (11)	2.7 (15)	1.9 (9)	1.1 (4)	1.6 (6)
	2012 to 2018	1.3 (6)	−6.1 (10)	−1.3 (9)	2.7 (6)	−3.4 (17)	1.7 (12)	1.6 (5)	−5.4 (13)	−0.6 (12)
	1994 to 2018	1.5 (4)	−1.2 (7)	0.5 (8)	2.6 (11)	0.6 (17)	2.2 (15)	1.7 (7)	−0.9 (11)	0.9 (11)
Tamil Nadu	1983 to 1994	0.9 (17)	1.2 (12)	1.0 (15)	2.9 (12)	3.1 (12)	2.9 (11)	1.6 (16)	1.6 (11)	1.6 (14)
	1994 to 2000	−0.8 (17)	−2.2 (16)	−1.4 (17)	3.2 (6)	2.6 (4)	3.0 (4)	0.7 (15)	−1.1 (15)	0.0 (16)
	2000 to 2012	0.5 (14)	−0.5 (9)	0.1 (14)	2.9 (12)	2.1 (13)	2.7 (14)	1.6 (13)	0.3 (6)	1.1 (12)
	2012 to 2018	−0.4 (12)	−3.5 (6)	−1.6 (11)	1.7 (13)	2.8 (11)	2.0 (9)	0.6 (11)	−0.9 (4)	0.1 (7)
	1994 to 2018	0.0 (16)	−1.7 (10)	−0.7 (16)	2.7 (8)	2.4 (10)	2.6 (9)	1.1 (14)	−0.4 (6)	0.6 (14)
Uttar Pradesh	1983 to 1994	2.8 (1)	0.5 (14)	2.1 (8)	2.7 (14)	3.9 (8)	2.9 (12)	2.8 (1)	0.8 (14)	2.2 (9)
	1994 to 2000	0.6 (14)	0.8 (5)	0.7 (8)	3.1 (7)	1.6 (9)	2.9 (5)	1.1 (13)	0.9 (6)	1.1 (9)
	2000 to 2012	1.8 (4)	1.0 (3)	1.6 (3)	2.9 (9)	3.3 (6)	3.0 (9)	2.0 (7)	1.2 (3)	1.8 (4)
	2012 to 2018	1.0 (7)	−8.4 (15)	−1.3 (8)	1.7 (12)	−2.6 (16)	1.0 (15)	1.1 (7)	−7.4 (16)	−0.8 (14)
	1994 to 2018	1.3 (7)	−1.5 (9)	0.6 (6)	2.7 (7)	1.4 (15)	2.5 (13)	1.6 (9)	−1.1 (13)	1.0 (9)
West Bengal	1983 to 1994	2.7 (3)	1.5 (10)	2.4 (5)	2.4 (15)	3.5 (10)	2.6 (15)	2.6 (3)	1.9 (10)	2.4 (6)
	1994 to 2000	0.8 (11)	−0.8 (14)	0.4 (12)	2.2 (13)	−1.3 (14)	1.6 (13)	1.2 (11)	−0.9 (14)	0.8 (13)
	2000 to 2012	1.6 (8)	2.2 (1)	1.8 (1)	2.8 (13)	6.3 (2)	3.4 (8)	2.0 (8)	3.3 (1)	2.3 (1)
	2012 to 2018	0.9 (8)	−2.9 (4)	−0.1 (5)	1.3 (15)	2.9 (10)	1.6 (14)	1.0 (9)	−1.1 (5)	0.5 (5)
	1994 to 2018	1.2 (9)	0.2 (2)	1.0 (4)	2.3 (16)	3.5 (4)	2.5 (12)	1.5 (10)	1.1 (1)	1.4 (4)

Source: Same as Table 33

Note: The figures in parentheses are ranks among seventeen major states.

When considering both rural and urban areas combined, Uttar Pradesh is the top performer in terms of growth in employed males, while Punjab ranks lowest. Regarding the growth of employed females, Jammu & Kashmir and Punjab are the best and worst performers, respectively. Jammu & Kashmir continues to hold its position, and Punjab remains the lowest performer in terms of growth in employed persons across all areas (rural and urban). Other states (apart from Uttar Pradesh) that perform relatively better in male employment growth across combined areas include Himachal Pradesh, West Bengal, Rajasthan, Haryana, and Madhya Pradesh. Regarding female employment growth, the better performers (besides Jammu & Kashmir) are Assam, Haryana, Andhra Pradesh, Himachal Pradesh, and Odisha. As for overall employment growth among persons (apart from Jammu & Kashmir), the better performers are Haryana, Assam, Himachal Pradesh, Andhra Pradesh, and West Bengal.

4.8.3.2 Period: 1994 to 2000

This is the first sub-period of the post-globalisation era. During this sub-period, the growth rates of employed males, females, and persons in rural areas have been highest in Jammu & Kashmir, Punjab, and Gujarat, respectively. Conversely, the lowest growth rates have been observed in Tamil Nadu (for rural males and females) and Haryana (for rural females). Other states performing relatively better in employment growth for rural males during this sub-period include Haryana, Assam, Gujarat, Bihar, and Kerala. For rural females, the states with stronger performance are Bihar, Gujarat, Kerala, Uttar Pradesh, and Assam. Regarding rural persons, the better-performing states are Punjab, Jammu & Kashmir, Bihar, Assam, and Kerala. Additionally, some states with weaker performance in terms of employment growth are Himachal Pradesh, Andhra Pradesh, Uttar Pradesh, Punjab, and Madhya Pradesh (for rural males); Tamil Nadu, Karnataka, West Bengal, Jammu & Kashmir, and Maharashtra (for rural females, all experienced negative growth rate); and Himachal Pradesh, Karnataka, Andhra Pradesh, Maharashtra, and West Bengal (for rural persons).

In urban areas, the growth rate of employed males during this period has been highest in Haryana and lowest in Andhra Pradesh. Other states performing well in this regard include Himachal Pradesh, Madhya Pradesh, Punjab, Maharashtra, and Tamil Nadu; conversely, states with poorer performance are Kerala, Odisha, Bihar, West Bengal, and Rajasthan. When considering urban females, the best-performing and worst-performing states are Punjab and Jammu & Kashmir, respectively. Additionally, noticeable performers regarding the growth of urban female employment include Assam, Bihar, Tamil Nadu, Karnataka, and Odisha. At the same time, states with poorer outcomes are Himachal Pradesh, Haryana,

West Bengal, Maharashtra, and Andhra Pradesh. Regarding employment growth for urban persons during this period, Punjab holds the top position, while Andhra Pradesh remains at the bottom. States such as Assam, Madhya Pradesh, Tamil Nadu, Uttar Pradesh, and Gujarat demonstrate relatively better employment growth for urban individuals, while Kerala, Jammu & Kashmir, Odisha, West Bengal, and Himachal Pradesh are among the poorer performers in this respect.

When we consider rural and urban areas together, the growth rate of employed males has been highest in Jammu & Kashmir and lowest in Himachal Pradesh. Other states that have performed relatively well in terms of growth in employed males across all areas (rural plus urban) include Haryana, Gujarat, Assam, Maharashtra, and Bihar. In contrast, lower-performing states in this regard include Andhra Pradesh, Tamil Nadu, Odisha, Uttar Pradesh, and Kerala. Regarding the growth of employed females in combined areas, Punjab has been the top performer, while Haryana has been the lowest performer. Other states that showed relatively better performance in terms of the growth of employed females include Bihar, Gujarat, Assam, Kerala, and Uttar Pradesh; conversely, states that performed relatively poorly include Jammu & Kashmir, Tamil Nadu, West Bengal, Karnataka, and Maharashtra. The growth rate of employed individuals in combined areas has been highest during this period in Punjab and lowest in Himachal Pradesh. Additionally, states demonstrating relatively better performance in terms of growth in employed persons include Gujarat, Bihar, Assam, Jammu & Kashmir, and Haryana. In contrast, others that performed poorly in this regard include Tamil Nadu, Andhra Pradesh, Odisha, West Bengal, and Rajasthan.

4.8.3.3 Period: 2000 to 2012

During this period, rural males in Jammu & Kashmir recorded the highest employment growth rate, while those in Kerala exhibited the lowest. Other states that performed relatively better in terms of employment growth among rural males include Madhya Pradesh, Bihar, Uttar Pradesh, Odisha, and Haryana. In addition to Kerala, the states that performed poorly in this regard were Andhra Pradesh, Maharashtra, Tamil Nadu, Karnataka, and Gujarat. Regarding rural females, the employment growth rate is highest in West Bengal and lowest in Maharashtra. Other states demonstrating relatively better performance in employment growth among rural females are Himachal Pradesh, Uttar Pradesh, and Rajasthan (the rest of the states show negative growth rates). Conversely, the poorly performing states in this aspect (apart from Maharashtra) include Bihar, Kerala, Gujarat, Karnataka, Haryana, and Madhya Pradesh. Considering rural persons, it is observed that West Bengal topped the list of states for employment growth during this period, with Kerala ranking last. Besides West Bengal, other states showing relatively better performance in employment growth are Himachal Pradesh, Uttar Pradesh, Rajasthan, Jammu & Kashmir, and Assam. In contrast, the relatively poor-performing states (apart from Kerala) are Gujarat, Andhra Pradesh, Tamil Nadu, Karnataka, and Punjab.

The employment growth pattern in urban areas of the states varies significantly. While Kerala ranks first among the states in terms of growth for employed urban males, Maharashtra ranks last. Other states that performed better include Gujarat, Jammu & Kashmir, Odisha, Haryana, and Andhra Pradesh. Apart from Maharashtra, Rajasthan, Punjab, Assam, West Bengal, and Tamil Nadu also showed relatively poor performance. Regarding urban females, Jammu & Kashmir occupies the top position in terms of the growth of employed persons, followed by West Bengal, Himachal Pradesh, Kerala, Haryana, and Uttar Pradesh. The lowest growth is recorded in Bihar, with other underperforming states being Maharashtra, Assam, Karnataka, Tamil Nadu, and Andhra Pradesh. For urban persons, the employment growth rate during this period is highest in Kerala and lowest in Maharashtra. Other states demonstrating relatively better performance include Jammu & Kashmir, Gujarat, Odisha, Haryana, and Himachal Pradesh; conversely, the lower-performing states are Assam, Rajasthan, Tamil Nadu, Bihar and Punjab.

When we consider the rural and urban areas together, it appears that, for males, the growth rate of employment has been highest during this period in Jammu & Kashmir, with some other states, such as Haryana, Gujarat, Madhya Pradesh, Bihar, and Odisha, also displaying relatively better performance in this regard. Kerala is the state with the lowest growth rate of employment among males; other states that display relatively low performance include Maharashtra, Andhra Pradesh, Himachal Pradesh, Tamil Nadu, and Assam. While West Bengal has been the best performer for females in combined areas (rural plus urban), Himachal Pradesh, Uttar Pradesh, Rajasthan, Jammu & Kashmir, and Tamil Nadu follow it. The state with the lowest growth in the number of employed females is Bihar. Other states with low growth in the number of employed females include Maharashtra, Gujarat, Karnataka, Kerala, and Odisha. Considering the combined areas for males and females, it is found that the state that performed best regarding the growth rate of employment during 2000–2012 is West Bengal, followed by Jammu & Kashmir, Haryana, Uttar Pradesh, Himachal Pradesh, and Rajasthan. On the other hand, the lowest employment growth rates are recorded for males and females in Maharashtra; other low-performing states include Kerala, Andhra Pradesh, Karnataka, Bihar, and Tamil Nadu.

4.8.3.4 Period: 2012 to 2018

In the final sub-period of the post-globalisation phase of our current discussion, the employment growth rate for rural males is highest in Jammu & Kashmir, followed by Maharashtra, Madhya Pradesh, Assam, Himachal Pradesh, and Rajasthan. Conversely, it is lowest in Kerala (-4.7 %), relatively low in Andhra Pradesh, Odisha, Gujarat, Haryana, and Tamil Nadu, and negative in these states. Regarding rural females, employment growth is highest in Madhya Pradesh and lowest in Punjab. Apart from Madhya Pradesh, Maharashtra recorded only a positive, albeit negligible, growth rate. On the contrary, in fourteen states, including Punjab, the employment of rural women declined considerably during this sub-period. Among rural areas, Madhya Pradesh ranks first in employment growth; the state with the lowest growth rate is Kerala (-5.6 %). Jammu & Kashmir, Maharashtra, and Assam are other states showing relatively higher growth in the number of employed rural persons. In contrast, the rest of the states experienced negative growth rates.

In contrast to rural males, urban males in Kerala registered the highest employment growth rate during this period, while the lowest growth was recorded in Himachal Pradesh. Other states demonstrating relatively better performance regarding the growth of employed urban males include Haryana, Madhya Pradesh, Assam, and Jammu & Kashmir; the states with relatively low growth of employed urban males (besides Himachal Pradesh) are Odisha, West Bengal, Karnataka, Tamil Nadu, and Uttar Pradesh. For urban females, employment growth during this period was highest in Assam and lowest in Rajasthan. Other states that recorded relatively higher employment growth for urban females include Jammu & Kashmir, Bihar, Andhra Pradesh, Madhya Pradesh, and Maharashtra; those with relatively lower growth rates are Uttar Pradesh, Odisha, Himachal Pradesh, Punjab, and Gujarat. For urban persons, the highest employment growth was observed in Kerala, while the lowest was in Himachal Pradesh. Other states showing relatively better growth in employment for urban persons include Haryana, Assam, Andhra Pradesh, Madhya Pradesh, and Jammu & Kashmir. The states with relatively low growth in employed persons are Odisha, Uttar Pradesh, West Bengal, Gujarat, and Rajasthan.

In combined (rural plus urban) areas, the highest male employment growth has been observed in Jammu & Kashmir, while the lowest growth has been recorded in Kerala. The growth rate has also been relatively high in Madhya Pradesh, Maharashtra, Assam, Rajasthan, and Himachal Pradesh, while low in Odisha, Andhra Pradesh, Bihar, Karnataka, and Gujarat. The highest employment growth for females across combined areas is recorded in Madhya Pradesh, followed by Jammu & Kashmir and Maharashtra. The remaining fourteen states recorded negative growth rates, with Punjab being the lowest. When considering both males and females together, it is observed that employment growth during this period has been highest in Madhya Pradesh and lowest in Odisha. In addition to Madhya Pradesh, other states showing relatively better growth are Jammu & Kashmir, Maharashtra, Assam, West Bengal and Haryana. In contrast, those with lower (negative) growth rates, besides Odisha, include Punjab, Kerala, Uttar Pradesh, Himachal Pradesh, and Rajasthan.

4.8.3.5 Period: 1994 to 2018 (Entire Post-Globalisation)

Table 51 shows the employment growth rates across states during the post-globalisation period. The highest employment growth rate for rural males is observed in Jammu & Kashmir, while the lowest is in Kerala. Other states exhibiting relatively higher growth rates for employed rural males include Assam, Madhya Pradesh, Rajasthan, Bihar, and Haryana. In contrast, the comparatively lower growth rates are in Tamil Nadu, Andhra Pradesh, Karnataka, Punjab, and Gujarat. For rural females, the highest employment growth is recorded in Madhya Pradesh, while the lowest is in Bihar. Beyond Madhya Pradesh, only two states, West Bengal and Himachal Pradesh, reported positive employment growth for rural females during this period. The employment growth rate for rural persons during the post-globalisation era is the highest in Jammu & Kashmir and the lowest in Kerala. Other states that reported positive employment growth for rural persons during this period include Assam, Madhya Pradesh, West Bengal, Bihar, Uttar Pradesh, Himachal Pradesh, Rajasthan, Maharashtra, Haryana, Punjab, and Odisha (listed in descending order of growth rate). Conversely, apart from Kerala, four other states – Tamil Nadu, Andhra Pradesh, Karnataka, and Gujarat – exhibit negative growth rates in the employed rural persons during this period.

In urban areas, the growth rate of employment among males from 1994 to 2018 is highest in Kerala, followed by Haryana, Jammu & Kashmir, Gujarat, Madhya Pradesh, Assam, Uttar Pradesh, Tamil Nadu, Karnataka, Punjab, Rajasthan, Bihar, Andhra Pradesh, Odisha, Maharashtra, West Bengal, and Himachal Pradesh (in descending order of growth rate). Unlike rural areas, all states experienced positive growth in the number of employed urban males during this period. For urban females, the highest employment growth is also in Kerala, followed by Punjab, Assam, West Bengal, Jammu & Kashmir, Madhya Pradesh, Andhra Pradesh, Bihar, Karnataka, Tamil Nadu, Gujarat, Maharashtra, Haryana, Odisha, Uttar Pradesh, Himachal Pradesh, and Rajasthan (in descending order of growth rate). As with urban males, all states experienced positive employment growth for urban females during this period. Regarding urban persons, Kerala again leads the list, followed by Haryana, Jammu & Kashmir, Madhya Pradesh, Gujarat, Assam,

Punjab, Andhra Pradesh, Tamil Nadu, Bihar, Karnataka, West Bengal, Uttar Pradesh, Maharashtra, Rajasthan, Odisha, and Himachal Pradesh (in descending order of growth rate).

Considering the rural and urban areas together, it seems that for males, the highest growth in employment during this period occurred in Jammu & Kashmir, followed by Haryana, Madhya Pradesh, Gujarat, Assam, Maharashtra, Rajasthan, Bihar, Uttar Pradesh, West Bengal, Punjab, Karnataka, Odisha, Tamil Nadu, Himachal Pradesh, Andhra Pradesh, and Kerala (in descending order of growth rate). All of these states experienced positive growth in the number of employed males during this period. In contrast, only four states experienced positive growth in the number of employed females during this period, in descending order of their growth rates: West Bengal, Madhya Pradesh, Jammu & Kashmir, and Himachal Pradesh. Jammu & Kashmir led the list of states regarding the growth rate of employed individuals when all males and females in rural and urban areas are considered, followed by Madhya Pradesh, Assam, West Bengal, Haryana, Gujarat, Maharashtra, Punjab, Uttar Pradesh, Bihar, Rajasthan, Himachal Pradesh, Karnataka, Tamil Nadu, Odisha, Andhra Pradesh, and Kerala (in descending order of their growth rates).

4.8.4 Comparison of Employment Growth Rates During Pre- and Post-Globalisation Periods

When we compare the growth rates of employment in the states during the pre-globalisation (1983 to 1994) and the post-globalisation (1994 to 2018) periods, the following observations can be made:

- The post-globalisation period saw a decline in employment growth rates across most states, particularly in rural areas and among females. When comparing growth rates from 1983 to 1994 with those from 1994 to 2012, it is evident that all but one state experienced a decrease in rural employment growth during the latter period. The exceptions were Jammu & Kashmir for males and Madhya Pradesh for females. In urban areas, a similar decline is observed in fourteen states for males (with Bihar, Haryana, and Kerala as exceptions) and in nine states for females (the exceptions are Andhra Pradesh, Assam, Bihar, Jammu & Kashmir, Karnataka, Kerala, Madhya Pradesh, and Punjab).
- However, when comparing the pre-globalisation period with the entire post-globalisation period (1994 to 2018), it appears that the downward trend in employment growth continued unabated beyond 2012, to the extent that all states in India observed a decline in their employment growth rates in rural areas during the post-globalisation period compared to the pre-globalisation

period, for both males and females (except Jammu & Kashmir for male). In urban areas, a nearly identical trend is noted, with thirteen states witnessing declines in employment growth rates for both males and females during the post-globalisation period compared to the pre-globalisation period. When considering both rural and urban areas, it is found that the employment growth rates from 1994 to 2018 were lower than those from 1983 to 1994, except for males in Jammu & Kashmir and females in Kerala and Punjab. Nevertheless, when combining males and females across all areas, all states except Punjab experienced lower employment growth rates from 1994 to 2018 than from 1983 to 1994.

4.9 Determinants of Employment Status in India

In this section, we conduct logit regression analyses to identify the employment status (employed or unemployed) of individuals in India, separately for rural, urban, and all areas, using unit-level data from the PLFS 2018. In our logit regression exercises, the dependent variable is the employment status of the persons (labelled as 'empstat'), a binary variable that takes the value '1' if the person is employed and '0' if unemployed. The explanatory variables considered are the following:

Age of the person (age): A person's age is likely to affect the likelihood of participating in employment. This is because, as one grows older, they acquire more education and skills that may help them access employment opportunities in the market. Thus, we may hypothesise a positive relationship between 'empstat' and 'age'.

Sex of the person (sex): The sex of an individual is viewed as a determinant of employment status, as females are often discriminated against in the job market in a society dominated by males, ostensibly due to their superior education and skills acquisition. In this study, 'sex' is treated as a dummy variable taking the value '1' for males and '0' for females. We hypothesise a positive relationship between 'empstat' and 'sex'.

Household size (hsize): The size of a household is measured by the total number of family members. It is regarded as one of the determinants, as a person with a large family is more likely to feel compelled to seek employment, even with unremunerative wages and unfavourable working conditions, due to the need to cover substantial family expenses. Thus, we hypothesise a positive relationship between 'empstat' and 'hsize'.

Relation to head (relhead): If the person is the head of the family, she/he will feel more compelled to find employment to support the family's upkeep. We consider 'relhead' as a binary variable assigned the value '1' if the person is the head of the family and '0' otherwise. The relationship between 'empstat' and 'relhead' is hypothesised to be positive.

Marital status (marstat): Individuals' marital status will likely determine their employment status. Unlike unmarried individuals, married individuals are more likely to seek employment to support their families. We employ a dummy variable to measure marital status, assigning a value of '1' to currently married individuals and '0' to unmarried individuals. We hypothesise that a positive relationship exists between 'empstat' and 'marstat'.

Social groups (sg1, sg2, and sg3): The social group background of individuals is regarded as a significant determinant of their employment status, as those belonging to weaker groups (e.g. SCs and STs) are more likely to face discrimination in employment compared to the general caste individuals, given the dominance of upper-caste people in society. It is also true that individuals from upper castes benefit from a superior educational background, making them more suitable candidates in the job market. In both the employment/unemployment surveys and the Periodic Labour Force Survey, the social group is utilised as a categorical variable to represent four categories: Scheduled Tribe (ST), Scheduled Caste (SC), Other Backward Classes (OBC), and 'Others' (comprising general caste individuals). Using this information, and taking 'Others' as the base category, we have constructed three dummy variables: 'sg1', which is assigned a value of '1' if the individual is SC and '0' otherwise; 'sg2', which is assigned a value of '1' if the individual is ST and '0' otherwise; and 'sg3', assigned a value of '1' if the individual is OBC and '0' otherwise. We hypothesise that there exists a negative relationship between these social group dummies and 'empstat', implying that those belonging to the weaker groups (sg1, sg2, and sg3) are less likely to be employed compared to those drawn from the 'Others' category.

Religious groups (rel1 and rel2): Individuals' religion may also be a determinant of their employment status in India. There is a viewpoint that those belonging to the Islamic (Muslim) faith (and possibly other non-Hindu groups) lag behind their Hindu counterparts in terms of accessing employment opportunities. To examine the validity of this viewpoint (hypothesis), we have constructed two religious dummies considering three groups: Hindus, Muslims, and 'Others'. We regard Hindus as the base category. The two dummies are 'rel1', which takes on the value '1' if the individual's religion is Islam and '0' otherwise; and 'rel2', which takes on the value '1' if the individual belongs to the 'Others' category and '0' otherwise.

General education groups (gedu1, gedu2, gedu3, and gedu4): The importance of education and skills in securing employment, particularly 'high-end' jobs, needs no elaboration. The prevailing perception is that individuals with higher levels of education are more likely to secure employment than those with lower levels of education. However, more educated individuals may struggle to secure their desired positions in an environment with a scarcity of high-end, well-paid jobs. Still, they may be reluctant to accept lower-end, inadequately paid jobs. In such circumstances, their employment likelihood may be lower than that of less educated individuals. To analyse the impact of education on employment status, we have constructed four education dummies, with 'illiterates' as the reference category. These dummies are: 'gedu1', which is assigned a value of '1' if the education level is up to primary and '0' otherwise; 'gedu2', which equals '1' if the education level is above primary but up to secondary and '0' otherwise; 'gedu3', which equals '1' if the education level is above secondary but up to graduation and '0' otherwise; and 'gedu4', which equals '1' if the education level is post-graduation and above and '0' otherwise. We hypothesise that the relationship between these dummies and 'empstat' is negative.

Vocational training (vtraining): It is often stated that individuals with vocational training are likely to have better job prospects. Therefore, to understand the impact of such training on the likelihood of employment, we have included it as an explanatory variable in our logit regressions. We have utilised a dummy variable assigned the value '1' if the individual has received vocational training and '0' otherwise. We hypothesise that the relationship between 'empstat' and 'vtraining' is positive.

Poverty status (pstat): Individuals' poverty status is likely to influence their current employment status, as non-poor individuals are more likely to be employed than unemployed. We have used data on per capita monthly consumption expenditure from the Periodic Labour Force Survey, along with the state-level 'official poverty lines' for rural and urban areas for 2017–18, to determine the poverty status of individuals. We employed a dummy variable that was assigned a value of '1' if the individual was non-poor and '0' if poor. The hypothesis is that the probability of employment is higher for non-poor individuals than for their poor counterparts, indicating a positive relationship between 'empstat' and 'pstat'.

Region (region): In our regressions for the combined region (rural and urban), we have utilised this as one of the determinants of individuals' employment status. Rural individuals are likely to be economically weaker and, consequently, cannot afford to remain unemployed. In other words, the probability of rural individuals being engaged in some form of employment (even if those are not adequately remunerative) is likely greater than that of urban individuals. We employed a binary variable that assigned a value of '1' to persons residing in rural areas and '0' otherwise. A positive relationship is hypothesised between 'empstat' and 'region'.

4.9.1 Logit Regression Results

The logit regression results for rural areas in 2018 are presented in Table 52. It was found that the estimated coefficients for the explanatory variables such as 'age', 'sex', 'relhead', and 'marstat' have a positive relationship with 'empstat'. Moreover, all their coefficients are statistically significant. Thus, in rural areas, an older, male, married, and household head is more likely to be employed than to remain unemployed. The estimated coefficient for the first social group dummy is negative and statistically significant, indicating that, compared to individuals from general castes, the probability of employment is lower for individuals from the SC social group, partially supporting our hypothesis. The estimated coefficient for the first religion dummy is also negative and statistically significant, suggesting that Muslims are less likely to be employed than Hindus, which again supports our hypothesis. The coefficients of the four education dummies are all negative, and all except for 'gedu1' are statistically significant. Thus, individuals with more education have a relatively lower probability of being employed than the 'illiterates' (the reference category). However, vocational training enhances the likelihood of being employed, as indicated by the positive sign and statistical significance of the estimated coefficient for 'vtraining'. Another finding from the regression results for rural areas is that a positive and statistically significant relationship exists between 'empstat' and 'pstat', indicating that the probability of being employed is greater for 'non-poor' individuals than 'poor' individuals.

Table 52. Logit Regression Results of Determinants of Employment Status in India [Dep. Variable: empstat = 1 if employed; 0 if unemployed]

Explanatory vars.	Rural Areas			Urban Areas			Rural + Urban Areas		
	Est. coeffi-cient	*z*-value	*p*-value	Est. coeffi-cient	*z*-value	*p*-value	Est. coeffi-cient	*z*-value	*p*-value
age	0.10	27.30	0.00	0.08	28.25	0.00	0.09	39.01	0.00
sex	0.10	2.57	0.01	0.37	10.94	0.00	0.23	9.02	0.00
hsize	−0.01	−1.51	0.13	0.01	1.04	0.30	0.00	−0.05	0.96
relhead	1.61	19.58	0.00	1.22	21.79	0.00	1.36	29.86	0.00
marstat	1.44	30.45	0.00	1.09	27.54	0.00	1.27	42.05	0.00
sg1	−0.13	−2.54	0.01	−0.19	−3.77	0.00	−0.18	−5.14	0.00
sg2	0.17	2.91	0.00	−0.16	−1.96	0.05	0.09	1.96	0.05
sg3	0.03	0.63	0.53	−0.01	−0.36	0.72	0.01	0.17	0.86
rel1	−0.22	−3.85	0.00	−0.09	−1.95	0.05	−0.17	−4.68	0.00
rel2	0.11	1.57	0.12	−0.02	−0.31	0.76	−0.01	−0.16	0.87
gedu1	−0.05	−0.47	0.64	−0.26	−2.26	0.02	−0.18	−2.47	0.01

(Continued)

Table 52 *(Continued)*

	Rural Areas			Urban Areas			Rural + Urban Areas		
Explanatory vars.	Est. coeffi-cient	*z*-value	*p*-value	Est. coeffi-cient	*z*-value	*p*-value	Est. coeffi-cient	*z*-value	*p*-value
gedu2	−0.56	−6.67	0.00	−0.79	−7.72	0.00	−0.71	−11.15	0.00
gedu3	−1.62	−19.26	0.00	−1.55	−15.26	0.00	−1.62	−25.53	0.00
gedu4	−2.39	−21.62	0.00	−1.74	−15.98	0.00	−1.99	−27.22	0.00
vtraining	0.74	12.94	0.00	0.45	9.64	0.00	0.57	15.75	0.00
pstat	0.20	5.25	0.00	0.22	5.53	0.00	0.19	7.14	0.00
region	–	–	–	–	–	–	0.28	11.80	0.00
constant	0.34	2.14	0.03	−0.55	−3.51	0.00	−0.15	−1.35	0.18
35 state dummies	Estimated coefficients are not reported								
	Pseudo R^2 = 0.39			Pseudo R^2 = 0.30			Pseudo R^2 = 0.34		
	LR Chi-sq = 6666.92 (df = 51; p-value = 0.00)			LR Chi-sq = 5639.16 (df = 51; p-value = 0.00)			LR Chi-sq = 12800.96 (df = 52; p-value = 0.00)		
	No. of observations = 93,822			No. of observations = 68,042			No. of observations = 1,61,864		

Source: Author's computation using PLFS unit-level data for 2017–18

Notes: (i) z-values are calculated using White's robust standard errors; and (ii) Estimated coefficiens of 35 state dummies have not been reported

The results for urban areas are broadly consistent with those for rural areas. They suggest that the probability of employment is higher for older individuals, particularly married males who are household heads. Regarding the social group dummies, the evidence indicates that individuals from weaker social categories are less likely to be employed than those from the 'Others' (general caste) category. The relationship between the first religious group dummy and 'empstat' is negative and statistically significant, implying that Muslims in urban India are less likely to be employed compared to Hindus. The findings relating to general education dummies are consistent with those in rural areas. Specifically, illiterate individuals are more likely to appear employed than those with higher educational backgrounds. Moreover, the positive, statistically significant impact of vocational training on employment likelihood is evident in urban areas. Additionally, similar to rural areas, the relationship between 'empstat' and poverty status is positive and statistically significant.

When considering the regression results for combined (rural plus urban) areas, nearly identical conclusions emerge. Thus, being male, older, married, the head of the family, having vocational training, and coming from non-poor families increases the likelihood of employment. It was also found that individuals from the SC social group are less likely to be employed than those from the 'Others' category. However, the results for combined areas indicate that individuals in the ST category are more likely to be employed than those in the reference category, namely 'Others'. Similarly, the likelihood of employment is lower for Muslims compared to Hindus. Another important observation is that people from rural areas are more likely to be employed than those from urban areas.

4.10 Summary of Findings

Assessing the workforce size at the all-India level from 1983 to 2018, it is observed that both rural and urban areas experienced a steady increase in workforce size until 2012. However, rural India saw a significant decline in the workforce after 2012, with 20.14 million workers missing from the rural labour market between 2012 and 2018. This decline primarily occurred due to a drastic reduction in the number of rural female workers. Between 2012 and 2018, 24.76 million female workers in rural India were excluded from the workforce, while the number of male workers increased marginally by 4.66 million. The situation in urban areas was somewhat different, as both males and females saw workforce numbers increase from 2012 to 2018. A comparison of changes in the number of workers between the pre-globalisation period (1983–1994) and the entire post-globalisation period (1994–2018) reveals that rural females were significantly disadvantaged in the era of globalisation, with the average yearly increase in rural female workers dropping from 1.36 million in the pre-globalisation period to –1.17 million in the post-globalisation phase. In contrast, the average annual increase in the number of workers for urban females rose from 0.48 million during the pre-globalisation period to 0.59 million during the post-globalisation period. Following a severe decline in the number of rural female workers, their share of the total rural workforce in the country decreased significantly in 2018.

Analysing the trends in workforce participation rates (WPR) at the all-India level, we found that although both males and females in rural areas experienced a decline in the WPR during the post-globalisation period, this decline has been particularly severe for females, especially after 2000. In urban areas, while males appear to have recorded a marginal improvement in WPR during the post-globalisation period, females faced a decline. However, over the 2012–2018 sub-period, a decrease in WPR is evident among both males and females in urban areas. Overall, it can be concluded that WPR across India declined from 1983 to 2018, with the rate of deceleration accelerating during globalisation, notably among females in rural areas.

Our discussion of changes in WPR across age groups revealed that individuals aged 15–24, 25–34, and 60 and above experienced the most significant declines in WPR over time, particularly after 2012. This decline was notably higher in rural areas for males in the 15–24 and 60 and above age groups, and for females in the 15–24, 35–59, and 60 and above age groups. A decrease in WPR among younger age groups is also evident in urban areas for both genders. When we examined the ratio of workforce share to population share across age groups, we found that in India, except for the 35–59 age group, the workforce share decreased faster than the population share. The most substantial decline in the ratio of workforce share to population share occurred in the 15–24 age group, followed by the 5–14 and 60 and above age groups. This trend is consistent for both males and females in rural and urban areas.

Examining the WPR across educational groups reveals that in rural areas, the WPR for females is higher among those with educational levels classified as 'illiterate' and 'graduates & above', suggesting a U-shaped relationship between WPR and educational level. However, WPR for rural males increases with higher educational attainment when the 'below primary' category is not considered. In urban areas, however, the WPR appears to increase with higher levels of education. The pattern is broadly consistent for both males and females. It should also be noted that the WPR has declined over time for all educational groups, particularly for the 'secondary/H.S.' and 'below primary' categories. The overall picture emerging is that individuals with lower educational attainment suffer more over time due to declines in their WPR. This conclusion is further supported by the observation that the ratio of workforce share to population share has declined more for lower education groups (including 'secondary/H.S.') over time. This trend holds for both males and females in urban areas, but for males only in rural areas.

Our examination of the relationship between individuals' social status and the WPR revealed that in rural areas, those from weaker social groups (ST and SC) exhibit higher WPR than those from higher social groups (OBC and general castes). The overall picture appears similar in urban areas when focusing on the period up to 2012; after this, no significant difference in WPR is observed among various social groups. However, when considering both rural and urban areas combined, it becomes evident that the WPR has consistently been higher for the ST and SC categories than for the OBC and general castes throughout the period from 1983 to 2018. Another noteworthy point is that the difference in the WPR between males across caste groups is considerably smaller than the difference in the WPR between females across caste groups. More specifically, females from the ST and SC categories recorded a notably higher WPR than their counterparts from superior caste groups. Nevertheless, the WPR has declined over time for all social categories, with a more pronounced decline observed among the weaker social groups, notably females.

In terms of WPR for various religious groups, our observation is that Muslims have consistently lagged behind Hindus throughout 1983–2018. However, the gap in WPR between Hindus and Muslims has been narrowing, particularly since 2000 and in rural areas. Although the WPR for females is lower than for males across all religious groups, it is especially deficient for Muslim females in both rural and urban areas. Additionally, we found that the WPR for Muslims has declined over time at a much greater rate than that of Hindus. Upon examining the share of employed individuals and the overall population share, we discovered that both Muslim men and women have a lower employment share compared to their population share when contrasted with their Hindu counterparts, indicating discrimination against them in the labour market.

In analysing the growth rate of employment during the pre- and post-globalisation periods, we found that not only did the growth rate of employed individuals decline drastically for both males and females in the latter period compared to the former, but also that this growth rate turned negative for females in the post-globalisation period. It was also observed that in all sub-periods after 2000, the female employment growth rate in rural areas turned negative, with the most significant decline happening from 2012 to 2018 (annual growth rate of employed at −4.56 %). The decline in employment growth during the post-globalisation period was evident for both males and females, irrespective of the chosen region (rural or urban). However, the decline in employment growth during the post-globalisation period was less pronounced in urban areas than in rural areas. Ultimately, it can be concluded that rural India, in general, and rural women, in particular, have borne the harshest impact of globalisation on employment.

When we examined employment growth rates across age groups, we found that those in the 5–14 age group experienced the steepest decline in employment growth over the years, and this decline surged dramatically after 2000. This holds irrespective of the sex of individuals and the regions considered. In addition to this age group, a notable decrease in employment growth after 2000 is also apparent for the 15–24 age group in both rural and urban areas, affecting both males and females.

Regarding employment growth across educational groups, our primary finding is that, in rural areas, both males and females with lower educational attainment experienced the largest employment losses in the post-globalisation period. Consequently, the growth rates of employment for 'illiterates' and those with 'below primary' and 'primary' education became negative during this period. In contrast, employment growth during the post-globalisation period in urban areas remained positive for all educational groups except those with 'below primary' education. Overall, we can say that individuals at the bottom of the educational hierarchy suffered the greatest employment losses during the era of globalisation, particularly in rural areas.

In analysing employment growth rates across social groups and genders in rural areas, we found a general trend of declining employment growth in rural areas during the post-globalisation period, except for ST males. In urban areas, while all social groups experienced positive employment growth rates, STs saw an improvement in their employment growth rate during the recent sub-period of the post-globalisation era (2012–2018). Overall, it can be stated that although all social groups experienced a decline in the employment growth rate during the post-globalisation period compared to the pre-globalisation period, the extent of this decline has been relatively less severe for the weaker caste categories (STs and SCs).

Discussing the growth rate of employment amongst religious groups, it is observed that in rural areas, Muslims experienced a lower growth rate of employment compared to Hindus during the pre-globalisation period. From 1994 to 2012, rural Muslims experienced faster employment growth rates than Hindus. However, this improvement could not be sustained after 2012, when employment growth for rural Muslim males turned negative, whereas employment growth for Hindu males continued to be positive. Regarding rural females from both Hindu and Muslim groups, the employment growth rate became negative during 2012–2018. The overall situation in urban areas is quite similar: Hindus showed higher employment growth than Muslims during the pre-globalisation period, followed by an improvement in Muslims' employment growth rate from 1994 to 2012, but a failure to maintain this momentum after 2012. Overall, considering rural and urban areas combined, it is evident that Hindus performed better in terms of employment growth during the pre-globalisation period than Muslims. Muslims began to catch up with Hindus in this regard during the first sub-period (1994–2012) of the post-globalisation era, but fell behind Hindus again after 2012. Furthermore, although both Hindus and Muslims noted a decline in their employment growth rate from 2012 to 2018, the decline was markedly more significant for Muslims than for Hindus.

We examined changing employment scenarios across seventeen major states in India, considering two key indicators: workforce participation rates (WPR) and workforce growth from 1983 to 2018. Overall, it can be concluded that Himachal Pradesh, Andhra Pradesh, Tamil Nadu, Karnataka, and Madhya Pradesh performed better in terms of WPR during this period. Conversely, the lagged states are Bihar, Assam, Uttar Pradesh, Haryana, Kerala, and West Bengal. Additionally, we found that the ranking pattern of the states remained relatively unchanged from 1983 to 2018.

Examining the growth rates of the employed or workforce in the states during the pre-globalisation period (1983–1994), we identified Jammu & Kashmir as the top performer and Punjab as the bottom performer. Other states that performed relatively better in terms of employment growth during this period include Haryana, Assam, Himachal Pradesh, Andhra Pradesh, and West Bengal. In the post-globalisation period (1994–2018), Jammu & Kashmir maintained its first place in employment growth, while Kerala ranked last. Other states that achieved higher employment growth than the all-India level are Madhya Pradesh, Assam, West Bengal, Haryana, Gujarat, Maharashtra, Punjab, Uttar Pradesh, and Bihar. Employment growth during this period has been below the all-India level in the remaining states (Himachal Pradesh, Karnataka, Tamil Nadu, Odisha, Andhra Pradesh, and Kerala).

An important observation regarding employment growth in the states during the post-globalisation period is that the vast majority experienced lower growth rates than in the pre-globalisation period. This trend is particularly evident in rural areas and among females. In rural areas, the growth rates of employed individuals were lower during the post-globalisation period across all major states than during the pre-globalisation period. While this holds for males and females, the decline was more pronounced for females. A similar trend persisted in urban areas, with thirteen major states (out of seventeen) also recording lower employment growth for males and females combined during the post-globalisation period. Another striking observation is that the downward trend in the growth of employed persons in India and its states, which began with the implementation of globalisation policies in the early 1990s, continued unabated during the sub-period of 2012–2018. During this period, all states except Maharashtra, Madhya Pradesh, and Assam recorded lower growth rates of employed persons (rural and urban combined) than in the immediately preceding sub-period from 2000 to 2012.

We have identified the main determinants of employment status for individuals in India using the unit-level PLFS 2018 data. To achieve this, we conducted logistic regression analyses, with the dependent variable a binary variable coded '1' for employed and '0' for unemployed. Our main finding is that the likelihood of being employed increases for males, older individuals, married people, heads of families, those with vocational training, and individuals from non-poor families. Conversely, this probability decreases for individuals belonging to weaker social groups (SC and ST) and Muslims. These observations largely remain valid when considered separately for rural and urban areas. However, rural individuals are more likely to be employed than their urban counterparts.

India's Evolving Employment Landscape: The Qualitative Dimensions

5.1 Introduction

The neo-liberal economic policies adopted in India have dismantled the socialist elements of the economy. The state-controlled system that led to macroeconomic instability and a balance of payments crisis in India in the late 1980s has been replaced by the principle of market-based fundamentalism. This policy recognises the importance of a flexible and efficient market system for navigating and excelling in international competition. However, while firms endeavoured to improve efficiency by adopting modern technologies, they faced the challenge of labour market inflexibility caused by existing labour laws, trade unionism, the demand for a social security system, and job benefits aimed at protecting workers' interests. Under these circumstances, to compete in the globalised environment, firms sought to overcome these labour market challenges by hiring more contract and casual labour. Furthermore, to enhance competitiveness, they increasingly employed labour-saving technologies, resulting in a decline in the share of regular salaried workers and a rise in self-employed and casual workers.

The International Labour Organisation (ILO) aims to foster a global environment of decent work, and as a member nation, India has also embraced this goal. To achieve this objective, India seeks to implement a comprehensive package of social and economic policies across various sectors, specifically designed to improve work quality and increase employment opportunities. However, due to the pervasive issue of mass unemployment, many macroeconomic policies aimed at overall economic development primarily focus on the quantitative aspect of employment, relegating the quality of employment to the periphery. This governmental attitude has been evident in various ways. For instance, an initiative by the National Commission for Enterprises in the Unorganised Sector to improve the working conditions of informal sector workers (Government of India, 2007b) lacked adequate political backing. Similarly, various employment-generating schemes (e.g. the Mahatma Gandhi National Rural Employment Guarantee Scheme) aimed to tackle unemployment while neglecting to enhance employment quality.

A growing trend towards the informalisation and casualisation of the workforce has recently created issues across multiple levels. Informalisation is characterised by a decline in the proportion of regular salaried workers and an increase in the other two categories (self-employed and casual workers) within the total workforce. Conversely, casualisation refers to the increase in the proportion of casual workers among the overall workforce. While a regular salaried job is generally viewed as the most favourable for workers in terms of remuneration, security, and stability, casual employment is often regarded as the least desirable of the three types, particularly in terms of stability and additional benefits. Moreover, NSSO data indicate that wages in casual employment are the lowest. A comparison of the remuneration received by regular salaried and self-employed workers reveals that, in some instances, self-employed individuals may receive the highest remuneration (Glinskaya and Jalan, 2006; World Bank, 2010). Therefore, while the increase in the share of casual workers is typically perceived as a decline in employment quality, the rising proportion of self-employed individuals warrants careful examination for a quality analysis of employment. In this context, investigating the changing proportions of the 'poor' (those with a monthly per capita income below the 'poverty line') among the employed could provide insight into the quality of employment among the self-employed. Additionally, it should be noted that the casualisation of the workforce may not necessarily signify a deterioration in employment quality from the workers' perspective. A satisfactory method of assessing employment quality involves evaluating the proportion of workers living below the poverty line across different employment modes.

In this context, this chapter analyses the evolving modes of employment among workers over time to determine whether there have been any changes in the proportions of workers across various modes of employment and whether the quality of employment has deteriorated, potentially indicated by the increasing proportion of the 'poor' among the employed. Furthermore, the factors influencing workers' employment mode choices are identified.

Having introduced the chapter, Section 5.2 examines the distribution of workers across various modes of employment at the all-India level. Section 5.3 discusses the employment modes of different religious and social groups. Section 5.4 examines the employment modes of workers across seventeen major Indian states.

Section 5.5 analyses the growth rates of workers by employment modes in these states. In Section 5.6, we analyse the quality of employment by examining the incidence of poverty among workers across different employment modes. Section 5.7 identifies the factors influencing workers' choice of employment modes. Finally, the main observations from this chapter are summarised in Section 5.8.

5.2 Distribution of Workers by Employment Modes in India

In terms of employment mode, three distinct categories are observed among the employed. First, there are the 'regular salaried' workers who work outside (not in their own or domestic farm/enterprise) in farms or non-farm enterprises and earn a wage or salary on a fixed or regular basis. In general, they enjoy job security and other supplementary employment benefits. The second category comprises the 'self-employed' who are generally own-account workers. They are either unpaid family workers or self-employed employers. The third group includes those referred to as 'casual' workers. They are engaged in outside farms or non-farm enterprises and are given remuneration on a daily or periodic basis.

The information on the percentage distribution of usual principal and subsidiary workers (UPSS) by the above-mentioned modes of employment for our chosen time points at the all-India level is presented in Table 53. The following observations could be made in this regard:

- If we consider the period 1983 to 2012, in rural India, there is a clear trend of the percentage of self-employed workers decreasing and casual workers increasing, which suggests a clear trend of growing casualisation of rural workers. However, during this period, the share of regularly employed rural workers appeared to have increased marginally. From 2012 to 2018, the casualisation of workers in rural India seemed to have halted, with an increase in the shares of self-employed and regularly employed workers. Considering the entire period of 1983 to 2018, it may be said that the proportion of self-employed in rural India revealed a declining trend over time; that of causal workers revealed the pattern of an 'inverted-U' (increasing till 2000 and declining thereafter); and the proportion of regularly employed increasing continuously after 1994, but its share in employment is lagging far behind the other two categories of employment (13.1 % only in 2018).
- When we consider the males and females separately in rural areas, there is not much difference between them regarding the share of self-employed workers to total workers (it varied between 62 % and 54 % from 1983 to 2018). However,

the proportion of such workers declined over time for rural males and females. Table 53 also shows that, at all times, the proportion of casual workers was higher and the proportion of regular workers was lower among rural females than among rural males (except in 2012 for casual labourers). This implied that, in terms of employment quality, rural males held a superior position compared to their female counterparts. However, a rising tendency in the proportion of regularly employed individuals is observed for rural males and females. Regarding the proportion of casual workers, the pattern is more like an 'inverted-U' for both categories – increasing until 2000 and declining thereafter. Nevertheless, it is worth noting that, despite its decline in recent years, nearly 28 % of rural male workers and 32 % of rural female workers were employed as casual workers in India in 2018. On the other hand, about 14 % of rural male workers and 11 % of rural female workers worked as regular workers in the same year. The share of self-employed workers among the male and female workers in rural India was about 58 % in 2018.

Table 53. Percentage Distribution of the Workers (UPSS Basis) by Modes of Employment in India

Mode of employment	Year	Rural			Urban			Rural + Urban		
		Male	Female	Male + Female	Male	Female	Male + Female	Male	Female	Male + Female
Regular Employee	1983	10.3	2.8	7.6	43.7	25.8	40.0	17.9	5.5	13.8
	1994	8.5	2.7	6.4	42.0	28.4	39.1	17.1	6.3	13.6
	2000	8.8	3.1	6.8	41.7	33.3	40.1	17.9	7.5	14.6
	2012	10.0	5.6	8.7	43.4	42.8	43.3	20.6	13.5	18.7
	2018	14.0	10.5	13.1	45.7	52.1	47.0	23.4	21.0	22.8
Self-employed	1983	60.5	61.9	61.0	40.9	45.8	41.9	56.0	60.0	57.3
	1994	57.7	58.6	58.0	41.7	45.8	42.6	53.6	56.8	54.6
	2000	55.0	57.3	55.8	41.5	45.3	42.2	51.3	55.5	52.6
	2012	54.5	59.3	55.9	41.7	42.8	41.9	50.4	55.8	51.9
	2018	57.8	57.7	57.8	39.2	34.7	38.3	52.3	51.9	52.2
Casual Labour	1983	29.2	35.3	31.4	15.4	28.4	18.1	26.0	34.5	28.9
	1994	33.8	38.7	35.6	16.3	25.8	18.3	29.3	36.9	31.8
	2000	36.2	39.6	37.4	16.8	21.4	17.7	30.9	36.9	32.8
	2012	35.5	35.1	35.4	14.9	14.3	14.8	29.0	30.7	29.4
	2018	28.2	31.8	29.1	15.1	13.1	14.7	24.3	27.1	25.0

Source: NSSO unit-level data from Surveys on Employment/Unemployment for the years 1983, 1993–94, 1999–2000, 2011–Force Survey for 2017–18.

- The pattern of urban workers' employment modes is quite different from that of rural workers. As expected, in the urban areas, the proportion of regular employees among workers has been the highest in recent years, followed by self-employed and casual workers. In 2018, while 47 % of urban workers in all-India were regular employees, the corresponding figures for the self-employed and casual employed were 38 % and 15 %, respectively. It also emerges that while the proportion of those who were regularly employed increased from 1983 to 2018 for males and females, the proportions of those who were self-employed and casual employed declined. However, the decline in the proportion of self-employed and casual employees in urban areas has been greater among females than among males. It is indeed heartening to note that in 2018, as high as 52 % of urban female workers were engaged in regular employment, 35 % in self-employment and 13 % in casual employment. On the other hand, for urban males in 2018, the proportions of regular employees, self-employed individuals, and casual employees were 46 %, 39 %, and 15 %, respectively. Overall, it can be seen that urban females have narrowed the gap with their male counterparts in terms of employment quality, as demonstrated by their significant decline in casual employment and increase in regular employment. Consequently, in terms of employment quality, urban females held a superior position compared to their male counterparts in 2018.
- Considering rural and urban areas together, it is found that the percentage of self-employed workers declined over time in India for both males and females. The same trend is also evident in the percentage of casual workers. Conversely, the percentage of regularly employed individuals increased for both males and females. In 2018, while nearly 52 % of workers (males and females combined) in India were engaged in self-employed activities, the corresponding percentages of regular and casual employed were 23 % and 25 %, respectively. It is also worth noting that the percentage of casual workers has historically been higher among females than among males. Females also reported a higher percentage of self-employment than males until 2012, after which the gap narrowed substantially. Overall, it appears that males in India enjoyed a somewhat superior position in terms of employment quality compared to females during the period from 1983 to 2018.

5.2.1 Average Annual Changes in Worker Numbers by Employment Mode

In the context of the discussion on workers' modes of employment, it may be worthwhile to examine the average annual increase/decrease in the number of workers across different modes of employment. The information in this regard is presented in Table 54. The main points to be noted here are the following:

- Compared to the period from 1983 to 1994 (the pre-globalisation period), the number of regularly employed individuals increased faster from 1994 to 2018 (the post-globalisation period) for both males and females, as well as in rural and urban areas. During the former period, the number of regular workers in rural India rose by 0.01 million per year; in contrast, it increased by 2.05 million per year in the latter period. A similar pattern emerges in urban areas, where regular workers grew by 0.81 million and 2.32 million per year from 1983 to 1994 and 1994 to 2018, respectively. The observation that the absolute number of regular workers increased at a higher rate during the post-globalisation period is further supported by examining figures for different sub-periods of the post-globalisation era.
- It has been observed that although both males and females experienced a greater annual increase in the absolute number of regular workers during the post-globalisation period compared to the pre-globalisation period, this increase was more pronounced for males than for females and also for urban areas compared to rural areas (except for males during 2012 to 2018).
- While the total number of self-employed workers in rural India increased by 1.78 million per year (including males and females) from 1983 to 1994, it declined by 0.90 million per year from 1994 to 2018. The decline in rural female self-employment is the sole factor driving the decline in the number of self-employed workers in rural India. As shown in Table 54, while the number of self-employed workers among rural females increased by 0.51 million per year from 1983 to 1994, it declined by 2.65 million per year from 2012 to 2018. It has also been observed that the downward trend in the number of self-employed rural female workers began with the initiation of economic reform policies in India in the early 1990s. Thus, as we considered in each sub-period of the post-globalisation era, rural females experienced a decline in the absolute number of their self-employed workers.

Table 54. Average Yearly Increase/Decrease in Number of Workers (UPSS) Under Different Modes of Employment in India (in Million)

Mode of employment	Period	Rural			Urban			Rural + Urban		
		Male	Female	Male + Female	Male	Female	Male + Female	Male	Female	Male + Female
Regular Employee	1983 to 1994	-0.02	0.03	0.01	0.64	0.17	0.81	0.62	0.20	0.82
	1994 to 2000	0.25	0.07	0.33	0.72	0.20	0.91	0.97	0.27	1.24
	2000 to 2012	0.50	0.20	0.70	1.33	0.47	1.80	1.83	0.67	2.50
	2012 to 2018	1.66	0.40	2.05	1.55	0.77	2.32	2.34	0.89	3.23
Self-employed	1983 to 1994	1.26	0.51	1.78	0.75	0.22	0.97	2.01	0.73	2.75
	1994 to 2000	0.15	-0.14	0.01	0.73	0.06	0.79	0.88	-0.08	0.80
	2000 to 2012	1.55	-0.03	1.52	1.19	0.29	1.48	2.74	0.25	3.00
	2012 to 2018	1.75	-2.65	-0.90	0.52	-0.14	0.38	2.77	-2.63	0.14
Casual Labour	1983 to 1994	1.67	0.82	2.49	0.32	0.09	0.41	1.99	0.91	2.91
	1994 to 2000	1.41	0.22	1.63	0.36	-0.09	0.27	1.76	0.13	1.89
	2000 to 2012	0.95	-0.52	0.43	0.30	0.00	0.30	1.25	-0.52	0.73
	2012 to 2018	-2.63	-1.88	-4.51	0.41	0.03	0.44	-1.87	-1.72	-3.59

Source: Same as Table 53

- There has been a decline in casual workers since 2000 for rural females and 2012 for rural males. It is worth noting that this decline has been particularly pronounced in the recent sub-period, from 2012 to 2018. It appears that rural India has experienced a slower rate of casualisation for both male and female workers in recent years.
- In urban areas, during the sub-period from 2012 to 2018, the number of self-employed female workers decreased by 0.14 million per year, while the number for males increased by 0.52 million annually. It is also noticeable that the annual increase in self-employed workers (both males and females)

in urban areas was lower during the post-globalisation period compared to the pre-globalisation period. Conversely, the annual increase in the number of regular employees (males and females combined) in urban areas was nearly three times higher during the post-globalisation period than in the pre-globalisation period. Regarding the absolute number of casual workers in urban areas, a marginal expansion is evident during the post-globalisation period for males, whereas it is negligible for females.

- When considering rural and urban areas combined, it can be said that females in India experienced a significant decline in the absolute numbers of self-employed and casual workers, particularly during the sub-period from 2012 to 2018. However, males and females enjoyed a higher annual increase in their absolute numbers of regular workers during the post-globalisation period compared to the pre-globalisation period. As shown in Table 54, while the number of regular workers increased by 0.62 million per year for males (rural and urban combined) from 1983 to 1994, this figure rose to 2.34 million per year from 2012 to 2018. Conversely, for females, the increase was 0.20 million and 0.89 million per year during these two sub-periods, respectively. Furthermore, combining males and females, the number of regular workers grew by 0.82 million per year during the former sub-period. In contrast, it increased by 3.23 million per year during the latter sub-period, offsetting the gap created by the reduction in the absolute number of casual workers in the country.

5.2.2 Growth Rates of Workers by Employment Modes

Let us now focus on the annual (compound) growth rates of workers across various sub-periods, by mode of employment. Information in this regard is presented in Table 55. It has been found that, in rural India, the annual growth rate of the self-employed has been declining since 1994. Table 55 shows that the annual growth rate of self-employed individuals (including both males and females) in rural India was 1.11 % per annum from 1983 to 1994; however, it declined to 0.31 % per annum from 1994 to 2018. The decline in the growth rate of self-employed individuals in rural areas was more pronounced for females than males, to the extent that their growth rate became negative in all sub-periods after 1994. The declining trend in the growth rate of casual workers is also evident in rural India between 1994 and 2018. Once again, the growth rate for rural females turned negative during this period. Conversely, a different picture emerges concerning the growth rate of regular employees in rural India, as males and females experienced much higher growth rates from 1994 to 2018 (the post-globalisation period) than from 1983 to 1994 (the pre-globalisation period).

Table 55. Annual Growth Rates of Workers (UPSS) by Modes of Employment in India

Mode of employment	Growth Rate during	Rural			Urban			Rural + Urban		
		Male	Female	Male + Female	Male	Female	Male + Female	Male	Female	Male + Female
Regular Employee	1983 to 1994	−0.13	1.06	0.03	2.76	4.33	2.99	1.58	2.99	1.78
	1994 to 2000	1.53	2.48	1.67	2.49	3.65	2.67	2.14	3.23	2.31
	2000 to 2012	2.48	4.69	2.87	3.49	5.63	3.87	3.14	5.31	3.52
	2012 to 2018	6.06	6.02	6.06	3.03	5.71	3.48	3.06	4.56	3.33
	1994 to 2018	3.13	4.47	3.36	3.12	5.15	3.47	2.87	4.60	3.17
Self–employed	1983 to 1994	1.25	0.88	1.11	3.34	3.38	3.35	1.63	1.13	1.46
	1994 to 2000	0.14	−0.22	0.01	2.53	0.75	2.14	0.64	−0.11	0.39
	2000 to 2012	1.32	−0.05	0.85	3.18	2.96	3.14	1.77	0.36	1.33
	2012 to 2018	1.32	−4.98	−0.49	1.10	−1.20	0.54	1.54	−4.05	0.02
	1994 to 2018	1.02	−1.35	0.31	2.50	1.35	2.23	1.43	−0.88	0.77
Casual Labour	1983 to 1994	3.14	2.30	2.80	3.71	2.44	3.32	3.22	2.31	2.86
	1994 to 2000	2.10	0.53	1.51	3.13	−2.16	1.70	2.25	0.28	1.53
	2000 to 2012	−3.44	−6.13	−4.21	2.35	0.83	1.95	−1.97	−4.91	−2.79
	2012 to 2018	1.23	−1.34	0.37	2.12	0.03	1.67	1.37	−1.21	0.54
	1994 to 2018	0.26	−2.10	−0.52	2.43	−0.32	1.74	0.74	−1.78	−0.06

Source: Same as Table 53

The decline in the annual growth rate of self-employed and casual workers from 1994 to 2018, compared to the period from 1983 to 1994, is also evident in urban India for both males and females. However, the decline was more pronounced among females than among males. Conversely, urban males and females experienced higher growth rates in regular employment between 1994 and 2018 than between 1983 and 1994.

When considering rural and urban areas together, it can be observed that the annual growth rates of self-employed and casual workers, for both males and females, declined in India during the post-globalisation period compared to the pre-globalisation period. Conversely, the growth rate of regular employment exhibited an opposing trend, being higher during the post-globalisation period than in the pre-globalisation era. However, it must also be noted that females in India experienced a continuous decline in the growth rates of self-employed workers from 1994 to 2018, resulting in negative growth rates across all sub-periods of the post-globalisation era (except during 2000–2012). A nearly identical conclusion can be drawn regarding the growth rates of female casual workers (except the 1994–2000 sub-period).

5.3 Modes of Employment by Social and Religious Groups

In this section, we first examine the modes of employment for various social groups at the all-India level, followed by a discussion on the modes of employment among different religious groups.

5.3.1 Modes of Employment Among Social Groups

To understand the modes of employment across social groups, we examine the data for 2000, 2012, and 2018. For these years, the population has been categorised into four social groups: Scheduled Tribes (STs), Scheduled Castes (SCs), Other Backward Classes (OBCs), and 'Others'. We have excluded years such as 1983 and 1994 from our discussion, as no separate information is available on the OBCs for these years, which are grouped with the category 'Others', rendering the data from these years non-comparable to subsequent years. The information on the modes of employment for workers belonging to various social groups, as presented in Table 56, reveals the following essential points:

- In rural India, most workers in all social groups except the SCs were engaged in self-employment in 2018. In 2018, the proportion of self-employed workers to total workers was the highest for the 'Others' category, followed by the OBCs, STs, and SCs. In that year, as many as 66 % of rural workers in the 'Others' category (including both males and females) were engaged in self-employment activities, while the figures for the OBCs, STs, and SCs were 62 %, 59 %, and 42 %, respectively. Notably, while the percentage of self-employed workers in rural India increased over time (from 2000 to 2018) for the OBCs, STs, and SCs, it decreased for the 'Others' category. However, when examining the percentage of casual workers, it emerged that the SCs had the highest proportion of their rural workers engaged in casual employment (46 % in 2018), compared to 32 %, 25 %, and 18 % for the STs, OBCs, and 'Others', respectively.
- Regarding regular employment in rural India, it was found that the 'Others' category ranked first in 2018, with approximately 17 % of their workers engaged in this mode of employment, followed by the OBCs (13 %), SCs (12 %), and STs (9 %). Overall, it can be stated that in rural India, while individuals from weaker social groups (particularly SCs and STs) experience higher rates of casual employment, self-employment, and regular employment are more prevalent among the more advantaged social groups ('Others' and OBCs).
- If we consider males and females in rural areas separately, the proportion of self-employed workers is lower among females from weaker social groups, such as STs and SCs, while it is higher for females from more privileged social groups, like OBCs and 'Others'. Regarding regular employment, however, rural males hold a superior position compared to rural females across all social groups. Conversely, the proportion of casual workers is higher among females than males in rural areas for all social groups except 'Others'. Overall, rural females from higher social groups (OBCs and 'Others') tend to engage more in self-employment and regular employment. In contrast, individuals from lower social groups (SCs and STs) are likelier to engage in casual employment.

Table 56. Modes of Employment of Workers (UPSS) by Social Groups in India (% of All Workers)

Mode of employment	Social Group	Year	Rural			Urban			Rural + Urban		
			Male	Female	Male + Female	Male	Female	Male + Female	Male	Female	Male + Female
Regular Employee	Scheduled Tribe	2000	6.01	2.04	4.29	40.70	24.27	35.97	9.38	3.24	6.79
		2012	5.77	3.32	4.83	52.03	34.56	47.72	10.83	5.21	8.73
		2018	9.74	7.75	9.10	49.37	50.73	49.70	13.94	10.92	12.99
	Scheduled Caste	2000	7.80	2.97	6.04	35.70	26.32	33.34	12.92	5.68	10.41
		2012	8.92	5.02	7.68	44.30	48.84	45.35	16.78	11.85	15.31
		2018	12.49	10.35	11.97	44.72	55.37	47.27	19.65	20.25	19.80
	Other Backward Class	2000	7.99	3.07	6.27	35.93	25.27	33.61	14.29	5.97	11.59
		2012	9.43	5.59	8.28	38.79	34.88	37.99	17.60	11.08	15.80
		2018	14.01	10.07	13.07	41.83	46.08	42.71	22.08	19.21	21.42
	Others	2000	11.73	4.11	9.49	46.88	45.82	46.71	24.53	12.82	21.59
		2012	14.13	8.29	12.64	47.02	50.45	47.67	27.84	21.28	36.37
		2018	17.43	14.40	16.81	49.69	57.78	51.19	31.04	31.45	31.12
Self–employed	Scheduled Tribe	2000	49.45	52.65	50.83	29.02	33.39	30.27	47.46	51.61	49.21
		2012	55.71	57.41	56.37	23.68	34.61	26.38	52.21	56.04	53.64
		2018	59.85	57.51	59.09	28.15	20.42	26.27	56.49	54.78	55.95
	Scheduled Caste	2000	35.02	36.96	35.73	31.99	38.37	33.60	34.47	37.12	35.39
		2012	35.70	44.35	38.44	29.55	31.82	30.07	34.33	42.40	36.74
		2018	41.96	40.83	41.69	30.01	27.38	29.38	39.31	37.87	38.96
	Other Backward Class	2000	59.20	61.04	59.85	43.97	51.74	45.66	55.77	59.83	57.09
		2012	57.82	61.29	58.86	43.83	48.93	44.87	53.93	58.97	55.32
		2018	61.51	61.85	61.59	40.85	39.14	40.49	55.52	56.09	55.65

(Continued)

Table 56. *(Continued)*

Mode of employment	Social Group	Year	Rural			Urban			Rural + Urban		
			Male	Female	Male + Female	Male	Female	Male + Female	Male	Female	Male + Female
Self–employed	Others	2000	65.53	74.27	68.09	43.14	44.54	43.36	57.38	68.07	60.05
		2012	63.76	73.35	66.21	45.21	41.81	44.61	56.03	63.62	57.73
		2018	64.81	68.26	65.52	41.83	35.00	40.57	55.12	55.19	55.13
Casual Labour	Scheduled Tribe	2000	44.55	45.31	44.88	30.29	42.34	33.75	43.16	45.15	44.00
		2012	38.52	39.26	38.80	24.29	30.83	25.90	36.96	38.75	37.63
		2018	30.41	34.74	31.81	22.48	28.85	24.03	29.57	34.30	31.07
	Scheduled Caste	2000	57.18	60.07	58.23	32.31	35.30	33.06	52.57	57.19	54.20
		2012	55.38	50.63	53.88	26.15	19.34	24.58	48.89	45.75	47.95
		2018	45.55	48.83	46.34	25.27	17.25	23.35	41.04	41.88	41.24
	Other Backward Class	2000	32.81	35.88	33.89	20.10	23.00	20.73	29.94	34.20	31.33
		2012	32.74	33.12	32.86	17.38	16.19	17.14	28.47	29.95	28.88
		2018	24.48	28.08	25.34	17.32	14.78	16.79	22.40	24.70	22.93
	Others	2000	22.74	21.62	22.41	9.98	9.64	9.93	18.10	19.12	18.35
		2012	22.12	18.37	21.15	7.77	7.75	7.76	16.13	15.09	15.89
		2018	17.76	17.34	17.67	8.48	7.22	8.25	13.84	13.36	13.75

Source: Same as Table 53

- In urban areas, most workers appear to be engaged in regular employment, followed by self-employment and casual employment. This holds for all social groups. However, there is a clear tendency for casual employment to be higher among weaker social groups than among stronger ones. Conversely, the incidence of regular employment has been highest for the 'Others' category, followed by STs, SCs, and OBCs. Regarding self-employment, individuals from higher social groups ('Others' and OBCs) occupy a superior position compared to those from lower social groups (SCs and STs). In 2018, more than two-fifths of workers from higher social groups were self-employed in urban India, while the figure for lower social groups was slightly above 25 %.
- There is a general trend for urban females to report a higher incidence of regular employment compared to urban males. This applies to all social groups in the year 2018. Furthermore, both males and females in urban areas appear to have increased their proportions of regular employees across all social groups. In 2018, the proportion of regular employees among urban females was 58 % for the 'Others' category, while for SCs, STs, and OBCs, it was 55 %, 51 %, and 46 %, respectively. Conversely, in the same year, the figures for urban males from the 'Others', STs, SCs, and OBCs social groups were 50 %, 49 %, 45 %, and 42 %, respectively. Regarding the proportion of casual workers in urban areas, it is higher among males across all social groups except STs. In contrast, in urban areas, the proportion of self-employed workers is higher among males than among females across all social groups. Overall, it appears that both males and females across all social groups in urban areas are increasingly engaged in regular employment, with a stronger trend among females than males, regardless of social group. However, the incidence of self-employment and casual employment among urban females from all social groups has been lower than that of their male counterparts.
- When considering both rural and urban areas, it is evident that SCs have a lower percentage of self-employed workers and a higher percentage of casual workers compared to all other social categories. Furthermore, the proportion of regular employees rises as one moves from lower to upper social classes. Therefore, the percentage of regular workers is lowest among STs, followed by SCs, OBCs and 'Others'. Similarly, the percentage of casual workers rises as one moves from higher social groups ('Others' and OBCs) to lower ones (SCs and STs). This trend holds across all the years we considered. This observation generally

remains valid when analysed separately for males and females. However, it is noteworthy that females exhibit lower incidences of regular employment and higher incidences of casual work than males across all social categories, with a few exceptions. It is imperative to mention that for females from the SC group, the incidence of casual workers has been significantly high over the years (57 %, 46 %, and 42 % in 2000, 2012, and 2018, respectively) in comparison to other social categories, thus reflecting a lag in the percentage of self-employed workers. It is also clear that the disparity between males and females in the percentage of regular employees decreased over time across all social categories.

5.3.2 Modes of Employment Among Religious Groups

The information on modes of employment by religious groups in India at five time points is displayed in Table 57. This table outlines employment modes for Hindus, Muslims, and 'Others'. Our main observations are as follows:

- In rural India, the proportion of self-employed workers appears to be slightly higher among Hindus compared to both Muslims and 'Others'. However, this proportion seems to have declined across all religious groups over time. In 2018, the proportions of self-employed workers (considering both males and females) in rural India were 58 %, 56 %, and 52 % for Hindus, Muslims, and 'Others', respectively. The situation in urban India regarding the proportion of self-employed workers is quite the opposite, as it has been higher for Muslims than for Hindus and 'Others'. In 2018, the proportions of self-employed workers in urban India were 48 %, 37 %, and 35 % for Muslims, Hindus, and 'Others', respectively. Table 57 further indicates that, in rural and urban areas, the proportion of self-employed workers declined over time for all religious groups.
- Regarding the proportion of regular employees in rural India, those from the 'Others' category lead, followed by Muslims and Hindus. In urban areas, however, Hindus consistently hold a significantly higher proportion of regular employees compared to Muslims across all time points. Nevertheless, the 'Others' category has surpassed both Hindus and Muslims in terms of the proportion of regular employees in urban areas. In 2018, the percentages of regular workers in urban areas for 'Others', Hindus, and Muslims were recorded at 51 %, 49 %, and 33 %, respectively.

Table 57. Modes of Employment of Workers (UPSS) by Religious Groups in India (% of All Workers)

Mode of employment	Religious Group	Year	Rural			Urban			Rural + Urban		
			Male	Female	Male + Female	Male	Female	Male + Female	Male	Female	Male + Female
Regular Employee	Hindu	1983	9.7	2.5	7.0	46.0	26.0	41.7	17.5	5.0	13.1
		1994	8.5	2.5	6.3	44.9	29.6	41.6	16.7	5.8	13.0
		2000	8.8	3.0	6.7	43.8	34.0	41.8	17.2	6.9	13.8
		2012	9.8	5.3	8.4	46.3	43.9	45.8	19.9	12.2	17.7
		2018	13.6	9.8	12.7	48.2	52.5	49.1	23.4	20.2	22.6
	Muslim	1983	8.1	2.9	6.6	29.7	14.5	27.1	15.6	5.5	13.1
		1994	7.2	2.9	6.2	26.9	15.2	24.8	14.1	6.3	12.4
		2000	7.3	2.4	6.0	30.1	17.3	28.1	15.4	5.8	13.2
		2012	10.4	6.6	9.5	28.8	24.9	28.2	17.5	11.5	16.3
		2018	14.1	10.4	13.5	32.7	36.6	33.2	21.4	18.6	20.9
	Others	1983	14.5	6.2	11.3	50.3	44.5	48.9	24.0	12.3	20.0
		1994	10.9	5.9	9.0	44.7	51.7	46.3	19.4	13.7	17.4
		2000	12.3	5.9	10.0	42.9	52.2	45.2	21.0	14.5	18.9
		2012	14.4	9.2	12.7	47.0	60.1	50.4	25.0	21.9	24.0
		2018	18.5	21.8	19.4	46.2	65.9	51.0	26.9	35.0	29.0

(Continued)

Table 57 *(Continued)*

Mode of employment	Religious Group	Year	Rural			Urban			Rural + Urban		
			Male	Female	Male + Female	Male	Female	Male + Female	Male	Female	Male + Female
Self-employed	Hindu	1983	61.0	61.5	61.2	38.9	45.0	40.2	56.2	59.7	57.5
		1994	57.6	58.4	57.9	39.2	43.1	40.0	53.4	56.6	54.5
		2000	54.9	56.2	55.3	39.4	43.4	40.2	51.2	54.6	52.3
		2012	54.7	58.1	55.8	39.4	41.1	39.8	50.5	55.1	51.8
		2018	58.6	57.8	58.4	37.7	33.9	36.9	52.7	51.9	52.5
	Muslim	1983	60.3	67.1	62.2	51.9	54.7	52.4	57.4	64.4	59.1
		1994	59.8	63.3	60.7	54.7	61.5	55.9	58.0	62.8	59.1
		2000	54.9	70.9	59.0	50.6	67.0	53.1	53.4	70.0	57.1
		2012	52.2	68.2	55.9	52.8	61.3	54.1	52.4	66.4	55.3
		2018	53.5	65.7	55.6	47.3	50.5	47.7	51.1	61.0	52.6
	Others	1983	58.6	63.7	60.5	37.0	36.9	36.9	52.7	59.3	55.0
		1994	56.6	57.4	60.3	40.6	32.3	38.7	53.5	53.1	56.3
		2000	53.5	59.1	55.5	41.8	32.4	39.5	50.2	54.2	51.5
		2012	54.9	64.8	58.2	40.2	31.6	38.0	50.1	56.5	52.1
		2018	53.5	48.4	52.3	38.1	25.7	35.1	48.8	41.6	47.0

(Continued)

Table 57 *(Continued)*

Mode of employment	Religious Group	Year	Rural			Urban			Rural + Urban		
			Male	Female	Male + Female	Male	Female	Male + Female	Male	Female	Male + Female
Casual Labour	Hindu	1983	29.3	36.0	31.9	15.1	29.0	18.1	26.3	35.2	29.4
		1994	33.9	39.1	35.8	15.9	27.3	18.4	29.8	37.7	32.5
		2000	36.3	40.8	37.9	16.8	22.6	17.9	31.6	38.6	33.9
		2012	35.5	36.6	35.8	14.3	15.0	14.4	29.6	32.7	30.5
		2018	27.7	32.5	28.9	14.1	13.6	14.0	23.9	27.8	24.8
	Muslim	1983	31.6	30.0	31.2	18.3	30.7	20.5	27.0	30.2	27.8
		1994	33.0	33.7	33.1	18.4	23.3	19.3	27.9	30.8	28.5
		2000	37.8	26.7	35.0	19.3	15.7	18.8	31.3	24.2	29.7
		2012	37.3	25.2	34.5	18.4	13.7	17.7	30.1	22.1	28.5
		2018	32.4	23.9	30.9	20.0	12.8	19.1	27.5	20.5	26.4
	Others	1983	26.9	30.0	28.1	12.8	18.6	14.2	23.3	28.3	25.1
		1994	32.5	36.7	30.7	14.6	16.0	14.9	27.1	33.2	26.3
		2000	34.2	35.0	34.5	15.3	15.4	15.3	28.8	31.3	29.7
		2012	30.7	26.0	29.1	12.8	8.3	11.6	24.9	21.6	23.8
		2018	27.9	29.8	28.4	15.7	8.4	13.9	24.2	23.4	24.0

Source: Same as Table 53

- The percentages of casual workers among the three religious groups show a slight variation in rural India. However, in urban areas, Muslims appear to have a higher percentage of casual workers compared to Hindus and 'Others'. In 2018, the percentages of casual workers in rural areas were 29 %, 31 %, and 28 % for Hindus, Muslims, and 'Others', respectively; in urban areas, they were 14 %, 19 %, and 14 % for Hindus, Muslims, and 'Others', respectively.
- By combining rural and urban areas, it can be observed that the Hindus have a higher proportion of their workers engaged in regular employment than Muslims. On the other hand, Muslims show a more significant proportion of workers involved in self-employment compared to Hindus. Although Hindus are reported to have a higher proportion of casual workers than Muslims during 1983–2012, Muslims exhibited a higher percentage of casual workers (26.45 %) compared to Hindus (24.82 %) in 2018.
- When we consider males and females separately, it appears that in rural areas, Hindu males have a higher proportion of self-employed workers than Muslim males in all the years except 1994. Conversely, Muslim females have a higher proportion of self-employed workers compared to Hindu females. Regarding the proportion of regular employees, Hindu males appear to have held superior positions to their Muslim counterparts until 2000; since then, the latter have improved their standings. On the other hand, Muslim females are in a better position than their Hindu counterparts, except for the year 2000. However, regarding the proportion of casual labour, Muslim males dominate Hindu males (except in 1994). In contrast, the situation is reversed for females, with Muslim females having a lower proportion of workers in casual employment compared to Hindu females. Overall, it can be said that Muslim females have a higher incidence of self-employment and regular employment in rural India compared to Hindu females. In contrast, the opposite is true concerning casual employment.

- The picture depicted above appears to be relatively consistent in urban areas, where Muslim females demonstrate a higher proportion of self-employment and a lower proportion of casual employment in comparison to their Hindu counterparts. Furthermore, the advantage of Hindu females over Muslim females is evident in urban areas regarding the proportion of regular employees. Regarding the proportion of males in regular employment in urban areas, Table 57 indicates that Hindus have a higher proportion than Muslims. Conversely, a higher proportion of Muslim males in urban areas are engaged in self-employment and casual employment compared to their Hindu counterparts.
- Overall, when considering both rural and urban areas, it can be observed that Muslim males tend to engage more in self-employment and casual employment compared to Hindu males. However, the former lagged behind the latter in terms of the proportion of regular employees during the period studied. As for Muslim females, an even higher proportion of them are involved in self-employment compared to Hindu females, resulting in lower proportions of regular employees and casual labour compared to Hindu females.

5.4 Employment Modes for Workers in Major States

In this section, we examine the percentage distribution of workers (UPSS) across three modes of employment (self-employment, regular employment, and casual labour) in seventeen major states of India, separately for rural, urban, and combined rural and urban areas.

5.4.1 Percentage Distribution of Rural Workers in Self-Employment, Regular Employment, and Casual Labour Across States

Tables 58 and 59 present information on the percentage distribution of UPSS workers into three modes of employment in the rural areas of seventeen states at our chosen points of time (1983, 1994, 2000, 2012, and 2018), as well as the ranks of the states on this basis. Considering these two tables together, the following observations may be put forward:

Table 58. Percentage Distribution of Usually Employed (UPSS) by Status of Employment in Major States: Rural Areas

Sex	State	Regular Employee					Self-employed					Casual Labour				
		1983	1994	2000	2012	2018	1983	1994	2000	2012	2018	1983	1994	2000	2012	2018
Male	Andhra Pradesh	12.7	8.1	7.6	11.8	13.1	50.9	49.1	48.4	48.4	52.8	36.4	42.8	44.0	39.8	34.1
	Assam	17.5	13.4	15.7	10.4	18.1	64.2	60.0	59.0	71.1	62.7	18.3	26.6	25.3	18.5	19.2
	Bihar	7.5	4.7	4.2	4.1	10.5	56.8	55.4	53.9	55.4	58.1	35.8	39.9	41.9	40.5	31.4
	Gujarat	8.3	9.9	9.6	12.4	16.3	59.0	46.9	50.9	56.5	62.6	32.7	43.2	39.5	31.1	21.1
	Haryana	18.6	13.5	16.6	16.5	28.0	62.3	63.3	59.0	58.2	47.9	19.1	23.2	24.4	25.3	24.2
	Himachal Pradesh	9.2	12.2	16.7	22.1	23.9	81.1	75.1	62.9	54.7	55.5	9.7	12.7	20.4	23.2	20.6
	Jammu & Kashmir	9.2	16.2	12.2	19.5	23.9	75.4	72.0	73.3	51.1	53.2	15.4	11.8	14.5	29.4	22.9
	Karnataka	6.9	6.5	7.6	13.4	14.5	59.0	57.9	51.8	53.0	58.7	34.1	35.6	40.6	33.6	26.8
	Kerala	15.5	12.3	13.0	15.5	24.7	44.3	40.8	38.1	38.9	40.7	40.2	46.9	48.9	45.6	34.6
	Madhya Pradesh	9.2	5.9	4.9	5.8	9.4	66.2	62.4	58.0	60.2	64.1	24.6	31.7	37.1	34.0	26.5
	Maharashtra	13.7	11.9	11.8	12.3	14.6	51.7	49.3	44.1	53.8	57.6	34.5	38.8	44.1	33.9	27.8
	Odisha	11.8	6.2	5.8	8.2	11.3	53.4	56.6	48.4	60.6	61.6	34.8	37.2	45.8	31.2	27.1
	Punjab	12.7	13.2	17.5	20.1	22.1	65.9	54.7	54.0	46.0	50.1	21.4	32.1	28.5	33.9	27.8
	Rajasthan	6.5	7.4	7.8	9.6	15.6	80.8	71.8	73.3	61.8	64.6	12.7	20.8	18.9	28.6	19.8
	Tamil Nadu	12.4	12.5	15.3	17.0	24.5	44.6	41.4	35.8	31.5	35.1	43.0	46.1	48.9	51.5	40.4
	Uttar Pradesh	6.6	5.7	7.1	7.1	9.9	76.0	72.4	70.8	62.4	65.1	17.4	21.9	22.1	30.5	25.0
	West Bengal	11.4	10.3	7.5	8.2	12.1	49.7	54.7	49.2	43.1	49.0	38.9	35.0	43.3	48.6	38.9

(Continued)

Table 58 *(Continued)*

Sex	State	Regular Employee					Self-employed					Casual Labour				
		1983	1994	2000	2012	2018	1983	1994	2000	2012	2018	1983	1994	2000	2012	2018
Female	Andhra Pradesh	3.0	1.9	3.6	3.2	6.0	44.3	45.3	42.6	44.7	45.7	52.7	52.8	53.8	52.1	48.3
	Assam	26.4	18.2	19.8	17.5	58.8	50.8	49.1	54.8	64.3	18.5	22.8	32.7	25.4	18.2	22.7
	Bihar	1.5	1.2	1.5	4.6	16.6	56.1	41.9	47.7	62.7	58.2	42.4	56.9	50.8	32.8	25.2
	Gujarat	1.8	1.5	1.6	5.2	9.4	60.8	55.4	59.1	58.3	64.7	37.4	43.1	39.3	36.5	26.0
	Haryana	5.6	1.1	1.5	4.2	16.8	72.8	77.4	86.0	75.2	50.1	21.6	21.5	12.5	20.6	33.1
	Himachal Pradesh	1.1	1.7	2.9	6.0	6.8	97.7	96.7	95.9	87.9	89.8	1.2	1.6	1.2	6.1	3.4
	Jammu & Kashmir	1.0	2.0	2.1	5.7	9.8	97.8	96.2	97.4	90.4	89.5	1.2	1.8	0.5	3.9	0.6
	Karnataka	2.7	2.3	1.9	8.2	10.8	51.2	53.4	47.6	49.6	45.2	46.1	44.3	50.5	42.1	44.0
	Kerala	9.9	9.7	15.0	23.0	41.3	58.7	55.0	53.0	36.4	30.5	31.4	35.3	32.0	40.5	28.2
	Madhya Pradesh	2.9	1.2	1.5	2.4	4.3	66.3	61.2	54.4	57.8	66.4	30.8	37.6	44.1	39.7	29.3
	Maharashtra	1.3	2.5	1.5	3.1	6.2	50.2	48.1	44.5	53.6	52.2	48.5	49.4	54.0	43.3	41.5
	Odisha	1.8	1.3	1.3	3.4	9.5	52.2	56.2	49.2	66.1	52.6	46.0	42.5	49.5	30.5	38.0
	Punjab	2.8	3.2	3.7	8.6	31.0	90.2	85.0	88.9	77.8	47.8	7.0	11.8	7.4	13.6	21.3
	Rajasthan	0.8	0.9	1.0	2.6	4.0	89.4	88.4	89.0	76.4	84.8	9.8	10.7	10.0	21.0	11.3
	Tamil Nadu	3.7	5.2	6.9	9.5	15.9	43.9	41.9	38.0	27.8	34.5	52.4	52.9	55.1	62.7	49.6
	Uttar Pradesh	1.1	0.9	1.6	3.8	8.0	83.5	79.5	77.5	81.6	78.3	15.4	19.6	20.9	14.7	13.7
	West Bengal	5.3	7.3	5.1	10.3	18.5	60.6	59.0	62.4	57.5	46.0	34.1	33.7	32.5	32.2	35.5

(Continued)

Table 58 *(Continued)*

Sex	State	Regular Employee					Self-employed					Casual Labour				
		1983	1994	2000	2012	2018	1983	1994	2000	2012	2018	1983	1994	2000	2012	2018
Male + Female	Andhra Pradesh	8.5	5.3	5.9	8.2	10.4	48.1	47.4	45.9	46.8	50.0	43.4	47.3	48.3	45.0	39.6
	Assam	19.2	14.5	16.6	11.7	22.9	61.7	57.6	58.1	69.9	57.5	19.2	28.0	25.3	18.4	19.6
	Bihar	5.6	3.9	3.5	4.2	11.0	56.5	52.2	52.4	56.4	58.1	37.9	43.9	44.1	39.5	30.9
	Gujarat	5.6	6.6	6.4	10.2	14.9	59.8	50.3	54.2	57.0	63.0	34.7	43.2	39.4	32.7	22.1
	Haryana	14.6	9.3	12.5	13.8	26.3	65.5	68.0	66.3	61.9	48.2	19.9	22.6	21.2	24.3	25.5
	Himachal Pradesh	5.4	7.3	10.3	14.2	16.5	88.9	85.2	78.3	70.9	70.3	5.7	7.5	11.5	14.8	13.2
	Jammu & Kashmir	6.6	10.3	8.6	15.4	20.0	82.5	82.0	81.9	62.7	63.2	10.9	7.7	9.5	21.9	16.8
	Karnataka	5.3	4.8	5.4	11.8	13.6	55.9	56.1	50.2	51.9	55.1	38.8	39.2	44.4	36.3	31.3
	Kerala	13.3	11.5	13.6	17.7	29.2	50.1	45.3	42.8	38.2	38.0	36.7	43.2	43.6	44.1	32.9
	Madhya Pradesh	6.5	4.0	3.5	4.7	7.7	66.2	61.9	56.5	59.4	64.8	27.2	34.1	39.9	35.9	27.5
	Maharashtra	8.1	7.6	7.3	8.7	11.9	51.0	48.8	44.3	53.7	55.8	40.9	43.6	48.5	37.6	32.3
	Odisha	8.4	4.5	4.2	6.8	10.9	53.0	56.5	48.7	62.2	59.7	38.6	39.1	47.1	31.0	29.4
	Punjab	9.5	10.6	13.1	17.0	23.4	73.8	62.7	65.1	54.7	49.8	16.7	26.8	21.8	28.4	26.8
	Rajasthan	4.0	4.6	4.9	6.8	12.2	84.6	79.1	79.9	67.6	70.6	11.4	16.4	15.2	25.6	17.3
	Tamil Nadu	8.7	9.3	11.8	14.1	21.5	44.3	41.6	36.7	30.1	34.9	47.1	49.1	51.5	55.8	43.6
	Uttar Pradesh	4.8	4.4	5.6	6.2	9.6	78.4	74.3	72.6	67.3	67.3	16.8	21.3	21.8	26.5	23.1
	West Bengal	9.8	9.6	7.0	8.7	13.5	52.5	55.7	52.1	46.5	48.4	37.6	34.7	40.9	44.8	38.2

Source: Same as Table 53

Table 59. States' Ranks Based on Percentage of Usually Employed (UPSS) Under Self-Employment, Regular Employment and Casual Employment: Rural Areas

Sex	State	Regular Employee						Self–employed						Casual Labour					
		1983	1994	2000	2012	2018	Overall	1983	1994	2000	2012	2018	Overall	1983	1994	2000	2012	2018	Overall
Male	Andhra Pradesh	6	11	11	10	12	10	14	14	13	13	12	14	4	4	5	5	4	3
	Assam	2	3	4	11	7	7	7	7	5	1	4	3	13	12	12	17	17	14
	Bihar	14	17	17	17	15	17	11	10	9	8	8	9	5	5	7	4	5	5
	Gujarat	13	10	9	8	8	9	9	15	11	7	5	11	9	3	9	11	14	9
	Haryana	1	2	3	5	1	1	8	5	6	6	15	7	12	13	13	15	12	12
	Himachal Pradesh	11	7	2	1	5	6	1	1	4	9	10	4	17	16	15	16	15	17
	Jammu & Kashmir	10	1	7	3	4	5	4	3	1	12	11	6	15	17	17	13	13	15
	Karnataka	15	13	12	7	11	12	10	8	10	11	7	10	8	8	8	9	9	8
	Kerala	3	6	6	6	2	3	17	17	16	16	16	16	2	1	1	3	3	2
	Madhya Pradesh	12	15	16	16	17	15	5	6	7	5	3	5	10	11	10	6	10	10
	Maharashtra	4	8	8	9	10	8	13	13	15	10	9	13	7	6	4	7	6	6
	Odisha	8	14	15	14	14	14	12	9	14	4	6	8	6	7	3	17	8	7
	Punjab	5	4	1	2	6	2	6	11	8	14	13	12	11	10	11	8	7	11
	Rajasthan	17	12	10	12	9	13	2	4	2	3	2	2	16	15	16	14	16	16
	Tamil Nadu	7	5	5	4	3	4	16	16	17	17	17	17	1	2	2	1	1	1
	Uttar Pradesh	16	16	14	15	16	16	3	2	3	2	1	1	14	14	14	12	11	13
	West Bengal	9	9	13	13	13	11	15	12	12	15	14	15	3	9	6	2	2	4
	Kendall's W			0.789*						0.752*						0.845*			

(Continued)

Table 59 *(Continued)*

Sex	State	Regular Employee						Self-employed						Casual Labour					
		1983	1994	2000	2012	2018	Overall	1983	1994	2000	2012	2018	Overall	1983	1994	2000	2012	2018	Overall
Female	Andhra Pradesh	6	9	6	14	15	9	16	15	16	15	13	16	1	3	3	2	2	2
	Assam	1	1	1	2	1	1	14	13	9	8	17	12	11	11	11	13	12	12
	Bihar	12	13	13	10	6	12	11	16	13	9	7	11	6	1	4	8	11	5
	Gujarat	11	11	10	9	11	10	8	10	8	10	6	8	7	6	8	7	10	7
	Haryana	3	15	14	11	5	7	6	6	5	6	10	6	12	12	13	12	7	11
	Himachal Pradesh	15	10	7	7	13	11	2	1	2	2	1	2	16	17	16	16	16	16
	Jammu & Kashmir	16	8	8	8	9	8	1	2	1	1	2	1	17	16	17	17	17	17
	Karnataka	9	7	9	6	8	6	13	12	14	14	14	15	4	5	5	4	3	4
	Kerala	2	2	2	1	2	2	10	11	11	16	16	13	9	9	10	5	9	9
	Madhya Pradesh	7	14	15	17	16	16	7	7	10	11	5	7	10	8	7	6	8	8
	Maharashtra	13	6	`	15	14	13	15	14	15	13	9	14	3	4	2	3	4	3
	Odisha	10	12	16	13	10	14	12	9	12	7	8	9	5	7	6	10	5	6
	Punjab	8	5	5	5	3	5	3	4	4	4	11	5	15	14	15	15	13	15
	Rajasthan	17	16	17	16	17	17	4	3	3	5	3	3	14	15	14	11	15	14
	Tamil Nadu	5	4	3	4	7	4	17	17	17	17	15	17	2	2	1	1	1	1
	Uttar Pradesh	14	17	11	12	12	15	5	5	6	3	4	4	13	13	12	14	14	13
	West Bengal	4	3	4	3	4	3	9	8	7	12	12	10	8	10	9	9	6	10
	Kendall's W	**0.745***						**0.842***						**0.916***					

(Continued)

Table 59 *(Continued)*

Sex	State	Regular Employee						Self-employed						Casual Labour					
		1983	1994	2000	2012	2018	Overall	1983	1994	2000	2012	2018	Overall	1983	1994	2000	2012	2018	Overall
Male + Female	Andhra Pradesh	7	11	11	12	15	11	16	15	14	14	12	15	2	2	3	2	2	2
	Assam	1	1	1	8	4	2	8	8	7	2	9	6	12	11	11	16	14	14
	Bihar	13	17	16	17	13	16	10	12	10	10	8	11	6	3	6	5	7	4
	Gujarat	12	10	10	9	8	10	9	13	9	9	6	9	9	6	10	9	13	10
	Haryana	2	6	4	6	2	4	7	5	5	7	15	7	11	13	14	14	11	12
	Himachal Pradesh	14	9	6	4	7	8	1	1	3	1	2	1	17	17	16	17	17	17
	Jammu & Kashmir	10	4	7	3	6	6	3	2	1	5	5	3	16	16	17	15	16	16
	Karnataka	15	12	13	7	9	12	11	10	12	13	11	12	4	7	5	7	6	6
	Kerala	3	2	2	1	1	1	15	16	16	16	16	16	8	5	7	4	4	5
	Madhya Pradesh	11	16	17	16	17	17	6	7	8	8	4	5	10	10	9	8	9	9
	Maharashtra	9	8	8	10	12	9	14	14	15	12	10	14	3	4	2	6	5	3
	Odisha	8	14	15	14	14	13	12	9	13	6	7	10	5	8	4	10	8	8
	Punjab	5	3	3	2	3	3	5	6	6	11	13	8	14	12	13	11	10	11
	Rajasthan	17	13	14	13	11	14	2	3	2	3	1	2	15	15	15	13	15	15
	Tamil Nadu	6	7	5	5	5	5	17	17	17	17	17	17	1	1	1	1	1	1
	Uttar Pradesh	16	15	12	15	16	15	4	4	4	4	3	4	13	14	12	12	12	13
	West Bengal	4	5	9	11	10	7	13	11	11	15	14	13	7	9	8	3	3	7
	Kendall's W			**0.809***						**0.855***						**0.916***			

Source: Author's computation using data in Table 58

*Note: * implies significance at 1 per cent level.*

- The states in India showed considerable variation in the proportions of workers engaged in three types of employment: self-employment, regular employment, and casual employment. As shown in Table 58, in 2018, the percentage of self-employed workers among rural males ranged from 65.1 % in Uttar Pradesh to 35.1 % in Tamil Nadu. In that year, other states with relatively high percentages of rural male workers in self-employment included Rajasthan (64.6 %), Madhya Pradesh (64.1 %), Assam (62.7 %), and Gujarat (62.6 %). Conversely, other states (apart from Tamil Nadu) with relatively low percentages of rural male workers engaged in self-employment were Kerala (40.7 %), Haryana (47.9 %), West Bengal (49.0 %), and Punjab (50.1 %).
- In 2018, the percentage of self-employed rural women was highest in Himachal Pradesh at 89.8 % and lowest in Assam at 18.5 %. That same year, states with a relatively high proportion of rural female workers in self-employment included Jammu & Kashmir (89.5 %), Rajasthan (84.8 %), Uttar Pradesh (78.3 %), and Madhya Pradesh (66.4 %). Conversely, states with a relatively low percentage of rural female workers in self-employment included Kerala (30.5 %), Tamil Nadu (34.5 %), Karnataka (45.2 %), and Andhra Pradesh (45.7 %).
- When considering rural persons (males plus females), Rajasthan has the highest percentage of self-employed workers at 70.6 %, while Tamil Nadu has the lowest at 34.9 %. Among rural persons, other states reporting relatively high proportions of self-employed workers include Himachal Pradesh (70.3 %), Uttar Pradesh (67.3 %), Madhya Pradesh (64.8 %), and Jammu & Kashmir (63.2 %). Conversely, some states with relatively low proportions are Kerala (38.0 %), Haryana (48.2 %), West Bengal (48.4 %), and Punjab (49.8 %).
- The data presented in Table 58 indicates that between 1983 and 2018, nearly two-thirds of the states we examined experienced a decline in the percentage of rural workers in self-employment (with exceptions being Andhra Pradesh, Bihar, Gujarat, Maharashtra, and Odisha for rural males, and Andhra Pradesh, Bihar, Gujarat, Madhya Pradesh, Maharashtra, and Odisha for rural females). Nevertheless, the ranking pattern of the states regarding the percentage of self-employed workers did not change significantly during this period for both rural males and females, as indicated by the statistical significance of Kendall's W statistic (the coefficient of concordance). Examining the period from 1983 to 2018, the states with relatively higher proportions of self-employed rural workers are Himachal Pradesh, Rajasthan, Jammu & Kashmir, Uttar Pradesh, and Madhya Pradesh (a mix of underdeveloped and hilly states). In these states,

more than 60 % of rural persons were self-employed throughout the years studied, except for Madhya Pradesh in 2000 and 2012.

- Regarding the percentage of regular employees among rural males in 2018, Haryana (28.0 %) topped the list of states, followed by Kerala (24.7 %), Tamil Nadu (24.5 %), Jammu & Kashmir (23.9 %), and Himachal Pradesh (23.9 %). Madhya Pradesh (9.4 %) was at the bottom, closely followed by Uttar Pradesh (9.9 %), Bihar (10.5 %), Odisha (11.3 %), and West Bengal (12.1 %). The situation differs somewhat for rural females, as Assam, with nearly 59 % of rural females, was reported to have been engaged in regular employment in 2018, followed by Kerala (41.3 %), Punjab (31.0 %), West Bengal (18.5 %), and Haryana (16.8 %). States with relatively low percentages of regular workers among rural females in 2018 include Rajasthan (4.0 %), Madhya Pradesh (4.3 %), Andhra Pradesh (6.0 %), Maharashtra (6.2 %), and Himachal Pradesh (6.8 %). For rural persons, the highest percentage of regular employees in 2018 was in Kerala (29.2 %), followed by Haryana (26.3 %), Punjab (23.4 %), Assam (22.9 %), and Tamil Nadu (21.5 %). Conversely, Madhya Pradesh had the lowest percentage (7.7 %), followed by Uttar Pradesh (9.6 %), Andhra Pradesh (10.4 %), Odisha (10.9%), and Bihar (11.0%). Overall, in 2018, the percentage of regular employees among rural individuals was higher in the more developed states (except Assam) and lower in the less developed states (excluding Andhra Pradesh).
- By examining the ranks of the states at various time points, it can be noted that the percentage of regular employees among rural males during 1983–2018 appears to be higher in Haryana, Punjab, Kerala, Tamil Nadu, and Jammu & Kashmir. In contrast, it seems to be lower in Bihar, Uttar Pradesh, Madhya Pradesh, Odisha, and Rajasthan. Regarding rural females, the percentage of regular employees from 1983 to 2018 appears to be higher in Assam, Kerala, West Bengal, Tamil Nadu, and Punjab, while it is lower in Rajasthan, Madhya Pradesh, Uttar Pradesh, Odisha, and Maharashtra. The percentage appears higher among rural persons in Kerala, Assam, Punjab, Haryana, and Tamil Nadu, and lower in Madhya Pradesh, Bihar, Uttar Pradesh, Rajasthan, and Odisha.
- Another important observation regarding the percentage of rural workers in regular employment is that most states experienced an increase in their

share of regular employees from 1983 to 2018. This is true for all categories: rural males (except in Odisha), rural females, and rural persons. However, the ranking order of the states in terms of the percentage of regular employees did not undergo any statistically significant change across these categories during this period, as affirmed by the statistical significance of Kendall's W statistic.

- Considering the information presented in Tables 58 and 59, it can be observed that the states reporting a relatively high percentage of casual workers among rural males in 2018 are Tamil Nadu (40.4 %), West Bengal (38.9 %), Kerala (34.6 %), Andhra Pradesh (34.1 %), and Bihar (31.4 %). In contrast, the percentages are relatively low in Assam (19.2 %), Rajasthan (19.8 %), Himachal Pradesh (20.6 %), Gujarat (21.1 %), and Jammu & Kashmir (22.9 %). Regarding rural females, the states with a relatively high percentage of casual workers are Tamil Nadu (49.6 %), Andhra Pradesh (48.3 %), Karnataka (44.0 %), Maharashtra (41.5 %), and Odisha (38.0 %). Conversely, the state reporting the lowest percentage of casual workers for rural females in 2018 is Jammu & Kashmir (0.6 %). Other states with relatively low percentages of casual workers for rural females include Himachal Pradesh (3.4 %), Rajasthan (11.3 %), Uttar Pradesh (13.7 %), and Punjab (21.3 %). As for the percentage of casual workers among rural persons in 2018, Tamil Nadu (43.6 %) topped the list, followed by Andhra Pradesh (39.6 %), West Bengal (38.2 %), Kerala (32.9 %), and Maharashtra (32.3 %); the lowest percentage was observed in Himachal Pradesh (13.2 %), closely followed by Jammu & Kashmir (16.8 %), Rajasthan (17.3 %), Assam (19.6 %), and Gujarat (22.1 %).
- When we consider the entire period 1983–2018, it appears that, for rural males, while the states of Tamil Nadu, Kerala, Andhra Pradesh, West Bengal, and Bihar have a relatively higher percentage of casual workers, the opposite seems to be true in Himachal Pradesh, Rajasthan, Jammu & Kashmir, Assam, and Uttar Pradesh. Regarding rural females, during the period in question, Tamil Nadu, Andhra Pradesh, Maharashtra, Karnataka, and Bihar appear to have higher percentages of casual workers. In contrast, Jammu & Kashmir, Himachal Pradesh, Punjab, Rajasthan, and Uttar Pradesh seem to have lower

percentages. For rural individuals, the ranking pattern of the states for the entire study period remains relatively stable; the percentages of casual workers are higher in Tamil Nadu, Andhra Pradesh, Maharashtra, Bihar, and Kerala, and lower in Himachal Pradesh, Jammu & Kashmir, Rajasthan, Assam, and Uttar Pradesh.

- Between 1983 and 2018, eight states saw an increase in the percentage of casual workers among rural males: Assam, Haryana, Himachal Pradesh, Jammu & Kashmir, Madhya Pradesh, Punjab, Rajasthan, and Uttar Pradesh. Additionally, five states experienced an increase in the percentage of casual workers among rural females: Haryana, Himachal Pradesh, Punjab, Rajasthan, and West Bengal. However, when examining rural persons (males plus females), nine states – namely Assam, Haryana, Himachal Pradesh, Jammu & Kashmir, Madhya Pradesh, Punjab, Rajasthan, Uttar Pradesh, and West Bengal – showed an increase in the percentage of casual workers during this period. Nonetheless, changes in the percentage of casual workers have not substantially affected the ranking order of states by this measure in rural areas. This holds true for rural males, females, and persons, as the calculated Kendall's W statistics are statistically significant.

5.4.2 Percentage Distribution of Urban Workers by Self-Employment, Regular Employment, and Casual Labour Across States

The percentages of self-employed, regular, and casual workers in the urban areas of seventeen major states, along with the rankings of these states about these categories, are presented in Tables 60 and 61, respectively. Our main observations here are as follows:

- In 2018, the highest percentage of self-employed urban males was in Assam (50.7 %), while the lowest was in Tamil Nadu (29.5 %). For urban females, Himachal Pradesh had the highest percentage (48.3 %), and Bihar had the lowest (25.5 %). Among urban persons, Uttar Pradesh recorded the highest percentage of self-employed workers (48.6 %), whereas Tamil Nadu had the lowest (30.1 %). Other states with relatively high percentages of self-employed urban males include Uttar Pradesh, Bihar, Odisha, and Rajasthan. For urban females, notable states are Jammu & Kashmir, West Bengal, Uttar Pradesh, and Rajasthan. For urban persons, states with relatively high percentages of self-employed workers are Assam, Rajasthan, Bihar, and Odisha. In contrast, states with lower percentages of urban males in self-employment are Himachal Pradesh, Maharashtra, Andhra Pradesh, and Karnataka. The states with lower percentages for urban females include Haryana, Maharashtra, Kerala, and Punjab, while those with lower percentages for urban persons are Maharashtra, Himachal Pradesh, Karnataka, and Haryana.

- When we examine the entire period from 1983 to 2018, certain states display relatively high percentages of self-employed workers among urban males: Uttar Pradesh, Bihar, Assam, Jammu & Kashmir, and Punjab. Conversely, states with relatively low percentages of self-employed workers for urban males include Tamil Nadu, Himachal Pradesh, Maharashtra, Andhra Pradesh, and Kerala. The percentage of urban female self-employed workers appears higher in Uttar Pradesh, Rajasthan, Jammu & Kashmir, Himachal Pradesh, and Punjab. At the same time, it is lower in Maharashtra, Assam, Tamil Nadu, Karnataka, and West Bengal. Considering urban persons, the states reporting the higher percentages of self-employed workers from 1983 to 2018 are Uttar Pradesh, Rajasthan, Bihar, Jammu & Kashmir, and Assam. In contrast, those with a lower percentage include Tamil Nadu, Maharashtra, Himachal Pradesh, Karnataka, and Andhra Pradesh.
- Another point to emerge from Table 60 is that while eight out of seventeen major states (these are Assam, Gujarat, Karnataka, Kerala, Madhya Pradesh, Maharashtra, Odisha, and West Bengal) experienced an increase in the percentage of urban male workers in self-employment from 1983 to 2018, only two states saw similar growth for urban females (these are Himachal Pradesh and West Bengal). For urban persons, however, five states, namely Assam, Gujarat, Madhya Pradesh, Odisha, and West Bengal, increased the percentage of self-employed workers during this period.

Table 60. Percentage Distribution of Usually Employed (UPSS) by Status of Employment in Major States: Urban Areas

Sex	State	Regular Employee					Self–employed					Casual Labour				
		1983	1994	2000	2012	2018	1983	1994	2000	2012	2018	1983	1994	2000	2012	2018
Male	Andhra Pradesh	44.0	40.1	42.0	49.4	47.6	40.3	38.2	35.8	35.4	35.6	15.7	21.7	22.2	15.2	16.9
	Assam	46.0	42.0	40.5	35.3	39.8	45.3	47.8	48.3	54.9	50.7	8.7	10.2	11.2	9.8	9.5
	Bihar	37.0	36.7	31.0	28.4	31.6	48.0	48.4	54.1	54.1	46.8	15.0	14.9	14.9	17.5	21.7
	Gujarat	44.1	44.9	35.9	52.0	49.6	40.3	37.3	40.8	40.3	43.1	15.6	17.8	23.3	7.7	7.2
	Haryana	40.4	45.4	44.4	46.3	52.6	49.4	41.9	43.3	42.7	37.5	10.2	12.7	12.3	11.0	9.9
	Himachal Pradesh	56.6	57.5	54.3	61.1	53.4	34.9	33.7	33.7	28.4	30.8	8.5	8.8	12.0	10.5	15.8
	Jammu & Kashmir	38.8	51.6	40.4	39.1	45.9	54.0	44.5	48.9	49.9	42.7	7.2	3.9	10.7	11.1	11.4
	Karnataka	41.8	40.6	41.7	42.7	43.7	34.7	39.9	37.9	41.6	36.0	23.5	19.5	20.4	15.7	20.3
	Kerala	32.1	26.8	28.0	31.6	31.3	35.9	37.5	37.4	36.3	40.9	32.0	35.7	34.6	32.1	27.8
	Madhya Pradesh	46.0	42.1	36.9	35.0	41.1	40.0	40.7	45.2	45.5	41.6	14.0	17.2	17.9	19.5	17.3
	Maharashtra	54.2	52.5	54.0	54.7	55.1	33.4	36.7	33.0	36.8	34.3	12.3	10.8	13.0	8.5	10.6
	Odisha	46.9	48.1	39.9	36.4	40.5	37.2	37.1	41.9	49.6	45.9	15.9	14.8	18.2	14.0	13.6
	Punjab	44.2	39.8	40.4	46.5	45.9	46.7	48.7	47.4	45.2	42.2	9.0	11.5	12.2	8.3	11.9
	Rajasthan	34.0	43.2	40.4	41.7	43.7	53.9	47.2	46.1	41.8	45.4	12.1	9.6	13.5	16.5	10.9
	Tamil Nadu	40.4	40.3	45.4	43.7	48.0	33.7	34.5	33.0	32.4	29.5	25.9	25.2	21.6	23.9	22.6
	Uttar Pradesh	34.0	31.4	33.4	30.5	37.9	54.6	57.4	53.1	52.0	49.2	11.4	11.2	13.5	17.4	12.9
	West Bengal	50.6	47.6	39.9	37.5	41.4	35.7	37.4	43.1	44.8	39.3	13.7	15.0	17.0	17.7	19.3

(Continued)

Table 60 *(Continued)*

Sex	State	Regular Employee					Self-employed					Casual Labour				
		1983	1994	2000	2012	2018	1983	1994	2000	2012	2018	1983	1994	2000	2012	2018
Female	Andhra Pradesh	18.3	17.5	28.5	37.4	44.7	46.4	46.0	39.3	44.4	39.8	35.3	36.5	32.2	18.1	15.5
	Assam	50.9	50.0	55.6	44.9	62.8	36.8	28.3	25.1	46.9	32.3	12.3	21.7	19.3	8.2	4.9
	Bihar	18.7	26.5	25.2	36.4	53.3	50.7	42.6	51.3	43.5	25.5	30.6	30.9	23.5	20.1	21.2
	Gujarat	22.3	24.1	26.4	37.0	49.7	47.7	42.6	41.9	48.3	35.8	30.0	33.3	31.7	14.7	14.6
	Haryana	31.2	20.4	33.0	67.5	49.9	55.6	57.3	53.5	27.8	26.4	13.2	22.3	13.5	4.7	23.7
	Himachal Pradesh	49.0	36.3	40.6	59.0	48.2	43.9	53.7	53.3	36.0	48.3	7.0	10.0	6.1	5.0	3.6
	Jammu & Kashmir	28.9	44.6	41.3	50.8	51.3	68.4	47.7	41.0	43.0	45.8	2.7	7.7	17.7	6.2	2.9
	Karnataka	23.5	25.4	32.6	53.3	55.2	37.4	45.9	41.5	30.1	31.0	39.1	28.7	25.9	16.6	13.8
	Kerala	26.3	26.6	31.9	46.6	55.8	52.0	45.8	50.9	36.3	28.5	21.7	27.6	17.2	17.1	15.8
	Madhya Pradesh	29.5	23.9	17.2	35.7	41.3	42.9	45.1	50.4	42.6	38.3	27.6	31.0	32.4	21.7	20.4
	Maharashtra	29.3	39.1	41.0	54.3	61.1	33.6	36.7	37.4	33.4	27.1	37.1	24.2	21.6	12.3	11.8
	Odisha	20.7	29.1	21.2	27.1	46.5	42.7	37.7	46.0	58.0	34.8	36.5	33.2	32.8	14.9	18.7
	Punjab	34.7	41.5	43.4	54.3	64.2	56.4	50.0	49.1	41.1	30.3	8.9	8.5	7.5	4.6	5.5
	Rajasthan	7.2	20.2	20.9	26.9	43.0	78.5	63.8	65.3	60.2	44.1	14.3	16.0	13.8	12.9	12.8
	Tamil Nadu	22.4	30.1	40.7	41.8	53.7	40.5	39.7	39.4	39.8	31.7	37.2	30.2	19.9	18.4	14.6
	Uttar Pradesh	25.0	19.6	25.7	22.9	48.0	58.2	65.7	66.1	66.7	44.5	16.8	14.7	8.2	10.4	7.5
	West Bengal	45.9	44.1	40.1	40.4	44.7	35.2	36.4	43.6	46.2	45.6	18.9	19.5	16.3	13.5	9.7

(Continued)

Table 60 *(Continued)*

Sex	State	Regular Employee					Self–employed					Casual Labour				
		1983	1994	2000	2012	2018	1983	1994	2000	2012	2018	1983	1994	2000	2012	2018
Male + Female	Andhra Pradesh	37.5	34.2	38.6	46.6	46.8	41.8	40.2	36.7	37.5	36.7	20.6	25.5	24.7	15.9	16.5
	Assam	46.5	43.0	42.9	36.6	43.4	44.4	45.3	44.6	53.8	47.8	9.1	11.7	12.5	9.6	8.8
	Bihar	34.1	35.5	30.2	29.2	34.2	48.4	47.7	53.7	53.1	44.2	17.5	16.8	16.0	17.7	21.6
	Gujarat	40.0	40.9	34.2	49.6	49.6	41.7	38.3	41.0	41.6	41.9	18.3	20.8	24.8	8.8	8.5
	Haryana	39.0	40.4	42.8	49.3	52.2	50.3	45.0	44.7	40.6	36.0	10.7	14.6	12.5	10.1	11.8
	Himachal Pradesh	55.0	52.1	51.9	60.6	52.4	36.8	38.8	37.1	30.2	34.2	8.2	9.1	11.0	9.2	13.4
	Jammu & Kashmir	37.4	50.3	40.5	40.9	47.0	56.1	45.1	48.1	48.8	43.4	6.6	4.6	11.4	10.3	9.7
	Karnataka	37.0	37.0	39.6	45.0	46.4	35.4	41.3	38.7	39.2	34.8	27.6	21.7	21.7	15.9	18.8
	Kerala	30.3	26.7	29.1	35.7	37.8	40.9	39.8	41.1	36.3	37.6	28.8	33.5	29.8	28.0	24.6
	Madhya Pradesh	42.5	38.2	33.0	35.1	41.1	40.6	41.6	46.2	44.9	40.9	16.9	20.1	20.8	20.0	18.0
	Maharashtra	49.2	49.6	51.6	54.6	56.4	33.5	36.7	33.8	36.1	32.8	17.3	13.7	14.6	9.3	10.8
	Odisha	42.7	44.2	35.9	34.5	41.6	38.1	37.2	42.8	51.3	43.8	19.2	18.6	21.3	14.2	14.5
	Punjab	42.6	40.0	40.9	47.8	48.9	48.4	48.9	47.7	44.5	40.3	9.0	11.1	11.4	7.7	10.9
	Rajasthan	26.9	38.0	36.5	38.6	43.6	60.4	51.0	50.0	45.6	45.2	12.7	11.1	13.6	15.8	11.2
	Tamil Nadu	35.5	37.5	44.1	43.2	49.5	35.6	35.9	34.7	34.3	30.1	29.0	26.6	21.1	22.5	20.4
	Uttar Pradesh	32.8	29.6	32.3	29.4	39.2	55.1	58.7	55.0	54.2	48.6	12.2	11.7	12.7	16.4	12.3
	West Bengal	49.8	47.0	39.9	38.1	42.2	35.6	37.2	43.2	45.1	40.7	14.5	15.8	16.9	16.8	17.1

Source: Same as Table 53

Table 61. States' Ranks Based on Percentage of Usually Employed (UPSS) Under Self-Employment, Regular Employment and Casual Employment: Urban Areas

Sex	State	Regular Employee						Self-employed						Casual Labour					
		1983	1994	2000	2012	2018	Overall	1983	1994	2000	2012	2018	Overall	1983	1994	2000	2012	2018	Overall
Male	Andhra Pradesh	9	13	5	4	6	5	9	10	14	15	14	14	5	3	3	9	7	4
	Assam	6	10	7	13	14	12	7	4	4	1	1	3	15	14	16	14	16	17
	Bihar	14	15	16	17	16	16	5	3	1	2	3	2	7	8	9	5	3	6
	Gujarat	8	7	14	3	4	4	8	13	11	12	6	10	6	5	2	17	17	9
	Haryana	11	6	4	6	3	3	4	7	8	9	12	7	13	10	13	12	15	12
	Himachal Pradesh	1	1	1	1	2	1	14	17	15	17	16	16	16	16	15	13	8	15
	Jammu & Kashmir	13	3	9	10	7	7	2	6	3	4	7	4	17	17	17	11	12	16
	Karnataka	10	11	6	8	10	11	15	9	12	11	13	12	3	4	5	8	4	3
	Kerala	17	17	17	15	17	17	12	11	13	14	10	13	1	1	1	1	1	1
	Madhya Pradesh	5	9	13	14	12	14	10	8	7	6	9	8	8	6	7	3	6	5
	Maharashtra	2	2	2	2	1	2	17	15	17	13	15	15	10	13	12	15	14	13
	Odisha	4	4	11	12	13	10	11	14	10	5	4	9	4	9	6	10	9	8
	Punjab	7	14	8	5	8	8	6	2	5	7	8	5	14	11	14	16	11	14
	Rajasthan	16	8	10	9	9	13	3	5	6	10	5	6	11	15	10	7	13	11
	Tamil Nadu	12	12	3	7	5	6	16	16	16	16	17	17	2	2	4	2	2	2
	Uttar Pradesh	15	16	15	16	15	15	1	1	2	3	2	1	12	12	11	6	10	10
	West Bengal	3	5	12	11	11	9	13	12	9	8	11	11	9	7	8	4	5	7
	Kendall's W	0.681*						0.830*						0.745*					

(Continued)

Table 61 *(Continued)*

Sex	State	Regular Employee						Self-employed						Casual Labour					
		1983	1994	2000	2012	2018	Overall	1983	1994	2000	2012	2018	Overall	1983	1994	2000	2012	2018	Overall
Female	Andhra Pradesh	16	17	11	11	15	16	9	7	15	7	6	7	5	1	3	4	6	2
	Assam	1	1	1	8	2	1	15	17	17	5	10	16	14	11	9	13	15	13
	Bihar	15	10	14	13	7	11	7	11	5	8	17	11	6	5	6	2	2	4
	Gujarat	13	12	12	12	10	12	8	12	11	4	8	6	7	2	4	8	7	6
	Haryana	5	14	8	1	9	6	5	3	3	17	16	8	13	10	14	16	1	10
	Himachal Pradesh	2	6	6	2	11	4	10	4	4	14	1	4	16	15	17	15	16	17
	Jammu & Kashmir	8	2	3	6	8	5	2	6	13	9	2	3	17	17	10	14	17	15
	Karnataka	11	11	9	5	5	10	14	8	12	16	12	14	1	7	5	6	9	7
	Kerala	9	9	10	7	4	8	6	9	6	13	14	12	9	8	11	5	5	8
	Madhya Pradesh	6	13	17	14	17	14	11	10	7	10	7	9	8	4	2	1	3	1
	Maharashtra	7	5	4	4	3	3	17	15	16	15	15	17	3	9	7	11	11	9
	Odisha	14	8	15	15	13	13	12	14	9	3	9	10	4	3	1	7	4	3
	Punjab	4	4	2	3	1	2	4	5	8	11	13	5	15	16	16	17	14	16
	Rajasthan	17	15	16	16	16	17	1	2	2	2	5	2	12	13	13	10	10	12
	Tamil Nadu	12	7	5	9	6	9	13	13	14	12	11	15	2	6	8	3	8	5
	Uttar Pradesh	10	16	13	17	12	15	3	1	1	1	4	1	11	14	15	12	13	14
	West Bengal	3	3	7	10	14	7	16	16	10	6	3	13	10	12	12	9	12	11
	Kendall's W	**0.685***						**0.468****						**0.765***					

(Continued)

Table 61 *(Continued)*

Sex	State	Regular Employee						Self-employed						Casual Labour					
		1983	1994	2000	2012	2018	Overall	1983	1994	2000	2012	2018	Overall	1983	1994	2000	2012	2018	Overall
Male + Female	Andhra Pradesh	10	15	10	6	8	10	8	10	15	13	12	13	4	3	3	8	7	4
	Assam	4	6	4	12	11	7	7	5	8	2	2	5	14	13	13	13	16	14
	Bihar	14	14	16	17	17	16	5	4	2	3	4	3	7	8	9	4	2	5
	Gujarat	8	7	13	3	4	5	9	13	12	10	7	10	6	5	2	16	17	9
	Haryana	9	8	5	4	3	3	4	7	7	11	13	8	13	10	14	12	11	13
	Himachal Pradesh	1	1	1	1	2	1	13	12	14	17	15	15	16	16	17	15	9	15
	Jammu & Kashmir	11	2	7	9	7	6	2	6	4	5	6	4	17	17	16	11	15	17
	Karnataka	12	13	9	7	9	11	16	9	13	12	14	14	3	4	4	7	4	3
	Kerala	16	17	17	13	16	17	10	11	11	14	11	12	2	1	1	1	1	1
	Madhya Pradesh	7	10	14	14	14	13	11	8	6	8	8	7	9	6	7	3	5	6
	Maharashtra	3	3	2	2	1	2	17	16	17	15	16	16	8	11	10	14	14	11
	Odisha	5	5	12	15	13	12	12	14	10	4	5	9	5	7	5	10	8	7
	Punjab	6	9	6	5	6	4	6	3	5	9	10	6	15	14	15	17	13	16
	Rajasthan	17	11	11	10	10	14	1	2	3	6	3	2	11	15	11	9	12	12
	Tamil Nadu	13	12	3	8	5	9	15	17	16	16	17	17	1	2	6	2	3	2
	Uttar Pradesh	15	16	15	16	15	15	3	1	1	1	1	1	12	12	12	6	10	10
	West Bengal	2	4	8	11	12	8	14	15	9	7	9	11	10	9	8	5	6	8
	Kendall's W	0.020						0.008						0.013					

Source: Author's computation using data in Table 60

*Note: * and ** imply significance at 1 and 5 per cent levels respectively.*

- The overall picture in urban areas regarding the ranking of states based on the percentage of self-employed males and females remained unchanged from 1983 to 2018, as indicated by the statistical significance of Kendall's W statistic for these categories.
- Regarding the percentage of regular employees in urban areas, Tables 60 and 61 show that for males in 2018, the highest percentage was in Maharashtra (55.1 %) and the lowest was in Kerala (31.3 %). For urban females in the same year, these figures ranged from a high of 64.2 % in Punjab to a low of 41.3 % in Madhya Pradesh. For urban persons, although Maharashtra continued to rank first in the percentage of regular employees in 2018 (56.4 %), Bihar ranked last (34.2 %).
- Taking an overall view of the period from 1983 to 2018, it appears that the states reporting a relatively high percentage of regular employees for urban males include Himachal Pradesh, Maharashtra, Haryana, Gujarat, and Andhra Pradesh; for urban females, these states are Assam, Punjab, Maharashtra, Himachal Pradesh, and Jammu & Kashmir; and for urban persons, the states are Himachal Pradesh, Maharashtra, Haryana, Punjab, and Gujarat. Conversely, the states with relatively low percentages of urban male workers in regular employment are Kerala, Bihar, Uttar Pradesh, Madhya Pradesh, and Rajasthan; the states with relatively low percentages of urban female workers in regular employment are Rajasthan, Andhra Pradesh, Uttar Pradesh, Madhya Pradesh, and Odisha; and those with relatively low percentages of urban persons in regular employment are Kerala, Bihar, Uttar Pradesh, Rajasthan, and Madhya Pradesh. Furthermore, Table 61 shows that the ranking patterns of the states regarding the percentage of regular employees in urban areas did not change significantly over the period 1983–2018, as indicated by the statistical significance of the computed Kendall's W statistic. This holds regardless of the sex of the urban workers.
- It is also noteworthy that from 1983 to 2018, while ten out of the seventeen major states we considered improved their percentages of regular employees for urban males (the exceptions being Assam, Bihar, Himachal Pradesh, Kerala, Madhya Pradesh, Odisha, and West Bengal), all but two states (Himachal Pradesh and West Bengal) experienced such improvement for urban females. However, when examining urban persons, an increase in the percentage of regular employees is evident in all states except Assam, Himachal Pradesh, Madhya Pradesh, Odisha, and West Bengal.
- In 2018, the percentage of casual workers among urban males ranged from 27.8 % in Kerala to 7.2 % in Gujarat; for urban females, it ranged between

23.7 % in Haryana and 2.9 % in Jammu & Kashmir; and for urban persons, this ranged from 24.6 % in Kerala to 8.5 % in Gujarat. Additionally, other states reporting relatively high percentages of casual workers for urban males in 2018 include Tamil Nadu (22.6 %), Bihar (21.7 %), Karnataka (20.3 %), and West Bengal (19.3 %); similarly, states with high percentages of casual workers for urban females that year are Bihar (21.2 %), Madhya Pradesh (20.4 %), Odisha (18.7 %), and Kerala (15.8 %). Conversely, states with relatively low percentages of casual workers for urban males in 2018 are Assam (9.5 %), Haryana (9.9 %), Maharashtra (10.6 %), and Rajasthan (10.9 %); while those with low percentages for urban females are Himachal Pradesh (3.6 %), Assam (4.9 %), Punjab (5.5 %), and Uttar Pradesh (7.5 %). For urban persons, the states with low percentages are Assam (8.8 %), Jammu & Kashmir (9.7 %), Maharashtra (10.8 %), and Punjab (10.9 %).

- Overall, covering the entire period from 1983 to 2018, it appears that for urban males, the states reporting a relatively high percentage of casual workers include Kerala, Tamil Nadu, Karnataka, Andhra Pradesh, and Madhya Pradesh. Conversely, those with a relatively low percentage of male casual workers in urban areas are Assam, Jammu & Kashmir, Himachal Pradesh, Punjab, and Maharashtra. Among urban females, the states with a comparatively high percentage of casual workers are Madhya Pradesh, Andhra Pradesh, Odisha, Bihar, and Tamil Nadu. In contrast, the states with a relatively low percentage of female casual workers include Himachal Pradesh, Punjab, Jammu & Kashmir, Uttar Pradesh, and Assam. For urban persons, the percentage of casual workers appears to be comparatively high in Kerala, Tamil Nadu, Karnataka, Andhra Pradesh, and Bihar and relatively low in Jammu & Kashmir, Punjab, Himachal Pradesh, Assam, and Haryana. As with self-employed and regular workers, the rankings of states regarding the percentage of casual workers showed no statistically significant changes from 1983 to 2018 across all categories: urban males and urban females.
- However, upon examining the change in the percentage of casual workers in urban areas over time, it is apparent that, for males, nine states experienced an increase from 1983 to 2018, while only two states saw a rise for females and eight states for persons. Thus, it is evident that urban females experienced a lower rate of casualisation in their workforce across many states over time. Furthermore, it is essential to note that the percentage of casual workers among urban females in those states declined over time, generally following a systematic trend pattern.

5.4.3 Percentage Distribution of All (Rural Plus Urban) Workers Across Self-Employment, Regular Employment, and Casual Labour in States

We now examine the distribution patterns of workers based on their modes of employment across seventeen major Indian states, encompassing both rural and urban areas. The percentage distribution of workers in self-employment, regular employment, and casual employment across the states, along with their corresponding ranks, is presented in Tables 62 and 63, respectively. Our primary observations here are as follows:

- When considering rural and urban areas together, the percentage of self-employed workers in 2018 for males ranged from 61.7 % in Uttar Pradesh to 32.5 % in Tamil Nadu; for females, these figures are 88.1 % in Himachal Pradesh and 20.4 % in Assam; and for both genders combined, the percentages are 67.3 % in Himachal Pradesh and 32.8 % in Tamil Nadu.
- Overall (i.e. considering the entire period 1983–2018), it appears that, aside from Uttar Pradesh, the percentage of self-employed workers among males was higher in Assam, Rajasthan, Odisha, and Madhya Pradesh. Similarly, the percentage of females in self-employment was higher (apart from Himachal Pradesh) in Jammu & Kashmir, Rajasthan, Uttar Pradesh, and Madhya Pradesh. Regarding persons (males and females), apart from Himachal Pradesh, other states that reported a relatively high percentage of self-employed workers include Rajasthan, Uttar Pradesh, Madhya Pradesh, and Jammu & Kashmir. Conversely, some states reported relatively low percentages of self-employed workers among males, including Kerala, Haryana, West Bengal, and Andhra Pradesh; states with low percentages for females include Kerala, Tamil Nadu, Punjab, and Karnataka; while states reporting low percentages for persons include Kerala, Haryana, Andhra Pradesh, and Punjab.
- Overall, we may say that the incidence of self-employed workers is relatively higher in both backward and hilly states, namely Himachal Pradesh, Rajasthan, Jammu & Kashmir, Uttar Pradesh, and Assam. Additionally, it is noteworthy that the ranking of the states from 1983 to 2018 did not exhibit any statistically significant changes for males, females, or both combined. Furthermore, as shown in Table 62, the percentage of self-employed individuals declined in a considerable number of states (in twelve states for males and in all states for females) between 1983 and 2018.

Table 62. Percentage Distribution of Usually Employed (UPSS) by Status of Employment in Major States: Rural + Urban Areas

Sex	State	Regular Employee					Self-employed					Casual Labour				
		1983	1994	2000	2012	2018	1983	1994	2000	2012	2018	1983	1994	2000	2012	2018
Male	Andhra Pradesh	19.4	15.9	15.9	24.0	25.3	48.6	46.5	45.4	44.2	46.7	32.0	37.7	38.8	31.8	28.1
	Assam	20.6	16.9	18.9	14.0	20.3	62.2	58.5	57.6	68.8	61.5	17.3	24.6	23.5	17.3	18.2
	Bihar	11.2	8.5	7.5	7.4	12.8	55.7	54.6	53.9	55.2	56.9	33.2	36.9	38.6	37.4	30.4
	Gujarat	19.4	21.9	19.0	29.8	29.9	53.2	43.6	47.3	49.4	54.7	27.4	34.5	33.7	20.8	15.4
	Haryana	24.1	22.5	24.9	27.0	36.9	59.1	57.3	54.3	52.7	44.1	16.9	20.3	20.8	20.3	19.0
	Himachal Pradesh	13.3	15.9	20.4	26.7	27.3	77.1	71.7	60.0	51.6	52.7	9.6	12.4	19.6	21.7	20.1
	Jammu & Kashmir	15.6	24.6	18.7	24.9	28.4	70.8	65.5	67.6	50.7	51.1	13.6	9.9	13.6	24.3	20.5
	Karnataka	16.4	16.7	18.5	24.5	25.3	52.4	52.5	47.3	48.7	50.3	31.2	30.8	34.1	26.8	24.4
	Kerala	19.0	16.2	16.9	23.4	27.5	42.6	39.9	37.9	37.6	40.8	38.5	43.9	45.2	39.0	31.7
	Madhya Pradesh	16.1	13.4	12.4	13.2	16.3	61.3	57.9	55.0	56.5	59.2	22.6	28.7	32.6	30.4	24.5
	Maharashtra	28.0	28.1	30.0	31.3	31.7	45.3	44.3	39.3	46.2	47.8	26.7	27.7	30.7	22.5	20.6
	Odisha	15.8	11.8	10.4	13.0	15.7	51.6	54.0	47.5	58.7	59.3	32.6	34.2	42.1	28.3	25.1
	Punjab	21.2	21.5	25.4	30.2	31.5	60.8	52.8	51.7	45.7	47.0	18.1	25.6	22.9	24.1	21.5
	Rajasthan	11.9	15.2	15.4	17.6	22.4	75.5	66.5	67.0	56.8	59.9	12.6	18.4	17.6	25.6	17.7
	Tamil Nadu	21.2	22.5	27.8	29.9	35.5	41.2	38.9	34.6	31.9	32.5	37.7	38.6	37.6	38.1	32.1
	Uttar Pradesh	11.9	10.6	12.7	12.7	16.0	71.9	69.5	67.0	59.9	61.7	16.3	19.9	20.3	27.4	22.4
	West Bengal	22.7	20.8	17.2	17.8	20.7	45.7	49.8	47.4	43.7	46.2	31.6	29.4	35.5	38.5	33.2

(Continued)

Table 62 *(Continued)*

Sex	State	Regular Employee					Self-employed					Casual Labour				
		1983	1994	2000	2012	2018	1983	1994	2000	2012	2018	1983	1994	2000	2012	2018
Female	Andhra Pradesh	4.6	3.8	6.6	8.8	15.3	44.6	45.4	42.2	44.7	44.3	50.8	50.8	51.2	46.5	40.4
	Assam	27.9	20.3	23.1	20.5	59.3	50.0	47.7	52.0	62.4	20.4	22.2	32.0	24.8	17.1	20.3
	Bihar	2.4	2.6	2.9	7.6	22.6	55.8	41.9	47.9	60.8	52.9	41.8	55.5	49.2	31.6	24.5
	Gujarat	4.4	5.1	5.5	13.4	23.1	59.1	53.4	56.4	55.7	54.9	36.5	41.5	38.1	30.9	22.1
	Haryana	8.6	4.2	6.6	19.7	27.8	70.8	74.1	80.8	63.6	42.3	20.6	21.6	12.7	16.7	30.0
	Himachal Pradesh	2.4	2.9	3.9	8.1	8.5	96.3	95.3	94.8	85.8	88.1	1.4	1.9	1.3	6.1	3.4
	Jammu & Kashmir	3.4	5.9	4.3	12.2	15.8	95.2	91.7	94.3	83.6	83.3	1.3	2.3	1.5	4.2	1.0
	Karnataka	6.2	6.0	7.7	20.1	25.8	48.8	52.2	46.4	44.5	40.4	44.9	41.8	45.9	35.4	33.8
	Kerala	12.4	13.6	18.9	33.9	47.5	57.7	52.9	52.5	36.4	29.6	29.9	33.5	28.6	29.7	22.9
	Madhya Pradesh	5.0	3.3	3.1	7.5	9.6	64.5	59.7	54.0	55.5	62.4	30.5	37.0	42.9	37.0	28.1
	Maharashtra	5.3	9.1	8.5	16.3	21.8	47.8	46.0	43.2	48.4	45.1	46.9	44.8	48.2	35.3	33.1
	Odisha	2.7	3.2	2.8	6.0	14.2	51.8	55.0	49.0	65.2	50.3	45.5	41.9	48.3	28.8	35.5
	Punjab	7.1	9.2	10.8	20.4	45.2	85.6	79.5	81.8	68.4	40.3	7.3	11.3	7.4	11.3	14.5
	Rajasthan	1.4	2.7	2.9	5.5	8.6	88.3	86.1	86.7	74.5	80.0	10.2	11.2	10.4	20.0	11.4
	Tamil Nadu	7.2	10.6	16.0	20.4	30.1	43.3	41.4	38.4	31.8	33.5	49.6	48.0	45.6	47.8	36.4
	Uttar Pradesh	2.9	2.8	4.2	6.4	14.5	81.6	78.1	76.3	79.5	72.9	15.5	19.1	19.5	14.1	12.7
	West Bengal	12.9	15.4	12.6	19.4	27.2	55.8	54.0	58.4	54.1	45.9	31.3	30.6	29.0	26.5	26.9

(Continued)

Table 62 *(Continued)*

Sex	State	Regular Employee					Self-employed					Casual Labour				
		1983	1994	2000	2012	2018	1983	1994	2000	2012	2018	1983	1994	2000	2012	2018
Male + Female	Andhra Pradesh	13.5	10.9	12.1	18.3	21.8	47.0	46.0	44.1	44.4	45.9	39.6	43.1	43.8	37.3	32.4
	Assam	21.9	17.6	19.7	15.1	25.1	59.9	56.2	56.5	67.7	56.5	18.2	26.2	23.8	17.2	18.5
	Bihar	8.5	7.2	6.4	7.4	13.6	55.7	51.7	52.5	56.0	56.5	35.8	41.1	41.1	36.6	29.9
	Gujarat	14.0	16.2	14.4	25.8	28.6	55.3	46.9	50.4	50.9	54.7	30.7	36.9	35.2	23.3	16.8
	Haryana	19.9	16.9	20.6	25.6	35.6	62.2	62.4	60.5	54.8	43.8	17.9	20.7	18.9	19.6	20.6
	Himachal Pradesh	8.3	10.0	13.0	18.0	19.5	85.8	82.4	75.5	67.6	67.3	5.8	7.6	11.4	14.4	13.2
	Jammu & Kashmir	12.1	17.7	14.3	21.6	25.1	77.8	75.2	75.9	59.3	59.5	10.1	7.1	9.8	19.1	15.4
	Karnataka	12.7	12.8	14.8	23.3	25.5	51.1	52.4	47.0	47.5	47.8	36.2	34.8	38.1	29.2	26.8
	Kerala	16.4	15.4	17.5	26.4	32.9	48.4	43.9	42.3	37.3	37.8	35.2	40.7	40.1	36.3	29.3
	Madhya Pradesh	11.8	9.7	9.0	11.4	14.3	62.5	58.6	54.6	56.2	60.2	25.7	31.8	36.4	32.4	25.6
	Maharashtra	19.3	20.8	22.4	26.5	28.9	46.2	45.0	40.7	46.9	47.0	34.5	34.2	36.9	26.6	24.1
	Odisha	11.6	8.8	7.9	11.0	15.4	51.6	54.3	48.0	60.5	57.4	36.8	36.8	44.1	28.4	27.2
	Punjab	17.1	18.7	21.5	27.9	33.6	68.0	58.8	59.9	51.1	46.0	14.9	22.4	18.7	21.0	20.4
	Rajasthan	7.6	10.2	10.6	13.3	18.7	80.8	74.4	74.5	63.1	65.3	11.6	15.5	14.9	23.6	16.0
	Tamil Nadu	15.7	17.9	23.5	26.8	33.8	42.0	39.9	36.0	31.9	32.8	42.3	42.2	40.5	41.3	33.5
	Uttar Pradesh	9.3	8.7	10.6	11.2	15.7	74.7	71.7	69.3	64.5	63.4	16.0	19.7	20.1	24.3	20.9
	West Bengal	20.4	19.6	16.3	18.2	22.1	48.1	50.8	49.6	46.1	46.1	31.5	29.6	34.1	35.7	31.8

Source: Same as Table 53

Table 63. States' Ranks Based on Percentage of Usually Employed (UPSS) Under Self-Employment, Regular Employment and Casual Employment: Rural + Urban Areas

Sex	State	Regular Employee						Self-employed						Casual Labour					
		1983	1994	2000	2012	2018	Overall	1983	1994	2000	2012	2018	Overall	1983	1994	2000	2012	2018	Overall
Male	Andhra Pradesh	8	12	12	9	10	12	13	13	14	14	13	14	5	3	3	5	5	4
	Assam	6	8	7	13	13	10	5	5	5	1	2	3	12	12	11	17	15	13
	Bihar	17	17	17	17	17	17	9	8	8	6	6	7	3	4	4	4	4	3
	Gujarat	7	5	6	4	5	5	10	15	13	10	7	11	8	5	8	15	17	9
	Haryana	2	4	4	5	1	3	8	7	7	7	15	9	13	13	13	16	14	14
	Himachal Pradesh	14	11	5	6	8	8	1	1	4	8	8	4	17	16	15	14	13	17
	Jammu & Kashmir	13	2	8	7	6	6	4	4	1	9	9	5	15	17	17	11	12	15
	Karnataka	10	9	9	8	9	9	11	11	12	11	10	12	7	7	7	9	8	7
	Kerala	9	10	11	10	7	11	16	15	16	16	16	16	1	1	1	1	3	1
	Madhya Pradesh	11	14	15	14	14	14	6	6	6	5	5	6	10	9	9	6	7	8
	Maharashtra	1	1	1	1	3	1	15	14	15	12	11	15	9	10	10	13	11	10
	Odisha	12	15	16	15	16	15	12	9	10	3	4	8	4	6	2	7	6	6
	Punjab	5	6	3	2	4	4	7	10	9	13	12	10	11	11	12	12	10	11
	Rajasthan	15	13	13	12	11	13	2	3	3	4	3	2	16	15	16	10	16	16
	Tamil Nadu	4	3	2	3	2	2	17	17	17	17	17	17	2	2	5	3	2	2
	Uttar Pradesh	16	16	14	16	15	16	3	2	2	2	1	1	14	14	14	8	9	12
	West Bengal	3	7	10	11	12	7	14	12	11	15	14	13	6	8	6	2	1	5
	Kendall's W	0.851*						0.839*						0.836*					

(Continued)

Table 63 *(Continued)*

Sex	State	Regular Employee						Self-employed						Casual Labour					
		1983	1994	2000	2012	2018	Overall	1983	1994	2000	2012	2018	Overall	1983	1994	2000	2012	2018	Overall
Female	Andhra Pradesh	10	11	8	11	12	10	16	15	16	14	11	16	1	2	1	2	1	1
	Assam	1	1	1	2	1	1	13	13	11	8	17	12	11	10	11	12	12	11
	Bihar	15	17	15	13	9	14	11	16	13	9	7	11	6	1	2	6	9	4
	Gujarat	11	9	10	9	8	9	8	10	8	10	6	8	7	7	8	7	11	8
	Haryana	4	10	9	6	5	7	6	6	5	7	12	6	12	12	13	13	6	12
	Himachal Pradesh	16	14	13	12	17	15	1	1	1	1	1	1	16	17	17	16	16	16
	Jammu & Kashmir	12	8	11	10	11	11	2	2	2	2	2	2	17	16	16	17	17	17
	Karnataka	7	7	7	5	7	6	14	12	14	15	13	15	5	6	5	4	4	5
	Kerala	3	3	2	1	2	2	9	11	10	16	16	13	10	9	10	8	10	10
	Madhya Pradesh	9	12	14	14	15	12	7	7	9	11	5	7	9	8	7	3	7	7
	Maharashtra	8	6	6	8	10	8	15	14	15	13	10	14	3	4	4	5	5	3
	Odisha	14	13	17	16	14	16	12	8	12	6	8	9	4	5	3	9	3	6
	Punjab	6	5	5	4	3	5	4	4	4	5	14	5	15	14	15	15	13	15
	Rajasthan	17	16	16	17	16	17	3	3	3	4	3	3	14	15	14	11	15	14
	Tamil Nadu	5	4	3	3	4	3	17	17	17	17	15	17	2	3	6	1	2	2
	Uttar Pradesh	13	15	12	15	13	13	5	5	6	3	4	4	13	13	12	14	14	13
	West Bengal	2	2	4	7	6	4	10	9	7	12	9	10	8	11	9	10	8	9
	Kendall's W	**0.905***						**0.820***						**0.907***					

(Continued)

Table 63 *(Continued)*

Sex	State	Regular Employee						Self-employed						Casual Labour					
		1983	1994	2000	2012	2018	Overall	1983	1994	2000	2012	2018	Overall	1983	1994	2000	2012	2018	Overall
Male + Female	Andhra Pradesh	9	11	12	9	11	11	15	14	14	15	14	15	2	1	2	2	2	1
	Assam	1	6	5	12	9	7	8	8	7	1	8	5	11	11	11	16	13	12
	Bihar	15	17	17	17	17	17	9	11	9	8	7	10	5	3	3	3	4	3
	Gujarat	8	8	9	5	6	8	10	13	10	11	9	11	9	5	9	12	14	10
	Haryana	3	7	4	6	1	4	7	5	5	9	15	8	12	13	13	14	11	13
	Himachal Pradesh	16	13	11	11	12	12	1	1	2	2	1	1	17	16	16	17	17	17
	Jammu & Kashmir	11	5	10	8	8	9	3	2	1	6	5	3	16	17	17	15	16	16
	Karnataka	10	10	8	7	7	10	12	10	13	12	10	12	4	7	6	7	7	6
	Kerala	6	9	6	4	4	5	13	16	15	16	16	16	6	4	5	4	5	4
	Madhya Pradesh	12	14	15	14	16	14	6	7	8	7	4	6	10	9	8	6	8	9
	Maharashtra	4	1	2	3	5	1	16	15	16	13	11	14	7	8	7	9	9	8
	Odisha	13	15	16	16	15	16	11	9	12	5	6	9	3	6	1	8	6	5
	Punjab	5	3	3	1	3	2	5	6	6	10	13	7	14	12	14	13	12	14
	Rajasthan	17	12	13	13	13	13	2	3	3	4	2	2	15	15	15	11	15	15
	Tamil Nadu	7	4	1	2	2	3	17	17	17	17	17	17	1	2	4	1	1	2
	Uttar Pradesh	14	16	14	15	14	15	4	4	4	3	3	4	13	14	12	10	10	11
	West Bengal	2	2	7	10	10	6	14	12	11	14	12	13	8	10	10	5	3	7
	Kendall's W			0.845*						0.863*						0.898*			

Source: Author's computation using data in Table 62

*Note: * implies significance at 1 per cent level.*

- Regarding the percentage of regular employees among males, Haryana (36.9 %) ranked first among states in 2018, while Bihar (12.8 %) was last; for females, Assam (59.3 %) and Himachal Pradesh (8.5 %) held the highest and lowest positions, respectively. For the males and females combined, Haryana (35.6 %) and Bihar (13.6 %) were similarly at the top and bottom. The other states with relatively high percentages of male workers in regular employment in 2018 included Tamil Nadu, Maharashtra, Punjab, and Gujarat; for females, these states were Kerala, Punjab, Tamil Nadu, and Haryana. Additionally, Tamil Nadu, Punjab, Kerala, and Maharashtra reported relatively high percentages of regular employees among the persons that year. Conversely, states reporting low percentages of regular employees among males in 2018 included Odisha, Uttar Pradesh, Madhya Pradesh, and Assam; for females, Rajasthan, Madhya Pradesh, Odisha, and Uttar Pradesh; and for persons, Madhya Pradesh, Odisha, Uttar Pradesh, and Rajasthan. Evidently, regular employees were higher in advanced and industrially developed states and lower in backward states for both males and females in 2018. This observation remains largely valid even when considering state rankings of the percentage of regular employees at various time points. Consequently, the computed values of Kendall's W statistic were statistically significant across all categories (males, females, and persons), indicating that the ranking pattern of states by the percentage of regular employees was consistent throughout our study period. Nonetheless, a positive development in the states' labour markets is that many experienced an increase in the percentage of regular employees from 1983 to 2018 – visible among males in fourteen of seventeen states and among females across all states.
- In 2018, the percentage of casual workers among males was highest in West Bengal and lowest in Gujarat; for females, it was highest in Andhra Pradesh and lowest in Jammu & Kashmir; and for persons, it was highest in Tamil Nadu and lowest in Himachal Pradesh, respectively. Some other states with notably high percentages of casual workers include Tamil Nadu, Kerala, Bihar, and Andhra Pradesh for males; Tamil Nadu, Odisha, Karnataka, and Maharashtra for females; and Andhra Pradesh, West Bengal, Bihar, and Kerala for all persons. Conversely, some states with relatively low percentage of casual workers for males are Rajasthan, Assam, Haryana, and Himachal Pradesh; for females, the states with low percentage of casual workers are Himachal Pradesh, Rajasthan, Uttar Pradesh, and Punjab; while for persons, the states with lower percentage of casual workers are Jammu & Kashmir, Rajasthan, Gujarat, and Assam. From 1983 to 2018, nine out of seventeen major states experienced an increase in the percentage of casual workers for males (these are Assam,

Haryana, Himachal Pradesh, Jammu & Kashmir, Madhya Pradesh, Punjab, Rajasthan, Uttar Pradesh, and West Bengal); in contrast, only four states saw such an increase for females (namely, Haryana, Himachal Pradesh, Punjab, and Rajasthan). However, when considering males and females together, eight states demonstrated an increase in the percentage of casual workers to total workers during this period: Assam, Haryana, Himachal Pradesh, Jammu & Kashmir, Punjab, Rajasthan, Uttar Pradesh, and West Bengal.

- However, when we consider the entire period from 1983 to 2018, it appears that the percentage of casual male workers was highest in Kerala, followed by Tamil Nadu, Bihar, Andhra Pradesh, West Bengal, Odisha, Karnataka, Madhya Pradesh, Gujarat, Maharashtra, Punjab, Uttar Pradesh, Assam, Haryana, Jammu & Kashmir, Rajasthan, and Himachal Pradesh (in descending order of the percentage of casual workers to total workers). Among females, the percentage of casual workers was highest in Andhra Pradesh, followed by Tamil Nadu, Maharashtra, Bihar, Karnataka, Odisha, Madhya Pradesh, Gujarat, West Bengal, Kerala, Assam, Haryana, Uttar Pradesh, Rajasthan, Punjab, Himachal Pradesh, and Jammu & Kashmir. When considering both males and females together, it is observed that the percentage of casual workers to total workers during 1983–2018 was highest in Andhra Pradesh, followed by Tamil Nadu, Bihar, Kerala, Odisha, Karnataka, West Bengal, Maharashtra, Madhya Pradesh, Gujarat, Uttar Pradesh, Assam, Haryana, Punjab, Rajasthan, Jammu & Kashmir, and Himachal Pradesh (in descending order of the percentage of casual workers to total workers). It should also be noted that the ranking pattern of the states regarding the percentage of casual workers to total workers did not change significantly during this period for males, females, and persons (as indicated by the statistical significance of Kendall's W statistic).

5.5 Growth Rates of Workers by Employment Modes in Major States

In this section, we investigate the growth rates of workers across three employment modes (self-employment, regular employment, and casual labour) in seventeen major states of India during the pre-globalisation period (1983 to 1994) and various sub-periods of the post-globalisation era. This analysis is conducted separately for males and females, as well as for rural and urban areas. Tables 64 and 65, respectively, provide information on employment growth rates across the three employment modes in the states' rural areas and their ranks. The following observations may be made in this regard.

- In rural areas, the growth rate of self-employment among males during the pre-globalisation period (1983 to 1994) was highest in West Bengal (3.6 %) and lowest in Punjab (–0.9 %); for rural females, it peaked in Jammu & Kashmir (5.4 %) and declined to its lowest in Bihar (–4.2 %); for rural persons, it was highest in West Bengal (3.0 %) and lowest in Punjab (–1.5 %). In the first sub-period of the post-globalisation era (1994–2000), the highest growth among males occurred in Jammu & Kashmir (3.8 %), while the lowest was in Tamil Nadu (–3.2 %); for rural females, the maximum growth was observed in Punjab (6.1 %) and the minimum in Tamil Nadu (–3.8 %), while for rural persons, it ranged from a maximum of 3.3 % in Gujarat to a minimum of –3.5 % in Tamil Nadu. In the next sub-period of the post-globalisation era (2000–2012), however, the trend of self-employment growth shifted for all categories – males, females, and persons. For males during this period, Odisha (3.7 %) led the list, while Kerala (–2.3 %) recorded the lowest; for females, the highest and lowest were Odisha (2.0 %) and Kerala (–6.1 %), respectively; for persons, these positions were held by Odisha (3.1 %) and Kerala (–3.6 %), respectively. In the final sub-period of the post-globalisation era (2012–2018), West Bengal (3.0 %) topped the states in terms of growth rates of self-employment for rural males, while Kerala (–4.0 %) remained at the bottom; for rural females, Madhya Pradesh (4.5 %) secured the highest position, and Assam (–22.9 %) the lowest; for rural persons, the highest and lowest positions were held by Madhya Pradesh (3.4 %) and Haryana (–5.8 %), respectively.
- A close examination of the growth rates of self-employed individuals in rural areas reveals that the number of states experiencing negative growth increased during various sub-periods of the post-globalisation era compared to the pre-globalisation period. This trend is particularly evident among rural females. As illustrated in Table 64, the number of states reporting negative growth of self-employed rural males from 1983 to 1994, 1994 to 2000, 2000 to 2012, and 2012 to 2018 are 2, 7, 4, and 4, respectively; for rural females, the figures are 3, 10, 10, and 15; and for rural persons, these numbers stand at 3, 8, 4, and 13, respectively. Consequently, in rural areas, many states have observed females lag significantly behind males in terms of growth in self-employment over time. This trend is especially pronounced in the sub-period 2012–2018.

Table 64. Annual Growth Rates of Workers (UPSS) by Employment Status in Major States: Rural Areas

Sex	State	Regular Employee				Self-employed				Casual Labour			
		1983 to 1994	1994 to 2000	2000 to 2012	2012 to 2018	1983 to 1994	1994 to 2000	2000 to 2012	2012 to 2018	1983 to 1994	1994 to 2000	2000 to 2012	2012 to 2018
Male	Andhra Pradesh	–2.3	–0.5	3.9	1.0	1.7	0.3	0.2	0.6	3.6	1.0	–0.6	–3.3
	Assam	–0.4	4.7	–1.9	11.5	1.5	1.7	3.1	–0.5	5.9	1.1	–1.1	2.2
	Bihar	–2.1	–0.2	1.8	17.0	2.1	1.2	2.3	0.9	3.4	2.5	1.8	–4.1
	Gujarat	3.7	1.4	3.4	4.2	–0.3	3.3	2.1	1.2	4.7	0.4	–0.8	–6.7
	Haryana	–1.0	5.9	1.7	8.7	2.2	1.1	1.6	–3.6	4.0	3.2	2.1	–1.2
	Himachal Pradesh	5.5	5.3	3.7	2.8	2.0	–3.0	0.1	1.7	5.4	8.1	2.4	–0.5
	Jammu & Kashmir	7.2	–1.3	6.2	5.6	1.1	3.8	–1.0	2.9	–1.0	7.1	8.3	–2.1
	Karnataka	1.2	3.5	5.9	1.3	1.6	–1.0	1.2	1.7	2.2	3.1	–0.5	–3.7
	Kerala	–0.8	2.3	–1.1	3.0	0.6	0.2	–2.3	–4.0	2.9	2.1	–3.1	–9.0
	Madhya Pradesh	–2.0	–2.4	3.5	10.3	1.6	–0.5	2.4	2.8	4.7	3.4	1.3	–2.4
	Maharashtra	0.2	0.7	2.1	3.5	1.1	–1.0	3.5	1.6	2.7	3.0	–0.4	–2.8
	Odisha	–4.6	–0.3	4.7	5.0	2.0	–1.7	3.7	–0.2	2.1	4.4	–1.4	–2.8
	Punjab	1.3	5.5	2.4	1.5	–0.9	0.5	–0.1	1.4	4.9	–1.3	2.7	–3.3
	Rajasthan	3.5	2.0	3.5	9.8	1.0	1.4	0.3	2.0	7.1	–0.5	5.3	–4.7
	Tamil Nadu	1.0	2.6	1.4	5.9	0.2	–3.2	–0.5	1.4	1.6	0.2	1.0	–4.4
	Uttar Pradesh	1.3	4.4	1.7	6.8	2.3	0.3	0.7	1.7	5.0	0.8	4.6	–2.4
	West Bengal	1.7	–4.4	2.4	7.6	3.6	–0.9	0.5	3.0	1.7	4.5	2.6	–2.8

(Continued)

Table 64 *(Continued)*

Sex	State	Regular Employee				Self-employed				Casual Labour			
		1983 to 1994	1994 to 2000	2000 to 2012	2012 to 2018	1983 to 1994	1994 to 2000	2000 to 2012	2012 to 2018	1983 to 1994	1994 to 2000	2000 to 2012	2012 to 2018
Female	Andhra Pradesh	-1.8	11.1	-1.2	6.9	2.8	-1.2	0.2	-3.3	2.6	0.2	-0.5	-4.8
	Assam	0.6	2.1	-1.3	16.1	3.9	2.6	1.1	-22.9	7.9	-3.4	-3.0	-1.6
	Bihar	-3.6	6.5	5.5	12.9	-4.2	4.8	-1.6	-10.0	1.3	0.7	-7.3	-12.9
	Gujarat	-0.7	3.4	7.8	2.1	0.2	3.4	-2.4	-5.9	2.4	0.7	-2.9	-12.6
	Haryana	-11.3	2.2	8.2	16.8	4.1	-1.2	-1.8	-13.4	3.4	-11.3	3.5	0.3
	Himachal Pradesh	6.9	9.1	8.5	-1.1	2.5	-0.3	1.4	-2.9	5.4	-4.8	16.9	-12.3
	Jammu & Kashmir	12.8	0.3	8.4	9.4	5.4	-0.3	-0.9	-0.2	9.7	-19.6	18.4	-26.0
	Karnataka	1.0	-4.0	11.2	0.3	3.0	-2.8	-1.2	-5.8	2.1	1.3	-3.0	-3.6
	Kerala	-2.3	8.7	0.4	2.1	-2.7	0.4	-6.1	-10.1	-1.0	-0.6	-1.2	-12.8
	Madhya Pradesh	-6.8	4.5	3.4	12.3	0.6	-1.3	-0.1	4.5	3.3	3.4	-1.5	-2.9
	Maharashtra	8.3	-8.4	6.3	8.0	1.2	-1.5	1.6	-4.3	1.8	1.3	-1.8	-4.6
	Odisha	-1.0	0.3	7.8	9.7	3.0	-1.9	2.0	-10.9	1.5	2.9	-4.4	-4.0
	Punjab	-0.7	7.9	6.6	8.2	-2.6	6.1	-1.7	-19.4	3.0	-2.6	4.6	-5.8
	Rajasthan	3.3	1.5	9.2	0.9	2.0	-0.1	-0.4	-4.4	3.0	-1.3	7.3	-15.3
	Tamil Nadu	4.6	2.5	2.1	5.2	0.8	-3.8	-3.1	0.0	1.3	-1.6	0.5	-7.2
	Uttar Pradesh	-1.4	11.0	8.4	4.0	0.1	0.4	1.4	-9.0	2.9	1.9	-2.0	-9.5
	West Bengal	4.7	-6.6	8.4	7.1	1.3	0.1	1.5	-6.4	1.4	-1.4	2.2	-1.3

(Continued)

Table 64 *(Continued)*

Sex	State	Regular Employee				Self-employed				Casual Labour			
		1983 to 1994	1994 to 2000	2000 to 2012	2012 to 2018	1983 to 1994	1994 to 2000	2000 to 2012	2012 to 2018	1983 to 1994	1994 to 2000	2000 to 2012	2012 to 2018
Male + Female	Andhra Pradesh	-2.2	1.8	2.8	2.1	2.1	-0.3	0.2	-0.9	3.1	0.6	-0.6	-4.0
	Assam	-0.1	4.0	-1.7	13.1	1.9	1.8	2.7	-2.2	6.4	0.0	-1.5	2.0
	Bihar	-2.2	0.4	2.3	16.7	0.5	2.0	1.5	-0.2	2.7	2.0	0.0	-4.7
	Gujarat	3.2	1.6	3.9	4.2	-0.1	3.3	0.4	-0.5	3.7	0.5	-1.6	-8.3
	Haryana	-1.8	5.8	2.0	9.2	2.9	0.3	0.6	-5.8	3.8	-0.4	2.3	-1.0
	Himachal Pradesh	5.7	5.7	4.5	1.7	2.2	-1.5	0.9	-0.9	5.4	7.1	3.9	-2.8
	Jammu & Kashmir	7.5	-1.1	6.4	5.9	2.9	1.9	-0.9	1.5	-0.4	5.7	8.6	-3.0
	Karnataka	1.2	2.3	6.8	1.0	2.1	-1.7	0.4	-0.4	2.2	2.3	-1.5	-3.7
	Kerala	-1.2	4.2	-0.5	2.6	-0.8	0.3	-3.6	-5.7	1.8	1.4	-2.6	-10.1
	Madhya Pradesh	-2.8	-1.4	3.5	10.9	1.2	-0.8	1.5	3.4	4.1	3.4	0.2	-2.5
	Maharashtra	1.0	-0.4	2.6	4.1	1.1	-1.2	2.7	-0.5	2.2	2.1	-1.1	-3.6
	Odisha	-4.3	-0.2	5.1	5.7	2.3	-1.8	3.1	-3.0	1.9	3.8	-2.4	-3.2
	Punjab	1.1	5.7	2.9	2.5	-1.5	2.7	-0.7	-4.4	4.6	-1.5	3.0	-3.7
	Rajasthan	3.4	1.9	4.2	8.6	1.5	0.7	0.0	-0.6	5.7	-0.8	5.9	-7.6
	Tamil Nadu	1.7	2.6	1.6	5.5	0.4	-3.5	-1.6	0.8	1.4	-0.6	0.8	-5.6
	Uttar Pradesh	1.2	4.8	2.5	6.1	1.6	0.3	0.9	-1.3	4.4	1.1	3.2	-3.5
	West Bengal	2.2	-4.8	3.7	7.5	3.0	-0.7	0.8	0.6	1.6	3.2	2.5	-2.7

Source: Same as Table 53

Table 65. States' Ranks Based on Annual Growth of Workers (UPSS) Under Self-Employment, Regular Employment and Casual Employment: Rural Areas

Sex	State	Regular Employee				Self–employed				Casual Labour			
		1983 to 1994	1994 to 2000	2000 to 2012	2012 to 2018	1983 to 1994	1994 to 2000	2000 to 2012	2012 to 2018	1983 to 1994	1994 to 2000	2000 to 2012	2012 to 2018
Male	Andhra Pradesh	16	14	4	17	7	8	12	13	9	12	13	11
	Assam	11	4	17	2	10	3	3	15	2	11	15	1
	Bihar	15	12	12	1	4	5	5	12	10	9	8	13
	Gujarat	3	10	8	11	16	2	6	11	7	14	14	16
	Haryana	13	1	14	5	3	6	7	16	8	6	7	3
	Himachal Pradesh	2	3	5	14	6	16	13	5	3	1	6	2
	Jammu & Kashmir	1	15	1	9	11	1	16	2	17	2	1	4
	Karnataka	8	6	2	16	8	13	8	6	13	7	12	12
	Kerala	12	8	16	13	14	10	17	17	11	10	17	17
	Madhya Pradesh	14	16	7	3	9	11	4	3	6	5	9	6
	Maharashtra	10	11	11	12	12	14	2	8	12	8	11	7
	Odisha	17	13	3	10	5	15	1	14	14	4	16	8
	Punjab	7	2	9	15	17	7	14	10	5	17	4	10
	Rajasthan	4	9	6	4	13	4	11	4	1	16	2	15
	Tamil Nadu	9	7	15	8	15	17	15	9	16	15	10	14
	Uttar Pradesh	6	5	13	7	2	9	9	7	4	13	3	5
	West Bengal	5	17	10	6	1	12	10	1	15	3	5	9
	Kendall's W	0.160				0.239				0.353			

(Continued)

Table 65 *(Continued)*

Sex	State	Regular Employee				Self-employed				Casual Labour			
		1983 to 1994	1994 to 2000	2000 to 2012	2012 to 2018	1983 to 1994	1994 to 2000	2000 to 2012	2012 to 2018	1983 to 1994	1994 to 2000	2000 to 2012	2012 to 2018
Female	Andhra Pradesh	13	1	16	10	6	11	7	5	9	8	8	8
	Assam	8	11	17	2	3	4	6	17	2	14	14	3
	Bihar	15	6	12	3	17	2	12	12	16	7	17	15
	Gujarat	9	8	9	14	13	3	15	9	10	6	13	13
	Haryana	17	10	7	1	2	12	14	15	4	16	5	1
	Himachal Pradesh	3	3	3	17	7	10	5	4	3	15	2	12
	Jammu & Kashmir	1	13	5	6	1	9	10	3	1	17	1	17
	Karnataka	7	15	1	16	5	16	11	8	11	4	15	5
	Kerala	14	4	15	13	16	5	17	13	17	9	9	14
	Madhya Pradesh	16	7	13	4	12	13	8	1	5	1	10	4
	Maharashtra	2	17	11	8	10	14	2	6	12	5	11	7
	Odisha	11	14	8	5	4	15	1	14	13	2	16	6
	Punjab	10	5	10	7	15	1	13	16	6	13	4	9
	Rajasthan	6	12	2	15	8	8	9	7	7	10	3	16
	Tamil Nadu	5	9	14	11	11	17	16	2	15	12	7	10
	Uttar Pradesh	12	2	6	12	14	6	4	11	8	3	12	11
	West Bengal	4	16	4	9	9	7	3	10	14	11	6	2
	Kendall's W	0.068				0.150				0.161			

(Continued)

Table 65 *(Continued)*

Sex	State	Regular Employee				Self-employed				Casual Labour			
		1983 to 1994	1994 to 2000	2000 to 2012	2012 to 2018	1983 to 1994	1994 to 2000	2000 to 2012	2012 to 2018	1983 to 1994	1994 to 2000	2000 to 2012	2012 to 2018
Male + Female	Andhra Pradesh	14	10	10	15	7	10	12	10	9	11	11	12
	Assam	11	6	17	2	8	5	2	13	1	13	13	1
	Bihar	15	12	13	1	13	3	4	5	10	8	10	13
	Gujarat	4	11	6	11	15	1	11	7	8	12	15	16
	Haryana	13	1	14	4	3	9	9	17	7	14	7	2
	Himachal Pradesh	2	2	4	16	5	14	7	11	3	1	3	5
	Jammu & Kashmir	1	15	2	8	2	4	15	2	17	2	1	6
	Karnataka	7	8	1	17	6	15	10	6	12	6	14	10
	Kerala	12	5	16	13	16	8	17	16	14	9	17	17
	Madhya Pradesh	16	16	8	3	11	12	5	1	6	4	9	3
	Maharashtra	10	14	11	12	12	13	3	8	11	7	12	9
	Odisha	17	13	3	9	4	16	1	14	13	3	16	7
	Punjab	9	3	9	14	17	2	14	15	4	17	5	11
	Rajasthan	3	9	5	5	10	6	13	9	2	16	2	15
	Tamil Nadu	6	7	15	10	14	17	16	3	16	15	8	14
	Uttar Pradesh	8	4	12	7	9	7	6	12	5	10	4	8
	West Bengal	5	17	7	6	1	11	8	4	15	5	6	4
	Kendall's W	0.155				0.208				0.333			

Source: Author's computation using data in Table 64

Note: None of the computed Kendall's W-statistics is statistically significant.

- The decline in the growth rate of self-employment in rural areas for both males and females is accompanied by an increase in the growth rate of regular employees. Once again, this trend is more evident in the sub-period 2000–2012, during which ten states for rural males and eight states for rural females experienced an increase in the growth rate of regular employees compared to the previous sub-period, 1994–2000. Even in the sub-period 2012–2018, almost two-third states observed an increase in the growth rate of regular employees both for males (these are Assam, Bihar, Gujarat, Haryana, Kerala, Madhya Pradesh, Maharashtra, Odisha, Rajasthan, Tamil Nadu, Uttar Pradesh, and West Bengal) and females (these are Andhra Pradesh, Assam, Bihar, Haryana, Jammu & Kashmir, Kerala, Madhya Pradesh, Maharashtra, Odisha, Punjab, and Tamil Nadu)) in rural areas compared to the preceding period.
- Between 2012 and 2018, the highest and lowest growth rates of regular employees among rural males were recorded in Bihar (17.0 %) and Andhra Pradesh (1.0 %), respectively. For rural females, the corresponding figures were 16.8 % in Haryana and –1.1 % in Himachal Pradesh. Notably, ten states (in alphabetical order: Assam, Bihar, Haryana, Jammu & Kashmir, Madhya Pradesh, Odisha, Rajasthan, Tamil Nadu, Uttar Pradesh, and West Bengal) experienced an annual growth rate of over 5 % in regular employees among rural males. Eleven states (Andhra Pradesh, Assam, Bihar, Haryana, Jammu & Kashmir, Madhya Pradesh, Maharashtra, Odisha, Punjab, Tamil Nadu, and West Bengal, in alphabetical order) achieved similar growth for rural females. When considering rural persons, ten states (Assam, Bihar, Haryana, Jammu & Kashmir, Madhya Pradesh, Odisha, Rajasthan, Tamil Nadu, Uttar Pradesh, and West Bengal, in alphabetical order) demonstrated more than 5 % growth in regular employees during 2012–2018.
- Regarding the growth rates of casual labour in rural areas, Table 64 indicates a general trend of declining growth rates from 2000 to 2012 compared to 1994 to 2000; this decline has been observed in twelve states for males and nine for females. Furthermore, from 2012 to 2018, a declining trend in the growth rate of casual workers was observed in sixteen states for males and fifteen states for females. For rural persons, all states (except Assam) also experienced a decrease in the growth rate of casual workers during 2012–2018 compared to the prior period (2000–2012).
- During the sub-period 2012–2018, Assam recorded the highest growth rate of casual workers among rural males at 2.2 %, while Kerala observed the lowest at –9.0 %. For rural females, Haryana showed the highest growth rate at 0.3 %, while Jammu & Kashmir had the lowest at –26.0 %. Similarly, Assam experienced the highest growth rate of casual workers among rural persons

at 2.0 %, compared to Kerala's low of –10.1 %. It is important to note that all the other states were undergoing a negative growth rate of casual workers (for males, females, and all persons) during this last sub-period.

- It is evident that there is no concordance among the ranks of the states regarding the growth rates of employment under various modes in rural areas across different sub-periods. This is highlighted by the statistical non-significance of the computed Kendall's W statistics across all categories – males, females, and persons.

The annual growth rates of workers across three modes of employment during various sub-periods in urban areas for males, females, and persons, along with their corresponding ranks, are presented in Tables 66 and 67, respectively. The key observations in this respect are as follows:

- During the sub-period of 2012–2018, the annual growth rate of self-employed workers among urban males was highest in Kerala (7.0 %) and lowest in West Bengal (–0.9 %). For urban females, the highest and lowest growth rates were recorded in Jammu & Kashmir (7.3 %) and Odisha (–10.1 %), respectively. The highest and lowest growth rates for urban persons were observed in Kerala (5.1 %) and Odisha (–2.7 %), respectively. Throughout this period, only three states for urban males, three for urban females, and two for urban persons recorded annual growth rates of 3 % or more of self-employed workers.
- Over time, the percentage of self-employed workers appears to have declined in urban areas across most states for all categories – males, females, and persons. For example, the growth of self-employed workers among urban males decreased in fifteen out of seventeen major states from 2012 to 2018 when compared to the period from 2000 to 2012 (the exceptions being Kerala and Rajasthan); a similar trend occurred in twelve states for urban females (the exceptions being Andhra Pradesh, Haryana, Himachal Pradesh, Karnataka, and Madhya Pradesh). This trend was observed among urban persons in fifteen states (excluding Himachal Pradesh and Kerala).
- Regarding the growth of regular male employees in urban areas during 2012–2018, Haryana (6.1 %) ranked highest among the states, while Himachal Pradesh (–2.7 %) held the lowest position. For urban females, Bihar (13.1 %) registered the highest growth, with Himachal Pradesh (–5.2 %) the lowest. Regarding urban persons, Assam recorded the maximum growth of regular employees at 6.7 %, while Himachal Pradesh again showed the lowest rate at –2.7 %.

Table 66. Annual Growth Rates of Workers (UPSS) by Employment Status in Major States: Urban Areas

Sex	State	Regular Employee				Self-employed				Casual Labour			
		1983 to 1994	1994 to 2000	2000 to 2012	2012 to 2018	1983 to 1994	1994 to 2000	2000 to 2012	2012 to 2018	1983 to 1994	1994 to 2000	2000 to 2012	2012 to 2018
Male	Andhra Pradesh	2.7	1.1	5.1	2.0	3.1	−0.8	3.6	2.7	6.9	0.7	0.5	4.4
	Assam	2.7	2.1	1.5	5.3	4.1	2.9	3.8	1.8	5.2	4.3	1.5	2.7
	Bihar	1.8	−0.7	2.3	3.9	2.0	4.1	3.0	−0.3	1.8	2.2	4.4	5.9
	Gujarat	3.5	−0.7	7.4	1.3	2.6	4.6	4.0	3.2	4.6	7.8	−5.0	1.0
	Haryana	4.7	3.5	4.2	6.1	1.9	4.4	3.7	1.7	5.7	3.3	2.8	2.1
	Himachal Pradesh	2.3	2.4	3.9	−2.7	1.8	3.4	1.5	0.8	2.5	8.9	1.8	6.5
	Jammu & Kashmir	5.6	−1.1	3.8	5.6	0.9	4.7	4.3	0.1	−3.0	22.0	4.4	3.2
	Karnataka	2.8	3.1	3.4	1.9	4.5	1.7	4.0	−0.9	1.3	3.4	1.0	6.0
	Kerala	3.0	1.3	7.0	4.7	5.2	0.5	5.7	7.0	5.9	0.1	5.3	2.4
	Madhya Pradesh	2.5	1.1	2.5	6.1	3.5	5.2	3.0	1.8	5.4	4.1	3.7	1.2
	Maharashtra	3.1	3.7	2.5	1.8	4.3	1.4	3.3	0.5	2.1	6.4	−1.2	5.4
	Odisha	3.3	−1.8	3.2	2.7	3.0	3.4	5.4	−0.5	2.4	4.8	1.7	0.3
	Punjab	2.0	3.5	3.8	1.8	3.4	2.8	2.2	0.8	5.4	4.3	−0.6	8.2
	Rajasthan	5.8	1.4	2.9	3.5	2.2	2.2	1.7	4.1	1.2	8.5	4.3	−4.2
	Tamil Nadu	2.8	5.2	2.6	3.3	3.1	2.4	2.7	0.1	2.6	0.5	3.8	0.8
	Uttar Pradesh	1.9	4.1	2.2	5.5	3.2	1.7	2.8	0.8	2.6	6.3	5.2	−3.2
	West Bengal	1.8	−0.8	2.3	3.0	2.8	4.6	3.2	−0.9	3.3	4.3	3.2	2.8

(Continued)

Table 66 *(Continued)*

Sex	State	Regular Employee				Self-employed				Casual Labour			
		1983 to 1994	1994 to 2000	2000 to 2012	2012 to 2018	1983 to 1994	1994 to 2000	2000 to 2012	2012 to 2018	1983 to 1994	1994 to 2000	2000 to 2012	2012 to 2018
Female	Andhra Pradesh	3.6	8.0	5.2	9.1	4.0	-3.0	3.9	4.0	4.4	-2.5	-2.0	3.2
	Assam	5.1	8.8	-0.6	12.5	2.7	4.7	6.6	-0.1	11.1	4.8	-5.8	-2.3
	Bihar	2.0	3.3	3.4	13.1	-2.9	7.5	-1.1	-2.9	-1.2	-0.4	-1.1	7.1
	Gujarat	4.4	3.4	5.9	6.7	2.5	1.6	4.2	-3.4	4.7	1.0	-3.4	1.4
	Haryana	3.0	4.8	10.2	-2.0	7.5	-4.4	-1.7	2.2	12.7	-11.0	-4.9	35.1
	Himachal Pradesh	1.9	-2.8	9.5	-5.2	6.9	-4.7	2.8	2.9	8.5	-12.1	4.4	-7.3
	Jammu & Kashmir	10.7	-10.4	10.7	6.4	2.6	-11.5	9.2	7.3	17.5	4.3	-0.3	-6.4
	Karnataka	2.7	6.7	6.4	4.0	3.9	0.6	-0.6	3.9	-1.0	0.6	-1.6	0.3
	Kerala	3.2	4.0	9.2	7.0	1.8	2.6	2.9	-0.3	5.5	-6.8	5.7	2.5
	Madhya Pradesh	1.3	-3.5	9.8	7.1	3.8	3.8	1.9	2.7	4.5	2.7	-0.1	3.5
	Maharashtra	7.4	0.2	6.5	2.5	5.3	-0.2	3.1	-3.0	0.3	-2.4	-0.7	-0.2
	Odisha	9.6	-3.1	5.4	7.1	4.9	5.6	5.3	-10.1	5.2	1.9	-3.3	1.7
	Punjab	1.3	9.1	5.2	3.5	-1.6	8.0	1.8	-4.3	-0.9	6.1	-0.8	3.8
	Rajasthan	12.0	0.6	5.1	4.5	-0.5	0.4	2.2	-8.2	2.6	-2.4	2.3	-3.4
	Tamil Nadu	6.1	7.9	2.4	7.2	3.0	2.4	2.2	-1.0	1.1	-4.3	1.5	-1.1
	Uttar Pradesh	1.5	6.3	2.3	10.2	5.1	1.7	3.4	-9.0	2.5	-7.8	5.4	-7.9
	West Bengal	3.1	-2.8	6.3	4.7	3.9	1.7	6.8	2.7	3.8	-4.2	4.6	-2.6

(Continued)

Table 66 *(Continued)*

Sex	State	Regular Employee				Self–employed				Casual Labour			
		1983 to 1994	1994 to 2000	2000 to 2012	2012 to 2018	1983 to 1994	1994 to 2000	2000 to 2012	2012 to 2018	1983 to 1994	1994 to 2000	2000 to 2012	2012 to 2018
Male + Female	Andhra Pradesh	2.8	2.1	5.1	3.5	3.4	–1.4	3.7	3.0	5.9	–0.5	–0.3	4.1
	Assam	3.0	3.2	1.1	6.7	4.0	3.1	4.1	1.6	6.3	4.4	0.2	2.2
	Bihar	1.8	–0.3	2.4	5.2	1.3	4.5	2.6	–0.6	1.1	1.6	3.6	5.9
	Gujarat	3.6	–0.2	7.2	1.7	2.6	4.0	4.1	1.8	4.7	5.9	–4.6	0.9
	Haryana	4.5	3.6	5.0	4.8	3.0	2.5	3.0	1.7	7.3	–0.1	2.0	6.5
	Himachal Pradesh	2.3	1.6	4.9	–2.7	3.3	0.9	1.8	1.8	3.8	4.9	2.1	6.2
	Jammu & Kashmir	6.3	–2.3	4.8	5.2	1.2	2.4	4.8	0.8	–0.1	17.7	3.9	1.6
	Karnataka	2.8	3.7	4.0	2.3	4.4	1.4	3.0	–0.2	0.5	2.5	0.3	4.6
	Kerala	3.1	2.1	7.7	5.5	4.0	1.2	4.8	5.1	5.8	–1.3	5.3	2.3
	Madhya Pradesh	2.3	0.6	3.5	6.2	3.6	4.9	2.7	1.8	5.1	3.6	2.6	1.6
	Maharashtra	3.7	3.1	3.2	1.7	4.5	1.0	3.3	–0.5	1.4	3.4	–1.0	3.7
	Odisha	4.0	–2.0	3.5	3.0	3.4	3.8	5.4	–2.7	3.3	3.8	0.3	0.2
	Punjab	1.9	4.3	4.1	2.1	2.6	3.5	2.1	0.0	4.6	4.4	–0.6	7.8
	Rajasthan	6.4	1.3	3.1	3.8	1.3	1.7	1.9	1.5	1.6	5.5	3.9	–3.9
	Tamil Nadu	3.5	5.8	2.5	4.3	3.0	2.4	2.6	–0.3	2.1	–0.9	3.2	0.3
	Uttar Pradesh	1.9	4.4	2.2	6.0	3.5	1.7	2.9	–0.8	2.6	4.3	5.2	–3.8
	West Bengal	2.0	–1.1	3.0	3.3	3.0	4.1	3.8	–0.1	3.4	2.7	3.4	1.9

Source: Same as Table 53

Table 67. States' Ranks Based on Annual Growth of Workers (UPSS) Under Self-Employment, Regular Employment and Casual Employment: Urban Areas

Sex	State	Regular Employee				Self-employed				Casual Labour			
		1983 to 1994	1994 to 2000	2000 to 2012	2012 to 2018	1983 to 1994	1994 to 2000	2000 to 2012	2012 to 2018	1983 to 1994	1994 to 2000	2000 to 2012	2012 to 2018
Male	Andhra Pradesh	10	12	3	12	8	17	8	4	1	15	14	6
	Assam	11	8	17	5	4	9	6	5	6	9	12	9
	Bihar	16	13	14	7	14	6	11	14	14	14	4	4
	Gujarat	4	14	1	16	12	4	4	3	7	4	17	13
	Haryana	3	4	4	1	15	5	7	7	3	13	9	11
	Himachal Pradesh	13	7	5	17	16	7	17	9	11	2	10	2
	Jammu & Kashmir	2	16	7	3	17	2	3	12	17	1	3	7
	Karnataka	9	6	8	13	2	14	5	16	15	12	13	3
	Kerala	7	10	2	6	1	16	1	1	2	17	1	10
	Madhya Pradesh	12	11	13	2	5	1	12	6	5	11	7	12
	Maharashtra	6	3	12	14	3	15	9	11	13	5	16	5
	Odisha	5	17	9	11	10	8	2	15	12	7	11	15
	Punjab	14	5	6	15	6	10	15	8	4	10	15	1
	Rajasthan	1	9	10	8	13	12	16	2	16	3	5	17
	Tamil Nadu	8	1	11	9	9	11	14	13	9	16	6	14
	Uttar Pradesh	15	2	16	4	7	13	13	10	10	6	2	16
	West Bengal	17	15	15	10	11	3	10	17	8	8	8	8
	Kendall's W	0.250				0.194				0.084			

(Continued)

Table 67 *(Continued)*

Sex	State	Regular Employee				Self-employed				Casual Labour			
		1983 to 1994	1994 to 2000	2000 to 2012	2012 to 2018	1983 to 1994	1994 to 2000	2000 to 2012	2012 to 2018	1983 to 1994	1994 to 2000	2000 to 2012	2012 to 2018
Female	Andhra Pradesh	8	3	12	4	6	14	6	2	9	11	13	5
	Assam	6	2	17	2	11	4	3	8	3	2	17	12
	Bihar	13	10	14	1	17	2	16	11	17	8	11	2
	Gujarat	7	9	9	9	13	10	5	13	7	6	15	8
	Haryana	11	7	2	16	1	15	17	7	2	16	16	1
	Himachal Pradesh	14	13	4	17	2	16	10	4	4	17	4	16
	Jammu & Kashmir	2	17	1	10	12	17	1	1	1	3	8	15
	Karnataka	12	5	7	13	7	11	15	3	16	7	12	9
	Kerala	9	8	5	8	14	6	9	9	5	14	1	6
	Madhya Pradesh	16	16	3	6	9	5	13	5	8	4	7	4
	Maharashtra	4	12	6	15	3	13	8	12	14	9	9	10
	Odisha	3	15	10	7	5	3	4	17	6	5	14	7
	Punjab	17	1	11	14	16	1	14	14	15	1	10	3
	Rajasthan	1	11	13	12	15	12	11	15	11	10	5	14
	Tamil Nadu	5	4	15	5	10	7	12	10	13	13	6	11
	Uttar Pradesh	15	6	16	3	4	9	7	16	12	15	2	17
	West Bengal	10	14	8	11	8	8	2	6	10	12	3	13
	Kendall's W	**0.089**				**0.144**				**0.111**			

(Continued)

Table 67 *(Continued)*

Sex	State	Regular Employee				Self-employed				Casual Labour			
		1983 to 1994	1994 to 2000	2000 to 2012	2012 to 2018	1983 to 1994	1994 to 2000	2000 to 2012	2012 to 2018	1983 to 1994	1994 to 2000	2000 to 2012	2012 to 2018
Male + Female	Andhra Pradesh	10	8	3	10	8	17	7	2	3	15	14	6
	Assam	9	6	17	1	4	7	5	7	2	5	13	9
	Bihar	17	14	15	6	16	2	13	15	15	13	5	4
	Gujarat	6	13	2	16	14	4	4	5	6	2	17	13
	Haryana	3	5	4	7	11	8	10	6	1	14	10	2
	Himachal Pradesh	13	10	5	17	9	16	17	4	8	4	9	3
	Jammu & Kashmir	2	17	6	5	17	10	2	9	17	1	4	11
	Karnataka	11	4	8	13	2	13	9	12	16	12	12	5
	Kerala	8	9	1	4	3	14	3	1	4	17	1	8
	Madhya Pradesh	12	12	9	2	5	1	12	3	5	9	8	12
	Maharashtra	5	7	11	15	1	15	8	14	14	10	16	7
	Odisha	4	16	10	12	7	5	1	17	10	8	11	15
	Punjab	15	3	7	14	13	6	15	10	7	6	15	1
	Rajasthan	1	11	12	9	15	12	16	8	13	3	3	17
	Tamil Nadu	7	1	14	8	10	9	14	13	12	16	7	14
	Uttar Pradesh	16	2	16	3	6	11	11	16	11	7	2	16
	West Bengal	14	15	13	11	12	3	6	11	9	11	6	10
	Kendall's W	**0.196**				**0.217**				**0.125**			

Source: Computed by the author using data in Table 66

Note: Same as Table 65

- Another important point to note is that during the sub-period 2000–2012 of the post-globalisation era, thirteen of the seventeen major states for urban males, eleven for urban females, and thirteen for urban persons experienced higher growth in regular employment than in the previous sub-period 1994–2000. Even during the last sub-period, 2012–2018, nine states for urban males and seven states for urban females recorded a higher growth of regular employees compared to the period 2000–2012, which appears to represent the most impressive sub-period in terms of the growth of regular employees across the states.
- It is further noted from Table 66 that during the sub-period 2012–2018, the growth rate of regular employees surpassed 5.0 % in five states for urban males (Assam, Haryana, Jammu & Kashmir, Madhya Pradesh, and Uttar Pradesh), ten states for urban females (Andhra Pradesh, Assam, Bihar, Gujarat, Jammu & Kashmir, Kerala, Madhya Pradesh, Odisha, Tamil Nadu, and Uttar Pradesh), and six states (Assam, Bihar, Jammu & Kashmir, Kerala, Madhya Pradesh, and Uttar Pradesh) for urban persons.
- Shifting our focus to the growth rate of casual workers in urban areas, it is found that during the sub-period from 2012 to 2018, urban males in Punjab experienced the highest growth at 8.2 %, while Rajasthan recorded the lowest at –4.2 %. For urban females, Haryana reported the highest growth at 35.1 %, whereas Uttar Pradesh saw a decline of –7.9 %. Additionally, for urban persons, the highest growth was again in Punjab at 7.8 %, with Rajasthan showing the lowest at –3.9 %. It is worth noting that during this period, alongside Punjab, the states of Himachal Pradesh, Karnataka, Bihar, and Maharashtra each recorded over 5.0 % growth in casual workers for urban males. Bihar and Haryana have recorded over 5.0 % growth in casual employment among urban females. At the same time, Bihar, Haryana, and Himachal Pradesh are the states, in addition to Punjab, that have observed more than 5.0 % growth in casual workers among urban persons.
- A thorough examination of the growth rates of casual workers in urban areas reveals that these rates have declined in many states over time, especially after 1994. This observation applies to both males and females in urban regions.

- However, similar to rural areas, there is no consistent ranking of the states in urban areas regarding the growth rates of employed individuals across different modes of employment during various sub-periods for males, females, and persons.

State-level information on the growth rates of workers across three employment modes for combined areas (rural plus urban), along with their corresponding ranks, is presented in Tables 68 and 69, respectively. Once again, the overarching trend is a declining growth rate of workers within the self-employed category over time. This trend is more pronounced among females than among males. During the latest sub-period, from 2012 to 2018, Madhya Pradesh recorded the highest growth in self-employed workers among males, while Haryana reported the lowest. It is also noteworthy that, across all states, the growth rate of self-employment for males (considering both rural and urban areas) was below 3.0 % during this period. For females, only one state (Madhya Pradesh) recorded growth exceeding 3.0 % in the self-employed persons during this timeframe. Furthermore, fifteen of the seventeen states experienced negative growth in the number of self-employed female workers during 2012–2018, whereas only three states (Haryana, Odisha, and Assam) reported negative growth for males. Considering both genders together, it is evident that the growth rate of self-employed persons was negative in eleven states during this period. Compared with the growth rate in the preceding period (2000–2012), thirteen states saw a decline in self-employed worker growth, with Jammu & Kashmir, Kerala, Madhya Pradesh, and Tamil Nadu being the exceptions.

In contrast to the picture obtained for the growth rate of self-employed workers, the broader trend for regular employees during the initial sub-periods of the post-globalisation era indicates an increasing growth rate in most states, particularly for females. However, in the last sub-period (2012–2018), the growth rate of regular female employees was lower in most states compared to the preceding sub-period (2000–2012). For males, nine states recorded a lower growth of regular employees during the last sub-period than earlier. Additionally, a reduction in the growth of regular employees was noted in nine states between 2012 and 2018, compared to the period from 2000 to 2012. Among the states in India, during the sub-period 2012–2018, the highest growth rate of regular male employees was observed in Bihar (10.0 %) and the lowest in Gujarat (0.6 %). The highest and

Table 68. Annual Growth Rates of Workers (UPSS) by Employment Status in the States: Rural + Urban Areas

Sex	State	Regular Employee				Self-employed				Casual Labour			
		1983 to 1994	1994 to 2000	2000 to 2012	2012 to 2018	1983 to 1994	1994 to 2000	2000 to 2012	2012 to 2018	1983 to 1994	1994 to 2000	2000 to 2012	2012 to 2018
Male	Andhra Pradesh	0.4	0.5	4.7	1.2	1.9	0.1	0.9	1.2	4.0	1.0	−0.5	−1.8
	Assam	0.4	3.9	−0.8	8.4	1.8	1.8	3.2	−0.1	5.8	1.3	−0.9	2.7
	Bihar	−0.3	−0.4	2.1	10.0	2.1	1.5	2.4	0.9	3.3	2.5	1.9	−3.1
	Gujarat	3.6	−0.1	6.3	0.6	0.5	3.7	2.7	2.3	4.7	1.9	−1.7	−4.3
	Haryana	1.8	4.6	3.1	6.5	2.1	1.8	2.2	−1.9	4.2	3.2	2.2	0.0
	Himachal Pradesh	4.5	4.5	3.8	1.7	2.0	−2.7	0.2	1.6	5.2	8.2	2.4	−0.1
	Jammu & Kashmir	6.4	−1.2	5.1	4.6	1.1	4.0	0.2	2.5	−1.2	9.0	7.7	−0.5
	Karnataka	2.4	3.2	4.2	1.2	2.2	−0.3	2.0	1.1	2.0	3.2	−0.2	−1.0
	Kerala	0.7	1.9	3.3	2.5	1.6	0.3	0.5	1.1	3.5	1.6	−0.7	−3.7
	Madhya Pradesh	0.6	0.0	2.8	5.8	1.9	0.4	2.5	2.9	4.8	3.5	1.7	−1.4
	Maharashtra	2.2	3.0	2.4	1.2	2.0	−0.2	3.4	1.6	2.6	3.6	−0.6	−0.5
	Odisha	−1.2	−1.1	4.0	2.9	2.1	−1.2	3.9	−0.1	2.1	4.4	−1.2	−2.3
	Punjab	1.7	4.4	3.2	1.4	0.2	1.1	0.7	1.2	4.9	−0.4	2.2	−1.2
	Rajasthan	4.8	1.6	3.1	5.8	1.2	1.5	0.5	2.5	6.2	0.7	5.2	−4.5
	Tamil Nadu	2.1	4.3	2.2	3.5	1.0	−1.2	0.9	0.9	1.8	0.3	1.7	−2.2
	Uttar Pradesh	1.7	4.2	2.0	5.1	2.4	0.5	1.1	1.6	4.7	1.5	4.6	−2.2
	West Bengal	1.7	−2.0	2.3	3.5	3.5	0.4	1.3	1.9	1.9	4.4	2.7	−1.5

(Continued)

Table 68 *(Continued)*

Sex	State	Regular Employee				Self-employed				Casual Labour			
		1983 to 1994	1994 to 2000	2000 to 2012	2012 to 2018	1983 to 1994	1994 to 2000	2000 to 2012	2012 to 2018	1983 to 1994	1994 to 2000	2000 to 2012	2012 to 2018
Female	Andhra Pradesh	0.8	9.4	2.6	7.9	2.9	–1.4	0.7	–1.8	2.7	0.0	–0.6	–3.9
	Assam	1.2	3.4	–1.1	14.9	3.9	2.7	1.4	–20.1	8.0	–3.0	–3.2	–1.0
	Bihar	–0.9	4.8	4.5	11.4	–4.1	5.0	–1.6	–9.3	1.2	0.6	–7.0	–11.0
	Gujarat	2.9	3.4	6.4	4.5	0.4	3.2	–1.4	–4.8	2.7	0.8	–3.0	–9.7
	Haryana	–2.8	4.3	9.8	1.4	4.5	–1.6	–1.8	–10.5	4.5	–11.3	2.5	5.6
	Himachal Pradesh	4.5	4.9	8.8	–2.5	2.5	–0.4	1.4	–2.7	5.9	–5.9	16.0	–12.0
	Jammu & Kashmir	11.3	–6.4	9.7	5.9	5.3	–0.7	–0.5	1.4	11.5	–8.7	9.9	–20.7
	Karnataka	2.1	3.8	7.6	2.3	3.1	–2.3	–1.1	–3.4	1.7	1.2	–2.9	–2.6
	Kerala	–0.2	6.7	4.8	3.5	–1.9	0.9	–3.2	–5.4	0.0	–1.6	0.2	–6.3
	Madhya Pradesh	–2.2	–0.6	7.5	7.2	0.8	–0.9	0.1	4.9	3.4	3.3	–1.4	–1.8
	Maharashtra	7.6	–1.4	6.5	2.5	1.7	–1.3	1.8	–3.5	1.7	0.9	–1.7	–3.4
	Odisha	4.0	–1.7	6.5	7.6	3.0	–1.5	2.3	–10.7	1.7	2.8	–4.4	–3.4
	Punjab	0.6	8.8	5.6	4.8	–2.5	6.3	–1.3	–16.0	2.4	–1.3	3.8	–4.3
	Rajasthan	8.5	0.9	6.6	2.0	1.8	–0.1	–0.2	–4.3	2.9	–1.5	6.8	–13.8
	Tamil Nadu	5.5	6.0	2.3	5.8	1.2	–2.3	–1.3	0.0	1.3	–1.9	0.7	–5.2
	Uttar Pradesh	0.6	7.7	4.8	6.1	0.4	0.5	1.6	–8.7	2.9	1.3	–1.5	–8.9
	West Bengal	3.7	–4.1	7.0	4.7	1.6	0.4	2.6	–3.7	1.7	–1.8	2.5	–0.8

(Continued)

Table 68 *(Continued)*

Sex	State	Regular Employee				Self-employed				Casual Labour			
		1983 to 1994	1994 to 2000	2000 to 2012	2012 to 2018	1983 to 1994	1994 to 2000	2000 to 2012	2012 to 2018	1983 to 1994	1994 to 2000	2000 to 2012	2012 to 2018
Male + Female	Andhra Pradesh	0.5	2.0	4.3	2.5	2.3	−0.5	0.8	0.1	3.3	0.5	−0.5	−2.8
	Assam	0.6	3.8	−0.9	10.3	2.1	1.9	2.9	−1.7	6.4	0.2	−1.3	2.5
	Bihar	−0.3	0.0	2.3	10.3	0.6	2.2	1.7	−0.1	2.6	2.0	0.2	−3.6
	Gujarat	3.5	0.3	6.3	1.2	0.5	3.5	1.4	0.6	3.9	1.5	−2.1	−5.9
	Haryana	1.3	4.5	3.8	5.7	2.9	0.7	1.1	−3.6	4.3	−0.3	2.3	0.9
	Himachal Pradesh	4.5	4.5	4.6	0.6	2.3	−1.5	0.9	−0.8	5.3	7.0	3.8	−2.2
	Jammu & Kashmir	6.9	−1.8	5.6	4.5	2.7	2.0	−0.1	2.0	−0.3	7.5	7.8	−1.6
	Karnataka	2.3	3.3	4.9	1.3	2.5	−1.0	1.1	−0.1	1.9	2.3	−1.2	−1.6
	Kerala	0.5	3.3	3.8	2.8	0.1	0.5	−0.7	−0.7	2.5	0.9	−0.5	−4.4
	Madhya Pradesh	0.2	−0.1	3.5	6.3	1.5	−0.1	1.7	3.6	4.2	3.4	0.5	−1.5
	Maharashtra	2.9	2.3	3.1	1.3	1.9	−0.6	2.9	0.0	2.1	2.3	−1.1	−1.7
	Odisha	−0.7	−1.2	4.3	3.6	2.4	−1.3	3.4	−2.8	1.9	3.8	−2.2	−2.7
	Punjab	1.6	4.9	3.6	2.0	−0.7	2.9	0.0	−2.9	4.6	−0.5	2.4	−1.6
	Rajasthan	5.2	1.5	3.5	5.2	1.5	0.8	0.2	−0.1	5.1	0.1	5.6	−6.9
	Tamil Nadu	2.8	4.7	2.2	4.0	1.1	−1.7	0.1	0.5	1.6	−0.7	1.3	−3.4
	Uttar Pradesh	1.6	4.6	2.3	5.0	1.8	0.5	1.2	−1.0	4.2	1.4	3.5	−3.3
	West Bengal	2.0	−2.3	3.2	3.8	3.0	0.4	1.6	0.5	1.8	3.2	2.7	−1.5

Source: Same as Table 53

Table 69. States' Ranks Based on Annual Growth of Workers (UPSS) Under Self-Employment, Regular Employment and Casual Employment: Rural + Urban Areas

Sex	State	Regular Employee				Self-employed				Casual Labour			
		1983 to 1994	1994 to 2000	2000 to 2012	2012 to 2018	1983 to 1994	1994 to 2000	2000 to 2012	2012 to 2018	1983 to 1994	1994 to 2000	2000 to 2012	2012 to 2018
Male	Andhra Pradesh	14	11	3	15	9	12	11	9	9	14	12	10
	Assam	15	6	17	2	11	4	3	15	2	13	15	1
	Bihar	16	14	15	1	6	5	6	14	11	9	8	14
	Gujarat	4	13	1	17	16	2	4	4	7	10	17	16
	Haryana	8	1	10	3	4	3	7	17	8	7	7	2
	Himachal Pradesh	3	2	6	12	8	17	16	8	3	2	5	3
	Jammu & Kashmir	1	16	2	7	14	1	17	3	17	1	1	5
	Karnataka	5	7	4	16	3	14	8	11	14	8	11	6
	Kerala	12	9	7	11	12	11	15	12	10	11	14	15
	Madhya Pradesh	13	12	11	4	10	9	5	1	5	6	10	8
	Maharashtra	6	8	12	14	7	13	2	6	12	5	13	4
	Odisha	17	15	5	10	5	15	1	16	13	4	16	13
	Punjab	10	3	8	13	17	7	13	10	4	17	6	7
	Rajasthan	2	10	9	5	13	6	14	2	1	15	2	17
	Tamil Nadu	7	4	14	9	15	16	12	13	16	16	9	11
	Uttar Pradesh	11	5	16	6	2	8	10	7	6	12	3	12
	West Bengal	9	17	13	8	1	10	9	5	15	3	4	9
	Kendall's W	0.160				0.224				0.277			

(Continued)

Table 69 *(Continued)*

Sex	State	Regular Employee				Self-employed				Casual Labour			
		1983 to 1994	1994 to 2000	2000 to 2012	2012 to 2018	1983 to 1994	1994 to 2000	2000 to 2012	2012 to 2018	1983 to 1994	1994 to 2000	2000 to 2012	2012 to 2018
Female	Andhra Pradesh	11	1	15	3	6	13	7	4	8	8	9	8
	Assam	10	11	17	1	3	4	5	17	2	14	15	3
	Bihar	15	7	14	2	17	2	15	13	16	7	17	14
	Gujarat	8	10	10	11	13	3	14	10	9	6	14	13
	Haryana	17	8	1	16	2	15	16	14	4	17	5	1
	Himachal Pradesh	5	6	3	17	7	9	6	5	3	15	1	15
	Jammu & Kashmir	1	17	2	7	1	10	10	2	1	16	2	17
	Karnataka	9	9	4	14	4	16	11	6	11	4	13	5
	Kerala	14	4	13	12	15	5	17	11	17	11	8	11
	Madhya Pradesh	16	13	5	5	12	11	8	1	5	1	10	4
	Maharashtra	3	14	9	13	9	12	3	7	13	5	12	7
	Odisha	6	15	8	4	5	14	2	15	14	2	16	6
	Punjab	12	2	11	9	16	1	12	16	10	9	4	9
	Rajasthan	2	12	7	15	8	8	9	9	6	10	3	16
	Tamil Nadu	4	5	16	8	11	17	13	3	15	13	7	10
	Uttar Pradesh	13	3	12	6	14	6	4	12	7	3	11	12
	West Bengal	7	16	6	10	10	7	1	8	12	12	6	2
	Kendall's W	**0.046**				**0.157**				**0.149**			

(Continued)

Table 69 *(Continued)*

Sex	State	Regular Employee				Self-employed				Casual Labour			
		1983 to 1994	1994 to 2000	2000 to 2012	2012 to 2018	1983 to 1994	1994 to 2000	2000 to 2012	2012 to 2018	1983 to 1994	1994 to 2000	2000 to 2012	2012 to 2018
Male + Female	Andhra Pradesh	13	10	6	12	6	10	12	6	9	12	12	11
	Assam	12	6	17	2	8	9	2	14	1	13	15	1
	Bihar	16	13	14	1	14	17	5	9	10	8	10	14
	Gujarat	4	12	1	16	15	6	7	3	8	9	16	16
	Haryana	11	4	8	4	2	2	9	17	5	15	7	2
	Himachal Pradesh	3	5	4	17	7	15	11	12	2	2	3	9
	Jammu & Kashmir	1	16	2	7	3	13	16	2	17	1	1	6
	Karnataka	7	7	3	15	4	11	10	10	14	6	14	5
	Kerala	14	8	7	11	16	8	17	11	11	11	11	15
	Madhya Pradesh	15	14	11	3	12	14	4	1	7	4	9	4
	Maharashtra	5	9	13	14	9	4	3	7	12	7	13	8
	Odisha	17	15	5	10	5	16	1	15	13	3	17	10
	Punjab	10	1	9	13	17	7	15	16	4	16	6	7
	Rajasthan	2	11	10	5	11	1	13	8	3	14	2	17
	Tamil Nadu	6	2	16	8	13	3	14	4	16	17	8	13
	Uttar Pradesh	9	3	15	6	10	5	8	13	6	10	4	12
	West Bengal	8	17	12	9	1	12	6	5	15	5	5	3
	Kendall's W		**0.116**				**0.185**				**0.253**		

Source: Author's computation using data in Table 68

Note: Same as Table 65

lowest growth rates for females were recorded in Assam (14.9 %) and Himachal Pradesh (–2.5 %), respectively. For all persons, the highest and lowest growth rates of regular employees were observed in Bihar (10.3 %) and Himachal Pradesh (0.6 %), respectively. It is also noteworthy that six states recorded more than 5.0 % growth of regular male employees during 2012–2018 (Assam, Bihar, Haryana, Madhya Pradesh, Rajasthan, and Uttar Pradesh). The same trend was observed in eight states among females (Andhra Pradesh, Assam, Bihar, Jammu & Kashmir, Madhya Pradesh, Odisha, Tamil Nadu, and Uttar Pradesh) and in six states among all persons (Assam, Bihar, Haryana, Madhya Pradesh, Rajasthan, and Uttar Pradesh).

When we examine the growth rates of casual workers across the states, most states in recent sub-periods have recorded negative growth rates for both males and females. In the latest sub-period, 2012–2018, all states except Assam and Haryana experienced negative growth among male casual workers; the same negative trend was observed across all states for females (except Haryana) and persons (except Assam and Haryana). Furthermore, compared to the preceding period (2000–2012), the growth rates of casual workers among males were lower in fifteen states between 2012 and 2018. These rates were lower in thirteen states for females and sixteen for persons. All these findings indicate a decline in the growth rates of casual workers in most states during the post-globalisation era.

Furthermore, it is noteworthy that, from 2012 to 2018, the highest growth of casual workers among males was observed in Assam (2.7 %), while the lowest was in Rajasthan (–4.5 %). The highest and lowest growth rates for females were recorded in Haryana (5.6 %) and Jammu & Kashmir (–20.7 %), respectively. Similarly, the highest and lowest growth rates for all persons were observed in Assam (2.5 %) and Rajasthan (–6.9 %), respectively. It is also important to note that, although all states registered a growth rate of casual workers of less than 3.0 % during 2012–2018 for both males and all persons, only one state (Haryana) exceeded a 3.0 % growth rate for females during this period.

As before, the rankings of states regarding the growth of workers across three employment modes during various sub-periods do not show any concordance, even when rural and urban areas are combined. This is evidenced by the statistical insignificance of Kendall's W statistics for the three categories – males, females, and persons.

5.6 Incidence of Poverty Across Various Employment Modes

In this section, we examine the incidence of poverty among employed workers, the unemployed, and individuals outside the labour force in India, as well as across various modes of employment. This discussion offers an alternative perspective on the quality of employment among workers.[1] The 'working poor' phenomenon is now well recognised, signifying that workers in less developed countries may be employed yet still classified as 'poor' due to insufficient earnings from their employment. Therefore, our discussion here enables us to assess the proportion of employed individuals across different employment modes who are poor, as well as the proportion of the poor among the unemployed and those outside the labour force.

For our current purpose, we utilise information on per capita monthly consumption expenditure generated by the NSSO surveys on employment and unemployment, as well as the Periodic Labour Force Survey. We employ state-level data on 'Tendulkar poverty lines' for rural and urban areas, which are compared with the monthly per capita expenditures of individuals within the states to classify them into 'poor' and 'non-poor' groups. The information on the percentages of poor individuals to the total population in rural and urban areas across India, categorised by employment status (employed, unemployed, and out of the labour force), is presented in Table 70. The following points arise here:

- In rural areas, in 2018, nearly 42 % of workers were classified as poor, down from 44 % in 1983. The proportion of the working poor in rural India increased between 1983 and 2000, then declined in 2012 before rising again in 2018. Notably, the proportion of individuals in poverty was highest among those who were out of the labour force from 1983 through 2018. Interestingly, the proportion of the poor was lower among unemployed individuals than among employed individuals in all the years.
- The pattern of working poor among the three categories remains consistent in urban India: those out of the labour force exhibit the highest incidence of poverty, followed by the employed and unemployed individuals. Once again, there was an increase in the incidence of poverty for these categories from 1983 to 2000, followed by a decline from 2000 to 2018. In 2018, 22.22 % of employed individuals, 21.94 % of unemployed individuals, and 27.36 % of those out of the labour force lived in poverty in urban India.

[1] Other ways to assess the quality of employment is by examining wage/earnings from employment, terms and conditions of employment, security of employment, etc.

Table 70. Percentage of Poor Persons Among the Employed, Unemployed, Out of Labour Force, and All Persons in India

Region	Year	Employed	Unemployed	Out of labour force	All Persons
Rural	1983	44.05	39.00	47.33	45.83
	1994	53.34	39.63	56.09	54.79
	2000	48.02	42.15	52.02	50.29
	2012	31.69	27.76	37.30	34.99
	2018	42.38	41.67	47.62	45.66
Urban	1983	39.93	38.47	42.73	41.70
	1994	34.27	29.19	36.34	35.50
	2000	45.62	43.13	47.56	46.83
	2012	16.21	13.80	18.43	17.58
	2018	22.22	21.94	27.36	25.46
Rural + Urban	1983	43.26	38.72	46.10	44.85
	1994	49.42	34.38	50.63	49.98
	2000	47.50	42.62	50.79	49.41
	2012	27.59	21.86	31.61	29.97
	2018	36.60	34.23	41.66	39.44

Source: Same as Table 53

- When considering both rural and urban areas together, it is evident that nearly 37 % of employed individuals were classified as poor in 2018, while the percentages of poor among the unemployed individuals and those out of the labour force stood at 34 % and 42 %, respectively. The fact that over one-third of employed persons are poor in India, even in 2018, highlights the low quality of employment for workers in terms of their earnings, as proxied by per capita consumption expenditure.

Let us examine the incidence of poverty among employed individuals across three distinct employment modes, as illustrated in Table 71. As expected, the highest rate of poverty is seen among casual workers, followed by self-employed workers and regular employees. In 2018, nearly half of the casual workers in rural areas and 41 % in urban areas were classified as 'poor'. When considering both rural and urban regions together, 48 % of casual workers were identified as 'poor' that year. For self-employed workers, the poverty rates in 2018 were

42 % in rural areas, 24 % in urban areas, and 38 % overall (rural and urban combined). Regarding regular employees, the percentages of those considered 'poor' in 2018 were 26 % in rural areas, 15 % in urban areas, and 20 % when combining both regions.

Table 71. Percentage of Poor Persons Among the Self-Employed, Regular Employees and Casual Labourers in India

Region	Year	Regular Employee	Self-Employed	Casual Labour	All Employed
Rural	1983	32.71	37.65	59.02	44.05
	1994	31.32	46.68	68.19	53.34
	2000	36.16	43.84	56.42	48.02
	2012	16.37	28.44	40.59	31.69
	2018	25.93	42.42	49.71	42.38
Urban	1983	26.10	42.85	63.59	39.93
	1994	20.05	36.43	59.88	34.27
	2000	36.68	46.16	64.49	45.62
	2012	8.00	18.06	34.98	16.21
	2018	15.08	23.61	41.46	22.22
Rural + Urban	1983	28.94	38.38	59.56	43.26
	1994	24.42	45.05	67.19	49.42
	2000	36.48	44.24	57.35	47.50
	2012	11.00	26.23	39.85	27.59
	2018	19.53	38.47	48.32	36.60

Source: Same as Table 53

It should also be noted that due to the predominance of self-employed workers in the overall workforce, more than 50 % of all 'poor' workers belonged to this category. As shown in Table 72, in 2018, 58 % of poor workers in rural areas, 41 % of poor workers in urban areas, and 55 % of poor workers in combined areas were self-employed. Meanwhile, in the same year, the proportion of casual workers among all poor workers in rural areas was 34 %; in urban areas, it was 27 %; and in combined areas, it was 33 %. Only about 8 % of all poor workers in rural areas were categorised as regular workers. In contrast, 32 % of all poor workers in urban areas belonged to this category, and 12 % of all poor workers in combined areas fell into it.

Table 72. Percentage Distribution of Poor Persons by Modes of Employment in India

Region	Year	Regular Employee	Self-Employed	Casual Labour
Rural	1983	5.32	52.34	42.34
	1994	3.79	50.72	45.49
	2000	5.14	50.90	43.96
	2012	4.49	50.19	45.32
	2018	8.03	57.87	34.10
Urban	1983	26.05	45.04	28.91
	1994	23.05	44.95	32.00
	2000	32.19	42.73	25.08
	2012	21.37	46.74	31.89
	2018	31.91	40.70	27.39
Rural + Urban	1983	9.01	51.03	39.96
	1994	6.53	49.91	43.56
	2000	10.75	49.20	40.05
	2012	7.12	49.65	43.23
	2018	12.18	54.88	32.94

Source: Same as Table 53

We also have data on the proportion of poor individuals among the workforce ('working poor') across various social and religious groups. Table 73 shows the percentages of poor workers from four social groups: ST, SC, OBC, and 'Others'. The findings here mirror those observed in rural areas and at various times, indicating that poverty is highest among workers in the ST group, followed by SC, OBC, and 'Others'. As shown in Table 73, in 2018, in rural areas, nearly 59 % of ST workers, 47 % of SC workers, 41 % of OBC workers, and 31 % of workers from the 'Others' category are classified as poor. In urban areas, the figures are 34 %, 31 %, 24 %, and 16 %, respectively, for ST, SC, OBC, and 'Others'. When combining rural and urban areas, as many as 56 % of workers from the ST group in 2018 are identified as poor; for SC, this stands at 43 %; for OBC, it is 36 %; and for 'Others', it is 25 %. Therefore, it is clear that the incidence of the 'working poor' in both rural and urban India has been higher among weaker social groups, and this trend has continued from 1983 to 2018. It is also noteworthy that although the 'working poor' incidence appears to have decreased over time for all social categories, this decline has been more significant (in percentage points) for the higher-caste group, namely 'Others', compared to the lower-caste groups.

Table 73. Percentage of Poor Among Employed Persons by Social Groups in India

Region	Year	Scheduled Tribe	Scheduled Caste	Other Backward Class	Others
Rural	1983	62.42	55.67	–	37.40
	1994	68.60	62.96	–	47.48
	2000	46.74	38.25	27.78	21.38
	2012	49.75	37.61	30.25	18.85
	2018	58.72	46.61	40.85	31.17
Urban	1983	56.10	53.00	–	37.04
	1994	45.27	51.52	–	31.12
	2000	46.16	41.66	33.80	18.54
	2012	26.90	24.38	18.24	10.17
	2018	34.33	30.80	23.66	16.27
Rural + Urban	1983	61.97	55.30	–	37.32
	1994	67.14	61.35	–	43.48
	2000	46.70	38.79	28.95	20.46
	2012	47.67	34.94	27.21	15.44
	2018	56.39	43.10	36.00	24.97

Source: As in Table 53

Note: For 1983 and 1993–94, 'Others' included 'other backward class'

The information on the incidence of the 'working poor' across religious groups is presented in Table 74. It was found that, in rural areas, the percentage of poor workers among Muslims was higher than that among Hindus until 2000, after which Hindus were reported to have a higher percentage of poor workers compared to Muslims. It was noted that while approximately 39 % of Muslim workers were poor in 2018, the corresponding figure for Hindus was 43 %. Another point to consider is that the incidence of working poor in rural areas has been the lowest in all years (except 2000) for the 'Others' category (comprising all those not belonging to the Hindu or Muslim groups). The situation is somewhat different in urban areas, where the percentage of the 'working poor' has been higher for Muslims compared to Hindus in all years. It was also observed that the 'Others' had a higher incidence of the 'working poor' compared to Hindus in all years (except 1983) in urban areas.

Table 74. Percentage of Poor Among Employed Persons by Religious Groups in India

Region	Year	Hindus	Muslims	Others
Rural	1983	44.82	46.67	27.91
	1994	53.74	55.15	49.41
	2000	30.66	37.22	45.37
	2012	32.23	31.36	27.47
	2018	43.21	38.57	36.85
Urban	1983	38.67	53.65	24.78
	1994	32.37	49.11	49.30
	2000	25.97	43.31	47.70
	2012	13.91	30.17	27.33
	2018	20.11	36.92	36.46
Rural + Urban	1983	43.73	48.86	27.18
	1994	49.67	53.13	49.06
	2000	29.72	39.20	47.05
	2012	27.67	30.93	27.14
	2018	36.89	37.95	36.44

Source: As in Table 53

Overall, when considering both rural and urban areas, Muslims across India show a higher incidence of poverty among their working population compared to Hindus. Furthermore, Muslims display a greater prevalence of the 'working poor' compared to 'Others' in all years, except for 2000. In 2018, the incidences of the 'working poor' across India were 36.89 %, 37.95 %, and 36.44 % for Hindus, Muslims, and 'Others' respectively.

5.7 Factors Influencing Workers' Choices of Employment Mode

In this section, we aim to identify factors that influence workers' choice of employment mode (i.e. regular employment, self-employment, or casual employment) in India. We estimate the multinomial logit regression model with casual employment as the base category to achieve this. We aim to understand the factors that influence workers' decisions between self-employment and casual employment, as well as the likelihood of choosing regular employment over casual employment. This analysis is conducted separately for rural, urban, and combined (rural plus urban) areas using the PLFS 2018 data.

In the multinomial logit regression exercises carried out, the explanatory variables considered as determinants of the workers' choice of employment mode are as follows: the age of the workers (age) in years; a sex dummy (sex) assigned the value '1' for males and '0' for females; household size (hsize), defined as the total number of members in the family; a relation to head dummy (relhead) assigned the value '1' for workers who are heads of their households and '0' otherwise; a marital status dummy (marstat) that takes the value '1' if the worker is married and '0' otherwise; social group dummies (sg1, sg2, and sg3: sg1 takes the value '1' for SC workers and '0' otherwise, sg2 takes the value '1' for ST workers and '0' otherwise, sg3 takes the value '1' for OBC workers and '0' otherwise), with the reference category being general caste workers; religious group dummies (rel1 and rel2: rel1 takes the value '1' for Muslim workers and '0' otherwise, and rel2 takes the value '1' for 'Others' (non-Muslim and non-Hindu) workers and '0' otherwise), with the reference category being Hindu workers; education group dummies (gedu1, gedu2, gedu3, and gedu4: gedu1 takes the value '1' for workers with education up to primary level and '0' otherwise, gedu2 takes the value '1' for workers with education above primary and up to secondary and '0' otherwise, gedu3 takes the value '1' for workers with education above secondary and up to graduation and '0' otherwise, and gedu4 takes the value '1' for workers with post-graduate and higher education and '0' otherwise), with illiterates serving as the reference category; a vocational training dummy (vtraining) that takes the value '1' if the worker has received any vocational training and '0' otherwise; a technical education dummy (techedu) assigned the value '1' if the worker has received any technical education and '0' otherwise; and a region dummy (region) assigned the value '1' if the worker belongs to rural areas and '0' otherwise. It is also important to note that we have used state dummies (the number of which equals the number of states in our sample minus one) to control for state-specific differences. Furthermore, we considered White's heteroskedasticity-corrected standard errors to address potential heteroskedasticity issues.

Table 75 presents the estimation results from our multinomial regression models. The main observations for rural, urban, and combined areas are given separately below.

Table 75. Determinants of Employment Mode of Workers (UPSS) in India: Results of Multinomial Logit Regressions

	Rural			Urban			Rural + Urban		
Base outcome: Casual Labour									
Status: Self-employed									
Explanatory variable	**Estimated coeff.**	***z*-value**	***p*-value**	**Estimated coeff.**	***z*-value**	***p*-value**	**Estimated coeff.**	***z*-value**	***p*-value**
_cons	−0.24	−3.27	0.00	−0.31	−2.78	0.01	−0.19	−3.04	0.00
age	0.03	30.56	0.00	0.03	21.45	0.00	0.03	38.10	0.00
sex	−0.30	−11.93	0.00	−0.66	−15.27	0.00	−0.39	−18.18	0.00
hsize	0.08	17.13	0.00	0.04	5.09	0.00	0.07	17.09	0.00
relhead	−0.10	−3.78	0.00	−0.02	−0.39	0.70	−0.08	−3.67	0.00
marstat	0.21	9.12	0.00	0.17	4.51	0.00	0.20	9.95	0.00
sg1	−1.39	−49.18	0.00	−1.00	−22.60	0.00	−1.31	−55.86	0.00
sg2	−0.64	−19.07	0.00	−0.99	−13.50	0.00	−0.61	−20.74	0.00
sg3	−0.44	−16.76	0.00	−0.34	−9.12	0.00	−0.42	−19.97	0.00
rel1	−0.35	−10.56	0.00	0.05	1.22	0.22	−0.22	−8.51	0.00
rel2	0.07	1.66	0.10	−0.09	−1.55	0.12	0.00	0.12	0.91
gedu1	0.33	13.02	0.00	0.54	12.08	0.00	0.36	16.55	0.00
gedu2	0.72	28.97	0.00	1.16	27.59	0.00	0.81	38.55	0.00
gedu3	1.27	34.24	0.00	2.21	39.91	0.00	1.54	51.11	0.00
gedu4	2.17	10.96	0.00	4.22	13.81	0.00	3.04	18.55	0.00
vtraining	0.49	18.98	0.00	0.37	9.94	0.00	0.45	21.34	0.00
techedu	0.29	2.52	0.01	0.47	3.85	0.00	0.50	6.04	0.00
region	–	–	–	–	–	–	−0.12	−7.17	0.00
35 state dummies	Estimated coefficients not reported								

(Continued)

Table 75 *(Continued)*

	Rural			Urban			Rural + Urban		
Status: Regular-employed									
_cons	−2.01	−19.95	0.00	1.01	8.91	0.00	0.36	5.02	0.00
age	0.02	13.70	0.00	0.01	7.09	0.00	0.01	12.94	0.00
sex	−0.40	−11.45	0.00	−0.93	−21.92	0.00	−0.59	−23.88	0.00
hsize	0.05	7.60	0.00	−0.05	−6.58	0.00	0.00	0.48	0.63
relhead	0.04	1.06	0.29	0.17	4.42	0.00	0.12	4.98	0.00
marstat	−0.05	−1.58	0.11	−0.09	−2.52	0.01	−0.09	−3.76	0.00
sg1	−0.85	−21.83	0.00	−0.61	−13.84	0.00	−0.80	−29.50	0.00
sg2	−0.53	−11.51	0.00	−0.49	−6.97	0.00	−0.49	−13.84	0.00
sg3	−0.32	−8.91	0.00	−0.43	−11.48	0.00	−0.42	−17.34	0.00
rel1	−0.18	−3.77	0.00	−0.26	−6.21	0.00	−0.29	−9.54	0.00
rel2	0.11	2.17	0.03	−0.11	−1.97	0.05	0.07	2.07	0.04
gedu1	0.89	17.79	0.00	0.61	12.73	0.00	0.69	21.91	0.00
gedu2	1.99	42.59	0.00	1.43	32.51	0.00	1.58	53.86	0.00
gedu3	3.56	65.94	0.00	3.03	53.76	0.00	3.06	85.41	0.00
gedu4	5.64	28.64	0.00	5.73	18.80	0.00	5.36	32.86	0.00
vtraining	0.22	6.08	0.00	0.06	1.59	0.11	0.16	6.17	0.00
techedu	1.00	9.07	0.00	0.97	8.22	0.00	1.02	12.80	0.00
region	–	–	–	–	–	–	−1.35	−70.09	0.00
35 state dummies				Estimated coefficients not reported					
	Pseudo R^2 = 0.15			Pseudo R^2 = 0.12			Pseudo R^2 = 0.17		
	LR (Chi–square) (102) = 20058.47*			LR (Chi–square) (102) = 11608.48*			LR (Chi–square) (102) = 40846.69*		
	No of observations = 88,190			No of observations = 61828			No of observations = 150,018		

Source: Author's computation using PLFS 2017–18 data

*Notes: * implies significance at 1 per cent level; z-values are calculated using White's robust standard errors.*

5.7.1 Factors Influencing Employment Mode Selection in Rural Areas

The likelihood of choosing self-employment over casual employment in rural areas increases with workers' age, particularly among married workers who have obtained vocational training or technical education. Conversely, the likelihood of selecting self-employment over casual employment is lower for males than for females, particularly among workers who are heads of their families. Concerning the impact of the workers' social status on the likelihood of engaging in self-employment instead of casual employment, our results indicate that, compared to the 'Others' category (i.e. general caste workers), those belonging to the SC, ST, and OBC categories have a lower likelihood of being engaged in self-employment, suggesting a higher propensity for casual employment. The estimated coefficients of the two religion dummies indicate that Muslim workers are less likely to be involved in self-employment compared to Hindu workers. However, when compared to Hindu workers, other non-Muslim workers exhibit a greater likelihood of choosing self-employment over casual employment. The coefficients of four education dummies suggest that, compared to illiterate workers, those with higher educational qualifications are more likely to pursue self-employment than casual employment. All these findings are robust, as all estimated coefficients are statistically significant and the overall model is statistically significant, as indicated by the significance of the LR statistic.

When analysing the probability of being engaged in regular employment rather than in casual employment in rural areas, it is observed that this probability increases with the age of the workers, larger family sizes, being drawn from the group of 'Others' (general castes), having higher educational qualifications, and possessing vocational and/or technical education. Conversely, the probability of opting for regular employment as opposed to casual employment is lower for males and workers belonging to the Muslim religious group. The estimated coefficients of two explanatory variables, 'relhead' and 'marstat', are statistically insignificant when considering the probability of choosing regular over casual employment.

Overall, it can be stated that the probability of choosing higher-quality employment (regular employment/self-employment) is greater in rural India among senior workers (in terms of age), females, individuals from larger households, workers from higher-caste/social groups, Hindu workers (compared to Muslim workers), those with higher educational attainment, and those possessing technical education and/or vocational training. Furthermore, when comparing self-employment with casual employment, it is noted that unmarried workers and those who are not heads of their families are more likely to be engaged in casual employment than in self-employment.

5.7.2 Factors Influencing Employment Mode Selection in Urban Areas

The factors influencing self-employment, regular employment, and casual employment in urban areas are also detailed in Table 75. The results regarding the choice of self-employment compared to casual employment among workers in urban areas indicate that senior workers, female workers, married workers, those with larger families, workers from general caste backgrounds, those with better education, and those with vocational training and/or technical education are more likely to opt for self-employment over casual employment. All these factors are statistically significant determinants of workers' preferences for self-employment instead of casual employment in urban areas. However, the religious status of the workers has become statistically insignificant as a determinant of the choice between self-employment and casual employment.

When examining the results regarding the choice between regular and casual employment in urban areas, it is observed that senior workers, females, heads of families, better-educated workers, those from general caste groups, workers from Hindu religious backgrounds, and individuals with technical education are more inclined to engage in regular employment rather than casual employment. However, married workers and those from larger households were more likely to opt for casual rather than regular employment. Furthermore, vocational training does not seem to be a statistically significant factor influencing urban workers' choice between regular and casual employment.

5.7.3 Factors Influencing Employment Mode Selection in Combined (Rural Plus Urban) Areas

Focusing on the results for both rural and urban areas combined, Table 75 reveals that older workers, female workers, married workers, those from larger households, non-heads of families, workers from the general caste group, Hindu workers, better-educated workers, and workers with vocational training and/or technical education are more inclined to choose self-employment over casual employment.

Regarding the workers' preference for regular employment instead of casual employment in the combined areas, it appears that the likelihood of choosing the former is higher for older (age-wise) workers, females, unmarried workers, family heads, workers from general castes, Hindu workers, better-educated workers, those with vocational or technical training, and residents of urban areas. However, the estimated coefficient for the household size variable is statistically insignificant.

The overall conclusion that emerges from the above discussion is that senior workers, female workers, those from larger families, heads of households, unmarried workers, individuals from higher (general) caste groups, Hindu workers, better-educated workers, and those with vocational training or technical education are more likely to select superior quality employment, such as regular employment or self-employment, rather than casual employment. Additionally, we found that workers are more inclined to choose regular employment or self-employment if they reside in urban areas.

5.8 Summary of Findings

We observed a clear trend of increasing casualisation of the workforce in India until 2000. This trend reversed after 2000, with a growing share of regular workers in the total workforce. Regarding the share of self-employed workers, the general trend is a decline over time. The overall picture remains largely unchanged in both rural and urban areas. However, while the predominant mode of employment among urban workers (both male and female) has been regular employment, followed by self-employment and casual employment, self-employment has been the most significant in rural areas, followed by casual employment and regular employment.

During 1983–2018, females in rural areas reported a higher incidence of casual workers (except in 2012) and a lower incidence of regular workers than males, indicating poorer employment quality for rural females compared to rural males. Although urban females have also lagged behind their male counterparts in employment quality, specifically in regular employment, they have made some progress over time, as evidenced by a sharp decline in the percentage of casual workers and an increase in the percentage of regular workers, surpassing their male counterparts in 2018.

Rural India experienced a notable decline in the percentages of casual and self-employed workers, accompanied by an increase in the percentage of regular workers during the post-globalisation period (1994–2018) compared to the pre-globalisation period (1983–1994). Although this trend is evident across all categories (rural males, rural females, urban males, and urban females) to varying degrees, the most significant declines in the absolute numbers and growth rates of casual and self-employed workers occurred among females, particularly in rural areas.

When examining employment modes across various social groups, it became evident that, in rural areas, workers from disadvantaged social groups (particularly SCs and STs) experience more casual employment. In contrast, workers from higher social groups (OBCs and 'Others') exhibit higher rates of self-employment and regular employment. This trend largely persists in urban areas. Consequently, workers at the lower end of the social spectrum face greater challenges in the quality of their employment. While this is true for both male and female workers, the poorer quality of employment for female workers is particularly apparent among lower-caste groups, especially the SCs.

Regarding modes of employment among religious groups, when considering both rural and urban areas, Muslims in India appear to lag behind Hindus in terms of regular employment, exhibiting a higher percentage of workers engaged in casual employment. However, it is worth noting that Muslim females have a greater incidence of self-employment and lower rates of both casual and regular employment compared to their Hindu counterparts. This pattern essentially holds for both rural and urban settings. Another significant observation is that, except for Muslim males in urban areas and 'Others' (non-Hindu and non-Muslim) category males in urban areas, the percentage of casual workers has decreased post–2000 in all other categories, including Muslim females.

We examined workers' employment modes in seventeen major states from 1983 to 2018. Our main finding is that the states reporting relatively high percentages of self-employed workers in rural areas during this period are Himachal Pradesh, Rajasthan, Jammu & Kashmir, Uttar Pradesh, and Madhya Pradesh; those with relatively low percentages are Tamil Nadu, Kerala, Andhra Pradesh, Maharashtra, and West Bengal, while the remaining states fall in between. However, over two-thirds of the states experienced a decline in the percentage of self-employed workers in rural areas during this time. We also observed that the degree of casualisation of the workforce in rural areas was relatively high in Tamil Nadu, Andhra Pradesh, Maharashtra, Bihar, and Kerala; it was relatively low in Himachal Pradesh, Jammu & Kashmir, Rajasthan, Assam, and Uttar Pradesh, with the other states falling into the middle category. Furthermore, the top five states by percentage of regular employees are Kerala, Assam, Punjab, Haryana, and Tamil Nadu. In contrast, the states with a relatively low percentage of regular workers are Madhya Pradesh, Bihar, Uttar Pradesh, Rajasthan, and Odisha.

In urban areas, states reporting a relatively high percentage of self-employed workers include Uttar Pradesh, Rajasthan, Bihar, Jammu & Kashmir, and Assam. In contrast, this percentage is comparatively low in Tamil Nadu, Maharashtra, Himachal Pradesh, Karnataka, and Andhra Pradesh. Regarding the percentage of regular employees, the leading five states are Himachal Pradesh, Maharashtra, Haryana, Punjab, and Gujarat. In contrast, the bottom five are Kerala, Bihar, Uttar Pradesh, Rajasthan, and Madhya Pradesh. Furthermore, the casualisation of the workforce in urban areas has been notably high in Kerala, Tamil Nadu, Karnataka, Andhra Pradesh, and Bihar.

When we examined the modes of employment for workers combining rural and urban areas, it became clear that developed states, including industrially advanced ones, such as Maharashtra, Punjab, Tamil Nadu, and Haryana, have a high percentage of their workforce engaged in superior (regular) employment. In contrast, this percentage is considerably lower in less developed states, such as Bihar, Odisha, Uttar Pradesh, Madhya Pradesh, and Rajasthan. However, regarding the prevalence of casual workers, a mix of developed and less developed states exists; Andhra Pradesh, Tamil Nadu, Bihar, Kerala, and Odisha exhibit a relatively high percentage of casual workers. Furthermore, the incidence of self-employment tends to be higher in hilly and less developed states such as Himachal Pradesh, Rajasthan, Jammu & Kashmir, Uttar Pradesh, and Assam. At the same time, it is lower in relatively advanced states such as Tamil Nadu, Kerala, Andhra Pradesh, Maharashtra, and West Bengal. It is essential to note that, despite some changes in the ranks of states over time concerning their percentages of workers in three modes of employment, these changes have not been statistically significant in rural, urban, and combined areas. This is evident from the statistical significance of all computed Kendall's W statistics.

When we examined employment growth rates under various modes, it became evident that, in rural areas, the growth rates of casual workers and self-employed workers continued to decline across a broad range of states during different sub-periods of the post-globalisation era. In the latest sub-period from 2012 to 2018, the growth rates of rural casual workers were negative in all but one state (Assam), while those of self-employed workers were negative in thirteen of seventeen states. Conversely, the growth rates of regular employees improved in most states, particularly after 2000. The most notable increase in regular employees in rural areas from 2012 to 2018 was observed in Bihar, Assam, and Madhya Pradesh, with all three states recording annual growth rates of over 10 % during this period.

The tendency for growth rates among casual and self-employed workers to decline, while those of regular employees increase, was also observed in urban areas across most states, particularly from 2012 to 2018, compared to earlier periods. Once again, some less developed states, such as Assam, Madhya Pradesh, and Uttar Pradesh, recorded annual growth of more than 5.0 % in regular employment in urban areas during this timeframe. In contrast, more developed states like Punjab, Haryana, Himachal Pradesh, and Karnataka, as well as the less developed state of Bihar, reported annual growth of over 4.0 % in casual workers in urban areas from 2012 to 2018.

When considering rural and urban areas together, the overarching trend across most states is a decline in growth rates for casual and self-employed workers, alongside increasing growth rates for regular workers. The less developed states of Bihar, Assam, Madhya Pradesh, Rajasthan, and Uttar Pradesh, as well as a more advanced state like Haryana, recorded growth rates of over 5.0 % per annum for regular employees during the last sub-period, 2012–2018. Conversely, all but two states (Assam and Haryana) experienced negative growth in casual workers during this period. Additionally, negative growth in self-employed workers was observed in eleven states during the same sub-period. Overall, regular employment is on the rise, and this trend has been at the expense of self-employment and casual work in recent years.

To assess the quality of employment, our study examined the incidence of the 'working poor' at various points in time. We found that as many as 42 % of workers in rural India and 22 % in urban India were categorised as 'poor' in 2018. Additionally, the incidence of the 'working poor' was highest among casual workers, followed by self-employed and regular workers. This trend holds in both rural and urban areas. When analysing the incidence of the 'working poor' among different social groups, it became evident that the most disadvantaged group, namely the STs, had the highest percentage of 'working poor' in rural and urban regions, followed by SCs, OBCs, and 'Others'. Thus, access to better-quality employment has been more pronounced for higher-caste workers than for those from weaker castes. In terms of the incidence of the 'working poor' among different religious groups, we found this to be higher for Muslim workers compared to Hindu workers across all years and regions (except in 2012 and 2018 in rural locations).

We aimed to identify factors influencing workers' employment choices in 2018. We estimated multinomial logit regression models separately for rural, urban, and combined areas. A significant finding was that older workers, female workers, family heads, individuals from larger families, unmarried workers, those with better education, workers from higher-caste groups, Hindu workers, and urban workers are more likely to secure better-quality employment, such as regular employment and self-employment, than casual employment.

Employment Diversification in India

6.1 Introduction

Employment diversification has been a significant topic of discussion for the past fifty years. Scholars such as Lewis (1954), Kuznets (1965, 1966), and Chenery and Syrquin (1975), among others, are credited with initiating this conversation. As Kuznets suggests, employment diversification involves workers moving from the agricultural to the manufacturing and service sectors (i.e. the non-agricultural sector), which is regarded as a key component of modern economic growth. He views manufacturing as the 'engine' of economic growth. Research conducted by him and others has revealed that the transition of labour from agriculture to industry and then to services followed the same path as that of high-income nations during their structural transformation (Sen, 2019). However, this structural transformation trajectory has not been observed in many developing countries, including India, despite the economy's increasing growth, thereby challenging Kaldor's 'growth laws' (Ghose, 2021). The pattern observed in India indicates that, although a majority of workers were engaged in agriculture during the early stages of development, the services sector has taken precedence in absorbing workers as the country progresses towards higher growth trajectories (increased GDP and per capita GDP), bypassing the manufacturing sector to accommodate workers transitioning out of agriculture – a phenomenon described as 'services-led' growth.

This chapter examines the pattern of employment diversification in India and its major states from 1983 to 2018.[1] This chapter is divided into seven sections. Section 6.2 examines the pattern of employment diversification at the all-India level, focusing on the one-digit and two-digit levels of the Industrial Classification of Workers. Additionally, this section discusses the sectoral distribution of workers in India by social and religious groups. Section 6.3 examines workers' growth rates across sectors to identify emerging sectors of the economy with potential to generate employment. Section 6.4 analyses the sectoral distribution of workers in seventeen major Indian states to understand their employment diversification patterns and discusses the sectoral growth of workers within these states. Section 6.5 evaluates the computed employment elasticities to comprehend the relationship between income growth and employment growth in the country. Section 6.6 aims to identify the factors influencing workers' choices of employment sector (non-farm/farm) in India. Finally, Section 6.7 summarises the main findings of this chapter.

6.2 Pattern of Employment Diversification in India

To understand the pattern of employment diversification that has been occurring at the all-India level during the period from 1983 to 2018, we first divided the workers (UPSS) into eight broad sectors of the economy: (i) agriculture, forestry, and fishing (hereafter referred to as the 'agriculture and allied' sector), (ii) mining and quarrying, (iii) manufacturing, (iv) electricity, gas, and water supply, (v) construction, (vi) wholesale and retail trade, (vii) transport, storage, and communication, and (viii) other services. All the sectors, except 'agriculture and allied', have been grouped to represent the non-agricultural or non-farm sector of the economy. The information on the sectoral distribution of workers at the all-India level is presented in Table 76, separately for rural and urban areas, as well as for males and females. The main observations regarding the changing sectoral composition of workers in the country are the following:

- The share of the 'agriculture and allied' sector has steadily declined in India throughout our study period, reducing from almost 69 % in 1983 to 44 % in

[1] Chapter 7 provides insight into changes in employment diversification patterns from 2018 to 2024.

2018 (considering rural and urban areas, as well as males and females together). This indicates a clear trend toward the growing importance of the non-agricultural sector, which accounted for 56 % of the country's total workers in 2018. It is also evident that employment diversification (from the 'agriculture and allied' sector to the non-agricultural sector) has accelerated from 2000 to 2018 compared to 1983 to 2000.

- The declining significance of the 'agriculture and allied' sector is evident in rural and urban areas. When considering both males and females, the share of this sector in rural areas decreased from 81 % in 1983 to 59 % in 2018. In urban areas, this share decreased from 15 % in 1983 to 6 % in 2018.
- A significant gap has persisted between males and females regarding the percentage of workers engaged in the non-agricultural sector. Table 76 shows that in 1983, 38 % of male workers were employed in the non-agricultural sector. In contrast, only 19 % of females participated in the same sector. By 2018, these percentages had increased to 60 % and 43 %, respectively, for males and females.
- The disparity between males and females concerning the percentage of non-agricultural workers has been more pronounced in rural areas than in urban areas, especially since 2000. According to Table 76, 45 % of rural male workers in 2018 were employed in the non-agricultural sector, compared with 27 % of rural female workers. When considering males and females together, the percentage of workers in the non-agricultural sector in rural areas is approximately 41 %, up from 19 % in 1983. Furthermore, while the rural workers in non-agricultural employment increased by only five percentage points between 1983 and 2000, it rose by nearly 17 percentage points between 2000 and 2018. Additionally, a notable increase in the percentage of rural non-agricultural workers is visible for both males and females in the latter period. However, a considerable gap between them persisted from 1983 to 2018. In contrast, the scenario in urban areas is different, as a substantial percentage of male and female workers are engaged in non-agricultural employment, and the difference between them has notably narrowed over time. In 2018, 95 % of urban male workers were employed in the non-agricultural sector, while 91 % of urban females were also in this sector.

Table 76: Sectoral Distribution of Workers (UPSS Basis) in India (Percentage)

Region	Sex of Workers	Year	Agrl. & allied	Mining & quarrying	Manufacturing	Electricity, gas & water	Construction	Wholesale & retail trade	Transport, storage and communication	Other services	Non-agri.
Rural	Male	1983	77.73	0.60	7.02	0.20	2.21	4.41	1.71	6.12	22.27
		1994	74.10	0.70	7.00	0.30	3.20	5.50	2.20	7.00	25.90
		2000	71.33	0.60	7.29	0.20	4.50	6.79	3.20	6.09	28.67
		2012	59.35	0.54	8.13	0.31	13.01	8.03	4.23	6.41	40.65
		2018	54.95	0.46	7.66	0.47	14.50	9.16	5.17	7.63	45.05
	Female	1983	87.76	0.30	6.42	0.00	0.70	1.91	0.10	2.81	12.24
		1994	86.11	0.40	6.99	0.00	0.90	2.10	0.10	3.40	13.89
		2000	85.23	0.30	7.58	0.00	1.10	2.00	0.10	3.69	14.77
		2012	74.94	0.29	9.79	0.07	6.59	2.95	0.16	5.21	25.06
		2018	73.19	0.17	8.14	0.03	5.34	4.01	0.27	8.85	26.81
	Male + Female	1983	81.40	0.49	6.80	0.13	1.66	3.50	1.12	4.91	18.60
		1994	78.40	0.59	7.00	0.19	2.38	4.28	1.45	5.71	21.60
		2000	76.16	0.50	7.39	0.13	3.32	5.13	2.12	5.26	23.84
		2012	64.06	0.46	8.63	0.24	11.07	6.50	3.00	6.05	35.94
		2018	59.40	0.39	7.78	0.36	12.27	7.90	3.98	7.92	40.60
Urban	Male	1983	10.32	1.20	26.85	1.10	5.11	20.84	9.92	24.65	89.68
		1994	9.01	1.30	23.52	1.20	6.91	21.92	9.71	26.43	90.99
		2000	6.59	0.90	22.36	0.80	8.68	29.34	10.38	20.96	93.41
		2012	5.64	0.86	22.37	1.37	10.65	25.99	11.72	21.39	94.36
		2018	5.38	0.56	22.39	1.30	11.73	24.45	12.70	21.48	94.62
	Female	1983	31.25	0.60	26.92	0.20	3.13	9.58	1.51	26.81	68.75
		1994	24.68	0.60	24.08	0.30	4.10	9.99	1.30	34.97	75.32
		2000	17.70	0.40	24.00	0.20	4.80	16.90	1.80	34.20	82.30
		2012	10.91	0.29	28.70	1.03	3.95	12.81	2.74	39.57	89.09
		2018	9.07	0.15	25.22	0.63	4.12	13.03	3.33	44.44	90.93

(Continued)

Table 76 *(Continued)*

Region	Sex of Workers	Year	Agrl. & allied	Mining & quarry-ing	Manufac-turing	Electricity, gas & water	Con-struc-tion	Wholesale & retail trade	Transport, storage and communication	Other ser-vices	Non-agri.
Urban	Male + Female	1983	14.64	1.08	26.87	0.92	4.70	18.51	8.18	25.10	85.36
		1994	12.31	1.15	23.64	1.01	6.32	19.41	7.94	28.22	87.69
		2000	8.75	0.80	22.68	0.68	7.93	26.92	8.71	23.53	91.25
		2012	6.69	0.75	23.64	1.30	9.31	23.36	9.93	25.03	93.31
		2018	6.14	0.48	22.97	1.16	10.17	22.11	10.78	26.19	93.86
Rural + Urban	Male	1983	62.31	0.74	11.56	0.41	2.87	8.17	3.58	10.36	37.69
		1994	57.44	0.85	11.23	0.53	4.15	9.70	4.12	11.97	42.56
		2000	53.52	0.68	11.44	0.36	5.65	13.00	5.17	10.18	46.48
		2012	42.28	0.64	12.66	0.65	12.26	13.74	6.61	11.17	57.72
		2018	40.24	0.49	12.03	0.72	13.68	13.69	7.41	11.73	59.76
	Female	1983	81.08	0.34	8.84	0.02	0.99	2.81	0.27	5.65	18.92
		1994	77.44	0.43	9.40	0.04	1.35	3.21	0.27	7.85	22.56
		2000	75.31	0.31	10.00	0.03	1.64	4.19	0.35	8.17	24.69
		2012	61.36	0.29	13.80	0.27	6.03	5.04	0.71	12.50	38.64
		2018	57.00	0.17	12.46	0.18	5.03	6.28	1.05	17.83	43.00
	Male + Female	1983	68.59	0.60	10.65	0.28	2.24	6.38	2.47	8.78	31.41
		1994	63.96	0.72	10.63	0.37	3.24	7.59	2.87	10.63	36.04
		2000	60.30	0.57	10.99	0.26	4.40	10.25	3.67	9.56	39.70
		2012	47.48	0.55	12.97	0.55	10.56	11.37	5.00	11.53	52.52
		2018	44.15	0.41	12.13	0.59	11.67	11.96	5.92	13.16	55.85

Source: Same as in Table 33

- Among the non-agricultural sectors, those showing the most impressive improvement in worker percentage are 'construction' and 'trade' (wholesale and retail). Considering both rural and urban areas, as well as males and females combined, the construction sector has seen a significant increase in the proportion of workers at the all-India level, rising from 2.24 % in 1983 to 11.67 % in 2018. The proportion of workers in the 'trade' sector has also increased from 6.38 % in 1983 to 11.96 % in 2018. It is also evident that the percentages of workers in 'other services' and 'transport, storage & communication' have significantly improved. Conversely, the 'manufacturing' sector has seen little change in its share of workers from 1983 to 2018, rising from 10.65 % to 12.13 %. Furthermore, the 'manufacturing' sector has recently experienced a slight decline in its share of workers, decreasing from 12.97 % in 2012 to 12.13 % in 2018.
- Table 76 also indicates that, among the non-agricultural sectors, the percentages of workers employed in 'construction' and 'trade' have been greater for males than for females. Conversely, a more significant percentage of female workers are involved in 'other services' than their male counterparts in the later part of the post-globalisation period, more specifically, since 2012.
- When examining rural and urban areas separately, it becomes clear that although the proportion of workers in 'manufacturing' within urban areas has decreased over time (dropping from 26.87 % in 1983 to 22.97 % in 2018), there has been a slight increase in rural areas (rising from 6.80 % in 1983 to 7.78 % in 2018). This trend is consistent for both males and females. Conversely, although rural and urban India saw an increase in the percentage of workers in 'construction' over time, this rise was more pronounced in rural areas than in urban ones. Regarding 'trade', we note that in 2018, more than one-fifth of urban workers were engaged in this sector, compared to around 8 % in rural areas. Nevertheless, both rural and urban regions experienced an increase in the percentage of workers in 'trade' over time.

6.2.1 Distribution of Workers by Sector at the Two-Digit Level of Industrial Classification

Using a two-digit classification of industrial economic activities, we have compiled data on the sectoral distribution of workers (UPSS) at the all-India level. This analysis encompasses rural and urban areas and is presented separately for males, females, and total persons for 2012 and 2018. Both years use the 2008 National Industrial Classification (NIC), thereby ensuring inter-temporal comparability of data. Table 77 displays the percentage of workers classified at the two-digit industrial level. The key points to note here are the following:

- Considering both males and females, the 'crop and animal production, hunting and related activities' sub-sector held the largest share of workers in the country in 2012 and 2018. However, this share exhibits a declining trend over time, decreasing from approximately 48 % in 2012 to 44 % in 2018. In 2018, other notable sub-sectors in terms of employment share include 'construction of buildings' (8.85 %), 'retail trade, except motor vehicles and motorcycles' (8.02 %), 'land transport and transport via pipeline' (4.49 %), 'education' (3.78 %), 'manufacture of wearing apparel' (2.10 %), 'manufacture of textiles' (1.76 %), 'food and beverage service activities' (1.71 %), 'public administration and defence: compulsory social security' (1.61 %), 'specialised construction activities' (1.48 %), 'civil engineering' (1.34 %), 'wholesale trade, except motor vehicles and motorcycles' (1.30 %), 'other personal service activities' (1.19 %), 'manufacturer of food products' (1.17 %), and 'activities of households as employers of domestic personnel' (1.08 %). Besides these fifteen sub-sectors, there are seventy-two other sub-sectors where the percentage of workers in the total workforce across India was less than 1 %.
- It has been noted that out of eighty-seven sub-sectors (at a two-digit level), as many as fifty-six sub-sectors observed an improvement in their respective shares of workers as a percentage of the total workforce (considering both males and females) during the period from 2012 to 2018, with the most significant increase occurring in 'construction of buildings' (rising by 1.17 percentage points). The other sub-sectors that experienced an increase of more than 0.5 percentage points in their percentage share of workers during this period include 'land transport and transport via pipeline', 'education', and 'retail trade, except motor vehicles and motorcycles'. Conversely, the percentage of workers to total workers declined in thirty-one sub-sectors during the same period, with the largest decline (–4.75 percentage points) occurring in 'crop and animal production, hunting and related activities'.
- When analysed separately for males, it is evident that five sub-sectors dominate in terms of employment share in both 2012 and 2018. These sub-sectors are 'crop production, hunting, and related activities', 'construction of buildings', 'retail trade, except motor vehicles and motorcycles', 'land transport and transport via pipeline', and 'education'. Their shares of the total male workforce across India in 2018 were 39.70 %, 10.74 %, 9.13 %, 5.80 %, and 2.62 %, respectively. Notably, these five sub-sectors accounted for 69 % and 68 % of the total male workforce in 2012 and 2018, respectively. Conversely, in 2018, over 78 % of all female workers at the national level were employed in 'crop production, hunting and related activities' (56.83 %), 'education' (7.60 %), 'retail trade, except motor vehicles and motorcycles' (4.35 %), 'manufacture of wearing apparel' (3.58 %), 'activities of households as employers of domestic personnel' (3 %), and 'manufacture of tobacco products' (2.76 %).

Table 77: Sectoral Distribution of Workers (UPSS) at Two-Digit Level of Industrial Classification in India (Rural & Urban Combined)

Sector	Code	Sub-sector	2012			2018		
			Male	Female	Male + Female	Male	Female	Male + Female
Agriculture, forestry & fishing	01	Crop and animal production, hunting and related service activities	43.05	62.53	48.43	39.70	56.83	43.68
	02	Forestry and logging	0.16	0.10	0.14	0.16	0.09	0.15
	03	Fishing and aquaculture	0.40	0.14	0.33	0.38	0.06	0.31
Mining and quarrying	05	Mining of coal and lignite	0.16	0.03	0.12	0.12	0.02	0.10
	06	Extraction of crude petroleum and natural gas	0.05	0.00	0.04	0.03	0.00	0.02
	07	Mining of metal ores	0.03	0.01	0.03	0.05	0.01	0.04
	08	Other mining and quarrying	0.39	0.25	0.35	0.28	0.13	0.25
	09	Mining support service activities	0.004	–	0.003	0.013	–	0.010
Manufacturing	10	Manufacture of food products	1.32	1.15	1.27	1.23	0.95	1.17
	11	Manufacture of beverages	0.10	0.05	0.09	0.11	0.07	0.10
	12	Manufacture of tobacco products	0.23	3.13	1.03	0.10	2.76	0.72
	13	Manufacture of textiles	1.62	2.82	1.95	1.55	2.47	1.76
	14	Manufacture of wearing apparel	1.65	3.01	2.03	1.65	3.58	2.10
	15	Manufacture of leather and related products	0.33	0.14	0.28	0.30	0.19	0.27

(Continued)

Table 77 *(Continued)*

Sector	Code	Sub-sector	2012			2018		
			Male	Female	Male + Female	Male	Female	Male + Female
Manufacturing	16	Manufacture of wood and products of wood and cork, except furniture; manufacture of articles of straw and plaiting materials	0.84	0.74	0.81	0.73	0.35	0.64
	17	Manufacture of paper and paper products	0.12	0.11	0.11	0.18	0.11	0.16
	18	Printing and reproduction of recorded media	0.16	0.05	0.13	0.17	0.06	0.15
	19	Manufacture of coke and refined petroleum products	0.04	0.00	0.03	0.05	0.01	0.04
	20	Manufacture of chemicals and chemical products	0.26	0.22	0.25	0.30	0.16	0.27
	21	Manufacture of pharmaceuticals, medicinal chemical and botanical products	0.20	0.07	0.17	0.20	0.07	0.17
	22	Manufacture of rubber and plastics products	0.27	0.14	0.24	0.25	0.14	0.23
	23	Manufacture of other non-metallic mineral products	1.19	0.70	1.05	0.97	0.57	0.87
	24	Manufacture of basic metals	0.41	0.06	0.32	0.49	0.06	0.39

(Continued)

Table 77 *(Continued)*

Sector	Code	Sub-sector	2012			2018		
			Male	Female	Male + Female	Male	Female	Male + Female
Manufacturing	25	Manufacture of fabricated metal products, except machinery and equipment	0.81	0.16	0.63	0.76	0.09	0.61
	26	Manufacture of computer, electronic and optical products	0.11	0.04	0.09	0.13	0.08	0.12
	27	Manufacture of electrical equipment	0.27	0.05	0.21	0.35	0.12	0.30
	28	Manufacture of machinery and equipment n.e.c.	0.28	0.02	0.20	0.35	0.08	0.29
	29	Manufacture of motor vehicles, trailers and semi-trailers	0.27	0.04	0.20	0.31	0.07	0.25
	30	Manufacture of other transport equipment	0.16	0.00	0.11	0.09	0.02	0.07
	31	Manufacture of furniture	0.69	0.01	0.50	0.61	0.01	0.47
	32	Other manufacturing	0.70	0.66	0.69	0.59	0.43	0.55
	33	Repair and installation of machinery and equipment	0.29	0.02	0.21	0.55	0.02	0.43
Electricity, gas, steam & air conditioning supply	35	Electricity, gas, steam and air conditioning supply	0.34	0.08	0.27	0.43	0.06	0.34

(Continued)

Table 77 *(Continued)*

Sector	Code	Sub-sector	2012			2018		
			Male	Female	Male + Female	Male	Female	Male + Female
Water supply, sewerage, waste management & remediation activities	36	Water collection, treatment and supply	0.08	0.00	0.06	0.12	0.01	0.09
	37	Sewerage	0.01	0.03	0.01	0.02	0.01	0.02
	38	Waste collection, treatment and disposal activities; materials recovery	0.18	0.14	0.17	0.14	0.09	0.13
	39	Remediation activities and other waste management services	0.01	0.00	0.00	0.00	0.01	0.01
Construction	41	Construction of buildings	9.69	2.37	7.67	10.74	2.59	8.85
	42	Civil engineering	1.36	3.39	1.92	1.05	2.32	1.34
	43	Specialized construction activities	1.26	0.33	1.01	1.89	0.13	1.48
Wholesale & retail trade; repair of motor vehicles & motorcycles	45	Wholesale and retail trade and repair of motor vehicles and motorcycles	0.91	0.09	0.68	0.98	0.12	0.78
	46	Wholesale trade, except of motor vehicles and motorcycles	1.47	0.22	1.12	1.59	0.36	1.30
	47	Retail trade, except of motor vehicles and motorcycles	9.01	3.59	7.51	9.13	4.35	8.02

(Continued)

Table 77 *(Continued)*

Sector	Code	Sub-sector	2012			2018		
			Male	Female	Male + Female	Male	Female	Male + Female
Transportation & storage	49	Land transport and transport via pipelines	5.05	0.12	3.69	5.80	0.17	4.49
	50	Water transport	0.04	0.00	0.03	0.04	0.02	0.03
	51	Air transport	0.02	0.00	0.02	0.02	0.00	0.02
	52	Warehousing and support activities for transportation	0.26	0.05	0.20	0.31	0.03	0.25
	53	Postal and courier activities	0.16	0.05	0.13	0.16	0.11	0.15
Accommodation & food service activities	55	Accommodation	0.17	0.17	0.17	0.16	0.17	0.17
	56	Food and beverage service activities	1.74	0.76	1.47	1.84	1.28	1.71
Information & communication	58	Publishing activities	0.08	0.06	0.08	0.09	0.06	0.08
	59	Motion picture, video and television programme production, sound recording and music publishing activities	0.03	0.00	0.02	0.04	0.00	0.04
	60	Broadcasting and programming activities	0.01	0.02	0.01	0.03	0.02	0.02
	61	Telecommunications	0.28	0.06	0.22	0.25	0.10	0.22
	62	Computer programming, consultancy and related activities	0.37	0.21	0.33	0.51	0.39	0.48
	63	Information service activities	0.12	0.07	0.11	0.15	0.15	0.15

(Continued)

Table 77 *(Continued)*

Sector	Code	Sub-sector	2012			2018		
			Male	Female	Male + Female	Male	Female	Male + Female
Financial & insurance activities	64	Financial service activities, except insurance and pension funding	0.62	0.33	0.54	0.79	0.65	0.76
	65	Insurance, reinsurance and pension funding, except compulsory social security	0.24	0.11	0.20	0.17	0.08	0.15
	66	Other financial activities	0.19	0.09	0.16	0.16	0.10	0.15
Real estate activities	68	Real estate activities	0.26	0.02	0.20	0.26	0.05	0.21
Professional, scientific & technical activities	69	Legal and accounting activities	0.32	0.11	0.26	0.49	0.24	0.43
	70	Activities of head offices; management consultancy activities	0.02	0.02	0.02	0.06	0.03	0.05
	71	Architecture and engineering activities; technical testing and analysis	0.05	0.02	0.04	0.08	0.04	0.07
	72	Scientific research and development	0.02	0.02	0.02	0.03	0.04	0.03
	73	Advertising and market research	0.04	0.04	0.04	0.04	0.02	0.03
	74	Other professional, scientific and technical activities	0.20	0.03	0.15	0.22	0.08	0.19
	75	Veterinary activities	0.04	0.00	0.03	0.03	0.01	0.03

(Continued)

Table 77 *(Continued)*

Sector	Code	Sub-sector	2012			2018		
			Male	Female	Male + Female	Male	Female	Male + Female
Administrative & support service activities	77	Rental and leasing activities	0.16	0.01	0.12	0.25	0.03	0.20
	78	Employment activities	0.02	0.02	0.02	0.05	0.03	0.04
	79	Travel agency, tour operator and other reservation service activities	0.12	0.02	0.09	0.07	0.03	0.06
	80	Security and investigation activities	0.20	0.00	0.15	0.40	0.04	0.31
	81	Services to buildings and landscape activities	0.06	0.06	0.06	0.10	0.15	0.11
	82	Office administrative, office support and other business support activities	0.24	0.13	0.21	0.51	0.32	0.47
Public admin & defense; compulsory social security	84	Public administration and defense; compulsory social security	2.03	0.73	1.67	1.80	1.01	1.61
Education	85	Education	2.33	4.67	2.98	2.62	7.60	3.78
Human health & social work activities	86	Human health activities	0.69	1.11	0.80	0.71	1.94	0.99
	87	Residential care activities	0.01	0.10	0.04	0.03	0.21	0.07
	88	Social work activities without accommodation	0.03	0.20	0.08	0.06	0.37	0.14
Arts, entertainment & recreation	90	Creative, arts and entertainment activities	0.18	0.07	0.15	0.24	0.05	0.19

(Continued)

Table 77 *(Continued)*

Sector	Code	Sub-sector	2012			2018		
			Male	Female	Male + Female	Male	Female	Male + Female
Arts, entertainment & recreation	91	Libraries, archives, museums and other cultural activities	0.02	0.01	0.02	0.01	0.03	0.02
	92	Gambling and betting activities	0.02	0.00	0.02	0.04	0.01	0.03
	93	Sports activities and amusement and recreation activities	0.04	0.00	0.03	0.05	0.02	0.04
Other service activities	94	Activities of membership organizations	0.31	0.05	0.24	0.28	0.09	0.23
	95	Repair of computers and personal and household goods	0.79	0.07	0.59	0.63	0.02	0.49
	96	Other personal service activities	1.15	1.68	1.30	1.08	1.55	1.19
Activities of households as employers of domestic personnel	97	Activities of households as employers of domestic personnel	0.38	2.00	0.83	0.50	3.00	1.08
Activities of extraterritorial organisations & bodies	99	Activities of extraterritorial organizations and bodies	–	0.002	0.001	0.005	–	0.004
Simpson Diversity Index			**0.791**	**0.600**	**0.749**	**0.815**	**0.663**	**0.788**

Source: Author's computation using unit-level data from NSSO 68th round employment/unemployment survey and PLFS 2017–18

Thus, by examining the changes in the percentage of workers across various sub-sectors from 2012 to 2018, it is observed that, apart from 'crop production, hunting, and related activities', females in the country have increasingly focused on sub-sectors such as 'education', 'retail trade, except motor vehicles and motorcycles', and 'manufacturer of wearing apparel'. In contrast, males have concentrated on 'retail and wholesale trade, excluding motor vehicles and motorcycles', 'construction of buildings', and 'land transport and transport via pipeline'. Another essential point to note is that although 'crop production, hunting, and related activities' remains the most dominant sector for employment for both males and females, the percentage of female workers in this sub-sector is significantly higher than that of male workers. Furthermore, there is a noticeable increase in diversification in India, as indicated by a rise in the Simpson Diversification Index (SDI) value. However, the calculated SDI values indicate that males exhibit greater employment diversification than females.

6.2.2 Sectoral Distribution of Workers by Social Groups

We now examine the distribution of workers across different social groups (ST, SC, OBC, and Others) within both rural and urban areas, while distinguishing between males, females, and persons. Table 78 presents information on this aspect. Focusing on males, it appears that lower social groups constitute a higher percentage of workers in the 'agriculture and allied' sector. In contrast, those from higher social groups account for a higher percentage of male workers in the non-agricultural sector. As indicated in the table, as many as 62 % of total male workers from the ST category were engaged in the 'agriculture and allied' sector in 2018, compared to 39.99 % for the SC category, 39.72 % for the OBC category, and 33.86 % for the 'Others' category. This trend is reversed in the non-agricultural sector as a whole and across various sub-sectors within it. For instance, while the manufacturing sector employed 14.14 % of total male workers for the 'Others' social category, the corresponding percentages for OBC, SC, and ST were 13.02, 10.25, and 5.08, respectively. A similar pattern is observable in other sub-sectors of the non-agricultural sector, except in construction, where the percentage of male workers in 2018 was highest for the SC category (22.69 %), followed by ST (14.38 %), OBC (12.80 %), and 'Others' (8.54 %).

The picture obtained for females is nearly identical: female workers from lower social categories are more engaged in the 'agriculture and allied' sector, while those from higher social categories represent a larger proportion of female workers in the non-agricultural sector. However, it should also be noted that the percentage of female workers in the 'agriculture and allied' sector has consistently been higher than for males across all social categories. Construction employs a higher proportion of female workers from lower social classes within sub-sectors of the non-agricultural sector. Conversely, a greater percentage of female workers from upper social groups are involved in trade and services.

Table 78: Sectoral Distribution of Workers (UPSS) by Social Groups (Rural & Urban Combined) in India (Percentage)

Sex	Sector	Year	ST	SC	OBC	Others	Total
Male	Agrl. & allied	2000	75.31	60.55	56.23	44.87	54.81
		2012	65.68	42.71	45.50	34.64	43.61
		2018	62.10	39.99	39.72	33.86	40.24
	Mining & quarrying	2000	1.19	0.70	0.75	0.43	0.67
		2012	0.71	0.91	0.58	0.51	0.63
		2018	1.32	0.32	0.53	0.27	0.49
	Manufacturing	2000	4.92	9.43	12.03	12.97	11.20
		2012	5.30	10.61	12.60	15.07	12.30
		2018	5.08	10.25	13.02	14.14	12.03
	Electricity, gas, water	2000	0.29	0.32	0.30	0.56	0.40
		2012	0.44	0.55	0.62	0.72	0.62
		2018	0.55	0.76	0.66	0.82	0.71
	Construction	2000	6.20	8.34	5.49	3.98	5.58
		2012	13.55	21.15	11.24	7.88	12.32
		2018	14.38	22.69	12.80	8.54	13.68
	Wholesale & retail trade	2000	3.05	6.67	10.95	15.95	11.15
		2012	4.08	6.88	11.41	16.45	11.38
		2018	5.10	9.49	15.00	17.55	13.69
	Transport, storage and communication	2000	2.72	5.30	4.62	5.84	5.01
		2012	3.15	6.54	6.43	7.34	6.43
		2018	4.05	7.01	7.40	8.83	7.41
	Other services	2000	6.31	8.68	9.63	15.40	11.18
		2012	7.10	10.65	11.61	17.38	12.70
		2018	7.44	9.50	10.87	16.00	11.74

(Continued)

Table 78 *(Continued)*

Sex	Sector	Year	ST	SC	OBC	Others	Total
Female	Agrl. & allied	2000	87.19	79.13	75.79	69.24	76.52
		2012	78.27	63.61	63.90	50.08	62.77
		2018	79.65	57.11	56.86	42.71	56.99
	Mining & quarrying	2000	0.42	0.31	0.35	0.14	0.30
		2012	0.36	0.44	0.32	0.05	0.29
		2018	0.12	0.10	0.30	0.02	0.17
	Manufacturing	2000	4.80	8.20	11.34	10.64	9.50
		2012	4.75	11.33	14.15	19.23	13.39
		2018	2.92	11.69	14.17	16.10	12.46
	Electricity, gas, water	2000	0.00	0.01	0.02	0.08	0.03
		2012	0.03	0.52	0.14	0.35	0.25
		2018	0.10	0.34	0.14	0.18	0.18
	Construction	2000	2.53	2.10	1.39	0.63	1.52
		2012	9.35	8.35	5.98	2.13	6.09
		2018	6.15	7.55	5.07	1.98	5.03
	Wholesale & retail trade	2000	1.33	2.66	3.73	4.56	3.35
		2012	1.96	2.86	4.25	5.39	3.90
		2018	2.36	5.50	7.25	7.72	6.28
	Transport, storage, communication	2000	0.07	0.23	0.21	0.65	0.31
		2012	0.22	0.46	0.55	1.31	0.65
		2018	0.10	0.69	0.96	2.13	1.04
	Other services	2000	3.66	7.37	7.16	14.06	8.47
		2012	5.05	12.44	10.71	21.47	12.66
		2018	8.62	17.03	15.25	29.16	17.84
Male + Female	Agrl. & allied	2000	80.33	66.99	62.59	50.97	61.67
		2012	70.37	48.95	50.58	38.11	48.90
		2018	67.64	44.12	43.67	35.59	44.14
	Mining & quarrying	2000	0.86	0.57	0.62	0.36	0.55
		2012	0.58	0.77	0.51	0.41	0.54
		2018	0.94	0.27	0.47	0.22	0.41
	Manufacturing	2000	4.87	9.00	11.81	12.38	10.66
		2012	5.09	10.83	13.03	16.01	12.60
		2018	4.40	10.59	13.29	14.53	12.13

(Continued)

Table 78 *(Continued)*

Sex	Sector	Year	ST	SC	OBC	Others	Total
Male + Female	Electricity, gas, water	2000	0.17	0.21	0.21	0.44	0.28
		2012	0.28	0.54	0.49	0.64	0.52
		2018	0.40	0.66	0.54	0.69	0.59
	Construction	2000	4.65	6.17	4.16	3.14	4.30
		2012	11.98	17.32	9.79	6.59	10.60
		2018	11.78	19.03	11.02	7.25	11.67
	Wholesale & retail trade	2000	2.32	5.28	8.60	13.09	8.69
		2012	3.29	5.68	9.44	13.97	9.32
		2018	4.23	8.53	13.21	15.62	11.97
	Transport, storage, communication	2000	1.60	3.54	3.18	4.54	3.52
		2012	2.06	4.72	4.81	5.99	4.83
		2018	2.80	5.48	5.92	7.51	5.93
	Other services	2000	5.19	8.23	8.83	15.06	10.32
		2012	6.34	11.19	11.36	18.30	12.69
		2018	7.81	11.32	11.88	18.58	13.16

Source: Same as Table 76

Considering both males and females, a significantly higher percentage of workers from weaker social groups (particularly ST) are engaged in the 'agriculture and allied' sector, even in 2018, compared to their counterparts from higher social groups ('Others'). A clear pattern is emerging regarding the employment of workers in the non-agricultural sector: weaker social groups are more prominently employed in the construction sub-sector, while the manufacturing, trade, and services sectors feature a higher percentage of workers from higher social groups.

6.2.3 Sectoral Distribution of Workers by Religious Groups

Table 79 presents the distribution of workers by religious groups at the all-India level, including both rural and urban areas. Regarding males, it appears that Hindus have a higher percentage of workers in the 'agriculture and allied' and 'other services' compared to Muslims. Conversely, in non-agricultural sectors such as 'manufacturing', 'construction', 'trade', and 'transport, storage, and communication', a higher percentage of male Muslim workers were engaged than their male Hindu counterparts. This pattern generally continued across all religious groups from 2000 to 2018, despite a decline in the percentage of workers in the 'agriculture and allied' sector and a corresponding increase in the percentage of non-agricultural workers.

Table 79 also revealed that, among all the sectors, the percentage of female workers has been highest in the 'agriculture and allied' sector for both Hindus and Muslims. It remained this way at all times, despite a decline in the percentage of female workers in the 'agriculture and allied' sector. However, comparing Hindus and Muslims, the percentage of Hindu female workers in the 'agriculture and allied' sector is higher than that of Muslim female workers, suggesting that involvement in non-agricultural employment is more significant for the latter than for the former. Additionally, Muslim women are predominantly concentrated in the manufacturing sector within the non-agricultural sub-sectors. In 2018, only about 11 % of female Hindu workers were employed in the manufacturing sector, whereas as high as 35 % of Muslim female workers were engaged in the same. Apart from manufacturing, 'other services' employed a considerable percentage (17 % to 18 %) of female workers from both groups in 2018.

Table 79: Sectoral Distribution of Workers (UPSS) by Religious Groups in India (Rural & Urban Combined) (Percentage)

Sex	Sector	Year	Hindu	Islam	Christian	Others	Total
Male	Agrl. & allied	2000	56.99	39.54	51.48	54.46	54.82
		2012	46.07	28.84	38.93	42.92	43.61
		2018	42.34	25.78	35.27	42.04	40.24
	Mining & quarrying	2000	0.69	0.56	1.26	0.16	0.67
		2012	0.68	0.42	0.92	0.08	0.63
		2018	0.53	0.21	1.12	0.14	0.49
	Manufacturing	2000	10.77	15.58	8.82	8.45	11.20
		2012	11.40	18.97	9.77	9.97	12.30
		2018	11.25	18.27	10.29	10.89	12.03
	Electricity, gas, water	2000	0.42	0.16	0.32	0.61	0.40
		2012	0.62	0.50	0.57	1.16	0.62
		2018	0.73	0.64	0.61	0.56	0.71
	Construction	2000	5.41	6.50	8.21	4.97	5.58
		2012	11.84	14.86	13.80	13.48	12.32
		2018	13.32	16.26	13.45	13.64	13.68
	Wholesale & retail trade	2000	9.81	20.71	8.79	14.14	11.15
		2012	10.41	17.53	10.88	11.80	11.38
		2018	12.95	19.70	11.43	12.59	13.69
	Transport, storage and communication	2000	4.60	7.28	6.53	6.55	5.01
		2012	6.00	9.01	7.46	6.31	6.43
		2018	7.02	9.82	9.70	7.17	7.41
	Other services	2000	11.31	9.66	14.58	10.66	11.18
		2012	12.98	9.88	17.66	14.27	12.71
		2018	11.86	9.32	18.14	12.96	11.74

(Continued)

Table 79 *(Continued)*

Sex	Sector	Year	Hindu	Islam	Christian	Others	Total
Female	Agrl. & allied	2000	78.42	56.28	61.21	82.36	76.52
		2012	65.40	40.46	42.53	69.81	62.77
		2018	59.32	36.11	40.88	54.10	56.99
	Mining & quarrying	2000	0.31	0.24	0.22	0.02	0.30
		2012	0.34	0.01	0.19	0.00	0.29
		2018	0.15	0.46	0.10	0.10	0.17
	Manufacturing	2000	8.20	28.22	9.44	3.99	9.50
		2012	10.91	40.21	13.16	7.42	13.39
		2018	10.89	34.85	7.28	10.12	12.46
	Electricity, gas, water	2000	0.03	0.00	0.03	0.09	0.03
		2012	0.25	0.31	0.32	0.14	0.25
		2018	0.17	0.29	0.09	0.27	0.18
	Construction	2000	1.60	0.69	1.82	0.95	1.52
		2012	6.47	3.23	7.83	1.90	6.09
		2018	5.27	2.42	4.31	4.94	5.03
	Wholesale & retail trade	2000	3.08	5.84	5.47	3.67	3.35
		2012	3.73	5.06	6.49	2.90	3.90
		2018	6.03	7.65	9.71	7.03	6.28
	Transport, storage, communication	2000	0.31	0.13	0.57	0.32	0.31
		2012	0.65	0.36	1.18	0.90	0.65
		2018	1.07	0.36	2.66	0.53	1.04
	Other services	2000	8.05	8.60	21.23	8.60	8.47
		2012	12.25	10.36	28.29	16.93	12.66
		2018	17.10	17.88	34.98	22.90	17.84
Male + Female	Agrl. & allied	2000	63.97	43.27	54.92	63.13	61.67
		2012	51.57	31.19	40.16	50.59	48.90
		2018	46.44	27.37	36.87	44.75	44.14
	Mining & quarrying	2000	0.57	0.49	0.89	0.12	0.55
		2012	0.58	0.33	0.67	0.06	0.54
		2018	0.44	0.25	0.83	0.13	0.41
	Manufacturing	2000	9.93	18.40	9.04	7.06	10.66
		2012	11.26	23.27	10.93	9.24	12.60
		2018	11.16	20.83	9.43	10.72	12.13
	Electricity, gas, water	2000	0.30	0.12	0.22	0.45	0.28
		2012	0.51	0.46	0.48	0.87	0.52
		2018	0.60	0.59	0.46	0.49	0.59

(Continued)

Table 79 *(Continued)*

Sex	Sector	Year	Hindu	Islam	Christian	Others	Total
Male + Female	Construction	2000	4.16	5.21	5.96	3.72	4.30
		2012	10.31	12.50	11.76	10.18	10.60
		2018	11.38	14.12	10.84	11.69	11.67
	Wholesale & retail trade	2000	7.61	17.40	7.62	10.89	8.69
		2012	8.51	15.00	9.38	9.26	9.32
		2018	11.28	17.84	10.94	11.34	11.97
	Transport, storage, communication	2000	3.20	5.69	4.42	4.61	3.52
		2012	4.48	7.26	5.31	4.77	4.83
		2018	5.59	8.36	7.69	5.68	5.93
	Other services	2000	10.25	9.42	16.93	10.02	10.32
		2012	12.77	9.97	21.29	15.03	12.69
		2018	13.13	10.64	22.95	15.20	13.16

Source: Same as Table 76

Considering the male and female workers together, it is observed that a higher percentage of Hindu workers are employed in 'agriculture and allied' and 'other services' sectors compared to the Muslim workers. On the other hand, in all other sectors, the percentage of Muslim workers exceeds that of Hindu workers (except in the 'mining & quarrying' and 'electricity, gas, water' sectors, where the difference is negligible). Among the non-agricultural sectors, Muslim workers have a much higher concentration in 'manufacturing' and 'trade' than Hindu workers. Even in 'construction' and 'transport, storage, and communication', the higher concentration of Muslim workers compared to the Hindu workers is visible.

6.3 Growth of Workers Across Various Sectors in India

In this section, we discuss the annual (compound) growth rates of workers across various sectors at the all-India level over different periods. The growth rates are calculated separately for rural and urban areas, as well as for males and females. The information in this regard is presented in Table 80, and our key observations are the following:

- In rural areas, the annual growth rate of workers in the 'agriculture and allied' sector has continuously declined for males. The growth rate of male workers in this sector in rural areas, which stood at 1.25 % per annum from 1983 to

1994, turned negative (–0.24 %) between 1994 and 2018. Notably, the growth rate of rural male workers in the 'agriculture and allied' sector turned negative after 2000. Conversely, similar to their rural male counterparts, the annual growth rate of workers in the 'agriculture and allied' sector for rural females was positive (1.22 %) from 1983 to 1994. However, in all sub-periods since 1994, the annual growth rates of rural female workers in the 'agriculture and allied' sector have been negative. Furthermore, it is observed that throughout all sub-periods from 1994 to 2018 (designated as the post-globalisation period), a significant decline in the growth of female workers within the 'agriculture and allied' sector became apparent, with the most substantial decline (–4.93 %) occurring between 2012 and 2018. When considering rural males and females together, the growth rate of workers has been negative since 2000, with no signs of a reversal of this trend by 2018. Overall, rural India's 'agriculture and allied' sector has experienced a decline in the number of workers, especially after 2000.

- It is also evident from Table 80 that, among the non-agricultural sectors, the two sectors that recorded an improvement in the growth rate of workers, both for the rural males and females, during the post-globalisation period (1994–2018) compared to the pre-globalisation period (1983–1994) are 'construction' and 'transport, storage and communication'. In the case of the rural males, the annual growth rate of construction workers increased from 5.37 % during the pre-globalisation period to 7.58 % during the post-globalisation period, while for the rural females increased from 3.82 % to 6.32 %. In the case of 'transport, storage, and communication', for males, the growth rate of workers increased from 4.21 % during the pre-globalisation period to 4.68 % during the post-globalisation period, and for females, from 1.37 % to 2.89 %. In all other non-agricultural sectors in rural areas, including sectors like 'manufacturing', 'trade' and 'other services', the growth rates of workers declined during the post-globalisation period compared to the pre-globalisation period, for both males and females. When considering all rural non-agricultural sectors together, it appears that while the growth rate of rural male workers improved slightly during the post-globalisation period (3.37 % per annum) compared to the pre-globalisation period (3.18 % per annum), the same for rural female workers declined in the latter period, from 2.64 % to 1.45 %. However, when considering rural males and females together, a marginal decline in the growth rate of workers in the non-agricultural sector is observed during the post-globalisation period compared to the pre-globalisation era.

Table 80: Annual Growth Rates of Workers (UPSS) in Different Sectors in India

Region	Sex of Workers	Period	Agrl. & allied	Mining & quarrying	Manufa-cturing	Electricity, gas & water	Constr-uction	Wholesale & retail trade	Transport, storage and communication	Other services	Non-agri.	All Sectors
Rural	Male	1983 to 1994	1.25	3.18	1.68	5.68	5.37	3.86	4.21	3.02	3.18	1.71
		1994 to 2000	0.30	−1.63	1.63	−5.67	6.83	4.56	7.43	−1.36	2.67	0.94
		2000 to 2012	−0.14	0.52	2.32	5.18	10.78	2.82	3.79	1.82	4.39	1.40
		2012 to 2018	−0.95	−2.31	−0.66	7.54	2.16	2.56	3.74	3.29	2.06	0.33
		1994 to 2018	−0.24	−0.74	1.40	2.92	7.58	3.19	4.68	1.38	3.37	1.02
	Female	1983 to 1994	1.22	4.18	2.24	–	3.82	2.34	1.37	3.26	2.64	1.41
		1994 to 2000	−0.02	−4.55	1.52	–	3.54	−0.68	0.13	1.55	1.19	0.15
		2000 to 2012	−1.40	−0.60	1.80	–	15.71	2.96	3.66	2.56	4.15	−0.34
		2012 to 2018	−4.93	−12.68	−7.45	−17.13	−7.84	0.45	4.14	4.26	−3.48	−4.56
		1994 to 2018	−1.96	−4.74	−0.66	–	6.32	1.41	2.89	2.73	1.45	−1.29
	Male + Female	1983 to 1994	1.24	3.42	1.88	5.68	5.15	3.58	4.13	3.07	3.05	1.60
		1994 to 2000	0.18	−2.30	1.59	−5.67	6.41	3.73	7.28	−0.70	2.34	0.66
		2000 to 2012	−0.61	0.29	2.14	6.00	11.49	2.84	3.79	2.01	4.34	0.83
		2012 to 2018	−2.26	−3.87	−2.72	6.08	0.69	2.26	3.75	3.53	1.00	−1.03
		1994 to 2018	−0.83	−1.41	0.77	2.97	7.42	2.91	4.64	1.70	2.99	0.32

(Continued)

Table 80 *(Continued)*

Region	Sex of Workers	Period	Agrl. & allied	Mining & quarrying	Manufa-cturing	Electricity, gas & water	Constr-uction	Wholesale & retail trade	Transport, storage and communication	Other services	Non-agri.	All Sectors
Urban	Male	1983 to 1994	1.83	3.93	1.86	4.00	6.16	3.65	2.94	3.84	3.30	3.15
		1994 to 2000	−2.61	−3.54	1.74	−4.14	6.60	7.72	3.76	−1.28	3.06	2.61
		2000 to 2012	1.82	2.77	3.15	7.89	4.91	2.11	4.19	3.32	3.23	3.14
		2012 to 2018	1.34	−4.91	2.16	1.25	3.80	1.11	3.52	2.21	2.19	2.14
		1994 to 2018	0.58	−0.79	2.55	3.10	5.05	3.23	3.92	1.88	2.93	2.76
	Female	1983 to 1994	1.08	3.29	2.29	7.36	6.08	3.80	1.89	6.03	4.28	3.38
		1994 to 2000	−4.50	−5.64	0.89	−5.64	3.64	10.18	6.58	0.57	2.44	0.94
		2000 to 2012	−0.65	0.70	4.99	18.58	1.77	1.08	7.12	4.70	4.12	3.44
		2012 to 2018	−0.79	−8.33	0.13	−5.74	3.03	2.60	5.69	4.31	2.66	2.31
		1994 to 2018	−1.66	−3.22	2.72	5.75	2.55	3.67	6.63	3.56	3.33	2.53
	Male + Female	1983 to 1994	1.50	3.86	1.95	4.18	6.15	3.67	2.90	4.36	3.47	3.20
		1994 to 2000	−3.38	−3.76	1.56	−4.23	6.22	8.00	3.86	−0.78	2.95	2.27
		2000 to 2012	0.92	2.59	3.56	8.92	4.59	1.99	4.33	3.73	3.39	3.20
		2012 to 2018	0.61	−5.17	1.58	0.12	3.58	1.13	3.48	2.84	2.16	2.06
		1994 to 2018	−0.25	−1.00	2.56	3.27	4.74	3.24	4.00	2.36	2.97	2.68

(Continued)

Table 80 *(Continued)*

Region	Sex of Workers	Period	Agrl. & allied	Mining & quarrying	Manufa-cturing	Electricity, gas & water	Constr-uction	Wholesale & retail trade	Transport, storage and communication	Other services	Non-agri.	All Sectors
Rural + Urban	Male	1983 to 1994	1.27	3.47	1.78	4.67	5.70	3.74	3.42	3.47	3.24	2.06
		1994 to 2000	0.19	−2.35	1.69	−4.77	6.73	6.44	5.29	−1.32	2.88	1.38
		2000 to 2012	−0.07	1.40	2.77	6.90	8.71	2.38	4.01	2.70	3.77	1.91
		2012 to 2018	0.10	−3.51	0.08	2.74	2.79	0.87	2.86	1.75	1.51	0.92
		1994 to 2018	0.04	−0.79	1.82	2.83	6.71	3.00	4.04	1.45	2.98	1.53
	Female	1983 to 1994	1.22	4.00	2.26	7.36	4.72	2.95	1.72	4.90	3.38	1.66
		1994 to 2000	−0.20	−4.76	1.29	−5.64	3.58	4.79	4.74	0.94	1.79	0.26
		2000 to 2012	−1.38	−0.35	3.05	20.82	11.81	1.89	6.39	3.93	4.14	0.32
		2012 to 2018	−4.07	−11.16	−4.52	−9.43	−5.78	0.74	3.73	3.04	−1.14	−2.89
		1994 to 2018	−1.77	−4.26	0.67	5.69	5.10	2.32	5.30	2.95	2.21	−0.50
	Male + Female	1983 to 1994	1.25	3.57	1.91	4.76	5.56	3.63	3.37	3.80	3.27	1.93
		1994 to 2000	0.04	−2.80	1.58	−4.80	6.33	6.22	5.28	−0.75	2.66	1.02
		2000 to 2012	−0.56	1.12	2.85	7.90	9.12	2.32	4.09	3.04	3.84	1.44
		2012 to 2018	−1.29	−4.73	−1.18	1.24	1.60	0.77	2.77	2.14	0.95	−0.08
		1994 to 2018	−0.59	−1.36	1.51	2.92	6.50	2.89	4.05	1.86	2.82	0.96

Source: Same as Table 76

- In urban areas, aside from 'manufacturing' and 'transport, storage and communication', the growth rate of workers decreased in all other sectors during the post-globalisation period compared to the pre-globalisation period for both males and females. As a result, the growth rate of non-agricultural workers also fell in urban areas for both males and females during the post-globalisation period compared to the pre-globalisation period.
- When examining rural and urban areas collectively, it is noted that the growth rates of male and female workers in the 'agriculture and allied' sector declined during the post-globalisation period compared to the pre-globalisation period at the all-India level. The growth rate of female workers in the post-globalisation period became negative, while that of male workers remained positive, albeit at a low level. It is also observed that in three sectors for males ('manufacturing', 'construction', and 'transport, storage, etc'.) and two sectors for females ('construction' and 'transport, storage, etc'.), the growth rates of workers were higher in the post-globalisation period than in the pre-globalisation period; across all other sectors, the growth rates were lower during the post-globalisation period for both males and females. When considering males and females together, the overall picture shows declining growth rates for workers across all sectors, except for the 'construction' and 'transport, storage, and communication' sectors.
- Overall, employment growth in India has been poor since the adoption of globalisation policies. Although non-agricultural employment continued to grow in all sub-periods of the post-globalisation era, agricultural employment turned negative from 2000 onwards, resulting in very low overall employment growth (0.96 % per annum) in the country from 1994 to 2018, compared to 1983–1994 (1.93 % per annum).

6.3.1 Shares in Total Workers and Growth Rates of Workers Across Different Sub-Sectors (Two-Digit Level)

Let us now examine the growth rates of workers in various two-digit sub-sectors of the NIC. For this purpose, we have considered data for two years (2012 and 2018), as mentioned above. To better comprehend the growth rate of workers from 2012 to 2018, we have prepared separate tables for the sub-sectors that experienced positive and negative growth rates during this period. Furthermore, for each category, we have arranged the sub-sectors in descending order by their share of total workers in 2018.

Table 81 presents information on the growth rates of workers (males and females, as well as rural and urban combined) in the sub-sectors (at the two-digit level) that experienced positive growth in worker numbers from 2012 to 2018. It was found that fifty-six sub-sectors (out of 87) accounted for around 42 % of the total workforce in India in 2018 and recorded positive growth rates during the period mentioned above. However, a close examination of growth rates reveals a trend where sectors with a very small share of the total workforce exhibit very high growth rates. Conversely, those with a larger share tend to show lower growth rates. For example, while 'construction of buildings' made up 8.85 % of India's workforce in 2018, its growth from 2012 to 2018 was only 2.32 %. In contrast, 'activities of extraterritorial organisations and bodies' recorded the highest growth rate (37.28 %) among all sub-sectors, despite its tiny share of just 0.004 % of the total workforce in 2018. Four other sectors employed more than 2 % of the workforce while also experiencing positive growth: these are 'retail trade, except motor vehicles and motorcycles' (employment share of 8.02 %; growth rate of 1.01 %), 'land transport and transport via pipelines' (employment share and growth rate of 4.49 % and 3.26 %, respectively), 'education' (employment share and growth rate of 3.78 % and 3.98 %, respectively), and 'manufacture of wearing apparel' (employment share and growth rate of 2.10 % and 0.50 %, respectively). Conversely, aside from 'activities of extraterritorial organisations and bodies', there are eight other sub-sectors – such as 'office administrative, office support and other business support activities', 'repair and installation of machinery and equipment', 'security and investigation activities', 'residential care activities', 'activities of head offices; management consultancy activities', 'employment activities', 'scientific research and development', and 'mining support service activities' – that recorded over 11 % growth in worker numbers despite having less than 0.50 % of the total workforce in the country.

Table 81: Shares in Total Workers and Growth Rates of Workers (UPSS) in Sub-Sectors Observing Positive Growth Rates During 2012–2018 in India (Males & Females and Rural & Urban Combined)

NIC Code	Sub-sector	% share in total workers in 2018	Annual growth rate of workers during 2012–2018
41	Construction of buildings	8.85	2.32
47	Retail trade, except of motor vehicles and motorcycles	8.02	1.01
49	Land transport and transport via pipelines	4.49	3.26
85	Education	3.78	3.98
14	Manufacture of wearing apparel	2.10	0.50

(Continued)

Table 81 *(Continued)*

NIC Code	Sub-sector	% share in total workers in 2018	Annual growth rate of workers during 2012–2018
56	Food and beverage service activities	1.71	2.43
43	Specialized construction activities	1.48	6.57
46	Wholesale trade, except of motor vehicles and motorcycles	1.30	2.43
97	Activities of households as employers of domestic personnel	1.08	4.53
86	Human health activities	0.99	3.47
45	Wholesale and retail trade and repair of motor vehicles and motorcycles	0.78	2.07
64	Financial service activities, except insurance and pension funding	0.76	5.67
62	Computer programming, consultancy and related activities	0.48	6.75
82	Office administrative, office support and other business support activities	0.47	14.04
69	Legal and accounting activities	0.43	8.74
33	Repair and installation of machinery and equipment	0.43	12.35
24	Manufacture of basic metals	0.39	3.65
35	Electricity, gas, steam and air conditioning supply	0.34	4.03
80	Security and investigation activities	0.31	13.17
27	Manufacture of electrical equipment	0.30	6.04
28	Manufacture of machinery and equipment n.e.c.	0.29	5.74
20	Manufacture of chemicals and chemical products	0.27	1.32
29	Manufacture of motor vehicles, trailers and semi-trailers	0.25	3.75
52	Warehousing and support activities for transportation	0.25	3.75
68	Real estate activities	0.21	1.35
77	Rental and leasing activities	0.20	8.74
90	Creative, arts and entertainment activities	0.19	3.95
74	Other professional, scientific and technical activities	0.19	3.51
21	Manufacture of pharmaceuticals, medicinal chemical and botanical products	0.17	0.21

(Continued)

Table 81 *(Continued)*

NIC Code	Sub-sector	% share in total workers in 2018	Annual growth rate of workers during 2012–2018
17	Manufacture of paper and paper products	0.16	5.97
63	Information service activities	0.15	5.73
02	Forestry and logging	0.15	0.68
18	Printing and reproduction of recorded media	0.15	1.40
53	Postal and courier activities	0.15	1.43
88	Social work activities without accommodation	0.14	9.47
26	Manufacture of computer, electronic and optical products	0.12	3.86
81	Services to buildings and landscape activities	0.11	9.28
11	Manufacture of beverages	0.10	2.08
36	Water collection, treatment and supply	0.09	7.32
58	Publishing activities	0.08	1.29
87	Residential care activities	0.07	11.13
71	Architecture and engineering activities; technical testing and analysis	0.07	9.74
70	Activities of head offices; management consultancy activities	0.05	17.82
19	Manufacture of coke and refined petroleum products	0.04	5.55
78	Employment activities	0.04	12.33
93	Sports activities and amusement and recreation activities	0.04	4.64
07	Mining of metal ores	0.04	6.79
59	Motion picture, video and television programme production, sound recording and music publishing activities	0.04	7.77
50	Water transport	0.03	1.38
72	Scientific research and development	0.03	11.26
92	Gambling and betting activities	0.03	9.60
60	Broadcasting and programming activities	0.02	8.53
37	Sewerage	0.02	6.28
09	Mining support service activities	0.010	24.27
39	Remediation activities and other waste management services	0.01	3.25
99	Activities of extraterritorial organizations and bodies	0.004	37.28

Source: As in Table 77

In Table 82, we provide information on thirty-one sub-sectors that account for 58 % of the country's total workers. All these sub-sectors experienced a negative growth rate of workers from 2012 to 2018. Notably, the most significant sub-sector, namely, 'crop and animal production, hunting and related service activities', which accounted for nearly 44 % of all workers in the country even in 2018, also recorded negative employment growth. This has primarily caused an overall decline in employment across the country. Other notable sectors that experienced negative employment growth during this period include 'manufacture of textiles', 'public administration and defence; compulsory social security', 'civil engineering', 'other personal service activities', 'manufacture of food products', 'manufacture of other non-metallic mineral products', and 'manufacture of tobacco products', among others.

Table 82: Shares in Total Workers and Growth Rates of Workers (UPSS) in Sub-Sectors Observing Negative Growth Rates During 2012–2018 in India (Males & Females and Rural & Urban Combined)

NIC Code	Sub-sector	% share in total workers in 2018	Annual growth rate of workers during 2012–2018
01	Crop and animal production, hunting and related service activities	43.68	-1.79
13	Manufacture of textiles	1.76	-1.76
84	Public administration and defense; compulsory social security	1.61	-0.65
42	Civil engineering	1.34	-5.86
96	Other personal service activities	1.19	-1.55
10	Manufacture of food products	1.17	-1.51
23	Manufacture of other non-metallic mineral products	0.87	-3.11
12	Manufacture of tobacco products	0.72	-5.90
16	Manufacture of wood and products of wood and cork, except furniture; manufacture of articles of straw and plaiting materials	0.64	-4.04

(Continued)

Table 82 *(Continued)*

NIC Code	Sub-sector	% share in total workers in 2018	Annual growth rate of workers during 2012–2018
25	Manufacture of fabricated metal products, except machinery and equipment	0.61	−0.68
32	Other manufacturing	0.55	−3.60
95	Repair of computers and personal and household goods	0.49	−3.14
31	Manufacture of furniture	0.47	−1.09
03	Fishing and aquaculture	0.31	−1.21
15	Manufacture of leather and related products	0.27	−0.28
08	Other mining and quarrying	0.25	−5.77
94	Activities of membership organizations	0.23	−0.64
22	Manufacture of rubber and plastics products	0.23	−0.98
61	Telecommunications	0.22	−0.35
55	Accommodation	0.17	−0.35
65	Insurance, reinsurance and pension funding, except compulsory social security	0.15	−4.82
66	Other financial activities	0.15	−1.93
38	Waste collection, treatment and disposal activities; materials recovery	0.13	−4.46
05	Mining of coal and lignite	0.10	−4.09
30	Manufacture of other transport equipment	0.07	−7.15
79	Travel agency, tour operator and other reservation service activities	0.06	−7.54
73	Advertising and market research	0.03	−2.77
75	Veterinary activities	0.03	−2.56
06	Extraction of crude petroleum and natural gas	0.02	−8.48
91	Libraries, archives, museums and other cultural activities	0.02	−0.36
51	Air transport	0.02	−0.15

Source: Same as Table 77

6.3.2 Shares of Various Sectors in Incremental Workers

We now examine the shares of different sectors in relation to the total change in the absolute number of workers across various sub-periods. This discussion helps clarify the sectors that experienced an increase or decrease in the absolute number of workers over time, and consequently, the sectors that are emerging or declining as employment providers. The relevant information for all-India, separately for males and females, and for rural and urban areas, is presented in Table 83. The main observations here are the following:

- In rural areas, the total number of workers in the 'agriculture and allied' sector decreased during the post-globalisation period (1994–2018) compared to the pre-globalisation period (1983–1994). Although this occurred for males and females, the drop in female workers in the 'agriculture and allied' sector was significantly higher than that of males. As shown in Table 83, the number of rural females in this sector decreased by 14.19 lakh per annum from 1994 to 2018, while the number of rural males declined by 3.19 lakh per annum. Additionally, it is noticeable that across all sub-periods, the most significant decrease in rural female workers in the 'agriculture and allied' sector occurred from 2012 to 2018, with a reduction of 33.16 lakh per annum; rural male workers in the same sector saw a decrease of 12.93 lakh per annum. Another notable point is that while rural females began to experience a decline in their numbers in the 'agriculture and allied' sector from the onset of the globalisation period, rural males did not begin to decline until 2000.
- Apart from the 'agriculture and allied' sector, the other significant sectors that witnessed a decline in rural workers in the recent sub-period (2012 to 2018) are 'manufacturing' for males and females and 'construction' for females only. However, when we compare the post-globalisation period with the pre-globalisation period, while rural males increased the absolute number of their workers in 'manufacturing' during the post-globalisation period, rural females declined. In the 'construction' sector, although both males and females in rural areas gained in terms of the increasing number of workers in the post-globalisation period compared to the pre-globalisation period, the increase was much higher for males (11.95 lakh per annum) than for females (1.31 lakh per annum).

Table 83: Per Year Increase/Decrease in Absolute Number of Workers (UPSS) in Different Sub-Periods in India (in Lakh)

Region	Sex	Period	Increase / Decrease in Number of Workers (in lakh) per year									
			Agri. & allied	Mining & quar-rying	Manufa-cturing	Electricity, gas & water	Constr-uction	Wholesale & retail trade	Transport, storage and com-munication	Other ser-vices	Non-agri.	Total Workers
Rural	Male	1983 to 1994	16.16	0.35	2.01	0.24	2.42	3.23	1.38	3.36	12.99	29.15
		1994 to 2000	4.25	−0.21	2.24	−0.28	4.87	5.28	3.70	−1.73	13.86	18.11
		2000 to 2012	−2.04	0.06	3.82	0.28	17.99	4.45	2.98	2.44	32.02	29.98
		2012 to 2018	−12.93	−0.28	−1.24	0.66	6.96	5.14	4.08	5.37	20.69	7.76
		1994 to 2018	−3.19	−0.09	2.16	0.23	11.95	4.83	3.43	2.13	24.65	21.46
	Female	1983 to 1994	10.30	0.14	1.45	0.00	0.29	0.45	0.01	0.97	3.31	13.61
		1994 to 2000	−0.20	−0.17	1.15	0.00	0.36	−0.15	0.00	0.58	1.78	1.58
		2000 to 2012	−11.70	−0.02	1.60	0.06	4.60	0.74	0.05	1.15	8.18	−3.53
		2012 to 2018	−33.16	−0.27	−6.15	−0.08	−4.32	0.14	0.07	2.50	−8.10	−41.27
		1994 to 2018	−14.19	−0.12	−0.45	0.01	1.31	0.37	0.04	1.35	2.51	−11.68
	Male + Female	1983 to 1994	26.46	0.49	3.45	0.24	2.71	3.68	1.40	4.33	16.30	42.75
		1994 to 2000	4.05	−0.38	3.39	−0.28	5.23	5.13	3.70	−1.16	15.64	19.69
		2000 to 2012	−13.74	0.04	5.42	0.33	22.59	5.19	3.02	3.60	40.20	26.46
		2012 to 2018	−46.02	−0.55	−7.37	0.57	2.60	5.22	4.15	7.83	12.44	−33.57
		1994 to 2018	−17.36	−0.21	1.71	0.24	13.25	5.18	3.47	3.47	27.12	9.76

(Continued)

Table 83 *(Continued)*

Region	Sex	Period	Increase / Decrease in Number of Workers (in lakh) per year									
			Agri. & allied	Mining & quarrying	Manufacturing	Electricity, gas & water	Construction	Wholesale & retail trade	Transport, storage and communication	Other services	Non-agri.	Total Workers
Urban	Male	1983 to 1994	1.68	0.47	4.46	0.44	3.46	7.40	2.74	9.29	28.26	29.94
		1994 to 2000	−0.85	−0.16	1.66	−0.17	2.08	7.96	1.55	−1.27	11.65	10.80
		2000 to 2012	0.75	0.16	4.75	0.56	3.18	3.93	3.12	4.74	20.44	21.19
		2012 to 2018	0.86	−0.41	5.57	0.19	4.87	3.24	4.92	5.47	23.85	24.70
		1994 to 2018	0.36	−0.06	5.25	0.35	4.21	6.75	3.95	4.00	24.44	24.80
	Female	1983 to 1994	0.76	0.05	1.46	0.05	0.54	0.93	0.07	4.60	7.70	8.45
		1994 to 2000	−1.02	−0.03	0.23	−0.02	0.17	1.36	0.10	0.21	2.02	0.99
		2000 to 2012	−0.15	0.00	2.17	0.15	0.13	0.26	0.26	2.86	5.84	5.69
		2012 to 2018	−0.23	−0.05	0.10	−0.14	0.35	0.97	0.49	5.19	6.91	6.68
		1994 to 2018	−0.59	−0.02	1.56	0.06	0.24	0.98	0.34	3.29	6.46	5.88
	Male + Female	1983 to 1994	2.43	0.52	5.92	0.48	4.01	8.33	2.81	13.90	35.96	38.39
		1994 to 2000	−1.88	−0.19	1.89	−0.19	2.25	9.32	1.66	−1.06	13.67	11.79
		2000 to 2012	0.60	0.17	6.92	0.71	3.31	4.19	3.38	7.60	26.28	26.87
		2012 to 2018	0.56	−0.46	5.30	0.02	4.97	3.72	5.14	10.42	29.12	29.69
		1994 to 2018	−0.24	−0.08	6.72	0.40	4.39	7.61	4.23	7.23	30.50	30.25

(Continued)

Table 83 *(Continued)*

Region	Sex	Period	Increase / Decrease in Number of Workers (in lakh) per year									
			Agri. & allied	Mining & quarrying	Manufacturing	Electricity, gas & water	Construction	Wholesale & retail trade	Transport, storage and communication	Other services	Non-agri.	Total Workers
Rural + Urban	Male	1983 to 1994	17.97	0.65	4.78	0.51	4.62	7.83	3.10	9.10	30.59	48.57
		1994 to 2000	8.47	–1.44	15.01	–1.70	25.03	55.63	18.86	–11.53	99.87	108.34
		2000 to 2012	–0.69	0.19	6.77	0.68	14.82	6.46	4.75	5.84	39.51	38.82
		2012 to 2018	1.40	–0.71	0.33	0.65	12.60	4.18	6.99	7.02	31.06	32.47
		1994 to 2018	0.54	–0.16	6.41	0.53	16.35	10.53	6.89	5.17	45.72	46.26
	Female	1983 to 1994	11.27	0.18	2.39	0.03	0.63	1.03	0.05	3.78	8.09	19.36
		1994 to 2000	–5.71	–0.66	4.58	–0.08	1.94	6.35	0.52	2.76	15.42	9.70
		2000 to 2012	–7.94	–0.01	2.99	0.18	3.18	0.73	0.27	3.31	10.64	2.71
		2012 to 2018	–29.08	–0.32	–7.18	–0.26	–3.88	0.49	0.37	5.28	–5.50	–34.58
		1994 to 2018	–13.70	–0.14	0.83	0.06	1.58	1.19	0.34	4.04	7.89	–5.81
	Male + Female	1983 to 1994	29.24	0.82	7.18	0.54	5.25	8.86	3.15	12.88	38.69	67.93
		1994 to 2000	2.76	–2.10	19.60	–1.78	26.96	61.98	19.39	–8.77	115.29	118.05
		2000 to 2012	–8.63	0.18	9.76	0.86	18.01	7.19	5.02	9.15	50.16	41.53
		2012 to 2018	–27.93	–1.09	–7.05	0.33	8.30	4.21	7.01	12.33	24.05	–3.89
		1994 to 2018	–13.23	–0.31	7.19	0.58	17.82	11.61	7.13	9.22	53.24	40.01

Source: Same as Table 76

- In rural areas, two other important sectors, namely, 'wholesale and retail trade' and 'transport, storage and communication', witnessed an increase in the absolute number of workers during the post-globalisation period compared to the pre-globalisation period for both males and females (except 'wholesale and retail trade' for females). The rise in the absolute number of workers was also evident in the 'other services' category. However, the expansion rate for rural males during the post-globalisation period was lower than that of the pre-globalisation period. In contrast, rural females improved their expansion rate in the number of workers in 'other services' during the post-globalisation period.
- When considering the entire non-agricultural sector, it can be observed that rural males nearly doubled the rate of worker expansion in this sector during the post-globalisation period, increasing by 24.65 lakh per year compared to 12.99 lakh per year in the pre-globalisation period. In contrast, rural females experienced a decline in the expansion rate of their non-agricultural workforce during the post-globalisation period, increasing by 2.51 lakh per year, compared with 3.31 lakh per year in the pre-globalisation period.
- When considered for rural persons (males and females), it is evident that, in contrast to the growth in the absolute number of workers in the 'agriculture and allied' sector during the pre-globalisation period (which increased by 26.46 lakh per year), there was a decline in the same sector during the post-globalisation period (falling by 17.36 lakh workers per year). This reduction in rural workers in the 'agriculture and allied' sector is somewhat offset by higher growth in the rural non-agricultural sector. As shown in Table 83, while the absolute number of rural non-agricultural workers grew by 16.30 lakh per year during the pre-globalisation period, this figure rose by 27.12 lakh per year during the post-globalisation period. The table also indicates that, for rural persons, the increase in the absolute number of workers was lower during the post-globalisation period compared to the pre-globalisation period in 'manufacturing' and 'other services'. Conversely, a different trend is observed in 'construction', 'wholesale and retail trade', and 'transport, storage, and communication'.
- In urban areas, the most noteworthy development during the post-globalisation period, compared to the pre-globalisation period, is the decline in the rate of expansion of workers in 'other services', for both males and females. However, in the post-globalisation period, the urban workforce's expansion rate in 'manufacturing' improved for both genders compared to the pre-globalisation period. Regarding 'construction', urban males experienced a higher workforce expansion

rate during the post-globalisation period than in the previous period, while females saw a decline. The two other non-agricultural sectors, namely 'wholesale and retail trade' and 'transport, storage, and communication', experienced higher expansion rates among urban female workers during the post-globalisation period than during the pre-globalisation period. However, a decline in the expansion rate of workers in 'wholesale and retail trade' has been observed for urban males during the post-globalisation period, although they improved the expansion rate of workers in 'transport, storage, and communication'. Despite diverse performances across sectors in the expansion of workers in non-agricultural sectors in urban areas during the post-globalisation period, the non-agricultural sector as a whole recorded a lower rate of worker expansion during this period than in the pre-globalisation period.

- When considering both rural and urban areas, it can be observed that while the 'agriculture and allied' sector experienced a significant decline in the absolute number of workers during the post-globalisation period compared to the pre-globalisation period, the 'non-agricultural' sector exhibited an opposing trend. Notably, there has been a considerable reduction in the absolute number of female workers in the 'agriculture and allied' sector during the post-globalisation period. According to Table 83, the country experienced a decrease of 1.37 lakh female workers per year during the post-globalisation period. This trend contrasts with the pre-globalisation period, when the total number of female workers increased by 1.13 lakh annually. It is also observed that while males in the country improved the growth rate of workers in the 'non-agricultural' sector during the post-globalisation period relative to the pre-globalisation period, females saw a decline. Examining the expansion and contraction rates of the absolute number of workers, it is notable that between 1994 and 2018, the emerging sectors employing males included 'construction', 'wholesale and retail trade', 'transport, storage, and communications', and 'manufacturing'. In contrast, sectors contributing to female employment during the same period included 'other services', 'construction', and 'wholesale and retail trade'. However, in all these sectors, the expansion rates in the absolute numbers of female workers in the post-globalisation period were lower than those of males.

Overall, across both males and females and rural and urban areas, the country's 'agriculture and allied' sector has experienced a significant decline in the number of workers during the post-globalisation period, by 11.32 lakh per year. This decline is somewhat offset by an increase in the 'non-agricultural' sector, which has risen by 5.32 lakh per year. Within the 'non-agricultural' sectors, the main contributors to the rise in the absolute number of workers during the post-globalisation period include 'construction', 'wholesale and retail trade', 'other services', 'manufacturing' and 'transport, storage and communication', listed in descending order of their contributions.

6.4 Pattern of Employment Diversification in Major States

In this section, we analyse the pattern of employment diversification in major states of India from 1983 to 2018. We achieve this by examining the proportion of non-agricultural or non-farm sector workers relative to the total workforce at various points in time, both for rural and urban areas combined and separately for rural areas. Additionally, we investigate the growth rates of farm and non-farm workers in the states during different sub-periods.

6.4.1 Employment Diversification (Combined Rural and Urban Areas)

Table 84 presents information on the degree of employment diversification across 17 major states, combining rural and urban areas. In this table, regarding employment diversification, we have established three notional categories of states: (i) states where over 50 % of workers (UPSS) are engaged in non-farm employment (termed 'high' diversification states); (ii) states where the percentage of non-farm workers is greater than or equal to 25 % but less than or equal to 50 % ('medium' diversification states); and (iii) states where the percentage of non-farm workers is below 25 % ('low' diversification states).

When considering both rural and urban areas, Table 84 shows that, in 1983, all seventeen states for males were classified as 'medium' diversification states. However, over time, male employment diversification increased significantly, such that by 1994, 8 out of the seventeen major states had transitioned to 'high' diversification states. This trend continued post–1994, with all but one state moving into the 'high' diversification category by 2018. The table also shows that, except in 1994, Kerala was the most diversified state in male employment every year. Conversely, the lowest proportion of male non-farm workers has consistently been reported for either Madhya Pradesh (in 1983, 2012, and 2018) or Bihar (in 1994 and 2000). Besides Kerala (79.86 %), other states with a notably high percentage of male non-farm workers in 2018 include Tamil Nadu (76.18 %), Haryana (76.01 %), Punjab (73.87 %), and Jammu & Kashmir (71.92 %). Apart from Madhya Pradesh and Bihar, other states that rank low in male employment diversification include Odisha, Assam, and Uttar Pradesh. It is worth mentioning that the ranking pattern of states regarding the degree of male employment diversification has remained consistent from 1983 to 2018, as evidenced by the statistical significance of Kendall's W.

Table 84: States Arranged in Descending Order of Percentage of Non-Farm Workers (NFW) to Total Workers (UPSS) in India: Rural & Urban Combined

Sex of Workers	Degree of Diversification	1983		1994		2000		2012		2018	
		State	NFW (%)	State	NFW (%)	State	NFW (%)	State	NFW (%)	State	NFW (%)
Male	> 50.0 (High)			1. TN	56.11	1. KER	66.50	1. KER	81.61	1. KER	79.86
				2. KER	55.25	2. TN	60.86	2. J&K	72.60	2. TN	76.18
				3. HARY	54.44	3. MAHA	56.51	3. PUN	71.47	3. HARY	76.01
				4. WB	52.25	4. HARY	56.46	4. TN	68.93	4. PUN	73.87
				5. MAHA	52.16	5. PUN	56.08	5. HARY	65.47	5. J&K	71.92
				6. GUJ	51.59	6. WB	52.42	6. HP	64.30	6. HP	64.32
				7. J&K	51.41	7. GUJ	51.54	7. RAJ	61.59	7. WB	63.17
				8. PUN	51.20	8. HP	51.11	8. WB	61.01	8. GUJ	60.93
								9. MAHA	60.06	9. RAJ	59.87
								10. GUJ	59.38	10. MAHA	59.28
								11. KAR	56.13	11. AP	58.70
								12. AP	55.46	12. KAR	57.27
								13. UP	55.02	13. BIH	55.69
										14. UP	54.63
										15. ASM	54.57
										16. ORI	52.80
	≥ 25.0 and ≤ 50.0 (Medium)	1. KER	49.88	9. RAJ	43.66	9. RAJ	46.79	14. ASM	49.24	17. MP	42.52
		2. TN	49.59	10. KAR	40.99	10. J&K	45.82	15. ORI	48.70		
		3. WB	47.00	11. AP	40.08	11. KAR	44.12	16. BIH	44.46		
		4. MAHA	45.72	12. HP	38.87	12. ASM	42.80	17. MP	43.39		
		5. HARY	43.11	13. UP	35.98	13. UP	41.98				

(Continued)

Table 84 *(Continued)*

Sex of Workers	Degree of Diversification	1983		1994		2000		2012		2018	
		State	NFW (%)	State	NFW (%)	State	NFW (%)	State	NFW (%)	State	NFW (%)
Male	≥ 25.0 and ≤ 50.0 (Medium)	6. GUJ	40.94	14. ASM	31.03	14. AP	41.76				
		7. PUN	40.59	15. ORI	30.02	15. MP	32.76				
		8. J&K	40.36	16. MP	28.21	16. ORI	32.07				
		9. AP	36.91	17. BIH	26.53	17. BIH	29.65				
		10. KAR	36.57								
		11. UP	34.17								
		12. RAJ	31.97								
		13. ORI	29.24								
		14. ASM	28.51								
		15. HP	28.26								
		16. BIH	27.30								
		17. MP	27.04								
Kendall's W = 0.88*; df = 16											
Female	> 50.0 (High)			1. WB	52.23	1. WB	57.09	1. KER	74.51	1. KER	80.96
						2. KER	50.67	2. WB	70.48	2. PUN	74.44
								3. TN	61.64	3. WB	64.45
										4. TN	63.75
										5. ASM	54.26
										6. HARY	52.88
	≥ 25.0 and ≤ 50.0 (Medium)	1. WB	36.55	2. KER	43.86	3. TN	40.48	4. PUN	40.94	7. KAR	45.57
		2. KER	33.41	3. TN	33.78	4. ASM	27.46	5. KAR	39.48	8. ORI	45.32
		3. TN	28.10			5. KAR	25.11	6. ORI	35.83	9. GUJ	43.65
								7. AP	34.55	10. BIH	41.31

(Continued)

Table 84 *(Continued)*

Sex of Workers	Degree of Diversification	1983		1994		2000		2012		2018	
		State	NFW (%)	State	NFW (%)	State	NFW (%)	State	NFW (%)	State	NFW (%)
Female	≥ 25.0 and ≤ 50.0 (Medium)							8. GUJ	34.24	11. AP	40.99
								9. HARY	31.97	12. UP	35.14
								10. MAHA	31.57	13. MAHA	34.50
								11. RAJ	29.55	14. MP	25.43
								12. ASM	28.69		
								13. UP	26.42		
								14. MP	25.76		
								15. BIH	25.54		
	< 25. 0 (Low)	4. ASM	22.21	4. KAR	24.18	6. ORI	24.08	16. J&K	23.33	15. RAJ	24.46
		5. AP	21.99	5. AP	22.70	7. AP	23.82	17. HP	15.77	16. J&K	23.37
		6. ORI	21.22	6. ASM	22.09	8. PUN	22.06			17. HP	16.05
		7. KAR	20.79	7. MAHA	21.80	9. MAHA	20.10				
		8. HARY	16.28	8. GUJ	20.46	10. UP	20.03				
		9. MAHA	15.83	9. ORI	18.91	11. GUJ	19.40				
		10. PUN	15.54	10. PUN	17.37	12. HARY	18.24				
		11. UP	15.29	11. HARY	16.86	13. BIH	18.10				
		12. BIH	14.97	12. UP	16.03	14. MP	14.82				
		13. GUJ	14.20	13. MP	12.22	15. RAJ	13.17				
		14. MP	9.60	14. BIH	12.17	16. J&K	10.52				
		15. RAJ	9.55	15. RAJ	11.84	17. HP	6.34				
		16. J&K	8.79	16. J&K	9.53						
		17. HP	4.18	17. HP	6.02						
Kendall's W = 0.88*; df = 16											

(Continued)

Table 84 *(Continued)*

Sex of Workers	Degree of Diversification	1983		1994		2000		2012		2018	
		State	NFW (%)	State	NFW (%)	State	NFW (%)	State	NFW (%)	State	NFW (%)
Male + Female	> 50.0 (High)			1. WB	52.24	1. KER	61.70	1. KER	79.58	1. KER	80.15
				2. KER	51.77	2. TN	53.43	2. TN	66.53	2. PUN	73.96
						3. WB	53.36	3. PUN	64.22	3. HARY	72.59
								4. WB	63.17	4. TN	72.26
								5. J&K	59.75	5. WB	63.44
								6. HARY	59.06	6. J&K	59.26
								7. GUJ	53.12	7. GUJ	57.57
								8. KAR	51.49	8. ASM	54.54
								9. MAHA	50.90	9. BIH	54.46
								10. RAJ	50.15	10. KAR	54.27
										11. AP	52.54
										12. MAHA	52.21
										13. UP	51.55
										14. ORI	51.24
										15. RAJ	50.43
	≥ 25.0 and ≤ 50.0 (Medium)	1. WB	44.53	3. TN	47.40	4. HARY	47.47	11. UP	48.36	16. HP	44.38
		2. KER	43.56	4. PUN	43.57	5. PUN	46.83	12. AP	47.65	17. MP	37.31
		3. TN	41.25	5. HARY	43.05	6. MAHA	43.68	13. ASM	45.71		
		4. HARY	35.85	6. GUJ	41.05	7. GUJ	40.70	14. ORI	45.14		
		5. MAHA	34.22	7. MAHA	40.58	8. ASM	39.66	15. BIH	41.94		
		6. PUN	33.29	8. J&K	35.87	9. KAR	37.60				
		7. J&K	31.30	9. KAR	34.82	10. UP	36.49	16. HP	41.58		
		8. GUJ	31.29	10. AP	32.94	11. J&K	34.86	17. MP	38.07		
		9. AP	30.91	11. UP	30.95	12. AP	34.56				
		10. KAR	30.88	12. RAJ	30.84	13. RAJ	34.01				

(Continued)

Table 84 *(Continued)*

Sex of Workers	Degree of Diversification	1983		1994		2000		2012		2018	
		State	NFW (%)	State	NFW (%)	State	NFW (%)	State	NFW (%)	State	NFW (%)
Male + Female	≥ 25.0 and ≤ 50.0 (Medium)	11. UP	28.67	13. ASM	29.13	14. HP	31.15				
		12. ASM	27.36	14. ORI	26.25	15. ORI	29.41				
		13. ORI	26.67			16. BIH	26.94				
						17. MP	26.21				
	< 25. 0 (Low)	14. BIH	23.59	15. HP	23.98						
		15. RAJ	22.72	16. BIH	23.30						
		16. MP	20.19	17. MP	22.26						
		17. HP	17.31								
Kendall's W = 0.91*; df = 16											

Source: As in Table 76

*Notes: AP = Andhra Pradesh; ASM = Assam; BIH = Bihar; GUJ = Gujarat; HARY = Haryana; HP = Himachal Pradesh; J&K = Jammu & Kashmir; KAR = Karnataka; KER = Kerala; MP = Madhya Pradesh; MAHA = Maharashtra; ORI = Odisha; PUN = Punjab; RAJ = Rajasthan; TN = Tamil Nadu; UP = Uttar Pradesh; WB = West Bengal; * implies significance at 1% level.*

Focusing on females (rural and urban combined), most states in India were categorised as having 'low' employment diversification until 2000. As illustrated in Table 84, while twelve of the seventeen major states fell into this category in 2000, only two states (West Bengal and Kerala) were classified as having 'high' diversification, and three as having 'medium' diversification. The degree of employment diversification for females appears to have begun improving after 2000 in most states. By 2012, three states were positioned in the 'high' diversification category, and twelve states were in the 'medium' diversification category. From 1983 to 2000, West Bengal ranked first in female employment diversification, followed by Kerala. However, this pattern shifted after 2000, with Kerala taking first place in 2012 and 2018, West Bengal second in 2012, and Punjab in 2018. Besides these three states, Tamil Nadu, Assam, and Haryana are notable for having a 'high' percentage of female non-farm workers. Conversely, in three states (Himachal Pradesh, Jammu & Kashmir, and Rajasthan), this percentage is still considered 'low' as of 2018. It is also worth noting that from 1983 to 2018, Himachal Pradesh recorded the lowest percentage of female non-farm workers. The ranking pattern of the states regarding the percentage of female non-farm workers remained essentially unchanged throughout the period from 1983 to 2018, as indicated by the statistical significance of Kendall's W.

The states' employment diversification picture, encompassing both urban and rural areas, alters when considering males and females together. In 1983, none of the states fell into the 'high' diversification category; by 2018, fifteen of the seventeen states had transitioned to this category. A rising trend among males has primarily driven this shift in employment diversification patterns, while females have lagged considerably behind. Kerala has consistently topped the list of employment diversification across all years since 2000, while West Bengal held that position before then. In 2018, besides Kerala, other states with a notably high percentage of workers (over 70 %) in non-farm employment included Punjab, Haryana, and Tamil Nadu. Conversely, Madhya Pradesh recorded the lowest non-farm employment percentage in all years except 1983. Alongside Madhya Pradesh, Himachal Pradesh also fell into the 'medium' category for employment diversification in 2018. Notably, there has been no significant change in the ranking pattern of states by the percentage of non-farm workers from 1983 to 2018, as shown by the statistical significance of Kendall's W.

Overall, the pace of employment diversification in most states accelerated after 2000. However, this advantage was realised more by males than by females, leading to the percentage of male workers in non-farm employment surpassing 50 % in sixteen of seventeen states in 2018, whereas this occurred in only six states for females.

6.4.2 Rural Employment Diversification

Table 85 shows that, for rural males, the diversification of employment from the farm to the non-farm sector accelerated after 2000. Initially, only one state fell into the 'high' diversification states category in 2000 (Kerala). By 2012, five states were classified in the same category (Kerala, Jammu & Kashmir, Himachal Pradesh, Punjab, and Rajasthan), and this number rose to eight states by 2018 (Kerala, Jammu & Kashmir, Haryana, Tamil Nadu, Himachal Pradesh, Punjab, Bihar, and Assam). The progress of other states towards employment diversification for rural males is also evident, as they have advanced along the path of diversification over time, ensuring that no state was classified as having 'low' diversification in 2012 and 2018. It is also important to note that Kerala ranked highest among states in terms of rural males' employment diversification, while Madhya Pradesh consistently ranked lowest. Furthermore, the ranking pattern of the states did not change significantly, as indicated by Kendall's W.

The pattern of employment diversification for rural females differs from that of rural males. In most states, the degree of diversification was considered 'low' for rural females until about 2012. As illustrated in Table 85, as many as thirteen states remained in the 'low' diversification group. At the same time, two were classified as 'medium' diversification states in 2012, and two were classified as 'high' diversification states. This picture changed slightly in 2018, when two states moved into the 'high' diversification category, while seven states remained in the 'medium' category. Among Indian states, Kerala ranked first in terms of employment diversification for rural females in 2018, while Maharashtra ranked last. In 2018, Punjab recorded a 'high' degree of employment diversification for rural females, while Tamil Nadu, Assam, West Bengal, Odisha, Haryana, Bihar, and Andhra Pradesh fell in the medium diversification category. Conversely, the states with 'low' employment diversification for rural females include Himachal Pradesh, Jammu & Kashmir, Madhya Pradesh, Rajasthan, Gujarat, Karnataka, and Uttar Pradesh. However, no statistically significant change in the states' ranking pattern is observed from 1983 to 2018.

Table 85: States Arranged in Descending Order of Percentage of Rural Non-Farm Workers (RNFW) to Total Rural Workers (UPSS) in India

Sex of Workers	Degree of Diversification	1983		1994		2000		2012		2018	
		State	RNFW (%)	State	RNFW (%)	State	RNFW (%)	State	RNFW (%)	State	RNFW (%)
Male	> 50.0 (High)					1. KER	57.24	1. KER	71.82	1. KER	73.15
								2. J&K	64.11	2. J&K	66.68
								3. HP	60.21	3. HARY	63.85
								4. PUN	56.46	4. TN	62.05
								5. RAJ	50.04	5. HP	60.32
										6. PUN	59.31
										7. BIH	51.18
										8. ASM	50.01
	≥ 25.0 and ≤ 50.0 (Medium)	1. KER	42.16	1. KER	46.91	2. HP	46.20	6. HARY	49.49	9. WB	49.63
		2. TN	31.27	2. HARY	38.98	3. HARY	40.40	7. TN	48.40	10. RAJ	48.31
		3. HARY	28.50	3. J&K	38.70	4. TN	37.74	8. UP	43.36	11. ORI	45.59
		4. J&K	27.40	4. TN	36.13	5. PUN	36.24	9. WB	43.16	12. UP	43.60
		5. WB	26.80	5. WB	35.24	6. ASM	35.30	10. ASM	41.41	13. AP	38.70
				6. HP	34.20	7. WB	33.53	11. ORI	40.74	14. GUJ	37.40
				7. PUN	31.90	8. J&K	33.10	12. BIH	36.69	15. KAR	36.23
				8. RAJ	30.33	9. RAJ	32.70	13. AP	36.03	16. MAHA	32.37
				9. GUJ	28.90	10. GUJ	28.60	14. KAR	34.09	17. MP	28.96
						11. UP	28.20	15. MAHA	30.25		
						12. MAHA	26.20	16. GUJ	30.08		
						13. AP	25.60	17. MP	27.71		

(Continued)

Table 85 *(Continued)*

Sex of Workers	Degree of Diversification	1983		1994		2000		2012		2018	
		State	RNFW (%)	State	RNFW (%)	State	RNFW (%)	State	RNFW (%)	State	RNFW (%)
Male	< 25. 0 (Low)	6. AP	22.60	10. MAHA	24.78	14. ORI	23.15				
		7. PUN	22.55	11. AP	24.48	15. KAR	21.58				
		8. HP	22.10	12. UP	23.70	16. BIH	21.08				
		9. ORI	21.80	13. ASM	21.80	17. MP	15.80				
		10. UP	21.00	14. ORI	21.22						
		11. ASM	20.68	15. KAR	21.12						
		12. GUJ	20.30	16. BIH	18.00						
		13. MAHA	20.28	17. MP	12.71						
		14. RAJ	19.16								
		15. BIH	18.60								
		16. KAR	18.28								
		17. MP	12.66								
Kendall's W = 0.83*; df = 16											
Female	≥ 50.0 (High)							1. KER	61.30	1. KER	73.91
								2. WB	58.30	2. PUN	59.43
	≥ 25.0 and ≤ 50.0 (Medium)	1. KER	29.13	1. WB	41.16	1. WB	45.95	3. TN	49.42	3. TN	49.05
				2. KER	36.94	2. KER	40.26	4. ORI	30.69	4. ASM	48.42
										5. WB	48.12
										6. ORI	38.16
										7. HARY	33.90
										8. BIH	30.97
										9. AP	25.05

(Continued)

Table 85 *(Continued)*

Sex of Workers	Degree of Diversification	1983		1994		2000		2012		2018	
		State	RNFW (%)	State	RNFW (%)	State	RNFW (%)	State	RNFW (%)	State	RNFW (%)
Female	< 25. 0 (Low)	2. WB	24.80	3. TN	21.42	3. TN	24.10	5. PUN	24.59	10. UP	24.51
		3. ORI	18.90	4. ASM	16.72	4. ASM	20.68	6. AP	23.35	11. KAR	23.45
		4. TN	18.18	5. AP	16.22	5. ORI	19.60	7. RAJ	22.61	12. GUJ	18.62
		5. ASM	17.92	6. KAR	15.32	6. AP	15.70	8. ASM	20.95	13. RAJ	17.27
		6. AP	16.30	7. ORI	15.08	7. BIH	14.30	9. KAR	20.64	14. MP	15.28
		7. BIH	11.71	8. UP	9.82	8. UP	12.41	10. BIH	19.30	15. J&K	14.29
		8. KAR	11.70	9. GUJ	9.31	9. KAR	12.11	11. UP	16.81	16. HP	13.72
		10. HARY	9.99	10. MAHA	8.71	10. PUN	9.40	12. MP	15.90	17. MAHA	11.55
		11. PUN	7.20	11. BIH	7.92	11. MP	8.58	13. J&K	14.94		
		12. GUJ	7.10	12. PUN	7.21	12. RAJ	8.01	14. GUJ	14.44		
		13. MAHA	7.00	13. RAJ	7.09	13. GUJ	7.91	15. HARY	13.99		
		14. RAJ	6.09	14. HARY	6.89	14. HARY	7.90	16. HP	13.04		
		15. MP	4.47	15. MP	6.19	15. J&K	6.59	17. MAHA	10.88		
		16. J&K	3.80	16. J&K	4.41	16. MAHA	6.10				
		17. HP	2.50	17. HP	4.31	17. HP	4.90				
Kendall's W = 0.85*; df = 16											
Male + Female	> 50.0 (High)					1. KER	51.94	1. KER	68.70	1. KER	73.34
										2. PUN	59.32
										3. HARY	59.25
										4. TN	57.49
										5. J&K	52.28

(Continued)

Table 85 *(Continued)*

Sex of Workers	Degree of Diversification	1983		1994		2000		2012		2018	
		State	RNFW (%)	State	RNFW (%)	State	RNFW (%)	State	RNFW (%)	State	RNFW (%)
Male + Female	≥ 25.0 and ≤ 50.0 (Medium)	1. KER	36.94	1. KER	43.75	2. WB	36.28	2. J&K	49.61	6. ASM	49.81
		2. WB	26.28	2. WB	36.65	3. ASM	32.21	3. TN	48.79	7. BIH	49.55
		3. TN	25.64	3. TN	29.68	4. TN	32.04	4. PUN	47.76	8. WB	49.35
				4. HARY	28.20	5. HARY	31.65	5. WB	46.71	9. ORI	44.00
				5. PUN	25.40	6. PUN	27.67	6. HARY	41.82	10. UP	40.42
						7. HP	26.98	7. RAJ	39.20	11. HP	40.13
								8. ORI	37.82	12. RAJ	39.11
								9. ASM	37.77	13. AP	33.45
								10. HP	37.14	14. GUJ	33.43
								11. UP	36.58	15. KAR	32.85
								12. BIH	34.28	16. MAHA	25.51
								13. AP	30.65		
								14. KAR	29.87		
								15. GUJ	25.30		
	< 25. 0 (Low)	4. HARY	22.87	6. J&K	24.56	8. UP	23.87	16. MP	23.83	17. MP	24.52
		5. ORI	20.82	7. GUJ	21.15	9. J&K	23.66	17. MAHA	22.71		
		6. ASM	20.16	8. AP	20.78	10. RAJ	22.35				
		7. J&K	19.88	9. ASM	20.66	11. ORI	21.91				
		8. AP	19.87	10. HP	20.27	12. AP	21.27				
		9. UP	17.54	11. RAJ	20.14	13. GUJ	20.30				
		10. PUN	17.53	12. UP	19.92	14. BIH	19.40				

(Continued)

Table 85 *(Continued)*

Sex of Workers	Degree of Diversification	1983		1994		2000		2012		2018	
		State	RNFW (%)	State	RNFW (%)	State	RNFW (%)	State	RNFW (%)	State	RNFW (%)
Male + Female	< 25. 0 (Low)	11. BIH	16.41	13. ORI	19.04	15. KAR	17.94				
		12. KAR	15.71	14. KAR	18.74	16. MAHA	17.36				
		13. GUJ	14.80	15. MAHA	17.45	17. MP	12.89				
		14. MAHA	14.26	16. BIH	15.61						
		15. RAJ	13.41	17. MP	10.08						
		16. HP	12.88								
		17. MP	9.19								
Kendall's W = 0.82*; df = 16											

Source: Same as Table 84
Notes: Same as Table 84

Considering rural persons, the pace of employment diversification accelerated in the vast majority of states from 2012 onwards. As illustrated in the table, while only one state belonged to the 'high' category for the percentage of non-farm workers (which was Kerala) in 2012, as many as fourteen states fell into the 'middle' category, contrasting with the situation in 2000 when six states were in the 'middle' category and ten states in the 'low' category. Conversely, by 2018, five states, namely, Kerala, Punjab, Haryana, Tamil Nadu, and Jammu & Kashmir, had advanced to the 'high' diversification category, and eleven states were in the 'middle' category. In 2018, among Indian states, Kerala recorded the highest percentage of rural non-farm workers at 73.34 %, while Madhya Pradesh recorded the lowest at 24.52 %. From 1983 to 2018, the ranking of states by the percentage of non-farm workers among rural persons did not change significantly.

The above discussion suggests that rural employment diversification has gained momentum across most states since 2012, although the relative rankings of the states remain unchanged overall. Moreover, rural males have outpaced rural females in terms of employment diversification.

6.4.3 Growth Rates of Farm and Non-Farm Workers (Combined Rural and Urban Areas)

We now analyse the growth rates of farm and non-farm workers across seventeen major states over various sub-periods, considering both rural and urban areas collectively and examining males, females, and persons separately. Information on this is presented in Table 86.

6.4.3.1 Growth of Farm Workers

The important points to note regarding the growth of farm ('agriculture and allied') workers in the states are the following:

- During the pre-globalisation period (1983–1994), among males, states such as Uttar Pradesh, Bihar, and Madhya Pradesh ranked high for growth in farm employment. In these states, the growth rates of farm employment exceeded 2 % per annum. Conversely, an agriculturally advanced state like Punjab was positioned last in this category. For females, Jammu & Kashmir and Kerala occupied the top and bottom positions in terms of growth in farm employment, respectively. When considering both males and females together, Assam demonstrated the highest growth rate of farm employment during this period, while Punjab recorded the lowest.

Table 86: Annual Growth Rates of Workers (UPSS) in Agriculture & Allied and Non-Agricultural Sectors in the States (Rural & Urban Combined)

Period	State	Male				Female				Male + Female			
		Agrl. & allied		Non-agri-culture		Agrl. & allied		Non-agri-culture		Agrl. & allied		Non-agri-culture	
1983 to 1994	Andhra Pradesh	1.87	(5)	3.18	(12)	2.64	(5)	3.04	(12)	2.22	(3)	3.14	(11)
	Assam	1.99	(4)	3.17	(13)	4.33	(2)	4.27	(7)	2.49	(1)	3.34	(9)
	Bihar	2.40	(2)	2.01	(16)	-1.18	(15)	-3.40	(17)	1.33	(10)	1.17	(17)
	Gujarat	0.47	(13)	4.67	(4)	0.71	(13)	5.03	(5)	0.57	(14)	4.73	(3)
	Haryana	0.29	(14)	4.74	(3)	3.95	(3)	4.37	(6)	1.73	(8)	4.70	(4)
	Himachal Pradesh	1.15	(9)	5.87	(1)	2.46	(6)	6.28	(2)	1.86	(6)	5.91	(1)
	Jammu & Kashmir	-0.12	(16)	4.22	(5)	5.55	(1)	6.45	(1)	2.40	(2)	4.42	(5)
	Karnataka	1.47	(8)	3.29	(9)	2.01	(7)	3.92	(10)	1.70	(9)	3.45	(8)
	Kerala	1.13	(10)	3.23	(11)	-2.71	(17)	1.48	(13)	-0.44	(16)	2.74	(15)
	Madhya Pradesh	2.26	(3)	2.83	(14)	1.29	(10)	3.93	(9)	1.84	(7)	3.04	(12)
	Maharashtra	1.01	(11)	3.53	(8)	1.38	(9)	5.25	(4)	1.20	(12)	3.86	(7)
	Odisha	1.55	(7)	1.91	(17)	2.75	(4)	1.34	(14)	1.98	(4)	1.77	(16)
	Punjab	-0.37	(17)	3.79	(6)	-1.98	(16)	-0.73	(16)	-0.93	(17)	3.27	(10)
	Rajasthan	0.62	(12)	5.53	(2)	1.81	(8)	4.17	(8)	1.21	(11)	5.31	(2)
	Tamil Nadu	0.22	(15)	2.75	(15)	0.83	(11)	3.42	(11)	0.51	(15)	2.93	(14)
	Uttar Pradesh	2.48	(1)	3.26	(10)	0.74	(12)	1.28	(15)	1.91	(5)	2.98	(13)
	West Bengal	1.58	(6)	3.64	(7)	-0.78	(14)	5.46	(3)	0.99	(13)	4.01	(6)
1994 to 2000	Andhra Pradesh	0.01	(11)	1.18	(17)	-0.41	(9)	0.63	(11)	-0.19	(12)	1.02	(17)
	Assam	-1.09	(14)	7.66	(1)	0.00	(7)	4.92	(3)	-0.83	(14)	7.24	(1)
	Bihar	1.01	(5)	3.65	(6)	1.48	(3)	9.68	(2)	1.14	(4)	4.46	(2)
	Gujarat	2.32	(2)	2.29	(12)	2.44	(2)	1.31	(10)	2.38	(1)	2.13	(12)
	Haryana	1.99	(3)	3.39	(7)	-3.28	(17)	-1.73	(17)	-0.17	(11)	2.84	(8)
	Himachal Pradesh	-3.46	(16)	4.89	(2)	-0.34	(8)	0.56	(13)	-1.65	(15)	4.44	(3)
	Jammu & Kashmir	5.31	(1)	1.45	(15)	-1.33	(14)	0.49	(14)	2.10	(2)	1.35	(15)
	Karnataka	0.49	(6)	2.66	(10)	-0.55	(11)	0.28	(15)	0.05	(8)	2.08	(13)
	Kerala	-3.62	(17)	4.32	(3)	-1.14	(13)	3.47	(7)	-2.70	(17)	4.11	(4)
	Madhya Pradesh	0.19	(10)	3.84	(4)	0.27	(4)	4.07	(6)	0.22	(6)	3.89	(5)

(Continued)

Table 86 *(Continued)*

Period	State	Male				Female				Male + Female			
		Agrl. & allied		Non-agri-culture		Agrl. & allied		Non-agri-culture		Agrl. & allied		Non-agri-culture	
1994 to 2000	Maharashtra	0.22	(9)	3.19	(8)	0.07	(6)	−1.62	(16)	0.14	(7)	2.29	(11)
	Odisha	0.41	(8)	2.03	(14)	−0.66	(12)	4.57	(5)	0.02	(9)	2.68	(9)
	Punjab	−0.26	(12)	3.06	(9)	4.79	(1)	10.11	(1)	1.54	(3)	3.80	(7)
	Rajasthan	0.45	(7)	2.59	(11)	−0.46	(10)	1.58	(9)	−0.01	(10)	2.44	(10)
	Tamil Nadu	−1.19	(15)	2.09	(13)	−2.82	(16)	1.96	(8)	−1.98	(16)	2.05	(14)
	Uttar Pradesh	−0.52	(13)	3.75	(5)	0.10	(5)	4.74	(4)	−0.33	(13)	3.88	(6)
	West Bengal	1.15	(4)	1.27	(16)	−2.66	(15)	0.58	(12)	0.36	(5)	1.11	(16)
2000 to 2012	Andhra Pradesh	−1.07	(13)	3.59	(10)	−1.07	(8)	3.34	(12)	−1.07	(12)	3.52	(13)
	Assam	0.68	(4)	2.88	(14)	−0.27	(4)	0.24	(16)	0.45	(2)	2.55	(16)
	Bihar	0.18	(7)	5.68	(3)	−4.28	(16)	−0.70	(17)	−0.80	(11)	4.92	(4)
	Gujarat	0.85	(2)	3.56	(11)	−2.91	(14)	3.54	(11)	−0.68	(8)	3.55	(12)
	Haryana	0.45	(5)	3.68	(9)	−1.32	(10)	5.00	(6)	−0.16	(7)	3.81	(9)
	Himachal Pradesh	−1.15	(14)	3.44	(12)	1.34	(1)	10.31	(1)	0.44	(3)	4.31	(6)
	Jammu & Kashmir	−3.07	(16)	6.61	(1)	−0.74	(7)	7.44	(3)	−2.01	(16)	6.69	(1)
	Karnataka	−0.25	(9)	3.85	(7)	−2.48	(13)	3.09	(15)	−1.10	(13)	3.68	(11)
	Kerala	−4.36	(17)	2.27	(17)	−5.51	(17)	3.10	(14)	−4.79	(17)	2.48	(17)
	Madhya Pradesh	0.81	(3)	4.69	(4)	−1.27	(9)	4.57	(8)	−0.01	(6)	4.66	(5)
	Maharashtra	1.33	(1)	2.57	(16)	−0.41	(5)	4.76	(7)	0.50	(1)	2.96	(15)
	Odisha	−0.28	(10)	5.70	(2)	−1.53	(11)	3.22	(13)	−0.71	(9)	5.09	(2)
	Punjab	−1.83	(15)	3.84	(8)	−2.06	(12)	5.53	(4)	−1.92	(15)	4.07	(8)
	Rajasthan	−0.79	(12)	4.30	(6)	−0.64	(6)	8.15	(2)	−0.71	(10)	4.98	(3)
	Tamil Nadu	−0.35	(11)	2.65	(15)	−3.34	(15)	3.84	(9)	−1.62	(14)	2.99	(14)
	Uttar Pradesh	−0.10	(8)	4.36	(5)	0.54	(2)	3.60	(10)	0.10	(5)	4.26	(7)
	West Bengal	0.31	(6)	3.29	(13)	0.10	(3)	5.10	(5)	0.27	(4)	3.71	(10)
2012 to 2018	Andhra Pradesh	−0.94	(13)	1.27	(10)	−3.31	(7)	1.21	(6)	−2.02	(11)	1.23	(7)
	Assam	−0.08	(11)	3.54	(3)	−10.63	(15)	7.02	(1)	−1.60	(9)	4.38	(1)
	Bihar	−3.33	(15)	4.21	(1)	−10.74	(16)	0.62	(7)	−4.23	(15)	4.17	(2)
	Gujarat	−0.05	(10)	1.04	(13)	−6.98	(11)	−0.62	(10)	−2.19	(12)	0.80	(9)
	Haryana	−4.90	(17)	3.59	(2)	−9.94	(14)	4.13	(2)	−6.39	(17)	3.58	(3)
	Himachal Pradesh	1.25	(6)	1.27	(9)	−3.18	(6)	−2.84	(14)	−1.54	(8)	0.35	(13)

(Continued)

Table 86 *(Continued)*

Period	State	Male				Female				Male + Female			
		Agrl. & allied		Non-agri-culture		Agrl. & allied		Non-agri-culture		Agrl. & allied		Non-agri-culture	
2012 to 2018	Jammu & Kashmir	2.78	(1)	2.20	(5)	1.44	(3)	1.47	(4)	2.13	(2)	1.79	(5)
	Karnataka	0.15	(8)	0.93	(15)	-3.60	(8)	0.49	(8)	-1.18	(6)	0.68	(11)
	Kerala	1.24	(7)	-0.64	(17)	-6.80	(10)	-0.79	(11)	-1.38	(7)	-0.79	(17)
	Madhya Pradesh	2.40	(2)	1.80	(6)	2.93	(1)	2.63	(3)	2.65	(1)	2.10	(4)
	Maharashtra	1.38	(4)	0.83	(16)	-3.05	(5)	-0.89	(12)	-0.54	(4)	0.33	(14)
	Odisha	-1.64	(14)	1.09	(12)	-9.19	(12)	-3.01	(16)	-3.89	(14)	0.11	(15)
	Punjab	-0.74	(12)	1.28	(8)	-20.20	(17)	1.37	(5)	-6.26	(16)	1.19	(8)
	Rajasthan	2.36	(3)	1.14	(11)	-4.30	(9)	-8.34	(17)	-0.72	(5)	-0.53	(16)
	Tamil Nadu	-3.73	(16)	2.31	(4)	-1.79	(4)	-0.30	(9)	-3.02	(13)	1.45	(6)
	Uttar Pradesh	1.27	(5)	1.01	(14)	-9.28	(13)	-2.85	(15)	-1.82	(10)	0.69	(10)
	West Bengal	0.05	(9)	1.59	(7)	2.05	(2)	-2.53	(13)	0.34	(3)	0.53	(12)

Source: Same as Table 76
Note: Figures in parentheses are ranks among seventeen major states.

- However, in the first sub-period (1994 to 2000) of the post-globalisation era, Jammu & Kashmir ranked first regarding male farm employment growth, followed by Gujarat and Haryana in second and third place, respectively. During this period, Kerala reported the lowest growth in male farm employment. For females, the highest and lowest growth rates in farm employment were observed in Punjab and Haryana, respectively. When considering males and females together, Gujarat ranked first and Kerala last among the states in terms of farm employment growth during this sub-period.
- From 2000 to 2012, the growth of farm employment for males was highest in Maharashtra and lowest in Kerala. For females, the highest and lowest growth rates of farm employment were observed in Himachal Pradesh and Kerala, respectively. Conversely, across both males and females, the highest and lowest growth rates in farm employment were observed in Maharashtra and Kerala, respectively.
- During the final sub-period of the post-globalisation era (2012 to 2018), Jammu & Kashmir demonstrated the highest growth rate of farm employment for males, whereas Haryana held the lowest position. The highest and lowest rates were observed for females in Madhya Pradesh and Punjab, respectively. When considering males and females combined, Madhya Pradesh had the highest growth in farm employment, while Haryana recorded the lowest.

To understand the performance of the states regarding the growth of farm and non-farm employment throughout the entire post-globalisation period (1994–2018), we have also calculated the ranks of the states based on the average of ranks in different sub-periods of this period (Table 87). Concerning the growth of male farm employment during the post-globalisation period, Gujarat appears to be the best performer, followed by Maharashtra, Madhya Pradesh, Jammu & Kashmir, and West Bengal. In contrast, the states that perform poorly in this regard include Tamil Nadu, Kerala, Punjab, Andhra Pradesh, and Himachal Pradesh. Madhya Pradesh ranks first in the growth of female farm employment during the post-globalisation period, followed by Himachal Pradesh, Maharashtra, Uttar Pradesh, and West Bengal. The underperforming states in terms of female farm employment growth during this period include Haryana, Kerala, Tamil Nadu, Odisha, and Bihar. Considering both males and females together, the state that ranks first in terms of growth of farm employment during the post-globalisation period is Maharashtra, followed by West Bengal, Madhya Pradesh, Jammu & Kashmir, and Gujarat. The state that ranks last in this regard is Tamil Nadu, with Kerala, Haryana, Andhra Pradesh, and Punjab following it.

Table 87: States' Ranks Regarding Growth of Employment During the Entire Post-globalisation Period: Rural & Urban Combined

State	Male		Female		Male + Female	
	Agriculture & allied	Non-agriculture	Agriculture & allied	Non-agriculture	Agriculture & allied	Non-agriculture
Andhra Pradesh	14	15	6	10	14	14
Assam	11	3	9	3	6	3
Bihar	10	1	13	6	11	1
Gujarat	1	13	10	13	5	11
Haryana	8	4	17	5	15	4
Himachal Pradesh	13	6	2	8	8	5
Jammu & Kashmir	4	5	7	4	4	6
Karnataka	7	11	12	17	9	12
Kerala	16	16	16	14	16	16
Madhya Pradesh	3	2	1	2	3	2
Maharashtra	2	17	3	16	1	17
Odisha	12	9	14	15	12	8

(Continued)

Table 87 *(Continued)*

State	Male		Female		Male + Female	
	Agriculture & allied	Non-agriculture	Agriculture & allied	Non-agriculture	Agriculture & allied	Non-agriculture
Punjab	15	8	11	1	13	7
Rajasthan	6	10	8	9	7	10
Tamil Nadu	17	12	15	7	17	13
Uttar Pradesh	9	7	4	11	10	9
West Bengal	5	14	5	12	2	15

Source: Same as in Table 76

Note: The ranks in this table are computed from the average of ranks in different sub-periods

6.4.3.2 Growth of Non-Farm Workers

Let us now examine the growth of non-farm workers across 17 major states, encompassing both rural and urban areas. The relevant information on this aspect is also presented in Table 86. Important observations concerning the growth of non-farm workers during various sub-periods are as follows:

- The growth rate of the non-farm workers (considering males and females together) was highest in Himachal Pradesh and lowest in Bihar from 1983 to 1994 (pre-globalisation). The states that followed Himachal Pradesh in terms of growth in non-farm workers were Rajasthan, Gujarat, Haryana, Jammu & Kashmir, and West Bengal. All these states recorded growth rates of more than 4 % per annum among non-farm workers during this period. On the other hand, apart from Bihar, other relatively low-performing states in terms of non-farm worker growth are Odisha, Kerala, Tamil Nadu, and Uttar Pradesh. However, when we consider the males separately, it is found that from 1983 to 1994, while Himachal Pradesh continued to be the best performer in terms of growth of non-farm workers, Odisha occupied the last position in this regard. On the other hand, for the females, the first and last positions went to Jammu & Kashmir and Bihar, respectively.
- The states' performances concerning the growth of non-farm workers have not been uniform during different sub-periods of the post-globalisation era. For instance, considering males and females together, from 1994 to 2000, the states that performed well in this regard were Assam, Bihar, Himachal Pradesh, and Kerala, each recording a growth rate of over 4 % per annum. In contrast, Andhra Pradesh, West Bengal, and Jammu & Kashmir displayed relatively low growth rates, below 4 %. During the following sub-period, from 2000 to 2012,

Jammu & Kashmir led the list of states, while Kerala ranked last. This trend shifted again between 2012 and 2018, with Assam ranked first in growth of non-farm workers, while Kerala ranked last. Notably, Bihar followed Assam during this sub-period, as both states achieved growth rates exceeding 4 % per annum for non-farm workers.

- When examining males separately, it is clear that from 1994 to 2000, Assam topped the list of states, while Andhra Pradesh ranked last. In the subsequent sub-period (2000–2012), Jammu & Kashmir and Kerala held the first and last positions, respectively, in terms of the growth rate of male non-farm workers. During the final sub-period of the post-globalisation era (2012–2018), the growth rate of male non-farm workers was highest in Bihar and lowest in Kerala. Among females, from 1994 to 2000, Punjab ranked first in the growth of non-farm workers, while Haryana ranked last. However, in the next sub-period (2000–2012), the first and last positions were assigned to Himachal Pradesh and Bihar, respectively. From 2012 to 2018, while Assam led in the growth of female non-farm workers, Rajasthan came last.
- To gain insight into the overall performance of the states concerning the growth of non-farm workers throughout the post-globalisation period, we have ranked the states by averaging their ranks across the three sub-periods of this era. Detailed information is presented in Table 87. Among all states during the post-globalisation period, when considering males and females combined, Bihar has excelled, followed by Madhya Pradesh, Assam, Haryana, Himachal Pradesh, Jammu & Kashmir, Punjab, and Odisha. Conversely, the weakest performer in this context has been Maharashtra. Other states experiencing low growth in non-farm employment include Kerala, West Bengal, Andhra Pradesh, Tamil Nadu, Karnataka, and Gujarat. When examining males separately, Bihar again ranks first, while Maharashtra ranks last. In contrast, Punjab emerged as the top performer in increasing the number of non-farm workers during the post-globalisation period, whereas Karnataka ranked lowest.

6.4.4 Growth of Farm and Non-Farm Workers in Rural Areas Alone

Now, let us focus on the growth rates of farm (agriculture and allied) and non-farm workers during various sub-periods, specifically in rural areas. Details on the growth rates of farm workers are presented in Table 88. Our main observations here are the following:

- From 1983 to 1994 (pre-globalisation), Bihar experienced the highest growth rate in farm employment for rural males, at 2.42 % per annum, followed closely by Uttar Pradesh, Madhya Pradesh, and Assam. All these states, recognised as relatively underdeveloped, recorded farm employment growth rates exceeding 2 % during this period. In contrast, an advanced state like Punjab recorded the lowest growth and experienced negative farm employment growth of –0.33 % during the same timeframe. Jammu & Kashmir was the other state to register negative growth in farm employment in this period. However, the situation changed from 1994 onwards. Between 1994 and 2000, Jammu & Kashmir ranked first in farm employment growth for rural males, while Himachal Pradesh ranked last. Notably, apart from Jammu & Kashmir, no other state recorded a growth rate of more than 2 % in farm employment for rural males during this period. Conversely, six states, including Himachal Pradesh, Kerala, Tamil Nadu, Assam, Punjab, and Uttar Pradesh, recorded negative growth rates in farm employment for rural males during this time. The situation worsened further regarding farm employment growth for rural males in subsequent sub-periods, as ten of the seventeen states considered experienced negative growth rates during both the 2000–2012 and 2012–2018 periods. In these sub-periods, while Maharashtra recorded the highest growth rate (albeit below 2 %), the lowest was observed in Kerala.

- Regarding rural females, it is noted that between 1983 and 1994, Jammu & Kashmir recorded the highest growth rate (5.51 % per annum) for farm employment. In contrast, Kerala experienced the lowest rate at –3.15 %. It is also significant that, apart from Jammu & Kashmir, seven other states achieved more than a 2 % growth in farm employment for rural females: Assam, Haryana, Odisha, Andhra Pradesh, Himachal Pradesh, Karnataka, and Rajasthan. Conversely, aside from Kerala, three states that experienced negative growth in farm employment for rural females during this period are Punjab, Bihar, and West Bengal.
- Farm employment for rural females began to decline after 1994, with ten out of seventeen major states reporting negative growth rates between 1994 and 2000. Punjab experienced the highest growth in rural female farm employment during this period, while Haryana saw the lowest. The situation deteriorated further from 2000 to 2012, as fourteen of seventeen states recorded negative employment growth for rural females. From 2012 to 2018, the circumstances regarding female farm employment remained relatively unchanged, with twelve states still reporting negative growth rates. While Kerala ranked last in terms of farm employment growth for rural females from 2000 to 2012 and from 2012 to 2018, Himachal Pradesh and Maharashtra led the way during these sub-periods.

Table 88: States Arranged in Descending Order of Annual Growth Rates of Farm (Agriculture) Employment in Rural Areas

	1983 to 1994		1994 to 2000		2000 to 2012		2012 to 2018	
Sex	State	Gr. Rate	State	Gr. Rate	State	Gr. Rate	State	Gr. Rate
Male	1. BIH	2.42	1. J&K	5.04	1. MAHA	1.31	1. MAHA	1.31
	2. UP	2.42	2. GUJ	1.97	2. GUJ	1.00	2. GUJ	1.00
	3. MP	2.18	3. HARY	1.91	3. MP	0.77	3. MP	0.77
	4. ASM	2.04	4. WB	1.25	4. ASM	0.70	4. ASM	0.70
	5. AP	1.76	5. BIH	1.04	5. HARY	0.35	5. HARY	0.35
	6. ORI	1.53	6. KAR	0.78	6. WB	0.29	6. WB	0.29
	7. WB	1.50	7. MAHA	0.54	7. BIH	0.19	7. BIH	0.19
	8. KAR	1.45	8. RAJ	0.50	8. UP	−0.22	8. UP	−0.22
	9. HP	1.11	9. ORI	0.44	9. KAR	−0.42	9. KAR	−0.42
	10. MAHA	0.98	10. AP	0.29	10. ORI	−0.43	10. ORI	−0.43
	11. GUJ	0.83	11. MP	0.10	11. RAJ	−0.75	11. RAJ	−0.75
	12. RAJ	0.75	12. UP	−0.38	12. TN	−1.03	12. TN	−1.03
	13. KER	0.61	13. PUN	−0.43	13. AP	−1.06	13. AP	−1.06
	14. HARY	0.53	14. ASM	−1.23	14. HP	−1.21	14. HP	−1.21
	15. TN	0.19	15. TN	−1.23	15. PUN	−1.90	15. PUN	−1.90
	16. J&K	−0.05	16. KER	−2.24	16. J&K	−3.08	16. J&K	−3.08
	17. PUN	−0.33	17. HP	−3.40	17. KER	−5.83	17. KER	−5.83
Female	1. J&K	5.51	1. PUN	4.89	1. HP	1.35	1. MAHA	0.49
	2. ASM	4.40	2. GUJ	2.55	2. UP	0.52	2. ASM	0.46
	3. HARY	3.84	3. BIH	1.36	3. WB	0.06	3. HP	0.43
	4. ORI	2.70	4. UP	0.35	4. ASM	−0.30	4. WB	0.25
	5. AP	2.56	5. MAHA	0.24	5. MAHA	−0.40	5. UP	0.02
	6. HP	2.39	6. MP	0.22	6. RAJ	−0.55	6. MP	−0.05
	7. KAR	2.13	7. KER	0.15	7. AP	−1.02	7. HARY	−0.20
	8. RAJ	2.02	8. AP	−0.03	8. J&K	−1.05	8. GUJ	−0.60
	9. MAHA	1.47	9. ASM	−0.10	9. HARY	−1.25	9. RAJ	−0.65
	10. MP	1.22	10. HP	−0.26	10. MP	−1.31	10. BIH	−0.79
	11. TN	0.85	11. KAR	−0.29	11. ORI	−1.70	11. ORI	−0.86
	12. GUJ	0.84	12. RAJ	−0.39	12. PUN	−2.11	12. AP	−1.04
	13. UP	0.57	13. ORI	−0.60	13. KAR	−2.37	13. KAR	−1.17
	14. WB	−0.81	14. J&K	−0.87	14. GUJ	−2.90	14. PUN	−1.98
	15. BIH	−1.10	15. WB	−2.19	15. TN	−3.84	15. J&K	−2.14
	16. PUN	−2.00	16. TN	−2.78	16. BIH	−4.30	16. TN	−2.23
	17. KER	−3.15	17. HARY	−3.13	17. KER	−6.55	17. KER	−6.10

(Continued)

Table 88 *(Continued)*

	1983 to 1994		1994 to 2000		2000 to 2012		2012 to 2018	
Sex	**State**	**Gr. Rate**	**State**	**Gr. Rate**	**State**	**Gr. Rate**	**State**	**Gr. Rate**
Male + Female	1. ASM	2.54	1. GUJ	2.24	1. MAHA	0.49	1. MP	1.80
	2. J&K	2.42	2. J&K	2.16	2. ASM	0.46	2. J&K	0.48
	3. AP	2.13	3. PUN	1.47	3. HP	0.43	3. WB	−0.91
	4. ORI	1.95	4. BIH	1.12	4. WB	0.25	4. RAJ	−1.30
	5. HARY	1.82	5. WB	0.54	5. UP	0.02	5. HP	−1.58
	6. UP	1.81	6. MAHA	0.39	6. MP	−0.05	6. MAHA	−1.73
	7. HP	1.81	7. KAR	0.33	7. HARY	−0.20	7. KAR	−2.06
	8. MP	1.76	8. MP	0.15	8. GUJ	−0.60	8. UP	−2.30
	9. KAR	1.74	9. AP	0.14	9. RAJ	−0.65	9. ASM	−2.54
	10. RAJ	1.37	10. ORI	0.06	10. BIH	−0.79	10. AP	−2.63
	11. BIH	1.37	11. RAJ	0.05	11. ORI	−0.86	11. GUJ	−3.97
	12. MAHA	1.22	12. HARY	−0.13	12. AP	−1.04	12. ORI	−4.04
	13. WB	0.93	13. UP	−0.16	13. KAR	−1.17	13. TN	−4.64
	14. GUJ	0.83	14. ASM	−0.96	14. PUN	−1.98	14. BIH	−4.99
	15. TN	0.51	15. KER	−1.36	15. J&K	−2.14	15. PUN	−6.82
	16. PUN	−0.91	16. HP	−1.58	16. TN	−2.23	16. HARY	−7.48
	17. KER	−0.92	17. TN	−1.97	17. KER	−6.10	17. KER	−8.11

Source: Same as in Table 76

Note: AP = Andhra Pradesh; ASM = Assam; BIH = Bihar; GUJ = Gujarat; HARY = Haryana; HP = Himachal Pradesh; J&K = Jammu & Kashmir; KAR = Karnataka; KER = Kerala; MP = Madhya Pradesh; MAHA = Maharashtra; ORI = Odisha; PUN = Punjab; RAJ = Rajasthan; TN = Tamil Nadu; UP = Uttar Pradesh; WB = West Bengal

- Table 88 also provides information on the growth of farm employment, considering rural males and females together across various sub-periods. It is observed that, compared to just two states (Punjab and Kerala) exhibiting negative growth in farm employment between 1983 and 1994, the number of states with negative growth rose to six between 1994 and 2000, twelve between 2000 and 2012, and fifteen between 2012 and 2018. While Tamil Nadu recorded the lowest growth in farm employment in rural areas from 1994 to 2000, Kerala held this position during the two subsequent sub-periods. In contrast, the best-performing state in this regard was Gujarat from 1994 to 2000, Maharashtra from 2000 to 2012, and Madhya Pradesh from 2012 to 2018.

We can now concentrate on the growth of rural non-farm employment during our selected periods in the states. Table 89 provides information on this aspect. The key observations are the following:

Table 89: States Arranged in Descending Order of Annual Growth Rates of Rural Non-Farm (Non-Agricultural) Employment

Sex	1983 to 1994		1994 to 2000		2000 to 2012		2012 to 2018	
	State	Gr. Rate	State	Gr. Rate	State	Gr. Rate	State	Gr. Rate
Male	1. HP	7.11	1. ASM	10.47	1. J&K	7.86	1. BIH	5.79
	2. RAJ	6.75	2. HP	5.03	2. MP	6.95	2. ASM	4.84
	3. GUJ	5.42	3. KER	4.77	3. BIH	6.87	3. HARY	3.86
	4. WB	5.41	4. MP	4.42	4. ORI	6.66	4. TN	3.80
	5. HARY	5.15	5. BIH	4.40	5. UP	5.49	5. WB	3.24
	6. J&K	4.96	6. UP	3.59	6. RAJ	5.41	6. GUJ	3.21
	7. PUN	4.29	7. HARY	2.92	7. PUN	5.08	7. J&K	2.81
	8. UP	3.95	8. PUN	2.83	8. KAR	4.96	8. MP	2.44
	9. MAHA	3.50	9. RAJ	2.36	9. WB	3.77	9. MAHA	1.65
	10. KAR	3.20	10. ORI	2.33	10. HP	3.57	10. HP	1.52
	11. AP	2.78	11. MAHA	1.81	11. HARY	3.48	11. ORI	1.39
	12. ASM	2.69	12. GUJ	1.73	12. AP	3.09	12. UP	1.05
	13. KER	2.47	13. AP	1.30	13. MAHA	3.01	13. KAR	1.01
	14. TN	2.29	14. KAR	1.24	14. ASM	2.89	14. PUN	0.77
	15. MP	2.22	15. J&K	0.85	15. TN	2.64	15. RAJ	0.70
	16. BIH	2.03	16. WB	−0.01	16. GUJ	1.60	16. AP	0.40
	17. ORI	1.19	17. TN	−0.08	17. KER	−0.64	17. KER	−4.41
Female	1. HP	8.05	1. BIH	13.20	1. HP	10.78	1. ASM	9.10
	2. J&K	7.09	2. PUN	10.08	2. RAJ	10.01	2. HARY	7.38
	3. WB	6.55	3. J&K	6.41	3. PUN	7.70	3. MP	1.44
	4. KAR	5.21	4. MP	6.28	4. J&K	6.76	4. PUN	1.27
	5. MP	4.61	5. UP	4.86	5. TN	5.60	5. J&K	−0.81
	6. MAHA	3.79	6. ORI	4.79	6. MAHA	4.98	6. BIH	−1.47
	7. GUJ	3.71	7. ASM	4.35	7. MP	4.62	7. KAR	−2.21
	8. RAJ	3.61	8. KER	2.52	8. WB	4.29	8. HP	−2.44
	9. ASM	3.57	9. HP	2.01	9. HARY	4.16	9. UP	−2.46
	10. TN	2.83	10. RAJ	1.81	10. UP	3.54	10. AP	−2.49
	11. AP	2.50	11. WB	1.04	11. ORI	3.31	11. MAHA	−2.93
	12. UP	0.18	12. TN	−0.28	12. AP	3.12	12. GUJ	−3.47
	13. KER	0.17	13. GUJ	−0.46	13. KAR	2.93	13. TN	−3.62
	14. ORI	0.08	14. AP	−0.67	14. GUJ	2.72	14. ORI	−4.05
	15. HARY	−0.09	15. HARY	−0.73	15. KER	0.35	15. KER	−4.42
	16. PUN	−1.99	16. KAR	−4.70	16. ASM	−0.16	16. WB	−5.91
	17. BIH	−5.10	17. MAHA	−5.98	17. BIH	−1.38	17. RAJ	−10.18

(Continued)

Table 89 *(Continued)*

Sex	1983 to 1994		1994 to 2000		2000 to 2012		2012 to 2018	
	State	Gr. Rate	State	Gr. Rate	State	Gr. Rate	State	Gr. Rate
Male + Female	1. HP	7.20	1. ASM	9.48	1. J&K	7.76	1. ASM	5.79
	2. RAJ	6.19	2. BIH	5.67	2. MP	6.38	2. BIH	5.59
	3. WB	5.70	3. MP	4.89	3. RAJ	6.26	3. HARY	4.05
	4. J&K	5.11	4. HP	4.75	4. BIH	5.81	4. GUJ	2.54
	5. GUJ	5.10	5. KER	4.20	5. ORI	5.74	5. MP	2.45
	6. HARY	4.58	6. UP	3.76	6. PUN	5.40	6. J&K	2.29
	7. KAR	3.83	7. PUN	3.47	7. UP	5.23	7. TN	1.10
	8. PUN	3.63	8. ORI	3.05	8. KAR	4.47	8. WB	0.86
	9. MAHA	3.56	9. HARY	2.65	9. HP	4.43	9. MAHA	0.81
	10. UP	3.34	10. RAJ	2.28	10. WB	3.92	10. PUN	0.72
	11. ASM	2.85	11. GUJ	1.36	11. TN	3.67	11. HP	0.52
	12. MP	2.76	12. J&K	1.32	12. HARY	3.53	12. UP	0.38
	13. AP	2.68	13. AP	0.64	13. MAHA	3.34	13. KAR	0.23
	14. TN	2.46	14. MAHA	0.29	14. AP	3.10	14. ORI	0.14
	15. KER	1.80	15. WB	0.28	15. ASM	2.53	15. AP	−0.52
	16. ORI	0.86	16. TN	−0.15	16. GUJ	1.79	16. RAJ	−1.37
	17. BIH	0.79	17. KAR	−0.56	17. KER	−0.39	17. KER	−4.58

Source: Same as Table 76
Note: Same as Table 88

- For rural males, the growth of rural non-farm employment from 1983 to 1994 was highest in Himachal Pradesh at 7.11 % per annum. Other states that exhibited significant growth in rural non-farm employment for males (over 5 % per annum) during this period include Rajasthan, Gujarat, West Bengal, and Haryana. Conversely, Odisha recorded the lowest growth of rural non-farm employment for males at 1.19 %. Additionally, states that reported relatively low growth in this regard (below 2.5 %) include Bihar, Madhya Pradesh, Tamil Nadu, and Kerala. From 1994 to 2000, Assam recorded the highest annual growth in non-farm employment for rural males at 10.47 %, while Tamil Nadu recorded the lowest at −0.08 %. In all but four states (Assam, Bihar, Kerala and Madhya Pradesh), the growth rate of non-farm employment for rural males declined from 1994 to 2000 compared to the preceding period (1983–1994). However, non-farm employment growth for rural males improved in all states except Assam, Gujarat, Himachal Pradesh, and Kerala from 2000 to 2012, compared with prior periods. Between 2000 and 2012, the highest growth in rural non-farm employment for males was recorded in Jammu & Kashmir at 7.86 %, while the lowest was recorded in Kerala at −0.64 %. Besides

Jammu & Kashmir, six other states achieved more than 5 % annual growth in non-farm employment for rural males during this period: Madhya Pradesh, Bihar, Odisha, Uttar Pradesh, Rajasthan, and Punjab. The situation shifted again from 2012 to 2018, when only Bihar experienced more than 5 % growth in rural male non-farm employment. In contrast, Kerala saw the lowest and negative growth rates. It is also noteworthy that rural non-farm employment growth rates for males were lower in all states during 2012–2018 than in the previous period, except in Assam, Gujarat, Haryana, and Tamil Nadu.

- Regarding rural females, from 1983 to 1994, the highest annual growth of non-farm employment occurred in Himachal Pradesh (8.05 %), while three other states, namely, Jammu & Kashmir, West Bengal, and Karnataka, also experienced impressive growth (exceeding 5 %). Conversely, Bihar exhibited the lowest and most negative growth at –5.10 %. During this period, non-farm employment growth for rural females was also negative in Punjab and Haryana. Notably, Bihar and Punjab experienced a remarkable turnaround in the growth of rural females' non-farm employment from 1994 to 2000, with growth rates of 13.20 % and 10.08 %, respectively, ranking first and second. Additionally, Jammu & Kashmir and Madhya Pradesh recorded impressive growth rates exceeding 6 % during the same period. In contrast, six states, namely, Maharashtra, Karnataka, Haryana, Andhra Pradesh, Gujarat, and Tamil Nadu, reported negative growth in non-farm employment for rural females. In the subsequent period (2000–2012), two states (Himachal Pradesh and Rajasthan) achieved non-farm employment growth above 10 % for rural females, while three states (Punjab, Jammu & Kashmir, and Tamil Nadu) recorded growth rates exceeding 5 %. Bihar's growth rate remained the lowest at –1.38 %, and Assam was another state that displayed negative growth in non-farm employment for rural females during this period. The situation deteriorated significantly from 2012 to 2018, during which thirteen states recorded negative non-farm employment growth for rural females, with Rajasthan experiencing the highest negative growth rate.
- When considering males and females together, we find that the annual growth of non-farm employment in rural areas has been highest in Himachal Pradesh (7.2 %) and lowest in Bihar (0.79 %) from 1983 to 1994. During this period, four other states (Rajasthan, West Bengal, Jammu & Kashmir, and Gujarat) recorded more than 5 % annual growth in rural non-farm employment. From 1994 to 2000, Assam (9.48 %) and Karnataka (–0.56 %) recorded the highest

and lowest growth rates of non-farm employment for rural persons. The only other state that recorded more than 5 % growth in rural non-farm employment during this period is Bihar (5.67 %). The situation seems to have improved from 2000 to 2012, when seven states recorded over 5 % growth in rural non-farm employment, with Jammu & Kashmir (7.76 %) leading, followed by Madhya Pradesh, Rajasthan, Bihar, Odisha, Punjab, and Uttar Pradesh. Conversely, during this period, Kerala recorded the lowest and most negative growth of non-farm employment for rural persons. The growth rate of rural non-farm employment declined significantly again from 2012 to 2018 compared to the previous period. During this period, only two states recorded more than 5 % growth in rural non-farm employment: Assam (5.79 %) and Bihar (5.59 %). Meanwhile, three states experienced negative growth: Kerala, Rajasthan, and Andhra Pradesh.

6.4.4.1 Overall Performance of the States Regarding Growth in Farm and Non-Farm Employment in Rural Areas

To understand the overall performance of the states regarding the growth of farm and non-farm employment in rural areas during the post-globalisation era (1994–2018), we have computed their ranks based on the average of the ranks in the sub-periods of the said era. Table 90 presents relevant information. During the post-globalisation era, Maharashtra emerged as the top performer in the growth of male employment in the farm ('agriculture and allied') sector in rural areas, followed by Gujarat, Madhya Pradesh, West Bengal, and Rajasthan. Conversely, Kerala ranks the lowest in rural male farm employment growth, with Tamil Nadu, Punjab, Andhra Pradesh, and Himachal Pradesh also among the low-performing states. Regarding the growth of farm employment for rural females in the post-globalisation era, Himachal Pradesh stands out as the best performer, followed by Madhya Pradesh, Maharashtra, Uttar Pradesh, and West Bengal. Kerala is the worst performer in this aspect. Other states that have performed poorly in terms of growth in farm employment for rural females during the post-globalisation era include Haryana, Tamil Nadu, Odisha, and Karnataka. West Bengal emerges as the best performer when considering males and females together. At the same time, Kerala is the worst performer in terms of growth in farm employment in rural areas during the post-globalisation era. States that are performing relatively better in terms of farm employment growth for rural persons include Maharashtra, Madhya Pradesh, Jammu & Kashmir, and Gujarat.

Table 90: States' Ranks Regarding Growth of Employment in Rural Areas During the Entire Post-Globalisation Period

State	Male		Female		Male + Female	
	Agriculture & allied	Non-agriculture	Agriculture & allied	Non-agriculture	Agriculture & allied	Non-agriculture
Andhra Pradesh	14	17	6	14	12	17
Assam	10	3	10	5	8	3
Bihar	11	1	12	6	11	1
Gujarat	2	13	8	17	5	11
Haryana	9	4	16	8	15	6
Himachal Pradesh	13	5	1	4	6	7
Jammu & Kashmir	6	6	7	2	4	4
Karnataka	7	14	13	15	10	15
Kerala	17	16	17	16	17	16
Madhya Pradesh	3	2	2	3	3	2
Maharashtra	1	12	3	12	2	14
Odisha	12	8	14	11	14	9
Punjab	15	9	11	1	13	5
Rajasthan	5	10	9	9	7	10
Tamil Nadu	16	15	15	10	16	13
Uttar Pradesh	8	7	4	7	9	8
West Bengal	4	11	5	13	1	12

Source: Same as in Table 76

Note: Same as Table 87

Regarding the growth of rural non-farm employment in the post-globalisation era, Table 90 indicates that among males, the top performer has been Bihar, followed by Madhya Pradesh, Assam, Haryana, and Himachal Pradesh. The poorest performance has been recorded in Andhra Pradesh, with Kerala, Tamil Nadu, Karnataka, and Gujarat also showing poor results. Concerning rural females, the growth of non-farm employment during the post-globalisation period has been most successful in Punjab and least successful in Gujarat; other states performing relatively better include Jammu & Kashmir, Madhya Pradesh, Himachal Pradesh, and Assam, while those performing worse are Kerala, Karnataka, Andhra Pradesh, and West Bengal. When considering rural persons (males and females combined), it is found that West Bengal has emerged as the best performer in farm employment growth in rural areas during the post-globalisation era, whereas Kerala has displayed the worst performance. Conversely, Bihar led the growth of rural non-farm employment during this period, followed by Madhya Pradesh and Assam, two other underdeveloped states. Notably, Madhya Pradesh (ranking third) also shows impressive growth in farm employment during the post-globalisation era.

6.5 Relationship Between Income and Employment Growth in India

This section examines the relationship between income growth (as indicated by gross value added (GVA) growth) and employment growth (on a UPSS basis) by calculating employment elasticities across various periods. Employment elasticity is the ratio of employment growth to income growth. Consequently, the employment elasticity indicates how much employment increases with a 1 % increase in income over a specific period. By comparing employment elasticities across sectors of the economy, we can identify the sectors that are more employment-intensive. Sectors with a higher employment elasticity value are more employment-intensive than those with lower employment elasticity values.

Table 91 presents information on the annual compound growth rates of employment and income, as well as employment elasticities, across sectors at the all-India level for various periods. Excluding the 'mining & quarrying' sector from comparison as it has a very low share in total employment and income, we observe that, during the period 1983–1994 (pre-globalisation), the 'construction' sector enjoyed the highest value of employment elasticity (1.05), which is followed respectively by 'wholesale and retail trade' (0.66), 'transport, storage, and communication' (0.59), 'electricity, gas & water' (0.57), 'other services' (0.51), 'agriculture and allied' (0.41), and 'manufacturing' (0.37). During this period, the employment elasticity of the non-agricultural sector was much higher (0.52) than that of the 'agriculture and allied' sector (0.41). Considering all the sectors together, however, the employment elasticity in India stood at 0.38.

Table 91: Annual Growth Rates of Employment and Income in Different Sectors and Sectoral Elasticities in India

Period	Agriculture & allied	Mining & quarrying	Manufa-cturing	Electricity, gas & water supply	Constr-uction	Wholesale & retail trade	Transport, storage and communication	Other services	Non-agriculture	All Sectors
Growth rate of employment (UPSS)										
1983 to 1994	1.25	3.57	1.91	4.76	5.56	3.63	3.37	3.80	3.27	1.93
1994 to 2000	0.04	−2.80	1.58	−4.80	6.33	6.22	5.28	−0.75	2.66	1.02
2000 to 2012	−0.56	1.12	2.85	7.90	9.12	2.32	4.09	3.04	3.84	1.44
2012 to 2018	−1.29	−4.73	−1.18	1.24	1.60	0.77	2.77	2.14	0.95	−0.08
1994 to 2018	−0.59	−1.36	1.51	2.92	6.50	2.89	4.05	1.86	2.82	0.96
Growth rate of income (GVA)										
1983 to 1994	3.07	6.76	5.11	8.36	5.29	5.49	5.72	7.38	6.30	5.13
1994 to 2000	3.22	5.03	6.74	6.64	6.08	8.39	11.03	7.57	7.30	6.08
2000 to 2012	2.75	4.02	7.83	5.96	9.54	6.51	11.02	5.90	7.03	6.07
2012 to 2018	3.08	5.21	7.83	6.27	3.74	4.82	13.37	13.75	9.56	8.43
1994 to 2018	2.88	3.54	7.01	5.77	7.68	6.58	11.45	6.75	6.99	6.05
Elasticity										
1983 to 1994	0.41	0.53	0.37	0.57	1.05	0.66	0.59	0.51	0.52	0.38
1994 to 2000	0.01	−0.56	0.23	−0.72	1.04	0.74	0.48	−0.10	0.37	0.17
2000 to 2012	−0.20	0.28	0.36	1.32	0.96	0.36	0.37	0.52	0.55	0.24
2012 to 2018	−0.42	−0.91	−0.15	0.20	0.43	0.16	0.21	0.16	0.10	−0.01
1994 to 2018	−0.21	−0.38	0.22	0.51	0.85	0.44	0.35	0.28	0.40	0.16

Source: Author's computation using data from NSSO employment/unemployment surveys (38th, 50th, 55th, and 68th rounds); PLFS 2017–18; and GVA data from RBI

Notes: (i) 'Other services' include banking & insurance, real estate, ownership of dwellings, business services and the remaining services, and (ii) Non-agriculture = All sectors excluding Agrl. & allied

Examining the entire post-globalisation period (1994–2018), it becomes evident that all sectors experienced a decline in their elasticity values. The most significant drop was observed in the 'agriculture and allied' sector, which turned negative (–0.21) due to a decrease in employment growth. The employment elasticity for the non-agricultural sector in the post-globalisation era stands at 0.40, which is also considerably lower than its pre-globalisation level.

If we consider the various sub-periods of the post-globalisation era, some intriguing facts emerge regarding sectoral employment elasticities. Firstly, the employment elasticity of the 'agriculture and allied' sector remained negative in all sub-periods after 2000. This, combined with the decline in the employment elasticity in the non-agricultural sector, resulted in the overall employment elasticity turning negative (–0.01) from 2012 to 2018. Secondly, due to a significant decrease in employment growth across sectors during 2012–2018, employment elasticity diminished in all sectors compared to the previous sub-period (2000–2012). Thirdly, in addition to the 'agriculture and allied' sector, two other sectors that recorded a negative employment elasticity during 2012–2018 were 'manufacturing' (–0.15) and 'mining & quarrying' (–0.91). Finally, during 2012–2018, the highest value of employment elasticity was observed in the 'construction' sector (0.43), followed by the 'transport, storage and communication' (0.21), 'electricity, gas, and water' (0.20), 'wholesale and retail trade' (0.16) and 'other services' (0.16).

6.5.1 Employment Elasticities Across the States

Considering all sectors, we have calculated employment elasticities for seventeen major states across two periods (1983–1994 and 1994–2018). This information is presented in Table 92. Jammu & Kashmir secured the highest employment elasticity in both the pre- and post-globalisation periods (1.19 and 0.41, respectively). At the same time, the lowest values were recorded by Punjab during 1983–1994 (0.13) and Kerala during 1994–2018 (0.03). Other states that demonstrated relatively better performance regarding employment elasticity in the later period include Assam, Madhya Pradesh, and West Bengal, with values above 0.25. The states with very low employment elasticities during 1994–2018 are Andhra Pradesh, Odisha, Tamil Nadu, and Karnataka, all of which have employment elasticities of 0.10 or less. Another striking observation from Table 92 is that all states (except Punjab) experienced a decline in employment elasticity from 1994 to 2018, compared to the period from 1983 to 1994. The highest rate of decrease was observed in Odisha (88 %), while Madhya Pradesh experienced the lowest decrease (39 %).

Table 92: Elasticity of Employment in Major States

State	Elasticity		Rank	
	1983–1994	1994–2018	1983–1994	1994–2018
Andhra Pradesh	0.42	0.06	10	16
Assam	0.89	0.34	2	2
Bihar	0.47	0.17	8	7
Gujarat	0.42	0.13	11	10
Haryana	0.48	0.16	7	8
Himachal Pradesh	0.50	0.10	6	12
Jammu & Kashmir	1.19	0.41	1	1
Karnataka	0.41	0.10	12	13
Kerala	0.23	0.03	16	17
Madhya Pradesh	0.46	0.28	9	3
Maharashtra	0.31	0.15	14	9
Odisha	0.55	0.06	3	15
Punjab	0.13	0.19	17	5
Rajasthan	0.38	0.13	13	11
Tamil Nadu	0.28	0.08	15	14
Uttar Pradesh	0.51	0.18	5	6
West Bengal	0.51	0.25	4	4

Source: Author's computation using data from NSSO employment/unemployment surveys (38th and 50th rounds), PLFS 2017–18, and state-level NSDP data from RBI

The decline in employment elasticity in India during the post-globalisation period (1994–2018), compared to the pre-globalisation period (1983–1994), has been relatively widespread, with all states (except one) experiencing such a decline, albeit at varying rates. This decrease may be attributed to a significant decline in the overall employment growth rate, particularly in the 'agriculture and allied' sector.

6.6 Choice of Sector of Employment by the Workers in India

In this section, we aim to identify some determinants of workers' choice of employment sector (non-farm or farm) in India, using unit-level data from the PLFS 2018. We have estimated logit regression models in which the dependent variable is a binary variable that takes the value of '1' if the worker opts for non-farm employment and '0' if farm employment is chosen. Table 93 presents a list of explanatory variables we considered. These variables encompass both individual and household-level characteristics of the workers. Individual factors include age, sex, marital status, and workers' formal and technical education. Household-level characteristics consist of household size, caste, and the religion of the households to which the workers belong. Workers' personal and household characteristics are assumed to affect their decisions between non-farm and farm employment.

Table 93: List of Explanatory Variables Used in Logit Regression

Variable name	Definition	
age	Age of the person (in years)	
sex	Sex dummy (1 = male; 0 = female)	
hsize	Size of household	
marstat	Marital status dummy (1 = currently married; 0 = otherwise)	
sg1	Social group dummy 1 (1 = SC; 0 = otherwise)	Base category: 'Others'
sg2	Social group dummy 2 (1 = ST; 0 = otherwise)	
sg3	Social group dummy 3 (1 = OBC; 0 = otherwise)	
rel1	Religious group dummy 1 (1 = Muslim; 0 = otherwise)	Base category: 'Hindu'
rel2	Religious group dummy 2 (1 = Others, excluding Hindu and Muslim; 0 = otherwise)	
attendcur	Current attendance of any educational institution (1 = yes; 0 = no)	
gedu1	General education dummy 1 (1 = up to primary; 0 = otherwise)	Base category: 'Illiterate'
gedu2	General education dummy 2 (1 = above primary & up to secondary; 0 = otherwise)	
gedu3	General education dummy 3 (1 = higher secondary & graduation; 0 = otherwise)	
gedu4	General education dummy 4 (1 = post-graduation & above; 0 = otherwise)	

(Continued)

Table 93 *(Continued)*

Variable name	Definition
vtraining	Vocational training dummy (1 = received; 0 = not received)
techedu	Technical education dummy (1 = received; 0 = not received)

Source: Generated by author using unit-level data from PLFS (2017–18)

We have estimated two logit regression models: one that considers both rural and urban areas and another that focuses solely on rural areas. When rural and urban areas are combined, the logit regression results (Table 93) indicate that the probability of selecting non-farm employment is higher for younger, unmarried, and male workers. This probability also increases for individuals with higher education levels, those not currently enrolled in formal education, those who have completed technical or vocational training, and those from larger households. Additionally, it was found that compared to 'Others' (general castes), the probability of choosing non-farm employment is lower for SCs, STs, and OBCs. Furthermore, the likelihood of opting for non-farm employment is higher for Muslims but lower for individuals of other religions compared to Hindus. All estimated coefficients for the explanatory variables are statistically significant, and the model itself is statistically significant, as indicated by the computed Chi-square.

The results regarding the determinants of workers' employment-sector choices in rural areas are nearly identical to those observed for rural and urban areas combined. The only difference is that SCs and OBCs in rural areas were likelier to choose employment in the non-farm sector than 'Others'. Moreover, the probability of selecting non-farm employment in rural areas is higher for those currently attending educational institutions, although the estimated coefficient is statistically insignificant. The estimated model remains significant overall.

Based on the results above, it can be asserted that the likelihood of choosing non-farm employment over farm employment is greater among males, younger individuals, and more educated, unmarried individuals who possess technical education and/or vocational training. This likelihood also appears to be higher among workers from the general caste and Hindu families, as well as those from larger households.

Table 94: Logit Regression Results of Determinants of Choice of Sector of Employment by the Workers in India [Dep. Variable: fnf = 1 if employed in non-farm sector; fnf = 0 if employed in farm sector]

Explanatory variables	Rural Areas Only						Rural and Urban Areas Combined					
	Model 1			Model 2			Model 1			Model 2		
	Est. coeff.	*z*-value	*p*-value	Est. coeff.	*z*-value	*p*-value	Est. coeff.	*z*-value	*p*-value	Est. coeff.	*z*-value	*p*-value
age	−0.02	−32.26	0.00	−0.02	−36.53	0.00	–	–	–	−0.01	−25.55	0.00
sex	–	–	–	0.52	27.59	0.00	0.73	58.67	0.00	0.41	29.13	0.00
hsize	0.01	4.45	0.00				0.01	5.25	0.00	–	–	–
marstat	–	–	–	−0.07	−3.23	0.00	–	–	–	−0.22	−13.71	0.00
sg1	0.27	11.92	0.00	–	–	–	−0.28	−15.84	0.00	–	–	–
sg2	−0.43	−16.11	0.00	–	–	–	−1.21	−55.46	0.00	–	–	–
sg3	0.15	7.49	0.00	–	–	–	−0.28	−18.44	0.00	–	–	–
rel1	–	–	–	0.48	18.75	0.00	–	–	–	0.78	38.35	0.00
rel2	–	–	–	−0.42	−13.16	0.00	–	–	–	−0.46	−19.52	0.00
attendcur	0.03	1.45	0.15	–	–	–	−0.33	−25.56	0.00	–	–	–
gedu1	–	–	–	0.35	15.24	0.00	–	–	–	0.49	26.80	0.00
gedu2	–	–	–	0.69	33.97	0.00	–	–	–	0.94	57.72	0.00
gedu3	–	–	–	1.21	46.49	0.00	–	–	–	1.72	83.97	0.00
gedu4	–	–	–	2.20	26.91	0.00	–	–	–	3.08	48.51	0.00
vtraining	–	–	–	0.13	6.26	0.00	–	–	–	0.06	3.55	0.00
techedu	–	–	–	0.81	10.72	0.00	2.17	37.87	0.00	1.08	18.21	0.00
35 state dummies	Estimated coefficients not reported						Estimated coefficients not reported					
	LR Chi-sq = 9048.19 (df = 41; p-value = 0.00)			LR Chi-sq = 13316.09 (df = 46; p-value = 0.00)			LR Chi-sq = 19372.28 (df = 41; p-value = 0.00)			LR Chi-sq = 25094.39 (df = 46; p-value = 0.00)		
	No. of obs. = 88,190			No. of obs. = 88,190			No. of obs. = 1,50,018			No. of obs. = 1,50,018		

Source: Authors' computation using unit-level data from PLFS 2017–18

Notes: (i) z-values are computed using White's robust standard errors; and (ii) Alternative models have been estimated to avoid multicollinearity problem.

6.7 Summary of Findings

Employment diversification from the 'agriculture and allied' sector to non-agricultural sectors occurred in India between 1983 and 2018, progressing slowly until around 2000 and then accelerating, particularly in rural areas. As a result, the percentage of non-agricultural workers (considering both rural and urban areas) rose from 31 % in 1983 to 40 % in 2000 and to 56 % in 2018. Among various non-agricultural sectors, the most notable expansion in the proportion of non-agricultural workers was recorded in 'construction' and 'trade (wholesale and retail)'. Conversely, 'manufacturing' not only failed to increase its workforce share over time but also experienced a slight decline in 2018 (12 %) compared to 2012 (13 %). More specifically, manufacturing in urban areas saw a decrease of 4 percentage points in its share of total workers from 1983 to 2018, while rural areas experienced a marginal improvement. In 2018, the shares of urban and rural manufacturing workers were 23 % and 8 %, respectively.

From 1983 to 2018, a significantly higher percentage of female workers were employed in the 'agriculture and allied' sector than males. Although the percentage of non-agricultural workers increased for males and females over time, a considerable gap between them persisted. In 2018, 60 % of male workers in the country were employed in the non-agricultural sector, compared to 43 % of females. We also found that 'construction' and 'trade' were the most important non-agricultural sectors for employment among males, while 'other services' were key for females.

When we examined the industrial classification of workers' economic activities at the two-digit level, it became clear that 'crop and animal production, hunting and related activities' was the most significant sub-sector, employing 44 % of the country's total workforce in 2018. That year, other notable sub-sectors in terms of employment included 'construction of buildings' (8.85 %), 'retail trade, except motor vehicles and motorcycles' (8.02 %), 'land transport and transport via pipeline' (4.49 %), 'education' (3.78 %), and 'manufacture of wearing apparel' (2.10 %). It was also found that seventy-two sub-sectors (out of eighty-seven at the two-digit level) accounted for less than 1 % of the total workers. Moreover, fifty-six sub-sectors experienced some growth in the percentage of workers in 2018 compared to 2012; the most significant increase was in 'construction of buildings', which rose by 1.17 percentage points. Additionally, three sectors – 'land transport and transport via pipeline', 'education', and 'retail trade, except motor vehicles and motorcycles' – saw an increase of more than 0.5 percentage points in their share of workers during this period.

Overall, there is clear evidence of increased employment diversification from 2012 to 2018, as indicated by the rising value of the Simpson Diversification Index

(SDI). When examining the data for males and females separately, it becomes apparent that the most significant sub-sectors for males have been 'crop production, hunting, and related activities', 'construction of buildings', 'retail trade, except motor vehicles and motorcycles', 'land transport and transport via pipeline', and 'education', which together accounted for 68 % of male workers in the country in 2018. Conversely, in the same year, the predominant sub-sectors for females were 'crop production, hunting, and related activities', 'education', 'retail trade, except motor vehicles and motorcycles', 'manufacture of wearing apparel', 'activities of households as employers of domestic personnel', and 'manufacture of tobacco products', which employed 78 % of female workers. Nevertheless, when SDI values are calculated separately for males and females, it is found that the degree of employment diversity was more pronounced among males than among females.

We examined the sectoral distribution of workers by socio-religious groups. In analysing the sectoral distribution of workers across various social groups, we observed that while workers from weaker social groups (ST, SC, and OBC) tend to find employment primarily in 'agriculture and allied', those from higher social groups ('Others') are more often employed in the non-agricultural sector. This pattern remains consistent when considering males and females separately. However, it also becomes evident that, among the non-agricultural sectors, the percentage of workers in 'construction' is higher among the weaker social groups than among 'Others'. Conversely, workers from higher social groups constitute a larger share of the workforce in manufacturing, trade, and services.

Regarding the sectoral distribution of workers by religious group, we note that 'agriculture and allied' and 'other services' are the sectors that employ a higher percentage of male Hindu workers than male Muslim workers. However, 'construction', 'trade', 'manufacturing', and 'transport, storage and communication' employ a higher percentage of male Muslim workers than their Hindu counterparts. For females as well, the percentage of workers in 'agriculture and allied' is higher for the Hindu group compared to the Muslim group. A significant percentage of Muslim female workers are employed in manufacturing (35 % in 2018, compared to 11 % for Hindu women). When considering males and females together, it is observed that while Hindus have a higher percentage of workers in 'agriculture and allied', and 'other services', Muslims have a higher share in 'non-agriculture'. Among the non-agricultural sectors, Muslim workers are more concentrated in 'manufacturing' and 'trade' than Hindu workers. Even in 'construction' and 'transport, storage and communication', the higher presence of Muslim workers is evident.

Examining the growth rates of workers in different sectors, we observed that in rural areas, the growth rate for 'agriculture and allied' has been declining continuously from 1983 to 2018 for both males and females. Thus, while the growth rate of male workers in rural areas was 1.25 % from 1983 to 1994, it became negative (–0.24 %) during the period from 1994 to 2018; the corresponding figures for rural females in the two periods were 1.22 % and –1.96 %, respectively. Another important observation is that the growth rate of rural female workers in the 'agriculture and allied' sector has declined sharply since 2000, with no indication of a reversal in this trend in the subsequent period. Among the rural non-agricultural sectors, the two sectors that recorded higher growth rates for male and female workers from 1994 to 2018 than from 1983 to 1994 are 'construction' and 'transport, storage and communication'. However, the rural non-agricultural sector registered a marginal decline in the growth rate of workers during the latter period compared to the former. Conversely, in urban areas, the growth rate of workers declined for both males and females from 1994 to 2018, compared with 1983 to 1994, in all sectors except 'manufacturing' and 'transport, storage and communication'. Overall, a dismal picture emerges regarding total employment growth in the country following globalisation. This decline can be attributed to the negative growth rate of agricultural employment after 2000, while the growth rate of non-agricultural employment remained positive.

While discussing the growth rate of workers across various sub-sectors at a two-digit level, we observed that fifty-six sub-sectors (out of a total of 87) accounted for approximately 42 % of the country's workforce in 2018 and experienced positive growth in workers from 2012 to 2018. However, among these sub-sectors, those with a lower share of total workers showed higher growth rates. For example, 'construction of building', which constituted 8.85 % of the total workforce in 2018, recorded an annual growth rate of 2.32 % from 2012 to 2018. Conversely, the 'activities of extraterritorial organisations and bodies' achieved the highest growth rate (37.28 %) during this period, despite their share of total workers being a mere 0.004 % in 2018. It is also important to note that 'crop and animal production, hunting and related service activities', which represented almost 44 % of all workers in the country in 2018, saw negative growth in employment during this timeframe, significantly contributing to the overall negative employment growth (when considering all sectors) from 2012 to 2018. Other notable sectors experiencing negative employment growth during this period include 'manufacture of textiles', 'public administration and defence; compulsory social security', 'civil engineering', 'other personal service activities', 'manufacture of food products', 'manufacture of other non-metallic mineral products', and 'manufacture of tobacco products'.

We have also examined the shares of various sectors in changes in total workers over time to identify which sectors create employment. Our observation is that although the absolute number of workers in the 'agriculture and allied' sector declined during the period from 1994 to 2018 (decreasing by 13.23 lakh per year), the number of workers in the 'non-agricultural' sector grew (increasing by 53.24 lakh per year), resulting in a total increase of workers by 40.01 lakh per year. Among the 'non-agricultural' sectors, the significant contributors to the rise in the number of workers during this period were 'construction', 'wholesale & retail trade', 'other services', 'manufacturing', and 'transport storage, etc.' (in descending order of their contributions). It is also important to note that the decline in the absolute number of workers in the 'agriculture and allied' sector during 1994 to 2018 was primarily due to a reduction in the number of female workers, which fell by 13.70 lakh per year – a trend that is in stark contrast to the increase of 11.27 lakh per year seen during the period from 1983 to 1994. When comparing the changes in the absolute number of workers across different sectors from 1994 to 2018, we can identify 'construction', 'wholesale & retail trade', 'transport, storage and communication', and 'manufacturing' as the emerging sectors employing males, while for females, the key sectors are 'other services' and 'construction'.

We have examined the employment diversification patterns across seventeen major states. Considering the rural and urban areas together, diversification accelerated after 2000 in most states. While none of the states reported having more than 50 % of their workforce in non-agricultural employment in 1983, three states reported the same in 2000 and 15 states in 2018. However, males benefited more from the diversification process than females, as their share of non-agricultural workers exceeded 50 % in sixteen of seventeen states in 2018, whereas this was achieved in only six states for females. As of 2018, Kerala ranked first in the percentage of non-agricultural workers, while Madhya Pradesh ranked last. Diversification in most states accelerated from 2012 to 2018, when we focused solely on rural areas. Thus, whereas only one state (Kerala) was reported to have more than 50 % of rural workers in non-farm employment in 2012, five states reported achieving this in 2018 (these are Kerala, Punjab, Haryana, Tamil Nadu, and Jammu & Kashmir). In 2018, Kerala again recorded the highest percentage of rural non-farm workers (73.34 %), with Madhya Pradesh (24.52 %) having the lowest. Another important observation is that despite the percentage of non-agricultural workers increasing in all states, their relative ranking did not change significantly from 1983 to 2018.

Our discussion of the employment growth rates in the 'agriculture and allied' (farm) sector compared to the non-agricultural sector (non-farm) across 17 major states indicates that between 1983 and 1994, Assam was the top-performing state in terms of farm employment growth, followed by Jammu & Kashmir and Andhra Pradesh, each with growth rates exceeding 2 % per annum. Conversely, Punjab and Kerala experienced negative growth rates during this period. Considering average growth rates across sub-periods from 1994 to 2018, Maharashtra emerged as the best performer, while Tamil Nadu was the worst. Regarding non-farm employment growth from 1983 to 1994, Himachal Pradesh was the leading state, whereas Bihar ranked the lowest. However, from 1994 to 2018, the situation changed significantly, with Bihar leading the growth in non-farm employment and Maharashtra falling to the bottom of the ranking.

Focusing specifically on rural areas and considering both males and females, we found that five states recorded more than 5 % growth in non-farm employment from 1983 to 1994: Himachal Pradesh, Rajasthan, West Bengal, Jammu & Kashmir, and Gujarat (in descending order of their growth rates). Conversely, Bihar and Odisha were the two states that recorded less than 1 % growth in rural non-farm employment during this period. However, over the entire period from 1994 to 2018, Bihar emerges as the best performer, while Andhra Pradesh is the poorest performer. It is also noteworthy that, in the sub-period from 2012 to 2018, while Assam and Bihar recorded more than 5 % growth in rural non-farm employment, Kerala, Rajasthan, and Andhra Pradesh experienced negative growth. During this period, the significant employment growth in the rural non-farm sector in Assam was attributed to the high growth of female workers (9.10 % per annum). In contrast, in Bihar, the growth was driven by male workers (5.79 % per annum).

One effective way to identify employment-intensive economic sectors is to examine their employment elasticities. Our analysis indicates that, at the all-India level, from 1983 to 1994, the 'construction' sector had the highest employment elasticity value at 1.05, followed by 'wholesale and retail trade' at 0.66, 'transportation, storage, etc.' at 0.59, 'electricity, gas, and water' at 0.57, 'other services' at 0.51, 'agriculture and allied' at 0.41, and 'manufacturing' at 0.37. The employment elasticity value for all sectors combined was 0.38 for this period. However, from 1994 to 2018, all sectors experienced declining employment elasticity values. During this period, the most significant drop occurred in the 'agriculture and allied' sector, where its employment elasticity value fell to a negative (–0.21). As a result, the employment elasticity across all sectors combined fell to 0.16 during this period. We also observed that adverse employment elasticity was a feature of the 'agriculture and allied' sector in all the sub-periods after 2000. Consequently, the employment elasticity became negative (–0.01) for all sectors combined from

2012 to 2018. Two other sectors experiencing negative employment elasticity during this period are 'manufacturing' and 'mining & quarrying'.

We examined employment elasticities across states and found that Jammu & Kashmir had the highest elasticity for both periods, at 1.19 and 0.41, respectively. In contrast, the lowest employment elasticity was observed in Punjab from 1983 to 1994 (0.13) and in Kerala from 1994 to 2018 (0.03). Another notable observation is that all major states (except Punjab) experienced a decline in employment elasticity from 1994 to 2018 compared to the earlier period from 1983 to 1994. While the significant drop in the employment growth rate in the 'agricultural & allied' sector can explain a large part of this trend, the decline in employment growth in the non-agricultural sector has also contributed.

We examined the factors influencing workers' choices between non-farm and farm employment using the PLFS 2018 data. To achieve this, we estimated two logit regression models: one combining rural and urban regions and another focusing solely on the rural region. In these models, the dependent variable is binary, taking the value '1' if a worker chooses non-farm employment and '0' if they decide on farm work. The explanatory variables include various personal and household characteristics of the workers. The results from both models are generally consistent. Overall, we found that the probability of choosing non-farm employment over farm employment is higher for individuals who are young, unmarried, male, better educated, and possess technical education or vocational training. Furthermore, this likelihood seems to be greater among workers from the general caste, those from Hindu families, and those from larger households.

Shifts in India's Employment Landscape (2018–2024)

7.1 Introduction

In the previous four chapters, we examined various changes in India's employment landscape from 1983 to 2018. We also compared the employment performance of different population segments during the pre-globalisation (1983–1994) and post-globalisation (1994–2018) periods. One conclusion that emerged strongly from the discussions in those chapters is that, while the country's employment performance deteriorated during the post-globalisation period compared to the pre-globalisation period across all population segments, this decline was especially pronounced among females and those living in rural areas. From a quantitative perspective, such deterioration became evident when we examined indicators such as the labour force participation rate, workforce participation rate, and employment growth rate, among others.[1] The quality of employment has been far from satisfactory, as fewer than one-fourth of all workers in the country were engaged in regular employment in 2018. More than two-fifths of rural and more than one-fifth of urban workers did not surpass the official poverty line, thus being classified as 'working poor'.

The present chapter further extends the discussion, utilising the most recent data to investigate whether there have been any changes in the employment landscape over the past six years, from 2018 to 2024, across the country and in its major states. For this purpose, we examine labour force participation rates, workforce participation rates, modes of employment, sectoral composition of

[1] Similar to previous chapters, this chapter follows the usual principal plus subsidiary status (UPSS) concept to measure the employed, unemployed, and those out of the labour force among individuals of all ages. We have utilised the Periodic Labour Force Survey (PLFS) data for 2017–18 and 2023–24. For brevity, these years are referred to as 2018 and 2024.

the workforce, labour force and workforce growth rates, the incidence of working poor, and other relevant aspects. These aspects have been examined across regions, genders, age groups, educational levels, and social and religious groups at the all-India level. For the state-level discussion, we considered indicators such as labour force and workforce participation rates, their growth rates from 2018 to 2024, modes of employment for workers, and the extent of employment diversification measured by the proportion of non-agricultural workers to the total workers. The employment-generating capacity of economic growth, as revealed by the growth rate of GVA/NSDP in the country and the states during this period, has been assessed by computing the employment elasticities. Additionally, we have employed a combination of quantitative and qualitative employment indicators to form a composite index. This index ranks states based on their overall employment performance in 2024, allowing us to compare these rankings with their 2018 employment performance rankings. This chapter specifically focuses on determining whether the current employment scenarios differ from those observed in 2018 or earlier.

The chapter is divided into five sections. The second section examines changes in the quantitative aspects of employment from 2018 to 2024, while the third section focuses on the qualitative elements during the same period. The fourth section examines the relative employment performance of the states in 2024 compared to their performance in 2018. The concluding section summarises the main findings of this chapter.

7.2 Changes in Quantity Aspects of Employment

7.2.1 Labour Force Participation Rates by Gender and Region in India

We begin by examining labour force participation rates (LFPRs) at the all-India level by gender and region. The data presented in Table 95 indicate that, as in previous years, the LFPR remains higher in rural areas than in urban areas, and for males than for females. In rural areas, the male LFPR was 57.9 % in 2024, while the female LFPR was 35.6 %. These figures are 59.0 % and 22.3 % in urban areas, respectively. Combining rural and urban areas, the female LFPR is 26.5 percentage points lower than the male LFPR, suggesting that females continue to lag significantly behind males in labour force participation.

Table 95: Labour Force Participation Rates (LFPR) by Region and Gender in India for 2024

Region	Gender	LFPR (%)	% pt change over 2018
Rural	Male	57.9	3.0
	Female	35.6	17.4
	Male + Female	46.8	9.8
Urban	Male	59.0	2.0
	Female	22.3	6.4
	Male + Female	41.0	4.2
Rural + Urban	Male	58.2	2.6
	Female	31.7	14.2
	Male + Female	45.9	9.0

Source: Author's computation using unit-level data from PLFS (2017–18 and 2023–24)

However, the most significant fact emerging from Table 95 is that the improvement in the LFPR for females in 2024 compared to 2018 was significantly higher than that for males, particularly in rural areas. In rural areas, the LFPR for males increased by only 3.0 percentage points from 2018 to 2024, while the improvement for females was nearly six times greater at 17.4 percentage points. Even in urban areas, females recorded a higher rate of improvement in the LFPR than males, as evidenced by the fact that the female LFPR increased by 6.4 percentage points from 2018 to 2024, while the male LFPR increased by only 2.0 percentage points. Combining rural and urban areas, females increased their LFPR by 14.2 percentage points, while males raised theirs by 2.6 percentage points from 2018 to 2024. Overall, although females still lagged behind males in LFPR in 2024, their improvement from 2018 to 2024 was significant, particularly in rural areas. This improvement in female LFPR led to a 9.0 percentage-point increase in the country's LFPR (combining males and females across rural and urban areas) during this period.

It is worth noting that the observed increase in LFPR in 2024, particularly among females, starkly contrasts with the trends observed in 2018. This increase has not occurred suddenly. Figure 2 illustrates the trends in the LFPR using data from all Periodic Labour Force Surveys conducted to date. It is observed that the LFPR has been consistently rising from 2018 to 2024 for both genders and regions. Of course, the increase in the LFPR has been more significant for females than for males.

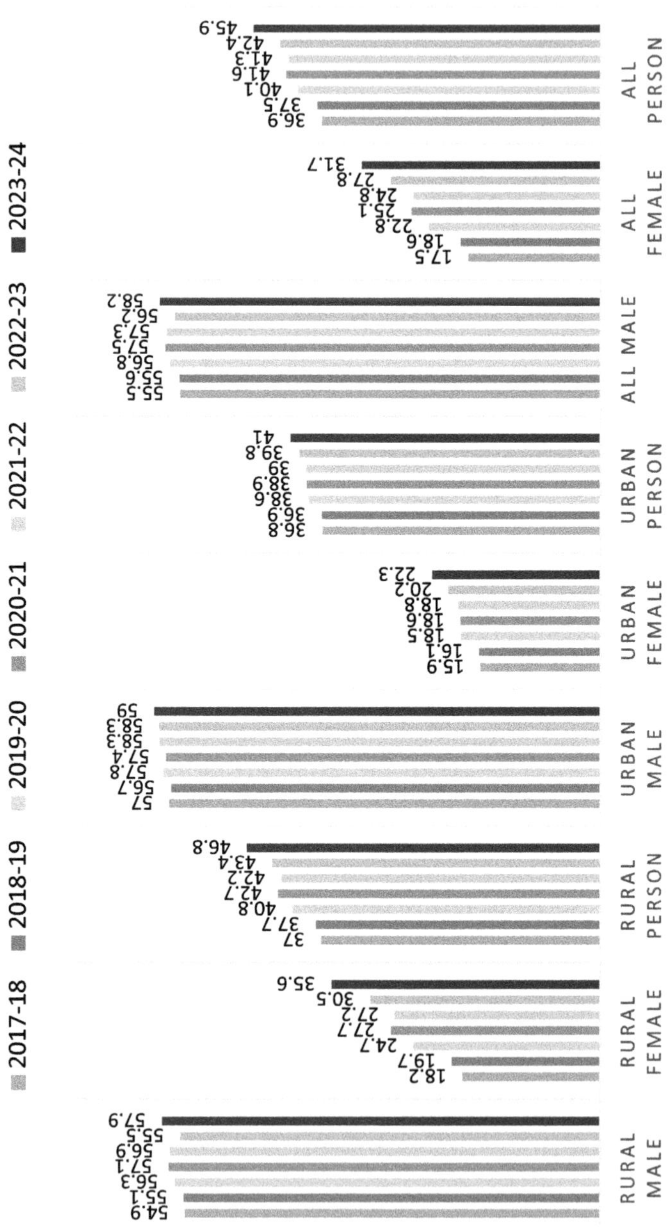

Figure 2: Labour Force Participation Rates in India from 2018 to 2024
Source: PLFS reports for 2017–18 through 2023–24

7.2.2 Labour Force Participation Rates by Age, Education, Social, and Religious Groups

Now, let us examine the LFPR across different age, educational, social, and religious groups in 2024 and observe the changes compared to 2018. Table 96 presents LFPR information for these categories. It is noted that, similar to the years before 2018, the LFPR in 2024 remains very low for males and females under 15. The LFPR gradually increases with age among individuals aged 15–59 and declines thereafter. This pattern holds for both genders. Among these individuals, the LFPR is highest for males aged 25 to 34 and females aged 35 to 59. In 2024, all age groups for males and females, except those under 15 years old, show improved LFPRs compared to 2018. However, the most significant increase in male LFPR in 2024 compared to 2018 occurred in the 15–24 age group (5.2 percentage points), while the most substantial increase for females was observed in the 35–59 age group (25.3 percentage points).

Table 96: Labour Force Participation Rates Across Age, Education, Social, and Religious Groups in India for 2024 (Rural & Urban Combined)

	Category	Male		Female		Male + Female	
		LFPR (%)	% pt change over 2018	LFPR (%)	% pt change over 2018	LFPR (%)	% pt change over 2018
Age Groups	0–4	0.0	0.0	0.0	0.0	0.0	0.0
	5–14	0.7	-0.5	0.6	0.3	0.7	-0.1
	15–24	49.5	5.2	23.4	11.5	36.9	8.0
	25–34	97.6	1.5	45.3	17.2	70.8	9.4
	35–59	97.1	0.6	57.4	25.3	77.1	12.9
	60 & above	51.4	4.0	22.0	11.6	36.3	7.2
Education Groups	Illiterate	41.1	-7.6	35.8	14.7	38.0	5.5
	Below Primary	23.7	-0.5	16.5	7.6	20.2	3.3
	Primary	54.7	0.9	31.8	16.7	43.6	8.5
	Middle	73.2	4.7	34.2	19.0	55.4	10.4
	Secondary / H.S.	68.9	6.6	27.8	13.7	50.8	8.6
	Graduate & above	87.0	5.3	41.5	8.1	67.2	5.5
Social Groups	ST	59.5	3.3	46.8	20.2	53.0	11.2
	SC	57.7	1.5	32.2	14.0	45.1	7.5
	OBC	57.5	2.9	31.2	14.1	44.4	8.2
	Others	59.6	3.4	26.2	11.5	43.2	7.3
Religious Groups	Hindus	58.7	2.8	33.3	14.7	46.2	8.5
	Muslims	54.9	2.8	21.4	11.5	38.2	7.0
	Christians	57.1	1.2	38.3	15.5	47.5	8.3
	Others	60.9	3.1	29.2	11.3	45.4	6.9

Source: Same as Table 95

Regarding various educational groups, the LFPR increases with higher educational levels among individuals (except for the 'secondary/H.S.' level). This observation is further solidified when we exclude the 'illiterates' from consideration. The LFPR is highest for males and females with a 'graduate' education or higher. When we compare the LFPR of different educational groups in 2024 with those in 2018, we find that, for males, the LFPR declined in 2024 for those who are 'illiterates' and those with 'below primary' education. However, none of the female educational groups experienced a decline in LFPR in 2024 compared to 2018. Among males, the most significant improvement in LFPR from 2018 to 2024 occurred in the 'secondary/H.S.' education group (6.6 percentage points). For females, the largest improvement was noted in the 'middle' education group (19.0 percentage points). When considering both males and females together, the 'middle' education group shows the largest improvement in LFPR between 2018 and 2024, rising by 10.4 percentage points.

Table 96 shows that, although there is no clear link between LFPR and social class background among males in 2024, LFPR continues to decrease among females as we move from lower to higher social groups. In 2024, the male LFPR was highest in the 'Others' category, while for females, it peaked in the ST category. Males and females across all social group categories improved their LFPR in 2024 compared to 2018. However, the rate of improvement was greater for females than for males. For males, the increase in LFPR ranged from 3.4 percentage points in the 'Others' category to 1.5 percentage points in the SC category. Conversely, the improvement in LFPR for females ranged from 20.2 percentage points in the ST category to 11.5 percentage points in the 'Others' category. When considering males and females combined, it is clear that the LFPR gradually declines as we move from lower to higher social groups. A similar pattern is observed in the percentage-point improvement in LFPR from 2018 to 2024, except for the OBC category.

When examining the LFPR for religious groups, we observe that, as in the past, Hindus have a higher LFPR in 2024 than Muslims. This pattern is evident for both males and females; however, the disparity in LFPR between Hindu and Muslim females is significantly more than between Hindu and Muslim males. Both Hindu and Muslim males saw their LFPR improve by 2.8 percentage points in 2024 compared to 2018. Conversely, for Hindu and Muslim females, the improvements in LFPR were 14.7 and 11.5 percentage points, respectively.

7.2.3 Workforce Force Participation Rates by Gender and Region in India

Table 97 presents data on workforce participation rates (WPR) by gender and region for 2024, highlighting changes since 2018. In line with the trend of higher LFPR for males compared to females, the WPR for males also remained higher than that of females. In rural areas, the female WPR is 34.8 %, compared to 56.3 % for males. The gap between male and female WPRs is wider in urban areas than in rural areas. Thus, while the WPR among males in urban areas was 56.4 %, it was 20.7 % among females. It was also found that the WPR is higher in rural areas than in urban areas among females, whereas among males, it is nearly the same in both rural and urban areas. When we examine changes in the WPR from 2018 to 2024, we observe that rural females increased their WPR by as much as 17.3 percentage points in 2024 compared to 2018. For rural males, this increase was only 4.6 percentage points. Although the rise in the WPR in urban areas from 2018 to 2024 was lower for both males and females, the increase in WPR for females was greater (6.5 percentage points) than for males (3.4 percentage points). When combining rural and urban areas and males and females, the all-India level WPR increased by 9.0 percentage points between 2018 and 2024, primarily driven by a rise in WPR among females. Furthermore, examining the data from 2018 to 2024 (Figure 3), it is evident that the upward trend in WPR across India has been consistent throughout this period.

Table 97: Workforce Participation Rates (WPR) by Gender and Region in India for 2024

Region	Gender	WPR (%)	% pt change over 2017–18
Rural	Male	56.3	4.6
	Female	34.8	17.3
	Male + Female	45.6	10.6
Urban	Male	56.4	3.4
	Female	20.7	6.5
	Male + Female	38.9	5.0
Rural + Urban	Male	56.4	4.3
	Female	30.7	14.2
	Male + Female	43.7	9.0

Source: Same as Table 95

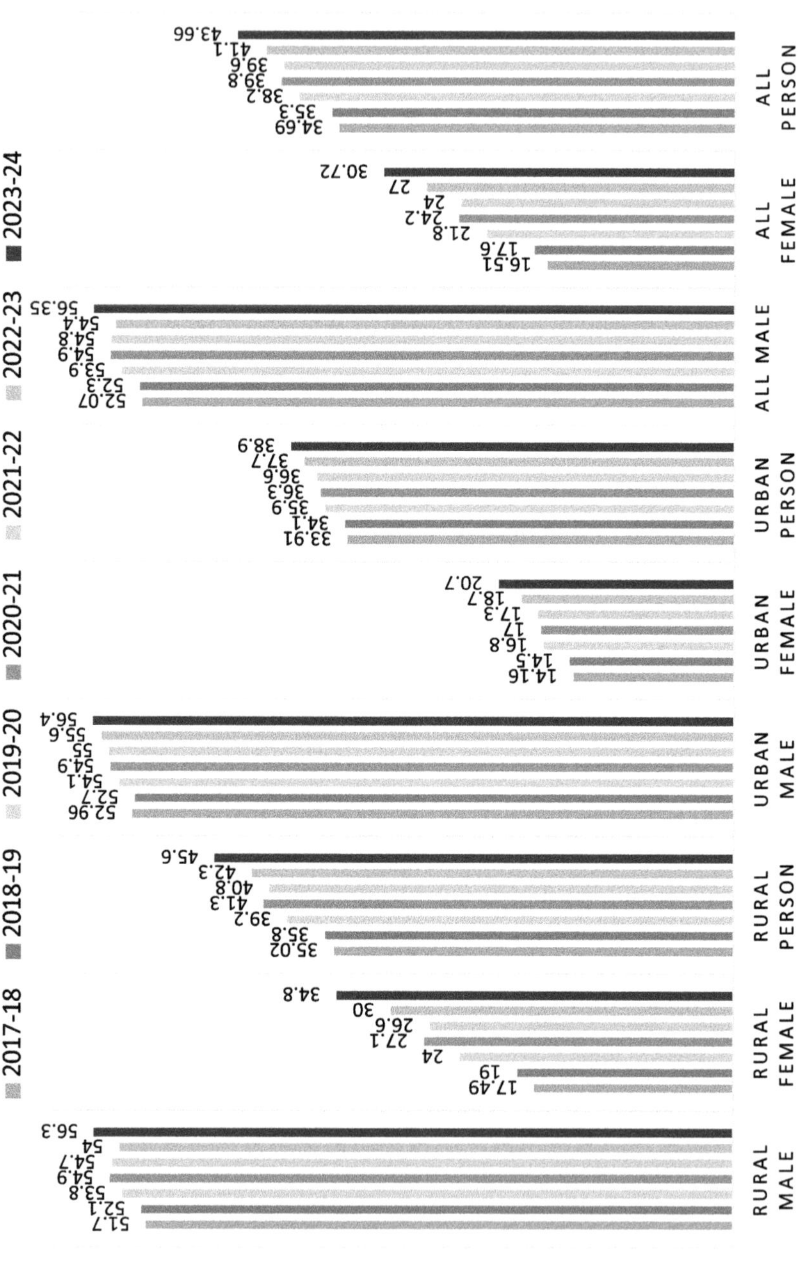

Figure 3: Workforce Participation Rates in India from 2018 to 2024
Source: Same as Figure 2

7.2.4 Workforce Participation Rates by Age, Education, Social, and Religious Groups

The information on workforce participation rates (WPR) by age, education, social, and religious groups in 2024 is presented in Table 98. Regarding the WPR by age group, the overall pattern is similar to that observed for the LFPR. For individuals aged 15 to 59, WPR increases with age. This is true for both males and females. In both sexes, the WPR is highest in the 35–59 age group. All age groups aged 15 and older showed an improvement in their WPR in 2024 compared to 2018. However, the highest increase is observed among males in the 15–24 age group (9.6 percentage points) and females in the 35–59 age group (25.4 percentage points). It is also worth noting that the rate of improvement in WPR value from 2018 to 2024 was higher for females than for males across all age groups.

Regarding the WPR of educational groups, Table 98 shows a trend of increasing WPR among males as they progress through the educational hierarchy (except for the 'secondary/H.S.' category). For them, the highest WPR value in 2024 is found in the 'graduate & above' education group. In contrast, there is no clear relationship between WPR and the education group for females, with the highest WPR recorded among the 'illiterates'. Additionally, it is worth noting that the WPR improved for all educational groups in 2024 compared to 2018, except for males with less than primary education and those categorised as 'illiterates'. Further, in line with the general trend, the extent of improvement in WPR for females was more significant than that for males in each educational group (except for 'graduate & above'). For males, the most significant improvement in WPR is observed among those with a 'secondary/H.S.' education (8.7 percentage points), while for females, it is noted among those with a 'middle' level education (19.3 percentage points).

Table 98: Workforce Participation Rates Across Age, Education, Social, and Religious Groups in India for 2024 (Rural & Urban Combined)

	Category	Male		Female		Male + Female	
		WPR (%)	% pt change over 2018	WPR (%)	% pt change over 2018	WPR (%)	% pt change over 2018
Age Groups	0–4	0.0	0.0	0.0	0.0	0.0	0.0
	5–14	0.7	−0.1	0.6	0.4	0.7	0.1
	15–24	43.1	9.6	20.4	11.4	32.2	10.3
	25–34	93.7	4.0	42.7	16.8	67.5	10.4
	35–59	96.8	1.2	57.2	25.4	76.8	13.2
	60 & above	51.3	4.2	22.0	11.6	36.3	7.3

(Continued)

Table 98 *(Continued)*

	Category	Male		Female		Male + Female	
		WPR (%)	% pt change over 2018	WPR (%)	% pt change over 2018	WPR (%)	% pt change over 2018
Education Groups	Illiterate	41.0	–5.2	35.8	15.1	37.9	6.9
	Below Primary	23.6	–0.1	16.5	7.7	20.1	3.5
	Primary	54.1	2.5	31.7	16.8	43.2	9.4
	Middle	71.9	7.4	33.9	19.3	54.5	12.1
	Secondary / H.S.	66.5	8.7	26.9	14.2	49.1	10.1
	Graduate & above	78.4	8.5	32.8	7.5	58.6	6.6
Social Groups	ST	58.2	4.8	46.0	20.1	52.0	12.1
	SC	55.6	3.2	31.3	13.9	43.6	8.4
	OBC	55.7	4.4	30.2	14.2	43.1	9.0
	Others	57.6	5.0	25.0	11.5	41.5	8.0
Religious Groups	Hindus	56.9	4.3	32.3	14.8	44.7	9.2
	Muslims	53.2	4.8	20.7	11.6	37.0	8.1
	Christians	54.6	3.0	36.3	16.0	45.2	9.4
	Others	58.0	3.7	27.4	10.7	43.0	7.0

Source: Same as Table 95

Examining the WPR across social groups, we observe that while there is no clear link between WPR and social groups for males in 2024, the WPR for females steadily decreases as we move from lower to higher social groups. However, the WPR is highest for both males and females in the 'ST' group. Although all social groups improved their WPR figures in 2024 compared to 2018, the degree of improvement was more substantial for females than males, regardless of their social class. An important point to note is that the most notable increase in WPR from 2018 to 2024 occurred in the 'Others' group for males (5.0 percentage points) and in the 'ST' group for females (20.1 percentage points).

When examining the WPR values for religious groups, it appears that Hindus had an advantage over Muslims in 2024. Furthermore, the gap in WPR values between these two groups has been more pronounced among females than males. Thus, while Hindu and Muslim males have WPR values of 56.9 and 53.2, respectively, the corresponding figures for Hindu and Muslim females are 32.3 and 20.7, respectively, in 2024. Again, while males and females from these religious groups improved their WPR in 2024 compared to 2018, the improvement was greater for females than for males. Another observation is that while Muslim males recorded a slightly higher improvement in WPR in 2024 compared to 2018 (4.8 percentage points) than their Hindu counterparts (4.3 percentage points), the rate of improvement for Hindu females was higher at 14.2 percentage points compared to Muslim females at 11.6 percentage points.

7.2.5 Absolute Numbers and Growth Rates of the Labour Force and Workforce in India

We will now examine the total number of males, females, and persons (males and females combined) in the labour force and workforce, along with their growth rates in India (Table 99). Notably, the number of males in the labour force rose from 386.5 million to 418.6 million between 2018 and 2024. However, the number of females in the labour force increased significantly during this period, rising from 115.3 million to 215.9 million. Thus, the proportion of females in the labour force increased from approximately 23 % in 2018 to 34 % in 2024. During this period, 5.4 million males and 16.8 million females joined the labour force each year, highlighting a significant increase in female participation. Correspondingly, the annual labour force growth rate during this period was 1.34 % for males and 11.02 % for females. Table 99 also illustrates a notable increase in the growth rate of the female labour force from 2018 to 2024, with a 11.32 percentage-point rise, compared to the growth rate recorded between 1994 and 2018. In contrast, males experienced a decline in growth rate of 0.37 percentage points from 2018 to 2024, relative to the previous period.

Table 99: Absolute Numbers and Annual Growth Rates of the Labour Force (UPSS) and Workers (UPSS) for India (Rural and Urban Combined)

Year / Growth rate	Labour force (in millions)			Workers (in millions)		
	Male	Female	Male + Female	Male	Female	Male + Female
2018	386.5	115.3	501.8	362.6	108.7	471.3
	(77.25)	(22.75)	(100)	(77.14)	(22.86)	(100)
2024	418.6	215.9	634.5	405.3	209.2	614.5
	(65.98)	(34.02)	(100)	(65.96)	(34.04)	(100)
Average annual change from 2018 to 2024 (in millions)	5.4	16.8	22.1	7.1	16.7	23.9
	(24.2)	(75.8)	(100)	(29.9)	(70.1)	(100)
Annual compound growth rate from 2018 to 2024	1.34	11.02	4.04	1.88	11.52	4.57
% pt change over growth rate from 1994 to 2018	−0.37	11.32	2.91	0.35	12.02	3.61

Source: Author's computation using NSSO unit-level data from Employment & Unemployment Survey (50th Round) and PLFS (2017–18 and 2023–24)
Note: The figures in parentheses show the percentage of males and females out of the total.

The patterns of change in workforce numbers and growth rates for males and females from 2018 to 2024 closely mirror those of labour force numbers and growth rates. Thus, the number of females in the workforce increased from 108.7 million in 2018 to 209.2 million in 2024, while the number of males in the workforce rose from 362.6 million to 405.3 million. The average annual increase in the workforce has been 16.7 million for females and 7.1 million for males. Notably, the share of females in the incremental workforce from 2018 to 2024 was 70.1 %. The female workforce grew at an annual rate of 11.52 %, compared to the male workforce's growth of only 1.88 %, less than one-sixth of the female workforce's growth. If we examine the change in the workforce growth rate between two periods (1994–2018 and 2018–2024), we find that the female workforce growth rate increased by 12.02 percentage points, while the male workforce growth rate improved by only 0.35 percentage points.[2]

In light of the above discussion, examining the proportion of subsidiary status workers to total workers (UPSS) may be beneficial, as it sheds light on the reason behind the significant workforce expansion during 2018–2024, particularly among women. The information presented in Table 100 shows that, in 2024, almost 31 % of female workers in rural India and 15 % in urban India worked in a subsidiary status. In contrast, the percentage of subsidiary status workers among males in rural and urban areas has been nearly 3 %. It is, therefore, evident that much of the increase in the number of women in the workforce in 2024 can be attributed to their employment in subsidiary roles.

Table 100: Percentage of Subsidiary Status Workers to Total (Principal + Subsidiary) Workers in India

Region	Year	Male	Female	Male + Female
Rural	2018	0.87	11.91	3.56
	2024	3.39	30.59	13.70
Urban	2018	0.52	5.68	1.58
	2024	1.51	14.59	4.92
Rural + Urban	2018	0.77	10.34	2.99
	2024	2.83	27.48	11.42

Source: Author's computation utilising unit-level data from Periodic Labour Force Surveys (2017–18 and 2023–24)

7.2.6 Activity Profile of Out-of-Labour Force Individuals

Having observed a significant rise in the labour force participation rate (LFPR) across India between 2018 and 2024, particularly among rural females, one may also be curious about the causes of this increase. Analysing the changes in the numbers and growth rates of individuals out of the labour force (OLF) and their activity

[2] In Chapter 4, we noted that the female workforce growth rate from 1994 to 2018 was negative, so the percentage-point change in their workforce during 2018–2024 is higher than the growth rate during this period.

profiles may provide some insight into this. Table 101 presents annual changes in the absolute number of OLF individuals and their growth rates by gender and region. Between 2012 and 2018, the absolute number of such individuals increased for both genders, although the rate of increase was higher for females than for males. This led to a larger proportion of females remaining outside the labour force in 2018 than in 2012, in both rural and urban areas. This trend reversed between 2018 and 2024, as more females entered or re-entered the labour force in 2024 than males, resulting in a significant decrease in OLF females. This phenomenon is primarily observed in rural areas, where the number of OLF females declined by 9.84 million per year between 2018 and 2024, compared to a decrease of 0.33 million per year for OLF males. In urban areas, during the same period, while the number of OLF females declined by 0.61 million per year, the number of OLF males increased by 0.20 million per year. Regarding the growth rates of OLF individuals, Table 101 shows that in rural areas, the number of OLF females increased by 2.71 % per annum, while the number of OLF males increased by 1.30 % per annum from 2012 to 2018. In contrast, OLF females and males decreased by 2.95 % and 0.16 % per annum, respectively, from 2018 to 2024. The trend is broadly similar in urban areas, with OLF males and females exhibiting growth rates of 2.39 % and 2.87 %, respectively, from 2012 to 2018. However, from 2018 to 2024, while the number of OLF females in urban areas declined by 0.33 % per annum, the number of males increased by 0.19 % per annum. When considering both rural and urban areas, it is evident that the number and growth rate of OLF individuals across India increased from 2012 to 2018 but decreased from 2018 to 2024. Of course, this change is more pronounced for females than males, particularly in rural areas.

Table 101: Average Annual Changes and Growth Rates of Out-of-Labour Force (OLF) Numbers by Gender and Region Across India

Region	Gender	Average annual change in OLF number (millions) during		Annual compound growth rate (%) of OLF number during	
		2012–2018	2018–2024	2012–2018	2018–2024
Rural	Male	2.60	−0.33	1.30	−0.16
	Female	8.85	−9.84	2.71	−2.95
	Male + Female	11.45	−10.17	2.17	−1.88
Urban	Male	2.22	0.20	2.39	0.19
	Female	4.84	−0.61	2.87	−0.33
	Male + Female	7.05	−0.41	2.70	−0.15
Rural + Urban	Male	4.81	−0.13	1.65	−0.04
	Female	13.69	−10.45	2.76	−2.02
	Male + Female	18.50	−10.59	2.35	−1.28

Source: Same as Table 99

Let us now examine the activity profile of OLF individuals in 2024 and compare it with that of 2018. The first point from Table 102 is that, for females outside the labour force in rural and urban areas, the most significant activities in 2024 have been attending to domestic duties (codes 92 and 93), followed by attending educational institutions (code 91). These two activities together represented nearly 80 % of out-of-labour-force females in rural areas and 85 % in urban areas. On the other hand, the most crucial activity for rural and urban males outside the labour force is attending educational institutions. Nearly 65 % of males in rural areas and 62 % in urban areas cited attending educational institutions as the reason for remaining outside the labour force. Another essential reason they are not part of the labour force is that many are rentiers, pensioners, remittance recipients, and so on (7 % in rural areas and 14 % in urban areas). Secondly, and importantly, the percentage of rural females in the out-of-labour force engaged in domestic duties decreased by 11.3 percentage points (codes 92 and 93) between 2018 and 2024, resulting in a 7.7 percentage-point increase in attendance at educational institutions. However, for urban females, the decline in attendance to domestic duties and the rise in attendance at educational institutions have been negligible. For rural and urban males, the percentage distribution of those out of the labour force into various activities has remained unchanged between 2018 and 2024. Considering both rural and urban areas, we can observe a clear trend: the attendance of out-of-labour force females in domestic duties is declining, while their attendance at educational institutions is increasing from 2018 to 2024. However, the activity profile of out-of-labour force males has undergone only minor changes. These observations, together with our previous insights into the changes in the numbers and growth rates of OLF individuals from 2018 to 2024 compared to 2012 to 2018, suggest that as more females are entering or re-entering the labour force by reducing their commitment to domestic duties, there is a clear trend of substituting domestic work with outside work in recent years in rural areas.[3] However, it cannot be precisely determined whether this shift in focus is due to the expansion of work opportunities outside their homes, the migration of more male members to urban areas for employment, or the economic hardships faced by their families, based on the NSSO survey data we used.

---

[3] This observation stands valid in spite of more females attending educational institutions in recent years. While the percentage of OLF females attending educational institutions increased in rural areas by 7.7 percentage points from 2018 to 2024 compared to 2012 to 2018, their attendance to domestic duties decreased by 11.3 percentage points between these periods.

Table 102: Percentage Distribution of Out-of-Labour-Force Persons (UPSS) Engaged in Different Activities in India in 2024

NSS Code	Activity	Rural			Urban			Rural + Urban		
		Male	Female	Male + Female	Male	Female	Male + Female	Male	Female	Male + Female
91	Attended educational institutions	64.5	37.7	48.3	62.0	30.1	41.4	63.8	35.2	46.2
	% pt change over 2018	–0.2	7.7	5.7	–1.3	0.6	0.2	–0.5	5.4	3.9
92	Attended to domestic duties only	1.0	28.1	17.3	2.2	48.1	31.8	1.3	34.7	21.9
	% pt change over 2018	–0.2	–9.2	–6.8	0.7	–3.1	–2.1	0.1	–6.8	–5.1
93	Attended to domestic duties and also engaged in free collection of goods, sewing, tailoring, weaving, etc. for household use	0.2	13.4	8.2	0.2	6.4	4.2	0.2	11.1	6.9
	% pt change over 2018	–0.5	–2.1	–1.9	0.0	2.1	1.3	–0.3	–1.0	–1.0
92+93	Attended to different domestic duties (incl. those engaged in free collection of goods, sewing, tailoring, weaving, etc. for household use)	1.2	41.5	25.5	2.4	54.5	36.0	1.6	45.8	28.8
	% pt change over 2018	–0.7	–11.3	–8.7	0.7	–0.9	–0.8	–0.3	–7.9	–6.2
94	Rentiers, pensioners, remittance recipients, etc.	7.4	5.4	6.2	14.0	5.7	8.6	9.3	5.5	6.9
	% pt change over 2018	0.3	1.4	1.1	1.6	1.2	1.4	0.7	1.3	1.2
95	Not able to work due to disability	3.1	1.3	2.0	2.9	0.7	1.5	3.0	1.1	1.8
	% pt change over 2018	0.3	0.3	0.3	0.0	–0.2	–0.2	0.2	0.1	0.2
97	Others (incl. beggars, prostitutes, etc.) plus those casual workers who did not work due to sickness	3.0	1.6	2.2	3.4	1.2	2.0	3.1	1.5	2.1
	% pt change over 2018	–1.8	–0.6	–1.0	–0.6	–0.7	–0.6	–1.5	–0.7	–0.9
99	Children of age 0–4 years	20.8	12.5	15.8	15.4	7.9	10.6	19.3	11.0	14.2
	% pt change over 2018	2.1	2.6	2.7	–0.4	0.0	0.0	1.4	1.7	1.8

Source: Same as Table 95

7.2.7 Labour Force Participation Rates in Major States

Now, let us examine the labour force participation rates (LFPR) in twenty-one major Indian states for 2024, along with the changes from 2018. The information presented in Table 103 indicates that among males, the LFPR in 2024 was highest in Chhattisgarh (64.9 %) and lowest in Bihar (48.1 %). Besides Chhattisgarh, thirteen other states had a male LFPR exceeding the national male LFPR of 58.2 %. These states, listed in descending order of LFPR value, include Himachal Pradesh, West Bengal, Gujarat, Punjab, Madhya Pradesh, Odisha, Assam, Maharashtra, Karnataka, Tamil Nadu, Telangana, Andhra Pradesh, and Kerala. Similarly, apart from Bihar, the states with a male LFPR below the national level are Jharkhand, Haryana, Uttar Pradesh, Jammu & Kashmir, Uttarakhand, and Rajasthan (in ascending order of LFPR). However, it is noteworthy that all states except Andhra Pradesh, Haryana, Jammu & Kashmir, and Tamil Nadu improved their male LFPR values in 2024 compared to 2018. Among the states, the largest improvement in the male labour force participation rate (LFPR) occurred in Chhattisgarh, with a 7.6 percentage-point increase. Additionally, two other states, Himachal Pradesh and Kerala, experienced increases of more than 5 percentage points in male LFPR during this period.

Table 103: Labour Force Participation Rates (LFPR) in Major States in 2024 by Gender (Rural & Urban Combined)

State	Male			Female			Male + Female		
	LFPR (%)	Rank	% pt change over 2018	LFPR (%)	Rank	% pt change over 2018	LFPR (%)	Rank	% pt change over 2018
Andhra Pradesh	59.5	13	−0.9	35.8	10	1.4	47.5	10	0.4
Assam	61.1	8	1.8	36.8	7	27.0	49.1	6	13.3
Bihar	48.1	21	2.7	20.3	20	17.6	34.5	21	9.1
Chhattisgarh	64.9	1	7.6	46.1	2	9.7	55.6	2	8.3
Gujarat	62.5	4	3.7	35.8	12	20.4	49.6	4	11.6
Haryana	53.5	19	−0.2	18.9	21	8.1	37.4	20	4.1
Himachal Pradesh	64.8	2	6.0	56.2	1	16.5	60.5	1	11.4
Jammu & Kashmir	56.2	17	−1.2	38.8	4	15.9	47.8	8	7.0
Jharkhand	52.9	20	2.5	35.8	11	24.9	44.4	17	13.3
Karnataka	59.9	10	0.2	30.5	17	10.1	45.4	16	5.3
Kerala	59.1	14	5.2	33.4	14	12.1	45.4	15	8.8
Madhya Pradesh	62.0	6	3.2	39.4	3	16.0	51.0	3	9.2
Maharashtra	61.0	9	3.4	32.1	15	7.9	46.8	13	5.6
Odisha	61.5	7	3.5	38.0	6	23.0	49.5	5	13.1
Punjab	62.5	5	3.2	24.5	19	12.2	43.7	18	7.0
Rajasthan	56.5	15	4.9	38.0	5	18.7	47.3	11	11.3

(Continued)

Table 103 *(Continued)*

State	Male			Female			Male + Female		
	LFPR (%)	Rank	% pt change over 2018	LFPR (%)	Rank	% pt change over 2018	LFPR (%)	Rank	% pt change over 2018
Tamil Nadu	59.9	11	−1.2	35.2	13	8.0	47.3	12	3.4
Telangana	59.8	12	1.6	36.5	8	10.4	48.0	7	5.5
Uttar Pradesh	55.2	18	4.2	25.2	18	15.8	40.4	19	9.7
Uttarakhand	56.4	16	4.0	35.9	9	22.2	46.2	14	13.0
West Bengal	63.8	3	2.5	31.7	16	15.4	47.7	9	8.6

Source: Same as Table 95

Table 103 shows that Himachal Pradesh ranked first in female LFPR in 2024, with a rate of 56.2 %, while Haryana ranked last at 18.9 %. This year, besides Himachal Pradesh, female LFPR values surpassed the national level (31.7 %) in fourteen other states: Chhattisgarh, Madhya Pradesh, Jammu & Kashmir, Rajasthan, Odisha, Assam, Telangana, Uttarakhand, Andhra Pradesh, Jharkhand, Gujarat, Tamil Nadu, Kerala, and Maharashtra (arranged in descending order of LFPR values). Conversely, besides Haryana, five other states reported a female LFPR below or equal to the national level: Bihar, Punjab, Uttar Pradesh, Karnataka, and West Bengal, in ascending order of LFPR. Another notable observation from Table 103 is that all states recorded improvements in their female LFPR values in 2024 compared to 2018. Furthermore, five states showed exceptionally high improvements in female LFPR values in 2024 relative to 2018, increasing by over 20 percentage points. These states are Assam, Jharkhand, Odisha, Uttarakhand, and Gujarat.

Combining data for males and females reveals that the highest LFPR in 2024 was recorded in Himachal Pradesh (60.5 %), while the lowest was in Bihar (34.5 %). In addition to Himachal Pradesh, thirteen other states exceed the national LFPR of 45.9 %. These states, listed in descending order of LFPR values, are Chhattisgarh, Madhya Pradesh, Gujarat, Odisha, Assam, Telangana, Jammu & Kashmir, West Bengal, Andhra Pradesh, Rajasthan, Tamil Nadu, Maharashtra, and Uttarakhand. Conversely, along with Bihar, the states of Haryana, Uttar Pradesh, Punjab, Jharkhand, Karnataka, and Kerala (in ascending order of their LFPR values) have LFPRs below the national average.

7.2.8 Workforce Participation Rates in Major States

Table 104 presents workforce participation rates (WPR) for males, females, and both genders combined in twenty-one major states for 2024, compared with those from 2018. It is noted that the rankings of the states regarding the WPR do not differ significantly from their rankings for the LFPR in 2024. Consequently, this year, the highest male WPR value is observed in Chhattisgarh (63.2 %), while the lowest is in Bihar (46.4 %). In addition to Chhattisgarh, thirteen other states report male WPR values that exceed the national average of 56.4 %. These states, arranged in descending order of their male WPR values, are Himachal Pradesh, West Bengal, Gujarat, Madhya Pradesh, Odisha, Punjab, Maharashtra, Assam, Karnataka, Tamil Nadu, Telangana, Andhra Pradesh, and Kerala. In addition to Bihar, other states with a male WPR below the national level include Haryana, Jharkhand, Uttar Pradesh, Uttarakhand, Rajasthan, and Jammu & Kashmir (in ascending order of their WPR values). The table also shows that all but two states (Andhra Pradesh and Jammu & Kashmir) improved their male WPR values in 2024 compared to 2018. The rate of improvement in male WPR varied from a high of 7.8 percentage points in Chhattisgarh to 1.3 percentage points in Karnataka.

Table 104: Workforce Participation Rates (WPR) in Major States by Gender in 2024 (Rural & Urban Combined)

State	Male			Female			Male + Female		
	WPR (%)	Rank	% pt change over 2018	WPR (%)	Rank	% pt change over 2018	WPR (%)	Rank	% pt change over 2018
Andhra Pradesh	57.0	13	−0.5	34.5	11	1.5	45.6	10	0.5
Assam	58.8	9	3.8	35.3	8	26.9	47.2	6	14.2
Bihar	46.4	21	4.3	20.1	20	17.4	33.5	21	9.9
Chhattisgarh	63.2	1	7.8	45.0	2	9.8	54.2	2	8.5
Gujarat	61.8	4	6.0	35.4	7	20.7	49.1	4	12.9
Haryana	51.5	20	2.1	18.4	21	8.9	36.1	20	5.6
Himachal Pradesh	62.6	2	7.6	51.8	1	13.9	57.2	1	10.8
Jammu & Kashmir	54.1	15	−0.9	35.1	9	14.1	44.9	13	6.3
Jharkhand	52.0	19	5.7	35.6	6	25.3	43.9	16	15.1
Karnataka	58.1	10	1.3	30.0	16	10.5	44.1	15	6.0
Kerala	56.5	14	6.0	29.5	17	13.1	42.1	17	9.7
Madhya Pradesh	61.4	5	5.6	39.1	3	16.2	50.6	3	10.6
Maharashtra	58.8	8	3.9	31.2	14	8.4	45.3	11	6.1
Odisha	59.4	6	5.7	36.9	4	22.9	47.9	5	14.1
Punjab	59.4	7	4.3	22.8	19	11.9	41.3	18	7.5
Rajasthan	54.1	16	5.6	36.5	5	17.7	45.3	12	11.1
Tamil Nadu	57.8	11	1.6	33.9	13	8.6	45.6	9	5.0
Telangana	57.0	12	3.3	34.7	10	10.4	45.7	8	6.4
Uttar Pradesh	53.4	18	5.9	24.6	18	15.4	39.2	19	10.5
Uttarakhand	53.8	17	5.0	34.5	12	22.2	44.2	14	13.6
West Bengal	62.2	3	4.1	30.8	15	14.9	46.4	7	9.2

Source: Same as Table 95

Focusing on the female WPR in 2024, we observe that the highest and lowest ranks in this regard are held by Himachal Pradesh (51.8 %) and Haryana (18.4 %), respectively. In addition to Himachal Pradesh, fourteen other states have a female WPR above the national level (30.7 %). The states listed in descending order of their WPR values are Chhattisgarh, Madhya Pradesh, Odisha, Rajasthan, Jharkhand, Gujarat, Assam, Jammu & Kashmir, Telangana, Andhra Pradesh, Uttarakhand, Tamil Nadu, Maharashtra, and West Bengal. Besides Haryana, other states with female WPR values below the national average include Bihar, Punjab, Uttar Pradesh, Kerala, and Karnataka, which are listed in order of their WPR values from lowest to highest. The most remarkable fact about the female WPR in 2024 is that all states have improved their WPR values compared to 2018, with the largest improvement of 26.9 percentage points in Assam and the smallest in Andhra Pradesh at 1.5 percentage points. Besides Assam, this improvement has also been significant (over 20 percentage points) in Jharkhand, Odisha, Uttarakhand, and Gujarat.

In 2024, when males and females are combined, Himachal Pradesh holds the top position in terms of WPR, with a value of 57.2 %, while Bihar ranks last, with a value of 33.5 %. Besides Himachal Pradesh, fifteen other states recorded WPR values exceeding the national level WPR of 43.7 %. These states, in descending order of WPR values, are Chhattisgarh, Madhya Pradesh, Gujarat, Odisha, Assam, West Bengal, Telangana, Andhra Pradesh, Tamil Nadu, Maharashtra, Rajasthan, Jammu & Kashmir, Uttarakhand, Karnataka, and Jharkhand. Conversely, apart from Bihar, the WPR fell short of the national level in Haryana, Uttar Pradesh, Punjab, and Kerala, in ascending order of WPR values. However, all states improved their WPR values (combined for males and females) in 2024 compared to 2018, with the highest improvement recorded in Jharkhand (15.1 percentage points) and the lowest in Andhra Pradesh (0.5 percentage points). Another noteworthy fact is that, apart from Jharkhand, eight other states experienced an increase of more than ten percentage points in WPR from 2018 to 2024: Assam, Odisha, Uttarakhand, Gujarat, Rajasthan, Himachal Pradesh, Madhya Pradesh, and Uttar Pradesh, listed in descending order of the magnitude of improvement.

7.2.9 Growth Rates of Labour Force in Major States

We examine labour force growth rates in major states from 2018 to 2024 and compare them with those of the preceding period, from 1994 to 2018. The information presented in Table 105 indicates that, for males, the highest annual labour force growth from 2018 to 2024 is recorded in Chhattisgarh (3.39 %), while the lowest is in Tamil Nadu (0.05 %). The male labour force growth rate was higher than the national average (1.34 %) during this period in thirteen other states, in addition to Chhattisgarh. These states, in descending order of growth rate, are Rajasthan, Uttar Pradesh, Bihar, Gujarat, Uttarakhand, Himachal Pradesh, Madhya Pradesh, Jharkhand, Kerala, Maharashtra, Odisha, Punjab, and Assam. Conversely, apart from Tamil Nadu, the states with labour force growth rates lower than the national average are Andhra Pradesh, Jammu & Kashmir, Karnataka, Telangana, West Bengal, and Haryana (in ascending order of growth rates). When examining the change in the male labour force growth rates from 2018 to 2024 compared to the rates from 1994 to 2018, we find that Kerala tops the list with a 1.74 percentage-point increase, while Jammu & Kashmir is at the bottom, where the growth rate declined by 2.29 percentage points from 2018 to 2024 compared to 1994 to 2018. It is also noted that a total of eleven states, out of nineteen for which a comparison is feasible, improved their labour force growth rates from 2018 to 2024, compared to the period from 1994 to 2018. Additionally, it is worth noting that, apart from Kerala, the growth rates of the male labour force increased by more than 1 % in Bihar, Odisha, Gujarat, and Jharkhand from 2018 to 2024, compared to the previous period (1994–2018).

The picture regarding the growth of the female labour force from 2018 to 2024 is drastically different from that observed for males, as many states experienced exceptionally high growth rates, and none reported negative growth during this period. Bihar ranked highest among the states, with a female labour force growth of 41.36 % per annum, while Andhra Pradesh occupied the lowest position, with a growth rate of 1.31 %. Besides Bihar, ten other states saw a female labour force growth rate exceeding the national average of 11.02 % from 2018 to 2024. These states, listed in descending order of growth rates, are Assam, Jharkhand, Uttarakhand, Uttar Pradesh, Odisha, Gujarat, Rajasthan, Punjab, West Bengal, and Haryana. It is also noteworthy that among these states, Assam and Jharkhand recorded female labour force growth rates of 26.01 % and 24.37 %, respectively. In addition to Andhra Pradesh, other states that experienced female labour force growth rates lower than the national average from 2018 to 2024 include Tamil Nadu, Maharashtra, Telangana, Chhattisgarh, Himachal Pradesh, Karnataka, Kerala, Jammu & Kashmir, and Madhya Pradesh (listed in ascending order of growth rates). However, all states improved their female labour force growth rates from 2018 to 2024 compared to 1994 to 2018, with the rate of improvement ranging from 50.75 percentage points in Bihar to 4.98 percentage points in Tamil Nadu. It is worth noting that, in addition to Bihar, six other states experienced an increase of over 20 percentage points in female labour force growth from 1994 to 2024, compared to the period from 1994 to 2018. These states are Jharkhand, Uttarakhand, Assam, Uttar Pradesh, Odisha, and Gujarat.

Table 105: Annual Compound Growth Rates of Labour Force in Major States from 2018 to 2024 (Rural & Urban Combined)

State	Male			Female			Male + Female		
	Growth rate from 2018 to 2024	Rank	% pt change over growth rate from 1994 to 2018	Growth rate from 2018 to 2024	Rank	% pt change over growth rate from 1994 to 2018	Growth rate from 2018 to 2024	Rank	% pt change over growth rate from 1994 to 2018
Andhra Pradesh	0.21	20	–	1.31	21	–	0.61	21	–
Assam	1.50	14	−0.79	26.01	2	28.29	6.50	4	4.52
Bihar	2.42	4	1.16	41.36	1	50.75	6.96	2	6.31
Chhattisgarh	3.39	1	0.98	6.26	17	5.77	3.72	14	1.28
Gujarat	2.40	5	1.03	16.58	7	20.57	5.95	8	5.77
Haryana	1.22	15	−0.73	11.39	11	14.05	3.16	16	2.07
Himachal Pradesh	2.23	7	0.05	6.60	16	9.23	4.15	11	4.16
Jammu & Kashmir	0.33	19	−2.29	10.12	13	8.19	3.53	15	1.29
Jharkhand	2.16	9	1.01	24.37	3	30.36	7.42	1	7.46
Karnataka	0.79	18	−0.35	7.71	15	9.10	2.88	18	2.55
Kerala	2.04	10	1.74	8.26	14	8.59	4.24	10	4.23
Madhya Pradesh	2.18	8	−0.71	10.20	12	5.72	4.85	9	1.69
Maharashtra	1.87	11	0.26	5.72	19	7.33	3.13	17	2.61
Odisha	1.65	12	1.08	17.68	6	23.71	6.12	6	7.29
Punjab	1.59	13	0.05	13.09	9	19.71	3.98	13	4.19
Rajasthan	2.68	2	0.28	13.46	8	18.61	6.04	7	6.02
Tamil Nadu	0.05	21	−1.60	4.85	20	4.98	1.74	20	0.75
Telangana	1.05	17	–	6.17	18	–	2.77	19	–
Uttar Pradesh	2.52	3	0.53	19.22	5	26.06	6.15	5	6.09
Uttarakhand	2.40	6	−0.58	19.54	4	28.57	6.61	3	6.60
West Bengal	1.20	16	−0.12	12.35	10	13.53	4.09	12	3.41

Source: Same as Table 95

Regarding the annual labour force growth rates for males and females combined from 2018 to 2024, Table 105 shows that Jharkhand (7.42 %) ranked first among the states, while Andhra Pradesh (0.61 %) ranked last. In addition to Jharkhand, eleven other states recorded growth rates exceeding the all-India level (4.04 %) for the combined male and female labour force. These states, listed in descending order of their growth rates, are Bihar, Uttarakhand, Assam, Uttar Pradesh, Odisha, Rajasthan, Gujarat, Madhya Pradesh, Kerala, Himachal Pradesh, and West Bengal. Along with Andhra Pradesh, the growth rates of the combined male and female labour force from 2018 to 2024 were below the all-India level in Tamil Nadu, Telangana, Karnataka, Maharashtra, Haryana, Jammu & Kashmir, Chhattisgarh, and Punjab, listed in ascending order of growth rates. Among the states, Jharkhand achieved the maximum improvement in the combined male and female labour force growth rate between 2018 and 2024, compared to the period from 1994 to 2018, with an increase of 7.46 percentage points. In contrast, Tamil Nadu recorded the lowest improvement at 0.75 percentage points. Other states that recorded appreciable improvement (more than 5.0 percentage points) in the combined male and female labour force growth rates from 2018 to 2024, compared to 1994–2018, are Odisha, Uttarakhand, Bihar, Uttar Pradesh, Rajasthan, and Gujarat.

7.2.10 Growth Rates of Workforce in Major States

Let us now examine workforce growth rates in the states from 2018 to 2024 and compare them with those from 1994 to 2018. Table 106 shows that, for males, the annual workforce growth rate from 2018 to 2024 was highest in Chhattisgarh (3.51 %) and lowest in Andhra Pradesh (0.30 %). In addition to Chhattisgarh, fourteen other states experienced higher growth rates in the male workforce than the all-India growth rate of 1.88 % during this period. These states, listed in descending order of growth rate, are Jharkhand, Uttar Pradesh, Bihar, Gujarat, Rajasthan, Madhya Pradesh, Uttarakhand, Himachal Pradesh, Odisha, Kerala, Assam, Maharashtra, Haryana, and Punjab. The states, apart from Andhra Pradesh, that fell below the all-India level regarding male workforce growth during 2018–2024 include Jammu & Kashmir, Tamil Nadu, Karnataka, Telangana, and West Bengal (in ascending order of growth rate). It is also observed that all states, except Jammu & Kashmir and Maharashtra, improved their male workforce growth rates between 2018 and 2024 compared to those from 1994 to 2018. The highest improvement in the male workforce growth rate is seen in Jharkhand (3.23 percentage points), while the lowest is in Tamil Nadu (0.21 percentage points). Apart from Jharkhand, other states that achieved more than a 2.0 percentage-point improvement in the growth rates of their male workforce from 2018 to 2024, compared to the previous period, are Odisha, Kerala, Bihar, Gujarat, and Uttar Pradesh.

For females, the highest annual workforce growth rate from 2018 to 2024 is in Bihar at 41.71 %, while the lowest is in Andhra Pradesh at 1.38 %. In addition to Bihar, ten other states exceeded the all-India female workforce growth rate of 11.52 %. These states, listed in descending order of their growth rates, are Assam, Jharkhand, Uttarakhand, Uttar Pradesh, Odisha, Gujarat, Punjab, Haryana, Rajasthan, and West Bengal. Among these states, Assam, Jharkhand, and Uttarakhand achieved growth of over 20.0 % in the female workforce from 2018 to 2024. On the other hand, besides Andhra Pradesh, the states that recorded lower growth in the female workforce than the all-India growth rate are Tamil Nadu, Himachal Pradesh, Maharashtra, Chhattisgarh, Telangana, Karnataka, Jammu & Kashmir, Madhya Pradesh, and Kerala. However, it is encouraging to note that none of the states experienced a decline in the growth rate of the female workforce between 2018 and 2024 compared to the period from 1994 to 2018. The improvement in the growth rate of the female workforce from 2018 to 2024, compared to the period from 1994 to 2018, varied from 50.02 percentage points in Bihar to 5.34 percentage points in Maharashtra. In addition to Bihar, six other states exhibited significant improvement in their female workforce growth rates, with increases exceeding 20.0 percentage points: Assam, Jharkhand, Uttarakhand, Uttar Pradesh, Odisha, Punjab and Gujarat.

When considering males and females together, the annual workforce growth rate from 2018 to 2024 was highest in Jharkhand (8.49 %) and lowest in Andhra Pradesh (0.60 %). Alongside Jharkhand, nine other states recorded workforce growth rates exceeding the national average of 4.57 %. These states, listed in descending order of growth rates, are Bihar, Assam, Uttarakhand, Odisha, Uttar Pradesh, Gujarat, Rajasthan, Madhya Pradesh, and Kerala. Among these states, nine experienced workforce growth rates over 5.0 % from 2018 to 2024. In contrast, the workforce growth rate during this period, along with that of Andhra Pradesh, fell short of the all-India growth rate in Tamil Nadu, Karnataka, Telangana, Maharashtra, Jammu & Kashmir, Chhattisgarh, Punjab, Himachal Pradesh, Haryana, and West Bengal (listed in ascending order of growth rates). However, for both males and females combined, none of the states reported a decrease in workforce growth rates from 2018 to 2024 compared to the growth rate from 1994 to 2018. Jharkhand (9.69 percentage points) and Jammu & Kashmir (1.39 percentage points) recorded the largest and smallest improvements in workforce growth rates from 2018 to 2024, respectively, compared to the previous period. It is also worth noting that, besides Jharkhand, nine additional states experienced significant improvements (more than 5.0 percentage points) in workforce growth rates from 2018 to 2024, compared to the period from 1994 to 2018. These states are Odisha, Uttarakhand, Bihar, Gujarat, Uttar Pradesh, Rajasthan, Assam, Kerala, and Punjab, listed in descending order of the magnitude of improvement in workforce growth rates.

Table 106: Annual Compound Growth Rates of Workers in Major States from 2018 to 2024 (Rural & Urban Combined)

State	Male			Female			Male + Female		
	Growth rate from 2018 to 2024	Rank	% pt change over growth rate from 1994 to 2018	Growth rate from 2018 to 2024	Rank	% pt change over growth rate from 1994 to 2018	Growth rate from 2018 to 2024	Rank	% pt change over growth rate from 1994 to 2018
Andhra Pradesh	0.30	21	–	1.38	21	–	0.60	21	–
Assam	2.12	12	0.34	28.30	2	32.07	7.27	3	5.92
Bihar	3.11	4	2.63	41.71	1	50.02	7.65	2	7.62
Chhattisgarh	3.51	1	1.37	6.43	17	6.34	3.73	15	2.40
Gujarat	3.09	5	2.49	17.19	7	21.74	6.58	7	7.13
Haryana	2.00	14	0.95	13.23	9	17.48	4.25	12	4.17
Himachal Pradesh	2.77	9	1.51	5.95	19	9.08	4.15	13	4.89
Jammu & Kashmir	0.41	20	–1.95	9.87	14	8.42	3.32	16	1.39
Jharkhand	3.33	2	3.23	25.39	3	31.65	8.49	1	9.69
Karnataka	1.11	18	0.52	8.23	15	10.11	3.23	19	3.43
Kerala	2.37	11	2.65	10.82	12	12.98	4.97	10	5.88
Madhya Pradesh	2.92	7	0.78	10.47	13	6.27	5.53	9	2.84
Maharashtra	2.05	13	–0.005	6.23	18	5.34	3.32	17	1.66
Odisha	2.38	10	2.65	18.41	6	25.14	6.75	5	8.73
Punjab	1.97	15	1.25	14.08	8	22.32	4.15	14	5.31
Rajasthan	2.98	6	1.36	13.13	10	18.54	6.10	8	6.72
Tamil Nadu	0.83	19	0.21	5.47	20	6.33	2.38	20	2.31
Telangana	1.60	17	–	6.57	16	–	3.25	18	–
Uttar Pradesh	3.18	3	2.11	19.34	5	26.51	6.60	6	7.12
Uttarakhand	2.82	8	0.58	20.99	4	31.03	7.04	4	8.08
West Bengal	1.66	16	0.66	12.38	11	13.44	4.32	11	3.86

Source: Same as Table 95

7.2.11 Factors Influencing Labour Force Participation

In Chapter 3 above, we conducted logit regression exercises to identify factors influencing labour force participation among individuals in India, utilising the PLFS 2018 data. Among the identified factors were the individuals' personal and household characteristics. More specifically, we considered age, sex, marital status, and the individuals' social, religious, and educational backgrounds as determinants of labour force participation. Similar exercises have been conducted in this chapter using the same set of variables to verify whether the conclusions drawn from our previous analysis, which utilised PLFS 2018 data, remain valid when using the PLFS 2024 data.[4]

The logit regression results presented in Table 107 indicate that, in rural areas, the probability of labour force participation increases with age, particularly among males and married individuals. It was also found that this probability is higher for individuals from SC, ST, and OBC families than those from the 'Others' category, i.e. individuals from general caste backgrounds. Regarding religion, the results show that individuals from Muslim families have a lower probability of participating in the labour force than those from Hindu families. Furthermore, increasing general education and obtaining technical education enhances the likelihood of participating in the labour force. However, individuals attending any educational institution are less likely to join the labour force. Another observation from Table 107 is that individuals from larger households are less likely to participate in the labour force. The estimated coefficients for all explanatory variables are statistically significant, and the model as a whole is statistically significant, as indicated by the likelihood ratio (LR) statistic.

The logit regression results for urban areas are nearly identical to those for rural areas, except that the probability of labour force participation appears to be higher among Muslim individuals than among Hindu individuals. However, the estimated coefficient of the corresponding religion dummy (rel1) is statistically insignificant. When considering both rural and urban areas, the findings align with those observed in the rural areas alone. These findings are consistent with those obtained from the PLFS 2018 data analysis.

Thus, overall, it can be stated that the probability of participating in the labour force in India is higher for individuals who are male, older, married, more educated, possess technical education, are not currently attending any educational institution, belong to smaller families, come from lower-caste families (compared to general caste), and are from Hindu families.

---

[4] For definitions of the variables and hypotheses, refer to Chapter 3.

Table 107: Logit Regression Results of Determinants of Participation in Labour Force in India [Dep. Variable: labf = 1 if participated in labour force; 0 otherwise]

Explanatory variable	Rural Areas			Urban Areas			Rural + Urban Areas		
	Est. coefficient	*z*-value	*p*-value	Est. coefficient	*z*-value	*p*-value	Est. coefficient	*z*-value	*p*-value
age	0.04	96.63	0.00	0.03	54.10	0.00	0.04	109.44	0.00
sex	1.38	111.06	0.00	2.03	139.30	0.00	1.63	176.90	0.00
hsize	−0.08	−27.84	0.00	−0.05	−17.42	0.00	−0.06	−30.21	0.00
marstat	2.04	150.98	0.00	1.54	92.21	0.00	1.84	179.91	0.00
sg1	0.37	19.89	0.00	0.54	27.16	0.00	0.52	39.26	0.00
sg2	0.76	36.65	0.00	0.54	15.48	0.00	0.91	56.51	0.00
sg3	0.30	18.19	0.00	0.28	17.70	0.00	0.37	33.45	0.00
rel1	−0.16	−8.73	0.00	0.01	0.35	0.73	−0.15	−12.22	0.00
rel2	−0.08	−3.15	0.00	−0.12	−4.40	0.00	−0.14	−7.42	0.00
gedu1	0.35	22.00	0.00	0.37	16.44	0.00	0.23	18.47	0.00
gedu2	0.94	64.08	0.00	0.86	42.31	0.00	0.70	62.24	0.00
gedu3	1.15	60.80	0.00	1.04	48.88	0.00	0.78	59.92	0.00
gedu4	1.59	20.99	0.00	1.62	40.33	0.00	1.10	32.70	0.00
techedu	1.04	16.85	0.00	1.15	31.73	0.00	1.09	34.73	0.00
attendcur	−1.01	−67.71	0.00	−1.33	−78.93	0.00	−1.14	−104.79	0.00
constant	−2.46	−62.36	0.00	−2.63	−58.39	0.00	−2.35	−81.60	0.00
35 state dummies	Estimated coefficients not reported								
	Pseudo R^2 = 0.35			Pseudo R^2 = 30			Pseudo R^2 = 0.31		
	LR Chi-sq = 50712.42 (df = 49; p-value = 0.00)			LR Chi-sq = 34821.85 (df = 49; p-value = 0.00)			LR Chi-sq = 93646.7 (df = 49; p-value = 0.00)		
	No. of observations = 2,35,773			No. of observations = 1,69,834			No. of observations = 4,05,607		

Source: Author's computation using unit-level data from PLFS 2023–24

Note: z-values are calculated using White's robust standard errors.

7.3 Changes in Quality Aspects of Employment

This section examines the changes in the quality dimensions of employment between 2018 and 2024. To achieve this, we consider three indicators: the modes of employment for workers, the sectoral composition of the workforce, and the incidence of the 'working poor'. Additionally, we examine sectoral employment elasticities from 2018 to 2024 to identify the employment-intensive sectors of the economy.

7.3.1 Modes of Employment by Gender and Region in India

Table 108 presents the percentage distribution of workers across three distinct employment modes (regular employees, self-employed individuals, and casual labourers) in India for 2024, along with the observed changes since 2018. In rural areas, among various employment modes, the incidence of self-employment is highest for both males and females. However, a more significant percentage of rural females are engaged in self-employment (73.5 %) than rural males (59.4 %) in 2024. Notably, the percentage of self-employed females in rural areas increased significantly from 2018 to 2024, rising by 15.77 percentage points. In contrast, the increase in the percentage of self-employed workers among rural males during this period was marginal, rising by only 1.57 percentage points. The next significant employment mode for males and females in rural areas has been casual labour; nearly 25 % of males and 19 % of females were employed as casual labourers in 2024. There is also a decline in the incidence of casual labour in 2024 compared to 2018 for both males and females. However, this decline was more significant for females (13.06 percentage points) than for males (3.31 percentage points). Table 108 also shows that the incidence of regular employment in 2024 was higher among rural males (15.8 %) than among rural females (7.8 %). Moreover, while rural males experienced an increase in the incidence of regular employment of 1.84 percentage points in 2024 compared to 2018, rural females experienced a decline of 2.72 percentage points. The rise in the incidence of self-employment among rural females from 2018 to 2024 is primarily attributed to a decrease in the proportion of workers in casual employment, as well as a reduction in the percentage of workers in regular employment. When considering both males and females, a clear trend of increasing self-employment rates is evident. In contrast, the percentages of regular workers and casual labourers decreased from 2018 to 2024.

Table 108: Modes of Employment (%) of Workers (UPSS) in India for 2024 by Gender and Region

Region	Mode of employment	Male	% pt change over 2018	Female	% pt change over 2018	Male + Female	% pt change over 2018
Rural	Regular employee	15.80	1.84	7.80	-2.72	12.70	-0.43
	Self-employed	59.40	1.57	73.50	15.77	64.70	6.89
	Casual labour	24.90	-3.31	18.70	-13.06	22.50	-6.57
Urban	Regular employee	46.80	1.10	49.40	-2.74	47.50	0.48
	Self-employed	39.80	0.59	42.30	7.56	40.40	2.10
	Casual labour	13.40	-1.68	8.30	-4.82	12.10	-2.58
Rural + Urban	Regular employee	24.90	1.52	15.90	-5.13	21.75	1.09
	Self-employed	53.60	1.29	67.40	15.48	58.43	6.21
	Casual labour	21.50	-2.81	16.70	-10.35	19.83	-5.12

Source: Same as Table 95

The modes of employment in urban areas differ from those in rural areas, with regular employment being the predominant form for both males and females. According to Table 108, urban females (49 %) have a higher proportion of regular workers than urban males (47 %). However, compared to the previous period in 2018, urban females experienced a decline of 2.74 percentage points in regular employment, while the share of urban males improved by 1.10 percentage points. In urban areas, self-employment ranks second after regular employment for both genders. In 2024, almost 40 % of male and 42 % of female workers were self-employed. It is also observed that, while the percentage of self-employed individuals in urban areas increased from 2018 to 2024 for both genders, the magnitude of the improvement was greater for females (7.56 percentage points) than for males (0.59 percentage points). The percentage of casual workers in urban areas was the lowest among the three employment modes for both males and females. In 2024, 13.40 % of male urban workers and 8.30 % of female urban workers were engaged in casual employment. Furthermore, both genders experienced declines in their share of casual employment in 2024 compared to 2018, with the decrease being more significant for females (4.82 percentage points) than for males (1.68 percentage points). Regarding males and females combined, 47.5 % of urban workers are engaged in regular employment, while the corresponding figures for self-employment and casual employment are 40.4 % and 12.1 %, respectively. Another observation for combined males and females is that the shares of regular employment and self-employment among total urban workers increased in 2024 compared to 2018, while the share of casual employment declined. However, the increase in the share of self-employment exceeded that of regular employment.

When we combine rural and urban areas, Table 108 indicates that nearly 54 % of males and 67 % of females were engaged in self-employment in 2024. These are 1.29 percentage points and 15.48 percentage points higher than the self-employment shares of males and females, respectively, in 2018. In 2024, regular employment accounted for approximately 25 % of males and 16 % of females. While the proportion of regular employment among males increased by 1.52 percentage points from 2018 to 2024, it fell by 5.13 percentage points for females during the same period. As for casual employment, the shares of males and females in 2024 are nearly 22 % and 17 %, respectively. These figures in 2024 are lower than those in 2018 by 2.81 percentage points for males and 10.35 percentage points for females. It appears that the increase in the share of females in self-employment has occurred at the expense of casual and regular employment. The males have gained higher shares of both regular and self-employment, resulting in a reduction in their share of casual employment. However, when considering both males and females together, a clear trend emerges: the shares of both regular and casual employment are declining, while the share of self-employment is increasing in the country from 2018 to 2024.

7.3.2 Growth Rates of Workers Under Different Modes of Employment

Table 109 presents growth rates for workers across various employment modes in India. Both regular employment and self-employment experienced positive growth rates from 2018 to 2024 for both males and females. However, the growth rates of these two types of employment are higher for females compared to males. According to the table, while males experienced a 2.95 % annual growth in regular employment, the corresponding figure for females is 6.44 %. On the other hand, concerning self-employment, the growth rates are 2.29 % for males and 16.48 % for females. When we compare the growth rates of these two modes of employment from 1994 to 2018 with those from 2018 to 2024, it shows that the growth rate of regular employment increased by 0.08 percentage points for males and 1.84 percentage points for females in the latter period compared to the former period. However, in the case of self-employment, females experienced a larger improvement in growth rate during the latter period (17.36 percentage points) than males (0.86 percentage points). The picture changes regarding the growth of casual employment from 2018 to 2024, with negative growth for males (–0.19 %) but positive growth for females (2.91 %). A comparison of casual employment growth for males and females from 1994 to 2018 and from 2018 to 2024 shows that the growth rate of such employment decreased by 0.93 percentage points for males but increased by 4.69 percentage points for females in the latter period.

Table 109: Annual Compound Growth Rates of Workers (UPSS) Under Different Modes of Employment in India from 2018 to 2024 by Gender (Rural & Urban Combined)

Mode of employment	Male	% pt change over growth rate from 1994 to 2018	Female	% pt change over growth rate from 1994 to 2018	Male + Female	% pt change over growth rate from 1994 to 2018
Regular employee	2.95	0.08	6.44	1.84	3.73	0.56
Self-employed	2.29	0.86	16.48	17.36	6.55	5.78
Casual labour	−0.19	−0.93	2.91	4.69	0.64	0.70

Source: Using information in Tables 99 and 108

Considering both males and females, self-employment in the country grew at the highest rate from 2018 to 2024, at 6.55 % per annum, followed by regular employment at 3.73 % per annum and casual employment at 0.64 % per annum. A comparison of the growth rates of workers under these modes of employment from 1994 to 2018 and from 2018 to 2024 shows that the self-employment growth rate increased by as much as 5.78 percentage points in the latter period compared to the former. In contrast, the growth rates of regular and casual employment increased by 0.56 percentage points and 0.70 percentage points, respectively, during the latter period compared to the former.

7.3.3 Modes of Employment in Major States

We now examine employment modes by gender across twenty-one major states (comprising both rural and urban areas) in 2024 and compare them with those in 2018. As shown in Table 110, the percentage of regular male employees in 2024 was highest in Haryana (41.4 %) and lowest in Bihar (10.3 %). In addition to Haryana, twelve other states recorded a percentage of male regular employees exceeding the all-India level of 24.9 %. These states, listed in descending order by percentage, are Tamil Nadu, Gujarat, Maharashtra, Punjab, Uttarakhand, Kerala, Himachal Pradesh, Telangana, Jammu & Kashmir, Karnataka, Rajasthan, and Andhra Pradesh. In contrast, along with Bihar, seven other states have a lower percentage of male regular employees than the national average. The states in descending order of the percentage of male regular employees are West Bengal, Chhattisgarh, Assam, Madhya Pradesh, Jharkhand, Odisha, and Uttar Pradesh. It is also noticeable that all states except Telangana, Bihar, Assam, and Uttar Pradesh increased the percentage of male regular employees in 2024 compared to 2018. Among these states, Gujarat recorded the largest increase in the percentage of male regular employees, rising by 7.7 percentage points. Other states, such as Andhra Pradesh, Haryana, Himachal Pradesh, Kerala, Maharashtra, Rajasthan, and Tamil Nadu (listed in alphabetical order), also recorded significant improvements (of more than 3.0 percentage points) in the percentage of male regular employees during this period.

Table 110: Modes of Employment in Major States in 2024 (Rural & Urban Combined)

Gender	State	Regular employee			Self-employed			Casual labour		
		%	Rank	% pt change over 2018	%	Rank	% pt change over 2018	%	Rank	% pt change over 2018
Male	Andhra Pradesh	25.4	13	4.5	49.4	14	3.4	25.2	7	−7.8
	Assam	19.8	16	−0.5	53.2	9	−8.3	27.0	6	8.8
	Bihar	10.3	21	−1.7	60.9	4	5.0	28.8	1	−3.3
	Chhattisgarh	20.3	15	2.4	62.1	3	−1.7	17.7	15	−0.8
	Gujarat	37.6	3	7.7	49.2	16	−5.5	13.2	21	−2.2
	Haryana	41.4	1	4.5	43.6	20	−0.5	15.0	18	−4.0
	Himachal Pradesh	31.0	8	3.7	50.8	12	−1.8	18.2	14	−1.8
	Jammu & Kashmir	29.5	10	1.1	53.0	10	1.9	17.5	16	−3.0
	Jharkhand	16.7	18	1.4	55.4	7	−4.4	27.9	5	3.0
	Karnataka	27.1	11	1.8	50.7	13	0.4	22.2	9	−2.2
	Kerala	31.3	7	3.8	43.6	19	2.8	25.1	8	−6.5
	Madhya Pradesh	17.2	17	1.5	63.0	2	5.5	19.8	12	−7.0
	Maharashtra	34.7	4	3.1	45.2	17	−2.6	20.1	11	−0.5
	Odisha	16.7	19	1.1	55.0	8	−4.3	28.3	2	3.2
	Punjab	33.6	5	2.1	44.7	18	−2.3	21.7	10	0.2
	Rajasthan	25.8	12	3.4	60.6	5	0.7	13.6	20	−4.0
	Tamil Nadu	38.8	2	3.4	33.1	21	0.6	28.1	4	−4.0
	Telangana	29.7	9	−2.2	55.7	6	8.0	14.6	19	−5.8
	Uttar Pradesh	15.0	20	−0.2	66.4	1	4.5	18.6	13	−4.3
	Uttarakhand	32.0	6	1.2	51.8	11	−4.4	16.2	17	3.3
	West Bengal	22.4	14	1.7	49.4	15	3.2	28.2	3	−5.0

(Continued)

Table 110 *(Continued)*

Gender	State	Regular employee			Self-employed			Casual labour		
		%	Rank	% pt change over 2018	%	Rank	% pt change over 2018	%	Rank	% pt change over 2018
Female	Andhra Pradesh	17.3	10	3.1	48.5	19	6.1	34.3	2	−9.2
	Assam	17.5	9	−41.8	75.3	9	54.9	7.2	16	−13.1
	Bihar	4.8	21	−28.0	83.5	5	49.6	11.7	14	−21.6
	Chhattisgarh	9.7	15	1.8	70.6	12	0.2	19.7	7	−2.0
	Gujarat	18.2	8	−4.9	68.9	13	14.1	12.9	11	−9.2
	Haryana	31.4	3	3.6	56.4	14	14.1	12.3	13	−17.7
	Himachal Pradesh	12.6	13	4.1	84.6	4	−3.6	2.8	20	−0.6
	Jammu & Kashmir	10.0	14	−5.8	89.5	1	6.3	0.5	21	−0.4
	Jharkhand	7.3	18	−6.8	86.8	2	18.2	5.9	18	−11.4
	Karnataka	24.0	6	−1.8	51.8	16	11.4	24.2	5	−9.6
	Kerala	41.2	1	−6.3	37.0	20	7.4	21.8	6	−1.1
	Madhya Pradesh	6.6	19	−4.0	76.9	8	19.3	16.6	9	−15.2
	Maharashtra	24.5	5	2.6	50.5	18	5.4	25.1	4	−8.0
	Odisha	8.8	16	−5.5	72.8	10	22.5	18.5	8	−17.1
	Punjab	36.1	2	−9.1	51.6	17	11.3	12.3	12	−2.2
	Rajasthan	8.5	17	−0.1	80.8	6	0.8	10.7	15	−0.7
	Tamil Nadu	27.3	4	−2.8	36.1	21	2.7	36.6	1	0.1
	Telangana	18.4	7	0.6	56.3	15	7.8	25.3	3	−8.4
	Uttar Pradesh	6.6	20	−7.2	86.6	3	13.3	6.8	17	−6.1
	Uttarakhand	17.2	11	−7.5	77.0	7	11.5	5.8	19	−4.0
	West Bengal	16.5	12	−10.7	70.6	11	24.7	12.9	10	−14.0

(Continued)

Table 110 *(Continued)*

Gender	State	Regular employee			Self-employed			Casual labour		
		%	Rank	% pt change over 2018	%	Rank	% pt change over 2018	%	Rank	% pt change over 2018
Male + Female	Andhra Pradesh	22.3	11	3.9	49.1	16	4.4	28.7	2	−8.3
	Assam	18.9	14	−6.1	61.4	11	4.9	19.7	9	1.2
	Bihar	8.7	21	−4.4	67.5	5	12.8	23.8	5	−8.4
	Chhattisgarh	15.9	16	1.8	65.6	8	−0.6	18.5	14	−1.1
	Gujarat	30.8	6	2.3	56.1	13	1.4	13.1	17	−3.6
	Haryana	39.0	1	3.5	46.6	18	2.8	14.4	16	−6.2
	Himachal Pradesh	22.6	10	3.1	66.2	7	−1.1	11.2	20	−2.0
	Jammu & Kashmir	22.2	12	−2.9	66.7	6	7.2	11.1	21	−4.3
	Jharkhand	12.9	19	−2.2	68.0	4	6.8	19.0	11	−4.6
	Karnataka	26.1	8	0.6	51.1	15	3.3	22.9	7	−3.9
	Kerala	35.0	2	2.1	41.1	20	3.4	23.9	4	−5.4
	Madhya Pradesh	13.2	18	−1.1	68.2	3	10.7	18.6	13	−9.6
	Maharashtra	31.3	5	2.4	47.0	17	0.0	21.8	8	−2.4
	Odisha	13.6	17	−1.8	62.0	9	4.6	24.4	3	−2.8
	Punjab	34.3	4	0.7	46.6	19	0.6	19.2	10	−1.3
	Rajasthan	18.8	15	0.1	68.8	2	3.5	12.5	18	−3.5
	Tamil Nadu	34.4	3	0.7	34.2	21	1.5	31.3	1	−2.1
	Telangana	25.4	9	−2.3	55.9	14	8.0	18.7	12	−5.7
	Uttar Pradesh	12.4	20	−2.6	72.7	1	9.0	14.9	15	−6.4
	Uttarakhand	26.3	7	−3.3	61.5	10	3.5	12.2	19	−0.1
	West Bengal	20.5	13	−1.6	56.5	12	10.4	23.1	6	−8.7

Source: Same as Table 95

In 2024, Kerala had the highest percentage of female regular employees at 41.2 %, while Bihar recorded the lowest at 4.8 %. The states with a female regular employee percentage above the all-India level this year include Punjab, Haryana, Tamil Nadu, Maharashtra, Karnataka, Telangana, Gujarat, Assam, Andhra Pradesh, Uttarakhand, and West Bengal, listed in descending order of female regular employee percentage. On the other hand, besides Bihar, the states with a lower percentage of female regular employees than the all-India level are Uttar Pradesh, Madhya Pradesh, Jharkhand, Rajasthan, Odisha, Chhattisgarh, Jammu & Kashmir, and Himachal Pradesh, listed in ascending order of their percentages. Another noteworthy observation from Table 110 is that, as at the all-India level, in fifteen of the twenty-one states we considered, the percentage of female regular employees declined in 2024 compared to 2018. Three states – Assam, Bihar, and West Bengal – experienced a decline of over 10 percentage points in the proportion of female regular employees. Among the states that increased the percentage of female regular employees during this period, Himachal Pradesh recorded the largest gain of 4.1 percentage points.

When combining data for males and females, the percentage of regular employees in 2024 ranged from 39.0 % in Haryana to 8.7 % in Bihar. Besides Haryana, eleven other states recorded a higher percentage of regular employees in 2024 than the all-India level of 21.8 %. These states, listed in descending order by the percentage of regular employees, are Kerala, Tamil Nadu, Punjab, Maharashtra, Gujarat, Uttarakhand, Karnataka, Telangana, Himachal Pradesh, Andhra Pradesh, and Jammu & Kashmir. Conversely, apart from Bihar, the states with a percentage of regular employees lower than the all-India level include Uttar Pradesh, Jharkhand, Madhya Pradesh, Odisha, Chhattisgarh, Rajasthan, Assam, and West Bengal, listed in ascending order of their percentage of regular employees. Another important point is that the percentage of regular employees declined in ten states from 2018 to 2024. Among the states that increased the percentage of regular employees during this period, Andhra Pradesh (3.9 percentage points) ranks first; two other states, Haryana and Himachal Pradesh, achieved improvements of over 3.0 percentage points. In contrast, the most significant decline in the percentage of regular employees occurred in Assam, by 6.1 percentage points. Two additional states that experienced a drop of more than 3.0 percentage points are Bihar and Uttarakhand.

Regarding self-employment, Table 110 indicates that for males, Uttar Pradesh had the highest percentage of workers in this mode of employment in 2024 at 66.4 %, while Tamil Nadu recorded the lowest at 33.1 %. In addition to Uttar Pradesh, seven other states had a higher percentage of workers in self-employment compared to the all-India level of 53.6 %. These states, listed in descending order of the percentage of self-employed workers, are Madhya Pradesh, Chhattisgarh, Bihar, Rajasthan, Telangana, Jharkhand, and Odisha. On the other hand, apart from Tamil Nadu, the states with a percentage of male self-employed workers lower than the national level, listed in ascending order of self-employment rates, are Haryana, Kerala, Punjab, Maharashtra, Gujarat, West Bengal, Andhra Pradesh, Karnataka, Himachal Pradesh, Uttarakhand, Jammu & Kashmir, and Assam. It is also observed that ten out of twenty-one states we considered registered declines in the percentage of male self-employed workers in 2024 compared to 2018. The largest improvement in this percentage from 2018 to 2024 occurred in Telangana, with an 8.0 percentage-point increase, followed by notable increases of over 4.0 percentage points in Madhya Pradesh, Bihar, and Uttar Pradesh.

The percentage of female self-employed workers in 2024 ranged from 89.5 % in Jammu & Kashmir to 36.1 % in Tamil Nadu. In addition to Jammu & Kashmir, twelve other states have female self-employed worker percentages that exceed the national level of 67.40 %. These states, in descending order of the percentage of self-employed workers, are Jharkhand, Uttar Pradesh, Himachal Pradesh, Bihar, Rajasthan, Uttarakhand, Madhya Pradesh, Assam, Odisha, West Bengal, Chhattisgarh, and Gujarat. In contrast, the states with a lower percentage of female self-employed workers than the national level, arranged in ascending order, are Kerala, Andhra Pradesh, Maharashtra, Punjab, Karnataka, Telangana, and Haryana. Another striking observation is that all states except Himachal Pradesh recorded an improvement in the percentage of female self-employed workers in 2024 compared to 2018. The extent of this improvement varied from 54.9 percentage points in Assam to 0.2 percentage points in Chhattisgarh. Additionally, Bihar, Odisha, and West Bengal experienced a significant improvement (over 20 percentage points) in the share of female self-employed workers.

In 2024, considering both males and females, Uttar Pradesh ranked highest among states in terms of the percentage of self-employed workers, while Tamil Nadu ranked lowest. In addition to Uttar Pradesh, ten other states had percentages of self-employed workers exceeding the all-India level of 58.4 %, listed in descending order: Rajasthan, Madhya Pradesh, Jharkhand, Bihar, Jammu & Kashmir, Himachal Pradesh, Chhattisgarh, Odisha, Uttarakhand, and Assam. Besides Tamil Nadu, other states with percentages of self-employed workers lower than the all-India level, listed in ascending order, include Kerala, Punjab, Haryana, Maharashtra, Andhra Pradesh, Karnataka, Telangana, Gujarat, and West Bengal. However, all states except for Himachal Pradesh and Chhattisgarh observed increases in the percentage of self-employed workers between 2018 and 2024. The states that showed the most significant improvement (over 10 percentage points) in the percentage of self-employed workers are Bihar, Madhya Pradesh, and West Bengal.

Focusing on the percentages of casual workers in the states in 2024, Table 110 shows that for males, the highest percentage was in Bihar (28.8 %), while the lowest was in Gujarat (13.2 %). In addition to Bihar, nine other states had a higher percentage of male casual workers than the all-India level (21.50 %). In descending order of this percentage, those states are Odisha, West Bengal, Tamil Nadu, Jharkhand, Assam, Andhra Pradesh, Kerala, Karnataka, and Punjab. Conversely, the states with male casual worker percentages lower than the all-India level, listed in ascending order, are Rajasthan, Telangana, Haryana, Uttarakhand, Jammu & Kashmir, Chhattisgarh, Himachal Pradesh, Uttar Pradesh, Madhya Pradesh, and Maharashtra. In all states except Assam, Uttarakhand, Odisha, Jharkhand, and Punjab, the percentage of male casual workers decreased in 2024 compared to 2018.

The percentage of female casual workers in 2024 is highest in Tamil Nadu (36.6 %) and lowest in Jammu & Kashmir (0.5 %). In addition to Tamil Nadu, other states with a female casual worker percentage above the all-India level (16.7 %) are listed in descending order: Andhra Pradesh, Telangana, Maharashtra, Karnataka, Kerala, Chhattisgarh, and Odisha. Conversely, apart from Jammu & Kashmir, the states with a lower percentage of female casual workers than the all-India level, arranged in ascending order of their percentages, are Himachal Pradesh, Uttarakhand, Jharkhand, Uttar Pradesh, Assam, Rajasthan, Bihar, Haryana, Punjab, Gujarat, West Bengal, and Madhya Pradesh. It is also noted that in every state except Tamil Nadu, the percentage of female casual workers decreased in 2024 compared to 2018. The most significant decline occurred in Bihar, down by 21.6 percentage points. The reduction was also substantial in six other states, exceeding 10.0 percentage points: Haryana, Odisha, Madhya Pradesh, West Bengal, Assam, and Jharkhand.

In 2024, Tamil Nadu had the highest percentage of casual workers, combining males and females, at 31.3 %, while Jammu & Kashmir had the lowest at 11.1 %. In addition to Tamil Nadu, seven other states exceeded the national average of 19.8 % of casual workers this year. These states, listed in descending order of their casual worker percentages, are Andhra Pradesh, Odisha, Kerala, Bihar, West Bengal, Karnataka, and Maharashtra. Conversely, apart from Jammu & Kashmir, the states reporting a lower percentage of casual workers than the national average, arranged in ascending order, are Himachal Pradesh, Uttarakhand, Rajasthan, Gujarat, Haryana, Uttar Pradesh, Chhattisgarh, Madhya Pradesh, Telangana, Jharkhand, Punjab, and Assam. It is also noteworthy that all states except Assam recorded a decline in the percentage of casual workers between 2018 and 2024. In some of these states, the decrease in the percentage of casual workers was significant, exceeding 8.0 percentage points. These states are Madhya Pradesh, West Bengal, Bihar, and Andhra Pradesh.

7.3.4 Sectoral Composition of Workers in India by Gender and Region

We now examine the sectoral composition of workers in 2024 to understand the country's employment diversification pattern. We also look at changes in employment diversification patterns from 2018 to 2024. Table 111 presents information for the entire country, categorised by gender and region. In rural areas, the percentage of male workers involved in non-agricultural employment (50.57 %) is marginally higher in 2024 than that of those employed in the agriculture and allied (for brevity, henceforth referred to as agriculture) sector (49.43 %). However, the situation for rural females is drastically different, as more than three-fourths are engaged in agriculture. When considering males and females together, agriculture remains the dominant sector in rural areas in 2024, with nearly three-fifths of the workforce employed in it. Another critical point is that there has been no progress in diversifying rural employment (for males and females combined) from agriculture to non-agriculture from 2018 to 2024. The percentage of agricultural employment rose by 0.44 percentage points during this period, thus decreasing the percentage of non-agricultural employment by a similar amount. However, the picture changes when rural males and females are considered separately. While rural males showed some evidence of diversifying their employment, with non-agricultural employment increasing by 5.53 percentage points from 2018 to 2024, the percentage of non-agricultural employment declined for rural females by 3.70 percentage points during this period.

Table 111: Sectoral Distribution of Workers (UPSS) in India by Gender and Region in 2024 (Percentage)

Region	Sector	Male	% pt change over 2018	Female	% pt change over 2018	Male + Female	% pt change over 2018
Rural	Agriculture & allied	49.43	–5.53	76.89	3.70	59.84	0.44
	Mining and quarrying	0.30	–0.16	0.04	–0.13	0.20	–0.19
	Manufacturing	8.10	0.43	8.53	0.39	8.26	0.48
	Electricity, gas and water supply	0.50	0.03	0.12	0.09	0.36	0.00
	Construction	17.72	3.22	3.90	–1.44	12.48	0.21
	Trade, hotels and restaurants	10.91	1.75	3.90	–0.10	8.25	0.35
	Transport, storage and communication	5.93	0.76	0.14	–0.13	3.74	–0.25
	Other services	7.12	–0.51	6.48	–2.37	6.88	–1.05
	Non-agriculture	50.57	5.53	23.11	–3.70	40.16	–0.44

(Continued)

Table 111 *(Continued)*

Region	Sector	Male	% pt change over 2018	Female	% pt change over 2018	Male + Female	% pt change over 2018
Urban	Agriculture & allied	4.76	−0.62	12.30	3.23	6.73	0.59
	Mining and quarrying	0.40	−0.16	0.13	−0.02	0.33	−0.15
	Manufacturing	19.27	−3.12	24.09	−1.13	20.53	−2.44
	Electricity, gas and water supply	1.28	−0.02	0.53	−0.11	1.08	−0.08
	Construction	13.19	1.45	3.03	−1.10	10.54	0.37
	Trade, hotels and restaurants	26.65	2.21	14.97	1.94	23.60	1.50
	Transport, storage and communication	13.22	0.52	4.85	1.53	11.04	0.26
	Other services	21.23	−0.26	40.11	−4.34	26.15	−0.04
	Non-agriculture	95.24	0.62	87.70	−3.23	93.27	−0.58
Rural + Urban	Agriculture & allied	36.29	−3.95	64.36	7.37	46.07	1.93
	Mining and quarrying	0.33	−0.16	0.06	−0.11	0.23	−0.18
	Manufacturing	11.38	−0.65	11.55	−0.91	11.44	−0.69
	Electricity, gas and water supply	0.73	0.02	0.20	0.02	0.54	−0.05
	Construction	16.39	2.71	3.73	−1.30	11.98	0.31
	Trade, hotels and restaurants	15.54	1.85	6.04	−0.24	12.23	0.26
	Transport, storage and communication	8.07	0.66	1.06	0.01	5.63	−0.30
	Other services	11.27	−0.47	13.01	−4.83	11.87	−1.29
	Non-agriculture	63.71	3.96	35.64	−7.37	53.93	−1.93

Source: Same as Table 95

In 2024, 'construction' was the most crucial non-agricultural sub-sector for rural males, accounting for 17.72 %, while 'manufacturing' was the most significant for rural females, comprising 8.53 %. In the same year, rural males' next critical non-agricultural sub-sectors were 'trade, hotels and restaurants', 'manufacturing', and 'other services', absorbing 10.91 %, 8.10 %, and 7.12 %, respectively. Besides 'manufacturing', the other non-agricultural sub-sector for rural females to absorb more than 5 % of workers was 'other services'. For rural males, the non-agricultural sub-sectors experiencing an increase in the percentage of workers from 2018 to 2024 include 'construction' (3.22 percentage points), 'trade, hotels, and restaurants' (1.75 percentage points), 'transport, storage and communication' (0.76 percentage point), 'manufacturing' (0.43 percentage point), and 'electricity, gas, and water supply' (0.03 percentage point); meanwhile, 'other services' and 'mining and quarrying' are the sub-sectors seeing a decline in this regard. In contrast, for rural females, all non-agricultural sub-sectors witnessed a decline in the percentage of workers in 2024 compared to 2018, except for 'manufacturing' and 'electricity, gas, and water supply', which saw improvements of 0.39 percentage points and 0.09 percentage points, respectively, in the share of workers. However, considering the males and females together, only three non-agricultural sub-sectors displayed improvement in the percentage of rural workers during this timeframe, which are 'manufacturing' (0.48 percentage point), 'trade, hotels, and restaurants' (0.35 percentage point), and 'construction' (0.21 percentage point).

In urban areas, the most significant sub-sector for males in 2024 was 'trade, hotels, and restaurants', which employed 26.65 % of them. This was followed by 'other services' (21.23 %), 'manufacturing' (19.27 %), 'transport, storage, and communication' (13.22 %), and 'construction' (13.19 %). However, only three sub-sectors – namely, 'trade, hotels, and restaurants', 'construction', and 'transport, storage, and communication'– improved their percentage of workers from 2018 to 2024. For urban females, the three most significant non-agricultural employment sub-sectors in 2024 are 'other services', 'manufacturing', and 'trade, hotels, and restaurants', accounting for 40.11 %, 24.09 %, and 14.97 % of workers, respectively. Another noteworthy point is that none of the sub-sectors, except for 'trade, hotels, and restaurants' and 'transport, storage and communication', showed improvement in the percentage of urban female workers in 2024 compared to 2018. Combining males and females, the key sub-sectors in urban areas are 'other services', 'trade, hotels and restaurants', 'manufacturing', 'transport, storage, and communication', and 'construction'. These sub-sectors absorbed 26.15 %, 23.60 %, 20.53 %, 11.04 %, and 10.54 % of urban workers in 2024, respectively. However, only three of these sectors experienced improvement in the percentage of workers from 2018 to 2024: 'trade, hotels and restaurants' (1.50 percentage points), 'construction' (0.37 percentage points), and 'transport, storage, and communication' (0.26 percentage points).

When combining rural and urban areas, nearly 64 % of male workers were engaged in non-agricultural employment in 2024, while the corresponding figure for females was about 36 %. Moreover, while the share of male workers in non-agricultural employment increased by 3.96 percentage points from 2018 to 2024, the share of female workers declined by 7.37 percentage points. The picture is reversed in the case of agricultural employment: the female share increased by 7.37 percentage points from 2018 to 2024, while the male share decreased by 3.95 percentage points over the same period. Combining males and females from rural and urban areas, it appears that while the share of non-agricultural employment declined by 1.93 percentage points from 2018 to 2024, the share of agricultural employment increased by the same amount. Another observation is that, for the combined areas, the percentage of male employment in non-agricultural sub-sectors such as 'construction', 'trade, hotels and restaurants', 'transport, storage, and communication', and 'electricity, gas and water supply' increased in 2024 compared to 2018. In contrast, for females, the share of non-agricultural employment declined in all non-agricultural sub-sectors except 'electricity, gas and water supply' and 'transport, storage, and communication', where there was a minuscule increase. However, when considering males and females together in combined areas (rural plus urban), only two non-agricultural sub-sectors have seen an improvement in the percentage of workers in 2024 compared to 2018: 'construction' and 'trade, hotels and restaurants'.

7.3.5 Growth Rates of Workers in Different Sectors in India

Table 112 provides annual growth rates for males, females, and both genders combined across sectors in the combined rural and urban areas from 2018 to 2024, and compares these rates with those from 1994 to 2018. It is observed that, for males, agricultural employment grew at an annual rate of only 0.14 % from 2018 to 2024, while non-agricultural employment grew by 2.97 %. In contrast, females experienced significant growth in agricultural (13.80 %) and non-agricultural (8.08 %) employment during this period. Among the non-agricultural sub-sectors, the highest employment growth for males during this period is witnessed in 'construction' (4.99 %), followed by 'trade, hotels and restaurants' (4.05 %), 'transport, storage, and communication' (3.33 %), 'electricity, gas and water supply' (2.27 %), 'other services' (1.18 %), and 'manufacturing' (0.94 %). For females, the highest non-agricultural employment growth is recorded by 'electricity, gas and water supply' (13.08 %), followed by 'transport, storage, and communication' (11.72 %), 'trade, hotels and restaurants' (10.80 %), 'manufacturing' (10.12 %), 'construction' (6.08 %), and 'other services' (5.80 %). Employment growth has been negative for both males and females in the 'mining and quarrying' sub-sector. It is also important to note that in all non-agricultural sub-sectors, the employment growth rates for females exceeded those of males (except 'mining and quarrying' where employment declined more rapidly for females than males). Furthermore, when we compare the employment growth rates of the non-agricultural sub-sectors from 1994 to 2018 with those from 2018 to 2024, it is observed that while males improved their growth rates in the latter period only in the case of 'trade, hotels and restaurants', females did so in all the sub-sectors except 'mining and quarrying'. The non-agricultural sub-sector in which females recorded maximum improvement in growth rate is 'manufacturing' (9.45 percentage points), which is followed by 'trade, hotels and restaurants' (8.48 percentage points), 'electricity, gas and water supply' (7.39 percentage points), 'transport, storage, and communication' (6.42 percentage points), 'other services' (2.85 percentage points) and 'construction' (0.98 percentage points).

Table 112: Annual Compound Growth Rates of Workers (UPSS) in Different Sectors in India from 2018 to 2024 by Gender (Rural & Urban Combined)

	Male		Female		Male + Female	
Sector	Gr. Rate (%)	% pt change over growth rate from 1994 to 2018	Gr. Rate (%)	% pt change over growth rate from 1994 to 2018	Gr. Rate (%)	% pt change over growth rate from 1994 to 2018
Agriculture & allied	0.14	0.10	13.80	15.57	5.32	5.91
Mining and quarrying	-4.60	-3.81	-6.59	-2.33	-5.02	-3.66
Manufacturing	0.94	-0.88	10.12	9.45	3.55	2.04
Electricity, gas and water supply	2.27	-0.56	13.08	7.39	3.17	0.25
Construction	4.99	-1.72	6.08	0.98	5.03	-1.47
Trade, hotels and restaurants	4.05	1.05	10.80	8.48	4.95	2.06
Transport, storage and communication	3.33	-0.71	11.72	6.42	3.66	-0.39
Other services	1.18	-0.27	5.80	2.85	2.79	0.93
Non-agriculture	2.97	-0.01	8.08	5.87	3.96	1.14
All sectors	1.88	0.35	11.52	12.02	4.57	3.61

Source: Computed using information in Tables 99 and 111

However, combining males and females, the 'construction' sub-sector displayed the maximum growth rate (5.03 %) among non-agricultural sub-sectors from 2018 to 2024, followed by 'trade, hotels and restaurants' (4.95 %), 'transport, storage, and communication' (3.66 %), 'manufacturing' (3.55 %), 'electricity, gas and water supply' (3.17 %), and 'other services' (2.79 %). A comparison of growth rates of these sub-sectors from 1994 to 2018 and 2018 to 2024 reveals that the biggest improvement in the growth rate in the latter period happened in 'trade, hotels and restaurants' (2.06 percentage points) followed by 'manufacturing' (2.04 percentage points), 'other service' (0.93 percentage point) and 'electricity, gas and water supply' (0.25 percentage points). On the other hand, the growth rates from 2018 to 2024 declined compared to those from 1994 to 2018 for the sectors of 'construction', 'transport, storage, and communication', and 'mining and quarrying'.

7.3.6 Employment Diversification in Major States

To assess employment diversification across states in 2024, we compiled data on the proportion of non-agricultural workers among total workers, including both rural and urban areas. We also analysed changes in employment diversification from 2018 to 2024. The information in Table 113 shows that Kerala was the most diversified state in the country for male employment in 2024, with 78.6 % of male workers engaged in non-agricultural activities. In contrast, Chhattisgarh had the least diversification in male employment, with only 45.5 % of workers involved in non-agricultural activities. Besides Kerala, fourteen other states reported higher percentages of male non-agricultural workers than the all-India average of 63.71 %. These states, listed in descending order of their percentages of non-agricultural workers, are Tamil Nadu, Jammu & Kashmir, Haryana, Punjab, Uttarakhand, Assam, West Bengal, Jharkhand, Gujarat, Himachal Pradesh, Maharashtra, Rajasthan, Odisha, and Telangana. Conversely, the states that had a lower percentage of male non-agricultural workers than the all-India average, apart from Chhattisgarh, include Madhya Pradesh, Uttar Pradesh, Bihar, Karnataka, and Andhra Pradesh. It is also noteworthy that all states, except for Kerala, showed an improvement in the percentage of male non-agricultural workers in 2024 compared to 2018. Among these states, the most significant improvements were seen in Assam, with a 14.5 percentage-point increase in male non-agricultural workers, followed by Odisha with an 11.8 percentage-point increase and Jharkhand with an 11.2 percentage-point increase.

Table 113: Percentage of Non-agricultural Workers to Total Workers (UPSS) in Major States in 2024 (Rural & Urban Combined)

State	Male			Female			Male + Female		
	%	Rank	% pt change over 2018	%	Rank	% pt change over 2018	%	Rank	% pt change over 2018
Andhra Pradesh	60.1	16	3.1	43.5	7	4.6	53.7	11	3.5
Assam	69.1	7	14.5	25.3	14	–29.0	52.9	13	–1.7
Bihar	57.2	18	1.9	17.9	21	–28.5	45.8	18	–9.1
Chhattisgarh	45.5	21	6.5	23.0	17	1.3	36.2	21	3.7
Gujarat	67.6	10	6.6	38.9	10	–4.8	57.6	7	0.0
Haryana	78.2	4	2.2	54.1	4	1.2	72.5	3	–0.1
Himachal Pradesh	66.5	11	2.2	21.6	19	5.5	46.1	17	1.7
Jammu & Kashmir	78.3	3	6.4	22.2	18	–1.1	57.2	9	–2.1
Jharkhand	67.9	9	11.2	23.4	15	–13.7	50.0	15	–3.3
Karnataka	59.5	17	2.3	41.6	8	–4.0	53.5	12	–0.8
Kerala	78.6	1	–1.2	63.6	2	–17.3	73.0	1	–7.1
Madhya Pradesh	47.6	20	3.7	23.2	16	–4.5	38.4	20	–1.0
Maharashtra	64.8	12	5.5	41.0	9	6.5	56.8	10	4.6
Odisha	64.6	14	11.8	30.5	12	–14.8	51.1	14	–0.1
Punjab	75.3	5	1.4	66.0	1	–8.4	72.8	2	–1.2
Rajasthan	64.6	13	4.7	25.8	13	1.3	49.0	16	–1.5
Tamil Nadu	78.5	2	2.4	61.4	3	–2.4	72.0	4	–0.2
Telangana	64.1	15	2.7	46.9	6	1.4	57.5	8	0.9
Uttar Pradesh	55.6	19	1.5	18.2	20	–17.3	44.1	19	–7.2
Uttarakhand	73.8	6	9.7	32.0	11	1.3	57.7	6	0.2
West Bengal	68.1	8	5.0	49.2	5	–15.2	61.8	5	–1.6

Source: Same as Table 95

In 2024, Punjab emerged as the most diversified state for female employment, with 66.0 % of workers in the non-agricultural sector. In contrast, Bihar was the least diversified, with only 17.9 % of female workers engaged in this sector. Apart from Punjab, nine states had a higher percentage of female non-agricultural workers in 2024 than the all-India average of 35.64 %. These states, listed in descending order of their percentage of non-agricultural workers, are Kerala, Tamil Nadu, Haryana, West Bengal, Telangana, Andhra Pradesh, Karnataka, Maharashtra, and Gujarat. Conversely, besides Bihar, the states that reported lower percentages of female non-agricultural workers than the all-India average, listed in ascending order, are Uttar Pradesh, Himachal Pradesh, Jammu & Kashmir, Chhattisgarh, Madhya Pradesh, Jharkhand, Assam, Rajasthan, Odisha, and Uttarakhand. It was also noted that thirteen of the twenty-one states included in our analysis experienced a decline in the percentage of female non-agricultural workers from 2018 to 2024. Additionally, seven of these states experienced a significant decrease (more than 10.0 percentage points) in the percentage of female non-agricultural workers: Assam, Bihar, Jharkhand, Kerala, Odisha, Uttar Pradesh, and West Bengal (in alphabetical order).

Table 113 also provides insights into employment diversification across Indian states, combining data for both males and females. In 2024, Kerala emerged as the most diversified state, with 73.0 % of its workers engaged in non-agricultural employment. Conversely, Chhattisgarh ranks as the least diversified state, with only 36.2 % of its workers involved in non-agricultural employment. The other states with higher non-agricultural employment percentages than the all-India average (53.93 %) are arranged in descending order: Punjab, Haryana, Tamil Nadu, West Bengal, Uttarakhand, Gujarat, Telangana, Jammu & Kashmir, and Maharashtra. On the other hand, apart from Chhattisgarh, the states with lower percentages of non-agricultural employment compared to the all-India average, arranged in ascending order of these percentages, are Madhya Pradesh, Uttar Pradesh, Bihar, Himachal Pradesh, Rajasthan, Jharkhand, Odisha, Assam, Karnataka, and Andhra Pradesh. Another important observation is that in fourteen of twenty-one states, the percentage of non-agricultural employment declined from 2018 to 2024. Notably, three states, Bihar, Uttar Pradesh, and Kerala, experienced a decline of over 7.0 percentage points during this period. The states that saw an increase in the percentage of non-agricultural employment from 2018 to 2024, listed in descending order of improvement rate, are Maharashtra, Chhattisgarh, Andhra Pradesh, Himachal Pradesh, Telangana, and Uttarakhand. In contrast, Gujarat's percentage remained unchanged.

7.3.7 Incidence of Working Poor in India

We now examine the incidence of the working poor in India, considering their activity status, employment modes, and social and religious backgrounds in 2024, and observe changes compared to 2018. As before, to identify individuals experiencing poverty among this population, we used the Tendulkar poverty lines for states in both rural and urban areas, adjusting them with appropriate price deflators to derive state-specific poverty lines for 2018 and 2024. We then compared their per capita monthly consumption expenditures, as reported in the Periodic Labour Force Surveys, with the specific poverty lines to identify the poor. Individuals are classified as poor if their monthly per capita expenditures fall below the poverty line.

Table 114 indicates that the incidence of the working poor in the country (combining rural and urban areas) in 2024 is approximately 21 %. However, when examined separately, the incidences are nearly 23 % and 16 %, respectively. The incidence of the working poor declined from 2018 to 2024 in both regions, with a more pronounced decrease in rural areas (19.0 percentage points) than in urban areas (6.8 percentage points). Overall, the incidence of working poor declined by 15.3 percentage points in the combined regions during this period. Additionally, 16.3 % of the country's unemployed population was classified as poor in 2024, a decrease of 17.9 percentage points from the corresponding figure in 2018. However, the incidence of poverty is highest among individuals not in the labour force, standing at 27.6 % in 2024, although this is 14.1 percentage points lower than its percentage in 2018. According to the PLFS 2024 data, the poverty incidence among the entire population is 24.7 %, which is 14.7 percentage points lower than in 2018.

Table 114: Incidence of Working Poor in India in 2024

Percentage of poor among	Region	% of poor in 2024	% pt change over 2018
Employed / Workers	Rural	23.4	–19.0
	Urban	15.5	–6.8
	Rural + Urban	21.4	–15.3
Unemployed	Rural + Urban	16.3	–17.9
Out of labour force	Rural + Urban	27.6	–14.1
All persons	Rural + Urban	24.7	–14.7
Regular employee	Rural	14.9	–11.07
	Urban	10.7	–4.4
	Rural + Urban	12.5	–7.0

(Continued)

Table 114 *(Continued)*

Percentage of poor among	Region	% of poor in 2024	% pt change over 2018
Self-employed	Rural	22.4	–19.98
	Urban	16.5	–7.1
	Rural + Urban	21.4	–17.1
Casual labour	Rural	31.0	–18.71
	Urban	30.5	–10.9
	Rural + Urban	30.9	–17.4
ST workers	Rural + Urban	33.6	–22.8
SC workers	Rural + Urban	25.2	–17.9
OBC workers	Rural + Urban	21.0	–15.0
Other workers	Rural + Urban	12.5	–12.4
Hindu workers	Rural + Urban	21.3	–15.6
Muslim workers	Rural + Urban	23.9	–14.1
Other-religions workers	Rural + Urban	15.8	–14.3

Source: Same as Table 95

When examining the incidence of the working poor by employment mode, it is clear that casual workers have the highest rates, followed by self-employed individuals and regular employees. This trend is consistent in both rural and urban areas. In 2024, the poverty incidence among casual workers, self-employed individuals, and regular employees in rural areas was 31.0 %, 22.4 %, and 14.9 %, respectively. The combined figures for rural and urban areas are 30.9 % for casual workers, 21.4 % for self-employed individuals, and 12.5 % for regular employees. Notably, across all these categories, poverty decreased in 2024 compared to 2018, with the largest reduction among casual workers, followed by self-employed and regular employees.

Regarding the incidence of the working poor among different social groups, Table 114 indicates that workers from lower social groups experience higher poverty rates than those from higher social groups. The highest incidence of poverty is found among Scheduled Tribe (ST) workers, followed by Scheduled Castes (SC), Other Backward Classes (OBC), and 'Others' groups. Across all categories, the incidence of the working poor declined in 2024 compared to 2018, with a larger decrease among lower-caste groups than among higher-caste groups. Additionally, Table 114 shows that the incidence of working poor is slightly higher among Muslims (23.9 %) compared to Hindus (21.3 %) in 2024, with both groups experiencing a decline in poverty rates compared to 2018. However, the decrease for Hindu workers was marginally higher than that for Muslim workers.

7.3.8 Elasticities of Employment in Different Sectors

We start by examining employment elasticities across various sectors at the all-India level from 2018 to 2024 and comparing them with those recorded from 1994 to 2018. The information in Table 115 indicates that the highest elasticity value recorded from 2018 to 2024 is 2.21 for the 'wholesale & retail trade' sector. This is followed by 'agriculture & allied' with an elasticity value of 1.31, 'transport, storage and communication' at 1.11, 'manufacturing' at 1.07, 'construction' at 0.78, 'electricity, gas & water supply' at 0.66, and 'other services' at 0.53. Considering all non-agricultural sectors together, the elasticity value is 0.94, lower than that of the 'agriculture and allied' sector. However, the most significant fact here is that all sectors of the economy, except 'construction', have increased their employment elasticity values from 2018 to 2024, compared to the period from 1994 to 2018. Deviating from the situation observed from 1994 to 2018, when employment elasticity was negative, the 'agriculture & allied' sector registered an improvement in elasticity value of 1.52 points from 2018 to 2024, compared to the period from 1994 to 2018. Another sector that significantly improved elasticity value is 'wholesale & retail trade', which recorded an increase of 1.77 points in the latter period compared to the former. Even in 'manufacturing' and 'transport, storage and communication', the improvement in elasticity values has been quite impressive.

Table 115: Annual Growth Rates of Employment and Income and Sectoral Elasticities Across Various Sectors from 2018 to 2024 in India

Sector	Growth rate: 2018–2024		Elasticity	
	Employment	GVA	1994–2018	2018–2024
Agriculture & allied	5.32	4.07	−0.21	1.31
Mining & quarrying	-5.02	0.00	−0.38	-
Manufacturing	3.55	3.33	0.22	1.07
Electricity, gas & water supply	3.17	4.79	0.51	0.66
Construction	5.03	6.47	0.85	0.78
Wholesale & retail trade	4.95	2.24	0.44	2.21
Transport, storage and communication	3.66	3.31	0.35	1.11
Other services	2.79	5.25	0.28	0.53
Non-agriculture	3.96	4.23	0.40	0.94
All sectors	4.57	4.21	0.16	1.09

Source: Author's computation using data from PLFS (2017–18 and 2023–24), Gross Value Added (GVA) data from RBI, and elasticity information for 1994–2018 from Table 91 above.

In our state-level discussion, we compared employment elasticity values (for all sectors combined) across seventeen states (including four undivided states that were subsequently bifurcated) from 1994 to 2018 and from 2018 to 2024. Additionally, we have examined the employment elasticities from 2018 to 2024 for the states following their bifurcation and the newly created states. Table 116 shows that from 2018 to 2024, the top five states regarding employment elasticity values are Bihar (undivided), Uttar Pradesh (undivided), Kerala, Rajasthan and Haryana (in descending order of elasticity values). In contrast, in ascending order of elasticity values, the five states at the bottom in this regard are Andhra Pradesh (undivided), Tamil Nadu, Karnataka, Maharashtra, and Gujarat.

When we include the bifurcated states, the top five states, ranked by employment elasticity values from 2018 to 2024, are Uttarakhand, Bihar, Jharkhand, Kerala, and Uttar Pradesh, in descending order. Conversely, in ascending order of elasticity values, the five states at the bottom are Andhra Pradesh, Tamil Nadu, Karnataka, Telangana, and Chhattisgarh. However, from an overall perspective, economically weaker states exhibited relatively better employment elasticity values than richer states from 2018 to 2024. This is because employment growth in poorer states has surpassed richer states (including those attaining high growth of NSDP). By comparing the rankings of these states for the periods of 1994–2018 and 2018–2024, we can further observe that the less developed states have enhanced their employment elasticity rankings from 2018 to 2024, in contrast to the period from 1994 to 2018.

Table 116: Elasticity of Employment in Major States from 2018 to 2024

State	Growth rate: 2018–2024		Elasticity: 2018–2024	Rank	
	Employment	NSDP		1994–2018	2018–2024
Andhra Pradesh (U)	1.71	5.05	0.34	16	17
Assam	7.27	5.67	1.28	2	6
Bihar (U)	8.00	3.78	2.12	7	1
Gujarat	6.58	6.06	1.09	10	13
Haryana	4.25	3.27	1.30	8	5
Himachal Pradesh	4.15	3.72	1.12	12	12
Jammu & Kashmir	3.32	2.70	1.23	1	8
Karnataka	3.23	5.06	0.64	13	15
Kerala	4.97	2.80	1.77	17	3
Madhya Pradesh (U)	5.02	4.43	1.13	3	11
Maharashtra	3.32	3.22	1.03	9	14

(Continued)

Table 116 *(Continued)*

State	Growth rate: 2018–2024		Elasticity: 2018–2024	Rank	
	Employment	NSDP		1994–2018	2018–2024
Odisha	6.75	5.87	1.15	15	10
Punjab	4.15	3.50	1.19	5	9
Rajasthan	6.10	4.58	1.33	11	4
Tamil Nadu	2.38	4.99	0.48	14	16
Uttar Pradesh (U)	6.79	3.79	1.79	6	2
West Bengal	4.32	3.41	1.27	4	7
Andhra Pradesh	0.60	5.11	0.12	–	–
Telangana	3.25	4.99	0.65	–	–
Bihar	7.65	3.40	2.25	–	–
Jharkhand	8.49	4.39	1.93	–	–
Madhya Pradesh	5.53	3.86	1.43	–	–
Chhattisgarh	3.73	5.66	0.66	–	–
Uttar Pradesh	6.60	4.15	1.59	–	–
Uttarakhand	7.04	1.60	4.40	–	–

Source: Author's computation using data from PLFS (2017–18 and 2023–24), state-level NSDP data from RBI and information in Table 92 above.

Note: U stands for undivided state

7.4 Employment Performance by the States

This section analyses the employment performance of twenty-one major states in India for the years 2018 and 2024. We calculated the composite scores for each state using data on selected employment quantity and quality indicators. These composite scores rank the states to identify which excel in employment performance. For this analysis, we specifically considered four indicators for each dimension. The quantity indicators include: (i) the worker-population ratio (WPR), (ii) the ratio of female WPR to male WPR, (iii) the employment rate of individuals with secondary education and above, and (iv) the youth employment rate.[5] The quality indicators considered are (i) the percentage of regular employees among total workers, (ii) the percentage of non-farm workers among total workers, (iii) the percentage of non-poor workers among total workers, and (iv) the percentage

5 The youth are those in the age bracket 15-29 years. The employment rate is calculated using the formula: $\left[\frac{number\ of\ employed}{number\ of\ employed + unemployed}\right]*100$

of workers with any social security benefits. The data for these indicators at the state level have been normalised using the 'max-min formula'[6] to compute the scores for each indicator. After obtaining the individual scores, we calculated the unweighted average to derive the composite score. Using the composite scores, we ranked the states to conclude their employment performance. The composite scores are calculated separately for quantity indicators, quality indicators, and all indicators combined. This distinction is important because some states may excel in employment quantity but not quality. This disaggregated information facilitates effective policy design at the state level.

The composite scores for the states, along with their rankings in 2018 and 2024, are presented in Table 117.[7] In 2018, the top one-third of states performing well in the quantity dimension of employment, ranked in ascending order, were Chhattisgarh, Himachal Pradesh, Madhya Pradesh, Maharashtra, Andhra Pradesh, Gujarat, and Karnataka. By 2024, the top seven states, based on their performance in the quantity aspect of employment, are Madhya Pradesh, Chhattisgarh, Gujarat, Jharkhand, Himachal Pradesh, Uttarakhand, and West Bengal. In contrast, according to the quantity dimension of employment, the seven states at the bottom in 2018, arranged in descending order, are Kerala, Bihar, Assam, Uttarakhand, Odisha, Jharkhand, and Haryana. The set of states lying at the bottom in 2024, based on the quantity aspect of employment, in descending order, are Kerala, Punjab, Bihar, Haryana, Jammu & Kashmir, Andhra Pradesh, and Uttar Pradesh. It is worth noting that the ranking patterns of states based on their composite scores for the quantity dimension of employment in 2018 and 2024 have remained essentially unchanged, indicating that the states that performed relatively better on the quantity aspect of employment in 2018 have continued to do so in 2024. This observation is supported by Spearman's rank correlation coefficient (0.53), indicating a positive relationship between the ranks in 2018 and 2024. This relationship is also statistically significant at the 1 % level.

---

6 The formula is: $X_{score} = (X_{actual} - X_{minimum}) / (X_{maximum} - X_{minimum})$

7 Tables 118 and 119, presented at the end of this chapter, provide data on individual indicators and their respective score values.

Table 117: Composite Score of Employment Performance in States

State	Quantity indicators				Quality indicators				All indicators			
	Composite score		Rank		Composite score		Rank		Composite score		Rank	
	2018	2024	2018	2024	2018	2024	2018	2024	2018	2024	2018	2024
Andhra Pradesh	0.75	0.42	5	16	0.39	0.51	14	14	0.57	0.46	10	17
Assam	0.35	0.51	19	12	0.58	0.51	7	13	0.47	0.51	17	13
Bihar	0.33	0.36	20	19	0.18	0.12	18	20	0.25	0.24	21	21
Chhattisgarh	0.95	0.78	1	2	0.02	0.12	21	21	0.48	0.45	14	18
Gujarat	0.69	0.77	6	3	0.52	0.63	11	7	0.60	0.70	7	1
Haryana	0.44	0.38	15	18	0.73	0.88	5	1	0.58	0.63	8	5
Himachal Pradesh	0.88	0.71	2	5	0.41	0.59	13	10	0.64	0.65	4	3
Jammu & Kashmir	0.66	0.39	8	17	0.66	0.60	6	9	0.66	0.49	3	15
Jharkhand	0.40	0.75	16	4	0.22	0.28	16	17	0.31	0.52	18	12
Karnataka	0.68	0.56	7	8	0.56	0.57	10	12	0.62	0.57	5	9
Kerala	0.20	0.19	21	21	0.78	0.86	3	2	0.49	0.53	13	11
Madhya Pradesh	0.78	0.81	3	1	0.18	0.27	17	18	0.48	0.54	16	10
Maharashtra	0.75	0.55	4	9	0.58	0.60	8	8	0.67	0.58	1	7
Odisha	0.39	0.55	17	10	0.17	0.41	19	15	0.28	0.48	20	16
Punjab	0.48	0.27	13	20	0.73	0.73	4	4	0.60	0.50	6	14
Rajasthan	0.63	0.48	10	13	0.34	0.38	15	16	0.48	0.43	15	19
Tamil Nadu	0.53	0.51	12	11	0.79	0.83	1	3	0.66	0.67	2	2
Telangana	0.54	0.47	11	14	0.58	0.72	9	5	0.56	0.59	11	6
Uttar Pradesh	0.48	0.44	14	15	0.14	0.16	20	19	0.31	0.30	19	20
Uttarakhand	0.38	0.57	18	6	0.78	0.72	2	6	0.58	0.64	9	4
West Bengal	0.66	0.57	9	7	0.44	0.58	12	11	0.55	0.57	12	8

Source: Computed using information in Tables 118 and 119 below.

The ranking of states based on composite scores calculated from employment quality indicators indicates that the top one-third of states in 2018 included Tamil Nadu, Uttarakhand, Kerala, Punjab, Haryana, Jammu & Kashmir, and Assam. In contrast, the seven states that performed poorly on the employment quality front in 2018, ranked in descending order, are Chhattisgarh, Uttar Pradesh, Odisha, Bihar, Madhya Pradesh, Jharkhand, and Rajasthan. The situation did not change much in 2024 regarding states' rankings of employment quality. This year's top seven states, in ascending order of ranks, are Haryana, Kerala, Tamil Nadu, Punjab, Telangana, Uttarakhand, and Gujarat. In descending order of ranks, the states from below are Chhattisgarh, Bihar, Uttar Pradesh, Madhya Pradesh, Jharkhand, Rajasthan, and Odisha. Thus, we observe a highly positive, statistically significant correlation between the rankings of states in 2018 and 2024 regarding the quality of employment. The states that did well in terms of employment quality in 2018 also continued to do so in 2024. This conclusion is based on Spearman's rank correlation coefficient, which is 0.90 and statistically significant at the 1 % level.

Table 117 also provides rankings of states based on all indicators (both quantity and quality), offering insight into their overall employment performance. In 2018, the seven leading states, ranked in ascending order, were Maharashtra, Tamil Nadu, Jammu and Kashmir, Himachal Pradesh, Karnataka, Punjab, and Gujarat. In 2024, the leading states, ranked in ascending order, are Gujarat, Tamil Nadu, Himachal Pradesh, Uttarakhand, Haryana, Telangana, and Maharashtra. Conversely, in descending order, the bottom seven states based on overall employment performance in 2018 are Bihar, Odisha, Uttar Pradesh, Jharkhand, Assam, Madhya Pradesh, and Rajasthan. In 2024, the seven states listed in descending order of rank were Bihar, Uttar Pradesh, Rajasthan, Chhattisgarh, Andhra Pradesh, Odisha, and Jammu & Kashmir. Once again, the data suggest that the ranking patterns of these states in terms of overall employment performance have remained essentially unchanged from 2018 to 2024. The value of Spearman's rank correlation coefficient, calculated using the states' ranks based on composite scores for all indicators in 2018 and 2024, is 0.64 and statistically significant at the 1 % level. This implies some continuity in the patterns of employment performance across states in India over the period from 2018 to 2024, leading to little change in their relative rankings.

Another intriguing point is that, in any given year, the sign of Spearman's rank correlation coefficient, calculated from the ranks of states based on their performance in terms of the quantity and quality of employment, is negative, though statistically insignificant. For 2018 and 2024, these values are –0.27 and –0.34, respectively. This suggests that, in a given year, states that excel in the quantity of employment often perform poorly in terms of the quality of employment. Conversely, states that perform better in terms of employment quality in a given year do not necessarily excel in terms of employment quantity. Therefore, to enhance state employment performance, some require policy intervention on the quantity front, while others need to focus on improving quality.

7.5 Summary of Findings

Our analysis of labour force participation rates revealed that, despite significantly lagging behind males even in 2024, females had made remarkable progress in their participation from 2018 to 2024. This improvement is particularly evident among rural females, who experienced a 17.4 percentage-point increase in labour force participation in 2024 compared to 2018. As a result, the country's overall labour force participation rate, encompassing both rural and urban areas, increased by 9.0 percentage points over the six years from 2018 to 2024, reaching 45.9 %. This trend of increasing labour force participation has been consistent since 2018, as confirmed by our data review covering all years between 2018 and 2024.

When examining labour force participation rates by age groups, we found that participation was very low for males and females under 15. Generally, labour force participation increases with age. However, in 2024, it was highest among males aged 25 to 34 and females aged 35 to 59. Between 2018 and 2024, the most significant increases in labour force participation rates were observed among males aged 15–24 and females aged 35–59. Additionally, there is a general trend for the labour force participation rate to rise with improvements in individuals' educational levels (except for the 'secondary/H.S.' level). Between 2018 and 2024, males with secondary or higher secondary education and females with middle-level education experienced the largest improvements in labour force participation rates.

This chapter also examined labour force participation rates by individuals' social and religious backgrounds. A key finding is that labour force participation rates tend to decrease as we move from lower to higher social groups. Notably, while all social groups experienced improvements in their labour force participation rates from 2018 to 2024, the increase was particularly significant among individuals from lower social groups, especially those belonging to Scheduled Tribes (STs). This trend applied to both males and females, but the improvement for females was notably greater than for males. When examining labour force participation rates by religious groups, we found that Hindus generally have higher participation rates compared to Muslims. This trend holds for both genders, but even in 2024, Muslim females lagged significantly behind their Hindu counterparts in terms of labour force participation rates. Nevertheless, both genders improved their participation rates from 2018 to 2024, with the improvement being more pronounced for Hindus than for Muslims in general and for females in particular.

Similar to the labour force participation rate, the workforce participation rate in the country increased significantly from 2018 to 2024, primarily due to the rise among rural females. It is also noted that nearly 31 % of the female workforce in rural areas and 15 % in urban areas were employed as subsidiary status workers in 2024, which are considerably higher than the corresponding percentages in 2018. Despite this, rural and urban females continued to lag significantly behind their male counterparts in workforce participation rates in 2024. Across age groups, we observed that the workforce participation rate increases as we move to higher age groups, up to the 35–59 age range. In 2024, the workforce participation rate is highest among individuals aged 35–59, for both males and females. While all age groups experienced increased workforce participation rates from 2018 to 2024, the largest increase occurred in the 35–59 age group. Generally, workforce participation increases with workers' educational levels, particularly for males (except for the 'Secondary/H.S.' level). In 2024, the highest rates are for males who are 'graduate & above' and for females who are 'illiterates'. All educational groups of males and females (except males without primary education) experienced increases in workforce participation rates from 2018 to 2024, and the magnitude of this increase was notably higher for females than for males.

The picture regarding workforce participation rates by social and religious groups closely resembles the trends seen in labour force participation rates. Both males and females across social groups improved their workforce participation rates from 2018 to 2024. However, the increase in the workforce participation rate was more significant for females and those in the ST category than for males. Further, considering both males and females, we observed a tendency for the workforce participation rate to decline as we move from lower to higher social groups. Regarding religious groups, although both Hindus and Muslims improved their workforce participation rates from 2018 to 2024, the workforce participation rate remained higher for Hindus than for Muslims in 2024. Notably, the gap between these two religious groups has been more prominent among females than males.

As the labour force participation rate in the country, especially among females, has increased significantly, the total labour force has risen from approximately 500 million in 2018 to 635 million in 2024. Notably, almost 76 % of this increase can be attributed to females. The annual growth rate of the labour force for females from 2018 to 2024 is 11.02 %, while for males, it is only 1.34 %. Similarly, the total workforce has grown from 471 million in 2018 to 615 million in 2024, with females accounting for 70 % of this growth. As a result, females have experienced an annual growth rate of 11.52 % in workforce numbers, compared to just 1.88 % for males.

We have also investigated the changes in the numbers and growth rates of out-of-labour force males and females from 2018 to 2024. It was found that, deviating from the past trend observed from 2012 to 2018, the absolute number and the growth rate of out-of-labour force females declined in the country, especially in rural areas, from 2018 to 2024. A similar trend is evident among males, though less pronounced than among females. Examination of the activity profile of the out-of-labour force males and females in 2024 revealed that while attendance at educational institutions has been the primary reason for remaining out of the labour force for males, for females, the most important reason for staying outside the labour force is attending to domestic duties, followed by participation in educational institutions. However, compared to 2018, the proportion of females engaged in domestic duties declined significantly in 2024, particularly among rural females, while the proportion attending educational institutions increased. Overall, there is a clear trend of females, especially in rural areas, substituting domestic work for outside work, which explains the significant rise in their labour force participation rates from 2018 to 2024, as noted earlier.

Moving the discussion to labour force participation rates in the states in 2024,[8] and comparing them to 2018, we found that for males, all but four states (Andhra Pradesh, Haryana, Jammu & Kashmir, and Tamil Nadu) improved their labour force participation rates in 2024 compared to 2018. In contrast, all states experienced improvements in female participation rates between 2018 and 2024. Nevertheless, the significant gap between males' and females' labour force participation rates persisted in 2024. For males, labour force participation rates in 2024 ranged from 64.9 % in Chhattisgarh to 48.1 % in Bihar; for females, the highest and lowest rates were observed in Himachal Pradesh (56.2 %) and Haryana (18.9 %), respectively. It is also worth noting that three states (Chhattisgarh, Himachal Pradesh, and Kerala) recorded significant improvements (of more than 5 percentage points) in male labour force participation rates from 2018 to 2024. The increase in female labour force participation rates during this period was even more noteworthy in all states except Andhra Pradesh. Moreover, five states recorded increases of more than 20 percentage points in female labour force participation rates between 2018 and 2024, namely Assam, Jharkhand, Odisha, Uttarakhand, and Gujarat.

---

8 For the state-level discussions spanning from 2018 to 2024, we analysed data from twenty-one major states in India, combining rural and urban areas. The tables are based on unit-level data from the PLFS surveys conducted in 2017–18 and 2023–24.

The changes in workforce participation rates across states from 2018 to 2024 mirror the trends in labour force participation. While all states, except for Andhra Pradesh and Jammu & Kashmir, experienced an increase in male workforce participation rates by 2024 compared to 2018, all twenty-one states also saw improvements in female participation rates. In 2024, male workforce participation rates varied from 63.2 % in Chhattisgarh to 46.4 % in Bihar. The highest participation rate among females was recorded in Himachal Pradesh at 51.8 %, while the lowest was in Haryana at 18.4 %. When considering males and females together, workforce participation rates improved across all states from 2018 to 2024. The most significant increase in workforce participation during this period occurred in Jharkhand, rising by 15.1 percentage points. Additionally, eight other states reported improvements of over 10.0 percentage points in combined workforce participation rates for males and females during the same timeframe.

Regarding the growth rates of the male labour force from 2018 to 2024, Chhattisgarh led the states with an annual increase of 3.39 %, while Tamil Nadu remained at the bottom with a modest growth rate of 0.05 % per year. For females, the labour force growth rates during this period were highest in Bihar (41.36 %) and lowest in Andhra Pradesh (1.31 %), respectively. The most notable observation is that while only five states (Kerala, Bihar, Odisha, Gujarat, and Jharkhand) improved between 1 to 2 percentage points in their male labour force growth rates from 2018 to 2024 compared to 1994 to 1998, all states experienced a remarkable improvement (ranging between 50.75 percentage points to 4.98 percentage points) in their female labour force growth rates. Furthermore, while the highest rate of progress in male labour force growth is recorded in Kerala at 1.74 percentage points, many states saw exceptionally high female labour force growth rates. Specific mention may be made of Bihar, Jharkhand, Assam, Uttar Pradesh, Odisha, and Gujarat, where female labour force growth rates improved by more than twenty percentage points from 2018 to 2024, compared to the period from 1994 to 2018. When considering both males and females combined, the picture shows that the annual labour force growth rates from 2018 to 2024 are highest in Jharkhand (7.42 %) and lowest in Andhra Pradesh (0.61 %). Furthermore, seven states experienced an improvement of over 5.0 percentage points in the combined growth rates of the male and female labour force during 2018–2024 compared to 1994–2018. These states are Jharkhand, Odisha, Uttarakhand, Bihar, Uttar Pradesh, Rajasthan, and Gujarat.

Like the male labour force growth rate from 2018 to 2024, Chhattisgarh stands out as the top performer in workforce growth among the states, achieving an annual growth rate of 3.51 %. In contrast, Andhra Pradesh records the lowest male workforce growth at just 0.30 %. For females, the states recording the highest and lowest workforce growth rates from 2018 to 2024 are the same as those observed for labour force growth rates: Bihar (41.71 %) and Andhra Pradesh (1.38 %), respectively. Another important observation is that in three more states, apart from Bihar, the growth rate of the female workforce from 2018 to 2024 exceeded 20.0 %. It is also worth noting that while seventeen states recorded improvements in male workforce growth rates between 2018 and 2024, compared to 1994 and 2018 (with the exceptions of Jammu & Kashmir and Maharashtra), all states recorded such improvements for females. In fact, in eight states, the female workforce growth rates increased by more than 20.0 percentage points in the latter period compared to the former. These states are Bihar, Assam, Jharkhand, Uttarakhand, Uttar Pradesh, Odisha, Punjab and Gujarat. Combining males and females, the highest- and lowest-ranking states regarding workforce growth rates during 2018–2024 are Jharkhand (8.49 %) and Andhra Pradesh (0.60 %), respectively; furthermore, none of the states experienced a decline in workforce growth rates during 2018–2024 compared to 1994–2018. On the contrary, ten states improved their workforce growth rates by more than 5.0 percentage points between 2018 and 2024, compared to the period from 1994 to 2018. In descending order of the magnitude of improvement, these states are Jharkhand, Odisha, Uttarakhand, Bihar, Gujarat, Uttar Pradesh, Rajasthan, Assam, Kerala, and Punjab.

Regarding the factors influencing individuals' labour force participation decisions, our results using the PLFS 2024 data are broadly similar to those observed in Chapter 3 above, which utilised 2018 data. The results indicate that individuals' household and personal characteristics influence their decisions to join the labour force. Specifically, the probability of joining the labour force is higher among individuals identified as male, older, married, possessing higher levels of education, having received technical training, not currently enrolled in any educational institution, coming from small families, belonging to lower castes, and being of the Hindu religion.

One qualitative indicator of changes in the employment landscape is the employment mode of workers. We found that self-employment was the predominant form of employment in the country in 2024, across both rural and urban areas. It accounted for 54 % of male and 67 % of female workers. In contrast, nearly 25 % of male workers were engaged in regular employment, and 22 % were engaged in casual employment during the same year; for females, the percentages of regular and casual workers were 16 % and 17 %, respectively. We also noticed that the percentage of casual workers declined in 2024 compared to 2018 for males and females. However, the rate of decline in casual worker incidence was much higher among females than among males. This decline in the incidence of casual workers contributed to increases in self-employment and regular employment for males. Among females, the decrease in the percentages of casual and regular workers led to a significant increase in the percentage of self-employed workers in 2024 compared to 2018. Another noteworthy point is that the rates of decline in the percentage of casual workers and the rise in self-employed workers for females during 2018–2024 are much higher in rural areas than in urban areas.

Moving to the state level for males and females combined, we observed that the percentage of regularly employed workers in 2024 ranged from 39.0 % in Haryana to just 8.7 % in Bihar; the percentage of self-employed workers varied from 72.7 % in Uttar Pradesh to 34.2 % in Tamil Nadu; and the percentage of casual workers ranged from 31.3 % in Tamil Nadu to 11.1 % in Jammu & Kashmir.

Among males, the states leading in regular employment, self-employment, and casual employment in 2024 are Haryana (41.4 %), Uttar Pradesh (66.4 %), and Bihar (28.8 %), respectively. In contrast, the percentages of regular employment, self-employment, and casual employment among males are lowest in Bihar (10.3 %), Tamil Nadu (33.1 %), and Gujarat (13.2 %), respectively. Regarding females, the leading states in regular employment, self-employment, and casual employment are Kerala (41.2 %), Jammu & Kashmir (89.5 %), and Tamil Nadu (36.6 %); the states with the lowest percentages of female workers in regular employment, self-employment, and casual employment are Bihar (4.8 %), Tamil Nadu (36.1 %), and Jammu & Kashmir (0.5 %). Another critical point is that the decline in the percentage of casual workers from 2018 to 2024 has been widespread, with sixteen states witnessing such a decline among male workers and all states (except Tamil Nadu) experiencing a decline among female workers. This is associated with the increase in self-employed workers in eleven states for males and as many as twenty states for females. Regarding the change in the percentage of regular workers, we observed a somewhat contrasting picture: while seventeen states increased the percentage of males in regular employment from 2018 to 2024, fifteen states experienced declines in the percentage of females in regular employment.

Examining sectoral employment diversification in India (combining rural and urban areas), we observed that 64 % of male workers, 36 % of female workers, and 54 % of all workers were engaged in non-agricultural employment in 2024. Furthermore, employment diversification from the agriculture and allied sector to the non-agricultural sector appears to have stalled in recent years, as evidenced by a decline in the share of non-agricultural workers by 1.93 percentage points from 2018 to 2024. This decline is solely due to a 7.37 percentage-point decrease in the proportion of female non-agricultural workers among total female workers. In comparison, the share of male non-agricultural workers to total male workers increased by 3.96 percentage points during this period. We also found that among the non-agricultural sub-sectors for males, the most significant has been 'construction', followed by 'trade, hotels and restaurants', 'manufacturing', and 'other services'. Together, these four sectors accounted for nearly 55 % of all male workers (rural and urban combined) in the country in 2024. For females, the non-agricultural sub-sectors, in descending order of their share of total workers in 2024, are 'other services', 'manufacturing', and 'trade, hotels and restaurants', collectively accounting for nearly 31 % of total female workers. It also appeared that, for males, aside from agriculture and allied activities, three other non-agricultural sub-sectors recorded a decline in their share of total workers from 2018 to 2024: 'other services', 'manufacturing', and 'mining and quarrying'. In contrast, such a decline is visible for females in all non-agricultural sub-sectors, except for two minor sectors from the perspective of employment, which are 'electricity, gas and water supply' and 'transport, storage, and communication'.

However, the growth rates of workers in different sectors from 2018 to 2024 appeared to differ. The most significant point is that both the 'agriculture and allied' and 'non-agricultural' sectors (rural and urban areas combined) registered positive growth rates of male and female workers during 2018–2024. Of course, the growth rates for females were substantially higher than those for males in both sectors. In contrast to a mere 0.14 % yearly growth in the 'agriculture and allied' sector and 1.88 % growth in the 'non-agricultural' sector of male workers, during this period, females registered impressive growth rates of 13.8 % and 8.08 % in these two sectors, respectively. The rapid increase in female workers resulted in a 5.32 % annual growth in the 'agriculture and allied' sector and a 3.96 % increase in the 'non-agricultural' sector across the country (combining males and females) from 2018 to 2024. Another significant finding is that, while all non-agricultural sub-sectors (except 'trade, hotels and restaurants') experienced declines in growth rates of male workers from 2018 to 2024, all non-agricultural sub-sectors (except 'mining and quarrying') recorded increases in growth rates of female workers during this period.

We examined the extent of employment diversification across states in 2024 by considering the percentage of non-agricultural workers among total workers (rural and urban combined). We observed that while Kerala is the most diversified state for males, with nearly 79 % of workers employed in the non-agricultural sector, Chhattisgarh is the least diversified, with 46 % of workers in this sector. Additionally, Madhya Pradesh is the only other state where less than half of male workers are engaged in non-agricultural employment. We also observed that, except for Kerala, all states showed improvements in the percentage of male workers in non-agricultural employment in 2024 compared to 2018. States like Assam, Odisha, and Jharkhand saw increases of more than 10 percentage points. Among females, the most diversified state in 2024 is Punjab, with 66 % of female workers employed in the non-agricultural sector, while Bihar is the least diversified, at just 17.9 %. Unlike the trend among males, thirteen states experienced a decline in the percentage of non-agricultural workers among females compared to 2018. In seven states, the decline has been more than 10 percentage points, with the highest being Assam (–29 percentage points). When examining the combined data for males and females, Kerala remains the most diversified state, with 73 % of the workforce engaged in the non-agricultural sector. On the other hand, Chhattisgarh is the least diversified, with only 36.2 % of its workforce in this sector. Alarmingly, two-thirds of states experienced declines in the percentage of non-agricultural workers between 2018 and 2024, with the largest decline observed in Bihar, which decreased by 9.1 percentage points.

We also evaluated employment quality by examining the percentage of workers in poverty. Our calculations indicate that more than 21 % of the country's workers are projected to be poor in 2024, a 15.3 percentage-point reduction from 2018. As expected, the percentage of poor workers is higher in rural areas (23.4 %) than in urban areas (15.5 %). Moreover, the percentage of poor workers is highest among casual workers at 30.9 %, followed by self-employed workers at 21.4 %, and regular workers at 12.5 %. Farm workers also experience a higher rate of poverty, with 24.5 % classified as poor, compared to 20.5 % for non-farm or non-agricultural workers. The percentage of poor workers varies among social and religious groups, generally decreasing from lower to higher social strata. Additionally, it is lower among Hindu workers compared to Muslim workers. Notably, the highest percentage of the poor in India is found among individuals not in the labour force, at nearly 28 %, whereas the lowest is among unemployed individuals, at 16 %.

Considering all sectors, we found that the country's employment elasticity for the period 2018–2024 is 1.09, which is quite impressive compared to the very low elasticity value of 0.16 observed during 1994–2018. During 2018–2024, the employment elasticity in the 'agriculture and allied' sector was notably higher at 1.31 compared to 0.94 in the non-agricultural sector. This contrasts with the 1994–2018 period, during which the elasticity value for the 'agriculture and allied' sector was negative. Among the non-agricultural sub-sectors during 2018–2024, the highest employment elasticity was found in 'wholesale and retail trade' (2.21), followed by 'transport, storage and communication' (1.11), 'manufacturing' (1.07), 'construction' (0.78), 'electricity, gas, and water supply' (0.66), and 'other services' (0.53). Additionally, all non-agricultural sub-sectors, except 'construction', experienced an increase in employment elasticity during 2018–2024 compared to 1994–2018. At the state level, considering all sectors combined, our overall finding indicates that relatively poorer states exhibited higher elasticity values than richer states during 2018–2024. Furthermore, these poorer states also exhibited greater improvements in elasticity values during this period than during the 1994–2018 period.

In this chapter, we also ranked the states based on their overall employment performance using indicators that capture both employment quantity and quality dimensions. The data for these indicators have been used to construct a composite index that serves as the basis for their ranking. We ranked the states based on their performance in terms of employment quantity, employment quality, and a combined measure of quantity and quality. This approach is necessary because some states may excel in employment quantity but not necessarily in quality. Understanding their performance disaggregated will help set appropriate policy interventions to enhance the employment performance of the states. Employment performance was assessed for 2018 and 2024.

We found that, from an employment quantity perspective, the top performer in 2024 is Madhya Pradesh, followed by Chhattisgarh, Gujarat, Jharkhand, Himachal Pradesh, Uttarakhand, and West Bengal. In contrast, the worst performer in this regard is Kerala; the states above it in terms of employment quantity performance are Punjab, Bihar, Haryana, Jammu & Kashmir, Andhra Pradesh, and Uttar Pradesh. The remaining seven states demonstrate a medium level of performance in terms of employment quantity. Regarding employment quality in 2024, the best performer is Haryana, followed by Kerala, Tamil Nadu, Punjab, Telangana, Uttarakhand, and Gujarat. Chhattisgarh is the worst-performing state in terms of quality, followed by six other states at the bottom: Bihar, Uttar Pradesh, Madhya Pradesh, Jharkhand, Rajasthan, and Odisha. The states falling between these two sets are the medium performers in terms of employment quality in 2024. The overall performance of the states, based on the combined aspects of quantity and quality of employment, indicates that in 2024, the top seven states, in ascending order of rank, are Gujarat (the best performer), Tamil Nadu, Himachal Pradesh, Uttarakhand, Haryana, Telangana, and Maharashtra. In contrast, the seven states at the bottom, in descending order of rank, are Bihar (the worst-performing state), Uttar Pradesh, Rajasthan, Chhattisgarh, Andhra Pradesh, Odisha, and Jammu & Kashmir.

Our overall observation is that developed states perform relatively better in terms of employment quality and the combined aspects of quantity and quality. However, employment performance based on the quantity dimension appears relatively stronger in less developed states. Another interesting finding from this analysis is that the ranking patterns of states based on employment quantity in 2018 and 2024 do not differ significantly. The same observation applies if we consider the correlation between their ranks in these years based on the quality aspect of employment or the combined aspects of quantity and quality. In other words, the states display continuity in employment performance from 2018 to 2024. Another important finding is an inverse relationship between the ranks of states based on their performance in the quantity and quality aspects of employment in a given year, implying that states excelling in the quantity aspect of employment are not necessarily the same ones excelling in the quality aspect.

Table 118: Quantity Indicators Used to Calculate the Composite Score of Employment Performance in Major States

Year	State	WPR (%)			Ratio of female WPR to male WPR			Employment rate of persons with secondary & above education (%)			Youth employment rate (%)		
		Indicator value	Score	Rank	Indicator value	Score	Rank	Indicator value	Score	Rank	Indicator value	Score	Rank
2024	Andhra Pradesh	45.56	0.51	10	0.61	0.52	10	89.25	0.19	18	82.55	0.45	19
	Assam	47.16	0.58	6	0.60	0.51	11	90.97	0.36	14	85.91	0.58	14
	Bihar	33.51	0.00	21	0.43	0.15	19	93.07	0.56	10	90.14	0.73	8
	Chhattisgarh	54.16	0.87	2	0.71	0.75	2	93.76	0.63	8	93.68	0.86	4
	Gujarat	49.08	0.66	4	0.57	0.45	13	97.61	1.00	1	96.93	0.98	2
	Haryana	36.14	0.11	20	0.36	0.00	21	94.65	0.71	5	89.32	0.70	10
	Himachal Pradesh	57.17	1.00	1	0.83	1.00	1	91.09	0.37	13	83.67	0.50	16
	Jammu & Kashmir	44.91	0.48	13	0.65	0.61	5	87.29	0.00	21	82.63	0.46	18
	Jharkhand	43.89	0.44	16	0.69	0.69	3	96.74	0.92	2	96.43	0.96	3
	Karnataka	44.13	0.45	15	0.52	0.33	16	95.04	0.75	4	89.84	0.72	9
	Kerala	42.12	0.36	17	0.52	0.35	15	87.69	0.04	20	70.14	0.00	21
	Madhya Pradesh	50.55	0.72	3	0.64	0.59	7	96.70	0.91	3	97.43	1.00	1
	Maharashtra	45.28	0.50	11	0.53	0.36	14	94.06	0.66	7	89.20	0.70	11
	Odisha	47.92	0.61	5	0.62	0.56	8	90.89	0.35	15	88.88	0.69	12
	Punjab	41.32	0.33	18	0.38	0.05	20	90.36	0.30	17	81.17	0.40	20
	Rajasthan	45.26	0.50	12	0.67	0.67	4	88.56	0.12	19	87.63	0.64	13
	Tamil Nadu	45.59	0.51	9	0.59	0.48	12	92.73	0.53	11	84.65	0.53	15
	Telangana	45.70	0.51	8	0.61	0.53	9	90.89	0.35	16	83.42	0.49	17

(Continued)

Table 118 *(Continued)*

Year	State	WPR (%)			Ratio of female WPR to male WPR			Employment rate of persons with secondary & above education (%)			Youth employment rate (%)		
		Indicator value	Score	Rank	Indicator value	Score	Rank	Indicator value	Score	Rank	Indicator value	Score	Rank
2024	Uttar Pradesh	39.19	0.24	19	0.46	0.21	18	93.08	0.56	9	90.91	0.76	6
	Uttarakhand	44.22	0.45	14	0.64	0.60	6	92.40	0.50	12	90.18	0.73	7
	West Bengal	46.44	0.55	7	0.49	0.29	17	94.31	0.68	6	91.01	0.76	5
2018	Andhra Pradesh	45.04	0.94	3	0.57	0.81	3	85.98	0.47	17	83.92	0.77	9
	Assam	32.92	0.41	15	0.15	0.14	20	86.31	0.50	15	73.05	0.36	19
	Bihar	23.64	0.00	21	0.06	0.00	21	89.96	0.80	8	77.21	0.52	15
	Chhattisgarh	45.65	0.97	2	0.64	0.91	2	91.44	0.92	3	89.91	1.00	1
	Gujarat	36.20	0.55	11	0.26	0.32	13	92.45	1.00	1	86.74	0.88	4
	Haryana	30.50	0.30	18	0.19	0.20	18	88.23	0.66	13	79.28	0.59	13
	Himachal Pradesh	46.38	1.00	1	0.69	0.99	1	90.30	0.82	7	81.65	0.69	11
	Jammu & Kashmir	38.62	0.66	8	0.38	0.50	9	88.55	0.68	12	84.95	0.81	7
	Jharkhand	28.77	0.23	19	0.22	0.25	16	86.31	0.50	16	79.62	0.61	12
	Karnataka	38.10	0.64	9	0.34	0.44	10	90.88	0.87	5	84.19	0.78	8
	Kerala	32.39	0.38	16	0.32	0.41	11	80.17	0.00	21	63.67	0.00	21
	Madhya Pradesh	39.97	0.72	5	0.41	0.55	7	91.42	0.92	4	87.98	0.93	2
	Maharashtra	39.22	0.69	7	0.42	0.56	6	91.96	0.96	2	85.04	0.81	6
	Odisha	33.79	0.45	14	0.26	0.31	14	83.93	0.31	20	76.42	0.49	17

(Continued)

Table 118 *(Continued)*

Year	State	WPR (%)			Ratio of female WPR to male WPR			Employment rate of persons with secondary & above education (%)			Youth employment rate (%)		
		Indicator value	Score	Rank	Indicator value	Score	Rank	Indicator value	Score	Rank	Indicator value	Score	Rank
2018	Punjab	33.83	0.45	13	0.20	0.21	17	88.60	0.69	11	78.40	0.56	14
	Rajasthan	34.13	0.46	12	0.39	0.51	8	88.67	0.69	10	85.71	0.84	5
	Tamil Nadu	40.55	0.74	4	0.45	0.61	5	84.61	0.36	19	74.37	0.41	18
	Telangana	39.26	0.69	6	0.45	0.61	4	84.73	0.37	18	76.70	0.50	16
	Uttar Pradesh	28.72	0.22	20	0.19	0.20	19	89.11	0.73	9	83.30	0.75	10
	Uttarakhand	30.67	0.31	17	0.25	0.30	15	87.15	0.57	14	72.55	0.34	20
	West Bengal	37.28	0.60	10	0.27	0.33	12	90.49	0.84	6	86.83	0.88	3

Source: Same as Table 95

Table 119: Quality Indicators Used to Calculate the Composite Score of Employment Performance in Major States

Year	State	% of regular employees			% of non-farm workers			% of non-poor workers			% of workers with any social security benefit		
		Indicator value	Score	Rank	Indicator value	Score	Rank	Indicator value	Score	Rank	Indicator value	Score	Rank
2024	Andhra Pradesh	22.28	0.45	11	53.72	0.48	11	91.30	0.87	5	17.20	0.24	18
	Assam	18.94	0.34	14	52.85	0.45	13	80.99	0.64	9	28.37	0.61	10
	Bihar	8.67	0.00	21	45.76	0.26	18	62.35	0.24	19	9.96	0.00	21
	Chhattisgarh	15.90	0.24	16	36.16	0.00	21	51.29	0.00	21	17.19	0.24	19
	Gujarat	30.83	0.73	6	57.58	0.58	7	78.35	0.59	12	28.89	0.62	9
	Haryana	39.03	1.00	1	72.50	0.99	3	78.05	0.58	13	39.18	0.96	2
	Himachal Pradesh	22.60	0.46	10	46.05	0.27	17	80.86	0.64	10	40.34	1.00	1
	Jammu & Kashmir	22.15	0.44	12	57.19	0.57	9	78.45	0.59	11	34.38	0.80	4
	Jharkhand	12.92	0.14	19	49.98	0.37	15	67.58	0.35	18	17.79	0.26	16
	Karnataka	26.06	0.57	8	53.51	0.47	12	74.86	0.51	15	32.33	0.74	6
	Kerala	34.99	0.87	2	73.03	1.00	1	97.47	1.00	1	27.77	0.59	11
	Madhya Pradesh	13.20	0.15	18	38.44	0.06	20	77.60	0.57	14	18.86	0.29	14
	Maharashtra	31.27	0.74	5	56.78	0.56	10	70.91	0.42	17	30.55	0.68	7
	Odisha	13.59	0.16	17	51.11	0.41	14	90.03	0.84	6	17.10	0.23	20
	Punjab	34.27	0.84	4	72.78	0.99	2	89.97	0.84	7	17.28	0.24	17
	Rajasthan	18.80	0.33	15	48.95	0.35	16	72.97	0.47	16	21.33	0.37	12
	Tamil Nadu	34.44	0.85	3	72.02	0.97	4	91.54	0.87	4	29.44	0.64	8

(Continued)

Table 119 *(Continued)*

Year	State	% of regular employees			% of non-farm workers			% of non-poor workers			% of workers with any social security benefit		
		Indicator value	Score	Rank	Indicator value	Score	Rank	Indicator value	Score	Rank	Indicator value	Score	Rank
2024	Telangana	25.40	0.55	9	57.51	0.58	8	94.86	0.94	2	34.29	0.80	5
	Uttar Pradesh	12.41	0.12	20	44.06	0.21	19	53.58	0.05	20	18.05	0.27	15
	Uttarakhand	26.27	0.58	7	57.67	0.58	6	86.57	0.76	8	38.32	0.93	3
	West Bengal	20.45	0.39	13	61.84	0.70	5	92.35	0.89	3	20.30	0.34	13
2018	Andhra Pradesh	18.42	0.24	15	50.22	0.37	18	82.82	0.88	3	16.67	0.09	16
	Assam	25.07	0.53	11	54.53	0.46	11	74.71	0.71	7	32.12	0.63	5
	Bihar	13.05	0.00	21	54.90	0.47	10	50.75	0.21	17	14.75	0.02	20
	Chhattisgarh	14.14	0.05	20	32.49	0.00	21	40.38	0.00	21	14.99	0.03	18
	Gujarat	28.57	0.69	7	57.58	0.53	7	67.57	0.56	12	22.30	0.28	12
	Haryana	35.55	1.00	1	72.59	0.84	3	65.32	0.51	13	30.40	0.57	6
	Himachal Pradesh	19.51	0.29	13	44.38	0.25	19	74.07	0.69	8	25.41	0.39	9
	Jammu & Kashmir	25.09	0.54	10	59.25	0.56	6	76.77	0.75	6	36.89	0.79	3
	Jharkhand	15.14	0.09	17	53.25	0.44	13	49.38	0.19	18	18.66	0.16	14
	Karnataka	25.45	0.55	9	54.28	0.46	12	63.73	0.48	14	35.86	0.76	4
	Kerala	32.90	0.88	4	80.15	1.00	1	85.84	0.94	2	22.95	0.31	10
	Madhya Pradesh	14.29	0.06	19	39.41	0.15	20	54.66	0.29	16	20.31	0.21	13
	Maharashtra	28.87	0.70	6	52.21	0.41	14	56.95	0.34	15	38.70	0.86	2
	Odisha	15.36	0.10	16	51.24	0.39	16	48.53	0.17	19	14.15	0.00	21
	Punjab	33.61	0.91	3	73.95	0.87	2	81.58	0.85	5	22.67	0.30	11

(Continued)

Table 119 *(Continued)*

Year	State	% of regular employees			% of non-farm workers			% of non-poor workers			% of workers with any social security benefit		
		Indicator value	Score	Rank	Indicator value	Score	Rank	Indicator value	Score	Rank	Indicator value	Score	Rank
2018	Rajasthan	18.72	0.25	14	50.46	0.38	17	68.03	0.57	11	18.66	0.16	15
	Tamil Nadu	33.77	0.92	2	72.26	0.83	4	88.86	1.00	1	26.32	0.42	8
	Telangana	27.70	0.65	8	56.57	0.51	9	72.50	0.66	9	28.36	0.50	7
	Uttar Pradesh	15.01	0.09	18	51.25	0.39	15	42.72	0.05	20	14.82	0.02	19
	Uttarakhand	29.61	0.74	5	57.47	0.52	8	82.41	0.87	4	42.83	1.00	1
	West Bengal	22.06	0.40	12	63.42	0.65	5	70.95	0.63	10	16.3	0.07	17

Source: Same as Table 95

Conclusions and Policy Implications

For any country, particularly those in the developing world, the primary aim is to stimulate rapid economic growth and generate sufficient employment opportunities. Achieving inclusive growth, where employment creation accompanies economic expansion, is essential. However, during India's early planning stages after independence, employment was regarded as a byproduct of economic growth. Consequently, policies prioritised GDP growth over employment creation. This approach led to several challenges, including a severe balance of payments crisis in the 1980s. In response, India introduced economic reforms in 1991 to reduce government intervention and encourage market competition through liberalisation and globalisation. The economic reforms and globalisation gradually implemented various measures, such as reallocating public spending towards infrastructure, tax reform, market-determined interest rates, a competitive exchange rate, trade liberalisation, openness to direct foreign investment, privatisation of state-owned enterprises, and deregulation. Advocates of economic reforms argued that this strategy would enhance economic efficiency and ultimately lead to higher GDP growth, thereby expanding employment in the country. Conversely, critics maintained that the environment created by liberalisation, privatisation, and globalisation would favour modern, capital-intensive production processes, decreasing labour demand and potentially hindering employment growth.

Several past studies have investigated the effects of liberalisation and globalisation policies in India, particularly concerning economic growth, regional or interstate disparity, employment, unemployment, and poverty. Evidence indicates that while the globalisation era saw the country's GDP growth rate surpassing pre-globalisation levels, it also exacerbated inequality among states regarding per capita net state domestic product (PCNSDP) growth. Furthermore, despite the higher

GDP growth rates of the Indian economy since the implementation of reforms and globalisation, employment growth has been inadequate, resulting in a period of jobless growth. After implementing economic reforms and globalisation policies, India's annual employment growth rate significantly declined. Additionally, rural areas have consistently lagged behind urban areas in terms of employment performance since liberalisation and globalisation. Ongoing concerns also exist about the nature and quality of employment in India during globalisation, especially in rural areas where many workers are self-employed or engage in casual work. The sluggish growth of the manufacturing sector and an overreliance on informal sector employment have further complicated efforts to generate stable, higher-quality jobs. Above all, employment performance varied across states, genders, age groups, educational backgrounds, and socio-religious groups, underscoring the need to address employment issues more nuancedly. This approach could facilitate targeted policies that more effectively safeguard the interests of those disproportionately affected by the labour market in the post-globalisation era.

Set against this backdrop, the current study aims to illuminate the processes of economic growth in India during the globalisation era, particularly investigating whether these growth trajectories can yield sufficient employment. By scrutinising national and state-level growth patterns and employment outcomes during globalisation and contrasting them with those of the pre-globalisation period, the study explores the connection between economic growth and employment, as well as the potential for increased economic growth to create meaningful employment opportunities. This study distinguishes itself from earlier research by analysing growth and employment trends in India and its states over more than forty years, using the most recent available data, and providing a detailed analysis of regional (rural/urban), sectoral, gender, age, educational, and social and religious demographics.

This study relies entirely on secondary data. Using GDP/NSDP data from the Reserve Bank of India (RBI) from 1980–81 to 2023–24, we examined issues such as income growth, interstate disparity, and sectoral performance. The analysis of employment-related problems covers the years 1983 to 2023–24. We utilise data from reports along with the 'unit-level' data from the employment and unemployment surveys for the 38th (1983), 50th (1993–94), 55th (1999–00), and 68th (2011–12) rounds, as well as Periodic Labour Force Surveys for 2017–18 and 2023–24, conducted by the National Sample Survey Office (NSSO). The NSSO concept we employ to measure employment or workers is the usual principal and subsidiary status (UPSS). Unlike some recent studies, our analysis considers the entire population rather than limiting it to individuals aged 15 and above. This approach helps us gain a more comprehensive and complete understanding of the shifting employment landscape in the country following globalisation. To understand the effects of reforms and globalisation on economic growth and interstate disparity, we have compared the pre- and post-globalisation periods, specifically 1981–1993 and 1994–2024, respectively. In analysing employment-related aspects, the pre-globalisation period, determined by data availability, extends from 1983 to 1994. In contrast, the post-globalisation period is divided into two phases: 1994–2018 and 2018–2024. It is essential to examine the country's employment landscape separately for these phases of the post-globalisation period, as significant changes in employment outcomes are observed in the later phase compared to the earlier one. By comparing these two sub-periods, we can gain a better understanding of the changes and continuities in employment across the country and its states in recent years, relative to the earlier phase of the post-globalisation period.

In the following, we present the major conclusions of this study relating to growth and interstate disparity between 1981 and 2024, changes in labour force participation patterns, shifts in employment scenarios across quantitative and qualitative dimensions, and employment diversification patterns from 1994 to 2018, compared with those from 1983 to 1994. Additionally, we outline conclusions regarding changes in all these aspects of employment during the sub-period from 2018 to 2024, emphasising the elements of change and continuity in comparison to the previous period. Finally, we draw important policy implications from this study's findings to enhance employment outcomes in current growth processes and address persistent labour-market inequalities.

8.1 Economic Growth and Interstate Disparity

- India's economic reforms and globalisation policies appear to have succeeded, as the country's GDP growth rates improved following globalisation, despite a slight decline towards the end of the post-globalisation period. The benefits of this increased economic growth have been shared among the states, though to varying degrees, with all major states experiencing growth in their NSDP during the post-globalisation period. However, more developed states such as Gujarat, Haryana, Tamil Nadu, Himachal Pradesh, Maharashtra, Karnataka, and Andhra Pradesh have gained more from the rise in their NSDP growth rates during the era of globalisation than others.
- Similar to the NSDP, the annual growth rate of per capita net state domestic product (PCNSDP) demonstrated significant improvement across the country and in all states during the post-globalisation period compared to the pre-globalisation phase. Nationally, it increased from 2.68 % in the pre-globalisation

period to 4.38 % in the post-globalisation period. When comparing the growth rates of PCNSDP across the two sub-periods of the post-globalisation phase, it was observed that sixteen out of twenty states examined experienced higher growth rates in the second sub-period than in the first. The former BIMARU states[1] and more developed states are included among these sixteen states.

- During our study period, the Indian economy experienced significant income diversification. This led to a decline in the share of the primary sector (agriculture and allied activities) in gross value added (GVA), from 41 % in 1981 to 14.5 % in 2024. In contrast, the shares of the secondary and tertiary sectors increased, rising from 27 % and 32 % in 1981 to 31 % and 55 % in 2024, respectively. There is a distinct shift towards a tertiary-based economy.
- When examining the growth rates of output from the primary, secondary, and tertiary sectors, it became evident that, at a national level, the primary sector experienced a decline in the first sub-period of the post-globalisation era compared to the pre-globalisation period. However, there was a recovery in the second sub-period. The situation varied across the secondary and tertiary sectors: output growth rates increased in the first sub-period of the post-globalisation era relative to the pre-globalisation period, but declined in the subsequent sub-period. During the post-globalisation period, the output growth rate in the secondary sector surpassed that of the primary sector in all states except Andhra Pradesh, Jharkhand, and Telangana. Nevertheless, all states recorded higher growth in the tertiary sector than in the primary sector during this time. We conclude that while the growth of the tertiary sector has primarily driven the increase in net state domestic product (NSDP) across most states in the post-globalisation period, the secondary sector has also contributed to this growth.
- Given the varying growth rates of PCNSDP across different states over time, we conducted comprehensive statistical analyses to examine whether signs of convergence in PCNSDP are evident in the post-globalisation era. Our results indicate divergence in PCNSDP across states both before and after globalisation, highlighting the growing interstate disparity within India.
- The factors that explain why some states achieve a higher level of PCNSDP than others require exploration to inform policy and reduce disparities between states. The econometric model we estimated concludes that states with higher urbanisation rates, a greater presence of the secondary and tertiary sectors, improved infrastructure, enhanced education, and better institutional support tend to achieve higher PCNSDP.

---

1 BIMARU stands for Bihar, Madhya Pradesh, Assam, Rajasthan and Uttar Pradesh.

8.2 Trends and Patterns of Labour Force Participation, 1983–2018

- The overall size of the labour force in India has increased over time, rising from 312 million in 1983 to 502 million in 2018. However, comparing the pre- and post-globalisation periods, it is evident that the annual increase in the labour force has significantly diminished in the latter period. The decline in the labour force size became even more pronounced after 2012 in rural areas. This decrease is primarily attributable to a drop in female participation in the rural labour force, with approximately 23.7 million rural women exiting the labour market between 2012 and 2018. Consequently, the female labour force participation rate (LFPR), which was 30.0 % in 1983, dropped to 17.5 % in 2018. In contrast, the LFPR for males, which was 56.1 % in 1983, remained virtually unchanged at 55.6 % in 2018. Another notable observation is that, although the labour force participation rate declined significantly in rural areas, it rose slightly in urban areas during 1983–2018, except in 2000.
- Labour force participation rates in India differ considerably across age groups, displaying a negatively skewed distribution that increases up to the 35–59 age bracket before decreasing. Nevertheless, LFPR has fallen across all age groups over time, with the largest reductions observed in the 5–14 and 15–24 age groups for both men and women. In 2018, the 35–59 age group made up around half of the country's labour force.
- A positive correlation exists between the labour force participation rate (LFPR) and education level in India. In 2018, those with graduate-level education had an LFPR nearly twice that of illiterate individuals. Illiterate males had a higher LFPR than illiterate females, and the proportion of female illiterates in the female labour force was greater than that in the male labour force. The female labour force in India tends to be less educated than its male counterparts. In 2018, approximately one-quarter of India's total labour force was illiterate, with 21 % of men and 43 % of women being illiterate.
- Our examination of the LFPR among different social groups highlights that individuals from lower social categories, such as Scheduled Tribes (ST), Scheduled Castes (SC), and Other Backward Classes (OBC), exhibit a higher LFPR compared to those in the 'Others' category, which includes individuals from the general castes.
- Examining the LFPR among religious groups, we find that from 1983 to 2018, the LFPR of Muslims was consistently lower than that of Hindus. However, the gap between these two groups has been narrowing over time. Additionally, Muslim females demonstrate a significant lag in terms of LFPR compared to their Hindu counterparts.

- The yearly growth rate of the labour force in rural India decreased from 1.60 % between 1983 and 1994 to 0.50 % from 1994 to 2018, with a notable decline of –0.44 % from 2012 to 2018. This decline was primarily due to the withdrawal of rural women from the labour force, resulting in a negative growth rate for women after 2000, particularly severe at –4.24 % between 2012 and 2018. However, in urban areas, both male and female labour force growth rates declined slightly from 1994 to 2018 compared to the previous period.
- All age groups experienced a decline in labour force growth rates after 1994, especially among those aged 5–14 and 15–24. Additionally, individuals with lower educational levels – primarily those who are illiterate or have less than primary education – experienced a larger drop in labour force growth rates during this period.
- The analysis of LFPR growth by social groups indicates that STs and SCs were in a stronger position than OBCs and 'Others' from 1983 to 1994. From 1994 to 2018, although the LFPR growth rate declined for all groups, the decrease was less pronounced for STs and SCs. Unlike males, females across all social groups experienced negative growth in LFPR during this period. Regarding religious groups, Hindus had an advantage over Muslims from 1983 to 1994 in terms of LFPR growth, but Muslims surpassed Hindus between 1994 and 2018.
- The analysis of the decline in female participation in the labour force was conducted by examining the composition of the women who are 'out of the labour force'. The conclusion is that until 2012, the primary reasons were education and domestic duties; however, after 2012, domestic responsibilities became the predominant factor for both rural and urban women. In contrast, men mainly withdrew from the labour force to pursue education.
- The analysis of the LFPR in the states from 1983 to 2018 revealed that in rural areas, the best-performing states are Andhra Pradesh, Himachal Pradesh, Tamil Nadu, Maharashtra, and Karnataka. In contrast, the lowest performers include Bihar, Uttar Pradesh, Haryana, Assam, and West Bengal. In urban areas, higher LFPR is found in Tamil Nadu, West Bengal, Himachal Pradesh, Kerala, and Karnataka, while Bihar, Uttar Pradesh, Rajasthan, Haryana, and Jammu & Kashmir have lower rates. Another notable conclusion is that labour force growth rates declined across all states (except Punjab) during the period from 1994 to 2018 (post-globalisation) compared to the period from 1983 to 1994 (pre-globalisation).
- From 1994 to 2018, the growth rate of the male labour force in fourteen of the seventeen major states decreased compared to 1983–1994, with Haryana, Jammu & Kashmir, and Punjab as exceptions. Meanwhile, growth in the female labour force declined in all states except Kerala and Punjab. This trend

suggests that the globalisation of the Indian economy has negatively affected women's labour-market participation, particularly in rural areas. Furthermore, the decline in female labour force growth persisted throughout the post-globalisation period and worsened after 2012.

- The econometric model aimed at identifying factors influencing labour force participation in India concludes that males, older individuals, married individuals, those with higher education, individuals with technical training, and those from poor families are more likely to participate in the labour force. Additionally, individuals from lower-caste backgrounds are more likely to participate than those from higher castes. However, the probability of participation is lower among Muslims and other minority groups in comparison to Hindus.

8.3 Quantitative Aspects of Employment Changes, 1983–2018

- The workforce size in India steadily increased in both rural and urban areas from 1983 to 2012. However, after 2012, there was a significant decline in rural areas, resulting in 20.14 million workers missing work opportunities in the rural labour market between 2012 and 2018. This decline was primarily due to a sharp decline in the number of female workers in rural areas. Specifically, between 2012 and 2018, 24.76 million female workers in rural India left the workforce, while the number of male workers increased by 4.66 million. In contrast, the situation in urban areas was somewhat different; both males and females saw an increase in workforce numbers from 2012 to 2018.
- The analysis of workforce participation rates (WPR) trends indicates that both males and females in rural areas experienced a decline in WPR during the post-globalisation period compared to the pre-globalisation period. This decline was particularly significant for females after 2000. In contrast, in urban areas, males saw a slight improvement in WPR during the post-globalisation period, while females faced a decline. During the 2012–2018 sub-period, WPR decreased for both males and females in urban areas. Overall, WPR across India has declined from 1983 to 2018, with the rate of decline accelerating during globalisation, especially for females in rural areas.
- The discussion on changes in the WPR for various age groups indicated that individuals aged 15–24, 25–34, and 60 and above experienced the most significant declines in WPR, particularly after 2012. This decline was especially pronounced in rural areas among males aged 15–24 and 60 and above, as well as females aged 15–24, 25–34, and 35–59. In urban areas, younger age groups

also displayed a decrease in WPR for both genders. Furthermore, except for the 35–59 age group, all other age groups in India experienced a faster decline in workforce share than in their population share. The most notable decrease in this ratio was observed in the 15–24 age group, followed by those aged 5–14 and 60 and above.

- The relationship between the WPR and educational level in rural India is U-shaped, exhibiting higher WPRs among those who are illiterate and those with graduate degrees or above. However, in urban areas, the WPR increases with higher education levels, a trend that is consistent across genders. Furthermore, individuals with lower levels of education experience a greater decline in WPR over time.
- In rural India, individuals from marginalised groups, specifically the STs and SCs, exhibit a higher WPR than those from OBCs and 'Others'. This trend was also observed in urban areas until 2012, after which the differences among social groups began to diminish. The disparity in WPR among males is smaller than that among females, with ST and SC females displaying a higher WPR than those from higher castes. Overall, we conclude that the WPR has declined across all social categories from 1983 to 2018, particularly among weaker groups, with females being especially affected.
- In analysing the WPR of various religious groups from 1983 to 2018, we conclude that Muslims have consistently lagged behind Hindus. However, the gap in WPR between Hindus and Muslims has narrowed, particularly since 2000 and in rural areas. While the WPR for females is lower than that for males across all religious groups, it is deficient for Muslim females in both rural and urban settings. Furthermore, the WPR for Muslims has declined over time at a significantly greater rate than that of Hindus. When comparing the share of employed individuals to the overall population share, it is evident that both Muslim men and women have a lower employment share relative to their population share compared to their Hindu counterparts. This indicates the continuation of discrimination against them in the labour market.
- The post-globalisation period (1994–2018) has seen a significant decline in the growth rate of employment in India for both males and females compared to the pre-globalisation period (1983–1994). However, females have been particularly affected, with their employment growth rate decreasing after globalisation. More specifically, in all sub-periods after 2000, the female employment growth rate in rural areas became negative, with the most severe drop occurring from 2012 to 2018, during which the annual growth rate was –4.56 %. The decline in employment growth during the post-globalisation period was evident irrespective of the region (rural or urban). Nevertheless,

the decline in employment growth was less severe in urban areas than in rural areas. Ultimately, rural India, especially rural women, has borne the most significant impact of globalisation on employment losses.

- When we analysed employment growth rates across different age groups, it became evident that the 5–14 age group experienced the most significant decline in employment growth over the years. This decline was particularly pronounced after 2000, irrespective of individuals' sex or the regions considered. Furthermore, the 15–24 age group also showed a notable decrease in employment growth after 2000, affecting both males and females in rural and urban areas.
- Our primary conclusion concerning employment growth among different educational groups is that, in rural areas, both males and females with lower educational attainment experienced the most significant employment losses following the onset of globalisation. Consequently, employment growth rates for illiterate individuals and those with below primary and primary education turned negative during this period. In contrast, employment growth remained positive in urban areas across all educational groups, except those with below primary education. Overall, we conclude that individuals at the lower end of the educational spectrum experienced the greatest employment losses during globalisation, particularly in rural regions.
- There is a general trend of declining employment growth rates in rural areas for all social groups and genders, except for ST males, during the post-globalisation period. In urban areas, all social groups experienced positive employment growth rates, with STs witnessing an improvement in their employment growth rate from 2012 to 2018. Our overall conclusion is that while all social groups faced a decline in employment growth rates during the post-globalisation period compared to the pre-globalisation period, this decline has been less severe for weaker social categories, specifically STs and SCs.
- The employment growth rates among religious groups reveal various trends. In rural areas, Muslims had a lower employment growth rate than Hindus during the pre-globalisation period. However, from 1994 to 2012, rural Muslims experienced improved employment growth rates and surpassed those of Hindus. This progress could not be sustained after 2012, as rural Muslim males experienced negative growth, while Hindu males continued to show positive growth. Similarly, rural females from both groups encountered declines in employment growth from 2012 to 2018. In urban areas, Hindus demonstrated higher growth rates than Muslims during the pre-globalisation period, followed by improved rates for Muslims between 1994 and 2012, which they were unable to maintain after 2012. Overall, Hindus outperformed Muslims in employment growth

rates during the pre-globalisation period. Muslims began to catch up with Hindus in this regard in the early years of the globalisation period. However, later in the globalisation period (2012–2018), both groups faced declines in growth rates, with Muslims experiencing a significantly larger fall.

- We examined how employment scenarios evolved across 17 major states in India, focusing on two key indicators: workforce participation rates (WPR) and the growth of the workforce/employed individuals from 1983 to 2018. Overall, Himachal Pradesh, Andhra Pradesh, Tamil Nadu, Karnataka, and Madhya Pradesh demonstrated superior WPR performance during this period. In contrast, the lagging states included Bihar, Assam, Uttar Pradesh, Haryana, Kerala, and West Bengal. We also found no statistically significant changes in the rankings of these states between 1983 and 2018.
- While reviewing the growth rates of employed individuals during the pre-globalisation period (1983–1994), we identified Jammu & Kashmir as the top performer, whereas Punjab ranked the lowest. Other states that performed relatively well in terms of employment growth during this period included Haryana, Assam, Himachal Pradesh, Andhra Pradesh, and West Bengal. In the post-globalisation period (1994–2018), Jammu & Kashmir retained its position as the leading state for employment growth, while Kerala ranked the lowest. Other states that achieved higher employment growth than the national average included Madhya Pradesh, Assam, West Bengal, Haryana, Gujarat, Maharashtra, Punjab, Uttar Pradesh, and Bihar. Conversely, states such as Himachal Pradesh, Karnataka, Tamil Nadu, Odisha, Andhra Pradesh, and Kerala experienced employment growth that fell below the all-India average.
- Another important conclusion regarding employment growth during the post-globalisation period is that most states experienced a decline in growth rates compared to the pre-globalisation period. In rural areas, employment growth rates decreased across all major states during the post-globalisation period relative to the pre-globalisation period. This trend was observed for both males and females, with a more pronounced decline among females. A similar pattern was evident in urban areas, where thirteen of the seventeen major states also recorded lower employment growth for males and females during the post-globalisation period. Another significant observation is that the downward trend in employment growth, which began with the introduction of globalisation policies in the early 1990s, continued uninterrupted during the sub-period of 2012–2018. During this period, all states, except Maharashtra, Madhya Pradesh, and Assam, reported lower growth rates in the number of employed persons (rural and urban combined) than in the preceding sub-period from 2000 to 2012.

- Our econometric analysis, which aimed to identify the key factors influencing employment status (i.e. whether individuals are employed or unemployed) in India, concludes that the likelihood of being employed is higher among males, older individuals, married individuals who are heads of their households, those who have received vocational training, and individuals from non-poor households. In contrast, this likelihood is lower for individuals from disadvantaged social groups (SCs and STs) and Muslims. This pattern holds when examining rural and urban areas separately; however, individuals living in rural areas are more likely to be employed than those in urban settings.

8.4 Qualitative Aspects of Employment Changes, 1983–2018

- One way to assess the quality of employment is by examining the modes of employment in which workers engage. Among the three modes of employment, regular employment is viewed as the most desirable, followed by self-employment and casual employment. Our analysis reveals a clear trend of increasing casualisation of the workforce in rural India until 2000. However, this trend reversed after 2000, with a growing proportion of regular workers in the total workforce. The percentage of self-employed workers has generally declined from 1983 to 2018.
- In rural areas, female employment experienced a higher rate of casualisation between 1983 and 2018, while regular employment was less common. This indicates lower-quality employment for women. In urban areas, women have also fallen behind men in terms of employment quality, particularly in regular employment, although some progress has been made over time.
- Regarding employment modes across various social groups, the conclusion is that the workers from disadvantaged social groups (SCs and STs) are more engaged in casual employment. In contrast, individuals from higher social groups (OBCs and 'Others') are more likely to participate in both self-employment and regular employment. While this holds for both male and female workers, the inferior quality of employment for female workers is particularly pronounced among lower-caste groups, especially the SCs.
- The overall conclusion regarding employment modes across religious groups is that Muslim males lag behind Hindu males in terms of regular employment, as they tend to engage more in self-employment and casual employment compared to their Hindu counterparts. However, an important point to note is that Muslim women are more involved in self-employment and have lower rates of casual and regular employment in comparison to their Hindu counterparts.

- The analysis of employment modes among workers in major states in India concludes that more developed states, such as Maharashtra, Punjab, Tamil Nadu, and Haryana, have a high percentage of regular employment workers. In contrast, less developed states, such as Bihar, Odisha, Uttar Pradesh, Madhya Pradesh, and Rajasthan, exhibit a significantly lower percentage of regular workers. Casual workers are present in developed and less developed states, with Andhra Pradesh, Tamil Nadu, Bihar, Kerala, and Odisha displaying relatively high percentages. Self-employment is more prevalent in less developed and hilly states, such as Himachal Pradesh, Rajasthan, Jammu and Kashmir, Uttar Pradesh, and Assam. It is comparatively lower in more developed states, including Tamil Nadu, Kerala, Andhra Pradesh, Maharashtra, and West Bengal. While some shifts in state rankings regarding employment modes have occurred over time, these changes have not reached statistical significance.
- The state-level analysis of employment growth rates, considering rural and urban areas combined, revealed a decline in casual and self-employment growth rates in rural areas across numerous states during various sub-periods of the post-globalisation era. From 2012 to 2018, the growth rates of rural casual workers were negative in all states except Assam. Likewise, the growth rates of self-employed workers turned negative in thirteen of the seventeen states studied. Conversely, the growth rates of regular employees improved in most states, particularly after 2000. Notably, Bihar, Assam, and Madhya Pradesh experienced significant growth in regular employment in rural areas between 2012 and 2018, with all three states achieving annual growth rates of over 10 % in this category. The growth of regular employment is generally similar across urban areas, as some less developed states, such as Assam, Madhya Pradesh, Uttar Pradesh, and Bihar, recorded an annual growth rate of over 5.0 % in urban areas between 2012 and 2018. In contrast, more developed states, such as Punjab, Haryana, Himachal Pradesh, and Karnataka, as well as the less developed state of Bihar, recorded annual growth rates of over 4.0 % in casual workers in urban areas from 2012 to 2018.
- The analysis of employment growth rates at the state level, encompassing both rural and urban areas, concludes that most states are experiencing a decline in growth rates for casual and self-employed workers. In contrast, growth rates for regular workers are steadily increasing. During the sub-period from 2012 to 2018, the less developed states of Bihar, Assam, Madhya Pradesh, Rajasthan, and Uttar Pradesh, alongside the more advanced state of Haryana, reported impressive growth rates of 5.0 % or more per annum for regular employees. In stark contrast, all but two states – Assam and Haryana – observed a significant decrease in the number of casual workers during the same period.

Furthermore, eleven states experienced negative growth in the number of self-employed workers.

- To evaluate the quality of employment, our study additionally examined the incidence of the 'working poor'. In 2018, 42 % of workers in rural India and 22 % cent in urban India were classified as 'poor'. We found that the occurrence of 'working poor' was highest among casual workers, followed by self-employed and regular workers. This trend was consistent in both rural and urban areas. When we analysed the prevalence of 'working poor' across social groups, it became evident that the most disadvantaged group, STs, had the highest percentage of 'working poor' in both rural and urban areas, followed by SCs, OBCs, and 'Others'. Therefore, we can conclude that higher-caste workers have superior access to higher-quality employment in India than lower-caste workers. Furthermore, the incidence of 'working poor' was greater among Muslim workers compared to Hindu workers.
- The conclusion drawn from the multinomial logit regression model, which was estimated to identify the factors influencing workers' employment mode choices, indicates that certain groups of workers are more likely to seek higher-quality employment, such as regular or self-employment, rather than casual employment. Specifically, older workers, women, heads of households, individuals from larger families, unmarried workers, those with higher levels of education, workers from higher-caste groups, Hindu workers, and urban workers are more likely to choose regular or self-employment over casual employment.

8.5 Trends and Patterns of Employment Diversification, 1983–2018

- From 1983 to 2018, India witnessed a diversification in employment from agriculture to non-agricultural sectors, with a significant acceleration post–2000, particularly in rural areas. Consequently, the proportion of non-agricultural workers rose from 31 % in 1983 to 40 % in 2000, reaching 56 % by 2018. Among non-agricultural sectors, the largest increase in the percentage of workers occurred in the construction and trade sectors. Meanwhile, the proportion of manufacturing workers declined from 13 % in 2012 to 12 % in 2018 across both rural and urban areas. In 2018, manufacturing workers accounted for 23 % of the urban workforce and 8 % of the rural workforce.
- The primary beneficiaries of the employment diversification process in India have been males, as an overwhelmingly high percentage of female workers remain involved in agriculture and allied sectors. Despite the acceleration of

diversification for both sexes, a considerable gap has persisted between them. In 2018, when combining rural and urban areas, 60 % of male workers in the country were employed in the non-agricultural sector, compared to 43 % of female workers. Among the various sub-sectors, 'construction' and 'trade' emerged as the most significant non-agricultural sectors for employment among males, whereas 'other services' played a crucial role for females.

- The analysis of the industrial classification of economic activities of workers at the two-digit level revealed that 'crop and animal production, hunting, and related activities' was the most significant sub-sector, employing 44 % of the total workforce in the country in 2018. That year, other notable sub-sectors for employment included 'construction of buildings' (8.85 %), 'retail trade, except for motor vehicles and motorcycles' (8.02 %), 'land transport and transport via pipeline' (4.49 %), 'education' (3.78 %), and 'manufacture of wearing apparel' (2.10 %). Additionally, it was found that there were seventy-two sub-sectors (out of a total of eighty-seven at the two-digit level) in which the percentage of workers was less than 1 % of the total workers. Furthermore, fifty-six sub-sectors experienced an increase in the percentage of workers in 2018 compared to 2012, with the most significant improvement occurring in the 'construction of buildings', which saw a 1.17 percentage-point increase. Moreover, three sub-sectors, namely, 'land transport and transport via pipeline', 'education', and 'retail trade, except for motor vehicles and motorcycles', also observed an increase of more than 0.5 percentage points in the percentage of workers during this period. Overall, there is clear evidence of increased employment diversification from 2012 to 2018, as confirmed by the rising value of the Simpson Diversification Index (SDI).
- In 2018, the main sub-sectors for male workers at the two-digit level included 'crop production, hunting, and related activities', 'construction of buildings', 'retail trade (excluding motor vehicles and motorcycles)', 'land transport and transport via pipeline', and 'education', accounting for 68 % of male employment. For females, the key sub-sectors were 'crop production, hunting, and related activities', 'education', 'retail trade', 'manufacture of wearing apparel', 'activities of households as employers of domestic personnel', and 'manufacture of tobacco products', which together represented 78 % of female employment. Notably, employment diversity has been greater for males than for females, as shown by their SDI values.
- The analysis of employment diversification patterns among various socio-religious groups concludes that marginalised communities, specifically STs, SCs, and OBCs, are more actively engaged in agriculture and related fields. In stark contrast, individuals from higher social groups, referred to as 'Others', are significantly more represented in the non-agricultural sector. Within these

non-agricultural sectors, marginalised groups account for a substantial share of employment in construction, while individuals from higher social groups dominate the manufacturing, trade, and services sectors. The analysis by religious affiliation reveals that a higher proportion of male Hindu workers are engaged in agriculture and allied activities compared to male Muslim workers, who are primarily concentrated in 'construction', 'trade', 'manufacturing', and 'transport'. Although a larger percentage of Hindu women are employed in agriculture, an impressive 35 % of Muslim women work in manufacturing, compared to only 11 % of Hindu women. In conclusion, the data highlights that Hindus maintain a dominant presence in agriculture, while Muslims are significantly more concentrated in non-agricultural sectors, particularly in manufacturing and trade.

- Regarding the growth rates of workers across various sectors, there is a clear and yet concerning trend. In rural areas, the growth rate of the 'agriculture and allied' sector has declined continuously from 1983 to 2018 for both males and females. Specifically, male workers in rural areas experienced a growth rate of 1.25 % from 1983 to 1994, which fell to –0.24 % from 1994 to 2018. Similarly, rural females exhibited growth rates of 1.22 % and –1.96 % during those two periods, respectively. Furthermore, the growth rate of rural female workers in the 'agriculture and allied' sector has declined significantly since 2000, with no signs of recovery since then. Among rural non-agricultural sectors, 'construction' and 'transport, storage and communication' have demonstrated notable improvements in growth rates for both male and female workers from 1994 to 2018, compared to the previous period from 1983 to 1994. However, the growth rate of rural non-agricultural workers has declined slightly from 1994 to 2018. In urban areas, the situation is equally troubling. The growth rate of male and female workers has consistently declined from 1994 to 2018, compared with the period from 1983 to 1994, across all sectors except 'manufacturing' and 'transport, storage, and communication'. The overall picture of employment growth in the country following globalisation is dire. This situation arises primarily from a substantial decline in agricultural employment after 2000, while non-agricultural employment has grown slowly, remaining the lowest among all sub-periods.
- The analysis of worker growth rates across various two-digit sub-sectors revealed that fifty-six out of eighty-seven sub-sectors comprised around 42 % of the country's total workforce in 2018. These sectors demonstrated favourable growth rates in the number of workers from 2012 to 2018. However, sectors with smaller workforce shares exhibited significantly higher growth rates. For instance, the 'construction of buildings' accounted for 8.85 % cent

of the total workforce in 2018 and achieved an annual growth rate of 2.32 % from 2012 to 2018. In contrast, the 'activities of extraterritorial organisations and bodies' achieved the highest growth rate at 37.28 %, despite employing only 0.004 % of the total workforce in 2018. Moreover, 'crop and animal production, hunting, and related service activities', which employed nearly 44 % of the workforce in 2018, experienced negative employment growth during the same period. Other notable sectors, each accounting for more than 1 % of the total workforce, that also experienced negative employment growth, included 'manufacture of textiles', 'public administration and defence; compulsory social security', 'civil engineering', 'other personal service activities', and 'manufacture of food products'.

- Examining the share of various sectors in new employment over different periods reveals emerging sectors crucial for employment creation. While the 'agriculture & allied' sector experienced a significant decline of 1.32 million workers per year during globalisation (1994–2018), the non-agricultural sector expanded its workforce by 5.32 million annually. This resulted in a net gain of 4 million workers each year. Among the non-agricultural sectors, the most significant contributors to this employment expansion are 'construction', 'wholesale & retail trade', 'other services', 'manufacturing', and 'transport, storage and communication', ranked in order of their impact. Furthermore, it is worth noting that the decrease in workers within the 'agriculture & allied' sector was primarily driven by a marked reduction in female workers, whose numbers fell by 1.37 million per year. This stark trend contrasts with the growth of 1.12 million female workers annually during pre-globalisation (1983–1994). When comparing employment changes across sectors from 1994 to 2018, the emerging employment-generating sectors for males are 'construction', 'wholesale & retail trade', 'transport, storage and communication', and 'manufacturing'. For females, the standout sectors are 'other services' and 'construction'.
- The analysis of employment diversification patterns in seventeen major states concludes that diversification accelerated after 2000 in most states, considering rural and urban areas together. In 1983, no state had more than 50 % of its workforce engaged in non-agricultural employment. By 2000, three states had reached this milestone; by 2018, that number increased to fifteen. Notably, males gained more from this diversification process than females. As of 2018, Kerala ranked first in the percentage of non-agricultural workers, while Madhya Pradesh ranked last. Focusing specifically on rural areas, diversification in most states accelerated between 2012 and 2018. In 2012, only one state, Kerala, had more than 50 % of its rural workers engaged in non-farm employment. By

2018, five states achieved this mark: Kerala, Punjab, Haryana, Tamil Nadu, and Jammu & Kashmir. In 2018, Kerala recorded the highest percentage of rural non-farm workers at 73.34 %, whereas Madhya Pradesh had the lowest at 24.52 %. Another noteworthy conclusion is that, despite the overall increase in the percentage of non-agricultural workers across all states, their relative rankings did not change significantly from 1983 to 2018.

- Employment elasticity values are considered to identify employment-intensive economic sectors. For the pre-globalisation period (1983–1994), we noted that the construction sector dominated with the highest employment elasticity value of 1.05, followed by 'wholesale & retail trade' (0.66), 'transport, storage and communication' (0.59), 'electricity, gas, & water' (0.57), 'Other services' (0.51), 'agriculture & allied activities' (0.41), and 'manufacturing' (0.37). The employment elasticity for the combined sectors during this period was 0.38. However, the situation changed markedly during the post-globalisation period (1994–2018), when employment elasticities declined across all sectors. Most alarmingly, the 'agriculture & allied' sector experienced the steepest decline, with employment elasticity plummeting to −0.21. This led to a decline in employment elasticity for the combined sectors. More importantly, the decline in the elasticity value for the country persisted in all sub-periods of the post-globalisation period, even becoming negative at −0.01 from 2012 to 2018. Furthermore, during this period, the 'manufacturing' and 'mining & quarrying' sectors experienced negative employment elasticity. In conclusion, the link between income and employment growth in the country has significantly weakened in the post-globalisation era across a wide range of sectors, with 'agriculture & allied activities' being the most impacted.
- The analysis of employment elasticities across various states revealed that Jammu & Kashmir had the highest employment elasticity in the pre- and post-globalisation periods, with values of 1.19 and 0.41, respectively. In contrast, Punjab recorded the lowest employment elasticity during the pre-globalisation period, at 0.13, while Kerala exhibited the lowest elasticity during the post-globalisation period, at 0.03. Another important conclusion is that all major states, except Punjab, experienced a decline in employment elasticity after globalisation compared to before globalisation. Although a notable decrease in the employment growth rate in the 'agriculture & allied' sector can account for much of this downturn, the drop in the non-agricultural sector has also contributed.
- The econometric exercises carried out to identify the factors influencing workers' decisions to choose between farm and non-farm employment lead to the conclusion that younger individuals who are unmarried, male, better educated,

and have received technical or vocational training are more likely to opt for non-farm employment over farm employment. Additionally, this likelihood is higher among workers from the general caste, those from Hindu families, and individuals from larger households.

8.6 Change and Continuity in Employment Landscape, 2018–2024

We now highlight the changes and continuities in India's employment landscape during the most recent phase (2018–2024) of the globalisation era, compared to the situation before. The subsequent points require particular attention:

- Deviating from past trends, women in India have experienced a substantial and rapid increase in their labour force and workforce participation rates from 2018 to 2024, compared to previous periods. Women's labour force and workforce participation rates, encompassing both rural and urban areas, have increased by 14.2 percentage points over these six years, which is notable given that the increase for men ranged from 3 to 4 percentage points. This rise in female participation rates (in both the labour force and the workforce) has elevated the country's overall participation rate by 9.0 percentage points. However, it is essential to note that much of this improvement is driven by increased participation rates of women in rural areas. The upshot of this development is that, compared to 1.07 million rural women who missed out on the labour force each year during the earlier phase of globalisation (1994–2018), an additional 16.8 million entered the labour force annually between 2018 and 2024. Similarly, while 1.17 million rural women left the workforce each year from 1994 to 2018, an additional 16.7 million joined the workforce each year from 2018 to 2024. These observations may lead one to suggest that the discrimination women have faced in the labour market appears to be easing somewhat in recent years, at least based on the indicators of their participation rates compared to men. However, this conclusion should be approached with due caution, as despite improvements in participation rates, women continue to lag significantly behind men in 2024. Furthermore, much of this increase in the female workforce is focused on subsidiary activities (31 % in rural areas and 28 % overall), which are typically short-term, intermittent, poorly paid, and insecure.
- The improvement in labour force and workforce participation rates from 2018 to 2024 is reflected in the growth rates of the labour force and workforce. The annual growth rates of the female labour force and workforce in

combined (rural plus urban) areas over the past six years were 11.02 % and 11.52 %, respectively, which are 11.32 and 12.02 percentage points higher than the corresponding growth rates achieved during 1994–2018. In contrast, the males attained growth rates of 1.34 % and 1.88 % only in the labour force and the workforce, respectively, during 2018–2024. This further reinforces the conclusion that females have recently improved their labour market outcomes.

- In line with previous trends, the labour force participation rate shows a rising tendency with the age and education of individuals. From 2018 to 2024, the labour force participation rate remained low, particularly for males and females under 15, while the largest increases occurred for males aged 15–24 and females aged 35–59. Males with secondary or higher education and females with middle-level education experienced the most notable improvements in labour force participation rates during this period. By 2024, the highest labour force participation rates are observed among males and females who are 'graduate & above'.
- Another striking similarity with the past picture is that the labour force participation rate between 2018 and 2024 was higher for lower social groups than for higher ones and for Hindus than Muslims. Although all social groups experienced an increase in labour force participation rates between 2018 and 2024, the increase was particularly notable among lower social groups, especially the STs. This trend was observed in both males and females, but the improvement in females was significantly more pronounced than in males.
- As in the past, the relationship between the workforce participation rate and the level of education remained positive during 2018–2024. However, in 2024, the highest rates were observed among males who were 'graduates and above', and among females who were 'illiterate'. All educational groups of males and females (except males without primary education) experienced increases in workforce participation rates from 2018 to 2024, with the rise notably greater for females than for males.
- Workforce participation rates among social and religious groups closely mirror trends observed in the past. Consequently, the workforce participation rate remains higher for individuals from lower social strata than for those from higher strata, and for Hindus than for Muslims. Across both genders, workforce participation rates have improved from 2018 to 2024. However, the increase has been more pronounced for females than males, particularly those in the ST category. Although both Hindus and Muslims have increased their workforce participation rates from 2018 to 2024, the rate for Hindus remains higher than that for Muslims in 2024. Notably, a significant gap persists between these two religious groups in female workforce participation rates.

- There was a noticeable shift in the composition of individuals outside the labour force between 2018 and 2024. Firstly, during this period, the absolute number and growth rate of out-of-labour-force females decreased significantly nationwide, particularly in rural areas. A similar, though less pronounced, trend was observed among males. Secondly, an analysis of the reasons for being out of the labour force in 2024 revealed that attending educational institutions was the primary reason for males, while for females, the main reasons were attending to domestic duties and participating in educational institutions. Thirdly, when comparing 2024 to 2018, there was a significant decrease in the proportion of females engaged in domestic duties, especially in rural areas, while the percentage attending educational institutions increased. Overall, there is a clear trend of females transitioning from domestic work to employment outside the home, particularly in rural areas. This shift partly explains the significant rise in their labour force and workforce participation rates from 2018 to 2024.
- In 2024, labour force participation rates exhibited significant changes compared to 2018. For males, all but four states – Andhra Pradesh, Haryana, Jammu & Kashmir, and Tamil Nadu – improved their rates. In contrast, all states reported increases in female participation. Male participation rates ranged from 64.9 % in Chhattisgarh to 48.1 % in Bihar, while female participation rates ranged from 56.2 % in Himachal Pradesh to 18.9 % in Haryana. Chhattisgarh, Himachal Pradesh, and Kerala saw improvements of over five percentage points for males. Female participation increased notably across all states except Andhra Pradesh, with Assam, Jharkhand, Odisha, Uttarakhand, and Gujarat achieving increases of over 20 percentage points. However, the gap in participation between men and women persisted despite these improvements.
- The changes in workforce participation rates across various states from 2018 to 2024 reflect the trends in labour force participation rates. While male workforce participation rates increased in all states except Andhra Pradesh and Jammu & Kashmir, female workforce participation rates improved in all twenty-one states analysed. In 2024, male participation rates ranged from 63.2 % in Chhattisgarh to 46.4 % in Bihar. Among females, the highest participation rate was recorded in Himachal Pradesh at 51.8 %, while Haryana had the lowest rate at 18.4 %.
- From 2018 to 2024, Chhattisgarh boasted the highest male labour force growth rate at 3.39 % per annum, while Tamil Nadu recorded the lowest at 0.05 %. Among females, Bihar recorded the highest growth rate of 41.36 %, while Andhra Pradesh recorded the lowest at 1.31 %. Only five states – Kerala, Bihar, Odisha, Gujarat, and Jharkhand – observed improvements in male labour

force growth of 1 % to 2 % compared to the 1994–1998 period. In contrast, all states experienced substantial growth in female labour force rates, ranging from 4.98 % to 50.75 %.

- Between 2018 and 2024, Chhattisgarh excelled in male workforce growth, achieving an annual rate of 3.51 %, while Andhra Pradesh registered the lowest growth at 0.30 %. For females, Bihar led with a remarkable growth of 41.71 %, starkly contrasting with Andhra Pradesh's 1.38 %. Moreover, four states, including Bihar, recorded female workforce growth rates exceeding 20 %. Seventeen states exhibited improvements in male workforce growth rates between 1994 and 2018, with Jammu & Kashmir and Maharashtra being the exceptions. All states demonstrated advancements in female workforce growth rates, with eight states recording increases exceeding 20 percentage points. Overall, Jharkhand achieved the highest combined growth in the male and female workforce at 8.49 %, whereas Andhra Pradesh had the lowest at 0.60 %. Notably, unlike in the previous phase of the globalisation era, no state experienced a decline in workforce growth rates, and ten states improved their growth rates by more than five percentage points, including Jharkhand, Odisha, and Uttarakhand.
- There have also been noticeable changes in the quality aspect of employment from 2018 to 2024. For the country as a whole, compared with 2018, the share of casual workers declined by 5.12 percentage points in 2024, while self-employment and regular employment increased by 6.21 percentage points and 1.09 percentage points, respectively. Although this development raises some hope regarding improvements in employment quality in recent years, there is also concern, given that not much progress has been made in increasing the share of regular employment. As of 2024, approximately 22 % of the total workforce is in regular employment, while as many as 58 % are engaged in self-employment, which may not generate sufficient earnings. Another noteworthy development is that much of the expansion in self-employment has been confined to females, particularly in rural areas. Furthermore, females have observed a decline in their share of regular employment in 2024 compared to 2018 in rural and urban areas.
- The state-level analysis for 2024 indicated that the percentage of regularly employed workers, combining both males and females, varied significantly across states. The percentage of regularly employed workers ranged from 39.0 % in Haryana to just 8.7 % in Bihar in 2024. The percentage of self-employed workers varied from 72.7 % in Uttar Pradesh to 34.2 % in Tamil Nadu. In comparison, the percentage of casual workers ranged from 31.3 % in Tamil Nadu to 11.1 % in Jammu & Kashmir. The picture is mixed regarding the change in the percentage of regular employees, as more than half of the

states benefited from its expansion, while others witnessed a decline during 2018–2024. The decline in casual employment has been widespread, with all states except Assam experiencing a decrease in the percentage of casual workers among total workers during this period. Regarding the change in the percentage of self-employed workers, while all but one state experienced an increase for females, the increase was larger in more than half of the states for males.

- In this study, the incidence of the working poor is regarded as an alternative measure of employment quality. We conclude that nearly one-fifth of workers in the country are poor in 2024, representing a decrease of approximately fifteen percentage points since 2018. This incidence is also higher in rural areas than in urban ones. Furthermore, casual workers experience the highest poverty rate at 30.9 %, followed by self-employed workers at 21.4 % and regular workers at 12.5 %. Overall, the incidence of the working poor decreases as we progress from lower to higher social strata. Additionally, Hindu workers have a lower incidence of the working poor compared to their Muslim counterparts.
- A significant change in the Indian labour market over the past six years is the decline in the employment diversification rate. In 2024, 54 % of all workers are engaged in the non-agricultural sector, representing a decrease of 1.93 percentage points from 2018. This decline primarily stems from a 7.37 percentage-point drop in the proportion of female workers in the non-agricultural sector, compared with a 3.96 percentage-point increase for male workers. In 2024, while 'construction', 'trade, hotels and restaurants', 'manufacturing', and 'other services' sectors comprised nearly 55 % of male workers, 'other services', 'manufacturing', and 'trade, hotels and restaurants' together accounted for around 31 % of female workers. Notably, during 2018–2024, the share of male workers declined in 'other services', 'manufacturing', and 'mining and quarrying', while females experienced decreases in nearly all sectors except for 'electricity, gas, and water supply', and 'transport, storage and communication'.
- The state-level picture regarding the degree of employment diversification revealed that Kerala led for males, with nearly 79 % employed in non-agricultural sectors, while Chhattisgarh recorded the lowest figure at 46 %. All states, except Kerala, have seen improvements in male non-agricultural employment since 2018, with Assam, Odisha, and Jharkhand recording increases of over 10 percentage points. For females, Punjab had the highest diversification at 66 %, while Bihar had the lowest at just 17.9 %. Thirteen states experienced a decline in the number of female non-agricultural workers since 2018, with Assam recording the largest drop, down 29.0 percentage points. Considering both genders, Kerala remained the most diversified state,

with 73 % of workers in non-agricultural work, while Chhattisgarh was the least diversified at 36.2 %. Alarmingly, two-thirds of states reported declines in non-agricultural employment compared to 2018, with Bihar recording the largest decrease of 9.1 percentage points.

- One of the most remarkable aspects of the recent changes in the country's employment situation is the significant increase in employment elasticity between 2018 and 2024, especially compared to the earlier phase of the globalisation era from 1994 to 2018. Between 1983 and 1994, the employment elasticity relative to income was 0.38. However, it dropped to 0.16 between 1994 and 2018. This figure rose to 1.09 from 2018 to 2024 in a remarkable turnaround. This increase is particularly noteworthy in light of the negative value –0.01 recorded between 2012 and 2018. All sectors of the economy contributed to this turnaround, except for 'construction', where the elasticity value declined during 2018–2024 compared to 1994–2018. Moreover, in four sectors, the value of elasticity exceeded 1.0, namely 'wholesale & retail trade' (2.21), 'agriculture & allied' (1.31), 'transport, storage and communication' (1.11), and 'manufacturing' (1.07). Another startling fact is that, deviating from the pattern of all sub-periods of 1994–2018, the elasticity value of the 'agriculture & allied' sector exceeded that of 'non-agriculture' during the most recent sub-period (2018–2024). Between 2018 and 2024, the overall employment elasticity improved significantly in many states, with sixteen of the twenty-one exceeding 1.0. During this period, the range varied from 4.40 in Uttarakhand to 0.12 in Andhra Pradesh.

8.7 Employment Performance Overview by State

In this study, we evaluated the overall performance of the states, recognising that no single state is expected to excel in every aspect of employment. Our assessment involved analysing the quantitative and qualitative dimensions of employment separately. This approach is crucial because some states may perform well in terms of employment quantity but do not achieve the same level of success regarding quality. For each aspect, we used data from four indicators. This data was then utilised to construct a composite index that ranks the states and assesses their relative positions in terms of employment performance. Our findings indicate that, from an employment quantity perspective, Madhya Pradesh is the best performer in 2024 among the twenty-one states we analysed. Chhattisgarh, Gujarat, Jharkhand, Himachal Pradesh, Uttarakhand, and West Bengal follow it. In contrast, Kerala is the worst performer, closely followed by Punjab, Bihar,

Haryana, Jammu and Kashmir, Andhra Pradesh, and Uttar Pradesh. The remaining seven states show medium performance in terms of employment quantity. Regarding the quality of employment in 2024, Haryana stands out as the best performer, followed by Kerala, Tamil Nadu, Punjab, Telangana, Uttarakhand, and Gujarat. Chhattisgarh, however, ranks as the worst state for employment quality, followed closely by Bihar, Uttar Pradesh, Madhya Pradesh, Jharkhand, Rajasthan, and Odisha. The states that fall between these two ends represent medium performers in terms of employment quality for 2024. However, when the quantity and quality aspects of employment are considered together, the top seven states in 2024, ranked in ascending order, are Gujarat (the best performer), Tamil Nadu, Himachal Pradesh, Uttarakhand, Haryana, Telangana, and Maharashtra. Conversely, the seven states at the bottom, ranked in descending order, are Bihar (the worst performer), Uttar Pradesh, Rajasthan, Chhattisgarh, Andhra Pradesh, Odisha, and Jammu and Kashmir. The obvious conclusion is that developed states tend to perform better in terms of employment quality. However, employment performance based on the quantity dimension appears relatively stronger in less developed states. Another interesting conclusion is that the ranking patterns of states based on employment quantity in 2018 and 2024 do not differ significantly. The same observation applies if we consider the correlation between their ranks in these years based on the quality aspect of employment. In other words, the states display continuity in employment performance from 2018 to 2024. Another vital conclusion is that there is an inverse relationship between the ranks of states based on their performances in the quantity and quality aspects of employment in a given year, implying that states excelling in the quantity aspect of employment are not necessarily the same ones excelling in the quality aspect.

8.8 Policy Implications

This study highlights two phases regarding changes in employment performance and the growth-employment relationship during the post-globalisation period (1994–2024). The first phase, spanning from 1994 to 2018, reveals a narrative of setbacks in employment expansion and a gradual decline in the capacity of significant economic growth to generate employment in India following the adoption of economic reforms and globalisation policies. Conversely, the second phase, from 2018 to 2024, indicates a shift that improves the employment outcomes of the growth process. It is also worth noting that the turnaround in employment outcomes from the current growth process is by no means an aberration from past trends, having continued, more or less uninterrupted, since 2018. It is encouraging to observe that the number of workers (UPSS) in the country grew by about 24 million annually from 2018 to 2024, a significant increase compared to a decline of 0.04 million per year in the six years before that (2012-2018) or a modest rise of 4 million annually during 1994-2018.

That said, it remains premature to conclude that all changes on the employment front are moving in the desired direction after prolonged setbacks in the country during globalisation. The primary concern is that the recent improvement in employment is predominantly quantitative, largely manifested by an increase in women's employment in subsidiary roles and less lucrative self-employed activities within the informal sector. Meanwhile, the qualitative aspect has fallen significantly short of the desired level. Concerns exist about the slowing of employment diversification from the agricultural to the non-agricultural sectors between 2018 and 2024, alongside ongoing labour market inequalities based on gender, caste, and religion; moreover, youth employment has not shown any appreciable improvement. Considering these realities, we propose policies to enhance employment outcomes in the future and address labour-market inequalities.

- The priority at this time should be that, in addition to efforts to increase the quantity of employment, there must be a greater focus on enhancing the quality of employment, particularly regarding female employment and employment for socially disadvantaged groups. The improvement of employment quality relies on several factors: diversification of the economy (both in terms of income and employment), growth in regular employment, expansion of the more productive segment of the self-employment sector, and strengthening of the role of the secondary sector, particularly its manufacturing component. Concerning employment diversification, more emphasis should be placed on rural diversification, particularly rural manufacturing, as urban manufacturing increasingly becomes capital-intensive and labour-displacing. Indeed, the large and continuously growing services sector in the country can also contribute to the enhancement of quality employment, provided there is growth in high-end services, which access depends on the education and skill levels of the workforce. Attention must focus on the continual enhancement of education and skill levels of prospective workers, especially women and those from disadvantaged social backgrounds, including Muslims. It is expected that the state governments, in tandem with the central government, focus more on diversifying the economy, which can be achieved by further strengthening the infrastructure base, greater urbanisation, adequate institutional support to the entrepreneurs, and enhancing the education and skill levels of the people, as our empirical analysis implied. Such an effort would also help to address the significant interstate disparity that persists today.

- To improve employment outcomes across the country, we advocate for a customised approach instead of relying on a uniform policy set by central authorities. This is essential due to the differences among the states in India regarding their specific needs for intervention. Some states require a greater focus on increasing employment quantity, while others need improvements in employment quality. Our study indicates that developed states currently perform better in creating quality employment, while less developed states are more successful at increasing the quantity of employment. This finding highlights the importance of developing state-specific policies to improve labour market outcomes in the years to come.[2]
- As mentioned in the introductory chapter, much of the employment policy in India has been shaped by the ideological perspectives of policy planners since the onset of planning after independence. For approximately three decades, the approach emphasised maximising GDP growth in the economy, which was intended to tackle issues such as unemployment and poverty through the operation of the so-called 'trickle-down mechanism'. Subsequently, as the objective of maximising GDP growth persisted with increasing intensity, shifting towards supply-side or neo-liberal economic policies within the macroeconomic policy framework, especially since the adoption of globalisation policies, the country managed, more or less, to sustain a satisfactory GDP growth rate. However, it also faced rising inequality among regions and communities, as well as adverse employment outcomes stemming from the so-called 'jobless growth' syndrome. In this context, some scholars advocate for pursuing a demand-led policy to enhance the purchasing power of the masses, thereby accelerating the production of mass consumption goods and services, ultimately boosting employment. There is certainly merit in this argument, as a country like India, with its 1.44 billion people, presents considerable potential for a robust domestic market to drive growth in the industrial and services sectors. This becomes even more significant due to the unforeseen shocks and uncertainties in the global market that characterise a globalised world, as illustrated by the current 'tariff war', initiated by the USA. However, we suggest that while India cannot abandon its growth objective or deviate from the policy of economic reforms and globalisation, by adopting a balanced approach that incorporates both demand-side and supply-side strategies within its macroeconomic policy package, the country could promote robust economic growth, create more employment opportunities, and enhance the quality of life for its citizens.

---

[2] We agree with Basole (2022), who underscores the necessity for a disaggregated analysis of India's labour market to facilitate effective improvements in employment outcomes, given the country's vast size and diverse nature.

Bibliography

Abraham, Vinoj, 'Employment Growth in Rural India: Distress-Driven?', *Economic and Political Weekly* 44/16 (2009), 97–104.

Abraham, Vinoj, 'Missing Labour or Consistent "De-Feminisation"'? *Economic and Political Weekly* 48/31 (2013), 99–108

Agresti, A., *Categorical Data Analysis* (New York: Wiley, 2002).

Ahluwalia, M. S., 'Economic Performance of States in the Post-Reforms Period', *Economic and Political Weekly* 35/19 (2000), 1637–1648.

Ahluwalia, M. S., 'State Level Performance under Economic Reforms in India', *Paper presented at the Centre for Research and Development and Policy Reform Conference on Indian Economic Prospects: Advancing Policy Reform* (Stanford: Stanford University, 2001).

Ahluwalia, M. S., 'Economic Reforms in India since 1991: Has Gradualism Worked?', *Journal of Economic Perspectives* 16/3 (2002a), 67–88.

Ahluwalia, M. S., 'State-Level Performance under Economic Reforms in India', in Anne O. Krueger, ed., *Economic Policy Reforms and the Indian Economy* (New Delhi: Oxford University Press, 2002b).

Ahluwalia, M. S., 'Prospects and Policy Change in the Twelfth Plan', *Economic and Political Weekly* 46/21 (2011), 88–105.

Ahluwalia, M. S. (2020), *Backstage: The Story Behind India's High Growth Years* (New Delhi: Rupa Publications, 2020)

Ahmed, Sadiq, *India's Long-term Growth Experience: Lessons and Prospects* (New Delhi: Sage Publications, 2007).

Aiyar, S., 'Growth Theory and Convergence Across Indian states: A Panel Study', In T. Collen (ed.), *India at the Crossroads: Sustaining Growth and Reducing Poverty* (Washington, D.C.: International Monetary Fund, 2001)

Bajpai, N. and J. D. Sachs, 'Trends in Interstate Inequalities of Income in India', Development Discussion Paper # 5 (Harvard: Harvard Institute for International Development, 1996).

Bakshi, S., Chawla, A. and Shah, M., 'Regional Disparities in India: A Moving Frontier', *Economic and Political Weekly* 50/1 (2017), 44–51.

Balakrishnan, Pulapre, Mausumi Das and M. Parameswaran, 'Growth Transitions in India: Myth and Reality', *Economic and Political Weekly* 56/11 (2021), 43–49.

Barrow, R. and X. Sala-i-Martin, *Economic Growth* (New York: McGraw-Hill, 1995).

Basole, Amit, 'Structural Transformation and Employment Generation in India: Past Performance and the Way Forward', *The Indian Journal of Labour Economics* 65/2 (2022), 295–320.

Bedi, Jatinder S. and Ajad Singh, 'Consistency in NSSO Employment-Unemployment Estimates Using NSS 68th Round and PLFS Data', *Economic and Political Weekly* 57/12 (2022), 37–44.

Bhaduri, A., 'Growth and Employment in the Era of Globalisation: Some lessons from the Indian Experience', ILO Asia-Pacific Working Paper Series (New Delhi: International Labour Organisation, 2008).

Bhaduri, A., ed., *Employment and Development: Essays from an Unorthodox Perspective* (New Delhi: Oxford University Press, 2006).

Bhaduri, A., *Development with Dignity: A Case for Full Employment* (New Delhi: National Book Trust, 2005).

Bhalla, G. S. and P. Hazell, 'Rural Employment and Poverty', *Economic and Political Weekly* 30/33 (2003), 3473–84.

Bhalla, S., 'Inclusive Growth? Focus on Employment' (Available at *www.macroscan.com*, 2007)

Bhandari, Laveesh and Sumita Kale, 'Sources of Growth in India', In Ashima Goyal, ed., *A Concise Handbook of the Indian Economy in the 21st Century* (New Delhi: Oxford University Press, 2019), 1–34

Bharti, Nitin Kumar, Lucas Chancel, Thomas Piketty and Anmol Somanchi, 'Towards Tax Justice and Wealth Redistribution in India', *Economic and Political Weekly* 59/21 (2024), 91–96.

Bhattacharya, B. B. and S. Sakthivel, 'Regional Growth and Disparity in India: Comparison of Pre- and Post-Reform Decades', *Economic and Political Weekly* 39/10 (2004), 1071–7.

Bhaumik, Sankar Kumar, 'Unemployment in India in Post-Liberalisation Era', *The Indian Journal of Labour Economics* 46/1 (2003), 69–94.

Bhaumik, Sankar Kumar, 'Growth and Composition of Rural Non-farm Employment in India in the Era of Economic Reforms', *The Indian Economic Journal* 55/3 (2007), 40–65.

Bhaumik, Sankar Kumar, 'The Changing Employment Scenarios in Rural India in the Era of Economic Reforms', *The Indian Journal of Labour Economics* 56/3 (2013), 349–71.

Bhaumik, Sankar Kumar, 'Labour Market Discrimination in the State of Bihar', In Sankar Kumar Bhaumik, ed., *Development with Justice: The Bihar Experience* (Oxon: Routledge, 2024).

Cashin, P. and R. Sahay, 'Internal Migration, Centre-State Grants and Economic Growth in the States of India', *IMF Staff Papers* 43/1 (1996).

Chadha, G. K., 'Youth Unemployment in India: Past Policy Gaps and Future Strategic Options', *The Indian Journal of Labour Economics* 43/4 (2000), 591–624.

Chadha, G. K., 'Impact of Economic Reforms on Rural Employment: No Smooth Sailing Anticipated', *Indian Journal of Agricultural Economics* 56/3 (2001), 491–524.

Chadha, G. K., 'Post-Reform Rural Employment Scenario in India', In Surjit Singh and V Ratna Reddy, eds., *Changing Contours of Asian Agriculture* (New Delhi: Academic Foundation, 2009).

Chadha, G. K. and P. P. Sahu, 'Post-Reform Setbacks in Rural Employment: Issues That Need Further Scrutiny', *Economic and Political Weekly* 37/21 (2002), 1998–2026.

Chandrasekhar, C. P., 'Erroneous Understanding of Macroeconomic Challenges: Reliance on Supply-side Responses', *Economic and Political Weekly* 52/9 (2017), 30–3.

Chenery, Hollis, and Moshe Syrquin, *Patterns of Development, 1950–1970* (Delhi: Oxford University Press, 1975).

Chikte, Rasika P., 'Income Divergence and Regional Growth in India: Before and After Economic Liberalisation', *South Asia Economic Journal* 12/2 (2011), 239–269.

Dasgupta, D., P. Maiti, R. Mukherjee, S. Sarkar, S. Chakrabarti, 'Growth and Interstate Disparities in India', *Economic and Political Weekly* 35/27 (2000), 2413–22.

Dholakia, R., 'Spatial Dimension of Acceleration of Economic Growth in India', *Economic and Political Weekly* 29/35 (1994), 2303–09.

Ghate, Chetan and Stephen Wright, 'Why Were Some Indian States So Slow to Participate in the Turnaround?', *Economic and Political Weekly* 48/12 (2013), 118–27.

Ghose, Ajit K., 'The Employment Challenge in India', *Economic and Political Weekly* 39/27 (2004), 5106–16.

Ghose, Ajit K., 'Globalization, Growth and Employment in India', *Indian Journal of Human Development* 10/2 (2016a), 127–56.

Ghose, Ajit K., *India Employment Report 2016: Challenges and the Imperatives of Manufacturing-Led Growth* (New Delhi: Oxford University Press, 2016b).

Ghose, Ajit K., 'Economic Growth and Employment in India', In Rajendra P. Mamgain and Preet Rustagi, eds., *Labour and Development: Essays in Honour of Professor T. S. Papola* (New Delhi: Academic Foundation, 2017), 105–28.

Ghose, Ajit K., *Employment in India: Oxford India Short Introduction* (New Delhi: Oxford University Press, 2019).

Ghose, Ajit K., *Structural Transformation of the Indian Economy* (New Delhi: Institute for Human Development, 2020).

Ghose, Ajit K., 'Structural Change and Development in India', *Indian Journal of Human Development* 15/1 (2021), 7–29.

Ghose, Ajit K., 'India's Exclusive Growth', *Economic and Political Weekly* 58/6 (2023), 35–42.

Ghose, Ajit K. and Abhishek Kumar, 'India's Deepening Employment Crisis in the Time of Rapid Economic Growth', *The Indian Journal of Labour Economics* 64/2 (2021), 247–78.

Ghosh, B., S. Marjit and C. Neogi, 'Economic Growth and Regional Divergence in India, 1960 to 1995', *Economic and Political Weekly* 33/26 (1998), 1623–30.

Ghosh, J., 'Macroeconomic reforms and a labour policy framework for India', Employment Strategy Paper # 2004/1 (Geneva: International Labour Office, 2004).

Ghosh, Soumya Kanti and Pulak Ghosh, 'Reading between the Lines: The PLFS Survey', *Business Standard* (13 June 2019).

Ghosh, Tania and Kaustubh, 'Growth Divergence between Indian States', *Economic and Political Weekly* 60/6 (2025), 50–57.

Glinskaya, E. and J. Jalan, 'Quality of Informal Jobs in India?', Conference Papers Series (Conference on Labour and Employment Issues in India, Institute of Human Development, New Delhi, 2006).

Goldar, Bishwanath, 'Growth in the Organised Manufacturing Employment in Recent Years', *Economic and Political Weekly* 46/7 (2011), 20–23.

Goldar, Bishwanath, 'India's Economic Growth Has Been Manufacturing-led, Not Services-led', *Economic and Political Weekly* 59/24 (2024), 12–14.

Government of India, *Report of the Expert Group on Unemployment Estimate* (Dantwala Committee Report, 1970).

Government of India, *Eighth Five-Year Plan (1992–1997)* (New Delhi: Planning Commission, 1992).

Government of India, *Report of Task Force on Employment Opportunities* (New Delhi: Planning Commission, 2001).

Government of India, *Special Group on Targeting Ten Million Employment Opportunities Per Year* (New Delhi: Planning Commission, 2002).

Government of India, *Towards Faster and More Inclusive Growth: An Approach Paper to the Eleventh Five-Year Plan* (New Delhi: Planning Commission, 2007a).

Government of India, *Report on Conditions of Work and Promotion of Livelihoods in the Unorganised Sector* (New Delhi: National Commission for Enterprises in the Unorganised Sector, 2007b).

Government of India, *The Challenge of Employment in India: An Informal Economy Perspective* (New Delhi: Government of India, 2009).

Government of India, *Annual Report to the People on Employment* (New Delhi: Government of India, Ministry of Labour and Employment, 2010).

Government of India, *Report of The Working Group on Employment, Planning and Policy for the Twelfth Five-Year Plan (2012–17)* (New Delhi: Planning Commission, 2011).

Gupta, S. P., *Globalisation, Economic Reforms and Employment Strategy in India* (New Delhi: Academic Foundation, 2006).

Himanshu, 'Changes in Workforce Structure among Social Groups in Rural India', *The Indian Journal of Labour Economics* 46/4 (2003), 1009–30.

Himanshu, 'Employment Trends in India: A Re-examination', *Economic and Political Weekly* 46/37 (2010), 43–59.

Hirway, Indira, 'Missing Labour Force: An Explanation', *Economic and Political Weekly* 47/37 (2012), 67–72

ILO-IHD, *India Employment Report 2024: Youth Employment, Education and Skills* (2024) <http://www.ilo.org/sites/default/files/2024–08/India%20 Employment%20-%20web_8%20April.pdf>, accessed 26 February 2025.

Institute for Human Development, *India Labour and Employment Report 2014: Workers in the Era of Globalization* (New Delhi: Academic Foundation and Institute for Human Development, 2014).

International Labour Organisation, 'Introduction to Special Issue on Decent Work', *International Labour Review* 142/2 (2003), 109–12.

International Labour Organisation (ILO), *Perspectives on Labour Economics for Development* (Geneva: International Labour Office, 2013).

Islam, Rizwanul, 'The Nexus of Employment Growth, Employment and Poverty Reduction: An Empirical Analysis', Discussion Paper # 14 (Geneva: International Labour Office, 2004).

Islam, Rizwanul, 'The Nexus of Economic Growth, Employment and Poverty Reduction: An Empirical Analysis', In Rizwanul Islam, ed., *Fighting Poverty: The Development-Employment Link* (New Delhi: Viva Books, 2006).

Islam, Rizwanul, 'Pattern of Economic Growth and Its Implications for Employment', In A. Dasgupta, ed., *Development. Equity and Poverty: Essays in Honour of Azizur Rahman Khan* (New Delhi: Macmillan, 2010).

Islam, Rizwanul, *Employment and Inclusive Development* (London: Routledge, 2015).

Jajoria, Deepika and Manoj Jatav, 'Is Periodic Labour Force Survey, 2017–18, Comparable with the Employment-Unemployment Survey, 2011–12?' *Economic and Political Weekly* 55/3 (2020), 12–16.

Jatav, Manoj and Deepika Jajoria, 'Household-Level Surveys on Labour Force, Employment and Unemployment in India: A Comparative Assessment', *Labour and Development* 26/2 (2022), 29–47.

Jha, Praveen, 'Labour, Capital and State in Neoliberal India: Some Reflections on Recent Developments', In K. R. Shyam Sundar, ed., *Perspectives on Neoliberalism, Labour and Globalization in India* (Singapore: Palgrave Macmillan, 2019), 99–121.

Kaldor, N., 'Alternative Theories of Distribution', *Review of Economic Studies* 23 (1955), 83–100.

Kalecki, M., 'Three ways to full employment', in *The Economics of Full Employment* (Oxford: Blackwell, 1944).

Kannan, K. P. and G. Raveendran, 'Growth Sans Employment: A Quarter Century of Jobless Growth in India's Organised Manufacturing', *Economic and Political Weekly* 44/10 (2009), 80–91

Kannan, K. P. and G. Raveendran, 'Counting and Profiling the Missing Labour Force', *Economic and Political Weekly* 47/6 (2012), 77–80.

Kannan, K. P. and G. Raveendran, 'From Jobless to Job-loss Growth: Gainers and Losers during 2017–18', *Economic and Political Weekly* 54/44 (2019), 38–44.

Kar, S. and S. Sakthivel, 'Reforms and Regional Inequality in India', *Economic and Political Weekly* 42/47 (2007), 69–77.

Keynes, J. M., *The Theory of Employment, Interest and Money* (London: Macmillan, 1936)

Khan, A. R., 'Employment Policies for Poverty Reduction', Issues in Employment and Poverty Discussion Paper # 1 (Geneva: International Labour Organisation, 2001).

Khan, A. R., *Asian Experience on Growth, Employment and Poverty: An Overview with Special Reference to the Findings from Some Recent Case Studies* (Geneva: International Labour Organisation, 2007).

Kotwal, Ashok, Bharat Ramaswami and Wilima Wadhwa, 'Economic Liberalisation and Indian Economic Growth', *Journal of Economic Literature* 49/4 (2011), 1152–99.

Kumar, Avinash and Nazia Iqbal Hashmi, 'Labour Market Discrimination in India', *The Indian Journal of Labour Economics* 63/1 (2020), 177–188.

Kuznets, Simon, *Economic Growth and Structure: Selected Essays* (Norton: New York, 1965).

Kuznets, Simon, *Modern Economic Growth: Rate, Structure and Spread (Vol. 2)* (New Haven: Yale University Press, 1965)

Lewis, Arthur, 'Economic Development with Unlimited Supplies of Labour', *The Manchester School* 22/2 (1954), 139–91.

Lingam, L., 'Gender, Households and Poverty: Tracking Mediations of Macro Adjustment Programmes', *Economic and Political Weekly* 41/20 (2006), 1989–99.

Mahapatra, Sushanta Kumar and Pareswar Sahu, 'Economic Development in the States: Convergence versus Divergence', *Economic and Political Weekly* 60/36 (2025), 59–66.

Majumdar, D. and S. Sarkar, *Globalisation, Labour Markets and Inequality in India* (New York: Routledge, 2008).

Margit. S and S. Mitra, 'Convergence in Regional Growth Rates: Indian Research Agenda', *Economic and Political Weekly* 31/33 (1996), 2239–42.

Mehrotra, Santosh, Jajati Parida, Sarmistha Sinha and Ankita Gandhi, 'Explaining Employment Trends in the Indian Economy: 1993–94 to 2011–12', *Economic and Political Weekly* 49/32 (2014), 49–57.

Mehrotra, Santosh and Jajati K. Parida, 'Stalled Structural Change Brings an Employment Crisis in India', *The Indian Journal of Labour Economics* 64/2 (2021), 281–308.

Mitra, Arup, *The Indian Labour Market: An Overview*, ILO Asia-Pacific Working Paper, Sub-regional Office for South Asia (New Delhi: International Labour Organisation, 2008).

Mosse, David, 'Caste and Development: Contemporary Perspectives on a Structure of Discrimination and Advantage', *World Development* 110 (2018), 422–436.

Nagaraj, R., A. Varoudakis and M. A. Veganzones, 'Long-Run Growth Trends and Convergence across Indian States', Paris: OECD Development Centre Working Paper 131(1998),1815–1949.

Nagaraj, R., 'Indian Economy Since 1980: Virtuous Growth or Polarisation?', *Economic and Political Weekly* 35/32 (2000), 2831–33.

Nath, Paaritosh and Amit Basole, 'Did Employment Rise or Fall in India between 2011 and 2017? Estimating Absolute Changes in the Workforce', *Economic and Political Weekly* 56/34 (2021), 44–52.

Nayyar, Deepak, 'Economic Liberalisation in India: Then and Now', *Economic and Political Weekly* 52/2 (2017), 41–48.

Nayyar, Deepak, *Growth and Development: Essays on a Changing World Economy* (Oxford: Routledge, 2017).

Nayyar, G., 'Economic Growth and Regional Inequality in India', *Economic and Political Weekly* 43/06 (2008), 58–67.

Neff, Daniel, Kunal Sen and Veronika Kling (2012), 'The Puzzling Decline in Rural Women's Labour Force Participation in India: A Re-examination', German Institute of Global and Area Studies (GIGA) Working Paper # 196.

Okun, A. M., 'Potential GNP', Its Measurements and Significance', *Proceedings of the Business and Economics Statistics Section, American Statistical Association* (Washington D.C., American Statistical Association, 1962).

Padhi, Balakrushna and Venkatanarayana Motkuri, 'Labour Force and Employment Growth in India Evidence from the EUS (2011–12) and PLFS (I and II)', *Economic and Political Weekly* 56/47 (2021), 58–63.

Panagaria, Arvind, *India: The Emerging Giant* (New Delhi: Cambridge University Press, 2008).

Panagariya, Arvind, Pinaki Chakraborty, and M. Govinda Rao, *State-level Reforms, Growth, and Development in Indian States* (Oxford: Oxford University Press, 2014).

Papola, T. S., 'Employment in India's Development Strategy', In Sankar Kumar Bhaumik, ed., *Reforming Indian Agriculture: Towards Employment Generation and Poverty Reduction* (New Delhi: Sage Publications, 2008, 363–80).

Papola, T. S., *Employment Challenge and Strategies in India*, ILO Asia-Pacific Working Paper series (New Delhi: ILO Sub-regional Office for South Asia, 2008).

Patnaik, Prabhat, 'Economic Growth and Employment', *Economic and Political Weekly* 46/26–27 (2011), 172–76.

Planning Commission, *Twelfth Five-Year Plan (2012–2017): Faster, More Inclusive and Sustainable Growth* (New Delhi: Sage Publications, 2013).

Purfield, C., 'Mind the Gap: Is Economic Growth in India Leaving Some States Behind?', Working Paper 06/103 (Washington, D.C.: International Monetary Fund, 2006).

Rajeev, M., 'Contract Labour in Karnataka: Emerging Issues and Options', *Economic and Political Weekly* 41/21 (2006), 2086–88.

Raju, S., 'Growth across States in 2000s: Evidence of Convergence', *Economic and Political Weekly* 67/23 (2012), 76–79.

Ramaswamy, K. V., 'Regional Dimension of Growth and Employment', *Economic and Political Weekly* 42/49 (2007), 47–56.

Rangarajan, C., P., Iyer Kaul and Seema, 'Where is the Missing Labour Force?', *Economic and Political Weekly* 46/39 (2011), 68–72.

Rangarajan, C. and Srivastava, D. K., 'Underlying Drivers of India's Growth', *Economic and Political Weekly* 52/25–26 (2017), 69–77.

Rao, M. G., R. T. Shand and Kalirajan, 'Convergence of Incomes across Indian States: A Divergent View', *Economic and Political Weekly* 34/13 (1999), 769–78.

Rustagi, Preet, 'Changing Patterns of Labour Force Participation and Employment of women in India', *Indian Journal of Labour Economics* 56/2 (2013), 215–41

Sanga, Prerna and Abdul Shaban, 'Regional Divergence and Inequalities in India', *Economic and Political Weekly* 52/1 (2017), 102–10.

Sen, Amitava, 'Employment', In Kaushik Basu and Annemie Maertens, eds., *The New Oxford Companion to Economics in India* (New Delhi: Oxford University Press, 2012, 124–26).

Sen, Kunal, 'Structural Transformation around the World: Patterns and Drivers', *Asian Development Review* 36/2 (2019), 1–31.

Sharma, Alakh N. and Balwant Singh Mehta, 'India's Growth and Employment Patterns: A Four-Decade Perspective (1983–2024)', *Economic and Political Weekly* 59/50 (2024), 38–53.

Sharma, Alakh N., 'Persistent Challenges of Employment and Decent Work', *Economic and Political Weekly* 59/50 (2024), 35–37.

Shetty, S. L., 'Growth of SDP and Structural Changes in State Economics', *Economic and Political Weekly* 38/41 (2003), 5189–5200.

Sikdar, Soumyen, *Contemporary Issues in Globalisation: An Introduction to Theory and Policy in India* (New Delhi: Oxford University Press, 2006).

Singh, Nirvikar, 'The Dynamics and Status of India's Economic Reforms', In Chetan Ghate, ed., *The Oxford Handbook on the Indian Economy* (New Delhi: Oxford University Press, 2012, 499–525)

Solow, R. M., 'A Contribution to the Theory of Economic Growth', *Quarterly Journal of Economics* 70 (1956), 65–94.

Srinivasan, T. N., *Eight Lectures on India's Economic Reforms* (*New Delhi:* Oxford University Press, 2000).

Srivastava, Nisha and Anjor Bhaskar, 'Back to Barracks: Changing Pattern of Women's Work Participation in India', In P. Jha, A. Kuar and Y. Mishra, eds., *Labouring Women: Issues and Challenges in Contemporary India* (New Delhi: Orient Blackswan, 2020).

Subramanian, Arvind and Utsav Kumar 'Growth in India's States in the First Decade of the 21st Century: Four Facts', *Economic and Political Weekly* 47/3 (2012), 48–57.

Sundaram, K., 'Employment-Unemployment Situation in 1990s: Some Results from NSS 55th Round Survey', *Economic and Political Weekly* 36/11 (2001), 931–33 and 935–40.

Thorat, Sukhadeo, S. Madheswaran and B. P. Vani, 'Caste and Labour Market: Employment Discrimination and Its Impact on Poverty', *Economic and Political Weekly* 56/21 (2021), 55–61.

Unni, J. and G. Raveendran, 'Growth of Employment (1993–94 to 2004–05): Illusion of Inclusiveness?', *Economic and Political Weekly* 40/3 (2007),196–200.

Verick, Sher S., 'What Employment Policy for a Globalized India?', In K. R. Shyam Sundar, ed., *Globalization, Labour Market Institutions, Processes and Policies in India* (India: Springer, 2019)

World Bank, *India's Employment Challenge: Creating Jobs, Helping Workers* (New Delhi: Oxford University Press, 2010).

Index

www.ingramcontent.com/pod-product-compliance
Ingram Content Group UK Ltd.
Pitfield, Milton Keynes, MK11 3LW, UK
UKHW020201290926
15471UKWH00005B/1012

9 781805 841388